PRACTICAL
SOCIAL WORK LAW

PEARSON

We work with leading authors to develop the
strongest educational materials in law and social
work, bringing cutting-edge thinking and best learning
practice to a global market.

Under a range of well-known imprints, including
Longman, we craft high quality print and electronic
publications which help readers to understand and
apply their content, whether studying or at work.

To find out more about the complete range of our
publishing, please visit us on the World Wide Web at:
www.pearsoned.co.uk

PRACTICAL
SOCIAL WORK LAW

Analysing Court Cases and Inquiries

Siobhan E. Laird

University of Nottingham

Longman
is an imprint of

Harlow, England • London • New York • Boston • San Francisco • Toronto
Sydney • Tokyo • Singapore • Hong Kong • Seoul • Taipei • New Delhi
Cape Town • Madrid • Mexico City • Amsterdam • Munich • Paris • Milan

Pearson Education Limited

Edinburgh Gate
Harlow
Essex CM20 2JE
England

and Associated Companies throughout the world

Visit us on the World Wide Web at:
www.pearsoned.co.uk

First published 2010

© Pearson Education Limited 2010

ISBN: 978-1-4058-4739-1

British Library Cataloguing-in-Publication Data
A catalogue record for this book is available from the British Library.

Library of Congress Cataloging-in-Publication Data

Laird, Siobhan Elizabeth.
  Practical social work law : analysing court cases and inquiries / Siobhan Laird.
    p. cm.
  Includes bibliographical references and index.
  ISBN 978-1-4058-4739-1 (pbk.)
1. Social workers–Legal status, laws, etc.–England.   I. Title
  KD3302.L35 2010
  344.4203'13–dc22

                                                    2010007213

10 9 8 7 6 5 4 3 2
13

Typeset in 9/12 pt Stone Serif by 73
Printed and bound by CPI Group (UK) Ltd, Croydon, CR0 4YY

The publisher's policy is to use paper manufactured from sustainable forests.

Brief contents

Contents

Preface

Why I wrote this book

I have taught law to postgraduate and undergraduate social work students for almost five years. During that period I had become increasingly frustrated by the lack of texts which assisted students to contextualise the law. There are comprehensive social work law books which provide considerable technical detail in a sequential fashion. Others focus on the value base of social work, but are deficient in the technical detail crucial to practising lawfully. As a lecturer I wanted a text which thoroughly integrated technical detail of the law with the value base of social work. I also wanted to move beyond the restriction of paragraph-sized scenarios to longer and more expansive explorations of the complexity of real-world social work activity within a legal context. But more than anything else, I wanted to write a text which would engage students in the narrative accounts of users, carers, parents, children and social workers caught up in the midst of legal action. In short, I wanted to make the law an interesting, stimulating and sometimes moving read for social work students. It is for this reason that my book centres on Serious Case Reviews, Public Inquiry Reports, Ombudsman Reports and judgements handed down by the courts to explore the realities of social work practice and the law which frames it.

Conventions used in this book

There has been a tendency in official documents to note the ethnicity of individuals if they are from ethnic minority communities and not if they are from the majority white community. Unfortunately this has meant that in many instances the ethnicity of parties to a court case has not been explicitly stated. However, it can be assumed that in most instances these people are in fact from the white majority community. As ethnicity has simply not been recorded in many of the documents upon which this book is based, regrettably I have been forced to adopt the same convention.

As a large number of the cases and inquiries cited in this text involve children or vulnerable adults, often anonymity was granted to these individuals and preserved by replacing their real names by letters in judgements and inquiry reports. In all the Local Government Ombudsman Reports, as required by statute, the ombudsman had already substituted pseudonyms for each of the complainants. Where Ombudsman cases are used, I have simply adopted the same pseudonyms as were assigned in the original ombudsman's report. As regards Public Inquiry Reports, where the names of people were not used in the original version, I have observed the anonymity this gave. I have done so even when those names have subsequently come into the public domain. Where real names have been used in court reports or inquiries I have also used them. Each case commences with a list of key people, some of whom will be denoted by letters, pseudonyms or their real names.

There are frequent quotations from the court judgements, inquiries and ombudsman reports which are the basis of discussion of about professional practice. These are referenced according to paragraph or page number depending on the format used in the original documentation. These references appear without authors' names and are easily distinguishable from citations of the research literature.

How to read this book

Chapter 1 brings together all the background detail necessary to comprehend the rest of the book and as such it is crucial to begin by reading this. Subsequent chapters bring together government guidance, national minimum standards, service standards and codes of practice to bear upon the workings of different areas of social work law. Precisely because this textbook draws upon real-life cases it illustrates the complexity of social work practice within a legal framework including the interrelationships between different areas of legislation and practice. Consequently, the later chapters in the book build cumulatively upon the knowledge base of the early ones. So, for example, a court case in Chapter 9 concerning a parent's mental health examines this in relation to child protection which refers back to knowledge contained in Chapter 3. Ideally this book should be read sequentially from start to finish.

Siobhan E. Laird

Guided tour

Overview of relevant legislation

As the statistics above reveal, there are in the region of 300,000–400,000 children who are in need due to being in the care system, having a disability or due to their offending behaviour. The vast majority of these children are being cared for by their families. A small number of these children, around 60,000, are actually in the care system and may either be living with their family or relatives or else being *looked after* by the local authority. In any year 26,000 children are placed on the child protection register because they are at risk of significant harm due to neglect or abuse. Each of these children will have a Child Protection Plan in place and an allocated social worker who regularly sees the child and his or her family. This large number of successfully protected children needs to be seen against the rare but extremely tragic deaths of children who are known to Children's Services. Local authority social workers will be involved in obtaining in the region of 20,000 court orders during public law

Guidance document	Outline content
Department of Health (1991a) *The Children Act 1989 Guidance and Regulations: Family Placement*	This statutory guidance provides instruction to practitioners placing children living away from home with relatives or friends.
Department of Health (2000d) *Framework for the Assessment of Children in Need and their Families*	This is policy guidance and details how practitioners should conduct multidisciplinary assessments and care plans for children.
Department of Health (2000e) *Framework for the Assessment of Children in Need and their Families: Core Assessment Records*	These documents are produced for specific age groups of children and provide detailed pro forma for gathering information about children and their families.
HM Government (2006a) *Working Together to Safeguard Children*	This is policy guidance which describes how agencies should collaborate with each other and share information. It also outlines the roles of different agencies in safeguarding children.

At the start of each chapter, the **Overview of relevant legislation** describes the key provisions that affect social work practice in that area, including summaries of the most important **guidance documents**.

Fact file

- Total child population – 11 million
- Number of vulnerable children – 3-4 million
- Number of *children in need* – 300-400,000
- Number of *looked after* children – 60,000
- Number of children on the child protection register – 26,000
- Average number of Emergency Protection Orders per year – 2,500
- Average number of Care Orders per year – 7,500
- Average number of Supervision Orders per year – 3,000

A **Fact file** provides useful, thought-provoking data relevant to the chapter topic.

CASE 1
R v. Tameside MBC ex parte J (A Child) [2000] 1 FLR 942

Importance of the case

It explores the limits of local authority power over a child whose parents have voluntarily placed him or her into public care. The case also examines the complexities of partnership working with parents when there are fundamental disagreements between them and social workers regarding a child's care.

History of the case

The local authority sought to transfer a voluntarily accommodated child from residential

Each chapter contains detailed examinations of a number of **actual court cases, inquiries** or **ombudsman reports** which aid the legal understanding of social work students and practitioners, by considering the facts, factors, impact and meaning of each case.

Discussion of the case

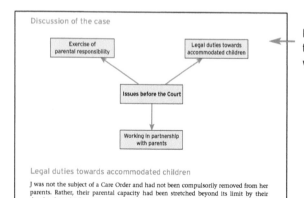

Legal duties towards accommodated children

J was not the subject of a Care Order and had not been compulsorily removed from her parents. Rather, their parental capacity had been stretched beyond its limit by their daughter's multiple severe learning difficulties and challenging behaviour. Unable to

Each case includes an in-depth **Discussion of the case** to identify all the legal, ethical and best practice issues which need to be considered.

Key guidance

Working Together to Safeguard Children

Para. 5.80 The initial child protection conference brings together family members, the child where appropriate, and those professionals most involved with the child and family, following s.47 enquiries. Its purpose is:

- To bring together and analyse in an inter-agency setting the information which has been obtained about the child's developmental needs, and the parents' or carers' capacity to respond to these needs to ensure the child's safety and promote the child's health and development within the context of their wider family and environment.

Key guidance assists the student or practitioner to identify what official documents are available to help them in their understanding and application of the law: what it contains, why it is important, and how the social worker can use it.

Background Information

Children and the Mental Health Act 1983

The Mental Health Act 1983 applies to children as well as adults. The Children Act 1989 and the Children Act 2004 will also be applicable at the same time. Therefore practitioners working with those under 18 years whether in hospital or in the community must operate within the legal frameworks of mental health and child welfare. Those with parental responsibility are normally required to give consent on behalf of their child to informal admission to hospital for treatment for a mental disorder. However, *Gillick* competent children under 16 years of

Background information enables students to gain a more detailed understanding of a particular legal term or concept, and how it impacts on social work.

 Critical questions

1 Government guidance and the GSCC *Code of Practice for Social Care Workers* demand that practitioners work in partnership with parents and carers. As the events surrounding Peter demonstrate, parents and carers can sometimes be manipulative, appearing compliant while frustrating intervention, or they can be overtly aggressive. As a practitioner how would you work with a parent who engages in these sorts of behaviour?

2 Poor supervision was one factor contributing to the failure to safeguard Peter. If you were experiencing poor supervision from your team leader how would you tackle it?

Critical questions at the end of each case encourage students and practitioners to think critically about the issues raised in each case and the implications for practice.

Perspectives

Lisa Arthurworrey on the Climbié Inquiry

The *Mail on Sunday* (15 June 2008) devoted three pages to an interview with Lisa Arthurworrey, the social worker, at the centre of the Climbié Inquiry in 2003. Lisa described her reaction to the telephone call informing her of Victoria's death, aged 8 years. 'When the call came I remembered an older social worker telling me that if a child dies on your watch, your own life will be destroyed. I nearly collapsed when I learned it was Victoria.' The media portrayal of Lisa Arthurworrey as primarily responsible for Victoria's death made her feel that 'I wanted to

Perspectives encourage students and practitioners to consider alternative viewpoints of a particular event, or stage in legal proceedings, or of a legal provision.

Critical commentary

Use of Emergency Protection Orders

Social workers acting to protect children in an emergency have several legal options. They can seek the consent of parents to the voluntary placement of a child with a relative or in local authority care under s.20 of the Children Act 1989. Where parental consent or voluntary arrangements are problematic, social workers can apply for an ex parte Emergency Protection Order under s.44 or request that an officer exercise a Police Protection Power under s.46. In two studies, covering 550 children in all, Masson (2005) examined how social workers decided which course of action to pursue in urgent situations.

Critical commentary looks deeper into the issues surrounding legal definitions and social work decisions, enabling students and practitioners to gain a critical understanding of processes and outcomes.

Learning points

- Children and young people who are the subject of criminal proceedings are entitled to a fair trial which may require the use of *special measures*.
- Sentences handed down to children must take account of their welfare in conjunction with the need to punish and protect the public.
- An assessment of risk of harm to the public can result in custodial sentences for children and young people being extended by Crown Court judges to take account of their dangerousness to the public.

The **Learning points** feature is a handy bullet-point list that summarises the key points to take away from the chapter.

Further reading

Arthur, R. (2005) 'Punish parents for the crimes of their children', *The Howard Journal* 44(3): 233-53. This article considers the controversy surrounding making parents accountable for the offending behaviour of their children.

Dugmore, P. and Pickford, J. (2006) *Youth Justice and Social Work*, Exeter: Learning Matters. This publication describes the role of social work within the youth justice system. It also focuses on social work practice with young offenders.

Smith, R. (2007) *Youth Justice: Ideas, Policy and Practice*, Cullompton: Willan. This publication examines the policy drivers behind legislation in relation to youth offending. It also provides an overview of the current youth justice system and critical commentary on recent developments.

Squires, P. and Stephen, D.E. (2005) *Rougher Justice: Anti-social Behaviour and Young People*, Cullompton: Willan. This book examines the political discourses surrounding youth justice and youth offending.

Useful websites

www.crimereduction.homeoffice.gov.uk/ Run by the Home Office this website provides statistics on the use of Anti-social Behaviour Orders and easy-to-read guides on these and other crime reduction strategies introduced by the Government.

An annotated list of **Further reading** and **Useful websites** is a helpful tool for further research and study, helping the student or practitioner to deepen his or her understanding of the topic.

Acknowledgements

I would like to thank Andrew Taylor, my editor, for his invaluable advice from conception through to completion of this text. Thanks are also due to the staff team at Pearson Education who have worked tirelessly to produce an accessible format for this book. Andrew White has assisted in reproducing several diagrams for the text which has relieved me of the need to become a technical wizard. I also wish to express my gratitude to Dorcas Boreland, my mother, who put her life on hold for a month to read and correct the initial manuscript. Hilary Pook at the Office of the Local Government Ombudsman, by generously making available their reports, has provided a wider choice of case studies than would otherwise have been possible in this book. I remain indebted to my colleagues in the Centre for Social Work at the University of Nottingham for their encouragement and many kindnesses. My work continues to be both a privilege and a pleasure. Finally, I want to thank the many social work students who have engaged with me during my lectures and taught me how to teach law.

Publisher's acknowledgements

We are grateful to the following for permission to reproduce copyright material:

Figures
Figures on page 119 and 122 from *Framework for the Assessment of Children in Need and their Families*, The Stationery Office (Department of Health 2000), reproduced with the approval of Royal Holloway University of London. Crown Copyright material is reproduced with permission under the terms of the Click-Use License.

Tables
Table on page 216 from *Children (Leaving Care) Act 2000: Regulations and Guidance*, The Stationery Office (TSO) (Department of Health 2001), Crown Copyright material is reproduced with permission under the terms of the Click-Use License; Tables on pages 408–9, pages 456–7 adapted from *Social Work Law*, Pearson Education (Brammer, A. 2007).

In some instances we have been unable to trace the owners of copyright material, and we would appreciate any information that would enable us to do so.

The publishers would like to thank the author for the dedication, skill and talent she's poured into the book and for being such a pleasure to work with.

The publishers would also like to thank the anonymous panel of reviewers whose generous and constructive comments on the draft material undoubtedly helped shape a better final text.

Table of cases

Table of statutes

Table of statutory instruments

Table of treaties and EU legislation

1

LEGISLATIVE FRAMEWORK

Fact file

- Number of qualified social workers in England and Wales GSCC (General Social Care Council) registered – 92,000
- MPs in House of Commons – 519 men, 126 women and 15 from ethnic minorities
- Primary legislation passed by Parliament annually – 50
- Secondary legislation passed by Parliament annually – 3,500
- Judges in House of Lords (Supreme Court) – 11 white men and 1 white woman
- Judges in Court of Appeal – 33 white men and 2 white women
- Judges in High Court – 94 men, 16 women and 3 from ethnic minorities
- District Judges (County Court) – 302 white male, 80 white female and 20 from ethnic minorities
- Circuit Judges (Crown Court) – 501 white male, 70 white female and 20 from ethnic minorities
- Lay Magistrates – 14,500 white male, 14,800 white female and 2,200 from ethnic minorities, 1,500 disabled and 25,000 over 50 years of age
- Practising solicitors – 100,000 of which 40% are women and 11% from ethnic minorities
- Practising barristers – 14,000 of which 33% are women and 11% from ethnic minorities
- Number of different types of tribunal – 80

Source: www.judiciary.gov.uk/keyfacts/statistics/index.htm, accessed on 19 June 2009.

Overview of chapter

Many of you will find law one of the most demanding and challenging aspects of your training as social workers. Some of you may not have encountered it before and those who have will almost certainly not have been required to study it in the detail necessary to qualify as social workers. Law can be a daunting subject because it cannot be fudged. It requires a comprehensive grasp of foundational concepts, an extensive knowledge of legislation and precision in its application. Moreover, practitioners can use knowledge of the law in ways which further oppress and disempower service-users, or exercise it in a manner which informs service-users of their entitlements, protects their rights and enhances their quality of life.

This chapter sets out the legal framework within which social work practice takes place. It describes statute law and case law and then explains the relationship between them. Also detailed are the different kinds of government-issued guidance which direct management and assist frontline professionals to implement new legislation. These are often neglected aspects of the law in mainstream textbooks, but are crucial documents for understanding the practice implications of legislation and case law. Moreover, Policy Guidance, Practice Guidance, Codes of Practice, Local Government Circulars and National Service Frameworks often articulate the guiding principles and purposes of legislation. In addition they commonly set out the standards and quality of professional work and service delivery. For these reasons government guidance is frequently referred to throughout this book.

Social workers as employees should be aware of the legal obligations owed to them by employers in terms of ensuring their health and safety. The GSCC *Code of Practice for Employers of Social Care Workers* imposes additional responsibilities upon organisations which employ social workers. The obligations of employers and the rights of social care professionals as employees are considered in this chapter. Without knowing their own rights as workers, practitioners will be unable to ensure that they operate in a safe environment.

Social workers have a legal duty of care towards service users and carers. This means that practitioners and their employers can be required to pay damages by those who avail of their services and suffer loss or distress as a result. If users or carers receive incorrect advice from professionals, or experience adverse consequences because of social work intervention, they may be entitled to sue in negligence. At the same time the law prevents social workers being sued when carrying out certain statutory functions, such as safeguarding children. Obviously practitioners need to know the circumstances under which they and their employers may be liable in negligence and when they are not.

Social workers not only assist users or carers to avail of services, but commonly are involved in helping them to assert their rights. In order to do this, social workers themselves have to be aware of the raft of legislation which protects people from discrimination on the grounds of their gender, sexual orientation, disability, age, religion or ethnicity. These domestic laws are complemented by the European Convention on Human Rights. This gives everyone in the United Kingdom basic protections against unjustified interference in their lives by the State. Parents, children, service users and carers are sometimes on the receiving end of interventions that they do not want by health and social care professionals. A resort to human rights law can often be an important means whereby individuals and families can protect their privacy and autonomy. Social workers need to be aware of the rights granted under the European Convention in order both to avoid violating them and to help individuals whose rights have been contravened to obtain justice.

Computerisation and the growing use of information technology in social work make it crucial for practitioners to understand the legislation which governs the use of personal information relating to users and carers. Much of contemporary social work consists of collecting information from different sources and using it to complete assessments. These may form the basis of a Child Protection Plan, a Community Care Plan or a risk assessment compiled as part of a wide-ranging multidisciplinary care plan. People about whom information is being gathered and processed have legal protections as to how that data is used. Social workers need to be aware of data protection legislation to ensure that they handle information correctly. They also need to be in a position to offer advice to users and carers when inaccurate or damaging information about them is being used to inform care plans or other professional activities.

Social workers are not lawyers and are not required to give legal advice to those they work with. However, social workers, regardless of whether they practise with adults or children, operate daily within a set of legal frameworks. They need to understand those frameworks in order to practise lawfully. But they also need to understand them if they are to assist parents, children, users and carers to protect their rights or to obtain redress when these have been violated. The law is at the heart of social work and a thorough working knowledge of relevant legislation supplemented by case law is at the heart of best practice. Reading this chapter provides all the background information that is necessary to be able to understand and engage with the discussion of real-life cases and professional decision making in the rest of the book.

Why law matters for social workers

Essentially the law comprises a set of rules that can be enforced by the police and courts through means of sanctions such as a prison sentence, compulsory community work, fine or injunction (court order preventing an action). However, the law is not the same as morality, which may or may not coincide with legal rules. For example, some people in Britain believe that abortion is immoral, but the Abortion Act 1967 permits abortion to be carried out in a number of circumstances, such as when pregnancy threatens the mother's life or is the result of a rape. Conversely, a section of the population believe that it is morally justified to help someone to die in certain circumstances, such as when they are experiencing severe chronic pain or a complete loss of dignity as the result of serious illness. Yet, the law in the United Kingdom makes euthanasia illegal and a number of people have been found guilty in court of either murder or manslaughter for assisting a suicide. On the other hand, almost all moral belief systems have sanctions against the taking of human life and this is also true of English law, with the handing down of long custodial sentences for murder and occasionally for manslaughter.

Consider the case study below and try to imagine how you would intervene in this situation if you had no knowledge of the law and only had your GSCC *Code of Practice for Care Workers* to guide your decisions and actions.

Case study

For the last five years Barbara aged 7 has lived with her father Luke, who is of African-Caribbean heritage, and his partner Debbie who is white and six months pregnant with Luke's child. Debbie's two children, Sheila aged 10 years and David age 12 years, also live with them. Both Luke and Debbie are unemployed. They rent a two-bedroom terraced house with one small living room and kitchen downstairs from a local housing association. The roof has leaked for the last eight months and there is rising damp in the kitchen.

A year ago Barbara was admitted to Borough Hospital with a broken arm after what her father tells the doctor was 'a fall down the stairs at home'. No concerns are raised by hospital staff although medical notes describe Barbara as being underweight for her age. A month ago

Barbara was admitted to Accident and Emergency at Central Hospital due to a gash in her arm which needed eight stitches. While the doctor could not determine whether the injury was non-accidental she alerts the hospital social worker to her concerns about Barbara. The hospital social worker asks Barbara and her father about the injury, but both of them maintain that she hurt herself while playing with friends. The hospital social worker makes a referral to your community based team to conduct an initial assessment.

Three weeks later when you make a first home visit, Debbie tells you that Barbara is in bed as she is off school with a cold and having an afternoon nap. You are not permitted to see her. You return to the house at about 3.00 pm five days later, but only catch a glimpse of Barbara through a glass-panelled door as her father takes her out of the house while you are talking to Debbie. Debbie complains to you that Barbara was not attended by the doctor at Accident and Emergency until everyone else, including patients who arrived after Barbara and her father, were treated first. Debbie insists this occurred because all the other patients were white. Debbie also tells you that Barbara's birth mother has contacted Luke to demand that Barbara comes to live with her.

A few days later the out-of-hours duty social worker for your team receives a telephone call from the hospital social worker at the Accident and Emergency Department of General Hospital requesting a home visit for David who has just been discharged home following treatment as an out-patient for several fractured ribs. David was not seen by a consultant paediatrician due to staff shortages, but the junior doctor who treated him accepted Debbie's explanation that he had been in a road traffic accident. The hospital social worker thinks the family needs support services and makes a referral to your team for an initial assessment. It is a further month before this referral is allocated to anyone because three social workers on your team are on long-term sick leave with stress-related illnesses. You are also beginning to feel unwell due to the relentless work pressures of covering for absent colleagues.

How might knowledge of the law help you as a qualified practitioner to work with this family?

This scenario raises a number of issues which you cannot effectively address without a working knowledge of the law. Consider the following in the light of the GSCC *Code of Practice for Social Care Workers*:

- Luke and Debbie are living in overcrowded social housing which is also in disrepair. Such circumstances are likely to detrimentally affect the welfare of their children and indeed their own health. Paragraph 3.1 of the Code requires social workers to promote the independence of service users by 'assisting them to understand and exercise their rights'. To help this family with their housing you would need to know: what their rights are in relation to housing; how they go about exercising their rights; and what you can do as a social worker to improve their housing situation.
- Debbie is convinced that Central Hospital is giving her family a poorer service because they are of African-Caribbean heritage. Paragraph 3.2 of the Code obliges social workers to challenge and report discriminatory practice alongside enabling service-users to exercise their rights. To assist Luke you would need to know: what law exists to protect people from racial discrimination; how Luke can use this to take action against the hospital for an act of discrimination; and what sources of funding or free legal advice are available to enable him to pursue his claim.
- Barbara and David have been treated in hospital and it is possible that their injuries are caused by physical abuse. Equally their injuries may be due to accidents and Barbara could have a medical condition which results in her being underweight for her age.

How can you establish which is true? Can you simply walk into people's homes because you are a social worker and demand to interview their children? Can parents simply refuse to let you speak to their children? In short, what are your powers as a social worker and what rights do parents have when they disagree with you? Paragraph 6.1 of the Code obliges social workers to work in a 'lawful, safe and effective way'.

- If you interview Luke and Debbie about the injuries to their children and they insist they do not want any further social work contact does that mean you should just end work with this family? To answer this question you would need to know what your legal duties are as a social worker as regards children's welfare. Paragraph 6.1 of the Code is again directly relevant in this situation as are paragraphs 4.2 and 4.3 which oblige social workers to conduct assessments and minimise the risk of harm to service-users.

- Barbara's birth mother has demanded to be given immediate custody of Barbara. What would be your response as a social worker if Luke and Debbie want to continue to look after Barbara and refuse to let her birth mother see Barbara again? How can you help to resolve this dispute as a social worker and what advice can you give to those involved? Paragraphs 1.2 and 2.2 of the Code oblige social care workers to respect and promote the views and wishes of service-users while 'communicating in an appropriate, open, accurate and straightforward way'. Putting this into practice would require knowledge of both relevant legislation and government guidance.

- It takes three weeks for a social worker to make a home visit after the referral for Barbara and a month for the referral for David to even be allocated to a practitioner. Paragraphs 2.4 and 2.5 of the Code require social care workers to be reliable and to honour work commitments. What might be an acceptable timescale for a social work response in these circumstances? To answer this you would need to be familiar with government guidance.

- What if Luke and Debbie were waiting for urgent assistance from Social Services which they only received after months of delay? How would they go about getting any kind of redress and what would be your responsibility to assist them? To answer this you would need to know the options for service-users wanting to make complaints and what responses they are entitled to. Paragraph 3.7 makes it clear that social care workers must be in a position to: help service users and carers to make complaints, ensure that they are taken seriously, passed to the correct person, and receive a proper response.

- A number of professionals have treated Barbara and David and it will be important to obtain information from them about the health of the two children. Paragraphs 6.5 and 6.7 require social care workers to collaborate with other professionals. What will you do if the doctors tell you the information is confidential or that they are too busy to speak to you? To answer this you would need to know what are the legal obligations of other agencies and professionals to work with you. This is set out both in legislation and government guidance.

- Colleagues who have gone off on sick leave have not been replaced by management and now you are yourself starting to experience illness. Paragraph 3.4 of the Code obliges workers to bring to the attention of their employers any 'resource or operational difficulties that might get in the way of the delivery of safe care'. Concomitantly, paragraphs 4.5 and 4.6 of the GSCC Code for Employers require them to 'promote staff welfare' and provide 'appropriate assistance to social care workers whose work is affected by ill health'. What rights do you have as an employee to work in a less stressful environment, and how can you enforce these rights? Once again the answer to this lies in knowing the relevant law and the legal responsibilities employers have towards their employees.

To summarise, it is not enough to have a working knowledge of the GSCC Code of Practice in order to address the issues and dilemmas raised by the case study. Knowledge of the law is necessary because it instructs practitioners as to:

- The rights and entitlements of service-users, carers, parents and children.
- How the rights and entitlements of service-users, carers, parents and children can be enforced.
- The rights and obligations of parents, guardians, partners, carers and others in relation to children and service-users.
- The legal responsibilities of social workers.
- The nature and limits of social workers' legal powers.
- The legal obligations of different agencies and professionals.
- The accountability of social workers to their service-users, employers and professional bodies.
- The legal responsibilities of employers to social workers as employees.

While the law relating to social work is extensive, it still leaves social workers with considerable discretion when making decisions and intervening. The circumstances which social workers encounter during their practice are simply too varied and numerous for the systematic application of prescriptive legal formulas. It is for this reason that the GSCC *Code of Practice for Care Workers* and professional judgement developed through post-qualifying practice are critical to good social work within the legal framework.

Statute law

This section details how law is actually created in the United Kingdom and how it is enforced. It also examines the impact of international legal frameworks which have an important and sometimes central role in the making and implementation of law in Britain.

Primary legislation

The United Kingdom has an unwritten constitution which means that Parliament, which comprises the House of Commons and the House of Lords (known together as the Houses of Parliament), can make any law it wishes. The House of Commons at any point in time tends to be dominated by just one political party which has the most Members of Parliament. The party with the majority of MPs forms the government and this means that normally it can successfully introduce laws by mustering the majority of votes from its own MPs to pass a new law. The majority of peers in the House of Lords also have to vote in favour for a government proposal to become law. But because the House of Commons has primacy in law making, even if the majority of peers reject a proposal they can only temporarily prevent it from becoming law. For this reason the House of Lords rarely votes against something which the majority of MPs in the House of Commons have voted to accept. A law created by Parliament is known as a statute or Act and is referred to as a piece of legislation.

The ability to create a statute which can repeal or supersede previous legislation is known as Parliamentary Sovereignty. In effect it means that one government can undo the Acts passed by a previous government. For instance the Conservative Government under Margaret Thatcher passed the Local Government Act 1988 of which section 28 prohibited Local Education Authorities from using material in schools which could be interpreted as promoting homosexuality. In the meantime homophobic bullying of school children continued unabated (Rivers, 2000, 2001). The Labour Government under Tony Blair passed a statute entitled the Local Government Act 2003 which repealed (cancelled) section 28 of the earlier legislation. Since this change in the law the Department for Education and Skills and the Department of Health (2004) have been able to produce clear policies to tackle the high incidence of homophobic bullying in schools.

There are a number of reasons why a government might introduce a particular piece of legislation. These are identified in the diagram below.

Political parties stand for election on a programme of what they consider to be improvements for the country. They achieve these improvements or changes through legislation. For example, the Conservative Party which won the general election in 1987 had an election manifesto entitled 'The Next Moves Forward' which promised to raise education standards. The Education Act 1988 fulfilled this undertaking by introducing into state schools the National Curriculum which outlined the knowledge and standards pupils should attain by the ages of 7, 11, 14 and 16 years of age. This was accompanied by a programme of national tests for pupils, performance indicators for education, and the creation of public league tables for schools. The Labour Party in their 1997 manifesto entitled 'New Labour because Britain Deserves Better' promised to introduce a welfare-to-work programme to get young people and the long-term unemployed into work. On being elected to office the Labour Government subsequently introduced a raft of legislation which reduced the welfare benefit entitlements of people who were not actively looking for work.

An influential report can also result in a government creating a new statute. For instance the Conservative Government asked Sir Roy Griffiths to chair a committee with terms of reference 'to review the way in which public funds are used to support community care policy'. In 1988 the Griffiths Report entitled *Community Care: Agenda for Action* set out a number of recommendations. These were to underpin the subsequent NHS and Community Care Act 1990 which introduced: care management; the mixed economy of care; needs-led service provision and the relocation of large numbers of vulnerable people from institutional settings to the community.

Scandals and public inquiries, often followed by a public outcry, can also be a key factor in a government's decision to introduce a new piece of legislation. For instance, newspapers widely reported the murder of 8-year-old Victoria Climbié at the hands of her great aunt and her partner during 2000. The adverse publicity surrounding Victoria's death, which largely blamed the tragedy on social workers and other professionals, prompted the Government to set up a public enquiry which reported in 2003. This investigation revealed that Victoria was known to: four social work departments; three housing authorities; two child protection teams of the Metropolitan Police; one NSPCC centre; and two hospitals which suspected Victoria's injuries where due to deliberate harm (Laming, 2003). All of these agencies failed to share vital information with each other that could have saved Victoria's life. These findings led Parliament to pass the Children Act 2004 which places legal duties on social services, housing authorities, health authorities and the police to cooperate with each other and share information to protect children.

Special interest or pressure groups may also lobby the government or try to sway public opinion to bring about legislative change. For example, the Joseph Rowntree Foundation and the Child Action Poverty Group are independent organisations which conduct research and campaign on poverty in the United Kingdom. They frequently lobby MPs to make legislative changes which improve poor people's lives. Based on their research, both groups campaigned for social policies to reduce the incidence of social exclusion through increasing benefits and childcare support to low income families generally and lone parents in particular. The Labour Government responded by passing legislation which introduced the Working Families Tax Credit and the minimum wage.

Finally, the government may respond to a change of circumstances. The Adoption Act 1976 was passed at a time when there were around 20,000 children adopted each year, a majority of whom were very young. Changes in morality have meant that most unmarried parents, particularly mothers, no longer experience stigma, and therefore bring up their own children rather than put them up for adoption. Consequently, there are now considerably fewer, and often only older children available for adoption. Currently half of all children adopted have been *looked after* by Social Services. Many of them want to have continued contact with their parents even though they can no longer live with their family because of abuse or neglect. The Adoption and Children Act 2002, which repealed the Adoption Act 1976, recognised this and created a new category of Special Guardianship which enables older children to acquire an additional legal relationship with an adult who has parental responsibility for them, without the children having to sever their legal or social ties with their birth parents.

 ## Critical questions

Look back at the Fact File at the very beginning of this chapter and notice the under-representation of women and people from ethnic minority communities in the House of Commons. In addition, there are only a handful of openly gay or disabled MPs and no trans-gendered Members of Parliament. How might the under-representation of these various minority groups influence what statute law is passed by the House of Commons?

Process for creating statute law

When a government wants to bring about changes it first engages in a process of consultation, often publishing what is known as a Green Paper which outlines its plans for new legislation. For example, in 2003 in the wake of the Climbié public inquiry the Labour Government issued a Green Paper entitled *Every Child Matters* which set out proposals for a new statute (to become the Children Act 2004) to ensure greater cooperation between agencies working closely with children. This Green Paper invited responses from a cross-section of interest groups and professional bodies which would be affected by planned changes to the law on inter-agency collaboration concerning child welfare and protection. After completing a consultation process the government often proceeds to develop and publish a White Paper which explains its proposed legislation.

White Papers are much more comprehensive than Green Papers and detail the legislation which the government intends to lay before Parliament. For example, the Department of Health (1989) published a White Paper entitled *Caring for People* which explained the rationale, objectives, underlying principles and organisational changes necessary for the reform of service delivery by the NHS and Social Services. This White Paper was the precursor to the NHS and Community Care Act 1990. Similarly, the White Paper entitled *Modernising Social Services* detailed the Labour Government's intention to introduce registration of the social care workforce alongside national minimum standards for social care provision. This was given legal expression in the Care Standards Act 2000. The publication of a White Paper is a further opportunity for interested parties to lobby MPs and the government on the proposed changes to the law. Both Green and White Papers are usually written in layman's terms. They are an important resource if you are trying to understand the reasoning and intentions behind a particular statute.

After the publication of a White Paper, specialists draft the associated legislation so that it can be put before Parliament for MPs and peers to vote on. During its passage through Parliament a piece of legislation is known as a bill because it has not yet become law. It is important to bear in mind that a bill may be rejected by Parliament if a majority of MPs vote against it. Recent mental health legislation was referred to as the Mental Health Bill during 2006 when it was being debated in Parliament and only became the Mental Health Act 2007 after it satisfactorily completed the parliamentary process. A bill is normally introduced into the House of Commons and goes through a number of stages which provide opportunities for MPs to debate and amend it. If the bill successfully passes these stages without being voted down, it then moves to the House of Lords where it goes through a similar process. Once agreed by the majority of peers, it passes to the monarch to receive her agreement, known as the Royal Assent. In practice the Queen as a constitutional head of state never refuses her consent to a bill becoming law.

It is essential to remember that even after receiving the Royal Assent and becoming an Act, different sections or provisions of the Act may come into force at different times. A statute cannot be enforced by the courts until it has been enacted. For example the Mental Health Act 2007 received the Royal Assent on 19 July 2007, but most of its legal provisions did not come into force until October 2008 and others not until April 2009. So there can be different dates for various provisions of the same Act to come into force. This may be because the changes produced by the Act require for example: money to be made available; organisational changes; or training for personnel implementing the new statute. All these were required for agencies and social workers administering the Children Act 1989, which received the Royal Assent in 1989, but did not come into force until 1992.

For recently created statutes, it will be necessary to double check which sections of the Act are currently in force and which will come into force at a later date. Occasionally even quite long-standing statutes can have provisions which were never enacted. For example, the Family Law Act 1996 received Royal Assent on 4 July 1996 and made provision under Part II for no-fault divorces, scheduled for implementation in 2000. In fact Part II was never enacted due in part to adverse media coverage which portrayed the new provisions as a quick faultless way to divorce, thus perpetuating family breakdown (Herring, 2007:117). The box below guides you through the different stages of a government proposal for new legislation, from its inception to completion of the parliamentary process and becoming legally binding statute law.

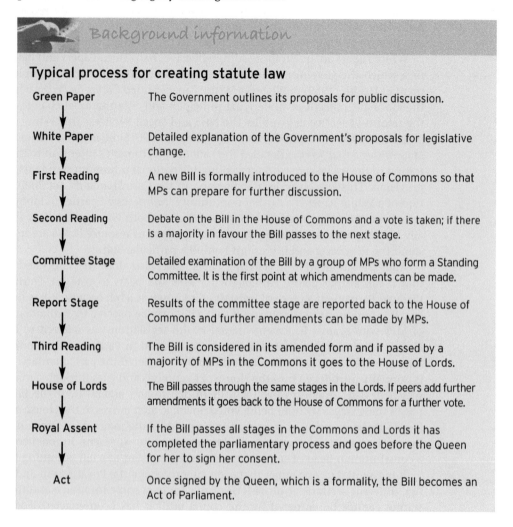

Typical process for creating statute law

Green Paper	The Government outlines its proposals for public discussion.
White Paper	Detailed explanation of the Government's proposals for legislative change.
First Reading	A new Bill is formally introduced to the House of Commons so that MPs can prepare for further discussion.
Second Reading	Debate on the Bill in the House of Commons and a vote is taken; if there is a majority in favour the Bill passes to the next stage.
Committee Stage	Detailed examination of the Bill by a group of MPs who form a Standing Committee. It is the first point at which amendments can be made.
Report Stage	Results of the committee stage are reported back to the House of Commons and further amendments can be made by MPs.
Third Reading	The Bill is considered in its amended form and if passed by a majority of MPs in the Commons it goes to the House of Lords.
House of Lords	The Bill passes through the same stages in the Lords. If peers add further amendments it goes back to the House of Commons for a further vote.
Royal Assent	If the Bill passes all stages in the Commons and Lords it has completed the parliamentary process and goes before the Queen for her to sign her consent.
Act	Once signed by the Queen, which is a formality, the Bill becomes an Act of Parliament.

Secondary legislation

Approximately 50 Acts of Parliament are created each year, many of them requiring extremely technical knowledge and/or detailed procedures to ensure that they are effectively implemented. For this reason many Acts delegate powers to a particular government minister who is tasked to instruct civil servants, assisted by experts and consultants, to produce a comprehensive set of regulations. Regulations created in this way are referred to as statutory instruments, secondary legislation or delegated legislation. These regulations have the same legal force as primary legislation, and in the region of 3,500 pieces of secondary legislation are generated each year. For example, the Care Standards Act 2000 s.22 delegates power to 'the appropriate Minister', meaning the head of a government department, to make detailed rules in relation to the management and standards of service for residential provision. The statutory instrument created under section 22 is the Care Homes Regulations 2001 SI No. 3965. Primary legislation which delegates power in this way is sometimes referred to as the Parent Act.

Critical questions

Go to **www.opsi.gov.uk** which is the website of the Office of Public Sector Information and provides full texts of statutes and statutory instruments. Download the Mental Capacity Act 2005.

What do you notice about how this primary legislation is structured? How easy or difficult is it to understand the wording of the Act or to comprehend what it would mean in your day-to-day practice as a qualified social worker? Describe the user group to which this Act would apply to.

Go back to **www.opsi.gov.uk** and download The Children's Homes Regulations SI2001/3967. This is secondary legislation. What specific areas of the care of children does this statutory instrument cover? How easy or difficult is this document to understand?

Government guidance

In addition to the production of detailed regulations through the use of statutory instruments the government also issues a variety of guidance documents. These instruct local authority social services departments, agencies and/or professionals on the day-to-day implementation of the law.

Policy guidance

The Local Authority Social Services Act 1970 established the framework for local authority social work functions. Section 7 of this Act states that Local Authority Social Services functions must be exercised under the general guidance of the Secretary of State. Policy guidance is therefore *formal guidance* issued by the Secretary of State under Local Authority Social Services Act 1970 s.7. This means that although the guidance is not legally binding (i. e. it is not legislation) it *must* be followed unless there are exceptional and justifiable reasons for departing from it. Government-issued guidelines will state in the introduction if they are issued under s.7 of the Local Authority Social Services Act 1970. Department of Health and Department for Education and Skills (2005) *Carers and Disabled Children Act 2000 and Carers (Equal Opportunities) Act 2004 Combined Policy Guidance*, which concerns services for carers, and Department of Health (2000a) *No Secrets*, which sets out procedures for protecting vulnerable adults, are both issued under this section. This type of guidance is directed at frontline staff and those with managerial and decision-making responsibilities. Although policy guidance is often very detailed it is also written in plain English and not technical legal jargon. It is an indispensable resource for understanding how to apply a piece of legislation in social work practice and ensuring that as a qualified professional you are acting correctly within the legal framework.

Critical questions

Go to **www.dh.gov.uk** which is the Department of Health website and download *No Secrets: Guidance on Developing and Implementing Multi-agency Policies and Procedures to Protect Vulnerable Adults from Abuse*. Compare the language in this to the language in the primary and secondary legislation you previously downloaded, what do you notice about this? If you were a qualified social worker how might you use this document to guide your practice?

Practice guidance

Practice guidance is *general guidance* which advises a local authority on how to go about implementing statutory provisions. The Local Authority does not have to follow the guidance to the letter but should have regard to it when reaching any decision. For example, Department of Health (2001a) *A Practitioner's Guide to Carers' Assessments under the Carers and Disabled Children Act 2000* directs social care professionals as to how to conduct the assessment of a carer. Similarly, Department of Health (2000b) *Assessing Children in Need and their Families: Practice guidance* provides guidance to social workers safeguarding and promoting the welfare of children from ethnic minority backgrounds and children with disabilities. These guidance documents are written for frontline staff and provide easy-to-follow explanations and instructions on performing social work roles and tasks. Social workers must endeavour to follow practice guidance unless there are very exceptional reasons for doing otherwise. It is important to appreciate that failure to follow practice guidance without justification is likely to result in a successful complaint by a service-user, or a court judgement against Social Services.

 Crítical questions

Go to **www.ecm.gov.uk** and download *The Common Assessment Framework for Children and Young People: Practitioner's Guide*. What are the main differences between this practice guidance and the *No Secrets* policy guidance you downloaded earlier? How easy or difficult would it be to use this document to guide your professional work with children?

Local authority circulars

Local authority circulars are issued by various government departments to local authorities giving them more detailed instructions on how to implement a piece of legislation. They may also be issued after a court judgement which alters the existing law, or because of a change in circumstances of some sort. For instance, many local authority circulars will be issued under the Local Authority Social Services Act 1970, s.7 and are therefore *formal guidance*. LAC (2002) 13 *Fair Access to Care Services* which instructs Local Authority Social Services on arrangements for prioritising service delivery to people with social care needs is issued under s.7. Not all circulars are issued under s.7, but they still constitute a form of government instruction and must be carefully adhered to unless there are compelling reasons for departing from them. While local authority circulars are essentially addressed to decision-makers and senior managers within a local authority they often have a direct bearing on the day-to-day work of frontline staff.

 Crítical questions

Go to **www.dh.gov.uk** and download LAC (2002) 13: *Fair Access to Care Services: Guidance on Eligibility Criteria for Adult Social Care*. What are the main implications of this local authority circular for social workers in Adult Social Services?

Codes of practice

Codes of practice are not legislation and do not have the force of law, but they are guidance as to good practice and are usually issued in relation to a specific statute. For example, the Mental Health Act 1983, s.118 provides a code of practice which directs practitioners in their work with service-users who have a mental disorder. Likewise, a code of practice has been issued under s.42 of the Mental Capacity Act 2005 to guide professionals working with mentally incapacitated adults. The Care Standards Act 2000 s.62 gives the General Social Care Council the legal authority to issue the *Code of Practice for Social Care Workers* by which all registered social work students and qualified practitioners are bound. Whilst breaching a code of practice is not an illegal act, doing so is likely to have adverse consequences for the service-user or patient, the professional involved in the breach and their employing agency. In particular, acting contrary to the *Code of Practice for Social Care Workers* may lead to de-registration as a social worker by the General Social Care Council. Where an incident involving a service-user reaches the courts, a breach of a code of practice by a social worker is likely to constitute evidence that the agency has failed in its statutory duties to the service-user.

 ### Critical questions

Go to **www.publicguardian.gov.uk** and download *Mental Capacity Act 2005: Code of Practice*. In what ways does the language and structure of the Code differ from the Act? How easy or difficult is it to follow the Code of Practice? What are the main areas covered by the Code of Practice? How does the Code define the 'best interests' of people who lack mental capacity?

National Service Frameworks

National Service Frameworks have been introduced by the Labour Government and are issued by the Department of Health. These cover the provision of health and social services to children, young people, older people and those with mental health problems or neurological long-term conditions. They are non-statutory in nature and while each framework sets out quality standards for service provision to a specific service-user group, these are not legally enforceable benchmarks. However, many of the objectives detailed in these National Frameworks are complemented by legislation, such as the Mental Health Act 1983 and the Care Standards Act 2000. Essentially, the frameworks are strategy documents which set out the Labour Government's aspirations for service delivery over a 10-year period. There are presently four National Service Frameworks in place which both care providers and inspection agencies are required to take into consideration in planning and inspecting services:

- National Service Framework for Mental Health.
- National Service Framework for Children, Young People and Maternity Services.
- National Service Framework for Older People.
- National Service Framework for Long-Term Conditions.

Although these Frameworks are ultimately addressed to those who commission, inspect and deliver services, they set out important performance standards which frontline health and social care workers are expected to follow.

European Union law

The Treaty of Rome 1957 established the European Economic Community (EEC) on the basis that there would be freedom of movement for goods, services, people and capital between the countries (referred to as Member States) that signed the treaty. Under the

European Communities Act 1972 the United Kingdom joined what is now known as the European Union and agreed to abide by the Treaty of Rome and all subsequent law created by the European Institutions. Under the European Communities Act 1972 s.2(4), Acts of Parliament are subject to the provisions of the European Community Treaties. This means that any legislation passed by the Westminster Parliament cannot contravene European Community law. Where there is a conflict between European Community Law and national legislation it is European Community law which prevails. It is important to realise that the supremacy of European Community law compromises the principle of Parliamentary Sovereignty. In other words the Houses of Parliament can no longer simply pass any law they want; it must comply with European Community law.

The European Union (EU) currently consists of 27 Member States, with the result that most countries of Europe operate within the same broad overarching legal framework. For example, article 141 (previously art.119) of the Treaty of Rome 1957 provides that men and women must receive equal pay for equal work. Thus in every EU Member State women are legally entitled to receive the same pay as men for similar work. They have this right even if the Member State in question has no equal pay legislation in force or introduces legislation which seeks to deprive women of this right. Since the first treaty was signed in 1957, subsequent ones have increased the social, political and economic integration of the European Union. Many of these more recent treaties contain provisions which expand the rights of citizens of Member States, particularly in relation to employment and protection from discrimination. Indeed, much socially progressive legislation introduced into the United Kingdom originates from the European Union. The different types of European Union law are described in the box below.

 Background Information

Sources of European Union Law

Treaties - Legislation introduced by national governments must be compliant with the articles of European Union Treaties. Member States which fail to abide by all the provisions of the treaties they sign can be taken to the European Court of Justice by other Member States and forced to meet their obligations under the treaty articles.

Regulations - These can be enforced in Member States as if they were national law. They are *directly applicable* and immediately become part of national law which can be enforced in British courts. For example, Regulation 1612/68 requires Member States to grant workers from other Members States the same rights as their own nationals. So an Italian man who comes to work in Britain is entitled to the same rights as a British worker. Therefore EU citizens living in the United Kingdom will have different rights and entitlements from nationals who come from outside the European Union.

Directives - These are binding on each Member State but are less detailed than regulations and are not *directly applicable*. Instead they require Parliament to develop legislation which will implement the directive. For example, the Equal Treatment at Work Directive 2000/78/EC required Member States to introduce legislation which protected people from discrimination in the workplace. The British Government passed secondary legislation in the form of statutory instruments which now protect employees against discrimination on the grounds of their age, sexuality or religion.

European Convention on Human Rights

It is important to appreciate that the European Convention on Human Rights is not part of the European Union and in fact pre-dates its creation. The Convention was actually signed in Rome in 1950 and ratified by the UK Government in 1951. The European Convention grants rights to individual citizens to protect them from the excessive, unwarranted or arbitrary exercise of state power. This is because the government of any country has control, to a greater or lesser extent, over all the security forces and public agencies which provide services to citizens. To take the United Kingdom as an example, it has no written constitution, so Parliament can pass oppressive or discriminatory legislation. For instance, the Immigration and Asylum Act 1999 and the Nationality Immigration and Asylum Act 2002 severely limited asylum seekers' rights to appeal against a refusal of asylum, and removed their rights to welfare benefits and social housing. On the other hand, public sector employees exercising their legal powers or duties can act in ways which result in oppression, harassment or discrimination against ordinary citizens. For example, a public inquiry concluded that the police had failed to properly investigate the murder of Stephen Lawrence, a black youth stabbed to death in 1993, due to institutional racism (Macpherson, 1999).

Action can only be taken under the European Convention on Human Rights if the State, meaning a public body (or a private or voluntary body carrying out public functions, such as a private security firm employed to staff a prison) infringes or violates the Convention Rights of an individual. Generally, the European Convention cannot be used by individuals who believe their rights have been violated by other citizens. For example, it would not be possible for a father to call upon the European Convention if a neighbour kidnapped his 10-year-old daughter and imprisoned her. This would be a matter for the police and the Crown Prosecution Service to proceed with a criminal charge and arraignment of the abductor before a court. But, if a police officer arrested his daughter and put her in a police cell without explanation or charge, the father could use the European Convention to take the police authority to court and to argue that one of its officers was acting in violation of Convention articles 5 and 6, and thus acting illegally. The box below lists the rights granted to the citizens of all signatory countries to the European Convention on Human Rights.

Key legislation

European Convention on Human Rights

Article 2 Right to life - Everyone's right to life shall be protected by law.

Article 3 Prohibition of torture - No one shall be subjected to torture or to inhuman or degrading treatment or punishment.

Article 4 Prohibition of slavery and forced labour - No one shall be held in slavery or servitude. No one shall be required to perform forced or compulsory labour (excludes those imprisoned).

Article 5 Right to liberty and security - Everyone has the right to liberty and security of person (excludes lawful detention).

Article 6 Right to a fair trial - Everyone is entitled to a fair and public hearing within a reasonable time by an independent and impartial tribunal established by law.

Article 7 No punishment without law – No one shall be held guilty of a criminal offence on account of any act or omission which did not constitute a criminal offence at the time when it was committed.

Article 8 Right to respect for private and family life – Everyone has the right to respect for his private and family life, his home and his correspondence.

Article 9 Freedom of thought, conscience and religion – Everyone has the right to freedom of thought, conscience and religion including the freedom to change religion or belief.

Article 10 Freedom of expression – Everyone has the right to freedom of expression. Includes freedom to hold opinions and to receive and impart information and ideas without interference by public authorities.

Article 11 Freedom of assembly and association – Everyone has the right to freedom of peaceful assembly and to freedom of association with others.

Article 12 Right to marry – Men and women of marriageable age have the right to marry and to found a family.

Article 14 – Provides that Convention rights 'shall be secured without discrimination on any ground such as sex, race, colour, language, religion, political or other opinion, national or social origin, association with a national minority, property, birth or other status.'

Most Convention rights are qualified or limited in some way rather than absolute. To take article 8, the right to respect for private and family life is subject to justified intervention by the State 'for the protection of health or morals, or for the protection of the rights and freedoms of others'. This exception permits social workers to intervene in extreme and persistent instances of abuse or neglect to remove children from their birth parents and into the care of the State. But it is important to appreciate that the presumption under the European Convention is against interference in family life, and the State has to present evidence in a court of law to justify its intervention.

In the past any citizen wishing to enforce their rights under the European Convention had to go to the European Court of Human Rights (ECHR), which is located in Strasbourg. This inevitably involved considerable time and costs to citizens trying to bring legal actions against their governments for violation of their Convention rights. However, the Human Rights Act 1998 incorporated the European Convention on Human Rights into national law and since this legislation came into force British citizens have been able to take their cases through the domestic courts. This means that they can have their case heard in a British court and are no longer forced to travel to Strasbourg to attend the ECHR. The Human Rights Act 1998 also made it unlawful for public authorities or their employees to act in a way which is incompatible with Convention rights.

The Human Rights Act 1998 also obliges Parliament to introduce legislation which is compatible with the European Convention. If the Government does pass a statute which is inconsistent with the Convention then a judge in a British court could make a Declaration of Incompatibility and so the Government would be under considerable pressure to amend or repeal the statute. Arguably this is another instance in which law from a source outside of the United Kingdom has eroded Parliamentary Sovereignty. Of course a future government could decide to repeal the Human Rights Act 1998, but this would have adverse consequences for the British Government's relations with its own citizens and with other European nations. In other words, as with withdrawal from the European Union, a government could in theory do it, but in practice the repercussions would be so grave that few would attempt it.

Critical questions

Find the Council of Europe website and download a copy of the *Convention for the Protection of Human Rights and Fundamental Freedoms*. Look at article 9 and list the circumstances under which it is lawfully permitted for the State to interfere with a person's freedom of thought, conscience or religion. Under what circumstances might it be justifiable to interfere in a person's freedom of thought, conscience or religion? Can you think of any instances in which the police, education authorities or social services have interfered in a person's article 9 rights in the United Kingdom? Did you agree or disagree with this action and why?

International law

When the UK Government enters into treaties with other countries or groups of countries these impose obligations on the part of the State in its relationship with those other states and sometimes in relation to its own citizens. Signing the European Convention in 1950 is a clear example. However, when the Government signs a treaty usually this does not automatically make it law and instead legislation has to be enacted to ensure that the UK complies with its treaty obligations. For example, the United Nations Convention on the Rights of the Child which the UK Government ratified in 1991 is reflected in national law by ensuring that statutes relating to children are consistent with this UN Convention and do not contravene any of its articles. The Children Act 1989 and the Adoption and Children Act 2002 were both drafted to comply with the UN Convention. A number of other international treaties have direct relevance to social work, such as the Hague Convention on Protection of Children and Cooperation in Respect of inter-country Adoption, which was formally ratified by the British government in 2003. The Hague Convention is given legal effect by the Adoption (Inter-country Aspects) Act 1999. This statute ensures that prospective adopters of children from abroad are subject to similar assessments as are those adopting British children and gives preference to children remaining in their country of origin with kin.

 Critical questions

Go to **www.unhchr.ch** which is the Office of the High Commissioner for Human Rights at the United Nations and download the *Convention on the Rights of the Child*. How does this convention actually define a child? What might be some of the advantages and disadvantages of having a universal charter of children's rights which the countries of the world are expected to abide by?

Common law

Common law is also known as case law or judge-made law. It consists of the reported judgements of cases coming before the courts. Parliamentary Sovereignty means that primary legislation cannot be dismissed, ignored or challenged by the courts. If there is conflict between a statute and common law, it is the Act of Parliament which will prevail and must be followed by the courts. The court system is crucial to the administration of justice for a number of reasons. First, the drafters who write statutes and the parliamentarians who pass them cannot foresee every possible circumstance which might fall under the provisions of the Act. Therefore, a system of enforcing statutes is needed which also accommodates new situations. This is known as statutory interpretation and it means that during the court case the judge decides how the statute is meant to apply in the unique circumstances.

The court case *Royal College of Nursing* v. *Department of Health and Social Security* [1981] 1 AER 545 involved a dispute over the interpretation of the Abortion Act 1967 which provided that abortions are only legal if performed by a 'registered medical practitioner'. However, by the late 1970s medical advances meant that qualified nurses were also able to assist in performing abortions. The court decided that the provision relating to a 'registered medical practitioner' should be interpreted so as to apply to a qualified nurse. In other words the judge sought to identify the true intention of Parliament in passing the Abortion Act 1967, which was to offer women safe and legal abortions under certain conditions. In this case statutory interpretation extended the classes of medical personnel to whom the provision could apply. Plainly this means that older legislation can be updated and applied to contemporary circumstances without Parliament having to pass new legislation every time there is a technological advance or some other kind of change.

Likewise Parliament cannot legislate for every single situation and consequently there are some unique situations in which there is actually no relevant legislation and therefore the courts have to make a decision. For instance in *Gillick* v. *West Norfolk and Wisbech Area Health Authority* [1986] 3 ALL ER 402 a mother went to court to object to her daughter, who was then under 16 years of age, being given contraceptive advice by her GP without the knowledge or consent of her parents. In the absence of a specific statutory provision the judge decided that if a child is of sufficient understanding they can receive medical treatment without parental knowledge or consent. The judgement stated that 'a minor's capacity to make his or her own decisions depends on the minor having sufficient understanding and intelligence to make the decisions and is not to be determined by reference to any judicially fixed age limit'. This became known as the 'mature minor principle'. The judgement was to have wide implications for social work as a 'Gillick competent' child is one of 'sufficient understanding' to make decisions independently of those with parental responsibility.

Common law comprises a collection of judgements based on the principle of *stare decisis* (stand by what has been decided) also referred to as judicial precedent. The box below outlines the main aspects of *stare decisis* and how it affects judgements by the courts.

Background information

Judicial precedent (*stare decisis*)

- Judicial precedent is a system of law-making by judges rather than Parliament.
- Future cases have to be decided in the same way as earlier ones if the facts before the court are similar.
- The part of the judgement which is binding on other courts is the legal reasoning for the decision, which is referred to as the *ratio decidendi*.
- Lower courts have to follow the decisions of higher courts because these have precedent-making powers, the House of Lords being the highest court and the Magistrates' Court the lowest.
- Where parties to a court case disagree with the verdict they may have an automatic right of appeal to a higher court or they may require permission of the higher court to hear the appeal.
- Precedent depends on the accurate reporting of judgements, these are contained in volumes of Law Reports which are now available on-line.
- Precedent is based on a recognised hierarchy of courts.

Most court cases are concerned with disputes over the facts, that is, did Mr X sexually abuse child Z. But, the courts also have a vital role in creating law through statutory interpretation and giving judgement in circumstances where there are no directly relevant statutory provisions. The system of judicial precedent ensures that like cases are decide alike, as this is the essence of justice. Judicial precedent also ensures consistency in decision-making between the different levels of courts. The court structure is diagrammatically represented below.

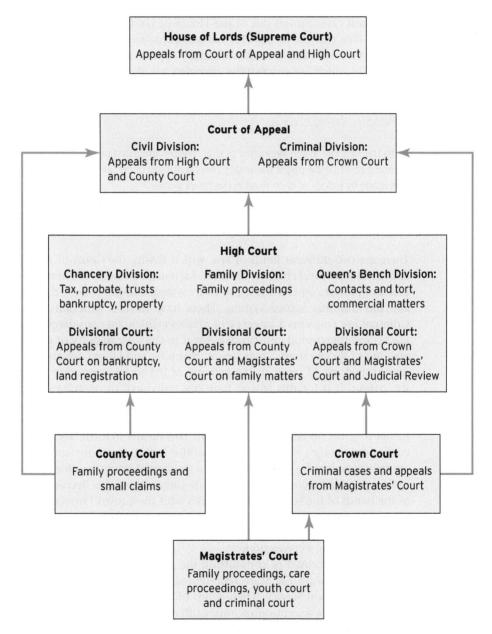

The diagram above illustrates the hierarchal relationships between the courts, with the lowest courts at the bottom and the highest courts at the top. These are connected through both a system of appeals from lower courts to higher courts and a system of precedent which requires lower courts in the system to follow the judicial decisions of higher courts. However, it needs to be appreciated that a party to a court case dissatisfied with a judgement often does not have an automatic right of appeal and has to obtain the permission of the higher court before their appeal can be heard.

It is possible therefore if permission is granted by each of the higher courts in succession to appeal a case from the Magistrates' Court to the High Court and from there to the Court of Appeal and then the House of Lords. In 2009 the Appellate Committee of the House of Lords was re-designated the Supreme Court, and the Law Lords who presided over appeal cases moved out of the House of Lords in order to increase their independence. Given that the House of Lords hears only around 60 cases a year, it becomes obvious that very few cases indeed are actually appealed up through the whole court system. Most cases which are successfully appealed are likely to be heard by just one appellate court before permission is refused by higher courts for any further hearings.

 ## Critical questions

Go to the Fact File at the very start of this chapter and examine the composition of judges in the different courts. How might the under-representation of certain social groups influence the rulings made by judges at each level in the court system?

Criminal law

There are two different kinds of law, which is why the Court of Appeal in the diagram above has a civil and criminal division. Each division hears different types of cases on appeal from lower courts. In fact the court system comprises both the Civil Justice System and the Criminal Justice System. These have distinct functions in law enforcement. Criminal law concerns a category of offences which are considered so serious that if left unchecked they would constitute a threat to the very stability of the State and even the viability of society itself. Theft, arson, maiming and killing are plainly acts which if left unpunished would result in the collapse of the social, economic and political fabric of the nation. It is for this reason that any individual or organisation engaging in these types of offences is regarded as committing a crime against the State. Hence, the State, in the form of the police and the Crown Prosecution Service take action to bring the offender to court on behalf of the victim. This means that the decision whether to prosecute or not is taken out of the hands of the victim. So for instance a service-user who is sexually assaulted by a care worker in a residential home for older people cannot decide against pursuing a court case against the care worker. This decision is entirely taken out of the hands of the service-user and rests with the Crown Prosecution Service. But if the victim of a crime, in this instance a service-user, is unwilling to provide evidence in court against the care worker, it may be very difficult for the Crown Prosecution Service to succeed in obtaining a conviction.

The person accused of committing the crime is known as the defendant, while the prosecutor is always the State represented in court by solicitors and barristers of the Crown Prosecution Service. These kinds of cases are heard through the Criminal Justice System. With the exception of minor offences, such as petty theft or common assault, which are heard before a Magistrates' Court, there is normally a jury present in criminal cases. Given that criminal acts can undermine the social and economic foundations of society, criminal offences are punishable by a custodial sentence, a community sentence and/or a fine. They can also be accompanied by a curfew or requirement to undertake a course of instruction or rehabilitation, for example attendance at a drug treatment centre. Since the punishment for a criminal offence can be the deprivation of liberty, sometimes for many years, a criminal court will require the Crown Prosecution Service to prove *beyond a reasonable doubt* that the defendant is guilty of the crime alleged.

Civil law

Civil law deals with breaches of the law that are regarded as less serious by the State and do not directly endanger the peace and stability of the nation. These types of breaches are regarded as essentially legal disputes between individuals or organisations. Therefore the law is enforced by the person who thinks they have suffered a harm or injury. In such instances the claimant (the injured party or victim) sues the defendant by taking him or her to court and demonstrating through the presentation of evidence that the defendant has caused the claimant some kind of detriment. No jury is present in a civil court except where an action concerns defamation (libel and slander) or fraud. In practice a jury sits in only 1 per cent of civil cases, the vast majority of them concerning defamation. A civil court is instead presided over by a judge or a bench of three judges who then make a decision based on the evidence before them. There are whole classes of actions which fall under the civil rather than the criminal law, some of which are listed below:

- *Law of contract* – concerns contracts between individuals or organisations relating to the provision of goods and services. It includes employment and property transactions as they are essentially agreements between parties to the transfer of goods or services. Where there has been a breach of contract the injured party sues the defendant for compensation. For example, the contract of employment between a social worker and a local authority or private residential home falls within the civil law.
- *Law of tort* – this has been developed through common law and has created a series of rights and corresponding duties between legal persons (people or corporations). A tort is an action which causes another party harm. It is based on the premise that people are not required actively to look after each other, only to avoid doing each other harm. When a tort is committed the law allows the victim to claim money, known as damages, to compensate for the commission of that tort. This is paid by the person who committed the tort (defendant) to the injured party (claimant). Damages are intended as far as possible to put the person who has suffered the harm back in the position they would have been in had the tort not occurred. While damages are the most common form of remedy in civil law the court may also issue an injunction which requires the defendant to refrain from a specified action, for instance to stop playing loud music during the night. There are a number of different types of torts, such as that of defamation and nuisance, but the tort of negligence is the subject of most litigation and is discussed in more detail later in this chapter.
- *Legislation creating civil law* – for example, divorce under the Matrimonial Causes Act 1973 or dissolution of a same-sex partnership under the Civil Partnership Act 2004 are civil matters. Under both statutes if a person deserts their partner for a continuous period of at least two years this is a ground for the legal termination of their marriage or civil partnership. However, this is dependent on one party deciding to take the other party to court. The police are not going to arrest a person for deserting his or her partner for two years. Nor will the Crown Prosecution Service take them to court. This is because desertion is not a criminal offence in the United Kingdom. Similarly, the Race Relations Act 1976 makes it illegal to discriminate against people on the grounds of their ethnic origins or colour in the provision of goods and services.

But if the owner of a restaurant refuses to serve food to an African-Caribbean couple he or she will not be arrested because this is a breach of civil law. In other words, the owner of the restaurant will get away with discrimination unless the couple who suffered it decide to take the proprietor to court for a breach of the Race Relations Act 1976. If the couple do take the proprietor to court they will be suing him or her for monetary compensation.

 ## Critical questions

Go to Westlaw on the internet, which is a database containing all the judgements of higher courts. In the field for 'parties to the case' type in *R (on the application of S)* v. *Plymouth City Council*, or in the field for 'citation' type in *[2002] EWCA Civ 388*. What is this judgement about? Who are the parties to this court case and how are they represented at the Court of Appeal hearing? Which statutes cited in the case are directly relevant to your practice as a social worker? What were the main arguments put forward by the local authority and the mother of C during the hearing? How might the judge's ruling in this case affect your own practice?

It should be clear from the examples above that civil law concerns acts between individuals or organisations which remain private matters and which the State will not step in to resolve. It is for the individuals or organisations affected to take legal action. Furthermore, the outcome of the court case will not be imprisonment or community service for the defendant who is found guilty, but the payment of compensation by the defendant to the claimant who is the victim of the breach of civil law. Since the consequences for a breach of civil law do not threaten the liberty of the defendant the standard of proof is set lower than that in criminal cases and only requires the claimant to prove the breach of law by the defendant on the *balance of probabilities*.

Summary of civil and criminal justice systems

	Civil law	*Criminal law*
Parties to the case	Claimant and defendant or applicant and respondent, appellant and respondent if appealed	Prosecution and defence appellant and respondent if appealed
Courts involved	Magistrates' Court County Court High Court Court of Appeal, Civil Division House of Lords	Magistrates' Court Crown Court High Court Court of Appeal, Criminal Division House of Lords
Composition of court	Usually judge only or a bench of judges	Judge and jury except in Magistrates' Court
Standard of proof	Balance of probabilities	Beyond reasonable doubt
Remedies	Monetary compensation and/or court order to refrain from or implement a course of action	Fine, custodial sentence, community sentence

Understanding the difference between the civil and criminal justice systems is essential for social workers. Many of their activities fall under one or other system or sometimes straddle both. For instance, family proceedings fall under the civil justice system. Family proceedings include court actions taken under the: Matrimonial Causes Act 1973; Civil Partnership Act 2004; Children Act 1989; and the Adoption and Children Act 2002. Care proceedings (court action to take children into the care of the State) under the Children Act 1989 are also within the civil justice system. In effect this means that when dealing with child abuse, social workers are taking court action under civil law. Consequently, when social workers seek an Emergency Protection Order to remove a child temporarily from his or her parent they have to prove that 'there is reasonable cause to believe that the child is likely to suffer significant harm'. But because this is a civil action they only have to prove this on the *balance of probabilities* and not *beyond a reasonable doubt*. Since the standard of proof is different as between the civil and criminal justice systems this can lead to the paradoxical situation whereby social workers are able to provide sufficient evidence of child sexual abuse to obtain an Emergency Protection Order, but not sufficient to convict the perpetrator in the Crown Court of a criminal offence. For, of course, within the Criminal Justice System social workers would have to prove *beyond a reasonable doubt* that the perpetrator sexually abused the child.

On the other hand, social workers may be either members of a Youth Offending Team or working closely with one in connection with a young offender. Plainly the contact of a social worker in this instance will be mainly with the criminal justice system and normally with the Magistrates' court sitting as a Youth Court. In this role the social worker could be required to produce a pre-sentence report, supervise a community sentence or appear as a witness. The passing into law of the Crime and Disorder Act 1998 has created an additional raft of court orders, such as Parenting Orders and Anti-Social Behaviour Orders, which are granted under the civil law, but fall under the criminal justice system if breached. So a social worker with responsibility for a young person engaging in anti-social behaviour will have to move between civil and criminal jurisdictions. Social workers initially involved in care proceedings can then find themselves acting as witnesses in a criminal case taking place in a Magistrates' Court or Crown Court if a crime against a child is suspected.

Even in instances where social workers are not directly involved in civil and criminal cases they are often working with vulnerable individuals who are subject to discrimination or violence. It is crucial that social workers who come into contact with service-users and carers who are experiencing discrimination or suffering harassment or violence are sufficiently conversant with the civil and criminal justice systems to be able to recognise when an offence or breach of the law is being committed. They also need to know the range of possible remedies and to advise the service-user or carer accordingly. Social workers are not qualified to give legal advice, but they are required under the GSCC Code of Practice 3.1 to assist those they work with to 'understand and exercise their rights'. The rights and entitlements of service-users, carers, parents and children are enshrined in legislation and common law. Social workers must have a working knowledge of them if they are to inform and empower the vulnerable people they assist.

Family Law Proceedings

Family Law Proceedings are usually heard by a bench of three lay magistrates, or it may be only one judge if heard in a higher court. Care Proceedings, which are brought by local authorities against parents and involve legal intervention to safeguard children, are also a form of Family Proceedings. All the parties to the court case (with the exception of the child) are normally present together with their legal representatives. Documents and witness statements are exchanged prior to the hearing so that the facts agreed and those in dispute can be identified. Evidence will only be heard on those matters on which there is disagreement, these are referred to as the *facts in issue*. The box below outlines the procedures involved in starting a court case and proceeding with it in court.

 Background information

Outline of procedures in Family Law Proceedings

Pre-hearing

1 Initial application outlines case - there are a number of standard pro forma which will differ depending on the civil case being pursued. This is lodged with the court.

2 Filing of witness statements - those who are to give evidence complete written statements of what they intend to say in court.

3 Filing of relevant documentation - other forms of evidence, for example copies of letters sent by a social worker to a parent, the photograph of an injury, correspondence exchanged between a divorcing couple.

4 Filing of reports - often specialists such as clinical psychologists or occupational therapists are commissioned to provide expert reports.

5 Exchange of statements and reports - the evidence above is exchanged between all the parties to the court case so everyone is aware of the evidence to be presented at the actual court hearing.

During hearing

6 Applicant's lawyer outlines case - for example in care proceedings the solicitor for the local authority will commence by explaining the local authority's reason for seeking to remove a child into care.

7 Eridence-in-chief - each party to the court case will have the opportunity to present their evidence, which normally involves highlighting the points they have already made in their witness statement.

8 Cross-examination - each party to the case can be cross-examined by the legal representative of another party. This consists of a close questioning of the evidence-in-chief and identifying any inconsistencies or requesting fuller explanations of particular points.

9 Re-examination - each party can then be re-examined by their own legal representative, who obviously is likely to be more sympathetic in their line of questioning.

10 Judgement - as Family Law Proceedings are within the Civil Justice System there is no jury and it is for the judge or bench of judges to weigh the evidence and make a ruling.

Youth Court

Youth Courts, which are part of the Magistrates' Court, try those aged 10–17 years. They deliberate on less serious criminal offences such as petty theft and minor physical assaults. Young people accused of more serious crimes, such as rape or murder, are committed to the Crown Court for trial. Youth Courts have no jury and so magistrates are required both to decide the guilt or innocence of a defendant and their sentence if found guilty. Parents are often required to attend court alongside the child who is accused of a crime. Where young people have an allocated social worker, he or she will normally attend court as well. The box below outlines the way in which a criminal case is instigated and how it proceeds once the matter comes before a Youth Court.

 Background information

Outline of procedures in Youth Court

Pre-hearing

1 Arrest for a criminal offence – person is arrested by the police for a criminal offence.

2 Charged with a criminal offence – the Crown Prosecution Service decides if there is sufficient evidence to pursue a successful prosecution and if this is in the public interest.

3 Committal hearing – Magistrates' Court decides whether the case will be tried in the Youth Court or the Crown Court.

4 Filing of evidence with the court.

5 Evidence is exchanged between the prosecution and the defence.

During hearing

6 Prosecution lawyer outlines case – a solicitor or barrister from the Crown Prosecution Service summarises the case against the defendant.

7 Evidence-in-chief – the prosecution calls witnesses and questions them about their evidence.

8 Cross-examination – the defence questions the evidence presented by the prosecution's witnesses.

9 Re-examination – the prosecution asks further questions of the witnesses it has called.

10 Defence presents case – the defence presents evidence to rebut that of the prosecution. The defence may also call witnesses including the testimony of the accused person.

11 Cross-examination and re-examination of defence witnesses.

12 Summing up by defence lawyer – the defence highlights the main points in the defence case.

13 Verdict – magistrates make a determination on guilt or innocence and decide the sentence if the accused is found guilty.

Alternatives to the courts

Tribunals

Tribunals are created by legislation and enable citizens to enforce many of their rights and entitlements without having to go to court. They are designed as alternatives to the enforcement of law through the court system and generally permit easy access to a prompt hearing at low cost. There are almost one hundred different types of tribunal, which collectively deal with more cases than the courts. Each tribunal is tailored to hear disputes in relation to specific legal rights and duties. The tribunal system is used to address an extremely wide range of matters. For example, the Mental Health Act 1983 set up a tribunal which has powers to review the compulsory detention of mental health patients in hospital. Employment Tribunals were created under the Employment Tribunals Act 1996 to settle disputes between employers and employees. The cases coming before an Employment Tribunal can include matters relating to discrimination at work as well as breaches of employment contracts in relation to conditions of service.

The make-up of tribunals differs depending on its statutory regulation and functions. For example the panel of an Employment Tribunal consists of three people: a chairperson, who must be a barrister or solicitor of seven years' experience, and two lay people, one representing employer interests and the other employee interests. Appeal is to the Employment Appeal Tribunal and from there further appeals are to the civil courts. Normally people represent themselves at tribunals and public funds are not available to meet costs. Exceptionally, for some tribunals state funding is available to the parties. For example, because the tribunal established under the Mental Health Act 1983 deals with the detainment of people in hospital against their will, a specialist solicitor represents mental health patients appearing before it. Originally appeal from what used to be called the Mental Health Review Tribunal was by way of a civil action in the High Court.

Tribunals make a range of decisions which may involve reversing an earlier decision if the tribunal is a form of appeal. For instance, the Housing Benefit Review Board hears appeals regarding the award of Housing Benefit. The Exclusion Appeal Panel hears appeals against the exclusion of a pupil from school. A number of tribunals have the power to award compensation to those wrongfully treated. For example, the Employment Tribunal can award damages, which have to be paid by the employer, to an employee who has suffered discrimination in the workplace. The function and powers of each tribunal depend on the primary or secondary legislation which established it and regulates its remit.

The ever-growing and ad hoc introduction of tribunals under different statutes and with different functions led to a lack of consistency in procedures and the administration of justice. This in turn spurred the government to enact the Tribunals, Courts and Enforcement Act 2007 in an effort to streamline the tribunal system and enforce standards. This statute covers most tribunals and introduces a two-level structure of First-Tier Tribunals which will hear matters at first instance and Upper Tribunals to which appeals can be made from First-Tier Tribunals. The new system will generally mean relatively minor administrative changes to existing tribunals and will create some name changes. For instance the Mental Health Review Tribunal becomes the First-Tier for Mental Health Review.

 Critical commentary

Tribunals

Originally conceived as offering informality, most tribunals now have a lawyer as the chair and often issues can be exceedingly technical. This reflects the growing amount of legislation and regulation in many areas presided over by tribunals. Increasingly, one party or both parties may choose to be legally represented by a solicitor at the tribunal, which plainly detracts from the rationale behind tribunals as being low-cost alternatives to the court system. Exacerbating this situation is the disadvantage and inherent unfairness which will ensue if only one party is legally represented while the other person is left to represent himself or herself (Brammer, 2007: 70-1).

Tribunals are specialist by nature, each being set up to adjudicate on a particular area of dispute, such as employment, social security or asylum applications. Yet, despite the considerable power of tribunals and the ramifications of their decisions, many do not have a system of precedent and therefore their decisions can occasionally be inconsistent. As not all panel members are trained professionals and strict rules of evidence are relaxed, a tribunal hearing can at times be inadequate resulting in some poor decision-making. For this reason a number of tribunal decisions have ended up in the court system as judicial review cases.

Access to tribunals is intended to be quick and easy, but can sometimes be hampered by the sheer number of cases being dealt with by a tribunal. Inevitably this leads to delays for individual applicants. The geographical accessibility of some tribunals has also been a factor in deterring people from pursuing their claims through them. For example, until recently there were approximately 150 Social Security Appeal Tribunals, but only about 10 Mental Health Review Tribunals (Leyland and Anthony, 2005: 191-2). As a result once an application is made to a tribunal, there can be many months of waiting before the matter is actually heard.

Alternative dispute resolution

There are a number of organisations which assist parties in dispute with each other to resolve their differences or agree to out-of-court settlements without having to access the tribunal or court system. Indeed, recent changes to the law in the administration of civil cases in the courts encourage the parties to consider arbitration or mediation before coming into court. For example, the Advisory, Conciliation and Arbitration Service (ACAS) can mediate between employers and employees during industrial disputes. Where individual workers appear to be the subject of unfair dismissal it can also negotiate between them and their employer before matters reach an Employment Tribunal. In the area of family law there are a number of voluntary sector organisations which offer out-of-court mediation services to divorcing or separating couples to help them resolve differences and agree on financial provision and the care of their children. Indeed, couples seeking a divorce or dissolution to a civil partnership are required to engage in some form of mediation before having their case heard in court. For those requesting public funds through legal aid, it is a mandatory requirement.

Complaints procedures

Service-users, carers, parents and children are on the receiving end of professional decision-making and service provision. Sometimes they may feel that the decisions made in relation to them are wrong or that social and healthcare professionals are ignoring basic facts in arriving at their conclusions. They may discover that the service they are receiving is of poor quality or infringes their dignity or privacy. In these circumstances those who come into contact with social services and social care workers may wish to complain about the treatment they are receiving. Social services and health services have separate routes for complaints.

Complaints against statutory social services by adults

The Health and Social Care (Community Health and Standards) Act 2003 gives the Secretary of State the power to make regulations concerning the complaints procedures set up by local authorities and the Commission for Social Care Inspection. The Local Authority Social Services Complaints (England) Regulations 2006 SI1681 sets out the regulations for complaints procedures for local authority social services. The related guidance issued by the Department of Health (2006) *Learning from Complaints: Social Services Complaints Procedure for Adults* stipulates that:

- The local authority appoint a complaints manager.
- Information on complaints procedures be publicised and available to service-users.
- Complaints can only be made by a person (or their representative) to whom the local authority has the power or the duty to provide services.
- A complaint must be made within twelve months of the matter complained of.
- The local authority investigates the complaint in the first instance.

Complaints may relate to any of the following:

- Disputed decision
- Quality of the service
- Cost of service
- Delay in decision making
- Behaviour of staff

The complaints procedure has three stages:

Stage one – local resolution

The complaint may be oral or in writing including electronically. It should be resolved if possible by the frontline manager. The service-user is entitled to take the complaint to the next stage if they do not wish it to be resolved at stage one. Service-users should be supported to make their complaint and advised of independent advocates, self-help groups, etc. Staff should endeavour to address the complaint within 10 working days, but not more than 20 working days. Where the issue is resolved at stage one a letter detailing the resolution should be sent to the service-user/representative.

Stage two – investigation

Where resolution cannot be achieved at stage one, or the complainant is dissatisfied with the outcome, or either party decides to skip stage one, then the complaint is dealt with through investigation. At stage two the complaint must be recorded in writing and the complaints manager must be made aware of it. The complaints manager, who should not be part of line management for social services, must arrange for a full investigation. An investigating officer may be appointed to conduct the enquiry, which should be completed within 25 days, or 65 days if there are extenuating circumstances. An investigation report must be produced and the outcome of this report sent in writing to the service-user and/or their representative.

Stage three – review panel

Where stage two has been concluded and the complainant is still dissatisfied he or she can ask for a review of the investigation report and the decision reached in stage two. The panel should be made up of three people and allow equal access to all parties to the complaint. No panel member can be an employee or the partner of an employee of the local authority considering the complaint. The panel must be held within 30 days of receiving a request for a review.

Complaints against statutory social services by children

Guidance for the complaints procedure for children is provided by Department for Education and Skills (2006) *Getting the Best from Complaints: Social Care Complaints and Representations for Children, Young People and Others*. There are three stages to the complaints procedure which are similar to those for adults. However, the procedure for children combines representations (positive comments on the service or ideas for improvement) which are not criticisms and complaints. All representations are dealt with at stage one.

Complaints may be made about:

- Services delivered to children.
- Decisions made about children.
- Assessments made on children.
- Reports written about children.
- Matters relating to adoption.

Complaints may only be made by:

- Any child or young person (or their parent or person with parental responsibility) looked after by the local authority.
- Any child or young person (or their parent or person with parental responsibility) who is not looked after by the local authority but is in need.
- Any local authority foster carer.
- Children leaving care.
- Special guardians.
- Any child or young person who may be adopted and their parents or guardians.
- Persons waiting to adopt a child.
- Adopted persons, their parents and natural parents.
- Any person which the local authority deems has 'sufficient interest' in the child.

Where a complaint is received on behalf of a child, the local authority must check that the child is in agreement and if the person acting for the child is suitable to act in this capacity. A child making a complaint on his or her own behalf will be entitled to advocacy support and should be informed of this and assisted to avail of it.

 Perspectives

Users on complaints procedures

The Commission for Social Care Inspection (2005) asked young people about their reactions to the new complaints procedure for children which was being introduced. Many children found it difficult to distinguish between the notion of an informal complaint and a formal procedure. As one child put it to the researchers, 'What are you asking us about complaining for? We all know how to do that.' Meaning that children know how to complain on a day-to-day basis about something they do not like.

Young people who were *looked after* by Children's Services expressed difficulty making more serious complaints because of anxiety about the consequences. One child said, 'Making a

▶

complaint makes you stressed and things just get worse.' Another, endorsing this viewpoint, added, 'The complaints system is intimidating and makes you worried about what will happen if you complain.' Added to this were concerns over some of the pro forma that children could use to voice a complaint. As one young person pointed out, using these would mean asking a foster carer to help fill out a form to complain about them (Commission for Social Care Inspection, 2005: 6).

Although many young people thought that their social worker was the best person to complain to, some found that either they were difficult to contact or took too long to react. A young person claimed, 'You leave a message and they don't call back' (Commission for Social Care Inspection, 2005: 6). One young person said in frustration, 'If it's not working out, it takes so long to find something else, so you say nothing.' In a similar vein another added, 'You make a complaint once and nothing happens, so you don't make another one.' A number of young people expressed exasperation with the complaints procedure. One said, 'All I see are bits of paper coming out.' Another young person described being ignored when trying to complain and being told, 'That is what you say, but this is what is going to happen' (Commission for Social Care Inspection, 2005: 7).

Complaints against the National Health Service

The National Health Service (Complaints) Regulations 2004 SI No. 1768 lays down the criteria for the NHS complaints procedure. This is available to patients or anyone 'who is affected by or likely to be affected by the action, omission or decision of the NHS body which is the subject of the complaint' (reg. 8). Therefore a close relative of a patient may also be entitled to make a complaint. The Department of Health's (2004) *Guidance to support implementation of the National Health Service (Complaints) Regulations, 2004* provides detailed instruction on the implementation of this secondary legislation. The NHS complaints procedure is separate from that of social care. Where part or all of the complaint relates to the actions of Social Services the NHS complaints manager must refer it to Social Services where it will be dealt with under the complaints procedures outlined above. Where a complaint is being dealt with under both the NHS and Social Services' complaints procedures, both agencies must liaise to ensure a coordinated response. The NHS procedure requires a complaint to be made within six months of the matter being complained about and consists of two stages.

Stage 1 Complaints can be made orally or in writing and must be recorded by the complaints manager. The complaint must be acknowledged and the complainant informed of the Independent Complaints Advocacy Services (ICAS) which help individuals to bring complaints against the NHS. The designated complaints manager in the organisation must thoroughly investigate the matter complained of and inform the complainant of the outcome of the investigation and any subsequent action which the NHS body intends to take.

Stage 2 If the complainant is dissatisfied with the response at stage 1 he or she can proceed to stage 2. This is the independent review stage and is conducted by the Healthcare Commission. The request for an independent review must normally be made within two months of completion of stage 1. On receiving a request the Healthcare Commission can: take no action; refer the matter back to the NHS body for further investigation; conduct a further investigation itself; or refer the matter to the Health Service Ombudsman or the General Medical Council for their deliberations.

Complaints against voluntary and private sector providers

Where the provider is from the private or voluntary sector, service provision is regulated by National Minimum Standards under the Care Standards Act 2000. These stipulate that service providers must have in place a complaints procedure. So, for example, an adult living in a private residential home who was dissatisfied with his or her care would avail of that care home's complaints procedure. Since putting in place a complaints procedure is a requirement of National Minimum Standards for residential care homes, a manager failing to establish a complaints procedure or to respond to a resident's complaint would be in breach of these standards. Consequently, the resident could report the care home to the Commission for Social Care Inspection, which ultimately could de-register the home for a breach of National Minimum Standards. The box below details the typical standards for complaints procedures taken from Department of Health (2003b) *Care Homes for Adults (18–65) and Supplementary Standards for Care Homes Accommodating Young People Aged 16 and 17: National Minimum Standards*.

 Key guidance

Care homes for adults (18–65): National Minimum Standards

Standard 22.1: The registered person ensures that there is a clear and effective complaints procedure, which includes the stages of, and time scales for, the process, and that service users know how and to whom to complain.

Standard 22.2: The registered manager and staff listen to and act on the views and concerns of service users and others, and encourage discussion and action on issues raised by service users before they develop into problems and formal complaints.

Standard 22.3: The home's complaints procedure has been given and/or explained to each service user in an appropriate language/format, including information for referring a complaint to the [Commission for Social Care Inspection] at any stage should the complainant wish to do so.

Standard 22.4: All complaints are responded to within 28 days.

Standard 22.5: Service users, if they wish, can make a complaint one-to-one with a staff member of their choice, and/or are helped to access local independent advocacy, independent interpreters/communication support workers and/or appropriate training.

Standard 22.7: A record is kept of all issues raised or complaints made by service users, details of any investigation, action taken and outcome; and this record is checked at least three-monthly.

Service-users or carers dissatisfied with the response of a private or voluntary sector service provider to their complaint may then refer this to Social Services. They can only do this if Social Services were responsible for the original assessment of need or arrangement of the service. Otherwise their only recourse is to the Commission for Social Care Inspection. Alternatively, if there has been a breach of contract relating to service provision to the person or the commission of a tort against him or her by the service provider, then the victim has recourse to the civil courts. Where a crime has been committed, such as a sexual assault by a care worker in a residential home, then the victim or their relatives can report this to the police who will investigate.

Local Government Ombudsman

Ombudsmen are commissioners appointed to oversee the proper administration of different aspects of central and local government functions. There are a number of different commissioners who deal with different aspects of the public sector. For example:

- Prison Ombudsman – deals with complaints against the prison service.
- Legal Services Ombudsman – deals with complaints against legal professionals.
- Health Services Ombudsman – deals with complaints concerning GPs, health authorities and trusts.
- Local Government Ombudsman (Commissioners for Local Administration) – deals with complaints against local authorities including housing, education and social services.

The Local Government Act 1974 Part III established the Commissioners for Local Administration in England and Wales. They are empowered under s.25 of this Act to investigate any local authority. Under s.29 they have the same powers as the High Court to require documentation, attendance and examination of witnesses. Their services are provided free of charge to the complainant, and the local authority must publicise the ombudsman's decision. The ombudsman may direct the local authority to put right the matter complained of and where this is not possible, or harm has been caused to the complainant, an amount of compensation may be suggested. The decisions of the Local Government Ombudsman (LGO) are not legally binding on the local authority, but generally local authorities do comply because of the public nature of the decision. Where a local authority fails to comply with the ombudsman's recommendations the LGO can issue a second report highlighting this failure, which in turn compels a local authority to respond publicly. However, certain statutory requirements must be met regarding the nature of the complaint before the Local Government Ombudsman can pursue an investigation on behalf of a complainant.

Key legislation

The Local Government Act 1974

- All complaints must be in writing and made by members of the public who claim to have sustained injustice due to maladministration by or on behalf of an authority (s.26).
- Normally the complaint must be made within 12 months of the incident which is the source of the complaint (s.26(4)). However, the Local Government Ombudsman does have discretion to accept complaints outside of this time limit.
- The ombudsman cannot investigate where there is a right of appeal to a tribunal or court unless it is unreasonable to expect the complainant to resort to such a course of action due to time and expense or for some other reason (s.26(6)).
- The ombudsman cannot investigate a complaint unless it has first been drawn to the attention of the local authority normally by means of an official complaint (s.26(5)).
- The ombudsman cannot investigate or question the decision of a local authority when the power or discretion to make that decision is vested in the local authority (s.34(3)).

Service-users, carers or parents who have pursued a formal complaint through the three stages of the statutory complaints procedure may still be dissatisfied with the outcome or indeed they may have a criticism about the complaints process itself. If an individual in this situation has exhausted the complaints procedure of the agency against which they are complaining they can take their complaint a stage further to the Local Government Ombudsman. In some circumstances, for example a complete breakdown of trust, the LGO will investigate even if a complainant has not gone through all three stages of the complaints procedure provided by Social Services. Complaints to the LGO cannot be solely on the grounds that the service-user, carer, parent or child disagrees with the decision of Adult Social Services or Children's Services or some other local government department. The ombudsman can only investigate a complaint which concerns how a decision was arrived at, as opposed to the decision itself. Maladministration concerns the manner in which decisions are reached and implemented by the local authority and includes:

- rudeness;
- delay;
- inconsistency;
- disregard of guidance;
- bias or discrimination;
- refusal to answer reasonable questions;
- failure to implement administrative rules and procedures.

Where the Local Government Ombudsman finds the local authority guilty of any of the above practices the LGO can make a number of recommendations. These can include requiring the local authority to change some aspect of its administrative procedures, provided these do not contravene statutory policy and practice guidance. The LGO may also request the local authority to carry out functions which it has failed to do, for example to conduct a carer's assessment or provide a suitable placement for a child excluded from school. Alternatively, or in conjunction with other recommendations, the LGO can require the local authority to pay compensation to those detrimentally affected by its flawed decision making. Most completed investigations together with the LGO's recommendations are published and accessible to the public. So although the LGO has no power to compel a local authority to comply with its recommendations, most do so on principle or because of the adverse publicity which a published report can attract (White, 2007: 81).

 Critical commentary

The Local Government Ombudsman

The Local Government Ombudsman receives in the region of 18,500 complaints annually and of these half relate to welfare matters such as benefits, social housing, education and social care. Around 10,000 of all complaints received by the LGO are rejected because they fail to comply in some way with the requirements necessary for them to be investigated. A further 5,500 investigations are discontinued due to insufficient evidence of maladministration. This leaves around 3,000 complaints to be fully investigated. Due to the practice of local settlements whereby a local authority can agree to remedial action at an early stage of the investigation very few reports are actually published by the LGO. On average only around 200 investigation reports a year are issued detailing maladministration by a local authority. Approximately 50% of the complaints accepted by the LGO are decided within three months and 80% within six months with just 3% outstanding after a year (Kirkham, 2005: 386, 391; White, 2007: 77).

Aside from the relatively small proportion of applications to the Local Government Ombudsman that are actually investigated, Kirkham (2005) found that a major problem was lack of awareness of the Local Government Ombudsman among members of the public. Even where there was awareness, this often went hand-in-hand with a lack of knowledge about what sort of complaints the LGO could actually investigate. Kirkham (2005: 385) reports the frustration of many complainants who find their application to the LGO refused on the grounds that it cannot consider grievances regarding local government decisions - only the manner in which they were made. For many members of the public this is not an easy distinction to comprehend. The practice of local settlements can also mean that complainants find themselves pressured into accepting LGO decisions on their case before an investigation has been completed. As Kirkham (2005: 391) observes, it can be difficult for complainants to resist a consensus between the LGO and the local authority as to how a matter is to be resolved. This means that a number of complainants who would prefer an investigation to be pursued to completion and the production of a public report are denied that satisfaction.

According to Local Government Ombudsman (2005: 15) during the period 2004-05 approximately 7.5% of decisions made by the LGO were formally complained of by the individual who had made the original application to the agency. Out of these complaints just eight resulted in the LGO investigation being reopened. As there is no formal appeal mechanism against decisions of the LGO for complainants dissatisfied with an LGO decision their only recourse is to judicial review. Of course judicial review is subject to the same limitations as the LGO, since this is a form of legal action reserved for investigation into allegations of maladministration in the process of decision making and not into the merits of the decision itself.

Judicial review

Like individuals and organisations, the government itself, at central and local level, is also subject to the rule of law. Government ministers cannot act beyond the powers granted to them by the provisions in a statute enacted by Parliament. For instance, when a Parent Act gives a secretary of state (head of a central government department) the power to make secondary legislation, he or she cannot create additional rules and regulations which are clearly outside the scope of the original legislation and therefore not sanctioned by Parliament. Similarly, at local government level, local authority employees cannot act beyond the powers given to them by legislation. For example, social workers can only remove a child from birth parents without their consent if they have a court order to do so. Local authority employees who act in ways amounting to maladministration are also acting unlawfully.

It is therefore necessary to have a system of justice which enables members of the public to challenge the decision making of local authority departments when these appear to be contrary to the law or made in such a way that they constitute maladministration. As with complaints to the ombudsman, judicial review cannot be used by a service-user, carer, parent or child solely because they disagree with the effect of a decision. An applicant for judicial review must have grounds for challenging the way in which a decision has been arrived at. In other words, a judicial review examines *how* a decision has been reached rather than the *outcome* of the decision. In court the applicant must produce evidence to show that the processes by which the decision was made amounted to maladministration or were unlawful in some way.

A case for judicial review always starts in the High Court (Divisional Court of Queen's Bench Division), but can be subsequently appealed to higher courts. When reviewing the lawfulness of decisions made by public bodies such as the police, NHS, local authorities, tribunals and even government ministers, the High Court can compel witnesses to appear before it and has powers to insist on the full disclosure of relevant documentation. Local authorities, like central government, must act reasonably in reaching decisions and since the introduction of the Human Rights Act 1998 they must also act in ways compatible with the European Convention on Human Rights. Thus, aside from maladministration, failure by central or local government to act in accordance with the Convention is also a ground for judicial review. This means in effect that social workers, as local government employees, are bound by the European Convention on Human Rights. Actions which contravene any of its articles leave practitioners and their public sector agencies open to litigation by service-users and carers.

Unlike local authority complaints procedures and appeal to the Local Government Ombudsman, an applicant taking a judicial review has to meet his or her own costs and may have to pay the legal costs of the other side if the applicant loses the case. Applicants on low income may qualify for public assistance with legal costs, but this is not an automatic entitlement and will depend on a number of factors. A court hearing for a judicial review, which must be in the High Court, will cost some tens of thousands of pounds and generally requires the services of a barrister as well as a solicitor. The average case may take up to a year before coming to court, although in very exceptional and urgent circumstances a case may be heard within 24 hours. On deciding in favour of the applicant, the High Court may quash a local authority decision and offer a remedy where it has caused an applicant injustice. These remedies can include ordering the local authority to: cease a particular action; act in a certain way; nullify the local authority's decision: and/or make a monetary payment for damages to the applicant. Usually when an applicant wins a case against a central or local authority agency or employee, the High Court also awards costs. This means that the government agency also has to pay the applicant's costs of taking the case to court as well as its own legal costs. Plainly, losing a judicial review could be extremely costly for a local authority. It can have an even more adverse financial impact on a service-user or parent if they lose.

In order to pursue a judicial review an applicant must show that:

- They have sufficient interest, that is that they are directly or indirectly (but substantially) affected by the matter.
- They have already pursued all other avenues to resolve the matter, such as complaints procedure, ombudsman, appeal to relevant tribunal.
- The local authority has acted 'unreasonably'.

The nature of unreasonableness, and therefore the grounds for a judicial review, were considered at length in *Associated Provincial Picture Houses* v. *Wednesbury Corporation* [1948] 1 KB 223. This judgement established the *Wednesbury* principles, which mean that a decision by a public authority is potentially unlawful if any of its staff in coming to that decision:

- Act beyond the legal powers they have actually been granted.
- Misapply the law because they do not fully understand it.
- Take into consideration irrelevant facts.

- Fail to take into consideration relevant facts.
- Act dishonestly or abuse their power.
- Introduce a blanket policy that limits the discretion that staff would normally exercise under the legislation governing their decisions.

Contravention of the European Convention on Human Rights was made a further ground for judicial review under the Human Rights Act 1998. Judicial review falls under civil law and therefore it is up to the individual to decide to enforce their rights by taking a central government or local government agency, such as Children's Services, to the High Court. As this form of legal action is taken through the civil justice system the standard of proof will be the *balance of probabilities* and not *beyond a reasonable doubt*.

Critical commentary

Judicial review

The number of cases which actually come before the court as judicial reviews is relatively small compared to the total of applications made. Every year on average between 5,000 and 6,000 applications (claims) are made for permission to avail of a judicial review. Of these claims around 50% will be refused permission. Of the remaining 50% only a small fraction actually result in substantive hearings. For example, in 2003-2004 out of 5,500 initial applications only 350 actually made it to a full court hearing (Leyland and Anthony, 2005: 240-1). Ultimately these statistics raise questions regarding the accessibility of judicial review as a form of redress for carers and service-users, many of whom are already vulnerable or managing considerable stress in their lives.

Application for a judicial review must be within three months of the date of the action by the public body which is the subject of the complaint. This is an excessively tight timescale as any prospective claimant is first required to avail of any complaints process, review by a tribunal or investigation by the ombudsman. Consequently, many claims are simply timed out. The delays caused when seeking legal aid and awaiting a decision can also make it difficult to apply for a judicial review on time. Conversely, those on middle-income levels do not qualify for legal aid and simply do not have the funds to conduct a judicial review, which can easily cost £50,000-£100,000. In addition to the costs of their own legal representation, should a claimant lose a case they may be ordered to pay the legal costs of the other party in addition to damages (Mandelstam, 2005: 96). Time constraints in conjunction with the huge financial liability for middle-income earners of taking a case before the High Court act to limit the use of judicial review in practice.

A judicial review can only be brought against a public agency. It cannot be brought against voluntary bodies or private sector agencies. For example, it is not possible for a child (or their representative) in a Barnardo children's home to take a judicial review against Barnardo, although they could against the Children's Services that arranged the placement. Likewise, it is not possible for a homeless person receiving assistance from Shelter, which is a charity, to take the organisation to judicial review because they refused a particular service to the homeless person. However, there are other protections under the law for individuals receiving assistance from the voluntary sector. To take the example of Citizens Advice Bureaux, which provide welfare rights and legal advice, as a voluntary body it cannot be the subject of a judicial review. Complaints against voluntary sector agencies must be taken under private law rights. So if a worker at a Citizens Advice

Bureau (CAB) gave incorrect advice on a person's welfare entitlement resulting in the loss of benefits, that person could sue the CAB for negligence. The tort of negligence falls under civil law and therefore nothing will happen unless the affected individual decides to pursue the matter through the civil courts or through an out-of-court settlement under threat of going to court.

An older person placed in a local authority residential home and dissatisfied with their care could potentially opt for a judicial review. While this is not an option for someone in a private residential home, he or she could take a judicial review against the local authority Adult Services Department which was responsible for the care assessment and the arrangement of services. An older person who arranged their own care in the private residential home would obviously not have recourse to judicial review; but such an individual can still avail of other legal solutions. Negligence can be committed by anyone who owes a duty of care to another individual, and a private sector residential home plainly owes a duty of care to its residents. So, for instance, if staff at a private residential home failed to obtain medical assistance for a female resident with dementia, resulting in a further deterioration of her physical health, they could be sued for negligence.

Alternatively, if a private sector residential home failed to provide the standard of accommodation described in the contract, then the resident could sue the proprietor for breach of contract and obtain compensation through the courts if a judge awarded damages in his or her favour. In addition, the same individual could rely on the breach of a specific statutory provision. In this instance private residential homes have to comply with National Minimum Standards under the Care Standards Act 2000. Any residential home failing to meet these standards can be reported to the Commission for Social Care Inspection and subsequently de-registered, thus forcing its closure. Clearly, it depends on the particular circumstances of service-users and their carers as to whether they have recourse to judicial review or not. Where they cannot obtain a judicial review, they may be able to rely on other legal options, for instance breach of contract, the commission of a tort such as that of negligence, or failure to meet a statutory requirement.

Access to justice

Social workers, as non-legal professionals, are not required to know in any detail how court cases are funded. As practitioners concerned with social justice they need to be concerned as to how funding can affect a person's access to, and experience of, the justice system. Furthermore, as professionals who may be involved in court proceedings, it is important to have an overview of how people obtain advice and representation within the legal system. To access the legal system people need to know:

- about their legal rights and entitlements;
- how the legal system works;
- how to obtain legal advice;
- how to access and arrange legal representation;
- how to obtain funding to obtain legal advice and representation in court.

Most civil disputes are actually settled out of court and often through the exchange of solicitors' letters and discussion between the parties. It is only a minority of civil disputes that actually go to court. For example, many separating couples come to an agreement about custody of their children and financial arrangements for child maintenance without resort to the courts. Care Proceedings, when a local authority seeks a court order to safeguard a child, by their very nature involve going to court. Likewise criminal cases always go to court, but a defendant may decide to plead guilty or (as often occurs in a Magistrates' Court) may not be legally represented.

State-funded legal services

The Access to Justice Act 1999 introduced major changes in the administration and organisation of publicly funded legal assistance. Often people in vulnerable groups are unaware of the financial assistance they might be entitled to or how to access it. Yet access to justice requires access to free or affordable legal assistance.

Legal Services Commission

This is a public body sponsored by the Department for Constitutional Affairs. It administers the Community Legal Services Fund and allocates public funds for the provision of legal services. The Legal Services Commission aims to ensure that the justice system is accessible and to this end it provides information on legal services mainly through **www.justask.org.uk.**

Community Legal Service

This provides advice and funding to the public on civil law matters. Such funding and advice is available for individuals availing of the courts, some tribunals (e.g. Tribunal for Mental Health Review) and some forms of alternative dispute resolution. A funding assessment is made and claims in the public interest are given priority – for example, human rights, social welfare and family and care proceedings. Funding is only provided to those on low income, and some types of claim will not receive funding at all, such as cases involving commercial transactions or personal injury (e.g. suing the driver of a car for injury to a pedestrian). Funding may be dependent on the applicant having pursued other courses of action. For instance in family proceedings such as divorce, public funding may only be awarded after the spouses have gone to a mediation service and tried to resolve outside of the court any dispute over child custody, maintenance or property. Even if the person is on low income, funding is not automatic and will not be awarded if it appears that the applicant has little chance of winning the case. As a general rule the probability of winning the case needs to be 60–80 per cent, and the potential damages need to be twice the costs of taking the case. In addition the case needs to fall into one of the high priority categories set out below:

- Challenges to the decisions of public bodies.
- Misconduct by the police.
- Violation of the European Convention on Human Rights.
- Housing.
- Social welfare.
- Child welfare.
- Domestic violence.
- Medical negligence.

Criminal Defence Service

This funds legal representation for defendants in criminal cases. Solicitors and barristers in the private sector are contracted by the Criminal Defence Service to provide public defenders in criminal cases. Funding from the Criminal Defence Service also provides duty solicitor schemes which provide free legal advice to people who have been taken to a police station. Funding of defendants is based on the 'interests of justice' and is targeted on criminal cases where there is a likelihood of a custodial sentence. To avail of funding from the Criminal Defence Service a financial assessment is conducted and where defendants are on higher incomes they are required to contribute to the costs of their legal representation. In the Crown Court, which tries the most serious cases, 95 per cent of defendants receive funding from the Criminal Defence Service. By contrast, many of those appearing before Magistrates' Courts, are either not legally represented or have no entitlement to public funding.

Community Legal Service Partnerships

These are funded by the Community Legal Service. They consist of local networks and one-stop-shops for legal services, which bring together sources of funding, legal service providers and special interest groups. Providers include agencies such as CAB, law centres, specialist solicitors and specialist advice centres such as those run by MIND and Shelter. Often the advice and assistance offered is free or at a low charge.

Alternatives to publicly funded legal assistance

Organisations, such as the Citizens Advice Bureaux, provide free legal advice on a wide range of rights and entitlements including those relating to: welfare benefits; special education; health; social care; housing; employment; and instances of discrimination. They also provide information on solicitors and other sources of legal advice or funding. Law centres also enable those who are disadvantaged or on low income to obtain information on their rights. Law centres may specialise in different areas, for example the Refugee Legal Centre provides legal services to asylum seekers, refugees and those with a variety of immigration statuses. Pro bono work may be undertaken by some solicitors, which means they offer free or reduced fees to people on low incomes. They are often accessed through organisations such as the local Citizens Advice Bureau which makes the initial referral.

Despite the existing provision regarding legal funding and free advice, many individuals may not be on sufficiently low income to avail of public legal funding, or they may not qualify for other reasons, for example because the Community Legal Service does not deem they have a high enough chance of winning. Others on average incomes may need more comprehensive legal advice than can normally be provided through a few consultations at a law centre or CAB. The cost of taking legal action is considerable. For instance a solicitor is likely to charge around £100–£200 per hour for work on a personal injury case. Normally a barrister will be required in the High Court (where judicial reviews must start) to present the applicant's case. He or she is entitled to a 'brief' fee to cover preparation of the case and the first day of the trial. For a Queen's Council (a senior and experienced barrister) this is likely to be in excess of £5,000. Thereafter the barrister is entitled to a 'refresher' for every additional day that the case is at court, which for a Queen's Council will be in excess of £1,000. Even a relatively simple judicial review is likely to cost in the tens of thousands of pounds to take to court. This means that even for those on average income, the costs of a judicial review are likely to be beyond their means.

Due to the excessive costs of taking a case to court some solicitors and barristers offer Conditional Fee Agreements also called 'no win, no fee'. These can be used in all civil cases except family proceedings, and cater for people whose income is not sufficiently low for them to receive State funding for their legal costs. A Conditional Fee Agreement means that if the client does not win the court case he or she does not have to pay the solicitor anything. However, even if the client does not have to pay his or her own solicitor he or she may have to pay all the legal costs of the other side if they lose the case. Conversely, under this type of agreement, if the client wins the case a considerable proportion of their award for damages may be claimed by their legal representatives in outstanding legal fees. Typically 25 per cent of any award for damages will be paid to the solicitor and/or barrister if the client wins the court case. It is possible for applicants taking a judicial review, or indeed any court case involving possible damages, to take out an insurance policy so that if they lose the case the insurance policy will pay the legal costs. These insurance premiums can be extremely expensive, sometimes amounting to almost half the total legal costs to the applicant.

 Critical questions

Consider the different ways in which funding is provided for criminal and civil cases. How might this affect the access of different groups of people in society to the justice system?

Professional accountability

The Care Standards Act 2000 was introduced to give additional protection to the public after a series of scandals which revealed that social care workers had abused or neglected vulnerable adults and children. This legislation made *social worker* a protected title, which means that it can only be used by those who have undertaken regulated training and whose names appear on a professional register. The General Social Care Council (GSCC), which was also created under the Care Standards Act 2000, has responsibility for accrediting social work training courses, maintaining a register of social care workers and producing a *Code of Practice for Social Care Workers* and their employers. A social worker who fails to abide by the *Code of Practice for Social Care Workers*, which sets out standards for professional conduct and practice, can be de-registered and thus debarred from employment as a social worker. The register is public and employers are required to check it before engaging staff as social workers. The Code of Practice also obliges employers of social care workers to enforce practice standards by disciplining those who fail to meet the requirements set out in the Code. Such disciplinary action may of course fall short of applying to the GSCC for their immediate de-registration.

 Critical questions

Go to **www.gscc.org.uk** and download a copy of the *Code of Practice for Social Care Workers*. Identify a few requirements of the Code which you personally think would be the most challenging to meet. Identify the kinds of practice situations which would make it more difficult to meet some of these standards. How would you endeavour to resolve these difficulties?

Accountability to the employer

Within local authorities, social workers normally work in teams which are increasingly multidisciplinary. The person responsible for day-to-day management of the quality of work will be the team manager. This could be a senior social worker or, in the case of a multidisciplinary team, a member of a different profession such as a community psychiatric nurse or occupational therapist. Above the team manager are middle managers of increasing seniority headed by a Director of Adult Services or a Director of Children's Services. Each of these directors is in turn responsible to a committee of councillors elected to run the local authority. This line of accountability from the frontline social worker up through various levels of management to a committee of elected councillors ensures that ultimately there is democratic accountability to the electorate. This is set out diagrammatically below.

Line management for Children's Services in a local authority

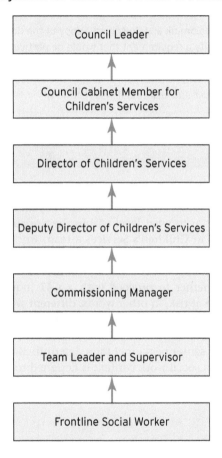

Aside from employment by the local authority, in what are often referred to as statutory social services because the local authority is required by law to provide them, a social worker may work for a private or voluntary sector organisation. Regardless of the size of the agency there will be a line management structure. This may differ as between small organisations which may have only one line manager and larger nationwide providers which have several layers of management. Above senior management in a voluntary agency will be a Board or the Trustees to whom management is ultimately accountable. Voluntary and private sector organisations providing social care such as day care, residential care or domiciliary services will be subject to the requirements of National Minimum Standards which include requirements relating to the working environment for social care staff.

Quite apart from the GSCC Code of Practice, which applies to all social workers, the contract of employment between an employee (social worker) and his or her employer (which could be a local authority, a private provider or a voluntary body) creates contractual obligations between the two parties. An employee can be disciplined or sacked for breach of his or her contract of employment. For example, persistent absenteeism or failure to complete routine tasks required by the job are likely to be grounds for dismissal. A contract of employment usually also obliges employers to provide some form of supervision, oversight or instruction to their employees.

 ## Critical questions

Go to **www.gscc.org.uk** and download a copy of the *Code of Practice for Employers of Social Care Workers*. Identify a requirement that would be particularly important to you as a social worker. If your employer was failing to fulfil this requirement how would you go about addressing this? What might be some of the main challenges or difficulties of bringing this matter to the attention of your employer and ensuring it was rectified?

Supervision in social work

Supervision formalises accountability within an agency and is the point at which agency policy and procedures are communicated by management to workers. It also serves to inform workers as to what level within their organisation various decisions are made. So, for example, in Children's Services a team working with children at risk might have a frontline worker deciding between high, medium and low risk referrals, but a senior social worker or team leader deciding whether to call a multidisciplinary strategy discussion to decide whether to proceed with a s.47 inquiry into the circumstances of a child deemed to be at risk. In other words, different workers within the hierarchy of an organisation have different competencies and authority regarding which decisions they can make on their own, which in consultation with others, or which decisions they must pass to more senior personnel for a determination. Alongside these broad functions, supervision in a social work context is designed to fulfil a wider range of functions, which are set out in the box below.

 ## Background information

Supervision in social work contexts

Supervision should:

1 Assist workers to make accurate assessments.
2 Assist workers to balance personal and professional responsibilities against agency requirements.
3 Monitor frontline workers by reviewing their decisions and activities.
4 Monitor individual workloads and change these when indicated.
5 Identify individual training needs.
6 Facilitate the professional development of workers.

7 Offer professional support.

8 Ensure high quality provision for service-users, carers, parents and children.

9 Share the responsibility of decision making in situations of risk within a clear framework of accountability.

Accountability to service-users and others

Social workers can be held to account by service-users and carers by virtue of the GSCC *Code of Practice for Social Care Workers*, which can form the basis of a complaint by a user or carer to the General Social Care Council. There are also aspects of common law which frame social work, just as they do for other forms of professional activity or interaction between citizens. In particular, the law relating to negligence can have an important bearing on the working relationship between practitioners and users.

The law of tort

As we saw earlier, a tort is an action by one person, which causes harm to another person. It falls within the civil justice system and is dependent on the injured person deciding to go to court to obtain redress (sue for damages) for commission of the tort. The principle behind tort is that generally people are not legally bound to look after each other, but they are required to avoid doing harm to each other. A person can only be expected to make amends for doing harm to someone if he or she could reasonably have foreseen the harm an action of his or hers might cause and could therefore with forethought have avoided doing the harm. The implication here is that if the harm could have been fore-seen and yet the person still commits the tort (or harm) this action is attributable to care-lessness. The law obliges each person to be mindful and to act with care towards their 'neighbour', which has a specific legal definition (see below). When a tort is committed, the law allows the victim to claim money known as damages to compensate for the com-mission of the tort. This is paid by the person who committed the tort (defendant) to the injured party (claimant). The amount of damages is based on a monetary equivalent of the harm done to the claimant. This could be physical, psychological or financial harm. It can include compensation for bodily injury, for mental distress or for the loss of employment or a business.

Tort of negligence

Although there are a number of different kinds of torts, for example that of nuisance and defamation, negligence is the tort that social workers are most likely to encounter in their practice and for this reason it is the one discussed in some detail. For a claimant to suc-cessfully sue a defendant in negligence he or she must prove.

(a) That the defendant owed the claimant a duty of care.
(b) That the defendant was in breach of this duty.
(c) That such a breach by the defendant caused the harm or injury to the claimant.

Donoghue v. *Stevenson* [1932] AC 562 550 was a defining judgement which established who owes a duty of care to whom by developing the legal concept of 'neighbour' widely known as *the neighbour principle*. Giving judgement in this case, Lord Atkin asserted that,

'You must take reasonable care to avoid acts or omissions which you can reasonably foresee would be likely to injure your neighbour.' At law a neighbour is a person 'so closely and directly affected by my act that I ought reasonably to have them in contemplation as being so affected when directing my mind to the acts or omissions which are called into question'. The neighbour principle creates a duty of care between the driver of a car and a pedestrian, or between a doctor and a patient, or indeed between a social worker and a service-user. It is because of this special relationship that when a driver is inattentive and injures a pedestrian, a doctor misdiagnoses a patient, or a social worker completes a slipshod assessment of a service-user's needs, all are potentially liable to be sued in negligence. For any one of these people could have foreseen that their carelessness would result in direct harm to their *neighbour*. It is now well established at common law that there is a duty of care between a professional and a client and also between an employer and an employee, this plainly includes social care workers and their professional relationships with service-users, carers, parents and children.

Negligence and social work

The application of the tort of negligence to social work is not straightforward and the case law on it can be confusing. Broadly speaking, common law draws a distinction between the duty of care which social workers owe to *looked after* children and foster carers on the one hand and on the other their statutory duties to investigate allegations of child abuse. For example, in *W* v. *Essex CC* [2000] 2 All ER 237, local authority Social Services placed a child who was known to have sexually abused others with a family of foster carers. The social workers responsible for placing the child withheld this information from the foster carers. The foster child went on to sexually abuse the children of the foster carers. The court found the local authority negligent for failing to disclose full information about the foster child as it was foreseeable that he might abuse members of his foster family.

A number of judgements also make it clear that social workers can be held liable in negligence for failing to safeguard children in their care. For instance in *S* v. *Gloucestershire County Council* [2000] 3 CCLR 294, a child was placed with foster parents who sexually abused the child. The judge found the local authority Social Services liable for negligently placing a child with foster parents who harmed the child. The local authority had to pay money in damages to the victims in both cases.

Conversely in *D* v. *Bury Metropolitan Borough Council* [2006] EWCA Civ 1, a four-month-old baby was discovered to have fractured ribs and it was believed that these had been caused by non-accidental injury. As a result the local authority sought and obtained an Interim Care Order which permitted it to remove the baby from the parents. It was later discovered that the baby had in fact brittle bone disease and the injuries were entirely accidental. The baby was returned to the parents and care proceedings against the parents terminated. The parents then sued the local authority in negligence for the psychological harm that they had suffered as a result of the unsubstantiated allegations against them and the removal of their baby. Despite acknowledgement by the court that the parents were entirely innocent of committing any abuse and had indeed suffered psychological harm as a consequence of the allegations, the case was held to be non-actionable in negligence. In other words, social workers where held not to owe a duty of care to the parents and therefore could not be sued.

The decision on whether it is fair, just and reasonable to impose a duty of care is known as judicial policy. This means that in deciding whether a duty of care arises the courts take into account not only the law of tort, but also whether society would benefit from the existence of the duty. In other words, judges are obliged to consider the 'public interest' in coming to their decisions. What distinguishes *D* v. *Bury Metropolitan Borough Council* [2006] from the other cases cited above is that social workers were exercising their statutory duties to protect children from neglect and abuse. The courts are reluctant to uphold claims for negligence when local authorities are exercising these statutory duties, because it would adversely affect decisions by social workers. If parents or guardians could sue social workers in negligence for initiating investigations or care proceedings in circumstances where the allegations of abuse later proved unfounded, practitioners would be fearful of taking action in the first place. Social workers would become overly cautious and perhaps even reluctant to intervene to protect children from abusive parents in case they were wrong in their suspicions. It is specifically to avoid this state of affairs that under judicial policy no common law duty of care is owed by Children's Social Services to parents or guardians and the child's interests remain paramount in the exercise of statutory duties under the Children Act 1989.

Although they cannot be held liable in negligence, social workers may be liable for their decisions under the European Convention of Human Rights if they fail to protect children who are being abused. In *Z* v. *United Kingdom* [2001] 2 FLR 612 children were subjected to severe long-term neglect and abuse in their family home. The neglect and abuse had been reported to Social Services on several occasions, but they only reacted four and a half years after the first complaint, when the children were eventually placed in emergency care at the insistence of their mother. The judge concluded that the local authority Social Services had failed to protect the children and art.3 of the European Convention on Human Rights had been violated. The State had failed in its positive obligation under art.3 to protect its citizens from 'inhuman or degrading treatment or punishment' of which it has or should have knowledge: in this instance the persistent ill-treatment of children. Damages were awarded to the children, payable by the local authority involved. Under the European Convention it is possible for social workers and their agencies to be sued in exceptional circumstances for failing to protect children within their families as well as children in the care of the local authority.

Employers' accountability and liability

An employer is considered to be responsible for many of the acts of his or her employees and is therefore held to be vicariously liable for their torts. This means that the employer is held liable for the negligent acts of an employee if these are committed during the course of their employment. To take an example, if a social worker employed by Adult Social Services made an incorrect assessment which resulted in a service-user's needs not being met culminating in a deterioration in their physical health, the social worker could be held negligent. However, in practice the service-user would actually sue the local authority as the social worker's employer and it is the local authority who would pay damages if these were awarded to the service-user by the court.

Employers of social care workers are bound by the GSCC *Code of Practice for Employers of Social Care Workers*. This Code sets out a number of responsibilities which employers have in relation to their staff and the delivery of quality services. The Code applies regardless of whether the employer of social care staff is in the voluntary, private or public sector. This Code can be used by social workers who are being asked to practise in unsafe working environments to report their employer to the General Social Care Council. In other words the GSCC Code of Practice for Employers can be used by social workers to hold their employers to account and to ensure that they meet the requirements of the Code.

Employers also have to meet a number of legislative duties to protect the health and safety of employees. These duties encompass the provision of adequate training and equipment and safe working practices. It includes ensuring that there are a sufficient number of employees to safely undertake the volume of work done by the agency or company. An employer can be held liable for failing to provide adequate supervision for a worker or endangering their health or safety. For example in *Walker* v. *Northumberland County Council* [1995] 1 All ER 737, Mr Walker, a social worker, was employed to manage four child protection teams. In 1986 he had a nervous breakdown due to stress caused by his work and was on sick leave for three months. Before his return the Local Authority agreed to provide support to reduce his workload, but inadequate assistance was provided and six months later the claimant experienced a second breakdown resulting in his resignation. The court held that the Local Authority, as an employer, had breached its duty of care to provide a safe system of work. The respondent employer had required the claimant to carry a workload which they could reasonably have foreseen would be detrimental to his health. Damages were awarded against the local authority which had to pay compensation to Mr Walker.

Overarching legislation

There are a number of key statutes which underpin social work practice across different social-care settings and work with all service-user groups. With the exception of the Human Rights Act 1998 and the Freedom of Information Act 2000, they also apply regardless of whether social workers are employed by a public, private or voluntary sector agency. These concern confidentiality, protection against discrimination and the standards of care provision.

The Data Protection Act 1998

This statute is designed to protect personal information and it applies to all data controllers, defined as any person who 'determines the purposes and manner in which personal data are processed' where 'processing' means the:

- organisation or alteration of data;
- retrieval, consultation or use of the data;
- compilation or destruction of data;
- disclosure of data.

The Data Protection Act 1998 is only concerned with information which identifies a living person. Data identifying people who have died or data which has been anonymised are not subject to the provisions of this statute. The 1998 Act covers data held in any medium on living individuals and encompasses electronic databases, microfiche, CCTV footage, audio recordings and information held in paper format. The legislation is equally applicable whether the information held identifies a living person directly, for example by virtue of their name, or indirectly, for example a service-user number. It also applies where information about a living person is held by an organisation in a set of documents which if brought together would identify the person. The Data Protection Act 1998 is an extremely comprehensive piece of legislation which will apply to most instances which involve social workers in handling information relating to service-users, carers, parents and children, including members of their families and wider social networks. The box below details the eight principles set out in the Data Protection Act 1998.

Key legislation

Data Protection Act 1998

1 **Data to be processed fairly and lawfully** - the individual giving the information must be informed as to how it will be used and must give their consent. There are exceptions to this where there is a legal requirement to process the data or to protect that individual or another person.

2 **Data only used for specific lawful purposes** - personal data can only be collected for specified lawful purposes and it cannot be further processed in any way that is incompatible with that original purpose.

3 **Data must be adequate and relevant** - personal information must be relevant and required for the purpose for which it is to be processed. Therefore agencies must not collect unnecessary information.

4 **Data must be accurate** - personal data must be correct and updated.

5 **Data must not be retained longer than necessary** - personal information must not be kept for longer than it is required and should be destroyed.

6 **Data must be processed according to the rights of data subjects** - which are:
   - Right of access to a copy of personal data held within 40 days of request (s.7).
   - Right to prevent processing (including disclosure of personal data) likely to cause damage or distress (s.10).
   - Right to prevent sole reliance on automated decision making where this significantly affects the individual (s.12).
   - Right to rectify, block, erase or destroy inaccurate data (s.14).
   - Right to compensation if an individual suffers damage by any breach of the Act (s.13).

7 **Data must be secure** - organisations which handle data must protect it from unauthorised or unlawful processing, accidental loss, or damage, e.g. password protection or storing manual files in locked filing cabinets. Data no longer required must be carefully destroyed.

8 **Data should only be transferred to certain countries** - personal data cannot be transferred to a country outside of the European Economic Area unless that country has a comparable level of data protection. Or unless: the individual concerned consents to the transfer of personal data; it is required by a contract; it is necessary to protect the public interest; it is vital to the safety of the individual concerned.

The Information Commissioner is responsible for overseeing the implementation of the Data Protection Act including enforcement proceedings and prosecutions if there are breaches of its provisions. Individuals who have been unsuccessful in enforcing any of their rights through application or complaint to an organisation processing their personal data can complain to the Information Commissioner who will take action on their behalf. Individuals who suffer harm as a result of unauthorised disclosure of information may sue the organisation concerned for damages.

Due to the special position which Adult Social Services and Children's Services occupy given their work with vulnerable groups and duties to safeguard children, secondary legislation entitled the Data Protection (Subject Access Modification) (Social Work) Order 2000 SI 2000/415 gives Social Services Departments of local authorities some exemption from s.7 of the Data Protection Act 1998. Department of Health (2000c) *Data Protection Act 1998: Guidance to Social Services* explains the implications of this for frontline social work. Broadly it means that Social Services does not have to comply with an individual's right to obtain a copy of their personal data or prevent processing likely to cause them harm in the following circumstances:

- Prevention or detection of a crime.
- If disclosure would be likely to cause serious harm to the physical or mental health of the individual concerned or another person.

It should be noted that compliance with all the principles set out in the Data Protection Act 1998 is the norm for social workers. It is only in the exceptional circumstances set out above that social workers should avail themselves of the exemptions granted to them under the Data Protection (Subject Access Modification) (Social Work) Order 2000 SI 2000/415.

 Critical commentary

Data protection

The Data Protection Act 1998 was introduced as a response to European Union Directive 95/46/EC which sought to protect the personal information of citizens held by organisations in the public, private and voluntary sectors. In the same year Parliament passed the Human Rights Act 1998, which incorporated into domestic law citizens' right to privacy under art.8 of the European Convention on Human Rights. While apparently strengthening the rights of citizens to control what information is held on them and how it is used, the coming into power of the Labour Government in 1997 also marked a policy commitment to greater data sharing between public sector agencies. This was aimed at stamping out benefit fraud; improving the protection of children; reducing risk of harm to the public; and more broadly improving quality of provision through better integration of services. The National Health Service, Social Services and the Social Security Benefits Agency have been particularly affected by the Labour Government's initiatives on information sharing.

Social policy under the Labour Government emphasises holistic and inter-agency approaches to welfare and public protection through the creation of Children's Trusts, integrated health and social-care provision for adults and the introduction of multidisciplinary Youth Offending Teams. Computerisation has also increased the potential for detailed information on large numbers of individuals to be held on national data bases where it can be accessed by many others. The creation of a national database for children under the Children Act 2004 is just one example of the increasing reliance on vast electronic data banks by public sector agencies. In tandem with this development has been the trend for health and social-care professionals to record information electronically as opposed to manually in paper files. The result is wider and easier accessibility of personal information to a greater number of professionals. Information sharing has actually become the means by which Government seeks to: reduce crime; safeguard children; protect the public; and target services. As a consequence much effort has been expended on improving the compatibility of computer systems used by different agencies to facilitate information sharing (Perri, et al., 2005).

The focus of social policy on risk reduction means that information is being shared on individuals even before identifiable problems arise. For example, Youth Offending Teams are required to identify, assess and put in place prevention programmes for young people deemed at risk of offending. This means sharing more information between agencies at an earlier stage (Perri, et al., 2005: 116-7). The Government has tended to use ad hoc statutory provisions and guidance to encourage ever greater sharing of data between agencies. This has been paralleled by governmental resistance to updating Data Protection legislation in order to ensure that citizens' privacy is protected in the face of growing information flows and ease of data sharing. Instead, central government has placed reliance on voluntary codes of practice concerning the sharing and matching of personal data between organisations (Perri, et al., 2005: 120-1).

Freedom of Information Act 2000

Members of the public, which obviously includes service-users, can obtain information from public sector organisations relating to policy or practice on request under the Freedom of Information Act 2000. This legislation can only be used to obtain information from public sector bodies and not voluntary or private sector organisations. However, it cannot be used to obtain personal data, for example the contract of employment of a social worker with a local authority or a care plan drawn up by a Community Mental Health Team. An individual must make a written application specifying the information requested. The public body is normally required to provide requested information within 20 days and can charge a fee to cover some of its costs. This means that a service-user or carer or indeed any interested member of the public can obtain information on the procedures or criteria which guide social work practice and decision making for a local authority. There are several grounds which permit a public body to refuse to disclose information which has been requested. These are where the request is for:

- Personal information.
- Documentation relating to an investigation.
- Court records or proceedings conducted by public authorities.
- Information which would prejudice the detection or prevention of a crime.
- Information which would endanger the United Kingdom's national security.

If a request for information under the Freedom of Information Act 2000 is refused, the applicant can appeal to the Information Tribunal which can investigate the reasons for the refusal and decide whether these fall within the exemptions permitted and listed above. Where a public body fails to comply with the Freedom of Information Act 2000 the Information Commissioner can take enforcement action against it. This has the effect of forcing the public body to disclose the information originally requested by the applicant.

Protection against discrimination

The Equality Act 2006 has set up a new single integrated body, the Commission for Equality and Human Rights (CEHR) to address discrimination and the protection of human rights. This body subsumes the functions of the former Equal Opportunities Commission, the Disability Rights Commission and the Commission for Racial Equality. The CEHR is required to:

- Monitor progress on equality, human rights and good relations between communities through publishing a regular 'state of the nation' report.
- Consult with all groups and ensure they have an opportunity to participate in its work.
- Promote good relations between and within communities across all sections of society.

- Combat prejudice and reduce crime affecting particular communities and to monitor hate crimes.
- Produce codes to guide good practice.
- Assist individuals to bring claims for discrimination.
- Conduct investigations of 'victimless' discriminatory activity such as advertisements.
- Issue a non-discriminatory notice against an organisation engaging in persistent discrimination and seek an injunction where there is non-compliance with the notice.

Since the 1970s a variety of primary and secondary legislation has been enacted to outlaw discrimination against an increasing number of social groups, such as women and those who have a disability. From time to time this legislation has been supplemented by

Statute	Groups covered	Type of discrimination outlawed	Contexts of unlawful discrimination
Sex Discrimination Act 1975	Men Women Trans-gendered people	Direct Indirect Harassment	Job recruitment Employment Housing Education Provision of goods, facilities and services
Race Relations Act 1976	Protects people on grounds of 'colour, race, nationality or ethnic or national origins'	Direct Indirect Harassment Segregation	Job recruitment Employment Housing Education Provision of goods, facilities and services
Disability Discrimination Act 1995 Special Educational Needs and Disability Act 2001 Disability Discrimination Act 2005	People with disabilities	Direct Requirement to make reasonable adjustment	Job recruitment Employment Housing Education Provision of goods, facilities and services Public transport
Employment Equality (religion or belief) Regulations 2003 and Equality Act 2006	Protects people on the grounds of their religion or belief	Direct Indirect Harassment	Job recruitment Employment Housing Education Provision of goods, facilities and services
Employment Equality (sexual orientation) Regulations 2003 and Equality Act 2006	Protects people on the grounds of their sexual orientation	Direct Indirect Harassment	Job recruitment Employment Housing Education Provision of goods, facilities and services
Employment Equality (Age) Regulations 2006	Protects people on grounds of age	Direct Indirect Harassment	Job recruitment Employment Education

case law which has further extended the applicability of anti-discriminatory statutes. The table opposite summarises this legislation and its key protections.

Direct discrimination occurs if one person is treated more favourably than another merely because they belong to one social group rather than another. For example, s.1(1)(a) of the Sex Discrimination Act 1975 prohibits *direct* discrimination which occurs if a woman on the grounds of her sex is treated less favourably than a man would be in her circumstances. To illustrate this: a local authority Adult Social Services arranges more services for male partners looking after a severely disabled female partner than for women in the same circumstances, despite similar assessments of need. Here women are being treated 'less favourably' as assumptions are made about their ability to care with less support than their male counterparts. This stems from the gendering of the caring role in society and the expectation that women, as opposed to men, provide hands-on care to dependants.

Indirect discrimination which is prohibited by s.1(1)(b) of the Sex Discrimination Act 1975 occurs if requirements or conditions are applied equally to men and women, but affect one group much more than the other. For example, more men than women will be able to comply with the requirement that applicants for a residential social work position undertake night shifts, due to the gendering of childcare responsibilities in the United Kingdom. Indirect discrimination of this kind will only be lawful if the employer can objectively justify the necessity for the condition. In this example, the employer would need to demonstrate that night shifts are an inherent aspect of the job and not a covert form of discrimination against female applicants. Similarly, an unnecessarily high English language requirement for a job could be a form of indirect discrimination against people from ethnic minority communities who may be less able to comply with this requirement than someone of British nationality. Indirect discrimination of this kind on the grounds of nationality or ethnic origins is prohibited by s.1 of the Race Relations Act 1976.

As regards people with disabilities, instead of a provision for indirect discrimination the Disability Discrimination Act 1995 requires employers or those providing goods and services to make a 'reasonable adjustment' to minimise the disadvantage caused to people with disabilities relative to those who are able-bodied. For instance, under s.6 of the Disability Discrimination Act 1995 reasonable adjustments mean changes to buildings, equipment, procedures or practices to enable a person with a disability to access employment and promotion opportunities on the same basis as those without that disability. An employer could be required to: construct a ramp between different floor levels within the building; alter working hours; modify equipment; reallocate tasks; or engage an interpreter. Under s.5(2) failure to make reasonable adjustments is defined as a form of discrimination against a person with a disability. Similar provisions apply to those providing goods and services to the general public.

The Equality Duty placed on public bodies by the Equality Acts is of particular relevance to social workers in the statutory sector. The introduction of this new duty requires local authorities when exercising their functions to endeavour to:

- Eliminate harassment and unlawful discrimination.
- Promote equality of opportunity.
- Promote positive attitudes towards people vulnerable to discrimination on the grounds of gender, disability, sexual orientation, ethnicity and religion.

The provision of quality services

National Minimum Standards

National Minimum Standards constitute the minimum standards for service delivery which are required by law and reflect good practice. They do not comprise 'best possible' practice, and many providers may exceed the mandatory criteria codified in the National Minimum Standards. The Care Standards Act 2000 also set up regulatory bodies to police these new provisions, with powers to de-register social care workers and care providers who fail to meet required standards. The regulations and standards introduced in the Department of Health White Paper (1998a) *Modernising Social Services* and legally defined in the Care Standards Act 2000 and associated statutory instruments apply equally to social workers and care providers in the public, private and voluntary sectors. *Modernising Social Services* moves away from concern with who provides care to ensuring the provision of good quality care.

The Care Standards Act 2000 also established the General Social Care Council which is charged to: accredit social work training programmes; register social care workers; and produce codes of practice for social care workers and their employers. It also set up the National Care Standards Commission to ensure that care providers were registered and met the criteria for care provision set out in the National Minimum Standards for service delivery in different care settings, including independent healthcare and nursing agencies, foster care, domiciliary, residential and day-care services. The National Care Standards Commission has now been amalgamated with the Social Services Inspectorate to form the Commission for Social Care Inspection (CSCI). Subsequently, Ofsted took over responsibility for the inspection and quality of services provided for children and the Care Quality Commission has now taken over the work of CSCI, which was abolished in 2009. These inspection agencies have the power to de-register providers who are failing to meet the National Minimum Standards.

 Critical questions

Go to **www.dh.gov.uk** and download *Children's Homes: National Minimum Standards, Children's Homes Regulations*. What areas of children's care does this document cover? Imagine that you are the named social worker for a child who is in a residential home run by a well-known national charity. The child is a wheelchair user and complains to you that residential staff are not taking him on many of the outings that the other children are going on. Which standard is this a contravention of? How would you go about resolving this matter? If there was no improvement in the situation for this child, how would you take the matter further?

Safeguarding adults and children

In addition to improving the quality of services, the Care Standards Act 2000 s.82 also protects adult service-users from abuse by creating a list of individuals considered unsuitable to work with vulnerable adults. This provision has now been superseded by the Safeguarding Vulnerable Groups Act 2006, which creates a single list of individuals barred from working with children and/or vulnerable adults in both social and healthcare settings. Employers of health and social care personnel are required to consult this list before offering employment to individuals. Individuals may be automatically listed on conviction of certain offences, for example a sexual offence against a mentally incapacitated adult. Others may subsequently be added to the list as the result of dismissal or disciplinary action connected with conduct which either harmed a child or vulnerable adult or put them at risk. The 2006 Act also establishes an Independent Safeguarding Authority which has the power to decide if an individual should be added to the list. The individual concerned has a right to make representations to the Independent Safeguarding Authority as to why they should not be included on the list.

Learning points

- The two main sources of legislation are statutory and common law. However, membership of the European Union means that law is also created through EU treaties, directives and regulations.
- Parliament creates primary legislation through the report and committee stages of a Bill as it is passed through the House of Commons and House of Lords before receiving the Royal Assent and being enacted.
- Legislation produced by Parliament is sometimes accompanied by Policy Guidance, Practice Guidance or a Code of Practice which directs managers and professionals as to how to implement the law in day-to-day practice.
- The court system depends on judicial precedent which means that similar cases are decided alike and lower courts have to follow the decisions of higher courts. There is also a system of appeal from lower courts to higher courts against a judge's ruling.
- Common law is divided into criminal and civil law which is administered by the criminal and civil court systems. Criminal law is invoked when a citizen commits more serious acts which potentially could undermine the stability of society. Civil law is invoked when disputes are essentially matters between individuals.
- The European Convention on Human Rights acts to curb and restrict the power and interference of the State in the lives of its citizens. In the United Kingdom this convention is given the force of domestic law through the Human Rights Act 1998.
- A raft of laws outlawing discrimination has been enacted in the United Kingdom and is central to protecting the rights and entitlements of people from minority groups.
- Parents, children, users and carers seeking to protect their rights have access to complaints procedures, the Local Government Ombudsman and the system of judicial review. These can be difficult to access for vulnerable individuals.
- The processing of personal information gathered on people by social care professionals during the course of their work is regulated by the Data Protection Act 1998. Social workers must only deviate from the principles set out in this statute in exceptional circumstances.
- National Minimum Standards, which apply to the majority of key service providers, set minimum requirements for the quality of care offered to adults and children in receipt of services.

Further reading

Department of Health (2000) *Data Protection Act 1998: Guidance to Social Services* (available for download at **www.dh.gov.uk**). This is an easy-to-follow guide for frontline social care professionals. It describes the major provisions of the Data Protection Act 1998 and explains the exemptions from some of its requirements granted to Adult Social Services and Children's Services.

Elliott, C. and Quinn, F. (2004) *English Legal System*, Harlow: Pearson. This is an easy-to-follow text which explains how statute and case law is made. It also describes the civil and criminal court systems and discusses aspects of judicial review.

Leyland, P. and Anthony, G. (2005) *Textbook on Administrative Law*, Oxford: Oxford University Press. This provides detailed and comprehensive discussion on the court, ombudsman and tribunal systems. It is devoted to administrative law and the oversight and limits placed on state power by the Convention on Human Rights and the process of judicial review.

Kirkham, R. (2005) 'A complainant's view of the Local Government Ombudsman', *Journal of Social Welfare and Family Law* 27(3–4): 383–4. This explores some of the difficulties people may encounter using the Local Government Ombudsman, and highlights the limitations of pursuing an action against local authorities for maladministration.

Useful websites

http://www.communitylegaladvice.org.uk is run by the Community Legal Service, which is funded by the government. It provides a wide range of easy-to-follow information on legal assistance for people on low incomes or in vulnerable groups who need to access the justice system.

http://www.direct.gov.uk is run by the government and offers a one-stop shop for information about the work of government. It offers a guide on central and local government work, policies and services. It also explains the workings of Parliament and the court system.

http://www.cehr.org.uk is run by the Commission for Equality and Human Rights and provides comprehensive and easy-to-follow guides on discrimination and the legislation which exists to protect people from it. It also provides a number of downloadable publications on discrimination in the United Kingdom.

http://www.gscc.org.uk is the official website of the General Social Care Council. It provides information on the Codes of Practice and other aspects of social care work. The site also permits access to the register of qualified social workers.

http://europa.eu/index_en.htm is the portal to the European Union and provides access to clear easy-to-read information on the European Union. It provides information on the law-making institutions of the European Union and how these relate to Members States.

2

THE FAMILY

Family life

Marriage and divorce: Approximately 300,000 marriages are contracted each year, of which around 40% are second or third marriages. This is just half the number of first-time marriages contracted in 1961. There are around 500 applications a year for annulments of marriage, compared to 150,000 petitions for divorce. The average marriage lasts 11 years. Around 25% of children will be the child of divorced parents by the time they are 16 years old.

Civil partnerships and dissolution: Civil partnerships could only be contracted from December 2005 onwards and therefore the number of dissolutions cannot be assessed at this early stage. During the first full year that civil partnerships were available around 16,000 took place. By 2007 this number had averaged out to 8,000 per year. There are currently 27,000 civil partnerships in the United Kingdom.

Cohabitation: Around 80% of heterosexual couples cohabit before marriage. Just over 12% of heterosexual couples are unmarried and of women aged 18-59 approximately 25% were cohabiting. The average union lasts 3 years. Around 40% of children are born to couples who are unmarried and roughly 6% of dependent children are currently being raised by couples in stable relationships outside of marriage.

Lone parenthood: Between 1972 and 2006 the number of lone-parent households had risen from 7% to 25% of all households in England and Wales. The average time spent as a lone parent is around 4 years and 25% of children live in a lone-parent family. The vast majority of lone parents are mothers and approximately 21% of non-resident fathers had not seen their children in the last year.

Reconstituted families: Approximately 17% of men will be stepfathers by the time they are aged 30 years. Just over 12% of children will live in a household with a step-parent at some point during their childhood.

Private law: As a result of the above trends private law affects a much greater number of parents and children than public law. For example, in 2005 approximately 97,000 Section 8 Orders were made compared to 6,500 Care Orders and 2,500 Supervision Orders.

Sources: Herring (2007); Ferri and Smith (2003); National Statistics Online (www.statistics.gov.uk).

Overview of relevant legislation

Look at the Fact File above which illustrates the high proportion of children who are currently being brought up by a lone parent or step-parent. Notice that annually the number of divorces is twice that of the number of marriages. Consequently the composition of many families changes over time as parents separate or divorce and spend time alone bringing up children or enter into other heterosexual or same-sex relationships. This often means that the legal relationships between children and the parental figures in their lives changes during their childhoods. As the Fact File reveals, private law cases (which only involve the individuals concerned) are far in excess of public law cases which necessitate intervention by Children's Services and the making of Care Orders or Supervision Orders. Even in private law cases, practitioners may be called upon to work with families where children are not at direct risk of harm, but whose parents are in conflict over the arrangements for their care.

Social workers may be involved in a private law proceeding to promote a child's welfare, for example if he or she has a disability. Sometimes a social worker needs to intervene to protect a child from abuse. On occasion, as the cases in this chapter will demonstrate, social workers have to intervene when the dispute between parents threatens to harm their child. A large proportion of professional practice involves work with parents or guardians and their children. Accordingly this chapter details the foundational legal concepts concerned with the family. It explores the legal implications of formal unions, cohabitation and the ending of relationships. Parental rights and responsibilities are explained both within the context of marriage or civil partnerships and when these break down. The cases used in this chapter highlight the complexity of reconciling parental rights, children's wishes and the best interests of children in the context of parental dispute.

The Children Act 1989 is the main legislation which frames social work activity with children, whether this is to promote their welfare or to protect them from harm. All children living in England and Wales fall under the provisions of the Children Act 1989 (those in Scotland and Northern Ireland are covered by comparable legislation). Section 105 of the Children Act 1989 defines a child as a person under the age of 18 years. The statute contains provisions which cover situations in which parents are in dispute and there is no social work intervention, and circumstances where Children's Services are involved. In short, any professional activity you undertake which concerns a child requires an understanding of the Children Act 1989 and an ability to work within this legislative framework. The table on next page provides a simple overview of the Children Act 1989 and its main provisions. This chapter will be concentrating on Parts I and II of the Children Act 1989.

The Children Act 1989 is underpinned by three main principles which are defined in s.1 of the statute and have the force of law. These principles direct the deliberations of judges presiding over hearings which involve children. Equally they apply to social work activity and professional decision making. The *welfare*, *no order* and *non-delay principles*, which are explained in the box below, are statutory requirements imposed on the court. Although these requirements under s.1 of the Children Act 1989 only refer to the court and do not mention Children's Services or local authorities they apply just as much to the conduct of social workers. Judges will question or criticise any social worker who fails to clearly demonstrate these principles in their evidence to the court and in the course of action they propose.

Children Act 1989	Key sections
Part I - Introduction	s.1 Definition of child's welfare
	ss.2-3 Definition of parental responsibility
	s.4 Acquisition of parental responsibility by the father
Part II - Orders with respect to children in Family Proceedings	s.8 Section 8 Orders
	ss.9-14 Matters related to making of s.8 Orders
	s.16 Family assistance order
Part III - Local authority support for children and families	s.17 Service for children in need
	s.18 Day care for children
	s.20 Providing accommodation for children
	ss.22-23 Duties concerning *looked after* children
	s.25 Secure accommodation
	s.29 Recovering costs of providing services
Part IV - Care and supervision	s.31 Care and Supervision Orders
	ss.32-34 Effect of Care Order
	s.35 Effect of Supervision Order
	s.36 Education Supervision Order
	s.37 Investigation by local authority in family proceedings
	ss.39-40 Matters relating to care and supervision orders
	ss.41-42 Children's representation in court
Part V - Protection of children	s.43 Child Assessment Order
	ss.44-45 Emergency Protection Orders
	s.46 Police protection power
	s.47 Investigation by local authority
Part VI, VII and VIII - Residential care for children	Repealed and now covered by Care Standards Act 2000
Part IX - Private arrangements for fostering children	s.66 Privately fostered children
	s.67 Welfare of privately fostered children
Part X - Childminding and day care	Repealed and now covered by Care Standards Act 2000
Part XI - Secretary of State's supervisory functions and responsibilities	s.80 Inspection of children's homes
	s.81 Inquiries
Part XII - Miscellaneous and general	s.85 Children accommodated by health authorities and local education authorities
	s.86 Children accommodated in residential care and nursing homes
	s.87 Welfare of children accommodated in independent schools
Schedules 1-15	These deal with a variety of related matters supplementary to the Act

Key legislation

Children Act 1989

Welfare principle

s.1(1) 'When a court determines any question with respect to the upbringing of a child . . . the child's welfare shall be the court's paramount consideration'

The court is required to place a child's welfare before that of the parents or guardians of the child and before any other consideration.

No order principle

s.1(5) 'Where a court is considering whether or not to make one or more orders under the Act with respect to a child, it shall not make the order or any of the orders unless it considers that doing so would be better for the child than making no order at all'

The court will not make an order unless it is convinced by the evidence that making an order would be more likely to improve the child's welfare than making no order at all.

Non-delay principle

s.1(2) the court 'shall have regard to the general principle that any delay in determining the question is likely to prejudice the welfare of the child'

The presumption is that delay in court proceedings is generally harmful to children. This presumption can be refuted if a party to the proceedings can show that a delay is likely to benefit the child. For example, a local authority might ask for the adjournment of a hearing until it conducts a vital interview to complete its investigation of child abuse and produce an improved Child Protection Plan.

There are a number of policy and practice guidance documents produced by the government which support social work practice in the area of private family law under the Children Act 1989. A number of these documents are referred to in this chapter and are summarised in the table below to provide a convenient reference.

Guidance document	Description of contents
Department for Education and Skills (2002) *National Minimum Standards for Private Fostering*	Sets out seven standards which local authorities are required to follow in administering private fostering arrangements.
Department for Education and Skills (2005a) *Replacement Children Act 1989 Guidance on Private Fostering*	This is statutory guidance which directs managers and professionals carrying out their duties under s.67 of the Children Act 1989 and the Children (Private Arrangements for Fostering) Regulations 2005.

Overview of the cases

This chapter explores the practical application of the three principles laid down in the Children Act 1989 through a discussion of five different private law Family Proceedings cases. A sixth case examines the responsibilities of Children's Services under the Children Act 1989 and secondary legislation when a parent makes an arrangement for his or her child to be looked after by someone else. All six of these cases came before the courts. The title of each case and the main issues it addresses are outlined below.

Case 1 *Re P (A Minor) (Parental Responsibility Order)* [1994] 1 FLR 578 explores the:

- Legal implications of cohabitation.
- Definition of parental responsibility.
- The welfare principle.
- Residence and Contact Orders.

Case 2 *Re D (A Child) (Intractable Contact Dispute: Publicity)* [2004] EWHC 727 explores the:

- Right to a fair trial.
- Intervention of Children's Services in private law proceedings.
- Non-delay principle.
- Use of expert witnesses in court.
- Children's representation in court.
- Use of Family Assistance Orders.

Case 3 *Re C (A Child) (Immunisation: Parental Rights)* [2003] EWCA Civ 1148 and *Re F (A Child) (Immunisation: Parental Rights)* [2003] EWCA Civ 1148 are two cases consolidated into a single court proceeding which explore the:

- Exercise of parental responsibility when held by both parents.
- Use of Specific Issue Order.
- Welfare principle.
- Children's representation in court.
- Conflicting expert evidence.

Case 4 *Re B (A Child) (Prohibited Steps Order* [2007] EWCA Civ 1055 explores the:

- Rights of the primary carer.
- No order principle.
- Prohibited Steps Order.

Case 5 *Re M (A Child) (Contact Domestic Violence)* [2001] Fam 260 explores the:

- Rights of a non-resident birth parent to contact with child.
- Wishes of child.
- Impact of domestic violence on parental rights.
- Status of expert evidence.

Case 6 *R (on the application of A)* v. *Coventry City Council* [2009] EWCA 34 explores the:

- Obligations of parents to maintain their children.
- Private fostering arrangements.
- Duty of local authorities to accommodate children in need.

CASE 1
Re P (A Minor) (Parental Responsibility Order) [1994] 1 FLR 578

Importance of the case

It examines the different legal consequences of marriage and cohabitation for parents and their rights and responsibilities towards children in the family. The case also explores how the *welfare principle* and its related list of considerations as set out in s.1(3) of the Children Act 1989 are actually applied by judges in practice to guide the decision of the court.

History of the case

An unmarried father applied to the Magistrates' Court (sitting as a Family Proceedings Court) for a Contact Order, Residence Order and Parental Responsibility Order in respect of his daughter. The applications for a Residence Order and a Parental Responsibility Order were dismissed by the magistrates. A Contact Order was granted and it was agreed that the father would have regular contact with his daughter. The father appealed to the Family Division of the High Court against the magistrates' decision to refuse his application for parental responsibility.

Facts of the case

At the time of the court hearing the father was 29 years old and the mother 26 years old. Their relationship began in 1985 and in 1988 their daughter was born. Throughout this period both the mother and father were residing with their own parents and therefore living apart. It was only with the allocation of a council flat in 1989 that the couple started to cohabit along with their infant daughter. The relationship ended within two months of taking up residence in the flat and the father moved out. The relationship between mother and father immediately deteriorated resulting in restricted contact between father and daughter. The father then applied to the Magistrates' Court for a Contact Order, which was granted, entitling him to regular contact with his daughter. A Residence Order was granted in favour of the mother, which meant that the daughter was to reside with her. Subsequently, there was a temporary improvement in relations between the parents and for some months during 1992 the father cared for his daughter four or five days a week, enabling the mother to take up part-time employment in a hair salon. The parents' relationship once more became acrimonious with the father pursuing a Residence Order for his daughter. The report submitted to the magistrates by the Family Court Welfare Officer (now Children and Family Reporter) made it clear that the child was well settled with the mother, who was providing a caring and loving environment. The magistrates concluded that the application for residence by the father was unsettling for both mother and child. Yet they also accepted, given the evidence before them, that the father had consistently demonstrated 'great love and concern' for his child. Alongside the application for a Residence Order, the father also sought a Parental Responsibility Order in respect of his daughter who was by then 5½ years old. At the time of the High Court hearing the father was cohabiting with a long-term partner near to the council flat where mother and child resided. Under the terms of the Contact Order he had his daughter to stay with him on alternate weekends and for longer periods during school vacations. The mother was engaged to be married and indicated to the High Court that she intended to change the child's surname to that of her husband's. The magistrates refused to make either a Residence Order or Parental Responsibility Order in the father's favour. The father did not pursue the Residence Order and the question before the High Court on appeal was solely whether the father should be granted parental responsibility.

Key people in the case

Father – unmarried birth father of 5-year-old daughter
Mother – unmarried birth mother of 5-year-old daughter
Ms Dooley – legal counsel representing the father
Mr Haycroft – legal counsel representing the mother
Justice Wilson – judge presiding over the High Court case

Discussion of the case

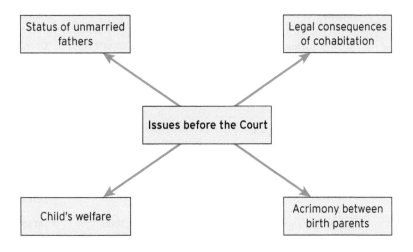

Legal consequences of cohabitation

In this case the father was not married to the mother of his child and subsequently moved to live with a new partner while the mother became engaged to be married. The father and mother mostly lived apart in the homes of their own parents and only cohabited for a few months in a council-owned flat before their relationship broke down. Cohabitation in this context refers to a heterosexual or homosexual couple in a sexual relationship living in the same household who have not been through the formalities associated with a marriage or civil partnership. Despite widespread references to *common-law marriage* (and *common-law wife*) in the media, and the assumption of almost 60 per cent of cohabiting heterosexual couples that common-law marriage exists, in fact legally there is no such thing (Probert, 2007; Barlow, et al., 2001). In other words, while marriage, civil partnership, divorce and dissolution are recognised legal statuses, which attract certain rights and obligations, this is not so in relation to common-law marriage. Thus cohabiting couples, even if they have lived in the same household for many years and had children together, often have no more legal rights or obligations in relation to each other than two friends who choose to share the same house.

By contrast, cohabiting couples have exactly the same obligations towards their biological children as those who are married. In these circumstances the parent who takes on the majority of childcare responsibilities may be entitled to remain in the family home with any dependent children for a specified period of time. In the present case the mother and child remained in the allocated council flat while the father moved out. Where a birth mother or birth father subsequently cohabits with another partner, that adult does not become responsible for maintaining his or her partner's children. This means that neither the father's cohabitee nor the mother's husband-to-be is responsible for supporting the 5-year-old girl at the centre of this court case, even if she were to live in their household. Generally, therefore, the rights which cohabiting partners have over each other rely on whether or not they had children together. This is in contrast to divorcing couples or those seeking dissolution of a civil partnership, where the court has wide-ranging powers to redistribute income and assets between the two parties. The table below summarises the main legal consequences of different living arrangements.

Implications for couples in different living arrangements

Issue	Marriage (heterosexual couple)	Civil partnership (homosexual couple)	Cohabiting (heterosexual or homosexual couple)
Occupation of family home	Right of partner to occupy the matrimonial home by virtue of marriage and can only be excluded by a court order	Right of partner to occupy the civil partnership home by virtue of civil partnership and can only be excluded by a court order	Only a right to occupy if the partner owns the property in part or whole
Taxation	Inheritance and capital gains tax exemptions	Inheritance and capital gains tax exemptions	No exemptions, treated as would transactions between strangers
Benefits	Benefits for a married couple	Benefits for a civil partnership same as those for a married couple	Generally treated similarly to couple in a marriage or civil partnership
Pension	Spouse has rights to receive pension or cash equivalent on death of partner or divorce	Civil partner has rights to receive pension or cash equivalent on death of partner or dissolution	On separation partner has no rights in relation to pension of other partner
Immigration	Entitlement of overseas spouse to apply for entry clearance to join spouse already settled in UK	Entitlement of overseas civil partner to apply for entry clearance to join civil partner already settled in UK	No entitlement of overseas partner to apply for entry clearance to join partner even if settled in UK
Inheritance	Entitlement of surviving spouse to all or part of the estate of a partner who dies without making a will	Entitlement of surviving civil partner to all or part of the estate of a partner who dies without making a will	No automatic entitlement of surviving partner to that of deceased partner's estate and any claim must be pursued through courts
Treatment of property	During marriage assets and income are owned by the spouse who acquired them, but on divorce or legal separation the court has the power to transfer the ownership of property between the spouses	During the civil partnership assets and income are owned by the civil partner who acquired them, but on dissolution or legal separation the court has the power to transfer the ownership of property between the civil partners	Assets and income are owned by whoever acquired them; on separation the court can only declare which property is owned by which partner, supplemented by trust law which in a few circumstances permits transfer of part value of a property from one partner to another

(Continued)

Issue	Marriage (heterosexual couple)	Civil partnership (homosexual couple)	Cohabiting (heterosexual or homosexual couple)
Maintenance of children	On divorce or legal separation, provision under the Matrimonial Causes Act 1973, Child Support Act 1991 and Children Act 1989. The ex-spouse may become responsible for maintaining a *child of the family*	On dissolution or legal separation, provision under the Civil Partnership Act 2004, Child Support Act 1991 and Children Act 1989. The ex-civil partner may become responsible for maintaining a *child of the family*	On separation, provision under the Child Support Act 1991 and Children Act 1989. There is no legal obligation for step-parent to maintain a *child of the family*.
Maintenance of partner	Entitlement to maintenance during marriage and on divorce, but depends on relative incomes of partners	Entitlement to maintenance during civil partnership and on dissolution, but depends on relative incomes of partners	No entitlement to maintenance

You will see from this table that the legal implications of marriage and a civil partnership are virtually identical. Partners in this situation have a right to occupy the family home and, on separation, divorce or dissolution of the union the partners have a right to maintenance for themselves and a responsibility to financially maintain their children. By contrast, partners who cohabit, regardless of their sexuality, have fewer rights over each other. In the first instance, a cohabiting partner can be made to leave the family home if he or she does not own it or is not the paying tenant. On separation, while both partners will continue to have financial responsibilities for any birth children, they will not have a duty to maintain each other. These differences in entitlements and obligations are crucial to understand when you are working with families. Not only can they fundamentally affect household income, but they can also underlie the motivations of parents caught up in disputes over the upbringing of children.

As revealed by the table above, cohabitees are not legally required to financially support each other's biological children. At the same time, if a partner's child is living in their household a cohabitee may well have practical day-to-day care of that child. In circumstances where an adult does not have parental responsibility, yet has the care of a child, for example as a teacher or foster carer, s.3(5) of the Children Act 1989 applies. This states that a person with care, but not parental responsibility 'may do what is reasonable in all the circumstances of the case for the purpose of safeguarding or promoting the child's welfare'. Hence cohabiting partners do have some responsibilities towards unrelated children living with them. In this particular court case the mother was living with a male partner who she intended to marry. This meant that initially the mother's partner would not have responsibilities towards her daughter beyond those identified in s.3(5) of the Children Act 1989. However, once married, it was likely that the mother's five-year-old daughter would then become a *child of the family*. If a couple are married or in a civil partnership and bring up an unrelated child as if he or she were their own child, then that child becomes a *child of the family*. As the table above illustrates, married partners or those in a civil partnership have financial obligations towards a *child of the family*.

If you apply the information in the table above to this particular court case it should lead you to conclude that:

- The unmarried birth father is responsible for financially maintaining his five-year-old daughter but not the birth mother.
- The unmarried birth mother is responsible for maintaining her five-year-old daughter but not the birth father.
- The prospective husband of the birth mother on marriage would become responsible for maintaining the birth mother and for maintaining her five-year-old daughter if she became a *child of the family*.

Status of unmarried fathers

The Children Act 1989 s.3(1) introduced the concept of parental responsibility which it defines as 'all the rights, duties, powers, responsibilities and authority which by law a parent of a child has in relation to the child and his property'. The rights of birth parents in relation to their children, and the obligations they have towards them, are set out in a number of different statutes, but they can be broadly summarised as follows:

Parental rights	Parental duties
• Choose a child's name	• Register the birth within six weeks
• Decide where a child lives	• Provide adequate food, clothing and lodgings
• Administer reasonable chastisement	• Provide access to medical aid
• Consent to medical treatment	• Ensure the child receives an adequate education
• Represent the child in private legal proceedings	
• Appoint a guardian by deed or will	
• Determine a child's religion	
• Take a child overseas temporarily or permanently	
• Refuse or agree to a child's adoption	
• Administer a child's property	
• Consent to a child's marriage or civil partnership if aged 16 or 17 years	

As you will appreciate from looking at the table above, parental responsibility carries with it a number of duties related to the financial and practical care of a child. It also bestows on those who hold parental responsibility a number of important legal rights. In this case, the mother intended to change the surname of her daughter to that of her prospective husband. If the child's birth father did not have parental responsibility then he could not prevent this from happening. For this particular birth father, who had cared for his daughter for up to five days a week at one point, the intention to change his daughter's surname to that of another man's must have been particularly hurtful and galling. The problem for the father in this case was that while a birth mother automatically obtains parental responsibility in relation to her child, a birth father does not. There are a number of circumstances specified in the Family Law Reform Act 1987, the Children Act 1989 and the Adoption and Children Act 2002 which enable a birth father to obtain parental responsibility. These are listed below:

- birth mother automatically (CA1989, s.2)
- birth father who is married to the mother at time of birth automatically (CA1989, s.2)
- unmarried birth father who subsequently marries the birth mother of his child (FLRA 1987, s.1)
- unmarried birth father obtaining a Residence Order for his own child (CA1989, s.4)
- unmarried birth father by entering into a Parental Responsibility Agreement with the birth mother or by obtaining a Parental Responsibility Order through the courts (CA1989, s.4)
- unmarried birth father who appears as the father on his child's birth certificate (A&CA2002, s.111)

In the present court case the father was not married to the mother at the time of his daughter's birth, nor did he subsequently marry her. Indeed, at the time of the court case the mother was engaged to marry another man. Due to the high level of animosity between the child's parents it had not been possible for the father to enter into a voluntary Parental Responsibility Agreement with the mother. Additionally, the Magistrates' Court had rejected his application for a Residence Order, which, as an unmarried birth father, would simultaneously have given him permanent parental responsibility for his own child. It was for these reasons and as a last resort that he sought a Parental Responsibility Order. During the High Court hearing, Mr Haycroft, representing the mother, conceded that there was commitment by the father towards his daughter and an attachment between them. Mr Haycroft noted that a Contact Order was in force and there was no intention to prevent the father spending time with his daughter. Ms Dooley, the barrister acting for the father, asserted that he wanted more that just contact with his daughter. He wanted to be recognised as the girl's father with a right to be consulted over her schooling, medical treatment and general welfare. These were the main issues put before the High Court.

Social workers intervene in many kinds of families comprising a variety of forms and child-caring arrangements. The increasing prevalence of family breakdown, short-term sexual relationships and reconstituted family units means that the legal relationships between adults and children living together within a household or between different households can be quite complex. Social workers involved in child protection routinely intervene in family life. To do so legitimately and effectively as a practitioner you must be conversant with the law on parental responsibility and how this can be varied or limited by the courts. As you read through the rest of this chapter and the following chapter it will become obvious just how central the concept of parental responsibility is to social work with children.

Child's welfare

Contact Orders and Residence Orders (which have been briefly mentioned) together with Specific Issue Orders and Prohibited Steps Orders are collectively known as Section 8 Orders because they are provided for under s.8 of the Children Act 1989. These four orders are normally used by the courts to settle disputes between parents or those with parental responsibility. All Section 8 Orders can specify the duration of the order, which may be for a period of months or until a child reaches the age of 16 years. They can also be applied for by Children's Services when social workers are involved in safeguarding a child. For example, a local authority might apply for a Residence Order to give a grandfather parental responsibility for a child removed from the parental home. The table below describes the effect of each of the Section 8 Orders available to the courts. This table will constantly be referred back to throughout the rest of the chapter.

Section 8 Orders	Effects of order
Residence Order	• determines the child's place of residence or periods of residence in specified places • gives the holder parental responsibility • gives the holder authority to decide all matters relating to the child's day-to-day care • holder cannot change the child's surname or remove him or her from UK for more than one month without consent of the court or written consent of everyone with parental responsibility
Contact Order	• requires the person living with the child to allow the child contact with the person named in the order • the contact can be direct, such as visits or stays with the person named in the order, or indirect, e.g. by telephone only • the type of contact can be specified, e.g. by letter only or a visit every Saturday or regular holidays with the named person
Specific Issue Order	• determines a specific issue where those with parental responsibility are engaged in an intractable dispute • does not remove parental responsibility from those with it, but delegates power to the court to make a decision on an issue which would normally be determined by those with parental responsibility
Prohibited Steps Order	• specifies actions which cannot be taken by those with parental responsibility without the consent of the court • prohibits the person with parental responsibility named in the order from exercising their authority in relation to the specified matter

When deciding whether to make a Section 8 Order or a Parental Responsibility Order the court must under s.1(1) of the Children Act 1989 ensure that the child's welfare is the 'paramount consideration'. This is the *welfare principle*, meaning that the court's first concern is the child's welfare and not the welfare, feelings or wishes of the parents. It is for this reason that when there is a dispute between parents over the arrangements for their children the court can request a report into the child's circumstances under s.7(1) of the Children Act 1989. Since the court is required to consider the welfare checklist before making any order under the Children Act 1989, the report should investigate and provide information to the court on the issues listed in the welfare checklist set out in the box on the next page.

This was a case in which Children's Services were not involved. There was no suggestion by any of the parties to the High Court case that the child would be harmed by either birth parent or indeed by the prospective partner of the mother. This was purely a dispute between parents as to the arrangements for their child's upbringing, specifically

Key legislation

Children Act 1989

Before making any order under the Children Act 1989 the court is required to consider all the matters set out in the welfare checklist which is also detailed in the statute.

s. 1(3)
   (a) the ascertainable wishes and feelings of the child concerned (considered in the light of his age and understanding);
   (b) his physical, emotional and educational needs;
   (c) the likely effect on him of any change in his circumstances;
   (d) his age, sex, background and any characteristics of his which the court considers relevant;
   (e) any harm which he has suffered or is at risk of suffering;
   (f) how capable each of his parents, and any other person in relation to whom the court considers the question to be relevant, is of meeting his needs;
   (g) range of powers available to the court under this Act in the proceedings in question.

the desire by the mother to change her daughter's surname in opposition to the father's wishes. Yet, as you will realise from the background information above and the summary of the facts at the start of this case, actually a social worker was involved. A Family Court Welfare Officer, now referred to as a Children and Family Reporter, provided a report to the Magistrates' Court which initially rejected the father's application for a Residence Order and a Parental Responsibility Order. This report described the child as settled and being provided with a loving environment by her mother. In other words this report described a situation in which the welfare needs of the child, as framed by the welfare checklist, were being met. Inevitably this report greatly influenced the magistrates' judgement. Children and Family Reporters, who are qualified social workers, normally undertake to make enquiries and produce reports requested by the court under s.7(1). The box below explains the background and role of Children and Family Reporters.

Background information

Children and Family Reporters

The Children and Family Court Advisory and Support Service (CAFCASS) was created in 2001 under the Criminal Justice and Court Services Act 2000. It is a publicly funded agency which is independent of the courts and social services. It safeguards the interests of children involved in family or care proceedings by ensuring that they have separate representation in court. CAFCASS has a remit to:

- Safeguard and promote children's welfare.
- Advise the court on children affected by family proceedings.
- Provide separate legal representation for children in family proceedings.
- Offer information and assistance to families.

Children and Family Reporters (formerly known as Family Court Welfare Officers) are trained social workers provided by CAFCASS when parents or those with parental responsibility who are separating or divorcing cannot agree on arrangements for their children. The Reporter will work with the family to resolve matters and reach an agreement (dispute resolution). Where agreement still cannot be reached the Children and Family Reporter will conduct enquiries (including discussion with a doctor, teacher, health visitor, social worker, etc., and family members) and write a report for the court, recommending a course of action in the best interests of the child.

The participation of a Children and Family Reporter in this case demonstrates how social work involvement with the court system is not confined to local authority intervention in situations where children are at risk of harm. The Children and Family Court Advisory and Support Service is staffed by qualified social workers who are appointed by the courts to perform a number of different functions. These range from mediation between parents to support for families experiencing difficulty to producing reports which assist judges deciding on the best living arrangements for children.

Returning to this particular High Court case. Justice Wilson, a presiding judge, had to decide whether the father should be granted parental responsibility and if his exercise of it would be in the child's best interests. There is judicial precedent to guide decisions of this nature. Judgement in *H (Minors) (Adoption: Putative Father's Rights) (No.3)* [1991] 2 All ER 185 set out three tests in deciding whether or not to grant parental responsibility to an unmarried father.

1 The degree of commitment which the father has shown towards the child.
2 The degree of attachment which exists between the father and the child.
3 The reasons of the father for applying for the order.

As legal council representing the mother had already conceded that the father had shown commitment and there was attachment, points 1 and 2 were not in dispute. Regarding point 3, an argument was put that if the father was granted parental responsibility he would use that authority to interfere in the mother's care and upbringing of the daughter. The magistrates had previously concluded that given the amount of acrimony between the parents, fierce disagreements would ensue. Under the *no order principle* contained in s.1(5) of the Children Act 1989, a court must not make an order 'unless it considers that doing so would be better for the child than making no order at all'. Epsom Magistrates' Court dismissed the father's application for parental responsibility because it could foresee no benefit to the child of granting the father parental responsibility. Both on the basis of the *welfare principle* and the *no order principle* the magistrates had rejected the father's application for parental responsibility. It was for the High Court, to which the father had appealed, to re-examine the magistrates' legal reasoning.

Acrimony between birth parents

Acting for the father before the High Court, Ms Dooley claimed that, as a parent, the father wanted his commitment formally recognised and wanted to be given the legal rights associated with parenthood, enabling him to play a fuller part in his child's life. However, if both father and mother had parental responsibility this raised the possibility of their disagreement over fundamental aspects of the child's upbringing. This is because under the Children Act 1989 s.2 any number of people can hold parental responsibility simultaneously and can exercise it independently of others with parental responsibility. Each person with parental responsibility has an equal legal relationship to the child in terms of exercising their parental rights and responsibilities – though, in practice, it is the residential parent who has day-to-day care and control of the child and therefore makes most of the decisions about his or her upbringing.

If the father possessed parental responsibility he could, strictly speaking, decide which school his daughter attended or what medical treatment she received, without requiring the agreement of the mother. In practical terms this would be difficult if the mother, as the resident parent, disagreed with these decisions. For example, how could the father compel his daughter to go to a school against the mother's wishes if she had day-to-day care and control of their daughter? So although those with parental responsibility are equal before the law in the exercise of their parental rights and responsibilities, in reality these are curtailed by the practical arrangements for everyday childcare.

Giving parental responsibility to the father plainly opens up potential for parental dispute. However, this does not place the father and mother in a fundamentally different position from say married birth parents who both automatically obtain parental responsibility. Deliberating on this aspect, Justice Wilson cited s.2(8) of the Children Act 1989, which provides that a person with parental responsibility cannot exercise it in a way 'incompatible with any order made with respect to a child under this Act'. Since the mother has a Residence Order under the Children Act 1989, which gives her day-to-day care and control of the child, the father can only exercise his parental responsibility subject to that of the mother's. Furthermore, as Justice Wilson observed, were there to be an intractable dispute between the parents, they could return to court and seek a Prohibited Steps Order or a Specific Issue Order to resolve it.

The parents' disagreement over a change to their daughter's surname was perhaps the lightning rod for wider tensions between the father and mother in this case. Social workers are constantly called upon to intervene in the midst of ongoing parental conflict. As this High Court case illustrates, such conflicts have a legal as well as a relational aspect. Parental responsibility in terms of who holds it, how they exercise it and how its exercise impacts on the child concerned are essential considerations for practitioners.

Judgement in *P (A Minor) (Parental Responsibility Order)*

On examining the father's past conduct, the child's evident attachment to him and his likely future conduct as a father, the High Court decided that it was in the child's best interests for both parents to be involved in their child's upbringing. A Parental Responsibility Order was granted in favour of the father.

 Critical questions

1 Unmarried fathers do not automatically gain parental responsibility. How fair do you think this is? The European Court of Human Rights has endorsed the legal position adopted by the United Kingdom. What do you think might be justifiable reasons for refusing to give unmarried fathers automatic entitlement to parental responsibility?

2 Go back over this case and examine the practical implications of different living arrangements between couples. What are the legal advantages or disadvantages for couples who are considering whether just to move in together or to marry or enter a civil partnership?

Critical commentary

Legal concepts of parenthood

The increasing prevalence of divorce, same-sex couples, short-term sexual relationships, cohabitation, family breakdown, repartnering and ultimately reconstituted families has split biological parenthood away from actually bringing up children. The law has endeavoured with uneven results to keep pace with these social changes.

Child Support Act 1991: Requires birth parents to financially maintain their children if the resident parent (usually the mother) claims non-contributory benefits. This legislation applies equally to married and unmarried fathers, but does not apply to step-parents. Biological parents, even if they have no contact with their child, remain financially responsible for them until they are 16 years old.

Matrimonial Causes Act 1973 and Civil Partnership Act 2004: These apply to spouses and civil partners or former spouses and civil partners making them financially responsible for both their own biological children and any step-children they treat as a *child of the family*. If a spouse or civil partner provides financial support or makes key decisions in respect of an unrelated child, he or she becomes a *child of the family*. By contrast there is no legal requirement for cohabitees or former cohabitees to financially support the children of their partner whether or not they treated any of their partner's children as a *child of the family*.

Children Act 1989: Treats married and unmarried fathers differently. While the biological relationship of the mother to her child always gives her parental responsibility, it is only married fathers who gain this automatically. There is a legal presumption that birth mothers and married fathers will become the social parents of their children, and their primary carers. This presumption is not extended to unmarried fathers because they can have many different kinds of association with their biological children. These can range from a child conceived by rape to a sexual liaison of a few weeks with no further contact with mother or child to cohabitation in a long-term relationship with both mother and child.

Children Act 1989 and Adoption and Children Act 2002: These enable adoptive parents and step-parents to gain parental responsibility through agreement with the birth parents or via court order. The legal procedure is the same regardless of whether the step-parent seeking parental responsibility is in a heterosexual or homosexual relationship, cohabiting, married or in a civil partnership. Parental responsibility can also be exercised by a range of carers who may or may not be related to the child. For example, a grandparent, a foster carer or a friend of the family could gain parental responsibility through a court order.

Taken altogether these legislative provisions disadvantage unmarried fathers, making them financially liable for their children, but often without giving them parental responsibility. Step-parents within marriages or civil partnerships are in a similar position. Indeed, a step-parent providing daily care for a partner's child has far fewer rights than a divorced father who sees them once a month. Despite increasing numbers of unmarried fathers in long-term committed relationships, step-parents within stable reconstituted families acting as primary carers, and same-sex couples, the law continues to favour biological parentage within marriage over other forms of parenthood.

CASE 2
Re D (A Child) (Intractable Contact Dispute: Publicity)
[2004] EWHC 727

Importance of the case

The majority of lone parents are mothers who are the primary carer for their child. This case examines the consequences for children when a resident parent refuses to comply with a Contact Order. It also demonstrates the damage which can occur to relationships when the *non-delay principle* is ignored.

History of the case

The father applied for a Contact Order in respect of his 2-year-old daughter in 1998 after he and his wife separated. The mother persistently frustrated the father's contact. Over a five-year period 43 separate court hearings were conducted before 16 different judges sitting in Magistrates', County and High Courts. In 2004, at a final hearing, the High Court delivered a public judgement having already handed down judgement in private to protect the anonymity of the parties to the case.

Facts of the case

The father and mother were married and in 1996 a baby daughter was born. During 1998 the couple separated and the mother petitioned for and was granted a divorce. In the same year a Residence Order was granted to the mother and a Contact Order to the father specifying that he was to have contact with his daughter from 10.00 am to 5.45 pm every Saturday. Within six months the mother had made it so difficult for father to meet his daughter under the Contact Order that the mother was threatened with imprisonment for defying a court order. Her recalcitrance persisted and she was given a seven-day suspended sentence by a County Court judge in April 2000. She continued to frustrate the father's contact and was given fourteen days' imprisonment in February 2001 by another County Court judge. At this point the mother reluctantly complied with the requirement for contact with the father which by then had been reduced by the court to only 2 hours a week at a contact centre. This followed a series of allegations by the mother against the father including: that he subjected her to domestic violence; threatened to remove the child from the UK; that he had broken contact arrangements; and that the child was frightened of him because he chastised her. All of these allegations proved unfounded over a series of subsequent court hearings. But the result of them was to lead judges to vary the Contact Order to reduce contact pending investigation. The father's response was to make several applications for a Residence Order in his favour. In a hearing on 20 February 2001 the acrimony between the parents and its detrimental affect on their child caused the judge to request a s.37 report under the Children Act 1989, which initiated Social Services involvement in the case. Expert reports were also obtained at different points in time from a Court Welfare Officer (Children and Family Reporter) on the child's welfare, a consultant clinical psychologist on the father and a consultant psychiatrist on the mother. Only during the 37th court hearing, in April 2002, was an order made to appoint a Children's Guardian to separately represent the best interests of the child in further hearings. Throughout this period there were repeated adjournments of scheduled hearings causing considerable delay in the progress of the litigation. Direct contact between father and daughter ceased in October 2001 and later variations of the

Contact Order only permitted minimal indirect contact through weekly and then fort-nightly cards and letters. Despite the complexity of the situation and the detrimental effect on both father and daughter, a Family Assistance Order requiring social work inter-vention with the family was not made until January 2003. By the time of the final High Court hearing in November 2003 the father had not seen his daughter for two years. It also appeared that the mother had prejudiced her daughter against her father with the re-sult that she refused to see him.

Key people in the case

Father – married father now divorced
Mother – birth mother divorced from father
Daughter – child aged 8 at the time of the court case
Justice Munby – presiding judge in the High Court case

Discussion of the case

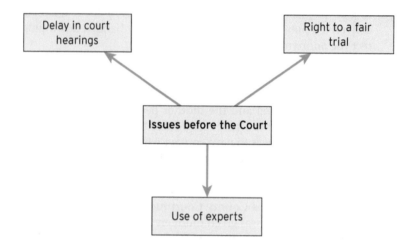

Delay in court hearings

In addition to the *welfare principle* and the *no order principle* codified respectively in s.1(1) and s.1(5) of the Children Act 1989, there is the *non-delay principle* contained in s.1(2). This requires courts to observe 'the general principle that any delay in determining the question is likely to prejudice the welfare of the child'. The courts have a system of case management which rationalises the way in which cases are listed for hearing and ensures that matters which are related are consolidated and heard before the same court. For ex-ample, if there was a complex divorce proceeding taking place in the Family Division of the High Court and an application for a Contact Order before magistrates in a Family Proceedings Court, both touching upon the same child, the two matters would be consol-idated and heard in the High Court. This case illustrates the devastating consequences for parent and child when there is a failure to follow the *non-delay principle*.

Common law assumes that it is in a child's best interest to have contact with both sep-arated parents. Directly quoting from persuasive precedent in *Kosmopoulou* v. *Greece* [2004] 37 EHRR 417 para.47 (decided in the European Court of Human Rights), Justice

Munby reiterated that 'the mutual enjoyment by parent and child of each other's company constitutes a fundamental element of family life, even if the relationship between the parents has broken down'. The five-year litigation between the mother and father in this case involved 43 separate hearings. It included a series of adjournments, which meant the postponement of court hearings, to the detriment of their daughter. The constant adjournments meant that the mother could persist over an extended period of time in preventing the father from seeing his daughter. This was despite the existence of a Contact Order expressly granting the father direct face-to-face contact with his daughter. To take just one example, on 4 March 1999 a final hearing to resolve the dispute between the parents was listed for 30 June 1999, this was then adjourned to 12 July 1999 and adjourned again until 27 September 1999 to be followed by yet another adjournment until 19 January 2000. Hence a hearing originally scheduled for 4 March did not actually take place until 19 January the following year. For a young child in particular this is an intolerably long time. Often these adjournments were simply the result of poor case management by the courts.

The frequent adjournments were exacerbated by further delays caused by the necessity of judges having to request a report to investigate what had happened in between court hearings. There were also delays in instructing expert witnesses. For example, the consultant clinical psychologist appointed to give expert evidence on the father's suitability to have continued contact did not report to the court until February 2001. That is almost three years after the father had first applied for a Contact Order. This was after a number of previous adjournments while the court awaited the consultant's evidence. The clinical psychologist's report stated:

> I found [father]'s interactions with [daughter] to be indicative of a warm caring relationship where there was clear evidence on his part of emotional sensitivity, reciprocity with [daughter], and appropriate attunement. This indicates a secure parent–child relationship, and that [the daughter] has indeed already formed a strong, significant attachment to her father . . .

Despite receiving the clinical psychologist's report, the court initiated a s.37 investigation on 20 February 2001 resulting in yet further adjournments while the court awaited the outcome of this enquiry by Social Services. The section of the Children Act 1989 which permits the court to request an investigation by the local authority in a private law case is reproduced in the box below.

Key legislation

Children Act 1989

s.37(1) Where, in any family proceedings in which a question arises with respect to the welfare of any child, it appears to the court that it may be appropriate for a care of supervision order to be made with respect to him, the court may direct the appropriate authority to undertake an investigation of the child's circumstances.

Most parental disputes are private law proceedings meaning that they only involve private individuals as parties to the court case. But a judge considering making an order under the Children Act 1989 may become concerned about a child's welfare. In this situation he or she can under s.37 of the Children Act 1989 require Children's Services to conduct an investigation into the child's circumstances. The local authority must decide whether there is a risk of significant harm to the child and, if so, whether to apply for a Care Order or Supervision Order (see Chapter 3). A social worker from Children's Services must produce a report for the court setting out the findings of this investigation. Even if there appear to be no grounds for involving the local authority any further in the family proceedings, by carrying out an assessment Children's Services may provide vital additional information upon which a judge can then make a ruling.

In this case the Local Authority did not deem it necessary to apply for a Care Order or Supervision Order. At the same time the behaviour of the mother was obviously a matter of grave concern. Not until six months after the s.37 report was requested by the court did a social worker become actively involved in trying to facilitate the father's contact with his daughter. More delays followed. The involvement of a social worker to facilitate contact between father and child in August 2001 was ad hoc and this initiative failed due to continued hostility from the mother. It was not until January 2003, 18 months later, that a social worker was formally appointed under a Family Assistance Order with the remit to facilitate contact between father and daughter. A Family Assistance Order can only be made where s.8 orders are being considered, as was true in this case. This order, which is described in the box below, cannot be applied for by parties to the proceedings and is solely at the discretion of the court. By the time the court decided to issue a Family Assistance Order, which was four years after the initial hearing, the family situation had greatly deteriorated.

Key legislation

Family Assistance Order

Under the Children Act 1989 s.16 the court of its own motion can make a Family Assistance Order. It can be made in any family proceedings, but predominantly is made during divorce and separation proceedings where there is dispute over contact with the child. The order is dependent on the consent of those named in the order, with the exception of the child. It can last up to one year. It is not widely used and only around 1,000 are issued each year.

A Family Assistance Order requires CAFCASS or the local authority to make an officer available, who may be a social worker, to 'advise, assist, befriend any person named in the order'. Children and Family Reporters are sometimes required to intervene with the family under a Family Assistance Order. The order is designed to provide short-term support to parents, or those with parental responsibility, who are experiencing distress and conflict due to family breakdown. The social worker appointed can also be required to report to the court on the arrangements for contact between parents or those with parental responsibility and any children.

The potential for section 37 investigations illustrates that there is no neat separation between private law cases concerning individuals involved in marital disputes or other forms of family breakdown and public law proceedings involving Children's Services. Angry and acrimonious parents in the throes of a bitter divorce or separation can inflict considerable harm on their children as they become convenient ammunition in a war of attrition. Social workers must be alert to the overlap between public law cases, which involve the State intervening in circumstances of child abuse or neglect, and private law cases which at first glance may seem to concern only a separating couple. Practitioners working with families in crisis can be confronted by embittered partners who routinely use their children against one another. In some situations this may be sufficiently grave to place children at risk of significant harm in terms of their emotional and psychological health.

The use of a Family Assistance Order in this case is yet another example of how social workers may become involved in private law cases. Like Children and Family Reporters they can also be called upon to report to the court regarding arrangements to promote the welfare of children in families experiencing difficulties. The use of Family Assistance Orders demonstrates how social care professionals can be used to intervene in private law disputes without the situation requiring the involvement of Children's Services. Unfortunately, for the father and daughter in this case the Family Assistance Order was issued too late in the litigation to be effective and little was accomplished through belated social work intervention.

Contravention of the *non-delay principle* pervades this case. There were interminable delays in bringing legal proceedings which contributed immensely to the deterioration in the relationship between father and daughter. Despite the positive role which the court acknowledged the father had to play in his daughter's life, persistent adjournments exacerbated by the mother's successful frustration of the Contact Order all but destroyed the father–daughter relationship. Although the delays in this case were mostly attributable to poor case management within the court system, the *non-delay principle* applies equally to social workers involved in court proceedings. Practitioners too are bound by the *non-delay principle*, which means that they must proceed on the basis that hold-ups in completing their investigations or submitting reports to the court potentially harm children.

Right to a fair trial

So endemic were the adjournments and delays in the litigation, protracting it over five years, that Justice Munby, presiding in the final High Court hearing, conceded that this was incompatible with article 6 of the European Convention. This article obliges States to ensure 'a fair and public hearing within a reasonable time'. Plainly the legal proceedings did not take place within a reasonable time. Citing persuasive precedent handed down by the European Court of Human Rights in *Hornsby* v. *Greece* [1997] 24 EHRR 250 and *Immobiliare Saffi* v. *Italy* [1999] 30 EHRR 756, Justice Munby acknowledged that article 6 also requires the judiciary to ensure that its decisions are enforced. In fact the reason for so many hearings was that the father had to return to the court time and again to ask for his original Contact Order to be enforced. Instead of enforcing the initial Contact Order, which specified contact between father and daughter as 10.00 am to 5.45 pm every Saturday, the courts' response to frustration of this by the mother was to reduce thefather's contact. In other words the effect of the mother's recalcitrance was punishment of the father. Not only did the court reduce the father's contact time with his daughter, but it also failed to expedite investigations of the mother's allegations against him which proved groundless.

The right to a fair trial under article 6 of the European Convention on Human Rights refers both to the process of the trial and to its outcome. The process of the trial was unfair because there were constant adjournments combined with a failure by the court and the local authority to speedily investigate allegations of abuse made by the mother against the father. In order to safeguard the 8-year-old child in the first instance, the father's contact with her was reduced. However, because investigations were not undertaken quickly and more court adjournments followed, the reduced contact between father and daughter became permanent. The combination of reduced contact and the mother's entrenched hostility towards the father resulted in the daughter being influenced against him. The likelihood is that both poor case management by the courts and poor prioritisation by social services resulted in drawing out the litigation to the point where justice was denied to the father with detrimental consequences for his daughter. More than any other case in this book the circumstances of this father and daughter illustrate the degree to which 'justice delayed is justice denied'.

Article 6 of the European Convention also requires the State to implement its decisions in order to enforce the rights of its citizens. In this case the father was also denied a fair trial because the court consistently failed to force the mother to abide by the original Contact Order. At the same time the court was caught on the horns of a dilemma. Previously the court had actually imprisoned the mother on one occasion and threatened her with a custodial sentence on others. A court is entitled to fine or imprison people for contempt of court, which means for defying its orders. However, in this particular case, the court also had to consider the welfare of the child concerned. Imprisoning a parent inevitably deprives a child of care and attention. It is this dilemma which makes it so difficult for justice to be done.

Social workers, by virtue of their being employed by local authorities or because of involvement in court cases, are acting on behalf of the State. As such their work is framed by the European Convention on Human Rights. If social workers unjustifiably delay carrying out investigations instigated by the court, or fail to follow through on court decisions, they may well be in violation of article 6. As you will now appreciate from reading through this case, delay and failure to implement decisions can also be destructive of a child's relationship with his or her parents to the detriment of both the child and the parent.

Use of experts

There were a number of professionals involved in giving evidence and writing reports for the court. These included the Court Welfare Officer, a consultant clinical psychologist, a consultant psychiatrist, an independent social worker and the social worker

 Background information

Children's Guardians

Children's Guardians are qualified social workers employed by CAFCASS to represent the interests of children during court cases involving social services or disputed adoptions. They are responsible for:

- Making enquiries of all those involved, e.g. child, family members, foster carer, other professionals.
- Attending meetings on behalf of the child, e.g. case conferences, court proceedings.
- Appointing a solicitor on behalf of the child.
- Informing the court of which other professionals or experts should be involved.
- Writing a report for the court detailing what outcome would be in the child's best interests. This must include a statement about the child's wishes and feelings and pay close attention to the requirements of the welfare checklist.

The court does not have to do what is recommended by the Children's Guardian, but it must give clear reasons why.

appointed as the Children's Guardian (see box below). While Justice Munby in his High Court ruling acknowledged the invaluable evidence a number of them had put before the courts, he criticised the restriction of expert witnesses to producing reports rather than being involved in resolving the dispute. The appointment of the independent social worker to facilitate contact between father and daughter was, in Justice Munby's opinion, far too late in the proceedings. As a result, the social worker was unable to save a situation which had by then deteriorated beyond the point of redress. The expertise of other professionals was not utilised by the courts in actively seeking an effective response to the animosity of the mother towards the father, which lay at the heart of this case.

Expert witnesses are commonly used to present specialist reports to the court in family proceedings and indeed in public law care proceedings. The main criticism of experts involved with this litigation was their ad hoc engagement to produce reports. This precipitated adjournments of court hearings and resulted in a lack of multidisciplinary work with the family. Even after the instigation of the s.37 inquiry in this case, Social Services still failed to develop a coherent plan of work with the family. As a result no coordinated intervention with the family ever took place. Preventive work with children and their families is an important aspect of social work. Good preventive work necessitates early intervention with a family, and certainly before it reaches the devastating breakdown in relationships which occurred in this case. Working in partnership with parents and acting as a mediator between hostile parties can deflect the worst effects of family breakdown from the children of the family.

Conversely, as the text box above describing Children's Guardians reveals, sometimes a social worker's role can be quite limited and specific. Despite the astute observation of Justice Munby regarding the plethora of experts appointed to produce reports but the lack of their actual engagement with the family, in fact not all experts are equally well placed to intervene. The Children's Guardian is required to represent the child's best interests to the court and to make recommendations for the child's upbringing having regard to the welfare checklist contained in s.1 of the Children Act 1989. Arguably if a Family Assistance Order had been made earlier in the litigation and a social worker involved through this route, the father's contact with his daughter (and hence their relationship) might have been preserved. But a Family Assistance Order is made at the court's discretion and cannot by applied for by Children's Services. This means that it is up to the court to decide whether to involve the local authority in a private law case.

Judgement in *D (A Child) (Intractable Contact Dispute: Publicity)*

In private judgement, due to the apparently irreparable damage done to the relationship between father and daughter caused by the protracted litigation and probable malign influence of the mother, the High Court ruled that the father was to be restricted to indirect contact with his daughter on just eight occasions a year. The father finally abandoned his five-year struggle for regular direct contact with his daughter, withdrew his most recent application for a Residence Order, and left the courtroom weeping.

In his public judgement, Justice Munby concluded his 14-page ruling recounting the long litany of omissions and errors by an apology to both father and daughter as he shamefully acknowledged, 'We failed them. The system failed them.'

Critical questions

1 In this case the court failed to enforce the Contact Order granting the father regular contact with his daughter. Campaign groups such as fathers-4-justice complain that the court system is biased against fathers in these types of situations. Re-examine this case and identify the difficulties that a court or Children's Services would face in trying to implement a Contact Order against a resident mother's wishes. How might these difficulties be addressed and overcome?

2 In his judgement, Justice Munby highlighted the paradox of many experts being commissioned to write reports rather than work with the family. This was a private law case and therefore not known to social services. The court has power under s.37 to involve Children's Services and under s.16 to make a Family Assistance Order. The court in this case exercised its powers very late in the litigation. What should the court's response have been regarding social work invention with this family?

3 Both CAFCASS and Children's Services became involved in this family proceeding. Identify the factors which could delay social workers in these organisations reporting to the court or assisting the family as directed by the court.

 Critical commentary

Public funding of private law family cases

Research studies reveal that solicitors acting for privately paying clients tend to encourage informal settlement of disputes over finance and arrangements for the children's care. By contrast, where clients are publicly funded through legal aid, solicitors are more likely to suggest court action. This pattern is also discernible when court action is initiated, with 60% of cases where couples are paying their own costs settled pre-trial compared to just 22% of cases funded by legal aid. A number of researchers have concluded that the legal aid scheme creates perverse incentives for divorcing and separating couples with children to engage in protracted legal battles over contact (Kemp, et al., 2005: 126).

In a combined qualitative and quantitative study of 280 private law family cases involving children, Kemp, et al. (2005: 128) found that solicitors' profits rose in proportion to the number of actual court hearings there were in relation to a specific case. On average, remuneration rates for publicly funded private family law cases are around half that of privately funded ones. This means that solicitors need to raise the number of hours worked on legal-aid supported cases to make them profitable. It is also significant that costs and profits rise the higher up the court system a case is heard. A dispute over post-separation arrangements for a child will cost the least if heard in a Family Proceedings Court, more in a County Court, and will be most expensive if brought before the High Court where barristers normally represent the parties. Plainly, as costs rise in order to appeal a decision up through the hierarchy of courts, couples funding their own private law disputes will be forced to settle, as continuing legal action will be prohibitively expensive. Those qualifying for legal aid encouraged by solicitors who are dependent on publicly funded private law cases for their profits are not subject to the same financial constraints.

Bitterness between the couples was cited by solicitors as a key reason for them fighting over residence and contact issues relating to children. Even when living and contact arrangements for the children were settled feuding could blow up again if one ex-partner then started another sexual relationship. In the Kemp, et al. study (2005: 132), a number of solicitors admitted to adopting a more conciliatory role in privately funded cases as opposed to publicly funded cases when being more adversarial meant that the case was likely to take up more time and climb higher up the court system thereby increasing profit margins. As for couples themselves, it was notable that when having to pay for their own legal services, they were found to be more likely to identify issues of real concern and to settle quickly on peripheral matters. This contrasted with many publicly funded separating couples who contested a large number of issues because they bore no economic costs in doing so (Kemp, et al., 2005: 133).

Not only do publicly funded private law cases involving children tend to be more protracted than privately funded ones, but a high proportion of repeat court hearings are actually over the same issue. Kemp, et al. (2005: 136) found that 50% of clients had returned to court in respect of the same relationship breakdown and, of these, three-quarters concerned the same residence or contact dispute which had been dealt with by a previous court hearing. Even where a court order is made, which appears to have settled a matter, in a high proportion of publicly funded cases one or other of the parties sought to reopen the issue. Solicitors in the study attributed this both to the apparent inability of the courts to enforce Contact Orders (predominately made in favour of fathers) and the tendency of some ex-partners to engineer repeated court hearings to punish a former partner.

CASE 3
Re C (A Child) (Immunisation: Parental Rights) [2003] EWCA Civ 1148 and *Re F (A Child) (Immunisation: Parental Rights)* [2003] EWCA Civ 1148

Importance of the case

It explores the relationship between parental responsibility and the *welfare principle* and illustrates why children need to be separately represented in court hearings. The case also explains how professionals and judges deal with situations where the expert evidence presented by different witnesses is contradictory.

History of the case

This was an appeal to the civil division of the Court of Appeal against a ruling of the High Court relating to a consolidated hearing in respect of two different families. These involved very similar circumstances and points of law. In each instance a father sought a Specific Issue Order to compel the mother to have their child immunised. The High Court granted Specific Issue Orders in each case, requiring that the two children be immunised. Both mothers appealed against these orders to the Court of Appeal, where the two cases were again heard together.

Facts of the case

In both instances the fathers were unmarried and had only cohabited with the mothers for a short period of time before the breakdown of their relationship. The mothers were each the primary carer of a girl, one aged 3 years and the other 9 years at the time of the High Court hearing. Neither child had ever received any form of vaccination. The fathers both had parental responsibility and contact with their daughters. They had asked the mothers of their children to have them vaccinated, but this had been refused. Both fathers and mothers engaged experts to give evidence as to the safety, health risks and benefits of vaccination. Given the complexity of the court case and its nature, the children involved were given separate legal representation in the High Court through the appointment of a Guardian ad Litem. The High Court had made Specific Issue Orders requiring both children to be immunised. The mothers were asking the Court of Appeal to overrule the High Court judgement.

Key people in the case

Fathers – two unmarried fathers holding parental responsibility
Mothers – two mothers residing with their daughters
Girls – aged 3 years and 9 years
Mr Cohen – barrister representing the fathers
Ms Gumbel – barrister representing the mothers
Dr Conway – consultant paediatrician instructed on behalf of the fathers
Professor Kroll – professor of paediatrics and infectious diseases instructed by
   CAFCASS Legal
Dr Donegan – General Practitioner instructed on behalf of the mothers
Dr Veasey – psychiatrist
Justice Sumner – judge in High Court case
Lord Justice Thorpe – judge in Court of Appeal case

Discussion of the case

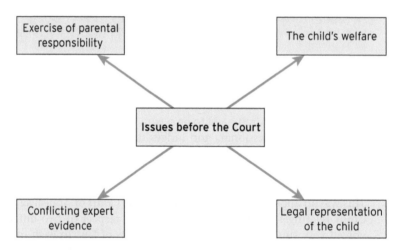

Exercise of parental responsibility

Under the Children Act 1989 s.2, parental responsibility is held equally by those who have it, and can be exercised independently of others holding parental responsibility. However, there are matters affecting children's welfare which require the mutual agreement of those holding parental responsibility, for example, life-saving or life-threatening medical treatment, a child's name and religion. Citing precedent for this position, Lord Justice Thorpe presiding in the Court of Appeal hearing referred to *Re J (A Minor) (Prohibited Steps Order: Circumcision), Re* [2000] 1 FLR 571 para. 577, which concluded that there is:

> a small group of important decisions made on behalf of a child which, in the absence of agreement of those with parental responsibility, ought not to be carried out or arranged by one parent carer although she has parental responsibility under section 2(7) of the Children Act 1989. Such a decision ought not to be made without the specific approval of the court. Sterilisation is one example. The change of a child's surname is another.

Immunisation belongs to this category of key decisions. In the two instances before the Court of Appeal the fathers could not independently of the mothers exercise their parental responsibility to have their children vaccinated.

When there are intractable disputes between those holding parental responsibility, application can be made to the courts for resolution. In these situations the court takes upon itself the authority that a parent with parental responsibility would normally exercise in relation to the particular issue in dispute. The court implements its decision through a Specific Issue Order, which directs a person with parental responsibility to carry out the action set out in the order. A Specific Issue Order does not remove parental responsibility from anyone, it merely directs the person with parental responsibility named in the order to do something decided by the court. The High Court had made Specific Issue Orders – directing each mother to immunise her daughter against a number of common diseases – which were now being appealed by the mothers.

Specific Issues Orders were applied for by two unmarried fathers who had gained parental responsibility by one of the means listed on page 65. This was not a situation in which Children's Services needed to become involved because failure to immunise children does not normally present a risk of significant harm to them. The important aspect of this case for social work practice is that the local authority or the NSPCC can also apply for a Specific Issue Order or indeed any Section 8 Order. For example, if a child was not receiving medical treatment for a life-threatening condition, but in all other respects his or her parents were providing a loving and caring environment, this is not a situation which necessitates the removal of the child into the care of the State. It is, however, a situation which requires very focused and limited social work intervention to ensure the child receives the life-saving medical treatment he or she needs. A local authority could obtain a Specific Issue Order which directs the parents to permit life-saving medical treatment to be administered to their child. It would then be for the court to ensure that this happened, through the threat of fines or imprisonment for contempt of court if necessary. In other words, a Specific Issue Order can be used by local authorities to direct those holding parental responsibility to carry out a particular action crucial to the welfare of their child without intensive social work involvement.

The child's welfare

The Children Act 1989 s.1(1) is unequivocally worded and provides that 'the child's welfare shall be the court's paramount consideration'. Ms Gumbel QC, acting as legal council for the mothers, sought to argue that immunisation was a form of non-essential invasive medical treatment. She also cited *Re T (A Minor) (Wardship: Medical Treatment), Re* [1997] 1 WLR 242; 1 FLR 502, a case in which the Court of Appeal refused to order life-prolonging surgery for a child because the mother was trenchantly against it and her emotional and mental well-being was crucial to the welfare of the child. In other words Ms Gumbel was using *Re T* as a precedent to argue that the immunisation was a form of invasive treatment which if given against the mothers' wishes would cause them distress and in turn harm the welfare of their daughters.

Lord Justice Thorpe denied that *Re T* was a precedent for judgement in the present case by distinguishing between the facts of both cases. Agreeing with Mr Cohen QC, representing the fathers, Lord Justice Thorpe asserted that immunisation was a form of preventative health treatment, not an invasive procedure. The judge also observed that the circumstances in *Re T* were very different. In that case the proposed life-prolonging surgery carried health risks to the child and in addition would have required the mother to return from residence overseas to live in the UK and provide long-term intensive care to her child. This was contrasted with vaccination, which was proven to carry low health risks, had positive health outcomes and would not necessitate any additional care-giving on the part of the mothers.

While the child's welfare is the court's paramount consideration, this is closely bound up with that of his or her parents. Ms Gumbel tried to argue that making a Specific Issue Order was counter-productive because it would induce so much distress in the mothers as to detrimentally affect their children. The impact of a court order on a parent has to be a consideration for social workers when deciding whether to resort to a Section 8 Order. Practitioners have to ask themselves, would the effect of enforcing the order have such a profoundly detrimental impact on the parent as to adversely affect the child? Lord Justice Thorpe acknowledged that the impact of implementing the Specific Issue Order on the mothers was a consideration. But this had to be weighed against the benefit to the child and the degree of interference in the life of the parent. Lord Justice Thorpe concluded that the benefit to the child was substantial and the inconvenience or burden to the mothers minimal. Social workers contemplating the use of Section 8 Orders must make similar calculations.

Legal representation of the child

When parents are in dispute with one another over some aspect of the upbringing of their child, they are not necessarily acting in the best interests of that child. Indeed, they may be acting in their own personal interests, or out of malice towards a former partner, to the detriment of their child's welfare. For this reason a solicitor or barrister acting for a parent is not automatically in a position to also represent the best interests of the child. A lawyer is ultimately before the court to advocate on behalf of the client, the parent, and what that parent perceives to be in their child's best interest. Of course an angry parent's perception of their child's best interest is not always a measured or objective one. To take account of this, where the court is confronted by a particularly complex case or has grounds to doubt that a parent will necessarily be acting in a child's best interest it can require a child to have separate legal representation before the court. At the initial hearing in the High Court it was decided, given the intricacy of the case and the intractability of the dispute between the two mothers and fathers, to appoint a Guardian ad Litem whose role is described in the box below.

 Background information

Guardians ad Litem

In more complex private family law proceedings, for example those involving, intractable disputes between parents, domestic violence, or allegations of child abuse, the child may be made a party to the proceedings and separately represented in the court. In these instances CAFCASS provides a Guardian ad Litem, who is a qualified social worker and will instruct a solicitor on behalf of the child, consult with the child and interview other relevant parties or professionals. The Guardian will then write a report for the court addressing the welfare checklist and recommending a course of action in the child's best interests. This provision for separate representation ensures that a child's interests are not routinely assumed to be identical to those of a parent or a person with parental responsibility.

Although a Guardian ad Litem was appointed and reported to the High Court, the Guardian was in agreement with the submissions made on behalf of the fathers. In others words, the representatives for the children in the High Court case agreed that the arguments and proposed course of action (a comprehensive series of vaccinations) put forward by the fathers' lawyers were in the best interests of the children. As judgement in the High Court hearing had established that the fathers' and children's interests in this case were essentially the same, it was decided that separate legal representation of the children before the Court of Appeal was not necessary. The submissions made by Mr Cohen QC for the fathers were accepted by CAFCASS as equally applicable to the children's best interests.

The appointment of a Guardian ad Litem in this case demonstrates yet another way in which social workers can be involved in private law cases where there are no child protection concerns and the local authority is not involved. In summary, social workers can be involved in family proceedings as:

- Children and Family Reporters
- Children's Guardians
- Guardians ad Litem
- Practitioners working under Family Assistance Orders

In these roles they may be reporting to the court, mediating, or providing assistance to a family experiencing difficulties caused by disputes between parents or other family members. As professionals operating within the context of family proceedings they are obliged to pay attention to the welfare checklist when reporting to the court and making recommendations for a child's upbringing. To this end, court reports prepared by social workers employed by CAFCASS should explicitly address all the aspects of a child's welfare listed in s.1(3) of the Children Act 1989.

Conflicting expert evidence

Dr Conway a consultant paediatrician with a specialism in immunology was instructed on behalf of the fathers. Professor Kroll, professor of paediatics and infectious diseases at Imperial College was instructed by CAFCASS Legal. Their expert opinions addressed the full range of vaccinations which were proposed, and demonstrated that the risk of not immunising each child carried considerably higher health risks than immunising them. Both experts demonstrated clear health benefits to each of the children of receiving a comprehensive programme of vaccinations, and they corroborated one another's evidence. Dr Donegan, a General Practitioner and homeopath, was instructed on behalf of the mothers and her evidence contradicted that of Dr Conway and Professor Kroll. Where expert opinion is divided it is for the court to weigh the evidence before it – of which expert evidence only forms one element – and then to make a decision.

In the High Court case, Justice Sumner, presiding, was extremely critical of the expert evidence presented by Dr Donegan and concluded that she had permitted her strongly held convictions against immunisation to erode her duty to the court to provide an objective opinion. Therefore Justice Sumner dismissed the evidence of Dr Donegan and, relying on the expert opinion of Dr Conway and Professor Kroll, concluded that a programme of vaccination against childhood diseases such as Diphtheria, Tetanus, Poliomyelitis, Meningitis C, Tuberculosis, Measles, Mumps and Rubella was in both children's best interest.

The Children Act 1989 s.1(1) requires that the child's welfare must be the court's 'paramount consideration'. A child's physical well-being, in terms of good preventative healthcare, is plainly one vital aspect of their overall welfare. A number of other aspects are contained in the welfare checklist. Particularly pertinent to this case is s.1(3)(f) which obliges the court to consider in relation to a child 'how capable each of his parents, and any other person in relation to whom the court considers the question to be relevant, is of meeting his needs'. This section directed the High Court to ask itself whether the mothers would be able to cope with a court order requiring their children's immunisation without this having a detrimental impact on each child's welfare. Expert evidence was ascertained from Dr Veasey, who produced a psychiatric report on one mother, while the High Court judge made an assessment of the other mother based on the evidence presented. In reviewing this, Justice Sumner concluded that both mothers would be able to accept the court's direction to have their children immunised without this adversely affecting their care by the mothers.

The use of specialists such as psychiatrists, paediatricians or educational psychologists has become commonplace in providing assessments of children or the parenting capacity of their carers. Reports from such experts are used to support the recommendation of a particular course of action. In this case medical experts presented evidence related to immunisation. The courts encourage the parties to a case to agree to the appointment of a single expert in a particular field, often referred to as a jointly appointed expert. Unfortunately in this case, the mothers and fathers commissioned different experts who presented conflicting medical evidence. When this occurs, the court must weigh up the contradictory medical evidence before it, just as the court would any other material presented in evidence. The local authority was not involved in this case because there were no child protection issues. However, social workers who become involved in private law disputes through a s.37 investigation may well decide to appoint their own expert to produce a report. Where the opinion of these expert witnesses conflicts with those commissioned by other parties to the court case, such as parents, it will be for the judge to decide which is the more convincing and robust expert opinion.

Judgement in C (A Child) (Immunisation: Parental Rights) and F (A Child) (Immunisation: Parental Rights)

The High Court made a Specific Issue Order requiring the two children to undergo a comprehensive programme of immunisation against common childhood diseases. The judges sitting in the Court of Appeal found that the case was correctly decided by the High Court and dismissed the mothers' appeal.

Critical questions

1 One aspect of this case examined the interdependence between the well-being of a mother as the primary care giver and the welfare of her child. Can you think of other examples where the mental and emotional well-being of a parent might be intimately linked to issues connected to the child's welfare? What is the potential for parents to abuse this interdependence by claiming that actions to promote their child's welfare would so detrimentally affect their own well-being as to result in poor parenting?

2 Usually children in family proceedings concerning private law parental disputes are not separately represented in court. Exceptionally in this case, because of the complex issues involved, the children were initially given separate legal representation. What are the advantages of children being separately legally represented in a court case involving a parental dispute?

3 There was disagreement between the experts in this case. What lessons do you draw from this case that might inform your practice if you had to engage experts to corroborate your evidence about a child's welfare?

Critical commentary

CAFCASS in private law hearings

The Children and Family Court Advisory and Support Service (CAFCASS) was set up in 2001 and is staffed by qualified social workers and solicitors to provide reports to the court on children's circumstances and provide separate representation for them where indicated. The vast majority of CAFCASS's work in private law cases relates to parental disputes over residence and contact. Within a few months of its creation, CAFCASS had a backlog of cases, with some parents having to wait for more than a year for the agency to complete welfare reports for the court (*The Times*, 15 February 2008). Concerted efforts since 2004 to divert parents away from the court and into forms of dispute resolution, requiring inputs from CAFCASS staff, has further overstretched the agency. Ofsted (2008a), which inspected CAFCASS in South Yorkshire, concluded that delays in allocating cases, inadequate record keeping and analysis combined with poorly evidenced recommendations to the court were putting vulnerable children at increased risk of harm.

Defending CAFCASS, its then Acting Head of the London Region, Steve Adams (2007), argued that there had been a widespread assumption that families involved in private law proceedings were only experiencing a temporary failure of parenting during a period of acute crisis. But research has revealed similar characteristics between families involved in private and public law proceedings, indicating that many experience long-term dysfunctional relationships and parenting failures (Buchanan, et al., 2001; Trinder, et al., 2006). It is therefore not surprising that the presumption of contact between a child and both parents frequently results in protracted litigation and multiple court hearings over a number of years. Adams (2007) notes that the presumption in favour of contact results in a Contact Order being granted by the court in 98% of cases.

Litigation itself has been found to cause high levels of stress in both the child and resident parent (Buchanan, et al., 2001). Indeed, a high proportion of children express a preference for ending contact with a non-resident parent rather than being subjected to continued parental conflict (Buchanan et al., 2001). Researchers have been unable to establish a

▶

positive correlation between healthy child development and contact with the non-resident parent. By contrast a number of studies demonstrate strong correlations between children's adjustment after separation and: household income; conflict between parents; resident and non-resident parents' capacity to parent (Trinder, 2006).

In view of these research findings Adams (2007) argues that CAFCASS's resources are being absorbed in reporting to the court or representing children often after several years of parental conflict. Frequently, it is being drawn into multiple court hearings concerning the same couple. He proposes that the agency's resources should instead be deployed in early in-tervention directed at therapeutic and educative work with parents in dispute. More contro-versially he suggests that if parents fail to heed the messages that their conflict is harming their child's health and development and to modify their behaviour in response, then contact should cease. Adams (2007: 2) asserts that 'the presumption of contact in effect obliterates the question of children's interests by assuming they are synonymous with parental contact'.

CASE 4
Re B (A Child) (Prohibited Steps Order) [2007] EWCA Civ 1055

Importance of the case

This examines the scope of the rights which a parent holds by virtue of having parental responsibility for a child. It also explores the difference between a Residence Order and Prohibited Steps Order in relation to where a child lives.

History of the case

The case was heard at first instance in the County Court where the father sought to pre-vent the mother from removing their child from the Huddersfield area to Northern Ire-land where she intended to settle. The County Court issued a Prohibited Steps Order which prevented the removal of the child to Northern Ireland on a permanent basis. There was an appeal by the mother to the Court of Appeal against the making of the Pro-hibited Steps Order.

Facts of the case

The father was originally from Huddersfield in Yorkshire and most of his immediate fam-ily still resided there. The mother was originally from Portaferry in Northern Ireland and likewise many of her family members were still living in or around that area. The mother moved to Huddersfield in 2000 and had a brief relationship with the father, which began in 2003 and ended in 2005. A boy, who was born in November 2004, is the only child of the couple, who did not marry. The mother proposed to return to Northern Ireland and reside there permanently with her son. The father endeavoured to prevent this by apply-ing to the County Court for a Residence Order and a Prohibited Steps Order. The mother made an application to the same court for permission to change the child's surname. The application to change the child's surname was refused and the father withdrew his appli-cation for a Residence Order. However, the County Court did issue a Prohibited Steps Order which prevented the mother from settling with her son in Northern Ireland, although she was permitted to take him there for holidays. Neither the father nor mother contested the court's refusal to give permission for a change of name or to make a Residence Order. But the mother did appeal to the Court of Appeal against the Prohibited Steps Order.

Key people in the case

Child – 3-year-old boy
Father – unmarried birth father of child
Mother – unmarried birth mother of child

Discussion of the case

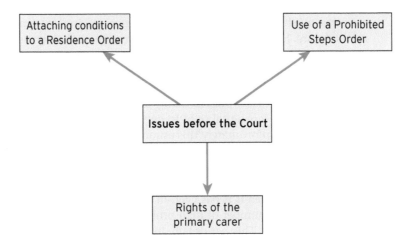

Attaching conditions to a Residence Order

The Children Act 1989 s.13 provides that where a Residence Order is in place the child's surname cannot be changed, nor can the child be removed from the United Kingdom 'without either the written consent of every person who has parental responsibility for the child or the leave of the court'. The County Court neither granted the father the Residence Order, nor did it make a Residence Order in favour of the mother. As the father did not contest the court's dismissal of his application and the mother was accepted as the primary carer by all the parties to the proceeding, the County Court followed the *no order principle*. In other words, since the father decided not to pursue his challenge to the mother's position as the resident parent, a Residence Order in favour of the mother would not have produced any positive benefit of the child. It would simply have given legal effect to a now accepted status quo.

Even if a Residence Order had been in force in the mother's favour this would not have prevented her from taking the child to settle in Northern Ireland without the father's or court's permission. This is because the legal condition attached to every Residence Order by virtue of s.13 is that the child cannot be *removed from* the United Kingdom. This does not in anyway prevent the child being *moved around within* the United Kingdom. However, s.11(7), which applies to all Section 8 Orders, permits the court to attach conditions. In relation to a Residence Order, such a condition could specify where a child is to live. In other words, the court could have made a Residence Order in favour of the mother and invoked s.11(7) to add a condition that the child must live in England or, indeed, Huddersfield. This was not a dispute between parents which necessitated the intervention of social services. A Residence Order can be used both to specify with whom a child is to live and where he or she is to live. This makes it an extremely useful Section 8 Order for social workers who may have to intervene to safeguard a child by specifying that the child lives in a particular place or is cared for by a particular person.

Use of a Prohibited Steps Order

The application for a Residence Order had been rejected by the County Court and none of the parties to the court case appealed this decision. Although a condition can be attached to a Residence Order, the order of itself has wide-ranging effects and gives parental responsibility to anyone who holds it. The dispute between the mother and father in this case was much narrower. The father was not seeking to remove the child from his mother's care. He simply wanted his son to remain in Huddersfield where he would have regular contact. It was for this reason that the father applied for a Prohibited Steps Order to prevent the mother moving to Northern Ireland with his son. A Prohibited Steps Order does not alter who holds parental responsibility. Instead it enables the court to prohibit a course of action which would normally be entirely lawful for someone holding parental responsibility. It is a parental right to decide where a child lives. Usually parents are able to agree on this. Unfortunately this estranged couple could not.

Children's Services were not involved in this case. However, they can apply for a Prohibited Steps Order where there is concern that a parental decision will adversely affect a child's welfare. When Children's Services have found it necessary to apply for a Prohibited Steps Order, often it is has been in connection with international custody disputes. There have been a number of high profile child abductions which have received extensive media coverage. This has usually involved one parent taking the child out of Britain and back to their own country of origin. Normally a person with parental responsibility would be legally entitled to take a child abroad, either on holiday or to emigrate. But when a child is taken abroad in the midst of a dispute over arrangements for his or her upbringing this becomes a child welfare issue. As the box below indicates, there are a number of international agreements in place which address these situations.

 Background information

Child custody in an international context

Globalisation in terms of faster, cheaper and more regular travel and communication between countries has resulted in the increased movement of people around the world. In the United Kingdom the recent expansion of the European Union to 27 Member States has meant increased migration from continental Europe. This has made it vital to ensure mutual recognition of judicial decisions in marital and child welfare matters across the European Union. Otherwise, for example, a divorced German husband refused direct contact with his child in a British court could return to Germany and apply for contact there, resulting in a German court overturning the decision of the British court. Plainly this would lead to chaos across the European Union with different jurisdictions able to overturn one another's decisions. To guard against this, EU Regulation 1347/2000 ensures that even if parents move with or without their children to another EU Member State they will still be subject to the original court decisions and these will be automatically enforced by all other EU Member States.

Beyond the EU the movement of people has meant that child custody disputes increasingly involve parents of different nationalities. A number of parents have circumvented court proceedings and unilaterally removed their children from the United Kingdom to the parent's country of origin on the Asian, African or American continents. Such circumstances are covered by the Hague Convention, which applies to children under 16 years of age who are habitually resident in one signatory country and wrongfully removed or held in another one. Not all countries have signed the Hague Convention, which means that if the abducted child has dual nationality and is removed to a non-Convention country, there is little the Foreign Office or the British justice system can do to bring them back to the United Kingdom. Conversely, where the child has been taken to a Convention country, its public authorities will endeavour to: find the child; prevent further harm to him or her; secure the child's voluntary return to the UK, and commence any necessary judicial proceedings.

Rights of the primary carer

In the present case the Court of Appeal considered the precedent created by *Re E (Minors) (Residence: Imposition of Conditions)* [1997] 2 FLR 638 in which it was requested by one party to the proceeding that the court should attach a condition to a Residence Order preventing the primary carer from relocating themselves and their child from Blackpool to London. Ruling against attaching such a condition in the case of E at the Court of Appeal, Lady Justice Butler-Sloss set out her reasoning at para 642(c):

> . . . where the parent is entirely suitable and the court intends to make a residence order in favour of that parent, a condition of residence is in my view an unwarranted imposition upon the right of the parent to choose where he/she will live within the United Kingdom or with whom. There may be exceptional cases, for instance where the court in the private law context has concerns about the ability of the parent to be granted a residence order to be a satisfactory carer, but there is no better solution than to place the child with that parent.

The judgement in *Re E (Minors) (Residence: Imposition of Conditions)* strongly defends the rights inherent to parental responsibility and the reluctance of courts to interfere with them unless there are pressing reasons which impinge significantly on a child's welfare. The question confronting the Court of Appeal in the present case was whether there were exceptional circumstances which would justify the interference in the mother's right as the primary carer to decide the place of residence of both herself and her child. None were presented before the court. Likewise, Children's Services will not be permitted by the courts to routinely interfere in decision making by those who hold parental responsibility. There have to be exceptional and pressing reasons as to why Children's Services might seek to use a Residence Order with attached conditions, or a Prohibited Steps Order, to prevent the movement of a child within the United Kingdom or abroad.

Judgement in *Re B (A Child) (Prohibited Steps Order)*

The Court of Appeal concluded that the judge at first instance in the County Court had misdirected himself by failing to apply the correct judicial precedents. These established that the imposition of restrictions on the place of residence of the child – whether through a Prohibited Steps Order or a condition attached to a Residence Order – was exceptional. The judge at first instance, by failing to ascertain from the evidence if there were exceptional circumstances, had not applied the correct legal principle. Consequently the Court of Appeal set aside the Prohibited Steps Order and ordered a retrial in the County Court.

Crítical questions

1 When parents split up, where a child lives can dramatically affect their contact with the non-resident parent. In this case the mother wanted to take her son to live in Northern Ireland, making it difficult for the father living in Huddersfield to continue regular contact with him. The court decided the mother was entitled to exercise her parental responsibility to move with her son to live elsewhere. Yet, reduced contact between a parent and child can be detrimental to a child's welfare. Do you think this case was correctly decided? If so, why and, if not, what ruling do you think the judge ought to have made?

2 This case involved two parents who both lived in the United Kingdom. Consider the situation if one parent originally came from Pakistan and wanted to return there to live with the child; how would this affect your judgement? What factors would influence you in coming to a decision?

3 How would you weigh the child's wishes and feelings, which are in the welfare checklist, against the rights of parents to make decisions of residence on their behalf?

CASE 5
Re M (A Child) (Contact: Domestic Violence) [2001] Fam 260

Importance of the case

It examines the effect of domestic violence on a child, and the impact on a child's welfare if he or she is required to have ongoing contact with a non-resident but previously violent parent or parent's partner. The case also describes the legal options available to parents who are experiencing domestic violence.

History of the case

This case was heard by the Court of Appeal alongside three other cases all involving domestic violence. In each situation a father had either threatened or perpetrated physical assaults against the mother. After separation each father then sought contact with his child, which was opposed by each of the mothers. In each case a lower court had issued a Contact Order specifying indirect contact only between father and child. In this particular case there had been a number of hearings in the County Court. A Contact Order was made in favour of the father, but restricted him to indirect contact with his child through letters, cards, Christmas and birthday presents. The father appealed to the Court of Appeal against the restriction imposed by the County Court as he wanted direct contact.

Facts of the case

The father and mother married in March 1987 and soon afterwards the father began physically assaulting the mother. At one point he was charged with grievous bodily harm although this did not result in criminal proceedings. The mother obtained an Ouster Order which required the father to leave the matrimonial home. Due to his violence she also obtained an injunction preventing him from approaching her. The couple separated in 1990 and in January 1991 their only child G, a son, was born. From March 1992 until

November 1997 G saw his father once a fortnight at a contact centre under the supervision of his mother. This arrangement ended after an argument between the couple in front of G, after which G refused to see his father. The report of a Court Welfare Officer (now a Children and Family Reporter) submitted to a court hearing in November 1998 was critical of the mother and stated that G had suffered emotional abuse due to the breakdown of contact with his father. The report recommended a phased reintroduction of the father into the child's life. The content of the Court Welfare Officer's report was disputed by the mother, who also made a complaint against the officer. At the court's request, both sides then agreed to jointly instruct a child psychiatrist to give expert opinion on contact between father and son. However, they could not identify a child psychiatrist and instead jointly instructed Dr Lowenstein, a psychologist. After interviewing both parents and child, Dr Lowenstein concluded that the son was suffering from Parental Alienation Syndrome and required therapy. Dr Lowenstein offered to conduct this therapy and then produce a further report. The mother, having divorced the father, remarried in 1997. At the time of the Court of Appeal hearing, the child by her first marriage G was 9 years old and lived with his mother who had remarried. He had not seen his father for 2 years. The Court of Appeal identified many relevant precedents, considered further expert advice, and in making its decision brought to bear findings from an extensive body of research on contact between non-resident fathers and their children against a background of domestic violence.

Key people in the case

G – 9-year-old boy
Father – divorced father of G
Mother – divorced mother of G
Dr Lowenstein – psychologist
Dr Sturge – child psychiatrist
Dr Glaser – child psychiatrist
Judge Rudd – judge in County Court case
Dame Butler-Sloss – judge in Court of Appeal case

Discussion of the case

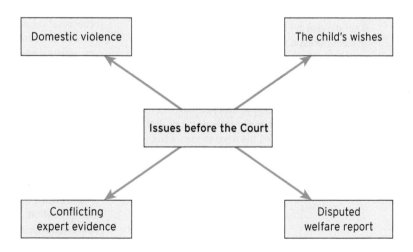

Domestic violence

At the time of the first court case, which dealt with the father's violence towards the mother, the court issued Ouster and Injunctive Orders intended to prevent the father from causing further physical harm to the mother. These were made under statutes which were subsequently repealed by the Family Law Act 1996. This later legislation introduced comparable orders, but ones which could be more easily and quickly obtained by the victim of domestic violence. These are summarised in the table below.

Court orders and offences in relation to domestic violence

Description of order	Effect of order
Occupation Order Under the Family Law Act 1996 the court can issue an order to exclude someone from the family home who is molesting or harming another member of the household. Can also be used to enable a household member to re-enter a dwelling. An application can only be made if the parties are 'associated', e.g. spouses, cohabitants, same-sex partners, relatives. An Occupation Order is a fundamental infringement of property rights and can result in one party being made homeless. It can only be granted if the 'significant harm test' is met under s.33(7). This requires the court to establish whether the applicant or any relevant child will suffer significant harm if it makes no order, and if it does make an order whether the respondent will suffer significant harm. The court has to balance the harm to different parties in coming to its decision.	• Only regulates who may occupy the property, it does not change the legal status of ownership or tenancy. • Can specify that the person named in the order is to leave all or part of the home, or not to approach the home, e.g. not to come within 100 metres of property. • Can be time limited or indefinite. • Court can specify which parties should contribute to payment of rent or mortgage. • Before making an order the court must consider the parties' finances and housing needs and the needs of the children. • These are exceptional orders and only used as a last resort. • Breach of the order is contempt of court and therefore the person in breach can be fined or imprisoned. • Court hearings in relation to FLA 1996 are defined as family proceedings
Non-molestation Order Under the Family Law Act 1996 the court can issue this order to prevent a person from approaching or molesting a member of the household. Molestation is not defined in FLA 1996, but at common law it includes harassing or threatening the applicant. Application can only be made if the parties are 'associated', e.g. spouses, cohabitants, same-sex partners, relatives. Under s.42(5) in deciding whether to make the order or not the court must 'have regard to all the circumstances including the need to secure the health, safety and well-being' of the applicant and any relevant child	• Requires the respondent not to approach or molest the applicant. • Can specify the particular acts of molestation which the person named in the order must desist from. • Protects the adult applicant together with any 'relevant child' from molestation. • Application can be made by a child, but only with the permission of the court. • Application can be by a court on its own motion or by a third party to protect the victim. • A Non-molestation Order may be time limited or indefinite. • Breach of the order is a criminal offence. • Police can arrest the respondent for a breach even if the applicant (victim) fails to take any action. • Court hearings in relation to FLA 1996 are defined as family proceedings.

(Continued)

Description of order	Effect of order
Restraining Order Under the Protection from Harassment Act 1997 s.1 it is a criminal offence to pursue a course of conduct which amounts to harassment. Under the Protection from Harassment Act s.4 and s.7 it is a criminal offence to cause a person to fear on at least two occasions, normally occurring within a few months, that violence will be used against him or her. On either conviction or acquittal for an offence under s.1 or s.7 the court can issue a Restraining Order prohibiting a person from further conduct which amounts to harassment of another. Action can be taken under the Protection from Harassment Act 1997 whether or not the persons involved are 'associated'.	• Harassment includes alarming or causing distress to a person. • A restraining order can specify the prohibited conduct. • A Restraining Order can be time limited or indeterminate. • Breach of the order is a criminal offence. • The victim can apply for a warrant of arrest if the order is breached. • Maximum penalty for a breach of the order is five years imprisonment. • A victim can apply for the award of damages against the perpetrator. • Court hearings in relation to PHA 1997 are defined as civil proceedings.

Conflict and violence characterise many of the families where social workers intervene to safeguard children. Consequently, practitioners may be required to assist victims of domestic violence to protect both themselves and their children from the perpetrator. To achieve this, social workers obviously need a working knowledge of the main legal options available to parents suffering violence at the hands of an intimate partner. The Adoption and Children Act 2002 s.120 amended the definition of 'harm' under the Children Act 1989 to include 'impairment suffered from seeing or hearing the ill-treatment of another'. Therefore a child who witnesses repeated physical assaults on a parent or sibling may be suffering harm of sufficient magnitude to justify the intervention of Children's Services. This means that a child does not have to be personally attacked by the perpetrator in order to suffer significant harm. The aftermath of domestic violence may also result in trauma to both adult and child victims. Social workers involved in safeguarding children need to be alert to the lasting effects on children of witnessing, or suffering, violence at the hands of a parent or parent's partner. As this case concerning a boy referred to as G will demonstrate, experiences of domestic violence can profoundly influence a child's willingness or interest in maintaining contact with a previously violent birth parent.

In the case of G, the couple had separated and while there had been a history of violence during their marriage this had abated. At the time of the Court of Appeal hearing the mother was living with her second husband. However, as Dame Butler-Sloss, presiding in the Court of Appeal case acknowledged, this protracted period of physical abuse had continued to detrimentally affect the mother even after it ceased. In coming to its judgement on all four cases the Court of Appeal turned to judicial precedents created by previous court cases which deliberated on parental contact after the breakdown of a relationship. Judgement from *Re O (Contact: Imposition of Conditions)* [1995] 2FLR 124 was quoted by Dame Butler-Sloss when she reiterated that 'the court is concerned with the interests of the mother and the father only in so far as they bear on the welfare of the child. Secondly, where parents of a child are separated and the child is in the day to day care of one of them, it is almost always in the interests of the child that he or she should have contact with the other parent' (p. 128). She also referred to *Re B (Contact: Stepfather's Opposition)* [1997] 2 FLR 579 in which Lord Woolf MR giving judgement asserted 'to deprive a father who bona fide wishes to have contact with his child of that contact is a drastic step. The court's general policy is clear: contact between a child and its natural parent is something which should be maintained wherever practical' (pp. 584–5). Neither of these cases involved domestic violence, and the judgements merely articulated general legal principles regarding contact.

As Dame Butler-Sloss observed there were far fewer precedents which dealt with contact in the context of domestic violence. One important judgement was that in *Re H (Contact: Domestic Violence)* [1998] 2 FLR 42 which asserted that '. . . domestic violence itself cannot constitute a bar to contact. Each case must inevitably be decided on its facts. Domestic violence can only be one factor in a very complex equation. There will be contact cases in which it is decisive against contact. There will be others in which it will be peripheral' (p. 56). A second key precedent identified by Dame Butler-Sloss in this area of law was *Re M (Minors) (Contact: Violent Parent)*, Re [1999] 2 FLR 321 from which she cited a crucial excerpt in which the judge in that case observed (p. 333):

> It is often said that, notwithstanding the violence, the mother must none the less bring up the children with full knowledge and a positive image of their natural father and arrange for the children to be available for contact. Too often it seems to me the courts neglect the other side of that equation, which is that a father, like this father, must demonstrate that he is a fit person to exercise contact; that he is not going to destabilise the family, that this is not going to upset the children and harm them emotionally.

The Court of Appeal also drew on research evidence contained in Lord Chancellor's Department (2000) *A Report to the Lord Chancellor on the Questions of Parental Contact in Cases where there is Domestic Violence* and Sturge and Glaser (2000) 'Contact and Domestic Violence – The Experts' Court Report' which was co-authored by two consultant child psychiatrists. The main issues highlighted by these authoritative accounts concerning contact between children and a previously violent partner are outlined in the box below.

 Key guidance

Expert reports

Lord Chancellor's Department (2000) recommends that the court should:

- Ensure that allegations of domestic violence are investigated and findings of fact made as early as possible in any family proceedings.
- Ascertain the short- and long-term impact of domestic violence on children as victims and witnesses.
- Ascertain the short- and long-term impact of domestic violence on the resident parent.
- Appraise the ongoing risk of further violence or threats of violence to the residential parent and child.
- Ensure that where indicated arrangements are put in place to protect the residential parent and child from further physical and emotional harm.

Sturge and Glaser (2000) focussed on the affects of domestic violence on the child and the likely impact of further contact with the abusive parent, and made the following key observations:

- A child can be as much affected by witnessing violence as being a victim of it.
- A child's mental health needs to be promoted in the midst of parental dispute and conflict.
- Contact should be considered in the context of each child and their particular circumstances.

- A child's need for contact can change in relation to developmental stages
- The purpose of the contact should be explicit and must benefit the child in some way.
- Contact with a father is important in terms of a child's developing identity.
- Direct contact can undermine a child's developmental needs if it: intensifies parental conflict; the child is bullied into taking sides; the child is frequently disappointed by inconsistent contact; the absent parent takes little interest in the child during contact or it is unstimulating; the contact is against the child's wishes; or the contact is stressful and there is little prospect of change.
- Where direct contact is harmful to the child, indirect contact can be important to demonstrate ongoing interest by the absent parent and preserve the possibility of a more constructive relationship developing in the future.

Applying both judicial precedent and the findings of authoritative research, Dame Butler-Sloss concluded that although domestic violence was a factor, it was just one consideration in determining whether there should be direct contact between the child and his father. She noted that the prolonged contact between father and son at the contact centre had: lacked stimulation; failed to develop as the child grew older; and was followed by several years without any contact at all. Furthermore, the child had a memory of domestic violence and enjoyed a satisfactory home life with his mother and stepfather. The consequence of all this was that while the mother and stepfather were prepared to facilitate contact, in fact the child was opposed to seeing his father. In these circumstances the mother was unwilling to force her son to have direct contact with his father. Yet, the court also concluded that the father had a genuine and well-meaning interest in re-establishing direct contact with his son.

By the time this case came to court the domestic violence had ceased. There were no ongoing child protection concerns and therefore no reason for social services to be involved. Looking beyond the immediate facts of this case, the precedents referred to by Dame Butler-Sloss and the authoritative research findings relied upon in her judgement have many implications for social work practice. Children's Services may be involved in applying for Residence or Contact Orders in situations of domestic violence, or be assisting victims to avail of court orders under the Family Law Act 1996. When negotiating contact with parents in circumstances of domestic violence, social workers need to follow both the law and the research evidence. On the one hand, there is a presumption at common law that it is in a child's best interest to have contact with both birth parents. On the other hand, research evidence reveals that there can be long-term psychological and emotional damage to children who witness domestic violence. This can weigh against contact with a previously violent parent. As the report of Sturge and Glaser (2000) suggests, such decisions have to made in relation to a particular child at a particular stage in his or her development. The needs of the resident parent who has been subjected to violence or is at risk of further violence must also be considered. This process of balancing benefits against adverse consequences has to pay attention to the effect on a resident parent of ongoing contact with a violent partner. Increased distress and fearfulness in a parent can in turn be detrimental to a child's welfare.

The child's wishes

By the time of the Court of Appeal hearing, the violence had ceased and the issue before the court was not domestic violence but contact between the child and his father in the aftermath of this violence. Matters relating to the custody of children and their contact with birth parents are regulated by the Children Act 1989 under which the child's welfare *is* paramount. There are seven considerations outlined in the supplemental welfare checklist set out in s1(3), four of which are directly applicable to this child's circumstances regarding contact. Namely, that the court must take into account: the child's wishes and feelings; his emotional needs; the ability of a parent to meet the child's needs; and any harm he has suffered or is likely to suffer. As the welfare checklist does not prioritise these considerations it is up to the court to weigh them against one another in coming to its decision.

The joint report produced by consultant child psychiatrists Sturge and Glaser (2000) concluded that continued contact with an absent father makes a vital contribution to a child's sense of identity, thereby meeting some of the child's emotional needs. The court found that the father had positive motives for wishing to re-initiate contact with his son and could be capable of meeting a number of the child's needs in his role as a non-resident parent. The court also established that the child did not wish to meet his father. The child's wishes are but one consideration among a number of others which the court must take account of before making any decision under the Children Act 1989. Nor are the child's feelings and wishes the overriding consideration of the court; in fact the overriding consideration is the child's welfare. The checklist also directs the court to consider any harm the child has suffered or is likely to suffer. So the son's wish not to see his father had to be weighed against the consequences of this in terms of the harm it might cause to the child presently or in the future. On this point there was disagreement between the experts giving evidence before the court.

As the welfare checklist illustrates, children's welfare encompasses more than their physical and mental well-being, it also includes their wishes and feelings. Courts recognise the emotional and psychological injury which can be caused to children by forcing them into situations against their will. This is not to deny that the safeguarding responsibilities of social workers will sometimes require them to remove children from families where they would much rather remain despite the abuse or neglect they are suffering. Even in these situations social workers are legally obliged to consider the effect of any course of action upon a child where it is in contravention of that child's expressed feelings on the matter. Certainly a court asked to take a decision regarding the future welfare of a child will want to know how he or she is likely to be affected by a course of action which is in opposition to the child's wishes.

Conflicting expert evidence

At the original County Court hearing, as directed by the judge both parents' solicitors agreed to jointly instruct a child psychiatrist to assess their son and give expert opinion to the court. The solicitors had difficulty identifying a willing child psychiatrist and instead appointed Dr Lowenstein, a forensic psychologist, to assess the child's mental state. In his report Dr Lowenstein asserted that the child was suffering from Parental Alienation Syndrome (PAS) triggered by his mother's hostility to the boy seeing his father. Dr Lowenstein also claimed that failure to re-initiate direct contact with his father would emotionally harm the child. He proposed that the child should be subject to a course of therapy in order to be treated for the syndrome. The judge presiding in the County Court case observed that some schools of PAS recommend immediate removal of the child from the alienating parent with no contact for a period thereafter. The judge decided to set aside Dr Lowenstein's expert evidence on several grounds. First, that the syndrome, on which Dr Lowenstein was one of the principal authorities, was not well recognised. Secondly, the judge was unwilling to subject an apparently mentally healthy child, who was then 8 years old, to therapy, particularly when his mother expressed her complete opposition to it or to compelling the child to see his father. Thirdly, the judge found the mother to be an entirely credible witness in court who expressed concern for her son and did not appear implacably hostile to him meeting with his father, as long as that was what he wished to do. It was this decision by the County Court to set aside expert evidence and concomitantly to make an order for indirect contact only, which constituted the main basis of appeal by the father.

The Court of Appeal had the advantage of commissioning a joint psychiatric report from Dr Sturge and Dr Glaser which, as Dame Butler-Sloss noted, 'incorporates the views of a distinguished group of consultants'. As expert evidence it therefore carried much more weight with the court than that produced by Dr Lowenstein. Commenting on this, Dame Butler-Sloss opined that 'Dr Lowenstein is at one end of a broad spectrum of mental health practitioners and that the existence of parental alienation syndrome is not universally accepted'. Indeed, this was a point alluded to by Dr Sturge and Dr Glaser in their report, when they observed that PAS was not recognised in the international classification of mental disorders. Dame Butler-Sloss also noted in her judgement that Dr Lowenstein was not in fact a child psychiatrist, but a psychologist. This called into question his expertise in relation to children, whereas the two child psychiatrists plainly had considerable experience of assessing them.

In effect the Court of Appeal heard further expert evidence and, recognising that there was conflict between experts, decided which was the more credible. Precedent for this approach comes from the judgement in *Re F (Mental Patient: Sterilisation)* [1990] 2 AC 1 in which Lord Goff of Chieveley asserted that while expert evidence is to be respected, ultimately it had to be evaluated and adjudged by the court. Dr Sturge and Dr Glaser specifically addressed instances of children refusing to see the non-resident parent. They made the following points:

- A child's views should be treated seriously.
- The child's age and understanding is an important consideration.
- The younger the child and the more reliant they are on a positive relationship with the resident parent, the more likely they are to be influenced by that parent's perspective.
- Acting against the child's wishes should only be contemplated if there are indications that the child may change his or her mind in the future.
- Regard must be had to the effect on the child of making a decision which pays little or no attention to his or her expressed wishes.

Taking all evidence into account it appeared unlikely to the Court of Appeal that the child would change his views about meeting his father in the foreseeable future. Therefore, forcing him to undergo therapy or see his father was likely to cause significant harm to his mental stability. An important aspect of this case is the decision of the Court of Appeal to endorse the decision of the County Court to set aside the expert evidence of Dr Lowenstein. Much emphasis has been placed on the production of expert reports by Children's Services when applying for court orders. But as this case illustrates, merely producing an expert for the court is not enough. The expert must have expertise in the right area. Here both the County Court and the Court of Appeal questioned the competence of Dr Lowenstein in relation to children because he was a psychologist and not a consultant child psychiatrist as were Dr Sturge and Dr Glaser. Furthermore, the expert evidence produced by Dr Lowenstein, like that of Dr Donegan in *Re C (A Child) (Immunisation: Parental Rights)* was not robust and represented a minority and not a well-recognised view within the discipline. Whether social workers become embroiled in private law cases or are applying for court orders in Care Proceedings they must identify experts who are indeed well recognised authorities in the area on which they are to give an opinion.

Disputed welfare report

Aside from the County Court's decision to set aside the expert evidence of Dr Lowenstein, the father also appealed on the grounds that it had then set aside the report of the Court Welfare Officer (now Children and Family Reporter). The judge presiding in the County Court had been faced with a difficult situation regarding the Court Welfare Officer's report. At an earlier hearing the offices had been instructed to produce a report recommending what course of action would be in this child's best interests. The report described the son as suffering serious emotional abuse due to the breakdown of contact with his father, it was critical of the mother, and proposed that direct contact between father and son be re-established, albeit in stages. The mother made a complaint against the Court Welfare Officer (Children and Family Reporter), which was duly investigated and partly substantiated. In consequence the Court Welfare Officer, with the endorsement of her line manager, refused to attend the court hearing. In her place another welfare officer attended court, but was unable to give reliable oral evidence because the officer had had no previous contact with the family. Being unable to effectively cross-examine the welfare officer's report in court, the judge initially accepted the report in evidence and then set it aside. He relied instead on the mother's presentation before the court as a credible witness. Since the welfare report supported the father's position, his legal representative appealed on the grounds of Judge Rudd's simply setting it aside as evidence.

Dame Butler-Sloss in her judgement was sympathetic to the argument presented by the barrister acting for the father and was herself critical of the position adopted by the judge. Effectively Judge Rudd had failed to obtain a welfare report on the best interests of the child. In Dame Butler-Sloss's opinion he should have compelled the original welfare officer to appear before the court and submit herself to cross-examination by the mother's legal counsel. This was particularly important where the contents of the report were disputed by an individual mentioned in it and where a complaint about the report had been upheld. Alternatively, the judge should have adjourned the hearing and ordered that a different welfare officer produce another report. This is a situation which plainly brings into play the *non-delay principle* under s.1(2) of the Children Act 1989. In these circumstances delay would have been justified on the grounds that it was essential to ascertain more information on the best interests of the child, including his wishes and feelings. Dame Butler-Sloss was also highly critical of the social worker acting as a welfare officer and her line manager who took it upon themselves not to attend a court hearing. This was patently poor practice.

In addition to concerns about the conduct of the welfare officer, Judge Rudd was critical of the written report itself. He noted that it made a number of unsubstantiated statements, including the assertion that the child had suffered emotional harm. There were a number of allegations in the report which lacked supporting evidence. It was for this reason that, although Judge Rudd initially accepted the welfare report as evidence, he later rejected it. In other words, the report did not constitute good evidence and was easily disputed on closer examination. Commenting on this decision by the County Court judge, Dame Butler-Sloss reiterated that judges are entitled to reject evidence brought before the court which is weak or flawed.

CAFCASS was created after the events of this case and is staffed by experienced social workers who represent the child's best interests in both private and public law proceedings. Reports submitted to the court by practitioners constitute evidence upon which a judge will rely before coming to his or her decision. As such, social workers producing court reports must provide detailed justification for their assertions in them. Practitioners cannot just state their opinion without the factual information to clearly support it. As witnesses, whether in connection with a private or public law matter, social workers can expect to be orally cross-examined about written evidence contained in their report to the court. In the case of the child G, the social worker both failed to produce a satisfactory welfare report and to appear in court to defend it. Such behaviour is clearly poor practice. Court decisions under the Children Act 1989 have to be taken in the light of the welfare checklist. This provides clear guidance to social workers employed by CAFCASS who are advising the court as to what areas need to be covered in their report. The welfare checklist is supplemented by more detailed guidance on report-writing for the court, issued by CAFCASS.

Judgement in *Re M (A Child) (Contact: Domestic Violence)*

Notwithstanding the problems encountered by the County Court in obtaining a reliable welfare report, the Court of Appeal upheld its decision permitting only indirect contact between father and son. Dame Butler-Sloss concluded her judgement with the comment that if the father persisted in sending his son interesting letters, postcards and presents, then over time as he grew older he might decide to seek direct contact with his father.

 ## Critical questions

1 This is another case in which the welfare of the child and parent is interdependent. Expert evidence shows that contact with a previously abusive partner can cause distress to the resident parent. Prolonged distress adversely affects parenting capacity and thus in turn the child's welfare. How does the expert evidence presented in this case seek to balance the child's welfare and the resident parent's welfare alongside the presumption that contact with both birth parents is in a child's best interests?

2 A number of legal options are available to parents experiencing violence from an intimate partner. Re-examine the table which summarises these options and identify the difficulties a parent might encounter trying to use each of these court orders.

 ## Perspectives

Children in private law proceedings

Each year Children and Family Reporters complete welfare reports on approximately 60,000 children in respect of applications for s.8 Orders, generally for residence or contact. Since Guardians ad Litem are only appointed in exceptional circumstances during private law proceedings, this means that for the vast majority of children their contact with the court is by way of the welfare report completed by the Children and Family Reporter. It is this report which comprises a statement of the child's wishes and feelings and ostensibly gives them a voice in court. Many children question: the degree to which Children and Family Reporters listen to them; the extent to which the welfare report accurately reflects their views; and how much notice the court actually takes of their wishes.

Bretherton (2002) found that children generally understood the role of the Children and Family Reporter and believed that they listened to them, but only one-third thought the Reporter actually understood what they felt and wanted. A large number of children felt that they had not been involved in the processes deciding their residence and contact with parents, even though they were the person most fundamentally affected by them. This is not to deny that there were a number of children who preferred such decisions to be taken by others to spare them the anguish of conflicted loyalties and guilt.

The same study revealed that some children were not aware that whatever they said to the Children and Family Reporter would be shared with other parties to the legal proceedings. This meant that children sometimes told the Reporter things in confidence only to find them appearing in the welfare report, a report to which they had very limited or no access. Some children subsequently found that their disclosure had damaged the relationship with a parent. The complexity of children's views and wishes could be simplified down to a few paragraphs in the welfare report, which consequently failed to fully articulate their perspective. At the same time many children were aware that their statements could be misinterpreted by parents in conflict and used as ammunition in an ongoing battle for residence or contact. Children were often also aware that they and the Children and Family Reporter had different agendas, with the Reporter having already decided what outcome was in the child's best interests. In short, many children felt excluded from basic decisions about their future.

CASE 6
R (on the application of A) v. *Coventry City Council* [2009] EWHC 34

Importance of the case

It explores the implications of a private fostering arrangement for a young person, which was informally agreed between his father and a friend. The case examines how Children's Services can become involved in situations that at first sight appear to be private matters between individuals.

History of the case

This was an application made by a young person to the Queen's Bench Division of the High Court for a judicial review of the refusal by the local authority to provide accommodation for him.

Facts of the case

Terry was born on 11 November 1991 and lived with his two older brothers Stephen and Mathew and his mother until the deaths of Stephen and his mother within a few weeks of each other during 2004. At this point Terry and his elder brother Mathew continued to look after themselves in their mother's home. After a few months Mathew left to stay with Ms Casey, the mother of a friend. Terry went to live with his elder married stepsister where he was treated as a member of the family. In 2005 Terry's father and his new partner Marie invited Terry to live with them. So Terry moved into a crowded three-bedroom house with his father, Marie and three children. Then in February 2007 when Terry was aged 15 years Marie demanded that he leave the house. Terry moved into

Ms Casey's home, where his older brother Mathew was already living. Terry was still residing with Ms Casey at the time of the court case. In March 2007 Ms Casey went to the offices of Coventry City Council to ask for financial assistance to support Terry. She told the official there that she did not want Terry taken into care by social services but was experiencing difficulty financially providing for him. At the time of this conversation she was in arrears with her rent and Council Tax. In June 2007 a social worker from the Fostering Team visited Ms Casey at her home and there were several further meetings between personnel from social services and Ms Casey. At each meeting Ms Casey emphasised her need for financial assistance in order to support Terry. Social workers gave Ms Casey the impression that she would receive financial assistance from the local authority to look after Terry. Terry's father permitted Ms Casey to claim child benefit for Terry, but provided no other assistance and took no interest in his son. In fact, neither Ms Casey nor Terry had any contact with the father. In September 2007 Ms Casey lost her job, and her financial position became even more precarious. She owed £900 in arrears of rent and Council Tax. She again approached Coventry City Council for financial support. In October 2007 Ms Casey received a letter from Children's Services stating that Terry was staying with Ms Casey under a private fostering arrangement and it was up to her to ask for money from Terry's father. At this point Ms Casey contacted the Coventry Law Centre, which assisted her and Terry to make an application for a judicial review of the Council's refusal to provide her with financial assistance to care for Terry.

Key people in the case

Terry – young person (aged 15 years at time of events) and claimant
Mathew – Terry's elder brother
Ms Casey – a friend of Terry and Mathew
Father – Terry's father
Marie – father's partner
Mr McGuire – barrister for local authority
Mr de Mello – barrister for the claimant
Mr Edward-Stuart – judge presiding in High Court

Discussion of the case

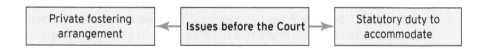

Private fostering arrangement

Birth parents and those holding parental responsibility are financially liable to maintain their children. This means that Terry's father, regardless of whether or not he was married to Terry's mother, is financially liable to maintain Terry until he is 18 years of age. As an unmarried father without parental responsibility Terry's father would have gained parental responsibility for Terry on the death of the birth mother, as otherwise no one would be responsible for his care. As a parent with parental responsibility, Terry's father was receiving child benefit for him. Although parental responsibility cannot be transferred to another adult the care of a child can be delegated to someone else by a parent with parental responsibility. Some parents may make arrangements for their children to live with someone else and be brought up by them. Where the person is not a member of the parent's immediate family this will be treated as a private fostering arrangement. The box below explains the legal definition of a private fostering arrangement.

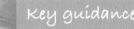

Key guidance

Replacement Children Act 1989 Guidance on Private Fostering

Para.1.6 A private fostering arrangement is essentially one that is made privately (that is to say without the involvement of a local authority) for the care of a child under the age of 16 (under 18, if disabled) by someone other than a parent or close relative with the intention that it should last for 28 days or more. Private foster carers may be from the extended family, such as a cousin or great aunt. However, a person who is a relative under the Children Act 1989, i.e. a grandparent, brother, sister, uncle or aunt (whether of the full or half blood or by marriage) or step-parent will not be a private foster carer. A private foster carer may be a friend of the family, the parent of a friend of the child, or someone previously unknown to the child's family who is willing to privately foster a child. The period for which the child is cared for and accommodated by the private foster carer should be continuous, but that continuity is not broken by the occasional short break.

Para.1.7 Private fostering arrangements can be a positive response from within the community to difficulties experienced by families. Nonetheless, privately fostered children remain a diverse and potentially vulnerable group.

Para.1.8 The private foster carer becomes responsible for providing the day-to-day care of the child in a way which will promote and safeguard his welfare. Overarching responsibility for safeguarding and promoting the welfare of the privately fostered child remains with the parent or other person with parental responsibility. Local authorities do not formally approve or register private foster carers. However, it is the duty of local authorities to satisfy themselves that the welfare of children who are, or will be, privately fostered within their area is being, or will be, satisfactorily safeguarded and promoted. It is the local authority in whose areas the privately fostered child resides which has legal duties in respect of that child.

Applying the definition of private fostering set out in the box above to Terry's situation, clearly Ms Casey was potentially acting as a private foster carer. She was a friend of Terry's elder brother Mathew in the first instance and was known to Terry's father. Terry's father had passed the child benefit claim book to Ms Casey, enabling her to obtain a very small weekly allowance for Terry. Ms Casey had day-to-day care of Terry, even though she did not have parental responsibility, which was held by Terry's father. Ms Casey had provided accommodation to Terry in her home for more than 28 days and she had expressed a willingness to continue looking after him. The house rented by Ms Casey was within the boundaries of the Coventry City Council area. Therefore this was the local authority responsible for overseeing any such private fostering arrangement.

Section 67 of the Children Act 1989 places a statutory duty on local authorities to safeguard and promote the welfare of children living in private fostering arrangements. The exercise of this duty requires the adults organising private fostering to notify the local authority of it, followed by visits from social care workers to interview those involved in the arrangement. Paragraph 1.8 reproduced in the text box above from Department for Education and Skills (2005a) *Replacement Children Act 1989 Guidance on Private Fostering*, which is statutory guidance, explains the duty of local authorities towards privately fostered children. These responsibilities are detailed in The Children (Private Arrangements for Fostering) Regulations 2005 which is reproduced in the box below. This piece of secondary legislation also sets out the legal requirement imposed on those involved in private fostering arrangements to notify the local authority.

Key legislation

The Children (Private Arrangements for Fostering) Regulations 2005

Reg.3(1) A person who proposes to foster a child privately must notify the appropriate local authority of the proposal -

(a) at least six weeks before the private fostering arrangement is to begin; or

(b) where the private fostering arrangement is to begin within six weeks, immediately

Reg.3(2) Any person who is involved (whether or not directly) in arranging for a child to be fostered privately must notify the appropriate local authority of the arrangement as soon as possible after the arrangement has been made.

Reg.4(1) Where a local authority have received notification under regulation 3 they must, for the purpose of discharging their duty under section 67(1) of the Act (welfare of privately fostered children), arrange for an officer of the authority within seven working days to -

(a) visit the premises where it is proposed that the child will be cared for and accommodated

(b) visit and speak to the proposed private foster carer and all members of his household

(c) visit and speak to the child, alone unless the officer considers it inappropriate

(d) speak to and, if it is practicable to do so, visit every parent of or person with parental responsibility for the child

Reg.8 (1) Each local authority must arrange for an officer of the authority to visit every child who is being fostered privately in their area -

(a) in the first year of the private fostering arrangement, at intervals of not more than six weeks; and

(b) in any second or subsequent year, at intervals of not more than 12 weeks

Reg.8(2) In addition to visits carried out in accordance with paragraph (1) the local authority must arrange for every child who is fostered privately in their area to be visited by an officer when reasonably requested to do so by the child, the private foster carer, a parent of the child or any other person with parental responsibility for the child.

As these regulations indicate, there is a duty on private foster carers and those involved in setting up, or who know of, private foster care arrangements to inform the local authority. The local authority in turn is obliged to visit the dwelling where it is proposed that the child will live, and interview those involved in the fostering arrangement. Thereafter, the local authority has a duty to visit that child at least once every six weeks during the first year and in subsequent years at least once every three months. These regulations are designed to safeguard and promote the welfare of children and young people in private fostering arrangements. Obviously any social worker who makes a visit or conducts an enquiry in connection with a private fostering arrangement which gives concern for a child's safety will take preventative action.

In the present case, Terry left his father's home and moved to live with Ms Casey. In turn Ms Casey went to the local authority to inform them that Terry had moved in with her and she urgently needed financial assistance to look after him. It is notable that although Ms Casey first informed the local authority in March 2007 that Terry was living with her, it was not until June 2007, that a social worker actually visited Ms Casey at home. Regulation 4(1) stipulates that an officer of the local authority should visit the premises within seven working days of receiving notice of a private fostering arrangement not, as in this case, three months later. But this was only one of a number of interactions between social workers and Ms Casey which created legal confusion as to whether she was actually providing private foster care for Terry. The local authority did not interview Terry's father and did not in fact carry out the regular visits required by regulation 8(1), which is also reproduced in the box above. For the High Court hearing this case, the conduct of Children's Services began to cast doubt on whether in actual fact Terry had ever been privately fostered by Ms Casey. Department for Education and Skills (2002) *National Minimum Standards for Private Fostering* sets out minimum requirements which a local authority must comply with in circumstances where there is a private fostering arrangement. These are outlined in the box below.

Key guidance

National Minimum Standards for Private Fostering

Standard 1: The local authority has a written statement or plan, which sets out its duties and functions in relation to private fostering and the ways in which they will be carried out.

Standard 2: The local authority promotes awareness of the notification requirements and ensures that those professionals who may come into contact with privately fostered children understand their role in notification.

Standard 3: The local authority determine effectively the suitability of all aspects of the private fostering arrangement in accordance with the regulations.

Standard 4: The local authority provides such advice and support to private foster carers and prospective private foster carers as appears to the authority to be needed.

Standard 5: The local authority provides advice and support to the parents of children who are privately fostered within their area as appears to the authority to be needed.

Standard 6: Children who are privately fostered are able to access information and support when required so that their welfare is safeguarded and promoted. Privately fostered children are enabled to participate in decisions about their lives.

Standard 7: The local authority has in place and implements effectively a system for monitoring the way in which it discharges its duties and functions in relation to private fostering.

Department for Education and Skills (2002) *National Minimum Standards for Private Fostering* is issued under s.7 of the Local Authority Social Services Act 1970 and is therefore statutory guidance. This means that in its dealings with Terry and Ms Casey the local authority was obliged to comply with the standards listed in the text box above unless there were exceptional reasons for departing from them. There were no exceptional circumstances in this case. Yet in its conduct, the local authority fell well short of these seven standards. In evidence to the High Court the local authority claimed that social workers had informed Ms Casey that she was providing private fostering and that Terry's father and not the local authority was financially liable for this arrangement. However, Ms Casey only received a formal response from Coventry City Council (in the form of a letter from the Children's Social Care Team) in October 2007 stating that she was a private foster carer. Indeed, not until November 2007 was a fostering assessment actually completed. Plainly the local authority had failed to properly determine the suitability of the fostering arrangement or to provide accurate advice and guidance to Ms Casey and Terry.

National Minimum Standards are not just applicable in relation to private fostering, but cover many areas of social work practice and that of other social care professionals. They are addressed both to management and frontline practitioners who are required to meet these minimum standards in their professional interactions with parents, children, users and carers. Plainly if the professionals involved with Ms Casey and Terry had been meeting the seven standards set out above there would not have been any confusion as to Terry's true position. National Minimum Standards assist practitioners to carry out their statutory duties and powers lawfully and in ways which best meet the needs of those they seek to assist or protect.

Statutory duty to accommodate

Ms Casey was under the impression between March 2007, when she first informed the local authority of Terry's presence in her home, and October 2007, when she received the letter from the Children's Social Care Team, that Coventry City Council would financially assist her to look after Terry. Ms Casey was actually looking after both Mathew and Terry at her own expense in a situation where she was herself in dire financial straits. Where children appear to be in need because they are not being properly provided with accommodation local authorities have a statutory duty to accommodate them under s.20 of the Children Act 1989, which is reproduced in the box below.

 Key legislation

Children Act 1989

s.20(1) Every local authority shall provide accommodation for any child in need within their area who appears to them to require accommodation as a result of –

(a) there being no person who has parental responsibility for him;

(b) his being lost or having been abandoned; or

(c) the person who has been caring for him being prevented (whether or not permanently, and for whatever reason) from providing him with suitable accommodation or care.

Section 20(1) describes three situations in which a local authority might have to provide accommodation for a child. The first circumstance is if there is no one with parental responsibility for the child. In this case, Terry's father held parental responsibility for him. The second circumstance is if the child has been lost or abandoned. Terry had certainly not been lost by his father, but it was arguable that his father had abandoned him. There had only been one contact between Ms Casey and Terry's father, which took place when she visited him to obtain the child benefit book. No contact at all had occurred between Terry and his father since he was asked to leave the house by Marie. The third situation where the local authority can be legally required to look after a child is if the person caring for him or her is unable to provide suitable accommodation. This was a crucial point of dispute in the High Court case. Mr McGuire acting for the defendant local authority argued that Ms Casey was providing Terry with suitable accommodation under a private fostering arrangement and therefore a duty to accommodate Terry under s.20(1)(c) of the Children Act 1989 did not arise.

Mr Edward-Stuart QC sitting as a Deputy Judge of the High Court and presiding over this case questioned whether the accommodation provided by Ms Casey could be correctly described as 'suitable'. As Mr Edward-Stuart pointed out, the accommodation provided by Ms Casey in February 2007 when Terry first came to live with her was of an unsure and possibly temporary nature. No formal agreement had been made between Terry's father and Ms Casey for Terry's care. The transfer of child benefit, which in 2007 was £12.10 a week, represented a trifling amount which clearly did not cover Terry's weekly living expenses. Although Ms Casey informed Coventry City Council that Terry was living with her, she did not complete formal notification as required by reg.3(1) and sch.1 of the Children (Private Arrangements for Fostering) Regulations 2005. In other words, Ms Casey was never registered with the local authority as a private foster carer. Had social workers really believed that this was the position Ms Casey was in, then they had a legal responsibility to inform her about the need to register Terry's living arrangement. In the light of all these factors, it appeared that as a 15-year-old boy forced to leave his father's house and arriving on Ms Casey's doorstep, a duty to accommodate Terry under s.20 arose. Reviewing the evidence before him Deputy Judge Edwards-Stuart came to the conclusion (para. 74) that:

> . . . accommodation which is uncertain as to duration because it is not founded on any secure financial footing is not accommodation that can be said to be suitable for a 15-year-old who is a child in need, however caring the prospective family may appear to be . . . on the facts of this case, leaving Terry in the care of Ms. Casey in circumstances where it was questionable as to how long she could afford to keep him would not have amounted to him having accommodation suitable for a 15-year-old – it was too precarious and insecure.

In effect the judge was saying that in February 2007 when Terry moved into Ms Casey's home, the local authority was wrong to assume that this automatically qualified as *suitable* accommodation. Ms Casey made it clear to the local authority from the outset that she was in serious debt and doubted her ability to continue to care for Terry without financial assistance. Since in fact Terry was a child that the local authority had a statutory duty to accommodate under s.20, it should have made appropriate arrangements to do so. In this particular case agreeing to pay Ms Casey a weekly allowance in order to accommodate Terry on behalf of the local authority would have been the most appropriate arrangement.

Terry's father had been unwilling to pay anything towards his son's living expenses when he moved to live with Ms Casey. Had the local authority accepted its statutory duty to accommodate Terry, it could have required Terry's father to contribute financially towards his care. This is because s.23 of the Children Act 1989 permits a local authority which is accommodating a child to recover a proportion of the costs from the child's parents. If Coventry City Council had complied with its legal obligation to provide accommodation for Terry, it could at the same time have ensured that his father paid towards Terry's maintenance.

Social workers invariably come across a wide variety of different living arrangements in the course of their day-to-day practice. As this case demonstrates, they need to be aware of the legal implications of the family arrangements they witness. Local authorities have a responsibility to safeguard and promote the welfare of children regardless of where they are living or in whose care. It could be argued that children who for one reason or another are not living with their parents require more vigilance from Children's Services. A legal framework to safeguard children in private fostering arrangements has been introduced by the Children (Private Arrangements for Fostering) Regulations 2005. But this is only effective if social workers and their local authorities correctly distinguish between a private fostering arrangement and a need for the local authority to intervene and accommodate a child.

Certainly the worst of all possible worlds is for social workers to be unclear as to their role or the law in relation to private fostering and the local authority's duty under s.20 of the Children Act 1989. The misleading information given to Ms Casey by social workers, and the contradictory way in which she was treated by the Children's Social Care Team, caused her considerable confusion, distress and financial hardship. Ms Casey's experiences of course are not unique. Belated assessments, inadequate communication by social care staff and different messages from the different practitioners can be replicated in other areas of practice if professionals are vague in their knowledge of the law.

Judgement in *R (on the application of A) v. Coventry City Council*

Deputy Judge Edwards-Stuart presiding over the High Court hearing for a judicial review concluded that a duty to accommodate Terry had arisen under s.20 of the Children Act 1989 and that the local authority had failed to assist Ms Casey to provide that accommodation. The judge ordered Coventry City Council to pay damages to Ms Casey equivalent to a weekly fostering allowance for Terry backdated to June 2007 and up to his 18th birthday. His judgement also recorded (para. 4) that since leaving the home of his father:

> Terry has remained with Ms Casey, with whom he has been very happy. She has cared for and supported him ever since, almost entirely at her own expense. He is now 17 and attending a carpentry course at a City College in Coventry. Ms Casey's kindness to Terry reflects enormous credit on her and her care has been beyond reproach.

 Critical questions

1 What are the problems associated with private fostering which emerge from this case?

2 Why do you think there was such confusion as to whether or not the local authority owed a duty to Terry under s.20 of the Children Act 1989 and what might be the implications for your own practice?

3 What aspects of poor social work practice are identified by the judge, and how would you avoid these in a similar situation?

 Perspectives

Children's experiences of private fostering

The Children's Rights Director for England canvassed the views of young people being privately fostered about the regulations which governed their care. His findings were published in Ofsted (2008b) *Children's Experience of Private Fostering*. A number of children expressed confusion as to whether their foster care had been organised by social workers or their parents. As Ofsted (2008b) notes this is not surprising as it can be difficult for children to distinguish between social workers organising their care and their involvement in monitoring the arrangement for their care. Of the 34 children interviewed by the Children's Rights Director most had lived with their carer for less than a year, but around one-quarter had lived in private foster care for three or more years.

Almost all the children participating in the research described receiving visits from social workers, although in some instances the number of statutory visits were fewer than stipulated in Reg.8(1) of the The Children (Private Arrangements for Fostering) Regulations 2005. One child complained that because there were only four visits during the second year that she was privately fostered this meant 'professionals thought I was happy, but a few months later when things went sour they weren't there any more' (Ofsted, 2008b: 11). Children generally welcomed visits by social workers with one explaining that 'we talk about how I feel living with my carer, am I OK, is everything fine, school and much more' (Ofsted, 2008b: 12). Yet, for many children, talking to their social worker about the negative aspects of being privately fostered could be difficult. One research participant pleaded for social workers to 'try really hard to get you to say what you are not allowed to say such as bullying'. For other children the problem was the way practitioners sometimes interacted with them. One thought that it was difficult to be really open with social workers because often they were 'not really having a conversation, just 21 questions' (Ofsted, 2008b: 12).

The legislation requires social workers to speak to children alone during visits to their home. However, a number of children said either they were spoken to in the presence of their carer or were asked if they wanted to be spoken to alone. There was consensus among the children participating in the study that 'asking "do you want to see me on your own?" is no good. It shouldn't be a choice. You should see the social worker on your own anyway.' One young person described a reluctance to speak about worries to a 'social worker you don't really know and the foster carer is there so you're intimidated and limited in what you can say' (Ofsted, 2008b: 12).

Reg.8(2) of the The Children (Private Arrangements for Fostering) Regulations 2005 requires social workers to visit children upon request. The children participating in the survey described a range of reactions when they tried to contact their social worker between statutory visits. Some social workers appeared not to respond, some only held a telephone conversation with the child and some came to visit the child at home as soon as possible. A number of children found it hard to contact their social worker, one described it as 'not easy at all, they're never there or put me on hold for a long time' (Ofsted, 2008b: 13). Despite their dissatisfactions with some aspects of private fostering, almost all children in the survey expressed a conviction that their substitute carer was the right person to look after them.

Learning points

- There are different legal rights and responsibilities attached to different forms of living arrangements between couples and children of the household.
- Parental responsibility is a key concept introduced by the Children Act 1989 and has major implications for the rights and obligations of parents and guardians.
- The *welfare, non-delay* and *no order principle* underpin the Children Act 1989 and guide the court's decisions in family law proceedings concerning children.
- Section 8 Orders are used in both private and public law proceedings to determine questions relating to children's welfare and care.

- The existence of domestic violence can affect the court's decision regarding ongoing contact between a child and a violent parent or parent's partner.

- Expert opinion can be controversial or contested by other experts during family proceedings. In these situations it will be up to the judge to weigh the evidence presented by different expert witnesses.

- Children in complex family proceedings will be given separate legal representation unless it can be clearly established that their interests are the same as their parents.

- Children in private fostering arrangements are still owed a number of statutory duties by local authorities, which includes ensuring that the accommodation is suitable and the arrangements promote the child's welfare.

Further reading

Collier, R. (2005) 'Fathers 4 Justice, law and the new politics of fatherhood', *Child and Family Law Quarterly* 17(4): 511. This article considers the perspectives of non-resident fathers regarding contact with their children.

Kemp, V., Pleasence, P. and Balmer, N.J. (2005) 'Incentivising disputes: the role of public funding in private law children cases', *Journal of Social Welfare and Family Law* 27(2): 125-41. This article investigates the way in which public funding of court action by parents can prolong legal disputes over residence and contact concerning their children.

Smart, C. and May, V. (2004) 'Why can't they agree? The underlying complexity of contact and residence disputes', *Journal of Social Welfare and Family Law* 26(4): 347-60. This article examines the underlying dynamics of disputes between parents and how the court system deals with these.

Sturge, C. and Glaser, D. (2000) 'Contact and Domestic Violence - The Experts' Court Report', *Family Law* 30: 615. This is the report produced by Dr Sturge and Dr Glaser, two eminent consultant child psychiatrists, to guide decisions regarding parent-child contact in circumstances of past or ongoing domestic violence.

Useful websites

www.cafcass.gov.uk This is the website of the Children and Family Court Advisory and Support Service. It provides information on the work of the organisation and easy-to-access guides on various aspects of family proceedings.

www.everychildmatters.gov.uk This is a government website which provides a wide range of documents on government policy and legislation in relation to children. It provides guidance on children's welfare, protection, education and private fostering.

www.womensaid.org.uk This site is run by the Women's Aid charity and provides information relating to domestic violence against women. It offers easy-to-read guides on the legal options available to parents experiencing domestic abuse.

www.fathers-4-justice.org/f4j/ This is the website of fathers campaigning for improved access to their children after the breakdown of a relationship.

3

PROMOTING WELFARE AND SAFEGUARDING CHILDREN

Overview of relevant legislation

As the statistics above reveal, there are in the region of 300,000–400,000 children who are in need due to being in the care system, having a disability or due to their offending behaviour. The vast majority of these children are being cared for by their families. A small number of these children, around 60,000, are actually in the care system and may either be living with their family or relatives or else being *looked after* by the local authority. In any year 26,000 children are placed on the child protection register because they are at risk of significant harm due to neglect or abuse. Each of these children will have a Child Protection Plan in place and an allocated social worker who regularly sees the child and his or her family. This large number of successfully protected children needs to be seen against the rare but extremely tragic deaths of children who are known to Children's Services. Local authority social workers will be involved in obtaining in the region of 20,000 court orders during public law proceedings in any given year. These will all be cases involving the safeguarding of children under the provisions of the Children Act 1989. As Children's Services are the lead agency in child protection, this area of work forms a large proportion of social work practice.

As you will have already seen in Chapter 2, the Children Act 1989 is the main legislation which frames social work activity with children living in England and Wales. As this chapter also explores social work with children, it will equally draw on the main precepts and provisions laid down in the Children Act 1989 (see the table on page 57 outlining the key sections of this Act). In addition, this chapter will explore the relevance of the Children Act 2004 to practice situations. The main provisions of this statute are set out in the table below.

Children Act 2004	Key sections
Part I - Children's Commissioner	ss.1-9 Creates separate children's commissioners to promote the rights and interests of children in England, Wales, Scotland and Norhteren Ireland
Part II - Children's Services in England	s.10 Places a duty on local authorities to put in place arrangements for cooperation between key agencies to improve the well-being of children
	s.11 Places a duty on key agencies to have regard to the need to safeguard and promote the welfare of children in exercising their functions
	s.12 Provides for the creation of a national databse to enable professionals working with children to share information
	ss.13-16 Establishment and function of Local Safeguarding Children Boards
	ss.19 Designation of a lead elected council member of the local authority for children's services
Part III - Children's Services in Wales	s.25 Places a duty on local authorities in Wales to put in place arrangements for cooperation between key agencies to improve the well-being of children
	s.28 Places a duty on key agencies in Wales to have regard to the need to safeguard and promote the welfare of children in exercising their functions
	ss.31-34 Setting up of Local Safeguarding Children Boards in Wales
Part IV - Advisory and Support Services for Family Proceedings	ss.35-43 Devolution of CAFCASS functions to the Welsh Assembly
Part V - Miscellaneous	ss.44-47 Regulation of private fostering
	s.52 Duty placed on local authorities to promote the educational achievement of *looked after* children
Part VI - General	ss.64-69 Deals with repeals by and commencement of the Act
Schedules 1-5	These deal with a variety of related matters supplementary to the Act

As already discussed in Chapter 2, the Children Act 1989 is underpinned by three main principles defined in s.1 of the statute. These principles direct the deliberations of judges presiding over hearings whether in private law or public law proceedings involving children. The *welfare, no order* and *non-delay* principles therefore apply to social work activity and professional decision making. For this reason they are once again set out in the box below for your reference.

Key legislation

Children Act 1989

Welfare principle

s.1(1) 'When a court determines any question with respect to the upbringing of a child . . . the child's welfare shall be the court's paramount consideration'

The court is required to place a child's welfare before that of the parents or guardians of the child and before any other consideration.

No order principle

s.1(5) 'Where a court is considering whether or not to make one or more orders under the Act with respect to a child, it shall not make the order or any of the orders unless it considers that doing so would be better for the child than making no order at all'

The court will not make an order unless it is convinced by the evidence that making an order would be more likely to improve the child's welfare than making no order at all.

Non-delay principle

s.1(2) the court 'shall have regard to the general principle that any delay in determining the question is likely to prejudice the welfare of the child'

The presumption is that delay in court proceedings is generally harmful to children. This presumption can be refuted if a party to the proceedings can show that a delay is likely to benefit the child. For example a local authority might ask for the adjournment of a hearing until it conducts a vital interview to complete its investigation of child abuse and produce an improved Child Protection Plan.

As Chapter 2 revealed, aside from these working principles which are designed to promote children's welfare, children in private law proceedings are sometimes given separate legal representation in court. This is an additional protection to ensure that children's best interests are not subsumed into the best interests of their parents. In public law cases involving children they are always separately legally represented in court by a Children's Guardian. As you read through this chapter, it will become evident that in public law cases conflicts can often emerge between the child, the parents and the local authority. Some of these cases demonstrate the conflict of rights between parents and children. Others highlight tensions and disagreements between the local authority and the children it is trying to protect. To assist managers and frontline professionals working in this challenging area of practice under the Children Act 1989, the government has produced a number of guidance documents. The policy and practice guidance referred to in this chapter are summarised in the table on the next page.

Guidance document	Outline content
Department of Health (1991a) *The Children Act 1989 Guidance and Regulations: Family Placement*	This statutory guidance provides instruction to practitioners placing children living away from home with relatives or friends.
Department of Health (2000d) *Framework for the Assessment of Children in Need and their Families*	This is policy guidance and details how practitioners should conduct multidisciplinary assessments and care plans for children.
Department of Health (2000e) *Framework for the Assessment of Children in Need and their Families: Core Assessment Records*	These documents are produced for specific age groups of children and provide detailed pro forma for gathering information about children and their families.
HM Government (2006a) *Working Together to Safeguard Children*	This is policy guidance which describes how agencies should collaborate with each other and share information. It also outlines the roles of different agencies in safeguarding children.
Social Services Inspectorate and Department of Health (1995) *The Challenge of Partnership in Child Protection: Practice Guidance*	This is practice guidance which focusses on partnership working with parents and collaboration with other agencies in safeguarding children.
HM Government (2006c) *The Common Assessment Framework for Children and Young People: Practitioners' Guide*	This provides a common standardised pro forma for recording information about children across different agencies working with children and young people.
HM Government (2008) *Safeguarding Children in whom Illness is fabricated or Induced*	This guidance provides advice and direction to practitioners who suspect that a child's illness may be induced or fabricated by a carer.

Overview of the cases

This chapter examines five cases. The first explores the findings of a Serious Case Review which is conducted by the Local Safeguarding Children Board whenever a child dies in a local authority area and abuse or neglect is a possible cause of the child's death. The other four cases all concern matters which came before the courts. A brief summary of all of these cases is provided below:

Case 1 Second Serious Case Review: Baby Peter, February 2009 explores the:

- Corresponding obligations of employers and employees in social care agencies.
- Challenges of multi-agency collaboration.
- Problems of investigation by police and social workers.
- Difficulties of working in partnership with parents.

Case 2 *Re C and B (Children) (Care Order: Future Harm)* [2001] 1 FLR 611 explores the:

- Thresholds for different court orders.
- Right to a private and family life.
- Concept of proportionality when interfering with a Convention Right.
- Rights of parents to apply for a variation of discharge of a court order.

Case 3 *X Local Authority* v. *B (Emergency Protection Orders)* [2005] FLR 341 explores the:

- Use of ex parte Emergency Protection Orders.
- Parents' right to a family life.
- Consideration to be given to children's wishes when safeguarding them.
- Challenges of working in partnership with parents while safeguarding children.

Case 4 *Re U (A Child) (Serious Injury: Standard of Proof)* [2004] EWCA Civ 567 explores the:

- Standard of proof in care proceedings.
- Status of medical evidence.
- Nature of fabricated or induced illness.

Case 5 *Re O (A Minor) (Care Proceedings: Education)* [1992] 1 WLR 912 explores the:

- Consideration to be given to the wishes of a *Gillick* competent child.
- Legal action available against parents who fail to send their children to school.
- Definition of significant harm.
- Threshold for a Care Order.

CASE 1
Second Serious Case Review: Baby Peter, February 2009

Importance of the case

This examines the role of social workers and healthcare professionals alongside inter-agency cooperation in relation to the failure to protect an infant from fatal physical abuse. It also explores the challenges of partnership working with an abusive parent.

History of the case

On 3 August 2007 a 17-month-old infant, known to the Children and Young People's Services of Haringey Council, died of injuries caused by months of physical abuse. A Serious Case Review, commissioned by Haringey's Local Safeguarding Board, into the events leading up to the infant's death reported in July 2008. This was deemed inadequate by Ofsted, and the Secretary of State for the Department of Children, Schools and Families directed that a second Serious Case Review should be conducted. The findings of the second Serious Case Review were published in February 2009.

Facts of the case

Mr A and Ms A married in 2002 and had three children together before the birth of Peter in March 2006. Shortly after Peter's birth the couple separated. Both Ms A and all her children were registered with the same General Practitioner in the London Borough of Haringey. Following Peter's birth Ms A received visits from a health visitor who initially reported that he was developing well. Ms A took Peter three times to her GP in the period September to December 2006 with a number of bruises, particularly to the head. Ms A explained that Peter bruised easily and had fallen down stairs. During the third consultation on 11 December 2006, the GP referred Peter to Whittington Hospital for further investigation. A number of bruises were discovered on Peter's body and identified on a body map. He was also found not to have any medical condition which would explain the bruising. A Strategy Discussion was held on 12 December and the notes of that meeting recorded that the bruises might have been caused by 'pummelling'. A consultant paediatrician concluded that the bruising was 'very suggestive of non-accidental injury'. Police and social workers interviewed the older children and Ms A but obtained no satisfactory explanation as to Peter's bruises. A Child Protection Conference was held on 22 December 2006 and Peter was placed on the Child Protection Register. Another of Ms A's children was also placed on the Child Protection Register at this time. Both of these children were, up until Peter's death, seen regularly by the health visitor, the children's social worker, the GP and a support worker from the Family Welfare Association. In April 2007 Ms A took Peter to the Accident and Emergency Department of North Middlesex University Hospital with swelling on the left side of his head. He was also found to have bruising on other parts of his body. Ms A informed medical staff that Peter had been pushed by another child. Peter was discharged home from hospital a few days later. Peter was again admitted to the same Accident and Emergency Department just over a month later where multiple bruises were again discovered on his body. A Strategy Meeting was held on 4 June 2007 at which it was agreed to commence a s.47 inquiry. There continued to be regular contact with the family by health and social care professionals who generally reported that all appeared well. On 1 August Ms A took Peter to the Child Development Centre where he was found to have suffered considerable weight loss and to be on the 9th centile. The doctor who saw Peter at the Centre diagnosed a viral infection. By this time Peter was known by professionals to have a history of hyperactivity, aggression and head banging. Two days later, on the morning of 3 August 2007 the London Ambulance Service responded to a 999 call from Ms A who reported that Peter was not moving. Peter was pronounced dead at 12.19 pm that same day.

Key people in the case

Peter – infant boy aged 17 months at time of death
Ms A – Peter's mother
Mr A – Peter's father
Ms M – mother's friend
Mr H – Ms A's boyfriend
Mr L – brother of Mr H
Ms F – Mr L's girlfriend

Discussion of the case

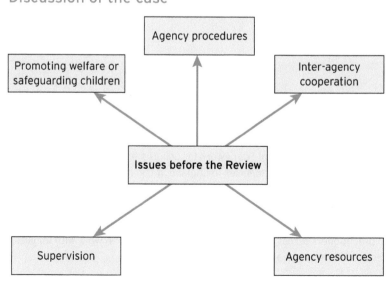

Agency resources

Ofsted, Healthcare Commission and HM Inspectorate of Constabulary (2008) *Joint Area Review: Haringey Children's Services Authority Area* was the report of an inspection into the operation of Haringey's Children's Services conducted a year after Peter's death. At paragraph 50, it noted,

> The high turnover of qualified social workers in some social care teams has resulted in heavy reliance on agency staff, who make up 51 of 121 established social worker posts. This results in lack of continuity for children and their families in care planning . . . currently there are four unfilled social work posts. Some social workers have heavy caseloads, exacerbated by the need for experienced staff to complete unfinished work for those staff who leave. Although a transfer protocol is in place to define when a case should transfer to long term social care teams, in practice there can be difficulty making timely transfers due to capacity issues within teams.

In fact at the time of Peter's death there were a high number of unallocated cases due to capacity issues at Haringey's Children and Young People's Service. By the completion of the Joint Area Review inspection in December 2008 there remained in the region of 400 unallocated cases. It is also noteworthy that during the six months that Peter was on the Child Protection Register he had one change of social worker, which likely reflects issues around staff turnover, alluded to by the Joint Area Review. In addition Ofsted, Healthcare Commission and HM Inspectorate of Constabulary (2008: para. 24) discovered that 'the use of the *Common Assessment Framework* as a tool for multi-agency assessment is not universally understood or effectively implemented by staff across agencies, despite them having been trained'. The Joint Area Review also expressed concern that most of the assessments completed using this online system were not in fact multidisciplinary. Often the Common Assessment Framework was simply used by practitioners as a means to refer a child to another agency. The contribution of the Common Assessment Framework to multi-agency work is explained in HM Government (2006c) *The Common Assessment Framework for Children and Young People: Practitioners' Guide*. This also provides instruction to frontline professionals working in health, education, social care, Connexions Service, Youth Offending Teams and other agencies that might be involved with a child's welfare. The main aspects of the Common Assessment Framework are described in the box below.

Key guidance

The Common Assessment Framework for Children and Young People: Practitioners' Guide

1.1 The Common Assessment Framework for children and young people (CAF) is a shared assessment tool used across agencies in England. It can help practitioners develop a shared understanding of a child's needs, so they can be met more effectively. It will avoid children and families having to tell and re-tell their story.

1.2 The CAF is an important tool for early intervention. It has been designed specifically to help practitioners assess needs at an earlier stage and then work with families, alongside other practitioners and agencies, to meet them.

3.2 A common assessment can help you work with the child and their family to identify what the needs are, when you are not sure. It provides a structure for recording information that you gather by having a conversation with them. It will also help you in getting other services to help, because they will recognise that your concern is based on some evidence, not just an assumption. Other services in your areas will also be using the common assessment and so they will recognise and expect an assessment in this format.

3.3 The CAF can be used to assess the needs of unborn babies, infants, children or young people. You do not have to be an expert in any particular area to do a common assessment. You do, however, need to have the right skills and to have been on a locally approved training course.

3.5 The CAF is an important tool for early intervention. It is designed for use when:

- You are concerned about how well a child is progressing. You might be concerned about their health, welfare, behaviour, progress in learning or any other aspect of their well-being. Or they or their parent may have raised a concern with you
- The needs are unclear, or broader then your service can address
- A common assessment would help identify the needs, and/or get other services to help meet them.

As practice guidance reproduced in the box above indicates, the Common Assessment Framework draws together the information held by professionals located in different agencies and with a variety of responsibilities towards children. HM Government (2006c: para. 3.7) *The Common Assessment Framework for Children and Young People: Practitioners' Guide* stresses that the CAF is only to be used when there are concerns that a child is not progressing well but it is not clear what exactly their needs are. Completion of a CAF is also dependent on permission being given by the child or parent. This is not a tool for use when it is clear that a child is at risk of significant harm which should trigger formal inter-agency child protection procedures. A CAF permits different agencies to complete a standardised pro forma so that all the information known about a child and his or her family can be drawn together. Local Safeguarding Children Board (2009) *Serious Case Review: Baby Peter: Executive Summary* noted (para. 4.3.1) that 'The CAF is not being used by social care staff in Haringey although it has been adopted by education and health services supporting children in universal settings.' As the events surrounding Peter were to reveal, the inadequate sharing of information between Children's Services and other agencies was a major factor in failing to protect him. CAF ought to have been an important tool in inter-agency communication.

The GSCC (2002b) *Code of Practice for Employers of Social Care Workers* sets out the obligations of employers to staff and service-users: para. 2.3 requires them to have 'systems in place to enable social care workers to report inadequate resources or operational difficulties which might impede the delivery of safe care and working with them and relevant authorities to address those issues'. In addition employers also have a duty of care to their employees which includes ensuring that there are sufficient resources to support safe working practices. Therefore frontline social workers who find their activity hampered, or are being put at risk, by inadequate staffing, insufficient administrative support, poor logistics, or deficient training, must bring this to the attention of management. Indeed para. 3.4 of the GSCC *Code of Practice for Social Care Workers* stipulates that social workers should bring 'to the attention of your employer or the appropriate authority resource or operational difficulties that might get in the way of the delivery of safe care'. It is plainly a requisite of the GSCC Code, and in some instances a statutory requirement, for shortcomings in working conditions to be rectified by senior management. Failure to address pressing problems within an agency, which in turn detrimentally affects the protection of children, can be reported to the General Social Care Council which will then be obliged to act.

Agency procedures

Department of Health (2000d) *Framework for the Assessment of Children in Need and their Families* sets out a flow diagram (reproduced on the next page) of the procedures and timescales involved in decision making for children in need.

On 11 December 2006 following a GP referral that day, Peter was admitted to Whittington Hospital with a swelling on the head. On examination by a paediatrician at the hospital Peter was discovered to have extensive bruising associated with non-accidental injuries. Correctly, the named doctor for child protection was informed and a referral was made immediately to Children and Young People's Services. In the meantime Peter was transferred to a paediatric ward to permit further investigation of his injuries and to ensure his safety. A Strategy Discussion was held the following day between key professionals at which it was agreed to hold a Child Protection Conference, scheduled for 22 December. The police officer who attended the Strategy Discussion was clear that Peter should not be allowed to return home to the care of Ms A until a s.47 inquiry had been completed under the Children Act 1989. This provision, which is set out in the text box below, permits social workers to carry out a detailed investigation where they suspect that a child may be at risk of significant harm.

Key legislation

Children Act 1989

s.47(1) Where a local authority –
- (a) are informed that a child who lives, or is found, in their area –
  - (i)   is the subject of an emergency protection order; or
  - (ii) is in police protection; or
- (b) have reasonable cause to suspect that a child who lives, or is found, in their area is suffering, or is likely to suffer, significant harm, the authority shall make, or cause to be made, such enquires as they consider necessary to enable them to decide whether they should take any action to safeguard or promote the child's welfare

31(9) gives further definitions to the terms used in s.47:
- 'harm' means ill-treatment or the impairment of health or development
- 'development' means physical, intellectual, emotional, social or behavioural development
- 'health' means physical or mental health
- ill-treatment includes sexual abuse and forms of ill-treatment which are not physical

Since action under s.47 involves a form of compulsory inquiry and assessment, social workers cannot launch an investigation at will. They must possess sufficient evidence to *have reasonable cause to suspect that a child who lives, or is found, in their area is suffering, or is likely to suffer, significant harm*. In the case of Peter, medical evidence

Maximum timescales for analysing the needs of child and parenting capacity

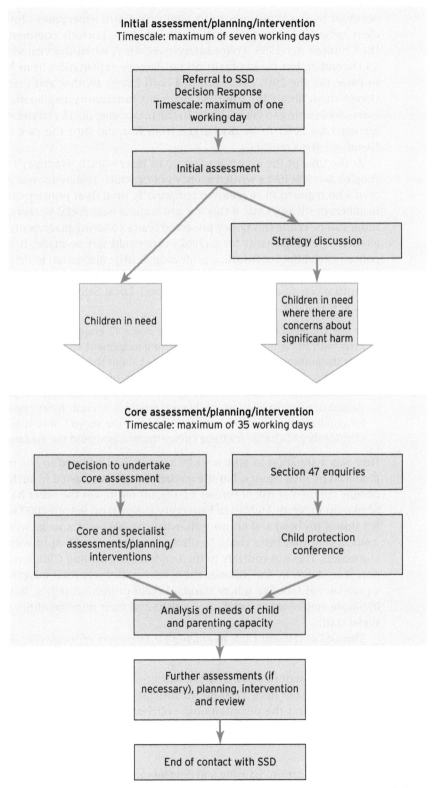

Initial assessment/planning/intervention
Timescale: maximum of seven working days

Referral to SSD
Decision Response
Timescale: maximum of one
working day

Initial assessment

Strategy discussion

Children in need

Children in need
where there are
concerns about
significant harm

Core assessment/planning/intervention
Timescale: maximum of 35 working days

Decision to undertake
core assessment

Section 47 enquiries

Core and specialist
assessments/planning/
interventions

Child protection
conference

Analysis of needs of child
and parenting capacity

Further assessments (if
necessary), planning, intervention
and review

End of contact with SSD

Source: Department of Health (2000) *Framework for the Assessment of Children in Need and their Families* London: Stationery Office, p. 33.

obtained by the Whittington Hospital's paediatric emergency clinic clearly gave sufficient cause for concern to reach the threshold to lawfully commence an inquiry under the Children Act 1989. Police interviewed Ms A when she visited Peter in hospital on 15 December, but could obtain no satisfactory explanation from her as to the injuries to Peter. On the 19th police arrested both Peter's mother and grandmother and questioned them about his injuries. Again no satisfactory explanation was given of the extensive bruising to Peter's body. In the meantime, on 15 December social workers had arranged for Peter to be discharged from hospital into the care of Ms M who was a friend of Peter's mother.

At the time of the events leading up to Peter's death, Haringey's Children and Young People's Services had a written agency policy which required social workers to place children who required to be removed temporarily from their primary carer with other family members or friends. Only if this was not feasible were social workers to place a child with foster carers. While this policy preserved scarce fostering placements for situations where alternative arrangements for a child's care could not be made, it introduced a blanket policy which afforded frontline professionals little discretion. In Peter's case, the fact that Ms M. was close friend of Peter's mother hardly offered Peter sufficient protection in the circumstances. Commenting on this aspect Local Safeguarding Children Board (2009: para. 4. 6.1) states:

> In the context of a police investigation and s.47 enquires by the social worker, to place Peter with the family friend was the wrong judgement and gave Ms. A the wrong message: that the authorities were not too concerned about the injuries to Peter. However, the managers were literally following the instructions in their own operational guidance of the time, which directs that before using one of the department's foster placements every effort should be made to place the child with family or friends. It does not qualify the guidance for children who are considered to have been the subject of non-accidental injuries. The practice should change for these circumstances, as should the guidance.

Here was a situation in which social workers had adhered to the operational guidance produced by their agency, but the guidance itself was flawed in such a way as to put vulnerable children at risk of further significant harm. On the other hand, following Peter's admission to North Middlesex University Hospital on 9 April 2007 with a swelling to the left side of his head and bruising elsewhere on his body, a social worker wrongly advised medical staff that Peter could be discharged home on 11 April without a prior Strategy Discussion. This was contrary to the London Safeguarding Children Board's child protection procedures. In one instance the agency policy was itself misguided and in the other a professional failed to follow standard child protection policy. Both of these instances implicate employers of social care workers and their responsibilities towards their professional staff.

The GSCC (2002b) *Code of Practice for Employers of Social Care Workers* requires that employers:

- Ensure that staff have suitable knowledge and skills for their job (para. 1.1).
- Ensure that staff have 'clear information about their roles and responsibilities, relevant legislation and the organisational policies and procedures they must follow in their work' (para. 1.4).
- Implement and monitor written policies on risk assessment and record keeping (para. 2.1).
- Provide 'induction, training and development opportunities to help social care workers do their jobs effectively' (para. 3.1).

Concomitantly, the GSCC (2002a) *Code of Practice for Social Care Workers* requires social workers to:

- Work in a 'lawful, safe and effective way' (para. 6.1).
- Maintain accurate records as required by agency procedures (para. 6.2).
- Train to maintain and improve professional knowledge and skills (para. 6.8).

Taken altogether these complementary aspects of the Codes of Practice place corresponding sets of responsibilities on employers and employees. These involve ensuring that: agency policies are lawful in the first instance; practitioners follow agency policy; compliance with agency policy is monitored; and, where this is lacking, additional instruction or training is provided. There were obviously a number of inadequacies at Haringey's Children and Young People's Services, which meant that not all the standards set down in the Codes of Practice were fully met.

Promoting welfare or safeguarding children

The GSCC Code for social care workers requires them to follow 'risk assessment policies and procedures to assess whether the behaviour of service users presents a risk of harm to themselves or others' (GSCC, 2002a: para. 4.2). *Framework for the Assessment of Children in Need and their Families* is policy guidance which sets out a comprehensive and detailed approach to assessing the care needs of children and developing care plans to meet these. There are two different types of assessment, an Initial Assessment and a Core Assessment. According to Department of Health (2000e: 4) an Initial Assessment should be used 'to decide whether the child is a child in need, the nature of any services required, from where and within what times scales, and whether a more detailed core assessment should be carried out'. An Initial Assessment Record, which comprises pro forma for the collection of information early on in the referral process, should be completed within 7 days of its commencement (Department of Health, 2000e: 4).

Department of Health (2000d: para. 3.11) defines a Core Assessment as 'an in-depth assessment which addresses the central or most important aspects of the needs of a child and the capacity of his or her parents or caregivers to respond appropriately to these needs within the wider family and community context'. Social workers are normally required to complete a Core Assessment within 35 days. Peter was known to Haringey's Children's Services and therefore once concerns had been raised about non-accidental injuries the correct approach was to commence a Core Assessment. Supplementary Core Assessment Records for different age groups of children are designed to facilitate information gathering for Core Assessments. These are tailored for children aged: 0–2; 3–4; 5–9; 10–14; and 15+. Core Assessment Records consist of comprehensive pro forma to help practitioners to collect detailed information from adults and children in a systematic and structured manner. Whether social workers are completing an Initial or Core Assessment, the Assessment Framework identifies three domains for the assessment of children and their families. These domains are further broken down into a number of elements which are fully described in the policy guidance and are reproduced in schematic form from Appendix A of the *Framework for the Assessment of Children in Need and their Families* in the figure on the next page.

The *Framework for the Assessment of Children in Need and their Families* emphasises that assessment is an ongoing process and not a one-off event, and the care needs of children may change over time. The Assessment Framework also makes clear that services should not be withheld from families pending completion of the assessment; instead temporary provision should be made available (Department of Health, 2000d: xi–xii). A pervasive theme in the circumstances surrounding Peter was uncertainty among a number of health and social

Framework for the assessment of children in need and their families

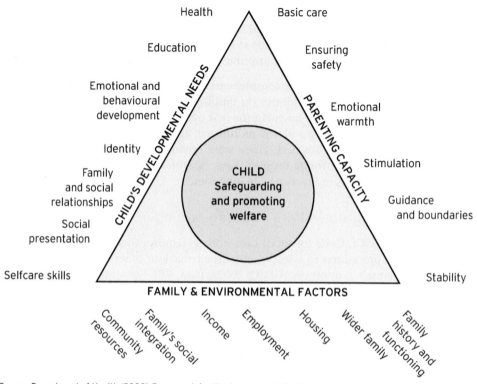

Source: Department of Health (2000) *Framework for the Assessment of Children in Need and their Families* London: Stationery Office, Appendix A.

care agencies as to whether he was a *child in need* or a child who was suffering or likely to suffer significant harm. In other words, did he require intervention by Children's Services to promote his welfare and counter poor and sometimes neglectful parenting by his mother or to protect him from abuse? The definition of a *child in need* and the correlating legal duties of local authorities towards them are set out in s.17 of the Children Act 1989.

Key legislation

Children Act 1989

s.17(1) It shall be the general duty of every local authority
  (a) to safeguard and promote the welfare of children within their area who are in need, and
  (b) so far as is consistent with that duty, to promote the upbringing of such children by their families, by providing a range and level of services appropriate to those children's needs.

s.17(10) a child shall be taken to be in need if –
  (a) he is unlikely to achieve or maintain, or to have the opportunity of achieving or maintaining, a reasonable standard of health or development without the provision for him of services by a local authority under this part;
  (b) his health or development is likely to be significantly impaired, or further impaired, without the provision for him of such services; or
  (c) he is disabled

Provisions under s.17 have several important implications. First, there are three categories of *children in need*, those who are unlikely to achieve or maintain a reasonable standard of health and development, those whose health and development may be impaired, and those who are disabled. Regardless of which category children fall into, the duty of the local authority is to provide services to promote their welfare and furthermore to promote care by their families. In this context *family* includes any person who holds parental responsibility for the child or with whom the child is living. It was known that Peter's mother had herself been subject to poor parenting. In 1991 aged 10 years she was placed on the Child Protection Register. The parenting she received was neglectful and at times abusive. Ms A had also been diagnosed with post-natal depression previously, and on the birth of Peter was referred to a Primary Care Mental Health Worker by her General Practitioner. Furthermore, Peter was Ms A's fourth child by her husband, from whom she had separated, which left her as the sole residential parent.

Given this family history the health visitor responsible for Peter placed him in a 'blue folder' which signalled to agency staff that he was a cause for concern. This of course did not mean that the health visitor was alleging that he was being abused. On the contrary, she was simply indicating that he was a child whose health and development could be at risk of impairment. In other words, Peter was an infant who fell under s.17(10)(a) of the Children Act 1989 and could at this very early stage of his life have been classed as a *child in need*. This would trigger a duty for Haringey Local Authority to provide services to Peter and his mother. Where primary carers require services to effectively discharge their parental responsibilities, local authorities can provide services directly to them. The different kinds of services which can be offered by a local authority once a s.17 duty had been triggered are listed in the box below.

 Key legislation

Children Act 1989

Local authority duties to provide services to *children in need*:

- s.17(3) services may be provided to members of the family as well as the child in need
- s.17(6) services may include accommodation, assistance in kind or in cash
- s.18 day care provision for those aged 5 years and under
- s.20 accommodation must be provided to a child where it appears nobody has parental responsibility for him or he has been abandoned or the person caring for him is unable to provide suitable accommodation or care
- s.17A and s.17B provide for direct payments or vouchers to be made available to parents of disabled children
- Schedule 2 provides for family centres, counselling, social and recreational activities, travel costs etc.

Clearly the Children Act 1989 empowers local authorities to provide a variety of services to *children in need* and their parents, which includes day care for the child and hands-on assistance for parents struggling with their caring responsibilities. The *Framework for the Assessment of Children in Need and their Families* makes clear that 'safeguarding children should not be seen as a separate activity from promoting their welfare' and that safeguarding children involves both 'a duty to protect children from maltreatment' and 'to prevent impairment' (Department of Health, 2000d: para. 1.15, 1.17). In other words, conducting an assessment must address both aspects of a child's circumstances regardless of whether it is initiated under s.17 or s.47. The *Assessment Framework* emphasises that the essential elements of a Core Assessment are the same regardless of whether a child's welfare is at hazard or abuse is suspected. It highlights the importance of clearly identifying the purpose of the assessment at the outset and agreeing 'an assessment plan with the child and family, so that all parties understand who is doing what, when and how the various assessments will be used to inform overall judgements about the child's needs and subsequent planning' (Department of Health, 2000d: para. 1.24). The box below outlines the principles which must underpin every Core Assessment regardless of the purposes for which it is being undertaken.

Key guidance

Framework for the Assessment of Children in Need and their Families

Para. 1.33 requires that assessments:

- Are child centred
- Are rooted in child development
- Are ecological in their approach
- Ensure equality of opportunity
- Involve working with children and families
- Build on strengths as well as identify difficulties
- Are inter-agency in their approach to assessment and the provision of services
- Are a continuing process not a single event
- Are carried out in parallel with other action and providing services
- Are grounded in evidence-based knowledge.

As these unpinning principles indicate, assessments should be multidisciplinary. Where professionals from other disciplines or agencies are required to contribute to the assessment, there must be agreement on which professionals are carrying out each element of the assessment and how they will contribute to the analysis of the information gathered and the resulting care plan (Department of Health, 2000d: para. 1.23). Evident in the events surrounding Peter was the failure to coordinate an effective multi-agency and interdisciplinary assessment under either s.17 or s.47 of the Children Act 1989. By December 2006 a paediatrician at the Whittington Hospital had identified extensive bruising to Peter's buttocks, face and chest together with a swelling to his forehead. Medical staff at the hospital concluded that these could not be satisfactorily accounted for by Ms A's explanation that Peter had fallen several times and bruised easily. Once the body map of these injuries had been sent through to Children and Young People's Services a Core Assessment should have been conducted according to the *Framework for the Assessment of Children in Need and their Families*, but under s.47 of the Children Act 1989. As already indicated, progressing a s.47 enquiry should not have prejudiced any services provided to Peter and his family under s.17.

Inter-agency cooperation

The section 47 enquiry initiated in December 2006 into the suspected non-accidental injuries to Peter should have involved a coordinated multidisciplinary approach to completing a Core Assessment underpinned by the Core Assessment Record for a child aged 0–2 years. Properly completed, this should have identified: Ms A's approach to parenting; Peter's developmental needs and his worrying behaviours; and the overall home environment in which Peter was growing up, including details on other household members. Multi-agency work does not cease on completion of a s.47 enquiry or the assessment of a *child in need*. It is integral to the care planning process which follows the completion of a Core Assessment. The Assessment Framework makes it clear that effective multi-agency work depends on following the principles set out in the guidance. These are reproduced in the box below.

Key guidance

Framework for the Assessment of Children in Need and their Families

Para. 1.23 The following principles should guide inter-agency, interdisciplinary work with children in need. It is essential to be clear about:

- The purpose and anticipated outputs from the assessment
- The legislative basis for the assessment
- The protocols and procedures to be followed
- Which agency, team or professional has lead responsibility
- How the child and family members will be involved in the assessment process
- Which professional has lead responsibility for analysing the assessment findings and constructing a plan
- The respective roles of each professional involved in the assessment
- The way in which information will be shared across professional boundaries and within agencies and be recorded
- Which professional will have responsibility for taking forward the plan when it is agreed.

The Strategy Discussion on 12 December had instigated a s.47 enquiry which resulted in police and social workers interviewing Peter's two eldest siblings, his mother and his grandmother. A detailed letter had been sent to social workers by the consultant paediatrician who examined Peter at Whittington Hospital. It stated that the bruising found on Peter's body 'is very suggestive of non-accidental injury'. On 22 December the initial Child Protection Conference concerning Peter was held. HM Government (2006a) *Working Together to Safeguard Children* is the definitive document on inter-agency working and sets out the purposes of a Child Protection Conference, which are reproduced in the box on next page. It also stipulates that 'cases where children are at risk of significant harm should not be allowed to drift. Consequently, all initial child protection conferences should take place within 15 working days of the strategy discussion' (HM Government, 2006a: para. 5.81). In fact the initial Child Protection Conference concerning Peter was held just 10 days after the Strategy Discussion and complied with the timescales set out in the guidance.

Key guidance

Working Together to Safeguard Children

Para. 5.80 The initial child protection conference brings together family members, the child where appropriate, and those professionals most involved with the child and family, following s.47 enquiries. Its purpose is:

- To bring together and analyse in an inter-agency setting the information which has been obtained about the child's developmental needs, and the parents' or carers' capacity to respond to these needs to ensure the child's safety and promote the child's health and development within the context of their wider family and environment.
- To consider the evidence presented to the conference, make judgements about the likelihood of a child suffering significant harm in future and decide whether the child is at continuing risk of significant harm; and
- To decide what future action is required to safeguard and promote the welfare of the child, how that action will be taken forward, and with what intended outcomes.

Para. 5.82 Those attending conferences should be there because they have a significant contribution to make, arising from professional expertise, knowledge of the child or family or both. The local authority social work manager should consider whether to seek advice from, or have present, a medical professional who can present the medical information in a manner which can be understood by conference attendees and enable such information to be evaluated from a sound evidence base.

Despite the stipulations of *Working Together* set out in the text box above, that the key professionals need to attend Child Protection Conferences to ensure that all the relevant information is shared and collectively considered, attendance was very poor on 22 December. The family's GP did not attend because he was not invited. Yet he had by this time seen Peter and his mother on a number of occasions and had a vital contribution to make. The consultant paediatrician from Whittington Hospital was invited, but could not attend due to an outpatient clinic – but she sent a detailed report of her findings. However, no representative attended from Whittington Hospital. The investigating police officer conducting ongoing enquiries under s.47 of the Children Act 1989 was in attendance, as was a legal representative from the local authority. Ms A had been asked to attend and came with her solicitor. At this first Child Protection Conference Ms A remained unable to account for the injuries to Peter. Consequently, the Child Protection Conference agreed to place Peter's name on the Child Protection Register for both physical abuse and neglect. The implications of placing a child's name on this register are explained in the box below.

Background information

The Child Protection Register

If a Child Protection Conference deems a child to be at continuing risk of significant harm then the child's name will be placed on the Child Protection Register and a Child Protection Plan will be devised. Registration requires that a named social worker be allocated to the child. This social worker then works with the child, coordinates multi-agency inputs for assessment and service delivery and monitors the situation. The Child Protection Register can be checked by other professionals with safeguarding responsibilities for children, quickly alerting them to wider child protection concerns and the agencies already involved. Children on the register will have a Child Protection Conference review meeting at least once every six months until such times as they are de-registered. The Child Protection Register has four categories of child maltreatment. These are defined in HM Government (2006a: paras 1.30-3) *Working Together to Safeguard Children*:

Physical abuse - may involve hitting, shaking, throwing, poisoning, burning or scalding, drowning, suffocating, or otherwise causing physical harm to a child. Physical harm may also be caused when a parent or carer fabricates the symptoms of, or deliberately induces illness in a child.

Emotional abuse - is the persistent emotional maltreatment of a child such as to cause severe and persistent adverse effects on the child's emotional development. It may involve conveying to children that they are worthless or unloved, inadequate, or valued only in so far as they meet the needs of another person. It may feature age or developmentally inappropriate expectations being imposed on children.

Sexual abuse - involves forcing or enticing a child or young person to take part in sexual activities, including prostitution, whether or not the child is aware of what is happening. The activities may involve physical contact, including penetrative (e.g. rape, buggery or oral sex) or non-penetrative acts. They may include non-contact activities, such as involving children in looking at, or in the production of, pornographic material, or watching sexual activities, or encouraging children to behave in sexually inappropriate ways.

Neglect - is the persistent failure to meet a child's basic physical and/or psychological needs, likely to result in the serious impairment of the child's health or development. Neglect may occur during pregnancy as a result of maternal substance abuse. Once a child is born, neglect may involve a parent or carer failing: to provide adequate food and clothing; to provide shelter, including exclusion from home or abandonment; to protect a child from physical and emotional harm or danger; to ensure adequate supervision, including the use of inadequate care-takers; to ensure access to appropriate medical care or treatment.

The legal advice given to Children and Young People's Services at this time was that Peter was at risk of significant harm and therefore met the threshold for care proceedings to be initiated through the courts by the local authority in order to take Peter into care. However, this did not happen. Instead of an authoritative Child Protection Plan to safeguard Peter, there were to be regular visits by social workers to his home. These were supplemented by a Family Welfare Association project worker who was assisting Ms A to improve her parenting skills. HM Government (2006a: para. 5.74) does recognise that:

In some cases, there may remain concerns about significant harm, despite there being no real evidence. It may be appropriate to put in place arrangements to monitor the child's welfare. Monitoring should never be used as a means of deferring or avoiding difficult decisions. The purpose of monitoring should always be clear, that is, what is being monitored and why, in what way and by whom.

It was not the situation that there was 'no real evidence' of significant harm to Peter. He had extensive bruising to his body which a consultant paediatrician had concluded was non-accidental. Moreover, legal advice given to Haringey's Children and Young People's Services deemed there to be sufficient evidence to commence court proceedings to remove Peter from his mother. Yet this did not happen. Commenting on the initial Child Protection Conference, Local Safeguarding Children Board (2009: para. 4.1.4–5) concluded that:

> Peter was the subject of a child protection conference in December 2006, with injuries so serious that they met the threshold for care proceedings. Although it cannot be known for certain how the injuries occurred, the medical view of the causes of the injuries went as far as it could in offering a non-accidental opinion – and it was gradually discounted. The likely explanation is that the injuries were not regarded as sufficiently serious and that there was over-identification with the parent whose account of possible explanations was perceived to be plausible . . . Neither the paediatrician nor a representative of the hospital medical team was at the child protection conference to advocate for the reality of the child's injuries. There was the real possibility that force had been used on Peter by an adult, that nobody was accepting responsibility, and that somebody was covering up. That was the reasonable inference and it should have guided the initial inter-agency response. It is difficult to understand how Peter could be returned to the family home after he has been seriously injured, possibly deliberately by an adult, and there is no resolution of who did it.

The implication of this excerpt from the report of the second Serious Case Review is that as a result of the absence of medical personnel from the Child Protection Conference other explanations of Peter's injuries were given sufficient credence for Peter to be allowed to return home from hospital back into his mother's care. This raises two issues; first the importance of following guidance and ensuring that key people are invited to Child Protection Conferences, and where necessary these are rescheduled to permit the attendance by crucial people. The second issue raised by this analysis of the case conference concerns the respect which professionals have for one another in a multidisciplinary context. The consultant paediatrician had produced a detailed report although she was not present at the Child Protection Conference to stand over it and answer questions about it. The GSCC (2002a) *Code of Practice for Social Care Workers* places a number of obligations upon social workers in relation to interdisciplinary and multi-agency work. These include:

- Working openly and cooperatively with colleagues and treating them with respect (para. 6.5).
- Recognising and respecting the roles and expertise of workers from other agencies and working in partnership with them (para. 6.7).
- Ensuring that relevant colleagues and agencies are informed about the outcomes and implications of risk assessments (para. 4.4).

Once a s.47 enquiry has been triggered under the Children Act 1989, s.47(9) obliges other agencies to assist Children's Services with their enquiries by 'providing relevant information and advice'. These agencies include health, education and housing authorities. This provision was strengthened and broadened by the introduction of the Children Act 2004, which imposed statutory duties on key agencies to cooperate with each other and to share information to safeguard and promote the welfare of children.

Key legislation

Major provisions of the Children Act 2004

s.8 Duty on key agencies to cooperate with local authority (key agencies include: police authorities, primary care trusts, NHS Trusts, youth offending teams, Connexions and education services).

s.10 Duty on local authorities to make arrangements for cooperation with relevant partners including voluntary organisations to improve the well-being of children. Children's well-being is defined in s.10(2) as comprising:

(a) physical and mental health and emotional well-being
(b) protection from harm and neglect
(c) education, training and recreation
(d) the contribution made by them to society
(e) social and economic well-being.

s.11 Duty on key agencies to have regard to need to safeguard children and promote their welfare in exercising their normal functions.

s.12 Creation of national database to hold information on children and young people and facilitate sharing of information between professionals.

s.13-14 Creation of Local Safeguarding Children Boards with representatives from all key agencies to coordinate the protection and promote the well-being of children in the local area (these replace Area Child Protection Committees).

s.18 Duty on local authority to appoint a Director of Children's Services to be accountable for education and social services provision to children (to improve integration of education and children's social services).

The Children Acts of 1989 and 2004 impose duties on professionals in other agencies to cooperate with Children's Services in assessment and care planning for children, which may involve activity to promote their welfare or to safeguard them. However, it remains the responsibility of social workers to respect the knowledge and expertise which other professionals bring to the area of child protection. Respect means more that just listening to the opinions of colleagues from other disciplines. It requires integrating the information and analysis they provide into assessment and care planning. This needs to be balanced against the clear statement in *Working Together* that a local authority's Children's Services will be the lead agency in safeguarding children. Section 47 of the Children Act 1989, which is reproduced in the box on the next page, sets out the statutory duty of local authorities to take action to protect children. Ultimately it is social workers and their line management who make the decision as to how to safeguard a particular child.

Partnership working with families

Department of Health (2000b: para. 1.34) highlights research evidence which reveals that parents involved with child welfare agencies value 'communication which is open, honest, timely and informative' in tandem with 'social work time with someone who listens, gives feedback, information, reassurance and advice, and is reliable'. This finding is

Children Act 1989

s.47(7) If, on the conclusion of any enquiries or review made under this section, the authority decide not to apply for an emergency protection order, a child assessment order, a care order or a supervision order they shall –

    (a) consider whether it would be appropriate to review the case at a later date; and

    (b) if they decide that it would be, determine the date on which that review is to begin.

s.47(8) Where, as a result of complying with this section, a local authority conclude that they should take action to safeguard or promote the child's welfare they shall take that action (so far as it is both within their power and reasonably practicable for them to do so).

consistent with the GSCC *Code of Practice for Social Care Workers* paras. 2.1, 2.2, 2.4 and 2.5 which require open, honest and clear communication with carers and service-users. Facilitating this process of open and cooperative working between professionals and family members is the principle underpinning the Assessment Framework which requires a focus on the strengths as well as weaknesses of a person's parenting capacity (Department of Health, 2000d: para. 1.48). This plainly helps to avoid situations in which parents and other primary carers find themselves on the receiving end of a relentless barrage of criticism: a state of affairs which is likely to contribute to resistance on the part of parents or carers to work with Children's Services and other agencies. At the same time, policy and practice guidance also recognise the limits of cooperative working with parents or carers where children are at risk of harm. Social Services Inspectorate and Department of Health (1995) *The Challenge of Partnership in Child Protection: Practice Guide* details how to work in partnership with parents and carers in the context of child protection concerns. This practice guidance explicitly acknowledges (para. 8.18) that:

> Continuing hostility towards professional intervention or total lack of motivation to be involved in planning for a child obviously precludes partnership unless these attitudes can be changed over time. A history of calculated and sadistic abuse of a child or children must raise doubts about the likelihood of partnership with the abuser unless there is unequivocal evidence of change. Persistent denial of abuse, when there is evidence that it has occurred, is not a good basis for a partnership.

A number of difficulties emerged around partnership working with Peter's mother. In the first instance social workers who came into contact with her were too willing to believe her version of events. After the initial Child Protection Conference, Peter returned home where he was frequently visited by his social worker. On 13 March the social worker interviewed Peter's father who had not been contacted since his son's admission to Whittington Hospital in December. Peter's father informed the social worker that he wanted more contact with his children. She advised him to seek legal advice. At this point Peter's father informed the social worker that Peter's mother had a boyfriend who frequented the family home. When the social worker confronted Peter's mother with this information she angrily denied it and inferred that he was a very peripheral figure. Neither the police nor the social worker pursued further enquiries to establish the truth.

Peter's parents were married at the time of his birth and therefore Peter's father held parental responsibility for him. Peter's father was known to have contact with his children and to have been involved in taking them to school. At around the time of the Strategy

Discussion on 12 December when it was decided not to permit Peter to return home until s.47 enquiries were completed, Peter's father offered to take time off work to look after his son. This offer was not taken up by social workers because Peter's mother claimed that he had previously slapped the children. In short, a series of assertions made by Peter's mother were treated as factual and true and never properly investigated. Yet, this was a woman who was known to be the primary carer for a child with non-accidental injuries for which she could not adequately account. As the Local Safeguarding Children Board (2009: para. 4.6.2) concluded,

> Peter's father was prepared to take time off from work and to get a reference from his employer. There had been no concerns about his care of the children in the past and he had parental responsibility and the right to care for his son. There should have been very good reasons before refusing his offer of temporary care and his rights should have been explained to him.

Instead of accepting the offer of care from Peter's father the social workers involved in this case instead decided to permit Peter to be discharged from hospital into the care of a friend of Peter's mother. This was not a placement which could be guaranteed to safeguard him. In other words, a number of professional decisions were based on statements by Peter's mother that were not independently verified, either by the police or by social workers. The difficulties of partnership work with Peter's mother also played out at the initial Child Protection Conference. This is succinctly explained in the findings of the Local Safeguarding Children Board (2009: 4.1.7):

> There may not have been sufficient awareness on the part of the participants, and particularly the Chair, of the dynamics of the relationships between the participants, and the part which procedures could play in minimising any adverse effects. Ms. A's presence in the meeting would have an influence on the agency representatives, who may feel that they need to protect their relationship with her as they have to work with her in the future. The impact of her presence would be compounded by the fact that she was accompanied by a solicitor. Ms. A was apparently a dominating and forceful personality who may have intimidated people in the meeting and certainly had done so outside of it.

The consequence of this collusion with Ms A was that a child protection plan was never properly conceived. According to the Local Safeguarding Children Board (2009: 4.1.12) 'what was required was an authoritative approach to the family, with a very tight grip on the intervention. Ms. A needed to be challenged and confronted about her poor parenting and generally neglectful approach to the home.' Of course the situation of facing a quite powerful and intimidating parent in the context of child protection is not uncommon. It is recognising the danger of over-focussing on the parent and of perceiving matters from that parent's perspective, to the detriment of a child-centred process of assessment and care planning supervision, which plays a crucial role in assisting frontline social workers to maintain professional objectivity.

 Perspectives

Parental participation in Child Protection Conferences

Research into the participation of parents at Child Protection Conferences revealed that around 90% of them were glad that they attended the meeting (Corby et al., 1996). Despite welcoming the opportunity to attend such conferences, many parents described difficulty in articulating their viewpoint, and general anxiety at being outnumbered by so many professionals. This was exacerbated by the fact that few parents attend Child Protection Conferences accompanied by an advocate or friend (Farmer and Owen, 1995: 109). Many parents experienced problems communicating in such large formal settings, in contrast to the professionals present who were used to multi-professional meetings in connection with children's welfare and protection (Cleaver and Freeman, 1995: 134). Parents also felt inhibited due to the embarrassment they often felt when sensitive or personal information was shared at the meeting, often in front of unknown professionals or people, such as teachers, whom they knew from everyday life (Farmer and Owen, 1995: 101). Generally, parents, fearful of their children being removed, tended to actively participate in deliberations only when asked a direct question (Corby, et al., 1996: 486; Farmer and Owen, 1996:116).

This state of affairs plainly advantages social workers when putting forward their understanding of events as it is exceptionally difficult for parents to dispute this professional presentation of the facts (Corby et al., 1996: 483). Parents found that the factual information they put before the Child Protection Conference was treated as less reliable than that of the professionals present and therefore frequently discounted. The overall experience of such meetings made parents behave in a defensive and sometimes hostile way (Farmer and Owen, 1995: 111). Taken together, research points to parental attendance at Children Protection Conferences being used by professionals to express their concerns to parents about childcare. There is little evidence that these are forums in which parents genuinely participate in decisions about their children's care (Hall and Slembrouck, 2001). Dale (2004: 146) captured the direct experience of parents attending Child Protection Conferences, with one mother epitomising the viewpoint expressed by many:

'An experience you'll never forget . . . very upsetting – it felt like everybody who was around that table was against you . . . everybody's looking at you, and then they are discussing you, your children, their recommendations – and you've not heard a word of what they've said before . . .'

Supervision

Department of Health (2000d: para. 3.36) *Framework for the Assessment of Children in Need and their Families* acknowledges that:

in a small number of instances, resistance to co-operation by a parent is accompanied by overtly aggressive, abusive or threatening behaviour or by more subtle underlying menace. Staff may be aware of the threat and in response either avoid family contact or unwisely place themselves in situations of danger. It is in these circumstances that access to available, skilled, expert supervision is essential so that the nature of the threat can be understood, the implications for the child and other family members identified and strategies found for maintaining work with the family. These may include co-working with experienced staff within or across agencies, changing times and venue for meetings with the family and other measures.

The *Code of Practice for Employers of Social Care Workers* requires employers to ensure that people entering the social care workforce understand their roles and responsibilities and are able to meet the standards of the GSCC code for social care workers. This entails employers:

- Managing the performance of staff and the organisation to ensure high quality service and care (para. 1.5).

- Effectively managing and supervising staff to support effective practice and good conduct and supporting staff to address deficiencies in their performance (para. 2.2).
- Responding appropriately to social care workers who seek assistance because they do not feel able or adequately prepared to carry out any aspects of their work (para. 3.4).

Both government guidance and the GSCC code of practice for employers explicitly recognise the crucial role of good supervision by team leaders and line managers. Despite this the Local Safeguarding Children Board (2009: 4.9.2–3) concluded that,

> The case supervision, particularly for one of the social workers in Peter's case, was ad hoc, inconsistent, and often cancelled. However, even if the supervision had taken place it is unlikely that it would have illuminated the deficiencies in the practice as in this instance the team managers were familiar with the case and themselves had insufficient concerns despite the frequency of injuries to Peter. Although consultation and supervision is useful in itself in providing support to the practitioner in their work, it will not improve the quality of the practice unless the manager has competent knowledge and skills which are relevant to the requirements of the case.

The supervisor of Peter's social worker believed that the mother's friend was living at the family home. It was on the basis of this mistaken understanding that Peter was returned home after yet another hospital admission in June 2007. It was thought by professionals that Peter would not be left alone unsupervised with his mother by the friend. In fact the mother's friend only occasionally visited Peter's family home and she did not stay there. This meant that decisions were being made by both Peter's social worker and her supervisor based on inaccurate information. As this situation illustrates, it is problematic if supervisors are unable to retain a degree of professional objectivity and an ability to question the quality of information gathered by frontline practitioners.

This extract from the second Serious Case Review highlights not just the need for good supervision, but also for supervisors themselves to be experienced, knowledgeable and competent professionals. The GSCC *Code of Practice for Social Care Workers* advises social workers to inform 'your employer or an appropriate authority where the practice of colleagues may be unsafe or adversely affecting standards of care'. It appears that the standard of supervision provided in relation to Peter lacked both rigour and expertise. Frontline professionals who find themselves in this position should raise the matter with their employer through line management structures. Social workers of course have the additional option of discussing matters of concern with the General Social Care Council.

Conclusions of the second Serious Case Review: Baby Peter

The combined shortcomings of individual professionals and failings in inter-agency work across the police, health, education and Children's Services meant that 'at no point did it occur to anyone that the injuries to the children were caused by someone else apart from their mother. On the basis of her observed interactions with her children it seemed to be incongruous and unlikely to be her' (Local Safeguarding Children Board, 2009: 4.8.1).

The police investigation which followed Peter's death discovered that the boyfriend of Peter's mother and his brother had been living in the family home. On 11 November 2008 the boyfriend of Peter's mother and his brother were both convicted in the Crown Court of causing or allowing Peter's death. This was a charge to which Peter's mother had already pleaded guilty. The second Serious Case Review concluded that the interventions by agencies involved with Peter were:

- Lacking urgency.
- Lacking thoroughness.
- Insufficiently challenging to the parent.
- Lacking action in response to reasonable inference.
- Insufficiently focussed on the children's welfare.
- Based on too high a threshold for intervention.
- Based on expectations that were too low.

 Critical questions

1 Government guidance and the GSCC *Code of Practice for Social Care Workers* demand that practitioners work in partnership with parents and carers. As the events surrounding Peter demonstrate, parents and carers can sometimes be manipulative, appearing compliant while frustrating intervention, or they can be overtly aggressive. As a practitioner how would you work with a parent who engages in these sorts of behaviour?

2 Poor supervision was one factor contributing to the failure to safeguard Peter. If you were experiencing poor supervision from your team leader how would you tackle it?

3 Peter's father was partly marginalised by professionals at Haringey's Children and Young People's Services. Both Peter's social worker and the team manager were women. How do you think issues of gender might have influenced social work practice in relation to Peter and his family?

4 Peter's father, as a parent holding parental responsibility, was not informed of his rights by social workers either when he asked to have more contact with his children or when he offered to look after Peter during the completion of s.47 enquiries. Identify the rights of Peter's father in these two situations. How might a social worker have supported Peter's father to exercise his rights?

 Perspectives

Lisa Arthurworrey on the Climbié Inquiry

The *Mail on Sunday* (15 June 2008) devoted three pages to an interview with Lisa Arthurworrey, the social worker, at the centre of the Climbié Inquiry in 2003. Lisa described her reaction to the telephone call informing her of Victoria's death, aged 8 years. 'When the call came I remembered an older social worker telling me that if a child dies on your watch, your own life will be destroyed. I nearly collapsed when I learned it was Victoria.' The media portrayal of Lisa Arthurworrey as primarily responsible for Victoria's death made her feel that 'I wanted to throw myself under a train. I stood so many times on the edge of the platform waiting for a Tube, thinking I should jump. I wanted to kill myself because I couldn't stand the pain, the feeling "I've killed a child". My photo was everywhere and I was recognized.'

Lisa criticised the excessive political correctness which prevented either the public inquiry or the media attributing some responsibility to Victoria's mother who gave her child into the care of Ms Kouau, a distant relative, whom she barely knew and had met on only two occasions. Lisa commented 'at the end of the day, parental responsibility begins and ends with her. She gave her daughter away.' In 2001 Ms Kouau was convicted of murdering Victoria.

Scrutinising the behaviour of her employer, Haringey Council, Lisa concluded that they had colluded with the media to make her a scapegoat. Haringey Council sacked Lisa for gross misconduct and later placed her name on the Protection of Children Act List (now the Vetting and Barring Scheme) thus preventing her from working with children. Lisa appealed against her inclusion on the list to the Care Standards Tribunal.

The Care Standards Tribunal noted that, 'there was a letter from a consultant paediatrician saying in unequivocal terms that Victoria's injuries were not non-accidental injuries . . . It would be difficult in the extreme for a junior social worker to contradict the opinion of such a senior professional.' The Tribunal also found that 'there was a pervasive culture of "close the file" from Lisa Arthurworrey's managers'. It concluded that, 'to blame everything on Ms Arthurworrey is, we believe, to make her a scapegoat for the failings of a number of people'.

The Care Standards Tribunal proceeded to criticise the public inquiry, observing that, 'a social worker is not a doctor and so has to defer to medical opinion. We are not sure that matters are quite as clear-cut as Lord Laming suggests they might be. The role played by the medical profession in this tragedy has, as far as we are aware, never been analysed in the same detail as the role of the social workers.' In June 2008 the Care Standards Tribunal removed Lisa Arthurworrey's name from the (now) Vetting and Barring Scheme permitting her, if she wished, to work with children again.

Reflecting on her experience, Lisa insisted that: 'child protection is so important. Yet, it's very clear to me now that I was set up to fail by my employer, just like the Government continues to set up social workers generally to fail. I wish we were gods or mind-readers, but we are not. Evil people kill children, not people like me.'

CASE 2
Re C and B (Children) (Care Order: Future Harm) [2001] 1 FLR 611

Importance of the case

This examines the legal thresholds for obtaining court orders to compulsorily intervene in family life. The case also investigates action taken under the Children Act 1989 in the context of human rights legislation. Finally, it explores the rights of parents facing care proceedings relating to their children.

History of the case

The County Court issued Care Orders in respect of two young children, one of whom was a newborn baby, on the grounds that the children were likely to suffer future harm. The County Court also gave permission for the local authority to refuse any contact between the parents and their two older children who were also subject to Care Orders. In addition the County Court barred both parents from making any further application to it in relation to their children for two years. The father and mother appealed against these decisions to the Court of Appeal.

Facts of the case

K was born in 1988 and CM in 1994. In 1996 their mother experienced a mental breakdown and was hospitalised for a month. She was also reported to have learning difficulties and appeared unable to understand concerns expressed by Social Services regarding her approach to parenting. K was discovered home alone on several occasions and it was agreed that both children would be accommodated by relatives. In 1997 Care Orders were made for both children on the grounds that K was suffering intellectual and emotional harm attributable to her mother's parenting and CM was likely to suffer such harm in the future. Both children were removed into foster care. Their mother was assessed as having learning difficulties in expert evidence presented during the care proceedings. The local authority sought to restrict contact between parents and children as it was claimed this was causing further harm to K. K, who was now aged 9, stated that she did not wish to have contact with her father or mother. Unofficial contact between parents and children continued as the family home and foster home were in the same vicinity. The parents applied for a Contact Order and the local authority issued a cross-application to refuse the parents any contact with K and CM, in March 1999. J was born in 1998 and neither the General Practitioner, midwife nor health visitor had any concerns regarding his care or development. The Guardian ad Litem (now a Children's Guardian) appointed for K and CM during the care proceedings expressed concern regarding the likelihood of harm to other children of the family. In response the court initiated a s.37 inquiry under the Children Act 1989. An independent social worker conducted the investigation and reported that J was likely to suffer significant harm in the future. Subsequently the local authority applied for an Interim Care Order for J which was granted along with a Recovery Order after a court hearing on 8 July 1999. Soon after this hearing the mother was admitted to hospital where she gave birth to C. On 22 July while the father and J were visiting the mother, J was recovered from the hospital. On the same day a Police Protection Power was exercised and an Emergency Protection Order obtained to remove the infant C into foster care. On 27 September 1999 the County Court issued an Interim Care Order for C, and on 20 October 1999, at a further hearing, the County Court made Care Orders for both C and J and granted an order to the Local Authority permitting it to refuse all contact between both parents and any of their four children. The same court also prohibited the parents from applying for discharge of the orders for a period of two years without the permission of the court.

Key people in the case

K – born in 1988 and aged 13 years old at time of Court of Appeal case in 2001
CM – born in 1994 and aged 7 years old at time of Court of Appeal case
J – born in 1998 and aged 3 years old at time of Court of Appeal case
C – born 1999 and aged 2 years old at time of Court of Appeal case
Mother – mother of K, CM, C and J
Father – father of K, CM, C and J
Mr Williams – independent social worker
Dr Adey – mother's GP
Mr Levy – barrister representing mother and father
Mr Dugdale – barrister representing local authority
Lady Justice Hale – judge presiding in Court of Appeal case

Discussion of the case

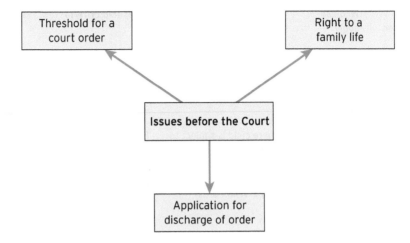

Threshold for a court order

When applying for a court order in relation to care proceedings, local authorities must demonstrate through presentation of the evidence before a judge that it meets the threshold criteria to trigger State interference in family life. Each order available for the protection of children under the Children Act 1989 has attached a set of evidential requirements which have to be met before a judge will grant that order. The question before the Court of Appeal was whether the local authority in applying for Emergency Protection and Care Orders on J and C had demonstrated in evidence that they met the threshold criteria and whether the judge at County Court level was correct in granting these orders.

Court orders available in care proceedings

Court order under Children Act 1989	Who can apply	When to apply	Threshold criteria	Effect of order
Child Assessment Order (s.43)	Local authority NSPCC	Non-emergency situations where assessment is needed to establish if child is suffering or likely to suffer significant harm.	Reasonable cause to *suspect* that the child is suffering or is likely to suffer significant harm.	• Maximum duration 7 days. • A person who can must produce the child. • Parental consent not required. • Child of sufficient understanding may refuse assessment.
Emergency Protection Order (s.44)	Anyone	Used in an emergency to protect a child who is likely to suffer significant harm. Used during an ongoing investigation by the social services or NSPCC when access to a child is being frustrated.	Reasonable cause to *believe* that the child is likely to suffer significant harm if not removed from or retained at the place in which he or she is presently accommodated.	• Maximum duration 8 days renewable once for 7 days. • Gives applicant parental responsibility. • Power to remove or prevent removal of child from present accommodation.

(Continued)

Court orders available in care proceedings *(continued)*

Court order under Children Act 1989	Who can apply	When to apply	Threshold criteria	Effect of order
			During a s.47 enquiry access to a child is being unreasonably refused.	• Authorises entry and search of premises. Obstruction of EPO is a criminal offence.
Care Order (s. 31)	Local authority NSPCC	Where child is subject to ill treatment by parent or carer and cannot be adequately protected by a supervision order.	The child *is* suffering or likely to suffer significant harm and this is attributable to the care given to the child, or the child is beyond parental control.	• Order in force until child reaches 18 years unless discharged. • Local authority gains parental responsibility. All s.8 Orders automatically discharged. • At common law local authority can authorise a doctor to use reasonable force to impose necessary medical treatment.
Supervision Order (s.31)	Local authority NSPCC	Where child is subject to ill treatment by parent or carer and there is parental or carer consent to supervision by a social worker which may be in conjunction with other services.	The child *is* suffering or likely to suffer significant harm and this is attributable to the care given to the child, or the child is beyond parental control.	• Maximum duration is one year but can be renewed. • Automatically discharged when child reaches 18 years. • Places child under the supervision of a designated social worker. • Parents retain parental responsibility. • Duty of supervisor to advise, befriend and assist the child. • Supervisor can call on assistance of police to gain access to child.
Interim Care and Supervision Orders (s.38)	Local authority NSPCC	Interim orders are made where there is an adjournment pending a full hearing of the court. Interim orders are also made where the court initiates a s.37 inquiry and pending its outcome.	Same criteria as for full Supervision and Care Orders and where there are reasonable grounds for *believing* that a full Care or Supervision Order will be required.	• Maximum duration is 8 weeks. • If first interim order was for 8 weeks then subsequent applications for interim orders are restricted to periods not exceeding 4 weeks. • Any number of successive interim orders may be made. Interim orders have the same consequences as full orders.

(Continued)

Court order under Children Act 1989	Who can apply	When to apply	Threshold criteria	Effect of order
Police Protection Power (s.46) (a court order is not required for its exercise)	Police constable	Used in an acute emergency where there is not time to apply for a court order to prevent significant harm to a child.	Where a constable has reasonable cause to *believe* that a child would be likely to suffer significant harm if not removed from or retained at the place where they are presently accommodated.	• Maximum duration is 72 hours. • Triggers s.47 enquiry. • Child must be moved to local authority-approved accommodation. • Does *not* give parental responsibility.
Recovery Order (s.50) (exercised only in conjunction with other orders)	Person with PR under an EPO or Care Order. Designated officer exercising a Police Protection Power	Used where a child is subject to a Police Protection Power, EPO or Care Order and made when the child has been unlawfully taken away, kept away or run away from the person designated to have care of the child under the Order.	Issued by court if it has reason to believe the child has been unlawfully taken away, kept away or run away from the person designated to have care of the child under a Police Protection Power, EPO or Care Order.	• Authorises removal of the child into the care of the person designated to have care of the child under the Police Protection Power, EPO or Care Order. • Police using reasonable force where necessary may enter premises specified in the Recovery Order and search for the child. • Any person with knowledge of the child's whereabouts is required to disclose this to the police.

When the Guardian ad Litem (now Children's Guardian) acting for K and CM in care proceedings expressed concern regarding the welfare of J, the court ordered a s.37 report in relation to 10-month old J. He was at that time the only child remaining with the parents. The local authority appointed an independent social worker, Mr Williams (a practitioner not employed by the local authority), to conduct the investigation and produce recommendations for J's future care. In his report dated 4 July 1999 Mr Williams concluded that:

> At the moment there is no evidence that [J] is suffering any harm. There is no suggestion that [the mother] and [the father] do not know how to meet an infant's physical needs . . . The Health Services, the only agency having direct contact with [J] do not have any current concerns for him. However, the fact that he appears to be thriving physically at the moment is not necessarily a reassurance. It is highly likely that [J] will suffer similar significant harm as his sisters [CM and K] in the future. Every indicator points to this likelihood.

The wording of s.31(2)(a) of the Children Act 1989 expressly permits the making of a Care Order or Interim Care Order on the grounds 'that the child is suffering or is likely to suffer, significant harm'. This means that a child can be removed from his or her parents or carer on the basis of the likelihood of future harm. The precise wording of s.31(2) permits preventative action to remove children from their caregivers where there is the prospect of significant harm occurring even though it has not as yet taken place. Relying on this element of s.31(2) and on the strength of the report produced by Mr Williams, the local authority applied for an Interim Care Order for J, which was granted on 8 July 1999 by the court together with a linked Recovery Order. This was despite the fact that Dr Adey, the mother's longstanding GP, her midwife and health visitor reported having no concerns regarding J's welfare. The Recovery Order was subsequently used on 22 July 1999 to remove J, then aged 10 months, from hospital premises during a visit with his father to see his mother who was at the time an inpatient. J was placed directly into foster care. Commenting on these events Lady Justice Hale presiding over the Court of Appeal hearing roundly criticised the decision of the local authority for seeking an Interim Care Order:

> On what basis could it possibly be appropriate to remove a ten-month-old baby from the only parents and home he had ever known, at a crucial stage in the development of his attachments, when there was no evidence that he was at immediate risk and, indeed, no evidence that he was at immediate emotional risk? All the evidence was that he was doing well. All the evidence was that there was no existing pointer to anything that might have been thought to indicate that he was not doing well at that time. Any evidence of a risk of harm was to his intellectual and emotional development at a considerably later stage.

This excerpt from the Court of Appeal judgement raises three key issues. First, the implication is that the local authority failed to take account of all the evidence before it, particularly that of healthcare professionals, which plainly confirmed that there were *no* concerns regarding J's welfare. Secondly, the Interim Care Order was issued on speculative grounds that future harm *might* occur and without a clear finding on the evidence that significant harm was *highly likely* to occur to J. Thirdly, the requirement that the harm must be *significant* raises the threshold for granting an Interim Care Order, or indeed any of the orders in the table above, from mere harm to harm of a significant magnitude. The Children Act 1989 deliberately avoids defining the word *significant* because what constitutes 'significant harm' will differ from child to child depending on their age, health and personal attributes. In the case of J the harm anticipated was at the lower end of the spectrum and, therefore, according to Lady Justice Hale, the lower court should have waited for a full court hearing to decide the matter rather than pre-emptively issuing an Interim Care Order. In other words, it was already established that there was no imminent risk of significant harm to J and therefore a decision on intervention could have been safely postponed until the court had before it all the evidence.

Turning to the issuance of an Emergency Protection Order for the infant C, Lady Justice Hale observed that these orders are designed to be used in a genuine emergency only and where a child is at risk of significant harm if not removed from, or kept at, the place where he or she is presently accommodated. In the instance before the Court of Appeal a Police Protection Power had been exercised to enable the local authority to gain sufficient time to make an application for an Emergency Protection Order to the court, which it did on the same day. The reasoning behind this is that a Police Protection Power can be exercised by a constable (as long as the threshold requirement is met) without recourse to the courts for permission. That is to say, it can be exercised with immediate effect, but only lasts up to 72 hours after which it automatically lapses. By contrast, an Emergency Protection Order, which lasts up to 8 days, can only be exercised by a social worker after the local authority has applied to the court for it and the court has heard the evidence and then decided to grant the Emergency Protection Order. In other words there can be situations of such urgency and immanent danger to a child that the initial use of a Police Protection Power is the single means of safeguarding the child having regard to the time required to go to court to obtain an Emergency Protection Order.

In the present case the court granted the Emergency Protection Order, and social workers exercised their powers under it, arriving at the hospital where the mother had recently given birth and removing her newborn daughter C. Lady Justice Hale in her judgement was critical both of the lower court for issuing the Emergency Protection Order and the local authority for making the application in the first instance. She also reproached social workers for the manner in which they then proceeded to exercise their powers under the order. The evidence presented to the lower court consisted principally of reports, not on C, but on the mother's other children. It was on the grounds of significant harm to K that CM was removed and then on the grounds of what was incorrectly asserted in Mr Williams' report as significant harm to K and CM that J was removed. In fact significant harm in terms of emotional and psychological harm was only ever established in relation to K. Now it appeared that the local authority was seeking to remove C on the grounds not of actual significant harm, but of the significant harm she was likely to suffer in the future. Again Lady Justice Hale criticised the use of an Emergency Protection Order in circumstances where there appeared to be no immediate risk of significant harm to the child in question. In this instance the mother had just given birth to C and both mother and child were in hospital and therefore in a protective environment from the standpoint of safeguarding the baby. Hence there was no emergency.

The requirement to meet a threshold criterion needed to trigger a particular legal action underpins many statutory provisions affecting social work. In this instance the Children Act 1989 sets out a number of different threshold criteria which vary depending on the court order being sought. These criteria are set at progressively higher levels as the related court orders increase in the magnitude of their interference in family life. So for example, under s.43(1) making a Child Assessment Order, which only involves compulsory examination of the child, requires that the applicant local authority has 'reasonable cause to *suspect* that the child is suffering, or is likely to suffer significant harm'. Therefore in court local authority social workers just have to produce sufficient evidence to prove that their *suspicions* are reasonable. By contrast, if a local authority wanted to apply for an Emergency Protection Order under s.44(1) it would have to prove to the court that it had 'reasonable cause to *believe* that the child is likely to suffer significant harm'. The most extreme interference in family life which is to remove a child for a potentially unlimited period from his or her family requires a Care Order which can only be issued by the court under s.31(2) if the applicant local authority is able to demonstrate in evidence that 'the child concerned *is* suffering or *is* likely to suffer, significant harm'. The legal requirement to prove that something *is* actually happening rather than that there is merely a *suspicion* of it happening constitutes a higher and lower criterion respectively. It is obviously easier to prove facts on the basis of a lower, as opposed to a higher, criteria. This means that less evidence is required to prove that the lower criterion has been satisfied.

Some provisions have more than one criterion which has to be met before a court order can be issued. For instance, a Care Order requires not only that the applicant local authority prove that 'the child concerned *is* suffering or *is* likely to suffer, significant harm' but that this harm is attributable to the care given to the child by their caregiver. In addition, for all the orders strictly related to public law care proceedings it must be proved not just that there is *harm* or likely *harm* but that it is *significant*. Social workers must not only provide evidence of harm, but they must show that this is of a degree of severity high enough to meet the threshold criterion of 'significant harm'. In short, practitioners who go to court to obtain a particular court order during care proceedings must produce evidence which demonstrates that multiple criteria have been met as set out in the related statutory provision of the Children Act 1989.

Right to a family life

Subsequent to the EPO an Interim Care Order was obtained for the baby C and, on 20 October 1999 in a final hearing before the County Court, Care Orders were made in respect of toddler J and baby C. As it is a statutory duty under s.34 of the Children Act 1989 for local authorities to promote contact between parents and children subject to a Care Order, a local authority requires permission from the court to refuse such contact. The local authority duly applied for this permission and it was granted by the County Court, permitting social workers to terminate contact between the parents and all four of their children. Turning to the decision to make Care Orders on J and C, Lady Justice Hale heard evidence presented by Mr Levy, legal counsel acting for the appellant parents, and from Mr Dugdale representing the respondent local authority. Mr Levy argued that there was no sound evidential basis from which to deduce that J and C were likely to suffer emotional harm at some future point in time. He observed that the only substantive evidence before the County Court was that K had suffered actual harm. Moreover, according to Mr Levy, in so far as harm to K had been established, professionals were unable to verify whether K's learning difficulties and developmental delay were attributable to parenting by her mother or not. This was a crucial point as one of the criteria for a Care Order is 'that the harm, or likelihood of harm, is attributable to the care given to the child . . . not being what it would be reasonable to expect a parent to give him'. Put more simply, it has to be established that the harm has been caused by the care given to the child by the parent and not for some other reason, for example a developmental delay caused by poor schooling. In relation to CM, no actual harm was proved. Indeed her removal from her parents was on the grounds that the eldest child K had suffered actual harm and this was used by social workers as a basis for concluding that CM was likely to suffer significant harm in the future. Mr Levy contended that the case put by the local authority for the removal of the two younger children J and C under Care Orders was too weak to meet the threshold criteria of s.31(2)(a) and that the County Court had been wrong in law to issue the orders on such inadequate evidence.

Bolstering his argument, Mr Levy cited precedent in *Re H and Others (Minors) (Sexual Abuse: standard of proof)* [1996] AC 563 p. 585F. This judgement makes clear that when giving consideration to future (rather than actual) harm as a grounds for making a Care Order the court must be satisfied not just that there is a chance of harm occurring in the future, but that 'there [is] a real possibility, a possibility that cannot be sensibly ignored, having regard to the nature and gravity of the feared harm in the particular case'. The legal reasoning in this short quotation establishes several principles. First, merely establishing that there is a *chance of future harm* is not sufficient grounds to meet the threshold of 'likely to suffer significant harm' set out in s.31(2) of the Children Act 1989. The local authority must do more than this. It must prove there is *a realistic probability of future harm* occurring. Furthermore, weight has to be given to the 'nature and gravity' of the anticipated harm to the child. This means that the harm anticipated needs to be of such severity as to justify removing a child from parents or guardians even though no harm has actually occurred.

Mr Levy contended in first place that the local authority had failed to produce sufficient evidence to establish the 'real possibility' of harm to the two younger children J and C in the future. Secondly, he asserted that even if Lady Justice Hale were to accept that the local authority had established a 'real possibility' of harm, the harm anticipated was that to intellectual and emotional development and was not at the grave end of the spectrum. Mr Levy's legal reasoning would mean that even if there were to be a finding of a likelihood of suffering harm of high enough probability to satisfy the s.31(2)(a) threshold, it was not serious enough (that is, *significant*) to justify the removal and severing of all ties between these children and their parents.

Mr Dugdale, acting on behalf of the local authority, drew the Court of Appeal's attention to the wide range of independent expert reports commissioned by Social Services. These had consistently alluded to the problematic parenting of the mother and the periodic absences of the father which meant that he was not always on hand to supplement her care of the children. Mr Dugdale also referred to several reports establishing actual harm to the eldest child K and describing her improvement since reception into foster care. He concluded his submission before Lady Justice Hale by insisting that the local authority's case was based on sound indications of the likelihood of future harm occurring to J and C as a result of the care they were receiving from their mother.

Lady Justice Hale in deciding between the arguments put to her by Mr Levy and Mr Dugdale invoked article 8 of the European Convention on Human Rights. She noted that this article gave both parents and children the right to have their private and family life respected. As a qualified right, any government seeking to interfere with this right could only do so lawfully if their action was: in accordance with the law; for a legitimate purpose; and necessary. Deliberating on the evidence put before her, Lady Justice Hale concluded that given the expert reports received by the local authority on both the children and the parents, it did have reasonable grounds to infer that future harm would occur to J and C. Therefore, the local authority in seeking the Care Orders was acting in accordance with the law and with a legitimate aim in view. However, the essential question was whether the Care Orders, together with the severing of all contact between parents and children, were a proportionate response to the anticipated harm to these children and the only means of safeguarding them.

Lady Justice Hale observed that the overarching aim of Social Services intervention is 'to support, and eventually to reunite, the family, unless the risks are so high that the child's welfare requires alternative family care' (para. 31). Indeed, even when children are subject to Care Orders and have been removed into residential or foster care, under s.34 of the Children Act 1989, local authorities are required to facilitate reasonable contact between child and parent in so far as this is consistent with the child's safety. Hence Lady Justice Hale was inclined to agree with Mr Levy's contention on behalf of the parents that the issuing of Care Orders and the severance of all contact was a disproportion response to the risk of harm at the lower end of the spectrum. She expressed scepticism that the only course of action open to the local authority at the time was the removal from home of J and C with a care plan for their adoption or else to take no action at all and leave the children at risk.

Notably, Mr Levy in his submission before the Court of Appeal proposed a support package for the parents to enable them to care more effectively for their children. In other words, should it be proved that the local authority could feasibly have offered a package of support to parents and children in their home which substantially reduced the risk of future harm to J and C, then the local authority would be found in breach of article 8. It would be in breach because the terms of the article 8 require the mode of interference in family life to be necessary and proportionate. Plainly, if the local authority could have followed an alternative less drastic course of action to safeguard J and C, the two younger children, then, by using Care Orders it was in violation of the parents' and children's Convention right to family life.

The protection of private and family life enshrined in article 8 of the Convention on Human Rights will constitute a key tension in any care proceedings, even if it is not the subject of dispute in the court case itself. In this Court of Appeal case there was recognition that interference in family life was, as it were, a necessary evil to safeguard the children concerned. This issue turned not on intervention of itself, which the court found was justified, but on the nature of that intervention. Often the legal argument at the heart of care proceedings turns not on whether the State, in the guise of Children's Services, should have interfered in family life, but *how* it should have interfered. Social workers must determine not only whether to intervene or not in a child's life, but the degree to which they should intervene. The legal concept of proportionality, which attaches to all qualified rights listed in the European Convention, requires practitioners to interfere as minimally as possible in family life to meet the lawful objective of protecting children from harm. It is this stipulation that is perhaps the most exacting on practitioners in terms of their professional judgement. This does not mean to say that social workers should use Emergency Protection Orders or Care Orders as a last resort and after trying other less invasive forms of intervention first. A dire situation and a child in imminent danger may require first recourse to an Emergency Protection or Interim Care Order. However, a proportionate response means that an Emergency Protection Order should only be sought in an emergency situation and a Care Order should only be sought when there is genuinely no other available course of action which will safeguard the child in question from significant harm.

Application for discharge of order

Where a court is deliberating on the making of an order under the Children Act 1989 parents and guardians have rights to appear in court and oppose the making of the order. Where an order has already been issued they are also entitled to go to court and apply for its discharge or variation. The parties directly affected by proceedings under the Children Act 1989 will have different rights to be heard in court depending on their relationship to the child. Respondents to the court case, who are automatically entitled to: be legally represented in court; present evidence; and cross-examine witnesses produced by the local authority or any other applicant for a court order, are:

- all those with parental responsibility;
- the child (normally represented by a Children's Guardian).

In addition to these respondents, notice of the court hearing must be served on specified others who do not have the automatic right to be parties to the proceedings, but can apply to the court for this status. These specified persons are:

- an unmarried birth father;
- any person caring for the child at the commencement of proceedings;
- any person with a Contact Order.

In the Court of Appeal case the mother had a mandatory right to appear in court as she was the birth mother of all four children concerned and therefore automatically had parental responsibility for each of them. However, as the father of the three younger children CM, J and C was not married to the mother of his children he did not automatically have parental responsibility and could only become a party to the proceedings with the permission of the court. This was given as the father was thoroughly involved in the care of these children, albeit that he was periodically absent from their lives. As mother and father were of the same mind, they were jointly represented by Mr Levy. Both parents had also attended the care proceedings at the previous County Court hearing. Of course had they disagreed on the future care of their children they would have been separately represented in court and their respective legal counsel would have presented evidence to support their conflicting positions. In addition to the right to be a party to the court proceedings which concern them, parents and children also have rights to apply for the variation or discharge of court orders once they are made. These rights vary depending on the nature of the order and are summarised in the table below.

Court order	Who can apply for discharge	Right to apply for discharge
Police Protection Power	None	No right of discharge
Emergency Protection Order	• Parents • Anyone with parental responsibility • Child • Anyone with whom the child is living	After first 72 hours
Child Assessment Order	• Determined under court rules	Determined under court rules
Care Order	• Anyone with parental responsibility • Child • Local authority	Once in every six month or earlier if permission given by court
Supervision Order	• Anyone with parental responsibility • Child • Local authority • Supervisor • Anyone with whom the child is living	Once in every six month or earlier if permission given by court

As regards the Care Orders, under s.39 of the Children Act 1989 the child, those holding parental responsibility, or the local authority have the right to apply for their discharge. If the court refuses to discharge the order the applicant is entitled to reapply under s.91(17) after six months. It was this right which the County Court sought to interfere with by debarring the parents from making such an application to the court for a two-year period. The court does have this power under s.91(14), but to be compliant with article 8 of the European Convention it has to be used in exceptional circumstances and not as a matter of routine. The two older children, K and CM, had been the subject of continuous court proceedings for four years by the time the Court of Appeal hearing took place in 2001. The County Court had taken the view that permitting six-monthly court hearings by parents who were opposed to both the Care Orders and the court order debarring them from contact with their children, would cause further harm to K and CM by denying them any certainty as to their future. Moreover, both children by this time were clearly indicating to their Guardian ad Litem (Children's Guardian) that they did not wish to have contact with their parents. Taking account of the two older children's wishes, the Guardian ad Litem concluded that it was detrimental to their welfare to be routinely asked their views regarding contact.

The concept of a fair trial underpins common law approaches to the dispensing of justice. Article 6 of the European Convention on Human Rights gives further legal expression to this principle. This concept is integrated into the Children Act 1989 through the right of certain individuals to be a party to care proceedings and the right of appeal against court orders once they are made. Such rights are afforded to the children concerned and the adults involved in their lives. The right of adults to oppose the State's interference in the lives of children has to be balanced by the need to protect children from distressful, destabilising and repeated court hearings. Consequently, the Children Act 1989 places restrictions on who has the automatic right to be represented or to appeal and who must seek the permission of the court.

Whether or not a person possesses parental responsibility or is living with the child prior to the court case fundamentally affects their entitlement to be represented in court. This makes it crucial that social workers establish who has parental responsibility, who is living with the child, and who has a Contact Order. It is a legal requirement that those automatically entitled to be parties to the care proceeding are notified and given sight of all the documentation and evidence related to the upcoming court hearing. Failure to do this can result in adjournment of the hearing and violation of the *non-delay principle*. The child is always a party to the care proceedings where they are normally represented by the Children's Guardian, who will also be responsible for giving instructions to the child's legal representatives.

Judgement in *Re C and B (Children) (Care Order: Future Harm)*

Having listened to all the evidence, Lady Justice Hale accepted that there was evidence to indicate that the two younger children J and C were 'likely to suffer significant harm'. However, the nature of this harm was not of sufficient gravity to justify the issuance of Care Orders. She concluded there were alternative courses of action open to the local authority to prevent the occurrence of harm to J and C at a future stage in their development. Accordingly Lady Justice Hale set aside the Care Orders on J and C and returned them home under an Interim Supervision Order. The threshold criteria for Supervision and Care Orders, whether on a full or interim basis, is exactly the same. In the judge's opinion this was another indicator that the local authority had the scope to choose a more proportionate form of interference in the family life of J and C and their parents.

In relation to the debarment of the parents from making applications for discharge of the orders relating to the older children K and CM, Lady Justice Hale came to a different set of conclusions. She had been convinced by the evidence put before her that K and CM would suffer further harm if forced against their wishes to have contact with their parents. Accordingly, Lady Justice Hale upheld the decision of the County Court both to grant permission to the local authority to refuse contact to the parents and to debar them from seeking discharge of either the Care Orders or the order effectively denying them the right of contact with their two older children. Yet, as Lady Justice Hale observed in her judgement, this did not mean that the mother and father would be prohibited from contacting K and CM for all time. It remained open for them and the local authority to work with K and CM at a later date to facilitate indirect contact initially and possibly direct contact thereafter if in future they had a change of mind in relation to seeing the mother and father.

 Critical questions

1 From what you know of the facts of this case, do you think it was correctly decided? Are there any statements by Justice Hale that you particularly agree or disagree with and why?

2 This case concerned a parent with learning disabilities. What might be the additional barriers that such a parent might confront in trying to avail of their rights in relation to care proceedings? As a social worker working in partnership with a parent with learning difficulties in the context of care proceedings, how would you support that parent to exercise their rights?

3 A disproportionately high number of parents with learning difficulties have their children removed from them by local authorities. Mr Levy, the barrister acting for the parents, proposed a support package for them. From what you know of the facts of this case, what kind of care plan might have improved their parenting capacity?

 Perspectives

Social workers involved in care proceedings

Beckett et al. (2007) and Taylor et al. (2008) asked four focus groups comprised of local authority social workers about their experiences of care proceedings. One practitioner responded 'these are judgements of Solomon at times, you know, and we do make them, and that is so scary' (Beckett et al., 2007: 59). Alongside this understanding of their work, social workers alluded to a pervasive anxiety, which the researchers characterised as a fantasy 'that somehow a "right decision" can be made if only there is enough assessment from expert enough professionals' (Taylor et al., 2007: 25).

Many social workers in the focus groups criticised the overemphasis on procedures and tick-box assessments at the expense of direct work with parents and children. They were also concerned by the greater weight given by judges to the evidence of expert witnesses and Children's Guardians who often had only a few interactions with the child or parent compared to sustained interaction by the allocated social worker or support worker. One research participant summed this up: 'there are situations when you get an expert or a specialist going in and doing a couple of contact sessions. The parents can be really ready for that and you end up with a report that is actually very positive for the parents. But it may be in total contrast to what you've been seeing or your family care worker has been seeing' (Beckett et al., 2007: 58). At the same time, focus group participants were quick to acknowledge the vital contribution of other professionals.

Social workers also felt concerned for children at the centre of care proceedings because as one practitioner explained, 'with all the red tape and everything else that comes with it now, you lose the children . . . I find that's the hardest part that they're the ones who are getting swept along with the process' (Taylor et al., 2008: 29). This was exacerbated by the adversarial nature of care proceedings which pitted legal representatives of the parents, children and local authority against one another. At times, according to another social worker, 'the solicitors and barristers and what have you, it's a contest between themselves, they don't really look at realistic things that can be managed. It's a case of winning a case so suggesting things that really aren't going to work. They're working on behalf of their clients and suggest unreasonable things' (Beckett et al., 2007: 59).

Beckett et al. (2007: 61) concluded that:

> As social workers choosing to resist the court route are also placing themselves in a position where failure could result in public disgrace – UK social workers do tend to see a media lynching as their likely fate if they fail to protect children – we do not find it hard to see why choosing care proceedings could, in borderline situations, be the more attractive option. Perhaps this is a dynamic that helps to account for the increasing numbers of care proceedings being brought to court.

CASE 3
X Local Authority v. *B (Emergency Protection Orders)* [2005] FLR 341

Importance of the case

It explores what constitutes a proportionate interference in family life to safeguard children; and the meaning of partnership working with parents. The case considers the degree to which children's wishes and feeling should influence decisions taken by local authorities to protect them.

History of the case

The case was transferred from a lower court to the Family Division of the High Court after Emergency Protection Orders (EPO) for four siblings D, J, W and N were issued by a lower court, followed by Interim Care Orders lasting 28 days for D, J and W. Further Interim Care Orders for J and W were then made by the High Court. After successful rehabilitative work with the children's family over the period of the Interim Care Orders, the local authority sought to withdraw its application for full Care Orders. A subsequent hearing in the High Court considered both this matter and the manner in which the local authority had arrived at its decisions and acted upon them.

Facts of the case

The family had been subject to Social Services involvement since 1988. The eldest child, 17-year-old N was seriously ill with an incurable disease, 15-year-old D had been diagnosed as suffering from Attention Deficit Disorder and Conduct Disorder, while child J suffered from Chronic Motor Disorder. There was ongoing concern within the local authority that the children's parents mismanaged medication, failed to act on medical advice and had disengaged from medical services. On 16 January 2003 two social workers made a pre-arranged home visit to discuss the situation. The mother asked the two social workers to leave when they suggested taking the children into local authority foster care. The next day the local authority commenced ex parte proceedings for Emergency Protection Orders for all four children, removing D, J, and W into foster care. N, who was then almost 18 years old, refused to leave the family home, and Social Services had little choice but to acquiesce. On 20 January 2003 the local authority applied for Care Orders for D, J, and W, and on 28 January 2003 a Children's Guardian was appointed after transfer of the matter to the Family Division of the High Court. Although the parents initially contested Interim Care Orders, they withdrew their objection when it was agreed that all three children would be placed with their maternal grandparents. At this time the eldest child N was admitted to hospital after her condition worsened, where she thereafter remained subject to detainment under s.3 of the Mental Health Act 1983. Successive Interim Care Orders were granted. On 26 June 2003 child D, who was 15½ years old, returned home to his parents against the wishes of the local authority. By the date of a High Court hearing on 20 October 2003 the local authority agreed that the best interests of all the children would be their return home to their parents under close supervision. A detailed care plan for each child was agreed between the parents and local authority with the involvement of health and education professionals. To facilitate rehabilitation, while safeguarding the children, the High Court sitting on 20 October 2003 granted Interim Care Orders for a period of up to 12 months and subject to review every 6 months for the children J and W. At the same hearing the previous Interim Care Order in respect of child D was discharged. Rehabilitation of the children proved successful and the local authority sought to withdraw the Interim Care Orders. The High Court hearing to consider this matter also deliberated on the local authority's decision-making process.

Key people in the case

Mother – mother of N, J, D and W
N – 17-year-old child at time of events
J – child at time of events
D – 15-year-old child at time of events
W – child at time of events
Ms R – social worker for N
Ms G – social worker for J, D and W
Mr C – key worker for J, D and W
Justice Munby – judge in High Court case

Discussion of the case

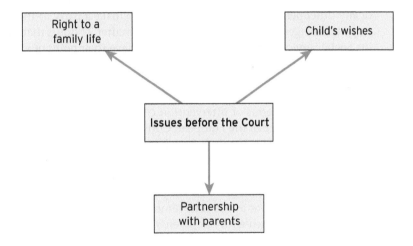

Right to a family life

Local authorities, which are local government bodies and therefore part of the State, are obliged to act in accordance with the requirements of article 8 of the European Convention on Human Rights which declares that 'everyone has the right to respect for his private and family life'. In exercising its legal duties and functions, including those of safeguarding children, local authorities must do so without violating the rights of parents and children under the European Convention. The question arose as to whether in seeking and exercising the Emergency Protection Orders and Interim Care Orders the local authority had violated article 8. This is of course a qualified right, and Social Services are legally justified in their intervention in family life if this is to protect the health of a child. Even in such situations the State is still obliged to act proportionately. This is a legal principle developed by the European Court of Human Rights and incorporated into domestic law by virtue of s.2 of the Human Rights Act 1998, which requires national courts to take into account precedents of the European Court of Human Rights.

Proportionality requires the State, when interfering with a person's Convention right, to act in a way that is manifestly necessary in order to achieve a legitimate objective, such as preventing the commission of a serious crime, or protecting an individual from harm. Hence social workers intervening in family life must not only do so according to the law, that is, the Children Act 1989, but their action must not interfere with a Convention Right beyond what is absolutely essential to prevent some kind of harm. This legal principle of proportionality applies to the use of ex parte Emergency Protection Orders. It is a fundamental tenet of the British justice system that both parties to a legal action must be given the opportunity to be heard in court. This principle is also enshrined in article 6 of the European Convention, which grants citizens the right to a fair trial.

However, in situations of extreme urgency, where a child is at immediate risk of significant harm, there is provision under court rules for a local authority to apply for an ex parte Emergency Protection Order which can be granted by a single magistrate without the prior knowledge of parents or guardians. This plainly deprives a child's carers of the opportunity to be represented in court should they wish to contest the making of the order. Where the court does issue an ex parte Emergency Protection Order, notice must be served on those holding parental responsibility (or carers with whom the child is living) within 48 hours of the EPO being made. A right to seek discharge (termination) of the order can be availed of after 72 hours by the child, those holding parental responsibility, or any other person which the court agrees to make a party to the proceedings. Under an ex parte Emergency Protection Order, it is only after 72 hours that a child or parent opposing Social Services intervention can actually have their point of view represented at court.

The draconian nature of ex parte orders and their exclusion of children and parents from the court during the initial stages of legal action mean that they must only be availed of in genuinely extreme and urgent circumstances. Routine use of ex parte orders when less drastic forms of intervention could have equally protected a child from harm contravenes article 8 of the European Convention. At an exporte court hearing on 16 January 2003, the local authority's Social Services Department applied for Emergency Protection Orders to last for 7 days (almost the maximum period) to remove each of the four children. The EPOs were issued on that day, resulting in the children D, J and W being placed with foster carers the following day. Although an EPO had been obtained for the eldest child N, she was at the time almost 18 years old and refused to be placed in care. She therefore remained with her parents. It is notable that a Children's Guardian was not appointed until 28 January, some 12 days after the ex parte court hearing. Consequently there was no independent representation of the children's interests or that of their parents' during the legal proceedings which resulted in the issuance of an EPO for the removal of all four children. The present court hearing sought to consider whether the employment of ex parte Emergency Protection Orders lasting 7 days was the only available course of action open to the local authority in January 2003.

In considering this aspect of the case, Justice Munby turned to the jurisprudence of the European Court of Human Rights, whose judgements are persuasive precedent. This means that they do not have to be strictly followed, as would a House of Lords decision, but they do have to be taken into account by national courts when deliberating on matters related to the European Convention. Justice Munby cited judgement from *Haase* v. *Germany* [2004] 2 FLR 39 heard in the European Court of Human Rights and which concerned both the exclusion of parents from decision making and the duration of children's removal from their home.

> The [European Court of Human Rights] must however be satisfied that the national authorities were entitled to consider that there existed circumstances justifying the abrupt removal of the child from the care of its parents without any prior contact or consultation.

In particular, it is for the respondent State to establish that a careful assessment of the impact of the proposed care measure on the parents and the child, as well as of the possible alternatives to the removal of the child from its family, was carried out prior to the implementation of a care measure. (para. 95)

In the above excerpt the European Court of Human Rights stipulates that even though the removal of children without notice can be justified under article 8 (which is a qualified right), the State can only proceed on this basis after assessing the impact of its action upon the parents and children and after considering alternative less drastic interventions. Turning to precedent established in the domestic courts, Justice Munby quoted from judgement in *Re S (Ex Parte Orders)* [2001] 1 FLR 308 (p. 320):

Those who seek relief ex parte are under a duty to make the fullest and most candid and frank disclosure of all the relevant circumstances known to them. . . It is an elementary principle of natural justice that a judge cannot be shown evidence or other persuasive material in an ex parte application on the basis that it is not at a later stage to be revealed to the respondent. The respondent must have an opportunity to see the material which was deployed against him at the ex parte hearing and an opportunity, if he wishes to apply for the discharge or variation of the [order] . . .

This precedent imposes two further obligations upon the local authority which seeks an ex parte Emergency Protection Order: that of obtaining all the available information; and of disclosing evidence which may be prejudicial to their application. In other words, because the parent or guardian is not present in court, the local authority is under an even greater duty to disclose facts which may support the parents' version of events and undermine rather than buttress the local authority's application for an EPO. Furthermore, whatever evidence is presented at the ex parte court hearing must be shared at the earliest opportunity with the parents or guardians of the children who have been the subject of removal under an EPO. The question before Justice Munby then was whether the local authority in applying for 7 day ex parte Emergency Protection Orders for all of the children had abided by these legal principles, established through precedent in the European Court of Human Rights and the British judicial system; namely, that social workers applying for an ex parte Emergency Protection Order or Interim Care Order:

- Must assess the impact of without notice court proceedings on the parents and children.
- Must consider less drastic alternatives to ex parte proceedings.
- Must make full disclosure in court of all the facts known to them, including those which undermine their case for an ex parte court order.
- Must make available to respondent parents all the information used in evidence during the original ex parte court hearing.
- Must ensure that parents are informed about the ex parte proceedings as soon as possible and of their rights to apply for a variation or discharge of the order.

To decide whether social workers had complied with these principles, Justice Munby examined the events leading up to the application for an ex parte EPO. On 8 January 2003 social workers from the different teams involved with the family met and agreed that assessments of all four children needed to take place under a s.47 enquiry and away from their parents. It was decided at the Strategy Discussion that should the parents refuse cooperation concerning their children's proposed clinical assessments then care proceedings would be considered. The parents were to be invited to attend a Child Protection Case Conference on 20 January 2003.

Ms G, the social worker for D, J and W, along with Ms R, the social worker for the eldest child N, visited the children's mother on 16 January 2003 to explain the intentions of Social Services and suggested that failure to cooperate could result in the children being taken into local authority care. The mother became angry and insisted that the social workers leave. Later the same day, the local authority applied for EPOs for all of the children. The following day, 17 January 2003, in the Magistrate's Court sitting as a Family Proceedings Court, the written evidence presented consisted of a report about N prepared by Ms R the day before and a short statement by Ms G dated the same day as the court hearing. This written statement drew particular attention to the mother's lack of praise or encouragement in relation to the education of J and W. However, this was in contradiction to a school report regarding child D in which the mother was mentioned as being pleased with D's school performance and cooperating with the school regarding concerns in relation to D's welfare. This report was not disclosed to the Family Proceedings Court. On the basis of the two social workers' reports the family proceedings court granted the four Emergency Protection Orders for the maximum eight-day period. The criteria for granting an Emergency Protection Order are set out in the box below.

Key legislation

Children Act 1989

Grounds for an Emergency Protection Order (EPO)

Under s.44 of the Children Act 1989 anyone can apply to court for an emergency protection order and the judge may make an EPO if satisfied that

s.44(1) (a) there is reasonable cause to believe that the child is likely to suffer significant harm if

    (i) he is not removed to accommodation provided by or on behalf of the applicant or

    (ii) he does not remain in the place in which he is then being accommodated

In the event, the three children, D, J and W, were collected from school and taken to the hospital where on arrival their blood and urine samples were taken. The three children, all of whom were distressed, were then placed with emergency foster parents. No other medical examination or assessment was ever carried out. Subsequently, at a further hearing on 21 January, the local authority obtained Interim Care Orders which were to last until 18 February 2003, with the proviso that the parents would have contact with their children for 1½ hours twice a week. Although a Children's Guardian had been appointed by this stage he had not had the opportunity to see the children and there was no CAFCASS report presented at the 21 January court hearing which issued the Interim Care Orders. On 31 January, Mr C was appointed as the key worker for D, J and W. He quickly identified that the maternal grandparents were able to care for the three children on a temporary basis and on 28 February 2003 they were moved out of foster care to live with these grandparents. Given these facts, Justice Munby identified six matters of concern:

1 The use of an ex parte application.
2 Application and grant of EPOs rather than CAOs.
3 Children removed from their parents into foster care.

4 Delay in approaching and placing the children with their grandparents.
5 Inadequacy of parental contact once the children were removed.
6 Delay in the appointment of a guardian.

Justice Munby accepted in evidence presented by the local authority that it was reasonable to believe that if the parents were warned beforehand of a clinical assessment they might have administered medication to disguise the children's actual medical condition. However, he made a number of criticisms regarding the way in which social workers had approached the court proceedings. In Justice Munby's opinion the failings listed below collectively made for an unacceptable state of affairs which contributed to poor decision making by the local authority.

- Lack of written evidence presented to the Family Proceedings Court despite the family being known to Social Services over many years.
- Failure to demonstrate before the court why an Emergency Protection Order rather than a Child Assessment Order was required.
- Insufficient evidence to justify the local authority obtaining parental responsibility and removing the children into foster care as opposed to a less interventionist course of action.
- Failure by social workers and their legal representatives at the original ex parte court hearing to make a proper note of deliberations there and to furnish the parents with a full report of the oral and written evidence presented.
- Delay in the appointment of a Children's Guardian and thus the lack of proper representation of the children during key court proceedings.

The initial decision to remove the children into foster care without first establishing the viability of placement with family members, in this instance the children's maternal grandparents, was a further contravention of article 8, since to remove children completely away from all their relatives into foster care is the most extreme interference in family life. The text box below provides excerpts from policy guidance to direct social workers when temporarily removing children from their home. Justice Munby also concluded that the decision to obtain a seven-day EPO when the actual medical examination of the children amounted to no more than taking blood and urine samples was disproportionate. In his view the same outcome could almost certainly have been achieved through Child Assessment Orders. The making of such orders could have provided for a short visit to the hospital for a medical examination and avoided the necessity of removing the children from their parents and home.

Key guidance

The Children Act 1989 Guidance and Regulations: Family Placements

Department of Health (1991a) *The Children Act 1989 Guidance and Regulations: Family Placements Vol. 3* is policy guidance issued under s.7 of the Local Authority Social Services Act 1970. Essentially it obliges local authorities who need to safeguard children by removing them from their parents or primary carer to endeavour to identify family placements for children with relatives or friends before opting for foster care. Of course any family placement needs to be consistent with the child's welfare and there may be circumstances in which foster care should be the first recourse. These points are elaborated by the guidance.

Para. 3.33 Possibilities for a child to be cared for within the extended family should have been investigated and considered as an alternative to the provision of accommodation by the responsible authority. However, even when it has become necessary for the responsible authority to arrange provision of accommodation, placement with a relative will often provide the best opportunities for promoting and maintaining family links in familiar settings.

Para. 3.37 Assessment of relatives as foster parents must include consideration of the extent to which the placement will affect the child's other family relationships, including contact with either or both parents. Where such contact has been terminated or restricted, the local authority will need to consider with the prospective foster parents any particular difficulties they may encounter in maintaining any conditions or restrictions on contact. Similarly, relatives may feel their loyalty strained where they are given confidential information not available to other family members, just as they may be reluctant to disclose to the authority information they already possess.

Proportionality is a legal principle which applies not only to article 8 of the European Convention on Human Rights, but to all qualified rights under the Convention. Even when a Convention right is qualified permitting the State to interfere with that right under certain circumstances (as set out in the Convention) such interference must be the minimum necessary to achieve a legitimate purpose. The mother and children in this case should have been subjected to the least draconian and extreme forms of intervention necessary to achieve the objective of assessing the children in the first instance and thereafter safeguarding them from further harm. In terms of assessment, the local authority was found to have acted disproportionately in seeking an Emergency Protection Order which gave it parental responsibility, instead of a Child Assessment Order which does not. In relation to safeguarding, removing the children into foster care was a disproportionate means of protecting them from harm, as a proper assessment would have revealed the ability of the children's grandparents to take care of them. Although this still meant removing the children from their mother and home it did not require that they be removed entirely from their family. Social workers whether working in the area of child protection or with vulnerable adults will often find themselves confronted by issues relating to qualified Convention Rights.

Child's wishes

It is also salutary that despite applying for four Emergency Protection Orders the local authority was only able to act on three of these because child N, then almost 18 years of age, simply refused to comply. Later, child D, who was nearly 16 years old at the time and subject to an Interim Care Order requiring him to live with his grandparents, returned to his parental home against the wishes of Social Services. In neither instance did social workers act to implement the court orders against the wishes of the children in question. In taking account of a child's wishes within the context of the welfare checklist, there is also a landmark judicial precedent established in *Gillick* v. *West Norfolk and Wisbech Area Health Authority* [1986] 3 ALL ER 402 which the courts must follow. This established that in certain circumstances the court will defer to a decision by a child even when this is opposed by those with parental responsibility. The facts of this case and the related judgement are briefly summarised in the box on the next page.

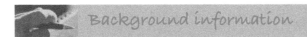

Background information

Gillick competent child

Gillick v. *West Norfolk and Wisbech Area Health Authority*
[1986] 3 ALL ER 402

A mother went to court to object to her daughter, then under 16 years of age, being given contraceptive advice by her GP without the knowledge or consent of her parents. The case was appealed all the way up to the House of Lords which held that if a child is of sufficient understanding he or she can receive medical treatment without parental knowledge or consent. The judgement stated that 'a minor's capacity to make his or her own decisions depends on the minor having sufficient understanding and intelligence to make the decisions and is not to be determined by reference to any judicially fixed age limit'. It concluded that 'parental rights yield to the child's right to make his own decisions when he reaches a sufficient understanding and intelligence to be capable of making up his own mind on the matter requiring decision'. Subsequent judgements have applied this reasoning beyond the area of medical treatment.

This means that as children develop and gain in understanding, parental authority needs to give way to their increasing capacity to make considered decisions for themselves. The case has wide implications for social work as a *Gillick* competent child is of 'sufficient understanding' to make decisions independently of those with parental responsibility. Under Emergency Protection Orders and Care Orders local authorities hold parental responsibility for minors and therefore the *Gillick* judgement had direct applicability to children *in care*.

The *Gillick* judgement taken together with the welfare checklist means that a child's wishes and feelings are of considerable importance when a court is deciding issues of residence and contact. Since child D was almost certainly *Gillick* competent it was unlikely that he could be forced to comply with the Care Order which Social Services had obtained for him. The fact that social workers went to court to obtain a court order which they later found themselves unable to implement speaks of a manifest failure to either consult with child D or take seriously his wishes and feelings. The eldest child N may well have been *Gillick* competent at the time that the Emergency Protection Order was obtained for her, and certainly the local authority was not willing to proceed against her refusal to comply with it. Evidently neither were the police, who could have been called upon, since refusing to comply with an Emergency Protection Order is strictly speaking a criminal offence. It is also true that events were overtaken by the subsequent deterioration in the eldest child N's mental health and her compulsory admission to hospital under s.3 of the Mental Health Act 1983. An outline of mental health provision for children is provided in the box on the next page. However, the refusal of N to comply with the EPO at the time it was served, and the weak position of the local authority in the face of her refusal, provides further evidence of inadequate consultation with the children or consideration of their wishes.

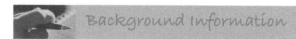

Background Information

Children and the Mental Health Act 1983

The Mental Health Act 1983 applies to children as well as adults. The Children Act 1989 and the Children Act 2004 will also be applicable at the same time. Therefore practitioners working with those under 18 years whether in hospital or in the community must operate within the legal frameworks of mental health and child welfare. Those with parental responsibility are normally required to give consent on behalf of their child to informal admission to hospital for treatment for a mental disorder. However, *Gillick* competent children under 16 years of age and young people aged 16-17 years may make these decisions for themselves. The decision to detain a child in hospital under the Mental Health Act 1983 must be made by at least one doctor or Approved Mental Health Professional specialised in Child and Adolescent Mental Health Services (CAMHS).

A child or young person being treated for a mental disorder in hospital must under s.131A(2) of the Mental Health Act 1983 normally be accommodated in a suitable environment relative to their age. Paragraph 36.68 of the *Mental Health Act 1983 Code of Practice* defines this as meaning the availability of:

- Appropriate physical facilities.
- Staff with the right training, skills and knowledge to understand and address their specific needs as children and young people.
- A hospital routine that will allow their personal, social and educational development to continue as normally as possible.
- Equal access to educational opportunities as their peers, in so far as that is consistent with their ability to make use of them, considering their mental state.

Giving consideration to the feelings and wishes of children subject to family or care proceedings under the Children Act 1989 is a requirement of the welfare checklist. Social workers applying for a court order can expect to be asked for evidence regarding the wishes and feelings of the children concerned. Practitioners need to bear in mind that it may be difficult to legally compel *Gillick* competent children, or that to do so may result in greater adverse consequences for their welfare. It is evident from this case that social workers having obtained an Emergency Protection Order for a 17-year-old and Interim Care Order for a 15-year-old then thought better of trying to implement these in the face of the children's defiance. Of course in situations where children and young people are at risk of significant harm there may be compelling reasons for proceeding with court orders even against older or *Gillick* competent children. However, it is important to recognise that such action may involve additional challenges and require a recalibration of the weight to be given to children's wishes and feelings as one factor of the welfare checklist.

Partnership with parents

Citing precedent in *Re G (Care: Challenge to Local Authority's Decision)* [2003] 2 FLR 42 (paras. 43–45) Justice Mumby quoted directly from that judgement noting that:

> In a case such as this, a local authority, before it can properly arrive at a decision to remove children from their parents, must tell the parents (preferably in writing) precisely what it is proposing to do. It must spell out (again in writing) the reasons why it is proposing to do

so. It must spell out precisely (in writing) the factual matters it is relying on. It must give the parents a proper opportunity to answer (either orally and/or in writing as the parents wish) the allegations being made against them. And it must give the parents a proper opportunity (orally and/or in writing as they wish) to make representations as to why the local authority should not take the threatened steps.

In both *Re G* and the present case, the local authority held a Care Order and therefore had parental responsibility for the children in question. The legal point made in *Re G*, and used as a precedent in the present case by Justice Munby was that, to be consistent with article 8, even when a local authority holds a Care Order it must exercise its powers in ways consistent with respect for private and family life. This involves continuing to work in partnership with parents and consulting them on decisions affecting their children and family life. In a statement placed before the court the father described being 'shocked, surprised and horrified at what the local authority have done and the manner in which they issued proceedings and sought an initial order behind our backs'.

It is therefore only in exceptional circumstances of extreme urgency that local authorities holding a Care Order should exclude parents from consultation and participation in decision making (*Re G* para. 58). In the present case, the local authority, which held Interim Care Orders on the children D, J and W, initially devised a care plan which stipulated that where possible at least 24 hours notice to remove the children from their parental home would be given to the parents. The issue before the court was whether this conditional and short period of notice to remove these three children from their family home was a disproportionate interference in family life to protect them from harm. Justice Munby considered that it was a disproportionate interference and insisted that the care plan should have made provision for consulting with the parents, and only permitted little or no notice by the local authority to remove D, J and W in circumstances of dire emergency. Government guidance as shown in the box below advises social workers on partnership working with parents when safeguarding children.

Key guidance

Framework for the Assessment of Children in Need and their Families

Para. 1.44 The majority of parents want to do the best for their children. Whatever their circumstances or difficulties, the concept of partnership between the State and the family, in situations where families are in need of assistance in bringing up their children lies at the heart of child care legislation. The importance of partnership has been further reinforced by a substantial number of research findings . . . In the process of finding out what is happening to a child, it will be critical to develop a co-operative working relationship, so that parents or caregivers feel respected and informed, that staff are being open and honest with them, and that they in turn are confident about providing vital information about their child, themselves and their circumstances.

Para. 1.45 Working with family members is not an end in itself; the objective must always be to safeguard and promote the welfare of the child. The child, therefore, must be kept in focus. It requires sensitivity to and understanding of the circumstances of families and their particular needs . . .

Partnership working requires social workers to proactively engage parents and children at every stage of intervention unless this would clearly jeopardise the child's welfare and safety. What this case reveals, is the danger of assuming that sharing information with parents subject to child protection procedures necessarily imperils the child in question. While Children's Services are charged with protecting children first and foremost, this can sometimes result in overreaction and disproportionate forms of intervention. Denying parents, and in this case the children also as the Children's Guardian was appointed late, the opportunity to be represented in court is a grave and extreme decision. It flies in the face of partnership working and such a course of action must be restricted to the most dire, urgent and exceptional of situations. Even in circumstances where social workers are compelled to act without the prior knowledge of parents or those with parental responsibility, they must thereafter abide by the underpinning tenet of partnership working. This includes sharing information (consistent with the child's welfare) and fully explaining the reasons for their actions.

Judgement in *X Local Authority* v. *B (Emergency Protection Orders)*

Justice Munby agreed to the withdrawal of the applications for Care Orders by the local authority while concluding that it had fallen short of its obligations under article 8 of the European Convention of Human Rights. In the concluding paragraph (para. 93) of his judgement he reiterates that:

> The summary removal of children from their parents in circumstances such as this is bound to be traumatic for all concerned. It needs to be handled with great care and sensitivity. Otherwise lasting damage may be done, both to the children and to their parents. And heavy-handedness is likely to be totally counter-productive, making it impossible for parents and local authority to 'work together' productively in the future.

 Critical questions

1 From what you know about this case and the difficulties encountered by social workers in making the two older children comply with the court orders, how might you work with a *Gillick* competent child in relation to pending care proceedings?

2 This case pitted the rights of parents to a private and family life guaranteed under article 8 of the European Convention on Human Rights against the duty of local authorities, as part of the State, to intervene in family life to safeguard children. Do you think this case was correctly decided and that Justice Munby identified the correct balance between these two imperatives? If not, why? Using your knowledge of child protection, what would be the challenges for social workers trying to follow the principles set out by Justice Munby when seeking court orders to remove children?

3 Compare this case with the issues relating to a family placement which emerged in the Serious Case Review of events surrounding Peter's death. In that case concern was expressed that placing Peter with a friend of his mother did not give him sufficient protection. In this case social workers were criticised for initially placing children in foster care rather than with their grandparents. What factors would you take into account in deciding whether to place a child removed from home with a local authority foster carer or with a relative?

Use of Emergency Protection Orders

Social workers acting to protect children in an emergency have several legal options. They can seek the consent of parents to the voluntary placement of a child with a relative or in local authority care under s.20 of the Children Act 1989. Where parental consent or voluntary arrangements are problematic, social workers can apply for an ex parte Emergency Protection Order under s.44 or request that an officer exercise a Police Protection Power under s.46. In two studies, covering 550 children in all, Masson (2005) examined how social workers decided which course of action to pursue in urgent situations.

Statutory guidance requires social workers to develop cooperative partnerships with families and avoid recourse to the courts where possible. However, voluntary agreements depend upon trust existing between social workers and parents. Practitioners must have confidence that parents or guardians will abide by a voluntary arrangement for the care of their child by a relative, foster carer or children's home. Research by Masson (2005) revealed that such agreements are sometimes coerced from parents under threat of an application for an Emergency Protection Order or Care Order. Parents threatened in this way give in to pressure from social workers without understanding what they are agreeing to, or why, or for how long. While court action can be exceptionally stressful for parents and children, avoiding it can result in parents being deprived of legal advice and the opportunity to challenge social work intervention through the judicial process.

No national statistics are compiled for the exercise of Police Protection Powers although their use is widespread. This is of concern as there is no appeal process against an officer's decision to invoke this power and remove a child from a parent for up to three days. Nor does the exercise of this power require a court order as it is exercised solely at the discretion of the police. This contrasts with an Emergency Protection Order which requires a social worker to make an application to the court. Masson (2005) in her study of several police forces found that in 75% of instances where a Police Protection Power was exercised, this had been at the request of Social Services.

Masson (2005) found evidence that Police Protection Powers were being used as an alternative to both with, and without, notice (ex parte) Emergency Protection Orders. The reliance on Police Protection Powers was commonly due to social workers and lay magistrates being unable to avail of legal advice on a 24-hour basis or delays in listing an EPO application for a court hearing. Masson (2005: 8) discovered that in the majority of cases where an Emergency Protection Order or a Police Protection Power was invoked, the family was known to Social Services and recourse to legal action was 'in response to an incident, the latest but not necessarily the most serious in a series that had raised concerns about the parents' ability to provide adequate care'. In other words an Emergency Protection Order or Police Protection Power was sometimes being used in non-urgent situations and often as a precursor to care proceedings.

In the Masson (2005) study almost all the applications for an Emergency Protection Order were decided by experienced lay magistrates. As lay magistrates, they were dependent on the opinion of their legal adviser who normally decided whether an EPO should be heard ex parte. In no instance did a magistrate reject the local authority's application for an Emergency Protection Order. As Masson (2005: 15) observed, the concern of magistrates 'was to get children into a position of safety and therefore they played safe and granted the EPO'. Reflecting on the findings of her research, Prof. Judith Masson (2005: 15) concluded that 'the dominant culture of rescue meant that magistrates did not refuse orders. Realistically, the courts could not hold local authorities to account.'

> **CASE 4**
> *Re U (A Child) (Serious Injury: Standard of Proof)*
> [2004] EWCA Civ 567

Importance of the case

It explores the concept of proof in court proceedings concerning the protection of children. The case also considers the status of medical evidence in relation to allegations of induced or fabricated illness.

History of the case

ML the mother of LU sought permission to appeal against a High Court's finding during initial care proceedings that she had harmed her infant daughter. This application for permission to appeal was heard by the Civil Division of the Court of Appeal.

Facts of the case

LU, a girl, was born to ML in July 2001. The mother ML was not married at the time of her daughter's birth, but married the child's father FL within a few weeks at a mosque, although no related civil ceremony took place. The families of both parents had originally migrated from the Indian subcontinent to live in Britain, and both ML and her husband had been born in the United Kingdom. When ML was eight-months pregnant she was forced to leave her parents' house and, after the birth of the child, went to live with her husband's family. On three separate occasions during August 2001 when the baby was alone with her, the mother claimed that the infant was having breathing problems and on each occasion admitted her daughter to hospital. In every instance medical staff could find no evidence of any respiratory problems, nor did clinical tests reveal any illness. In September 2001 a developmental check on the child found her to be 'healthy and progressing well'. During that same month the mother was admitted to hospital due to a drugs overdose. In October 2001, when ML was with a female relative in the home, ML alerted her to the baby having breathing problems and an ambulance was called. Ambulance staff reported the infant as being alert with no unusual signs and again no illness or medical explanation could be discovered at the hospital, where she remained for nearly two weeks. After consultation between medical staff and a social worker it was agreed to discharge the infant home to her maternal grandmother pending care proceedings. Shortly after being placed with her grandmother the baby appeared unwell and in November 2001 was again admitted to hospital. On this occasion doctors found that she had an infection and diagnosed retroviral enteritis. The baby returned to her grandmother's home where she was still living at the time of the Court of Appeal hearing. In November 2001 the health visitor assessed the mother as having post-natal depression which required support and monitoring. During initial care proceedings a year later, in November 2002, the judge concluded, based on the medical and non-medical evidence before her, that ML had obstructed the airway of her daughter on four separate occasions. She therefore found that the mother had caused *significant harm* to LU and consequently that the s.31 threshold had been crossed for a Care Order. The mother ML now sought permission from the Court of Appeal to agree to hear an appeal against this finding of having caused *significant harm* to her daughter. At the time of the Court of Appeal hearing the child was almost 3 years old.

Key people in the case

LU – a 2-year-old child
ML – mother of LU
FL – father of LU
Mr McFarlane – barrister representing ML
Mr Howard – barrister representing the local authority
Dame Butler-Sloss – judge presiding in Court of Appeal case

Discussion of the case

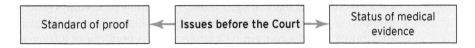

Standard of proof

Care proceedings, like adoption proceedings, divorce proceedings and proceedings under the Civil Partnership Act 2004, constitute forms of civil legal action and not criminal action. Yet care proceedings, despite being heard in a civil court, can result in the gravest of consequences for respondents, for example the removal of their children into the care of the State. It is on this ground that Mr McFarlane, legal counsel for ML set out to argue that so serious were the consequences for parents of a finding of *significant harm* against their child that it should be subject to a criminal law standard of proof. Since the standard of proof in criminal proceedings is *beyond a reasonable doubt*, this is a higher standard than that required by civil law, which is to establish the facts on *the balance of probabilities*.

The standard of proof is designed to ensure that the claimant in a civil case, or the prosecution in a criminal one, must prove allegations against the respondent or defendant up to a minimum level of reliability as to their truth. Otherwise people could be subject to civil orders or convicted of crimes on the basis of little or flimsy evidence. The standard of proof required by the court is one safeguard against innocent people being found guilty of criminal or civil wrongs. It is fundamental to the notion of a fair trial under article 6 of the European Convention on Human Rights. Lord Nicholls in the House of Lords case *Re H (Minors) (Sexual Abuse: Standard of Proof)* [1996] AC 563 at page 586 defined the civil standard of proof for family proceedings:

> The balance of probability standard means that a court is satisfied an event occurred if the court considers that, on the evidence, the occurrence of the event was more likely than not. When assessing the probabilities the court will have in mind as a factor, to whatever extent is appropriate in the particular case, that the more serious the allegation the less likely it is that the event occurred and, hence, the stronger should be the evidence before the court concludes that the allegation is established on the balance of probability . . .

Lord Nicholls elaborated on this statement by citing the example of an allegation that a stepfather lost his temper and slapped his young stepdaughter as against one that he repeatedly raped her. The first allegation is more likely to have happened than the second, because it is less serious. Many parents slap their children, very few parents rape them. If a local authority makes a grave allegation of neglect or abuse against a parent or carer, then it has to produce strong and convincing evidence to prove that this less probable event did in fact occur. According to Lord Nicholls, 'this approach also provides a means by which the balance of probability standard can accommodate one's instinctive feeling that even in civil proceedings a court should be more sure before finding serious allegations proved than when deciding less serious or trivial matters'. It was on this ground that legal counsel for the mother argued that the matters before the court were so serious that a heightened civil standard of proof should be applied. He claimed that to all intents and purposes, this heightened civil standard was virtually indistinguishable from the criminal standard of proof. It followed therefore that the allegations made against the mother of deliberately harming her child LU should have to be proved *beyond a reasonable doubt*.

The bench of judges hearing the application of the mother for permission to appeal took issue with the attempt by her barrister to introduce a criminal standard of proof into care proceedings which fall under the jurisdiction of civil law. Dame Butler-Sloss observed that criminal proceedings employ stricter rules on the admissibility of evidence, are more adversarial and are more formal than care proceedings and family proceedings generally. She restated the definition of *the balance of probabilities* and the flexibility inherent in this approach when adjudicating on cases concerning a range of issues from minor infringements of civil law to conduct causing serious harm to others. Accordingly the Court of Appeal reiterated that the House of Lords judgement in *Re H (Minors) (Sexual Abuse: Standard of Proof)* was binding judicial precedent and would be followed by the court in the present case.

Social workers employed in Children's Services must ensure that the evidence they present before the court meets the threshold criteria of the particular order they are seeking. In addition to this they must produce evidence which is sufficiently robust as to meet the requirements of the standard of proof. This means presenting evidence which is provided by credible witnesses and corroborated by expert opinions, and which shows that different sources of information point towards the assertion of the same facts. Another fundamental principle of common law is that 'he who alleges must prove'. This means that normally the *burden of proof* is on the claimant or applicant in a civil case or the prosecution in a criminal case. It is for the person who alleges wrongdoing to prove that it took place. The respondent or defendant does not have to prove they did nothing wrong, but they do have to rebut any evidence of wrongdoing produced by the claimant or prosecution. In the Court of Appeal case it was the local authority that was alleging that LU had tried to suffocate her child on a number of occasions. It was therefore for the local authority to provide evidence of this allegation, rather than requiring the mother to produce evidence that the allegation was unfounded.

The *standard of proof* and the *burden of proof* are elemental concepts which underpin the whole judicial system. They are also crucial aspects of a fair trial. The requirement for the person who makes an allegation to prove it and to prove it to an explicit standard offers further safeguards to prevent innocent people being found guilty, or in this case an innocent mother having her child removed from her care. The significance of this particular Court of Appeal judgement is the requirement for even more stringent standards to be applied to evidence within the *balance of probabilities* formula, when the consequence of proving an allegation in a civil court are particularly grave. In the Court of Appeal case the judge demanded not only that the local authority meet the *balance of probabilities* in a minimal way, but that it offer convincing evidence of a wrongful act that is highly unlikely to be committed by the vast majority of mothers. It was because social workers of the local authority were able to meet the stringent evidential demands of the court that the Care Order for the child LU was issued.

Status of medical evidence

Mr McFarlane on failing to convince the Court of Appeal that the criminal standard of proof should be applied to care proceedings then turned to the applicability of the decision in *R* v. *Cannings (Angela)* [2004] EWCA Crim 1. The Crown Court case concerning Angela Cannings and subsequent appeal to the Court of Appeal (Criminal Division) received considerable media coverage. Mrs Cannings was accused of murdering three of her four children who had all died in early infancy. The evidence against her at the trial consisted of contradictory medical expert opinion. However, she was still convicted by the Crown Court of murdering her infant children. On appeal, the Court of Appeal concluded that natural causes could not be ruled out to explain the deaths and quashed the decision of the lower court. In other words the charge of murder against Angela Cannings had not been proved *beyond a reasonable doubt*.

Mr McFarlane for the mother, sought to argue that despite being a criminal case, precedent in *R v. Cannings* was directly applicable to the present case. In particular, he drew the Court of Appeal's attention to the danger of relying on medical evidence when this was conflicting. Mr Howard, legal counsel for the respondent local authority, while acknowledging the applicability of some aspects of *R v. Cannings* to the present case, disputed the conclusions of the mother's barrister. Mr Howard contended that the present case did not involve criminal proceedings and was not concerned with the conviction or punishment of the mother. Instead it concerned child protection. According to Mr Howard, the local authority could not simply leave children exposed to risk of further significant harm because the exact cause of their injury could not be clearly identified. After hearing evidence from all parties Dame Butler-Sloss in her judgement then set out the elements of *R v. Cannings* which are applicable to care proceedings where medical evidence comprises a substantial component of the local authority's lawsuit for a Care or Supervision Order (para. 23):

(i) The cause of an injury or an episode that cannot be explained scientifically remains equivocal.
(ii) Recurrence is not in itself probative.
(iii) Particular caution is necessary in any case where the medical experts disagree, one opinion declining to exclude a reasonable possibility of natural cause.
(iv) The Court must always be on guard against the over-dogmatic expert, the expert whose reputation or *amour propre* [self-esteem] is at stake, or the expert who has developed a scientific prejudice.
(v) The judge in care proceedings must never forget that today's medical certainty may be discarded by the next generation of experts or that scientific research will throw light into corners that are at present dark.

Judges presiding over care proceedings must test the evidence presented by a local authority against these five stipulations, while at the same time determining whether the evidence also satisfies the threshold set out in s.31 of the Children Act 1989 for a Care or Supervision Order. Dame Butler-Sloss disagreed with the proposition put by the mother's barrister: that a local authority should not proceed against a parent if the medical evidence is equivocal or ambiguous. Instead she highlighted the importance of both medical and non-medical evidence. Dame Butler-Sloss observed (para. 26) that:

the judge invariably surveys a wide canvas, including a detailed history of the parents' lives, their relationship and their interaction with professionals. There will be many contributions to this context, family members, neighbours, health records, as well as the observation of professionals such as social workers, health visitors and children's guardian.

This means that even when medical evidence is equivocal, care proceedings must still continue because medical opinion is only one source from which evidence will be derived. The box on the next page explains the role of expert witnesses in care proceedings.

In evidence to the High Court all three medical experts agreed that the infant LU had 'probably either suffered induced upper respiratory obstruction or her symptoms were fabricated or they were described by an over-anxious mother' (para. 39). According to one doctor who gave evidence, while a one-off unexplained respiratory difficulty was not unusual,

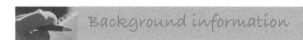
Background information

Expert witnesses

Statements of opinion

The law relating to the admissibility of evidence in court means that a witness may not give evidence on matters which require the special skill or knowledge of an expert. For example, a care worker can give evidence relating to the events they have witnessed, e.g. *'the service-user cannot dress himself without assistance'*. But the care worker does not have the expertise to speculate on whether or not an adult has mental capacity. However, as mental capacity is ultimately to be determined by the court and not a medical doctor, the judge will weigh the evidence of a care worker in coming to a final conclusion on the matter.

Expert opinion

Only expert witnesses are permitted to give an opinion in evidence rather than a statement of fact. The judge will want to hear the opinion of a specialist, for example a consultant psychiatrist who has expertise in assessing mental capacity. An expert opinion will only be required if on the proven facts it is impossible for the judge (or jury in criminal cases) to determine a matter without the opinion of an expert witness.

Experts giving evidence:

- Report on factors which tend to support a particular position.
- Must not misinform the court by failing to mention facts which detract from their overall conclusion.
- Must offer their considered opinion and not one which favours the party which appointed them to give evidence.

Examination by expert witnesses

Where it is necessary for expert witnesses, such as a consultant psychiatrist or paediatrician, to medically examine an adult or child in order to give their opinion, the parties to the court case should if possible agree on a single expert witness. This is designed to prevent an adult or child being subject to a series of unpleasant and invasive examinations.

an inability to medically explain repeated episodes was uncommon. The expert witnesses were of the opinion that as no medical cause for the baby's breathing difficulties could be identified on any of the four occasions it was reported, there must logically be a non-medical explanation. A non-medical explanation had to turn on some form of deliberate interference with the child's breathing. It was on this basis that during the original High Court hearing the judge concluded that on the medical evidence the most likely explanation of LU's repeated hospital admissions was smothering by her mother. The box on the next page excerpts the definition of fabricated or induced illness from HM Government (2008) *Safeguarding Children in whom Illness is Fabricated or Induced,* which is policy guidance.

The conclusion of the High Court judge did not rest solely on the medical evidence. Accounts of family members corroborated medical expert opinion. On three of the four occasions on which the mother reported her daughter as experiencing breathing difficulties there was a relative present in the house, though not in the same room as the mother. All three of these family members stated that the infant appeared to be unwell prior to being taken away in the ambulance. Each episode of breathing difficulty was followed by a

Key guidance

Safeguarding Children in whom Illness is Fabricated or Induced

1.5 There are three main ways of the carer fabricating or inducing illness in a child. These are not mutually exclusive and include:

- **Fabrication** of signs and symptoms. This may include fabrication of past medical history.
- **Fabrication** of signs and symptoms and falsification of hospital charts and records, and specimens of bodily fluids. This may also include falsification of letters and documents.
- **Induction** of illness by a variety of means.

4.5 Concerns may arise about possible fabricated or induced illness when:

- reported symptoms and signs found on examination are not explained by any medical condition from which the child may be suffering; or
- physical examination and results of medical investigations do not explain reported symptoms and signs; or
- there is an inexplicably poor response to prescribed medication and other treatment; or new symptoms are reported on resolution of previous ones; or
- reported symptoms and found signs are not seen to begin in the absence of the carer; or
- over time the child is repeatedly presented with a range of signs and symptoms; or
- the child's normal, daily life activities are being curtailed, for example school attendance, beyond that which might be expected for any medical disorder from which the child is known to suffer.

4.6 There may be a number of explanations for these circumstances and each requires careful consideration and review. A full developmental history and an appropriate developmental assessment should be carried out. Consultation with peers, named or designated professionals or colleagues in other agencies will be an important part of the process of making sense of the underlying reason for these signs and symptoms. The characteristics of fabricated or induced illness are that there is a lack of the usual corroboration of findings with symptoms or signs, or, in circumstances of proven organic illness, lack of the usual response to proven effective treatments. It is this puzzling discrepancy which alerts in particular the medical clinician to possible harm being suffered by the child.

dramatic recovery by LU and the absence of any symptoms or identifiable pathology. The High Court judge on examination of each witness in person concluded that all three family members were reliable witnesses in contrast to LU's mother, who gave contradictory accounts of events. When LU was admitted to hospital the mother failed to mention any of the previous episodes of respiratory difficulties which had resulted in the admission of the infant to hospital. The High Court judge found this to be incomprehensible behaviour for a mother concerned for the health of her child. The non-medical evidence produced in respect of the infant by family members and the mother's conduct appeared to corroborate suspicions that she was responsible for attempting to smother her own child.

Mr McFarlane, acting for the mother ML, submitted that all three medical experts had adopted a dogmatic approach and interpreted a medically inexplicable incident as evidence of child abuse on the basis of recurrence of the episodes. Mr McFarlane was claiming that the medical experts together with the original High Court judge were guilty of (i), (ii), (iv) and (v) above, as set out by Dame Butler-Sloss. Re-examination by the Court of Appeal of the reports submitted by the three doctors to the original High Court hearing revealed that each expert demonstrated open-mindedness and provided a thorough consideration of alternative explanations of the symptoms reported in the child. Having heard all the evidence, Dame Butler-Sloss concluded in her judgement that, 'the experts did not suggest that their explanation was certain, but only that it was established on the civil balance of probabilities elevated to recognise the gravity of its consequences' (para. 79).

As the approach of Dame Butler-Sloss to this Court of Appeal case demonstrates, expert opinion is not above scrutiny by the court and can itself be the subject of vigorous cross-examination. A judge in civil cases is required to probe the robustness of the evidence put before him or her. Simply because evidence is presented by an 'expert' witness does not preclude the court from questioning either the evidence itself or the credibility of the expert who produced it. Social workers relying on medical evidence have to ensure that it is produced by those who are competent to offer an opinion in that area. For example, a consultant psychiatrist is unlikely to be competent to offer an opinion on whether an injury to a 7-year-old child was non-accidental. However, his or her report on the mental health of the caregiver alleged to have caused the injury could corroborate the medical report of a consultant paediatrician or orthopaedic surgeon which claimed that the most likely cause of injury was a blow by a blunt instrument. So social workers need to ensure that expert evidence is produced by people who are not just medical doctors or consultants, but who have a particular expertise in the area of medicine upon which they are being called to offer an opinion. Where medical evidence is inconclusive or contested by the parents, as in this Court of Appeal case, it may be necessary to obtain a consensus of opinions from several expert witnesses. In this Court of Appeal case the local authority did just that and as a consequence the judge easily dismissed the contention of the mother's barrister that somehow the medical opinion was biased or flawed.

In summary, a number of family members were found by the judge to be reliable witnesses, each of whom corroborated the version of events presented by one another. The version of events presented by relatives was consistent with the medical evidence which was given by several experts who all agreed with each other. Finally, the local authority presented a report on the mother's personal history, including her mental health. As a different source of evidence this tended to support the version of events presented by other family members and the findings of the medical experts. In other words, the local authority produced in court a range of evidence both medical and non-medical of sufficient credibility to convince the court on *the balance of probabilities* that the mother had caused her daughter to stop breathing on four occasions.

Judgement in *Re U (A Child) (Serious Injury: Standard of Proof)*

On the basis of the evidence presented to the High Court at first instance and reconsidered by the Court of Appeal, permission for the mother to appeal against the finding that the s.31 threshold had been crossed was refused. The Court of Appeal concluded that the High Court judge had applied the correct standard of proof and given proper consideration to both the medical and non-medical evidence before her.

 ## Critical questions

1 The concept of induced or fabricated illness remains controversial, as does the medical evidence used to verify it. What is your own reaction to the facts of this case?

2 To what extent do you think that the standard of proof and the burden of proof in care proceedings provide parents and children with sufficient protection against unjustified intervention by Children's Services?

3 Having read through the legal arguments presented in this court case and the principles set out by Dame Butler-Sloss, what challenges do the standard of proof and the burden of proof present for social workers preparing an application for a Care Order to safeguard a child?

 Perspectives

Parents involved in care proceedings

Freeman and Hunt (1998) conducted research with 35 parents whose children were the subject of care proceedings under the Children Act 1989. They found that the majority of parents held very negative attitudes towards Social Services and denied that there had been any necessity for social work intervention. Parents with learning difficulties or mental health problems felt particularly stigmatised and deeply resented being categorised as child abusers. Commonly, parents perceived their problems as revolving around poor housing, domestic violence and their own abusive childhoods. Many acknowledged that these factors had impacted detrimentally on their parenting capacity, but claimed that social workers had failed to take account of their needs and were only focussed on the children.

Most parents described a lack of partnership working with Social Services throughout care proceedings. Although many parents did attend Case Conferences they reported feeling confused, intimidated and demeaned in ways which inhibited them from fully participating at the meeting. Estranged fathers and extended family members reported being marginalised by social workers. During the court hearing itself, parents felt poorly prepared and ill-informed about the legal proceedings. Their high levels of anxiety were increased by delays in the court system. Often parents were left devastated by care proceedings and found it difficult to engage positively with social workers thereafter.

Freeman and Hunt (1998) found that despite parents often denying they had harmed their children and holding negative views about social workers, they did react positively to professionals who were direct, truthful and sensitive. Surprisingly small acts by practitioners which demonstrated respect for parents could be extremely important in contributing to an effective working relationship.

CASE 5
Re O (A Minor) (Care Proceedings: Education) [1992] 1 WLR 912

Importance of the case

This examines the concept of *significant harm* in the context of education and the requirement for parents to ensure that their children receive full-time education. It is an example of the circumstances in which the wishes of *Gillick* competent children may be overridden so as to safeguard them.

History of the case

Maidenhead Magistrates' Court, sitting as a Family Proceedings Court, made a Care Order for a 15-year-old girl to remove her from her parents to a residential home for children. The girl appealed to the Family Division of the High Court to overturn the Magistrates' decision.

Facts of the case

A 15-year-old girl, referred to as O, was regularly absent from school over a two-year period commencing in 1989 when at times she missed full terms. At the beginning of 1991 O's parents were prosecuted and fined for not sending her to school. O's truancy continued and the local authority obtained an Interim Care Order in relation to her. This resulted in O attending school regularly for a month and then again being frequently absent. From January 1990 the Education Welfare Officer began to visit O and her parents frequently at the family home. Despite the offer of alternative schools and consultation O continued to miss school and appointments with the Education Welfare Officer. As a result of chronic absenteeism O's intellectual and social development was found to be suffering to a significant extent. Consequently, the local authority applied for a full Care Order, which was granted by the Family Proceedings Court. This was opposed by both O and her parents, resulting in an appeal by O to the High Court.

Key people in the case

O – 15-year-old girl and applicant
Mr Turner – legal counsel for O
Guardian ad Litem – representing O's best interests in High Court case
Justice Ewbank – judge in High Court case

Discussion of the case

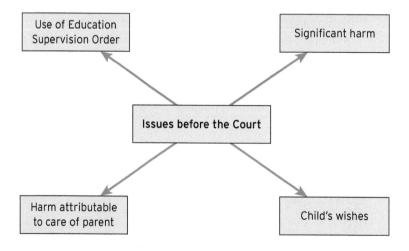

Child's wishes

Under s.39 of the Children Act 1989, the child, those holding parental responsibility or the local authority have the right to apply for the discharge or variation of a Care Order. This means returning to the court that made the order and applying for its alteration or termination. Under the provisions of s.91(17) an application can only be made six months after the court's initial decision unless it gives express permission for an earlier application. However, if an order under the Children Act 1989 was issued by the Magistrates' Court then, under s.94 of that Act, respondents have a right of appeal to the Family Division of the High Court. This right is not automatic and depends on the facts of each case. The High Court may refuse to hear an appeal against the decision of a Magistrates' Court if this appears to have been properly made and the arguments of the discontented parties lack merit. The denial of an automatic right of appeal is designed to prevent disgruntled parties to the original court case from miring the children concerned in endless litigation to the detriment of their welfare. In the present instance the High Court did grant a right of appeal from Maidenhead Family Proceedings Court where this case was initially heard.

In care proceedings the child and those holding parental responsibility are automatically entitled to be legally represented in court. In the present case, O who was 15 years old at the time, chose to oppose the Care Order on her own behalf. She was supported in this decision by her parents who were also legally represented in the High Court case. Generally courts seek to prevent children attending care proceedings in their own person and instead their 'best interests' are represented by a Children's Guardian who instructs a solicitor on the child's behalf. This means that children usually have separate legal representation at care proceedings from either those with parental responsibility or the local authority. Effectively this means that the Children's Guardian consults with the child and conveys to the court the child's wishes and feelings and recommends a course of action in the child's best interests. This is not the same as acting as the child's voice in court. For the primary responsibility of the Children's Guardian is not to do what the child wishes, but to recommend to the court what is in the child's best interests.

In the present case, the Children's Guardian, still referred to as a Guardian ad Litem at the time of the High Court case, was in direct disagreement with O. The Guardian ad Litem was of the same opinion as the local authority and both were of the view that a Care Order was the only way to ensure that O attended school. O sought to oppose the making of the Care Order and wished to remain at home with her parents. In these circumstances O, aged 15 years, could be considered *Gillick* competent, and consequently instructed her own solicitor who in turn engaged legal counsel to represent her at the High Court. The Guardian ad Litem was separately represented, as were the parents and the local authority. In other words there were four different parties to this court case, each with their own legal representative.

Use of Education Supervision Order

The Education Act 1944 s.35 introduced the compulsory school age of 5–15 years, raised to 16 years in 1972, thus making it a legal requirement for children to receive an education during this period. The Education Act 1996 consolidated previous legislation contained in disparate statutes and now constitutes the current framework for the delivery of education. Although not in force at the time of the present court case, the Education Act 1996 s.14 replicates duties set down in preceding legislation which require local education authorities to provide sufficient schools for the appropriate education of pupils in their area. This statute (as in previous legislation) also places a correlative duty on parents to send their children to school, which is reproduced in the box on the next page.

Education Act 1996

s.7 The parent of every child of compulsory school age shall cause him to receive efficient full-time education suitable:

(a) to his age, ability and aptitude

(b) to any special educational needs he may have, either by regular attendance at school or otherwise

s.576(1) 'Parent' means anyone who has parental responsibility for or care of the child

If parents fail to send their children to school the local education authority can take a number of remedial actions rising in severity and compulsion. In rank order these are from the least to the most intrusive:

- Provide support and advice to parents through the Education Welfare Service.
- Agree a Parenting Contract in which parents agree to ensure that their children regularly attend school, if necessary with specified support services.
- Issue a School Attendance Order (SAO) which requires the parents to assure the local education authority that their children are receiving appropriate education.
- Parents subject to a SAO who fail to arrange for their children to receive suitable education may be issued with a Penalty Notice and fined under s.444A and s.444B of the Education Act 1996.
- Parents who breach a SAO can also be prosecuted resulting in a fine or imprisonment under s.443 of the Education Act 1996.
- Magistrates can issue a Parenting Order requiring parents to attend guidance sessions and to ensure regular attendance of their children at school.

Continual absenteeism of children from school, and the apparent inability or unwillingness of parents to redress this, can result in the local education authority applying to court for an Education Supervision Order under s.36 of the Children Act 1989. This places the child under the supervision of the local education authority for a period of one year during which an Education Welfare Officer (usually a qualified social worker) is appointed 'to advise assist and befriend the parents of the child'. An Education Supervision Order can be extended up to a maximum of three years where it appears to the local education authority and the court that prolonged supervision is necessary. As it is an offence for parents not to comply with the direction of a social worker acting in this capacity, where children persist in truancy they are likely to face more intrusive intervention by Social Services. This is exactly what happened in the present case.

Mr Turner, counsel for O, contended that the use of a Care Order was an incorrect course of action to deal with the problem of truancy. Instead, he argued, the local education authority ought to have addressed the issue through application for an Education Supervision Order under s.36 of the Children Act 1989. Only if this intervention failed should recourse then be to Social Services. Justice Ewbank presiding over the High Court appeal conceded that in normal circumstances this would be the correct way to proceed. However, the judge identified an exceptional circumstance in this case. This centred on the fact that an Education Welfare Officer had essentially performed the same role of befriending and assisting the family over the previous three years as would have occurred had the officer been acting under the terms of an Education Supervision Order. The Guardian ad Litem (Children's Guardian) and the local authority took the view that 'everything that could be done has already been done' and therefore an Education Supervision Order would have no additional affect. Justice Ewbank concurred with this standpoint.

Since the judge agreed with the respondents that an Education Supervision Order was not required as a first step before applying for a Care Order to ensure school attendance, Mr Turner now sought to argue that the evidence submitted by the respondents was insufficient to establish that the harm suffered by O was 'significant'. This line of argument needs to be viewed in the light of the precise wording of the grounds for the making of a Care Order in the Children Act 1989, which is reproduced in the box below.

Key legislation

Children Act 1989

31(2) a court may only make a care order or a supervision order if it is satisfied –

    (a) that the child concerned is suffering or is likely to suffer, significant harm and;

    (b) that the harm, or likelihood of harm, is attributable to

        (i)   the care given to the child, or likely to be given to him if the order were not made, not being what it would be reasonable to expect a parent to give to him; or

        (ii) the child's being beyond parental control

31(9) 'harm' means ill-treatment or the impairment of health or development; including, for example, impairment suffered from seeing or hearing the ill-treatment of another; 'development' means physical, intellectual, emotional, social or behavioural development; 'health' means physical or mental health; and 'Ill-treatment' includes sexual abuse and forms of ill-treatment which are not physical.

31(10) where the question of whether harm suffered by a child is significant turns on the child's health or development, his health or development shall be compared with that which could reasonably be expected of a similar child.

The evidence presented by the respondents turned on a number of key reports. The Guardian ad Litem had requested an assessment of O from an educational psychologist. This report formed expert evidence at the original hearing of this case in the Magistrates' Court sitting as a Family Proceedings Court. The report concluded that O was of average general ability and that her 'prolonged absence from school at this crucial stage in her education will seriously hinder her ability to complete her coursework and take her exams'. The educational psychologist also gave oral evidence and stated: 'I am even more concerned about her social development. O is avoiding situations which make demands on her. She is avoiding basic requirements to adjust to work and obligations which the school presents.' The Guardian ad Litem concurred in her report which stated that:

> O has now missed such a substantial amount of basic secondary level learning. If the absenteeism is not arrested it will have a profound effect on O's ability to cope in adult life . . . it will also seriously impair her ability to relate to peers and adults in a more formal way. This will inhibit O's development because school is of course not only about intellectual learning, it also provides young people with necessary social and relationship skills.

This evidence, taken together, led Justice Ewbank to conclude that O was suffering and was likely to continue to suffer significant harm to her intellectual and social development.

It is not immediately evident that absenteeism from school could be so chronic as to so impair the 'intellectual, emotional, social or behavioural development' of a child as to meet the s.31(2) threshold to constitute a *significant harm* to the child. What this case demonstrates is that prolonged periods of absenteeism from school can start to affect not only a child's educational ability but also their emotional and social functioning. In this instance the young person's parents were not prepared to concede that their child's development was being seriously impaired by her non-attendance at school. It is undoubtedly exceptional for parents to continue to refuse to send their child to school even in the face of care proceedings. However, it is not uncommon for social workers to intervene with families to safeguard children where school attendance is an issue. As this case illustrates, there are a range of legal options available to practitioners working with families in these circumstances.

Harm attributable to care by parent

Mr Turner, O's legal counsel, then sought to argue 'that there was insufficient evidence to establish whether the care given or likely to be given to O if no order was made would be reasonable to expect a parent to give'. This final line of reasoning regarding the care given to O by her parents. Justice Ewbank was clear that 'where a child is suffering harm in not going to school and is living at home it will follow that either the child is beyond her parents' control or that they are not giving the child the care that it would be reasonable to expect a parent to give'. It should be noted that under s.31(2)(b) of the Children Act 1989 regardless of whether the harm to the child is attributable to the care they receive from their parents or because they are beyond parental control, each constitute grounds for a Care Order. It was in these circumstances that the local authority had applied for a Care Order with the intention of removing O to a children's home, there to establish a pattern of regular school attendance, before endeavouring to rehabilitate her back with her parents. The ultimate intention of Social Services was to facilitate family reunion as quickly as the problem of school attendance could be resolved.

Often there can be agreement between professionals and parents or guardians that harm has occurred to the child, but dispute as to whether this harm is *significant* in the legal sense. As this case demonstrates, harm is not restricted to direct abuse or neglect of children by caregivers. It can relate to the intellectual and social development of a child, as in the case of O. At first glance impairment to the intellectual and social development of a child may appear less serious than physical or sexual abuse. If the care of parents or guardians is consistently inadequate, it can over time result in severe and lasting developmental damage to a child. Schooling, whether in mainstream or special education, is a crucial component of a child's cognitive development.

Without formal educational inputs children are highly unlikely to develop comparable intellectual abilities or attain similar educational milestones as their peer group. At a certain point a child may fall so far behind their contemporaries that effectively their intellectual ability is limited to that of a much younger child. O had not attended school for over two years and had apparently begun to develop phobic tendencies in relation to attendance. Despite advice, support and information from educational professionals the child's parents were refusing to acknowledge the *significance* of the harm to O. Social workers may find themselves working with parents or guardians who are unwilling to recognise the harm which their care is doing to their children, regardless of the amount of evidence presented to them. At this point it may become necessary to have recourse to the courts in order to safeguard children.

Judgement in *Re O (A Minor) (Care Proceedings: Education)*

Justice Ewbank in giving judgement came to the conclusion that the local education authority had done all that it reasonably could over an extended period of time to persuade both O and her parents of the necessity for school attendance. These endeavours having failed, the Social Services Department of the local authority had presented sufficiently convincing evidence that O was now suffering significant harm to her intellectual and social development and this was attributable to the care provided to her by her parents. In view of this, Justice Ewbank upheld the decision of the Magistrates' Court and dismissed the appeal.

 ## Critical questions

1 The welfare checklist requires social workers to take into account the wishes and feelings of children when pursing legal action under the Children Act 1989. This case appears to illustrate the limits of complying with the wishes of *Gillick* competent children. How might you work with a *Gillick* competent child who was behaving in ways likely to cause him or her *significant harm*? What factors would inform your practice and decisions?

2 Do you think this case was correctly decided? Were there any other options which you think social workers could have explored before applying for a Care Order?

 ## Critical commentary

Implementation of the Children Act 1989

Department of Health (2001b) *The Children Act Now: Messages from Research* brought together the findings of 24 studies examining the implementation of the Children Act 1989. Major conclusions and recommendations arising from this collation of research remain pertinent to current social work practice with families. Department of Health (2001b) revealed that there was evidence of many local authorities using s.47 inquiries and concerns centring on the risk of abuse or neglect of children to enable families to access services. This was because a number of services, which should have been accessible under s.17, had high eligibility criteria due to local authority budgetary constraints and limits on service availability. Consequently, a number of parents and children who should have been facilitated to access support services under s.17 were subject to the invasiveness and stigmatisation of a s.47 inquiry in order to meet the high eligibility threshold for such provision. In other words 'children in need' is still very strongly correlated with children at risk of abuse even though the Children Act 1989 was designed to promote child welfare and not just protect children.

Research brought together by Department of Health (2001b) also found that despite the incidence of domestic violence in almost half of child protection cases this was rarely referred to in Child Protection Plans. Furthermore, parents often complained that social workers focused solely on the needs of their children with scant regard for the stresses that they, the parents, were under. Parental capacity was often detrimentally affected by a violent partner, addiction, or mental health problems. Many parents reported receiving little recognition from professionals of their own problems, or assistance to address them. A large proportion of parents felt prejudged and left without the help they needed. As the Department of Health (2001b) explicitly recognises, this is not to deny that a number of these parents simply refused to concede that social workers had legitimate concerns regarding their parenting and their children's health and safety.

Despite the *non-delay principle* enshrined in s.1(2) of the Children Act 1989 the studies included in the Department of Health (2001b) overview found that delay in care proceedings was endemic. Several factors contributed to this state of affairs. The transfer of cases between courts in order to consolidate proceedings, for instance an application for a Residence Order with one for a Supervision Order, when these had been started in two different courts, accounted for delay in a number of instances. The increasing use of expert witnesses and the difficulty of identifying willing experts or obtaining timely reports from them was a major contributing factor in the adjournment of care proceedings. Some parents obstructed court proceedings and employed delaying tactics which could result in hearings being rescheduled on consecutive occasions. Conversely, social workers sometimes failed to gather sufficiently reliable evidence or to produce well considered care plans before coming to court, which caused adjournments. The sheer numbers of family disputes and care proceedings coming before an overstretched court system also resulted in unnecessary delays which ultimately prolonged uncertainty for the children involved.

Learning points

- The GSCC Code of Practice places obligations on employers of social care workers to ensure that they receive the support, training and resources they require to carry out their responsibilities to the standards set out in the GSCC Code.

- Social work practice in the area of child protection is directed by government issued policy and practice guidance in relation to assessment, care planning and inter-agency collaboration.

- The Children Act 2004 places statutory duties on the Police, Health, Education and Social Services to collaborate with each other to promote the welfare of children and safeguard them.

- Intervention in families to safeguard children invokes article 8 of the European Convention on Human Rights. Although this is a qualified right permitting State intervention in family life, this must be proportionate and necessary to achieve a lawful objective.

- Partnership with parents, even in circumstances involving safeguarding their children, is a vital aspect of child protection work.

- Different court orders have different thresholds, and the standard of proof can be more stringent in situations involving grave allegations against parents or primary carers and the intention to permanently remove children from their parents or carer.

- Medical evidence alone will not normally determine the decision of the court and this will require it to be corroborated by evidence from other sources.

- Expert evidence presented in court will be scrutinised by the judge and the parties to the court proceeding. Experts engaged by the local authority must be competent in their field and their expertise be directly relevant to the matter they are asked to give an opinion on.

Further reading

Allen, N. (2005) *Making Sense of the Children Act 1989*, Chichester: John Wiley and Sons. This provides a comprehensive and detailed account of the Children Act 1989. It explains the legal ramifications of the key provisions in the statute.

Horner, N. and Krawczyk, S. (2006) *Social Work in Education and Children's Services*, Exeter: Learning Matters. This book provides a detailed overview of the interface between education and Children's Services. It also discusses issues surrounding the educational achievement of *looked after* children.

Masson, J. (2005) 'Research – Emergency intervention to protect children: using and avoiding legal controls', *Children and Family Law Quarterly* 171 (75). This article considers the implications of using and avoiding direct legal intervention with families. It explores the problems which arise if parents do not have recourse to legal redress.

Walsh, E. (2006) *Working in the Family Justice System: A Guide for Professionals*, Bristol: Family Law, Jordan Publishing. This book provides information about the roles and responsibilities of different professionals involved in safeguarding children. It provides useful insights into the operation of the legal system in relation to families.

Useful websites

www.nspcc.org.uk Run by the National Society for the Prevention of Cruelty to Children this website provides many easily accessible guides on the child protection and care systems. It also offers a number of research related publications on children's welfare and safeguarding.

www.everychildmatters.gov.uk Run by central government, this website provides information on children, ranging from the care system to education and health and youth offending. It provides easy to access guides in addition to free downloads of important policy documents.

http://publications.teachernet.gov.uk/ Run by central government, this website provides a wide range of material relating to education including issues around pupil absenteeism and school exclusion.

www.dh.gov.uk Run by the Department of Health, this website provides free downloads of a range of materials relating to the welfare and safeguarding of children. It also gives access to a number of crucial policy and practice guidance documents.

4

LOOKED AFTER CHILDREN

> ## Fact file
>
> - Number of *looked after* children - 60,000
> - Number of children in foster care - 42,000
> - Number of children in residential homes - 6,000
> - Number of *looked after* children placed with parents - 5,100
> - Number of children looked after under a Care Order - 39,000
> - Number of children voluntarily accommodated under s.20 - 17,800
> - Number of children in secure accommodation - 200
> - Number of children aged 16 years or over leaving care - 8,000
> - Number of children subject to a Placement Order - 2,400
> - Around 3,000 Adoption Orders are made annually
> - Around 400 Special Guardianship Orders are made annually
>   (Figures are for England and Wales for 2007.)
>
> *Source:* Hall (2008: 3), DCSF and Office for National Statistics (2007), SFR27/2007.

Overview of relevant legislation

The statistics in the box above illustrate the large number of children who are either in the care system or who leave it each year. It is notable that almost two-thirds of children who are in the care system are there by virtue of a Care Order. This means that they have been compulsorily removed from their family, predominantly because of abuse or neglect. Importantly, most children are in foster placements, with a much smaller number being looked after in residential homes and a very small, though significant number, in secure units. As children are cared for in a number of different settings, this chapter will explore the law in relation to each of these contexts. Relative to the total number of children in the care system only a small number of Adoption Orders and Special Guardianship Orders are made each year. However, social workers involved in safeguarding children are required to take a twin-track approach to intervention. This means that while trying to support parents to bring up their children, practitioners must also make longer term plans for children's care should rehabilitation with their family prove impossible. Therefore Special Guardianship and Adoption are relevant to a much greater number of practitioners than those working directly with adoption services.

As you will have already learnt from Chapter 2, the Children Act 1989 is the main legislation which frames social work activity with children living in England and Wales. As this chapter explores social work with children in a residential setting it will equally draw on the main precepts and provisions laid down in the Children Act 1989. But the focus of this chapter will be on the key sections contained in Part III. Residential and day-care provision for children was originally governed by Parts VI, VII, VIII and X of the Children Act 1989. These have now been replaced by amendments instituted by the Care Standards Act 2000, which is now the main statute dealing with the provision of care to children in residential and day-care facilities. The Children (Leaving Care) Act 2000 has also introduced amendments to the original Children Act 1989 to place additional duties on local authorities in preparing young people for leaving care and keeping in contact with them thereafter. Relevant provisions of the Care Standards Act 2000 and the Children (Leaving Care) Act 2000 are explored later in this chapter. The Adoption and Children Act 2002, like the Children Act 1989, is a major piece of primary legislation and governs social work activity related to adoption. For this reason a full summary of the key sections in the Adoption and Children Act 2002 is provided in the table below.

Adoption and Children Act 2002	Key sections
Part I – Adoption	s.1 Defines principles directing court
	s.3 Duty to maintain adoption service
	s.4 Adoption support services
	ss.8-11 Regulation of adoption agencies
	ss.18-20 Placement for adoption
	s.21 Placement orders
	s.22 Application for placement order
	ss.23-24 Change to placement orders
	s.25 Holding of parental responsibility
	ss.26-27 Contact with child
	ss.30-36 Restrictions on removal
	ss.37-40 Applications for adoption
	s.42 Placement of child with adopters
	s.45 Suitability of adopters
	ss.46-51 Adoption orders
	s.52 Parental consent
	s.56-62 Disclosure of information
	s.77 Adopted children register
	ss.83-91 International adoptions
Part II – Amendments of Children Act 1989	s.111 Parental responsibility of unmarried father
	s.115 Special guardianship s.14A-14G introduced to Children Act 1989
	s.121 Care plans s.31A introduced to Children Act 1989
Part III – Miscellaneous and Final Provisions	s.125 Adoption and Children Act register

As already discussed in earlier chapters, the Children Act 1989 is underpinned by three main principles defined in s.1 of the statute. Since these principles direct the deliberations of judges presiding over family proceedings, they are equally applicable to children for whom residential care is being considered or who are living in a Children's Home or fostering placement or who are leaving the care system. The *welfare, no order* and *non-delay* principles remain central to social work with children and young people in this context. As regards adoption, the *welfare, non-delay* and *no order principle* are also enshrined in s.1 of the Adoption and Children Act 2002. But there is some modification of these principles to take account of the effect of adoption on the child throughout his or her life. These three principles as defined in the Adoption and Children Act 2002 are reproduced in the box below.

Key legislation

Adoption and Children Act 2002

Welfare principle

s.1(2) The paramount consideration of the court or adoption agency must be the child's welfare, throughout his life

Non-delay principle

s.1(3) The court or adoption agency must at all times bear in mind that, in general, any delay in coming to the decision is likely to prejudice the child's welfare.

No order principle

s.1(6) The court or adoption agency must always consider the whole range of powers available to it in the child's case (whether under this Act or the Children Act 1989); and the court must not make any order under this Act unless it considers that making the order would be better for the child than not doing so.

There are a number of relevant policy and practice guidance documents which are central to social work activity with children and young people in the care system. These range from assessment to care provision to preparing children for leaving care and adoption. Where there are concerns that a child has been abused within the care system, gathering robust evidence for criminal proceedings is crucial. For this reason guidance of the evidential interviewing of children is also included. These are summarised in the table below.

Guidance document	Outline content
Department of Health (2000d) *Framework for the Assessment of Children in Need and their Families*	This is policy guidance and details how practitioners should conduct multidisciplinary assessments and care plans for children.
Home Office (2002) *Achieving Best Evidence in Criminal Proceedings: Guidance for Vulnerable or Intimidated Witnesses, including Children Vols 1 and 2*	This provides guidance to professionals working with children or vulnerable adults or witnesses in relation to court proceedings. It also describes the special measures available in court to protect such individuals.

(Continued)

Guidance document	Outline content
Home Office, Crown Prosecution Service and Department of Health (2001) *Provision of Therapy for Child Witnesses prior to a Criminal Trial: Practice Guidance*	This is practice guidance and advises professionals working with children in connection with court proceedings. It considers the potential conflicts between gathering evidence and providing therapy.
Department of Health (2001c) *Children (Leaving Care) Act 2000: Regulations and Guidance: Policy Guidance*	This is policy guidance which provides direction to both managers and frontline professionals responsible for children who are in the process of leaving local authority care or have left care.
Department for Education and Skills (2005c) *Adoption and Children Act 2002: Adoption Guidance*	This provides comprehensive guidance to the operation of the Adoption and Children Act 2002.
Department for Education and Skills (2005b) *Special Guardianship Regulations 2005: Special Guardianship Regulations*	This provides guidance to special guardianship which was introduced as a new provision into the Children Act 1989.
Department of Health (2003a) *Adoption: National Minimum Standards*	This sets out the National Minimum Standards for adoption services.
Department of Health (2002a) *Fostering Services: National Minimum Standards*	This sets out the National Minimum Standards for fostering services.
Department of Health (1999b) *Objectives for Children's Social Services*	This sets out the government's objectives in relation to children in the care of local authorities in relation to permanency planning and other aspects of *looked after* children's welfare.

Overview of the cases

This chapter explores the circumstances surrounding five different children. Four of these cases came before the courts and a fifth was the subject of an independent inquiry.

Case 1 *R* v. *Tameside MBC ex parte J (A Child)* explores the:

- Local authority duties towards accommodated children.
- Working in partnership with parents.
- Parental responsibility in relation to *looked after* children.

Case 2 Independent Inquiry Report into the Circumstances of Child Sexual Abuse by two Foster Carers in Wakefield explores:

- The importance of following procedures.
- National Minimum Standards for fostering services.
- Safeguarding *looked after* children.
- Evidential interviewing with children.
- Working with diversity.

Case 3 *Re C (A Child) (Secure Accommodation Order: Representation)* explores:

- Issues surrounding the use of secure accommodation.
- The right of a *Gillick* competent child to instruct a solicitor.
- The right to a fair trial when care proceedings are being taken.

Case 4 *R (on the application of J) v. Caerphilly County Borough Council* explores:

- Local authority duties towards young people leaving care.
- Working in partnership with children.
- Practitioners with a potential conflict between several professional roles.

Case 5 *Re MJ (A Child) (Adoption Order or Special Guardianship Order)* explores:

- The law on adoption and special guardianship.
- The meaning of parental consent to adoption.
- Dispensing with parental consent if necessary for the child's welfare.
- The welfare checklist in relation to adoption proceedings.

CASE 1
R v. *Tameside MBC ex parte J (A Child)* [2000] 1 FLR 942

Importance of the case

It explores the limits of local authority power over a child whose parents have voluntarily placed him or her into public care. The case also examines the complexities of partnership working with parents when there are fundamental disagreements between them and social workers regarding a child's care.

History of the case

The local authority sought to transfer a voluntarily accommodated child from residential accommodation to foster care against the wishes of her parents. An application was made on behalf of the child to the Queen's Bench Division of the High Court for a judicial review of this decision.

Facts of the case

J was 13 years old at the time of the court case and had multiple severe disabilities, exhibited challenging behaviour and frequently self-harmed. Her parents looked after her until she was aged 9 years, when they were no longer able to cope with her needs and asked the local authority to take on her care. The child was voluntarily accommodated under s.20 of the Children Act 1989 initially in a residential school and then from September 1997 at a residential home with attendance at a nearby day school for children with special needs. A psychologist's report indicated that her care needs were being fully met and commended the approach of residential staff to managing J's challenging behaviours. In August 1998 the local authority suggested moving her to foster care, to which J's parents objected in writing. At a Statutory Review meeting held on 13 May 1999, attended by staff from the residential home and her parents, the matter of foster care was again raised and the disagreement between the parties explicitly acknowledged in the minutes of the meeting. The minutes stated that the current care arrangements for the child were to continue and her introduction to prospective foster carers was to be deferred pending further consultation with J's parents. Eleven days later J's parents received a letter from the local authority stating that it had decided to go ahead and arrange introductory meetings between their daughter and the prospective foster carers. Contact between the girl and the prospective fosterers then took place. It was at this point that an application was made to the High Court for a judicial review of the local authority's decision to pursue a foster care placement.

Key people in the case

J – 13-year-old girl and applicant
M – J's mother
F – J's father
Mr Pleming – legal counsel for the parents
Mr Horowitz – legal counsel for the local authority
Justice Scott Baker – presiding judge in the case

Discussion of the case

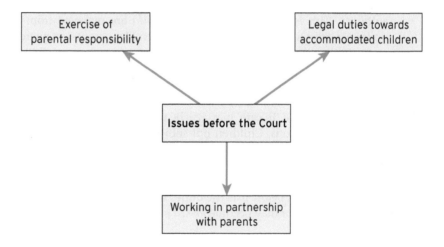

Legal duties towards accommodated children

J was not the subject of a Care Order and had not been compulsorily removed from her parents. Rather, their parental capacity had been stretched beyond its limit by their daughter's multiple severe learning difficulties and challenging behaviour. Unable to meet her care needs, when she reached the age of 9 years her parents asked the local authority to look after her.

In the present case M and F were married, as a result of which each held parental responsibility for their daughter J and both wished her to be looked after by the local authority as neither of them felt able to care for her at home. Applying the criteria in s.20(7) (see box on the next page), there was no one holding parental responsibility who objected to local authority care for the child and therefore she could be accommodated by Social Services. Since the provision of s.20 accommodation is by way of a voluntary agreement between parents or guardians and local authority Children's Services, parental

Key legislation

Children Act 1989

s.20(1) Every local authority shall provide accommodation for any child in need within their area who appears to them to require accommodation as a result of -

(a) there being no person who has parental responsibility for him

(b) his being lost or having been abandoned

(c) the person who has been caring for him being prevented (whether or not permanently, and for whatever reason) from providing him with suitable accommodation or care

s.20(7) A local authority may not provide accommodation under this section for any child if any person who

(a) has parental responsibility for him; and

(b) is willing and able to (i) provide accommodation for him; or (ii) arrange for accommodation to be provided for him, objects.

responsibility remains with the former and is not obtained or transferred to the local authority. This is in contrast to children who are removed from their parental home under a Care Order where, although the child's parents or guardians retain parental responsibility, the local authority also acquires parental responsibility. The law differentiates between these two types of circumstances.

Children who are in a residential home, with foster carers or placed with a family member or friend compulsorily under a Care Order are legally defined as being 'in care'. Sometimes children 'in care' may also be placed at home with parents or guardians under supervised conditions. Children not subject to a Care Order, but where their parents or guardians have entered into a voluntary agreement with the local authority to care for them, are referred to as being 'accommodated'. Both categories of children are 'looked after', a legal status which imposes a range of duties on the local authority in relation to their care. The box below lists the duties which local authorities owe to children that are either *looked after* or may become *looked after*.

Key legislation

Children Act 1989

When making decisions regarding 'looked after' children the local authority must:

1 Safeguard and promote the welfare of the child s.22(3)

2 Ascertain and consider the wishes and feelings of the child, parents, anyone with parental responsibility s.22(4)

3 Give due consideration to the child's racial origin, cultural and linguistic background s.22(5)

4 Give preference for a child to be placed with his or her parents, a person with parental responsibility, relative, friend, etc., unless not reasonably practicable or inconsistent with child's welfare s.23(6)

5 Give preference for accommodation near to the child's home if reasonably practicable and consistent with the child's welfare s.23(7)

6 Accommodate siblings together s.23(7)

7 Provide accommodation and maintain the child by placing him or her with a relative, foster carer or in a children's residential home 23(2)

8 Promote contact with parents, those holding parental responsibility, any friend, relative or person connected with the child if contact is reasonably practicable and consistent with the child's welfare Sch.2 para. 15(1)

9 Keep parents and those with parental responsibility informed of the child's whereabouts unless this is inconsistent with the child's welfare Sch.2 para. 15(2),(4)(b)

10 Consider representations from child, parent, person with parental responsibility, foster carers s.26(3) to (8)

11 Review *looked after* children within 4 weeks of initial placement, then within 3 months, then 6 months thereafter s.26(1), (2)

In the present case, J was accommodated by the local authority in a care home for disabled children and attended a day school. The residential unit was located near her parents' house and there was regular contact between the mother and father and their daughter, which included periodic holidays with them. So the duty on the local authority to promote and facilitate family contact laid down in s.23(7) and Sch.2, para. 15 of the Children Act 1989 was being met. According to a psychologist's report completed in 1999, staff at the residential home had 'developed a positive, consistent approach which builds on J's strengths'. Indeed, there was general agreement between professionals and the parents that the residential placement was meeting the child's needs. The residential home combined with day-school attendance alongside contact with the parents was therefore fulfilling the obligations imposed by s.22(3) on the local authority to promote the girl's welfare. There were also regular reviews of her care plan in accordance with s.26(1), (2) of the Children Act 1989. These are often referred to as statutory reviews because they are legally required to take place under a statute, in this instance the Children Act 1989. The box below explains the composition and purpose of statutory reviews for *looked after* children.

Background information

Looked After Children Reviews

Regular Review meetings are legally required by s.26 of the Children Act 1989. These are intended for professionals to share information with each other, to consult with the child and his or her parents and to make plans for the child's future care. Looked After Children Reviews also ensure that the current care plan is appropriate to the child's needs and consider any necessary changes to it. A Review meeting will be held whether the child is being *looked after* in a foster or residential placement or has been placed back with parents or relatives. The Review meeting normally takes place wherever the child is living.

Review meetings must be chaired and conducted by an Independent Review Officer who is a qualified social worker. Minutes of the meeting and decisions taken at it are recorded and circulated. Such meetings are normally attended by:

- The Independent Reviewing Officer
- Child if over 7 years of age
- Parents
- Child's carer
- Child's social worker
- A teacher, learning mentor or support worker may also attend

Looked After Children Review meetings consider a *looked after* child's progress, whether his or her needs are being met, the appropriateness of contact arrangements with parents and other important people in the child's life and if there have been any changes since the last Review, suggesting modification to the care plan.

As Justice Scott Baker observed, presiding in the High Court case, no evidence was presented to suggest that the existing care arrangements for the child were inadequate. He also astutely commented that 'scarcity of resources is of course an ever present problem for most local authorities'. It is considerably cheaper to accommodate a child with a foster family rather than in a residential care home. Additionally, arranging a long-term foster care placement was in line with Department of Health (1999b) *Objectives for Children's Services* which sets out the government's objectives for social services to children, and performance indicators to measure progress toward those objectives. Of particular relevance to the circumstances of J is the first of the government's objectives in this document, which is 'to ensure that children are securely attached to carers capable of providing safe and effective care for the duration of childhood' (Department of Health, 1999b: para. 1.0). To this end, local authorities are required 'to minimise the period children remain *looked after* before they are placed in long-term foster care' (Department of Health, 1999b: para. 1.5). Therefore local authorities are not only under financial pressures to place children in foster care rather than residential care, but they are also directed by government policy to increase the number of children in long-term foster care and reduce the numbers in residential care. Since April 2009 government policy for Children's Services has been most directly implemented through the Comprehensive Area Assessment which is explained in the box below.

 Background information

Comprehensive Area Assessment

Performance indicators for public services were introduced by the New Labour Government during the 1990s under the Performance Assessment Framework. These indicators measure progress towards improved quality, outcomes and value for money in public service provision. Specific indicators have been developed to measure particular public services, such as local authority activity and the National Health Service. Statistics are collected annually, collated and published so as to give the public information about the performance of local authorities in the delivery of services. Ofsted is responsible for inspecting Children's Services and uses the performance indicators to assess how well each council is performing.

The introduction of the Comprehensive Area Assessment for local authorities in April 2009 witnessed the development of a new annual rating scheme for Children's Services. This rating is based on a range of performance indicators. Some of the currently used indicators for Children's Services for which data has to be sent to Ofsted as part of its annual inspection are given below:

NI62 Stability of placement of *looked after* children: number of moves

NI63 Stability of placements of *looked after* children: length of placement

NI61-3 Percentage of *looked after* children (10-15) in foster placements or placed for adoption

NI66 *Looked after* children cases that were reviewed within required timescales

NI147 Care leavers in suitable accommodation

NI148 Care leavers in employment, education or training

As this aspect of the High Court case reveals, the social workers in this situation were caught in a difficult dilemma. On the one hand they were correctly proceeding with Statutory Review meetings and through them ascertaining that the child's needs were being met and her welfare promoted in her current residential placement. On the other hand, social workers were under some pressure from their agency to arrange a foster care placement – first, because this was a cheaper option than a residential placement and local authorities are always working within a finite budget; secondly, Department of Health (1999b) *Objectives for Children's Services*, which directs local authorities to increase the number of children in foster placements, measures progress towards this through a performance indicator which records the increase in the proportion of *looked after* children who have been in a foster placement for at least two years. The progress of each local authority towards different performance indicators relating to *looked after* children is made public. This situation is of course not unique to the social workers involved with arranging J's care. All social workers to a greater or lesser extent will be subject to budgetary and policy pressures in the conduct of their work in line with their statutory obligations.

Working in partnership with parents

Besides the girl's parents, the Review meeting in May 1999 was attended by the manager of the residential home, her key worker, her social worker and conducted by the Independent Review Officer. At this meeting both parents expressed their total opposition to their daughter being moved from her present residential placement to foster carers. This disagreement was clearly reflected in the minutes of the Review meeting which read:

[J's parents] remain implacably opposed to the care plan. They do not want a foster family for J and feel that her best interests would be served by her remaining at C. Avenue . . . Despite the differences of opinion the review meeting proceeded in an orderly manner and the working relationships between [J's parents] and staff at C. Avenue have been maintained. Under the circumstances it cannot be claimed that there is a meaningful partnership between [J's parents] and the Social Services Department.

The minutes concluded with several recommendations:

1 That the current arrangement for J's care continue.
2 That the plan for introductory visits for J to the prospective foster carers be deferred.

3 That the parties to the agreement either mutually consent to a way forward or another method of resolving the dispute is formulated. That this issue be clarified before introductory visits for J are commenced.

This document explicitly recognised the opposition of both parents to their daughter's move into foster care and reflected an agreement at the Review Meeting to postpone initiatives in this direction until further discussion with them. Despite the outcome of the Review Meeting, the parents received a letter from the local authority barely a fortnight later stating that the Social Services Department did not endorse recommendations 2 and 3 and was proceeding with the introductory meetings between the girl and already identified foster carers. These introductory meetings commenced in July 1999 despite continued opposition from both parents. Indeed, it was at this point that they felt they had no option but to seek a judicial review on behalf of their daughter.

Section 22(4) of the Children Act 1989 provides that when the local authority is making decisions in respect of *looked after* children it must ascertain and consider the wishes and feelings of the child, the parents and anyone else with parental responsibility. F and M are J's parents and in addition both have parental responsibility for her. Therefore they were entitled to be consulted and have their wishes considered by the local authority in coming to its decisions regarding their daughter's future care. The implications of s.22(4) for practice are elaborated in government guidance issued under s.7 of the Local Authority Social Services Act 1970. Department of Health (1991b: para. 2.10) *The Children Act 1989 Guidance and Regulations: Family Support, Day Care and Educational Provision for Young Children Vol. 2*, cited by Justice Scott Baker in his judgement, stipulates that:

> one of the key principles of the Children Act is that responsible authorities should work in partnership with the parents of a child who is being looked after and also with the child himself, where he is of sufficient understanding, provided that this approach would not jeopardise his welfare. A second closely related principle is that parents and children should participate actively in the decision-making process. Partnership will only be achieved if parents are advised and given explanations of the local authority's power and duties and the actions the local authority may need to take . . .

In the present instance the child had severe learning difficulties and was unable to participate meaningfully in decisions regarding her care. However, it was acknowledged in the minutes of the Review Meeting held in May 1999 that 'J would likely become confused and distressed if she became aware of her parents' reluctance to commit to the plan.' Although their daughter could not be involved in the actual decision-making process, it was recognised that the attitude of her parents towards her proposed move into foster care would have a significant impact on her welfare. The local authority is of course charged to promote the welfare of *looked after* children under s.22(3) of the Children Act 1989. Aside from the involvement of children, Department of Health (1991a: para. 2.10) makes clear that partnership with parents means their active participation in decision making and not merely consultation with them about their wishes and feelings. Furthermore, local authorities are required to explain the reasoning behind their decisions to both the parents and children affected by them. Neither parent could make out any justifiable or logical reasoning in the decision of the Department of Social Services (now Children's Services) to move their child into foster care, given that her present placement met all her needs including proximity to her parents' home.

Measuring the conduct of Social Services against the stipulations set out in the *Children Act 1989: Guidance and Regulations Vol. 2* reveals a failure by the local authority to work in partnership with the family. Despite acknowledging the total opposition of J's parents to the proposed foster placement and explicitly agreeing to postpone further action on this until after further consultation with them, social workers still went ahead to organise introductory meetings between their daughter and her prospective foster carers. Yet as the minutes recorded, notwithstanding the disagreement at the Review meeting, the working relationships between parents and professionals had been 'maintained'. In other words, there appeared to be still scope for negotiation and movement on the issue of fostering. It is also noteworthy that Justice Scott Baker observed, referring to M and F, that 'they are not implacably opposed to fostering but feel a good deal of care and research would be required if suitable foster parents are to be identified'. The opposition of the parents appears based on the entirely reasonable grounds that their daughter was doing well where she was currently placed and her needs were being met there. It is also salient that this opposition took place against a background of J's first placement in 1997 at a residential special school having broken down within a short space of time because the child was unable to cope.

The insistence of the local authority in proceeding hastily with a course of action in the face of parental disagreement undermined the principle of working in partnership and forced the parents to seek a judicial review as the only means of influencing decisions in respect of their daughter. Working in partnership with parents or guardians is not optional, to be dispensed with whenever carers have widely differing views from professionals or refuse to give their consent to a proposed course of action. In the case of J, her parents plainly had sound reasons for opposing the foster care placement. Indeed, it was the local authority that appeared unable to produce evidence to justify their proposed change in the child's care plan, which leads to the suspicion that is was based on agency imperatives rather than being child-centred.

Although all the procedures were correctly followed and the parents were invited to attend all the relevant Review meetings, ultimately their wishes and opinions were disregarded. Partnership working has to involve a two-way process of communication during which the opinions of parents are not merely heard, but acted upon. In the case of J, professionals at the Review meeting held in May 1999 proposed to address the open disagreement between the parents and the local authority by postponing preparation for the foster care placement. This was a decision that respected parental opinion without either ignoring it or capitulating to it. It was a strategy designed to preserve working relationships and buy time to hammer out a solution acceptable to both sides, while simultaneously meeting the child's needs. It was the decision of management to override the agreement reached by frontline staff which proved the breaking point for the parents and resulted in their resort to the court.

Paragraph 1.2 of GSCC *Code of Practice for Social Care Workers* emphasises the importance of 'respecting and where appropriate, promoting the individual views and wishes of both service users and carers'. This is complemented by paragraph 2.1 which requires a social worker to be 'honest and trustworthy'. Practitioners can find themselves acting in opposition to the wishes of users or carers, often for perfectly good reasons. Even in these situations the GSCC Code still obliges social care workers to articulate these disagreements and openly acknowledge them. Parents lulled into thinking they are being listened to only to discover matters proceeding surreptitiously behind their backs, will inevitably retreat from partnership working. This is not to deny that practitioners are sometimes in the very uncomfortable position of implementing an agency decision with which they disagree and in the face of parental opposition.

Exercise of parental responsibility

Parents of *accommodated* children (as opposed to those *in care*) retain all the rights pertaining to parental responsibility while the local authority does not gain parental responsibility. Under s.9(9) of the Children Act 1989 'a person who has parental responsibility for a child may not surrender or transfer any part of that responsibility to another but may arrange for some or all of it to be met by one or more persons acting on their behalf'. Put simply, parental responsibility cannot be reassigned, but it can be delegated. In effect this means that (with the exception of adoption) a parent or other person with parental responsibility cannot give it away to someone else, for example a grandparent, childminder or teacher who is taking care of their child. Thus, if a child was living temporarily with grandparents and failed to attend school, it would be the child's parents, not grandparents, who would be held accountable, pursued by Social Services and if necessary prosecuted under s.443 of the Education Act 1996 for failing to ensure that their child received efficient education. Conversely, a person with parental responsibility can delegate the care of their child to another adult. This effectively happens when a child is in school or when a relative or friend acts as a babysitter. To return to the present case; under the voluntary agreement between J's parents and the local authority, the parents retained full parental responsibility for their daughter while delegating her care to the local authority, which did not thereby gain parental responsibility.

Mr Pleming, counsel for the parents, argued that parental responsibility included the right to decide where a child lived, an assertion with which Justice Scott Baker concurred. Mr Pleming then reasoned that the local authority had entered into an agreement with the parents, thereby obtaining their consent, to place their daughter in a specified residential unit, referred to as C Avenue. By contrast, the local authority were now proposing to move the child to a foster home and thus to change her place of residence, a move to which her parents did not give their consent. Mr Pleming's point before the court was that if the local authority moved their daughter into foster care without the consent of her father and mother, it would in effect be infringing their parental responsibility.

In essence, Mr Pleming was contending that the local authority did not hold parental responsibility and therefore could not override the parental responsibility of the parents and the choices they were entitled to make by virtue of it concerning their daughter. Mr Horowitz, the barrister representing the local authority, challenged this supposition on the grounds that s.23(2) of the Children Act 1989 plainly gives Social Services discretion in placing a child either in foster care or a residential home. He maintained that it cannot be the case that parents can dictate exactly how their child should be looked after when they have voluntarily given him or her into the care of the local authority. Mr Pleming countered this argument by acknowledging that s.23(2) certainly gave the local authority discretion in placing a child, but this discretion was not boundless and was ultimately limited by the exercise of parental responsibility by parents opposed to where a child was to be placed.

Of course it was hypothetically possible for the local authority to gain parental responsibility through obtaining a Care Order. Since the criteria for a Care Order under s.31(2) requires that the court be satisfied 'that the child concerned is suffering or is likely to suffer significant harm' and that this is attributable to the care they are receiving, plainly this provision was inapplicable to J's situation. For she was in fact receiving care of the highest quality at the residential home where she lived and was progressing well as a result. Indeed, this was the crux of the matter for her parents and why they were seeking to ensure that she remained there.

A proportion of children are being accommodated in local authority care on a voluntary basis. Any practitioner working with a child or young person in this situation needs to be aware of the legal limits on their authority. Local authorities may have good reasons for moving a child from a residential setting into a foster placement or indeed from one foster placement to another. But as the arguments put forward in this case demonstrate, this has to be done subject to parents' rights not just to be consulted under s.22(4) of the Children Act 1989, but to give (or not) their consent as those holding parental responsibility. Plainly this can be an area of friction and difficulty for local authorities who have 24-hour care of a child and yet cannot make autonomous decisions as to where the child resides in order to receive that care. However, this is what partnership working means, it obliges practitioners to consult with parents along every step of the way and to involve them directly in the decision-making process about their children who are voluntarily accommodated under s.20 of the Children Act 1989. This may result in the work progressing more slowly than is ideal, or ultimately it may mean social workers have to accept frustration of what they believe to be in the better interests of the child concerned.

Judgement in *R v. Tameside MBC ex parte J (A Child)*

Having reviewed all the evidence before him in terms of legislative provisions and statutory guidance, Justice Scott Baker concluded that deciding where a child should be placed under s.20 was at the discretion of the local authority. But ultimately this discretion could not be successfully asserted against the rights of those holding parental responsibility to decide where their child lived. In short, a local authority providing accommodation under s.20 was not entitled to place a child against the express wishes of those holding parental responsibility for that child, even if they were not in a position to offer alternative accommodation to the child.

 Crítical questíons

1 In this case social workers were subject to a number of conflicting imperatives. First, they were required to promote J's welfare and contact with her family, which was successfully accomplished in the residential placement; secondly, there were budgetary pressures on the local authority to reduce costly residential placements; and thirdly, government policy favoured fostering as opposed to residential care. It was the difficulty of negotiating these multiple considerations that resulted in contradictory decisions to proceed with the fostering placement for J. How do you think the social workers in this case could have improved their handling of this challenging situation?

2 There was clearly disagreement between J's parents and professionals regarding plans for J's future care. It was also known that the attitude of J's parents would affect J's emotional stability and ultimately her capacity to adjust to a new placement. Social workers are required to work in partnership with parents. How might you have worked in partnership with the parents in this case?

3 The local authority was providing 24-hour care for J and meeting all her welfare and educational needs. Social care staff were praised by the judge for sensitively handling J's challenging behaviour. Yet, because J's parents still held parental responsibility for her and the local authority did not, they could effectively dictate to Children's Services how their daughter was looked after. The judgement in this case appears to endorse this position. What sort of issues does this raise for local authorities who are accommodating children under s.20 of the Children Act 1989, bearing in mind that there are around 18,000 children *looked after* under this provision?

CASE 2

Independent Inquiry Report into the Circumstances of Child Sexual Abuse by two Foster Carers in Wakefield 2007

Importance of the case

It explores an instance in which children were abused in a foster care placement. The case identifies the failings of social workers to identify the abuse and to take action to safeguard the children involved. The findings of this inquiry and their implications for practice are also discussed.

History of the case

Two registered short-term foster carers sexually abused a number of children placed in their care between August 2003 and January 2005. They were both convicted of sexual offences against children in June 2006 and given custodial sentences by Leeds Crown Court. Given the considerable media attention on the Crown Court proceedings, Wakefield Council decided to commission an independent inquiry into the events surrounding that abuse and the reasons why professionals failed to identify the abuse of the foster children at an early stage.

Facts of the case

CF was 29 years old and IW was 38 years old at the time of these events. They were both of white British descent and had purchased a house together early in their relationship. They had been living together in a stable relationship for seven years. In August 2002 the couple made an application to become foster carers. An assessment was undertaken and they were registered as short-term foster carers from July 2003 to take children aged 5–12 years. In September 2004 this was amended to children aged 5–16 years. In all, 18 children aged 11–15 years were placed with the couple between August 2003 and January 2005. In June 2004 a family support worker drove Child F and Child G from their foster placement at the home of CF and IW to their mother's home for a contact visit. During the car journey the children revealed that CF had taken a number of photographs of both of them urinating, defecating and washing in the bath and shower. The support worker informed both the children's mother and their social worker. The mother demanded that her children be immediately removed from the foster carers, which was duly done. The incident was also reported by the children's social worker to management and although the foster carers were challenged over their behaviour no further action was taken against the couple. Children who had previously suffered sexual abuse continued to be placed with the couple. There were several sexual incidents between two foster children, one in August and the other in October of 2004 while the children were staying with CF and IW. The relationship between social workers and the couple became increasingly strained resulting in a deterioration of collaborative working. In October 2004 the mother of Child F and Child G reported that she had seen CF and IW near her home and her children's school on a number of occasions. No action was taken regarding the couple's presence near the children's home. On 31 January 2005 Child T ran away from his foster care placement with CF and IW and informed his brother's girlfriend that he had been sexually abused by them. The police and Children's Services were alerted. A strategy meeting was convened the next day at which it was agreed to suspend all foster placements with the couple. Subsequently, other children placed with CF and IW also made allegations of sexual abuse. The couple were deregistered as foster carers in June 2005. After the Crown Court hearing in June 2006, which convicted them both of multiple sexual offences against children in their care, the independent inquiry commenced its investigation.

Key people in the case

CF – foster carer
IW – foster carer
Child F – a child aged 8 when first placed with CF and IW
Child G – a child aged 8 when first placed with CF and IW
Child T – a child aged 14 when first placed with CF and IW
Child B – a child aged 12 when first placed with CF and IW
Child P – a child aged 14 years when first placed with CF and IW
Child A – a child aged 12 when first placed with CF and IW

Discussion of the case

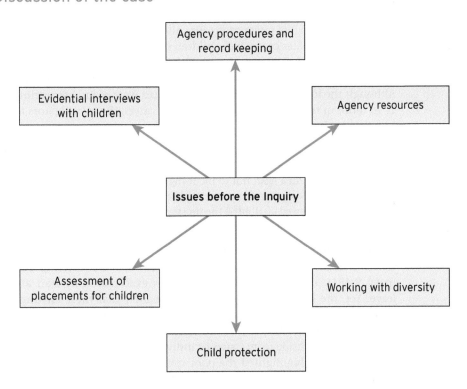

Agency resources

All aspects of fostering are regulated by the Fostering Services Regulations SI 2002/57 which is a statutory instrument issued under the Care Standards Act 2000. The implementation of these regulations is provided for by Department of Health (2002a) *Fostering Services: National Minimum Standards* which regulates both the placing of children in foster care and the placement itself. There are a number of National Minimum Standards set out in the box on the next page which impose obligations on those managing fostering services in relation to their staff.

key guidance

Fostering Services: National Minimum Standards

Standard 16: Staff are organised and managed in a way which delivers an efficient and effective foster care service.

Standard 17: The fostering service has an adequate number of sufficiently experienced and qualified staff and recruits a range of carers to meet the needs of children and young people for whom it aims to provide a service.

Standard 18: The fostering service is a fair and competent employer, with sound employment practices and good support for its staff and carers.

Standard 19: There is a good quality training programme to enhance individual skills and to keep staff up-to-date with professional and legal developments.

The Independent Inquiry acknowledged that in the Wakefield Council area there was an 'increasing shortfall of foster carers for children with particular problems or special needs, and that many foster carers had children for whom they were not approved placed with them' (para. 8.73). This, combined with a shrinking number of available foster carers overall, inevitably put greater pressure on the family placement team (para. 8.74). Although the local authority Fostering Services were plainly struggling to meet Standard 17 in terms of the number of available foster carers, the investigators for the Independent Inquiry concluded (para. 9.481):

> We do not believe financial or budget considerations had any major impact directly on the fostering service during this period. Undoubtedly, there were demand pressures on foster care resources and a wish not to incur higher costs of independent fostering agencies if the Council's own foster care resources could be stretched to the maximum. However, no social workers interviewed attributed the pressure on foster carer resources as due to any embargo on the use of independent sector foster placements.

In terms of human resources the Independent Inquiry observed that, 'there were significant workload pressures on social workers in both the fostering and children's teams' (para. 9.481). These pressures were at times exacerbated by staff absences due to sick leave. Yet, the Independent Inquiry did not infer that these circumstances had significantly affected the performance of personnel involved in the placement and supervision of foster children. This was instead attributed to other factors which the investigators were to uncover. Aside from issues of individual competency and performance, the Independent Inquiry highlighted the poor specialist training received by a number of social workers, which compromised Standard 19. A number of concerns around training were identified. First, when short in-service training courses were available, social workers were often not supported by management to apply for these, as they were given second place to day-to-day casework. Secondly, the local authority relied on dated training programmes which had changed little over the years and did not appear to meet the current training needs of staff. Thirdly, courses were not matched to the training needs of specific staff members in terms of their knowledge and skills.

Not only were National Minimum Standards compromised by some of the practices within Wakefield Council's Fostering Services, but arguably the agency was also failing to meet the requirements of the *Code of Practice for Employers of Social Care Workers*.

Specifically, para. 3.1 obliges management to provide, 'induction, training and development opportunities to help social care workers do their jobs effectively and prepare for new and changing roles and responsibilities'. By failing to meet this requirement the employing agency was at the same time impairing the ability of social work staff to comply with their own GSCC Code of Practice. Para. 6.1 requires social workers to practice 'in a lawful, safe and effective way'. Lack of knowledge of the legislative framework and lack of opportunity to develop skills through training were cited by the Independent Inquiry as contributory factors in the failure to identify the sexual abuse of foster children in Wakefield.

As previously discussed, the GSCC Code of Practice serves not only to ensure high quality practice with service-users and carers, but also to protect social workers as employees from inadequate or detrimental management practices which compromise their safety and health. Where fostering agencies, regardless of whether they are in the public, private or voluntary sectors, fall short of requirements set out in the Code of Practice, social workers can report these breaches to the General Social Care Council, who will then investigate. The Health Professions Council (HPC) will acquire GSCC functions from 2012. Social workers will also have recourse to the law of tort if their health has been damaged through unsafe management practices.

Agency procedures and record keeping

At the time of the events investigated by the Independent Inquiry, over the period 2002–2005, most of Wakefield Council's policies and procedures had last been updated in 2000. This meant that the new statutory framework introduced through the National Minimum Standards for fostering services in 2002 was not incorporated into agency policy or integrated into practice. However, *Inter-agency Procedures to Safeguard and Promote the Welfare of Children*, which implemented *Working Together to Safeguard Children* at local level, had been updated in 2004 to take account of the recommendations of the Public Inquiry into Victoria Climbié's death. This document included a section on inter-agency procedures where an allegation of abuse was made against a foster carer. It also referred to Joint Protocol arrangements established in 2000 between West Yorkshire Police and West Yorkshire local authorities on the conduct of inter-agency investigations by the police and Children's Services into such allegations. As the Independent Inquiry was to reveal, the procedures set out in this up-to-date and detailed documentation were not adhered to by Social Services' personnel.

As regards record keeping, the Independent Inquiry concluded that this was substandard across the teams involved in fostering provision. Indeed, the authors (and investigators) for the Independent Inquiry make frequent reference to the gaps in recording and documentation on fostering placements which at times made it difficult to establish the circumstances under which children had come to be placed with CF and IW or even when children had been placed with them and over what period. Significant incidents reported by the foster children or workers involved in their care were discovered to be poorly recorded. This state of affairs meant that the investigators for the Independent Inquiry were reliant on the sometimes contradictory recollections of those involved in the placement and supervision of the foster children. Some teams evidenced greater weaknesses in recording than others. At its worst, the Independent Inquiry found a 'failure of basic systems of recording, typing and filing' (para. 8.75). In the fostering team this was exacerbated by a very large change in personnel during the period 2003 to 2004. National Minimum Standards cover both record keeping and agency procedures.

Key guidance

Fostering Services: National Minimum Standards

Standard 20: All staff are properly accountable and supported

Standard 24: The fostering service ensures that an up-to-date, comprehensive case record is maintained for each child or young person in foster care which details the nature and quality of care provided and contributes to an understanding of her/his life events.

Standard 25: The fostering service's administrative records contain all significant information relevant to the running of the foster care services and as required by regulations

Standard 20 includes the requirement that 'all staff have clear written details of the duties and responsibilities expected of them, together with the policies and procedures of the organisation' (Standard. 20.2). This was plainly not true of Wakefield's Fostering Services, where most agency policy documents were out of date, as were the procedures flowing from them. Even where occasionally policies were up-to-date, such as for inter-agency working, staff failed to adhere to them. Both the *National Minimum Standards: Fostering Services* and the *Code of Practice for Employers of Social Care Workers* place the responsibility upon management to ensure that social workers are fully appraised of their role and tasks in conjunction with policies and procedures.

Standards 24 and 25 not only specify the records to be maintained and what should be in them, but the necessity of written instructions ensuring that staff know how to keep these records. Standard 25 also requires that any Fostering Service has management systems in place to monitor the quality of record keeping. The Independent Inquiry was of the opinion that record keeping was so inadequate, particularly with regard to the placement of children with CF and IW, that their investigation was actively hampered. The investigators were unable to identify any system of monitoring the quality of staff record keeping. This meant that poor practice was allowed to flourish unchecked within the agency. Aside from the National Minimum Standards, the GSCC *Code of Practice for Social Care Workers* charges social workers with 'maintaining clear and accurate records as required by procedures' (para. 6.2).

Procedures are often laid down in government guidance in more or less detail and must be followed unless there are compelling reasons to justify departure from them. Agencies in the public and private sector and larger voluntary sector organisations usually develop manuals of step-by-step instructions for frontline staff within the broader legal framework of their area of practice. Such procedures or instructions are not arbitrary, but designed to ensure the promotion of children's welfare and their protection from harm. Where agencies do develop their own documentation on procedures, management are responsible for ensuring that these are up-to-date, known to staff and in an easily accessible form. In this case some agency instructions had not been up-dated to reflect the changes in the law, and personnel lacked awareness of a number of standard procedures to safeguard children.

Under paragraph 6.1 of their GSCC Code of Practice, social workers are obliged to work 'in a lawful, safe and effective way'. Practitioners have a responsibility to familiarise themselves with the current law and the agency procedures which put it into practice. At the same time they also have an obligation under paragraph 3.4 to bring to the attention of an employer anything which impedes the delivery of safe care. Plainly out-of-date, poorly compiled or vague procedures contravene safe working practices and should be brought to the attention of management. Such a state of affairs also contravenes paragraph 1.4 of GSCC *Code of Practice for Employers of Social Care Workers* which requires employers to give 'staff clear information about their roles and responsibilities, relevant legislation and the organisational policies and procedures they must follow in their work'.

Assessment of placements for children

In all, 18 children were placed with IW and CF. Placement of children in foster care and the placement itself is regulated both by the Children Act 1989 and the National Minimum Standards for Fostering Services. There are a number of standards which are particularly relevant to the actual placement of children with IW and CF and are listed in the box below.

Key guidance

Fostering Services: National Minimum Standards

Standard 6: The fostering service makes available foster carers who provide a safe, healthy and nurturing environment.

Standard 7: The fostering service ensures that children and young people, and their families, are provided with foster care services which value diversity and promote equality.

Standard 8: Local authority fostering services, and voluntary agencies placing children in their own right, ensure that each child or young person placed in foster care is carefully matched with a carer capable of meeting her/his assessed needs. For agencies providing foster carers to local authorities, those agencies ensure that they offer carers only if they represent appropriate matches for a child for whom a local authority is seeking a carer.

Standard 9: The fostering service protects each child or young person from all forms of abuse, neglect, exploitation and deprivation.

Standard 10: The fostering service makes sure that each child or young person in foster care is encouraged to maintain and develop family contacts and friendships as set out in her/his care plan and/or foster placement agreements.

Standard 11: The fostering service ensures that children's opinions, and those of their families and others significant to the child, are sought over all issues which are likely to affect their daily life and their future.

Many of the children placed with CF and IW had previously been sexually abused and exhibited sexualised and challenging behaviour. A number of them had learning difficulties. Several had attention deficit hyperactivity disorder (ADHD), one had Asperger's syndrome, another had post-traumatic stress disorder and one of the other children suffered from depression. Two other children placed with the couple were incontinent. Another child with cerebral palsy had significant learning difficulties, was partially sighted and had limited speech. At least one of the children fostered by the couple was known to have previously sexually abused another child. Any one of these children would have presented considerable challenges in terms of their care even to the most experienced of foster carers. Yet, during the one-and-a-half year period from July 2003 to January 2005 these newly approved foster carers were to look after 18 different children each with substantial and complex needs. This raises the question as to what extent social workers at Wakefield Council were meeting Standard 8.

The Fostering Panel approved CF and IW as foster carers on 11 July 2003 and when visited by their fostering social worker just over two weeks later both complained that no children had been placed with them to date. The fostering social worker recorded her advice to CF and IW on file, noting that 'it may be worth them considering some respite placements until a more permanent placement is identified, that way they gain some experience'. Commenting on this very first interaction in relation to the placement of children with the couple, the Independent Inquiry observed that, 'This in our view is the first pivotal moment of the case following CF and IW's approval as foster carers. Priority appears to have been given to meeting the carers' needs (not to be kept waiting) rather than the needs of the children requiring placement.'

The actual approval status for fostering was 'short-term – one child male or two children of either sex if siblings in the age range of five to 12 years'. The rationale behind this was that CF and IW would provide short to medium term placements as part of a care plan, either designed to rehabilitate children back with their families or to facilitate a permanent placement away from their family home. The suggestion that CF and IW act as respite carers for children, rather than short-term fosterers, meant that from the very inception of their fostering career, placements were being contemplated which were in breach of their approved status. Later on, emergency placements and the placement of children outside of the age-range for which IW and CF had been approved were also to occur. The failure to focus on the needs of children in order to match them properly with CF and IW and the tendency to place children which breached the terms of the couple's approval as foster carers were to pervade the findings of the Independent Inquiry.

Of the 18 children placed with CF and IW, case records evidenced little or no matching for any of them. Generally the couple seem to have been identified as foster carers for each child because they could provide a placement or because the child had previously been placed with them. Often, poorly kept or missing records simply made it impossible for the investigators to ascertain why a particular child had been placed with the couple. Failure to assess children's needs prior to placing them, and lack of attention to the appropriateness of placing the children with CF and IW as recently approved short-term foster carers, proved detrimental to children's welfare.

To take just one typical example from the many children who came into the care of CF and IW. Child B aged 12 years was the second child to be placed with the couple. He was presenting challenging behaviour in his long-term foster placement and was thought to be suffering from post-traumatic stress disorder. CF and IW were suggested to provide respite care although they were not approved for respite placements and had only been foster carers for two months. Yet, Child B was presenting extremely challenging behaviour even for his permanent foster carers who knew him well. What is more, he had been sexually abused aged 7 years by a male babysitter. The Independent Inquiry questioned the judgement of social workers who placed a child evidencing challenging behaviour with such inexperienced foster carers and without considering the impact on the child of placement with two male carers when he had been sexually abused by a male carer in the past. The Independent Inquiry was of the opinion that no consideration had been given to the capability of CF and IW to care for a child with the complex needs of Child B (para. 9.128–33). In addition, it was discovered by the Independent Inquiry that the case file lacked information on the three separate respite placements which Child B spent with the couple, nor did it reveal the rationale for placing Child B with CF and IW.

Lack of matching in breach of Standard 8 plainly had implications for meeting Standard 6 and Standard 9. Recently appointed as foster carers, CF and IW could not possibly have been effective in meeting the needs of children in a safe and nurturing way when placements ignored their limitations in terms of both experience and approval status. Providing a 'safe, healthy and nurturing environment' depends not just on foster carers with good parenting capabilities, but also on caring for children within their range of ability. It seemed that once CF and IW gained a reputation as being effective foster carers for a few children, it was assumed they were able foster carers for any number of children. This was despite the very different ages, needs and circumstances of the vulnerable children placed with the couple.

The Independent Inquiry discovered that even when there was some initial good practice in terms of pre-placement meetings for the children involved and their parents or social worker, this gave way to poor assessment and record keeping. Initially there had been an over-focus on the needs of the foster carers to have placements, and once respite for some children was arranged with CF and IW they gained a reputation for being carers who could manage challenging behaviour. As a result children who fell outside their approval status as foster carers were regularly placed with them. This was compounded by the routine failure to match children to the capabilities of CF and IW or to accurately document incidents which called into question their competence as foster carers. In addition to these apparently widespread failings, which contravened National Minimum Standards for Fostering Services, no risk management strategy could be found for any child placed with CF and IW. For some children their care plan was not on file. This meant both that children were not properly safeguarded in foster care and that the purpose of the fostering placement in relation to each child's ongoing care needs was not stipulated. Ofsted, which is described in the box below, is the agency responsible for ensuring that Children's Services and Fostering Services meet the relevant National Minimum Standards.

 Background information

Ofsted

In April 2007 Ofsted became the *Office for Standards in Education and Children's Services and Skills* and took over inspection functions from the Commission for Social Care Inspection in relation to provision for children. Ofsted is charged to promote service improvement in terms of efficiency, value for money and meeting user needs. It is responsible for the regulation and inspection of:

- Adoption and fostering agencies
- CAFCASS
- Children's Services
- Day-care facilities
- Children's homes
- Educational provision across the public and private sectors

Ofsted is required by s.138 of the Education and Inspections Act 2006 to conduct an annual performance assessment of local authority Children's Services. This measures the outcomes of service provision for children, using specified performance indicators. For example, in terms of measuring how well local authorities keep children safe, they are required to submit figures to Ofsted showing the percentage of Initial Assessments completed within seven working days of referral and the percentage of children with a Child Protection Plan but no allocated social worker. Based on the data gathered for each performance indicator Ofsted then rates each local authority's Children's Services from 'outstanding' to 'inadequate'. The findings of each annual performance assessment are made public. Likewise, Ofsted inspects Fostering Services and assesses the quality of provision against the National Minimum Standards for this service. Ofsted has the power to require fundamental improvements to be carried out by a provider who falls short of the National Minimum Standards. Alternatively, if the quality of provision is so poor as to lead to concerns about the health and safety of children, Ofsted has the power to de-register a provider and thus shut down its service.

Matching children is a requirement of Standard 8 set out in the National Minimum Standards for Fostering Services, and social workers are obliged to implement it. But it is also an aspect of good practice for practitioners in other areas of work with children. Social workers involved in safeguarding children must maintain up-to-date Core Assessments which can be used to assist those in Fostering Services to ensure that the identified needs of children are met by suitable foster carers. Sometimes children are removed from their place of residence in an unexpected emergency. This is uncommon as usually there is a period of time to draw up a considered Child Protection or Child in Need care plan. Where there is a care plan in place, which will be in the vast majority of cases, this must inform decisions regarding the placement of the child. Matching is the process by which the care needs of a child are mapped onto the capabilities of the foster carers. These capabilities may be enhanced through specialist or advanced training. Where social workers identify shortcomings in the availability of appropriate foster care, this should be treated as a resource issue and brought to the attention of management, as required by the GSCC Codes of Practice.

Child protection

On 10 June 2004, while Child F and Child G were being driven from their foster placement with CF and IW to a contact visit with their mother, Child G showed a photograph of himself urinating to the family support worker who was driving them. According to Child G the photograph was taken by CF who had taken many others of them urinating, defecating and washing. Child G informed the support worker during the car journey that there was 'a whole drawer full of photos' of a similar nature (para. 9.180). The family support worker described being shocked by the photograph and promptly informed the children's mother on arriving at her house. She also left the photograph with the children's parent. The mother later telephoned CF and IW to complain about the photograph. As transpired during investigations by the Independent Inquiry, the support worker's decision to inform the mother before Social Services almost certainly resulted in CF and IW being tipped off and having time to destroy the rest of the photographs kept in the drawer referred to by Child G. The family support worker did, however, inform the children's social worker who in turn brought it to the attention of the team leader who agreed to discuss the matter with the fostering team manager. The team leader of the social worker for Child G and Child F wanted to call a Strategy Discussion immediately. In evidence to the inquiry, it appeared that a senior children's manager asked that the social worker responsible for supervising CF and IW and the named social worker for G and F first obtain more information about the matter from the couple and the two children.

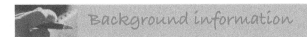

Strategy Discussion

Working Together to Safeguard Children details when and by whom a Strategy Discussion should be organised, who should attend and how it should be used. The Strategy Discussion can be conducted by telephone, but in complex situations should involve an actual face-to-face meeting of professionals. Paragraph 5.55 of the policy guidance sets out the purpose of a strategy discussion:

- Share available information.
- Agree the conduct and timing of any criminal investigation.
- Decide whether a core assessment under s.47 of the Children Act 1989 should be initiated or continued if it has already begun.
- Plan how the s.47 enquiry should be undertaken.
- Agree what action is required immediately to safeguard and promote the welfare of the child, and/or provide interim services and support.
- Determine what information from the strategy discussion will be shared with the family, unless such information sharing may place a child at increased risk of significant harm or jeopardise police investigations into any alleged offence.
- Determine if legal action is required.

Subsequently, it appeared that the photograph incident was treated as a 'standard of care issue' and not a child protection issue which would have invoked procedures under HM Government (2006a) *Working Together to Safeguard Children*. As a result the social worker for F and G visited them on her own at their mother's home. She interviewed the two children separately and asked them about their conversation with the family support worker. Both children repeated their story about the photographs and the existence of others at the home of CF and IW. The social worker did not gather any other information and no written record of the content of the interviews could be found by the Independent Inquiry. The social worker for G and F later visited the home of the foster carers to inform them that the children's mother had withdrawn Child G and Child F from the foster placement and to explain this was because of the discovery of the photograph. Neither dates of these two visits were recorded on file and could not be ascertained by the Independent Inquiry.

On 17 June 2004, that is a week after the photograph first came to light, the children's social worker together with the social worker responsible for supervising CF and IW made a joint visit to the couple's home. It was during this visit that the two social workers confronted CF and IW with the inappropriateness of the photograph. The couple maintained that they were trying to teach the children a lesson to get them to keep the toilet door shut. They denied the existence of any other photographs. The social workers checked the drawer where the children alleged the other photographs were kept. This was discovered to be empty. On reporting back to their respective team leaders, there were then differences of opinion among team leaders and senior managers as to whether a Strategy Discussion should be held or not. In the end no Strategy Discussion took place. Instead it was decided to convene an early foster carer annual review for CF and IW. Prior to the Crown Court hearing that convicted CF and IW for multiple sexual offences, the original photograph was lost. The only evidence of its existence was preserved in a fax sent between Social Services' offices within days of the photograph first coming to light. It was this facsimile which was presented in evidence before the Crown Court.

The social worker for Child G and Child F, who interviewed them shortly after the photograph was first seen by the family support worker, admitted to the Independent Inquiry that she had no training in either the interviewing of children or conducting witness interviews. The social worker also acknowledged that no manager either gave her instructions on how to go about the interview or raised questions about its timing or the way in which it was conducted. As the Independent Inquiry concluded, from start to finish no social worker or manager had treated the incident as a child protection issue and followed the procedures laid down both in agency policy and government guidance for dealing with such an eventuality (para. 9.207). Indeed, despite all that had transpired, two weeks after the photograph first came to light, both G and F were taken on a short visit to the home of CF and IW where for a period they were left alone with the couple. In effect Child G and Child F were put at risk of threatening behaviour or harm by the couple, given that from their perspective the children had brought the photograph to the attention of social workers. The Independent Inquiry revealed that there had been considerable reluctance on the part of the Children's Team Manager to permit this 'goodbye visit' to go ahead, but they reported coming under pressure from the Fostering Service who in turn appear to have been pressured by CF and IW. The Independent Inquiry noted that this was yet another example of foster carers' needs and wishes predominating over those of children (para. 9.210).

On examining agency documentation known as Wakefield Council Circular C11/2001 the Independent Inquiry discovered that agency policy in fact made clear when a complaint or concern about the standard of care should be treated under child protection procedures. It also detailed who was responsible for taking the final decision on how to proceed with the investigation. It appeared that team leaders and senior managers within the Children's and Fostering Services were not sufficiently conversant with this policy document and failed to act accordingly or to ensure that frontline workers did so (para. 9.217–23). Local policy guidance was compliant with child protection procedures laid down in *Working Together to Safeguard Children* and the *Framework for the Assessment of Children in Need and their Families* and it ought to have been followed. Had it been adhered to, a Strategy Discussion would have been triggered and professionals from both the Fostering and Children's teams would have met face-to-face. Such a forum would have facilitated the sharing of all available information on the couple while assisting professionals to explore and resolve their differences. Out of this, a jointly agreed plan of action could have emerged, which protected the children involved, preserved evidence and enabled an inquiry to proceed, if necessary under s.47 of the Children Act 1989. Instead a series of e-mails and telephone calls between different members of staff, often with opposing views, resulted in drift and indecisive action.

Closely connected to the issue of clear and properly publicised agency procedures is the matter of appropriate in-service training and agency support for professional development. In this case inexperienced social workers were left to assess situations where children were at considerable risk of harm. As the inquiry revealed, the combination of inexperience and inadequate in-service training led to poor assessment and feeble action to follow up allegations of abuse. Unfamiliarity with up-to-date procedures compounded the failings of frontline staff and their managers. Appropriate training and facilitation of professional development is an entitlement of social workers employed by social care agencies regardless of whether they are in the public, private or voluntary sectors. The GSCC *Code of Practice for Employers of Social Care Workers* para. 3.1 requires management to ensure that the agency provides 'induction, training and development opportunities to help social care workers do their jobs effectively'. It is the responsibility of social workers to bring to the attention of management any deficiencies in the provision of suitable training. At the same time, they are personally responsible for ensuring that they are familiar with agency procedures and are able to meet the requirements of para. 6.1 to 'practice and work in a lawful, safe and effective way'.

Evidential interviewing

Communication with children and gathering information from them, which is subsequently used as evidence in a court case, presents special challenges for all concerned. Practice guidance produced by the Home Office (2002) *Achieving Best Evidence in Criminal Proceedings: Guidance for Vulnerable or Intimidated Witnesses, including Children, Vols 1 and 2* provides instruction on conducting evidential interviews with children both as victims of and witnesses to crimes. In the circumstances surrounding the production of the photograph by Child G, the Youth Justice and Criminal Evidence Act 1999 is particularly pertinent. This statute extended *special measures* for children and vulnerable adults during pre-trial evidence gathering and the court hearing.

 Background information

Evidential interviewing of children

Section 27 of the Youth Justice and Criminal Evidence Act 1999 includes a *special measure* which allows for a pre-trial audio-visual taped interview of a child's oral evidence to be presented in court. This permits the formal gathering of information from a child through the videotaping of an evidential interview close to the time of an incident that could result in court proceedings. Such interviews must avoid contaminating evidence, for example through the interviewer asking leading questions, putting words in a child's mouth or intimidating the child into recalling a particular sequence of events. In circumstances where an interviewer appears to have coached a child or biased the interview the judge is likely to rule the taped interview inadmissible in court. Plainly this may result in either vital evidence being lost or additional stress to a child who has then to be re-examined by the court.

Precisely because of the crucial importance of obtaining uncontaminated evidence through objective questioning, such interviews must be carefully thought out and executed. Normally such interviews are planned and conducted jointly by a social worker and a police officer who are specifically trained to undertake this type of work. Detailed instruction on evidential interviewing is set out in Home Office (2002) *Achieving Best Evidence in Criminal Proceedings*, which also reiterates that the guidance should be used in conjunction with specialist professional training for investigative interviewing of children and vulnerable or intimidated adult witnesses. Where it is believed that the inclusion of a support person (usually an adult trusted by the child) would facilitate the gathering of best evidence by reassuring the child, Home Office (2002: para. 2.42) makes provision for this. However, the supporter must not participate actively in the interview otherwise this would be a source of contamination of the evidence (Home Office, 2002: para. 2.43). Any information collected in this manner may also be used as part of a s.47 enquiry under the Children Act 1989. In practice the preparation and conduct of evidential interviewing will often run in tandem with child protection procedures (Home Office, 2002: 9).

As is demonstrable from the conduct of the family support worker, the social worker for Child F and Child G and the failure of their line managers to call a strategy discussion, practice fell well short of Home Office (2002) guidance. The following actions by personnel either resulted in the destruction or contamination of evidence:

1 The decision of the family support worker to first bring the photograph to the attention of the children's mother instead of her own line manager resulted in CF and IW being tipped off and having the opportunity to destroy evidence in the form of other incriminating photographs.
2 The decision of the children's social worker to interview Child F and Child G on their own without videotaping the interview or recording its content potentially contaminated any later evidential interview.
3 The social worker who initially interviewed the children about the photograph had no training in evidential interviewing, thereby creating the danger of contaminating the children's evidence by asking leading questions.
4 The decision of the children's social worker to visit and inform CF and IW as to why Child F and Child G were being withdrawn from a foster placement with them, gave the couple yet another opportunity to destroy any remaining photographs. This also gave the couple ample time to concoct a credible explanation for the photograph of Child G urinating when later they were jointly visited by the social worker responsible for supervising them as foster carers and the social worker for Child F and Child G.
5 Poor record keeping by a number of professionals alongside the decision of management not to convene a Strategy Discussion meant that no coordinated investigation into the photograph incident was ever conducted and child protection procedures were never invoked. Consequently the police were not involved and no evidential interview in line with Home Office (2002) *Achieving Best Evidence in Criminal Proceedings* took place.

Evidential interviews serve a very specific purpose, which is to gather evidence for the court. However, they can also be crucial to managing risk and safeguarding children where more information is revealed about the circumstances of the abuse or neglect suffered by the victim. At first glance it may appear that the issue of evidential interviewing only affects a handful of specially trained social workers and police officers. This is far from being the case. Understanding the relationship between children's revelations about their abuse or neglect and how this fits into the production of evidence for the justice system is necessary for every social worker. Disclosures about abuse or neglect are not confined to those involved in direct work with children. Any social worker, regardless of their area of work, can be privy to a disclosure of child maltreatment. If they are to protect children and at the same time ensure that evidence is gathered for any subsequent court hearing, practitioners have to be alert to evidential requirements and the correct procedures to follow on disclosure.

As the Independent Inquiry discovered, in the case of Child F and Child G, neither were protected from the foster carers who had sexually abused them, nor was evidence collected from them which could then be used in court to convict IW and CF of their crime. Social workers need to know when to collect sufficient information from a child to ensure that they are immediately protected from any further harm, and yet prevent them from going into great detail about the events at a moment in time when there is not proper provision to record their evidence. This involves professional judgement which balances the child's therapeutic need to disclose, to be believed and to be reassured, as against the needs of the criminal justice system to punish offenders and protect the public from harm. Regardless of the circumstances in which a disclosure of abuse comes to light, practitioners must be child-centred in their decisions and actions. In practice this can also pose dilemmas.

The importance of gathering good evidence from children and doing so in ways which minimise their distress are not the only considerations for social workers mindful of subsequent criminal proceedings. Children who have been abused or neglected and are then subjected to child protection procedures involving examination, treatment, assessment and perhaps temporary or permanent removal from their home and family are often in desperate need of therapeutic support. The question arises as to how Children's Services in conjunction with the police can both collect and preserve crucial evidence while ensuring that children's psychosocial needs are met. There is a danger of denying children therapy by an exclusive focus on gathering evidence. Government guidance has endeavoured to address this issue and provide some direction to professionals faced with these kinds of dilemmas. The box below identifies the main pointers contained in practice guidance.

 Background information

Evidential interviewing and therapeutic work

The Home Office, Crown Prosecution Service and Department of Health (2001) *Provision of Therapy for Child Witnesses prior to a Criminal Trial: Practice Guidance* addresses this dilemma and sets out advice for frontline workers. This practice guidance makes reference to HM Government (2006a: para. 5. 125) *Working Together to Safeguard Children* (as revised) and reminds professionals that Child Protection Plans agreed at initial Child Protection Conferences should be based on the Core Assessment and 'describe the identified developmental needs of the child, and what therapeutic services are required'. *Provision of Therapy for Child Witnesses prior to a Criminal Trial* also advises (para. 1.9):

> If, during this planning stage, it is known that the child is to be a witness at a criminal trial, consideration should be given to the child's therapeutic needs, the possible impact the provision of therapy might have on the criminal trial and the consequences for the child of either proceeding with the therapy or deciding not to, having taken account of the implications for the criminal trial.

This statement is qualified in the very next paragraph (para. 1.10) which observes that:

> Therapy has not been encouraged before the video interview is recorded since lawyers have argued that the therapy might affect or taint the child's evidence. The likelihood of a prosecution being jeopardised is thought to be greater if therapy takes place before the video-recorded interview has taken place.

Although the practice guidance emphasises the importance of timely therapeutic support for children, it also cautions against this taking place before the recording of evidential interviews in preparation for a criminal prosecution against the child's alleged abuser. While it is not anticipated that therapy will be withheld until after the end of the criminal trial, which of course may take many months to come to court, there would have to be very pressing reasons for therapeutic support to take place before an evidential interview. In addition to these considerations, professionals must also bear in mind that where therapy is provided to children by local authority social workers or independent therapists they are compellable witnesses (para. 3.7-3.14).

In effect if the court has reason to believe that the child disclosed something during therapy which is directly pertinent to the criminal prosecution, the judge can demand that the social worker or therapist present that information in evidence. So a child cannot be guaranteed absolute confidentiality. The practice guidance advises professionals acting in a therapeutic role to ensure that they inform the child of the limits of confidentiality and the possibility of disclosure of information to the court given by the child in the course of therapy (para. 3.15).

Working with diversity

The Independent Inquiry stressed that its findings were not an indictment of same-sex foster carers and made no judgement regarding the suitability or otherwise of gay and lesbian fosterers (para. 1.4). However, the Independent Inquiry did reveal that the sexuality of CF and IW had impinged upon the professional judgement of social workers at frontline and management levels. Over the 18 months during which the couple were registered foster carers with Wakefield Council there were in fact a number of concerning incidents which are summarised in the table below.

Date	Description of incident
May 2004	CF audio-taped Child G saying adverse things about contact with his mother. Child G alleged at the time that he had been put under pressure to do so.
June 2004	Photograph of Child G urinating comes to light.
June 2004	Letter of complaint from mother of Child G and Child F alleging that CF and IW had used inappropriate strategies to manage the children's behaviour including: shouting at the children; threats to send the children to another carer; and saying that their toys would be sent to a charity shop. This letter also reiterated concerns about the audio-tape and existence of many photographs of the children naked.
July 2004	CF and IW fail to complete their section of the pro forma for their annual review and the meeting is adjourned. They are known to be increasingly difficult to manage, resistant to advice and hostile towards the social workers who came into contact with them.
August 2004	Sexual incident between Child A and Child P.
October 2004	Sexual incident between Child R and Child P.
October 2004	Report by the mother of Child F and Child G that CF and IW have been seen near the children's home and school.
August–November 2004	Social worker supervising CF and IW as foster carers records concern about their antagonism towards her and their insistence on focusing on financial matters at the expense of matters relating to foster children's care.
November 2004	Fostering team manager writes to CF and IW to express concern that they were not fulfilling aspects of their roles as foster carers.
December 2004	A second social worker in the fostering team also records concerns about the attitudes and behaviour of CF and IW towards personnel.

Despite these numerous incidents neither professionals' meetings nor Strategy Discussions were held to address the increasing difficulty of working with CF and IW as foster carers or in relation to incidents concerning the foster children in their care. There were persistent conflicting perspectives between social workers and team leaders in the children's and fostering teams. A number of the children's social workers and their team leaders believed that colleagues in the fostering team were unsympathetic to their concerns about CF and IW as competent foster carers. The Independent Inquiry sought to discover why, given the sheer number of concerns about CF and IW, ultimately no substantive action was ever taken. Not until a sexually abused foster child ran away from the couple at the end of January 2005, when the matter was reported to the police, did Social Services finally suspend placements with CF and IW. Giving evidence to the Independent Inquiry (para. 9.527) a children's social worker admitted:

> everyone was saying everything is not right . . . there is just something about them . . . their in-your-face eagerness to have children in their lives . . . they were viewed as important foster carers . . . you didn't want to be seen discriminating against a same sex couple and to be challenged that 'you were only saying that because we are a gay couple'.

Another social worker referring to CF and IW told the investigators that, 'by virtue of their sexuality they had a "badge" which made things less questionable'. A manager conceded that the couple were 'trophy carers' which had resulted in 'slack arrangements' in relation to placements (para. 9.529). According to the Independent Inquiry, 'the sexual orientation of CF and IW was a significant cause of people not "thinking the unthinkable" . . . It was clear that a number of staff were afraid of being thought homophobic' (para. 9.530). The Independent Inquiry concluded (para. 1.11) that:

> the effect on some social workers of working with deeply resistant and intimidating foster carers, alongside anxieties on their part about being or being seen as prejudiced against gay people. The fear of being discriminatory led them to fail to discriminate between the appropriate and the abusive.

The GSCC Code of Practice para. 1.6 requires social workers to respect diversity, which obviously includes homosexuality. Discrimination in the provision of services or performance of public functions on the grounds of sexual orientation is outlawed under the Equality Act 2006. Therefore social workers employed by the local authority were bound both by their professional code and by law to offer an equivalent quality of service to gay foster carers as to heterosexual fosterers. However, the fear of being labelled as homophobic or being accused of negatively stereotyping gay men as paedophiles resulted in social workers and their managers not being sufficiently self-assured to objectively examine the evidence before them. Had they done so, they might have directly challenged the questionable behaviour and actions of IW and CF.

The Independent Inquiry found that the sexuality of the foster carers had played a role in the failure to identify the abuse of children in their care at a much earlier stage. In their endeavour to be anti-discriminatory, social workers in Wakefield's fostering services had in fact turned a blind eye to some of the practices that they would almost certainly have challenged has they been committed by a heterosexual couple. In their anxiety to avoid being labelled homophobic they engaged in a form of positive discrimination. This phenomenon is not confined to heterosexual social workers engaging with homosexual foster carers, but to a whole range of diversity issues. For example white British social workers and managers working with colleagues and service-users from ethnic minority communities can make presumptions about their culture and background leading to inaccurate conclusions. In their anxiety to avoid an accusation of racism they apply different standards to childcare by a black parent as opposed to a white one, thus failing perhaps to challenge harmful parenting practices by a black father which they would challenge and possibly intervene to stop, were it a white father. Social workers must be alert to their own anxieties about being perceived as racist or homophobic and how this may detrimentally affect their professional judgement.

Recommendations of the Independent Inquiry Report into the Circumstances of Child Sexual Abuse by two Foster Carers in Wakefield

The Independent Inquiry made a number of key recommendations which included:

- Clear procedures for investigating allegations of abuse by foster carers.
- Clarity in decision-making responsibilities between different social work teams.
- Improvements in supervision and accountability.
- Foster carers should be recruited to care for specific groups of children and this should not be changed without formal reassessment.
- Matching and appropriate placing of children must be a priority.

 Critical questions

1 Poor record keeping was a major finding of this inquiry. How did the inadequate recording of information affect the process of matching children, tracking incidents which occurred while children were in the care of IW and CF, and sharing information with other teams or agencies? What factors might have contributed to poor record keeping in this case?

2 The failure of social care professionals to protect fostered children or to gather information on suspected sexual abuse was a major finding of the Independent Inquiry. How do you think the support workers and social workers involved with CF and IW should have acted in order both to protect Child F and Child G and yet obtain evidence about the abuse?

3 Home Office et al. (2001) *Provision of Therapy for Child Witnesses prior to a Criminal Trial: Practice Guidance* provides instruction to professionals involved in obtaining evidence from children. Do you think this practice guidance gets the balance right between the imperatives of gathering evidence from children and providing therapeutic support to them? If so, why; if not, what do you think the correct balance would be?

4 The sexual orientation of CF and IW appears to have inhibited social workers from acknowledging that they were abusing children in their care. Social workers were afraid of being perceived as homophobic. Practitioners from the white majority population who intervene with families from ethnic minority communities may similarly be frightened of articulating their concerns for fear of being accused of racism. How can social workers be anti-oppressive in their practice while not being hesitant to voice concerns in case they are accused of prejudice?

CASE 3
Re C (A Child) (Secure Accommodation Order: Representation) [2001] 2 FLR 169

Importance of the case

It examines the entitlement of a *Gillick* competent child to instruct her own solicitor and to have a fair trial. The case also explores the dilemmas posed for professionals when a young person wishes and chooses to act in ways which cause her significant harm.

History of the case

The local authority was granted an Interim Care Order and a Secure Accommodation Order by the Magistrates' Court enabling it to detain C, a 15-year-old girl, in a secure unit against her wishes. C appealed to the Family Division of the High Court against the Secure Accommodation Order on the grounds that it violated articles, 5, 6 and 8 of the European Convention on Human Rights. The High Court dismissed C's appeal and she then applied to the Civil Division of the Court of Appeal to overturn the decision of both the lower courts.

Facts of the case

C was born in 1985 and Social Services had been involved with her since she was 2½ years old when her parents separated, at which time C and her sister came into the care of her father. Around 1997 C dropped out of school and started using heroin and crack cocaine. In June 1999 C's father reported her missing from home and refused to have her back to live with him. In August 1999 she was admitted to an Accident and Emergency unit and found to be approximately 5-months pregnant. In March 2000 C gave birth to a baby boy R who became the subject of an application for a Care Order by Social Services. C returned to her father and was again reported missing by him in June 2002 when he again requested that Social Services accommodate his daughter. C and R were then accommodated in a mother and baby unit, but C was often absent and eventually abandoned R at the unit. R was then placed in foster care. It was suspected that C was prostituting herself in order to obtain money for hard drugs. In December 2000 police were called to an address where C alleged she was being threatened by a man with a knife. The police contacted Social Services and C was offered accommodation by them, which she refused. A few days later C told her mother that she had been beaten up by several men. Given C's continued high-risk behaviour, Social Services decided to apply for a Care Order. Before this application could be heard by the Family Proceedings Court, C arrived at her father's house in possession of cocaine. Her father informed Social Services, and social workers arrived at the house to escort C to a secure unit. At this point Social Services applied for a Secure Accommodation Order. In January 2001 the Family Proceedings Court granted both an Interim Care Order and a Secure Accommodation Order in respect of C to the local authority. C sought to appeal against both these orders on the grounds that they violated her human rights.

Key people in the case

C – 15-year-old girl
R – infant son of C
Father – father of C
Mother – mother of C
Ms Pattni – C's solicitor
Mrs Poole – C's Guardian ad Litem (now redesignated Children's Guardian)
Ms Phillipson – solicitor instructed by Guardian ad Litem
Lord Justice Thorpe – judge in Court of Appeal
Lord Justice Brooke – judge in Court of Appeal
Ms Johnson – solicitor for local authority in Family Proceedings Court
Mr De Mello – junior counsel representing C in Court of Appeal

Discussion of the case

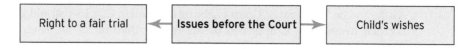

Child's wishes

Mrs Poole was appointed as the Guardian ad Litem (now Children's Guardian) for the upcoming hearing in the Magistrates' Court on 11 January 2001 regarding the Interim Care Order and Secure Accommodation Order. Notice of the application for these orders was served on C's parents and Mrs Phillipson who was the Guardian ad Litem's solicitor. Mrs Poole and Mrs Phillipson met with C at the secure unit on 10 January, the day before her case was due to be heard in the Family Proceedings Court. At this meeting C refused to accept that there was any necessity for her to remain at the secure unit or to agree with the contents of the care plan which had been drawn up by Social Services. This care plan stressed the hazards posed to C by her present lifestyle, while setting out the therapeutic, medical and educational provision available to her at the secure unit. C's parents were fully supportive of the care plan which incorporated arrangements for C to continue seeing her parents and sister. Once C rejected the care plan and the need for her to remain in the secure unit, it became plain to Mrs Phillipson that she was receiving diametrically opposed instructions from Mrs Poole as the Guardian ad Litem and C as the child at the centre of the upcoming court case. This situation is governed by rules 11 and 12 of the *Family Proceedings Courts (Children Act 1989) Rules 1991* which permit children of sufficient understanding, meaning *Gillick* competent, to instruct their own solicitor while permitting the Guardian ad Litem (Children's Guardian) to be separately represented and to continue as a party to the court proceedings. In this instance Mrs Poole continued to be legally represented by Mrs Phillipson while C chose to be represented by Ms Pattni who had acted for her in relation to the ongoing care proceedings concerning her infant son R.

C and her Guardian ad Litem, Mrs Poole were clearly at odds over what course of action was in her best interests. The Guardian ad Litem is legally required to determine the child's best interests and not simply to persuade the court to act on the basis of the child's wishes or preferences. Of course where there is disagreement between the views of the Guardian and the child these should be explicitly set out in the Guardian ad Litem's report to the court alongside a rationale as to why the child's wishes should not prevail or how they are accommodated to some extent where possible within the proposed care plan. Once C rejected the care plan, social workers decided that they had no option but to apply for an Interim Care Order under s.38(1) of the Children Act 1989. The grounds for this are the same as for a full Care Order except that an interim order can only be granted for a maximum of eight weeks and is renewable every four weeks thereafter. In this instance C was suffering significant harm which was attributable to 'the child's being beyond parental control'. C's circumstances therefore met the threshold criteria laid down in s.31(2)(b)(i) and consequently the Family Proceedings Court granted the order. This judgement was upheld both by the High Court and the Court of Appeal, thus fully endorsing the decision of the social workers involved.

As regards the local authority's application for a Secure Accommodation Order, in arriving at its judgement the court is normally obliged to consider all the items comprising the welfare checklist set out in s.1(3) of the Children Act 1989. Exceptionally, where a case concerns whether or not to place a child in secure accommodation the criteria which the court is obliged to apply under the Children Act 1989 is not s.1(3) but the threshold criteria set out in s.25(1) which relates to a child's likelihood of absconding. This section of the Children Act 1989 is reproduced in the box below.

Key legislation

Children Act 1989

Secure accommodation is defined under s.25 as 'accommodation provided for the purpose of restricting liberty'. Any such accommodation is required to meet the same National Minimum Standards as are Children's Homes. Local authorities are under a legal duty, set out in Sch. 2, para. 7(c) of the Children Act 1989, to avoid the need for children to be placed in secure accommodation. This is reiterated in policy guidance Department of Health (1991c: para. 8.5) *The Children Act 1989 Guidance and Regulations: Residential Care* Vol. 4 which states:

> Restricting the liberty of children is a serious step which must be taken only when there is no genuine alternative which would be appropriate. It must be a last resort in the sense that all else must first have been comprehensively considered and rejected – never because no other placement was available at the relevant time, because of inadequacies in staffing, because the child is simply being a nuisance or runs away from his accommodation and is not likely to suffer significant harm in doing so, and never as a form of punishment.

Section 25(1) defines the threshold criteria for placing children in secure accommodation:

25(1) a child may not be placed in secure accommodation unless:

    (a) it appears that the child has a history of absconding and;

    (b) is likely to abscond from any other type of accommodation; and

    (c) if the child absconds, he or she is likely to suffer significant harm;

    (d) if the child is kept in any other type of accommodation the child is likely to injure himself or other people.

The *Children (Secure Accommodation) Regulations 1991* restricts the length of time a child can be kept in secure accommodation to a maximum of 72 hours in any period of 21 days. For periods longer than 72 hours an application must be made to the court for a Secure Accommodation Order. This can be granted for a maximum initial period of 3 months and 6 months thereafter.

As s.22(3) of the Children Act 1989 places a duty on local authorities to safeguard and promote the welfare of *looked after* children this means that a judge must weigh up the child's welfare in conjunction with the criteria set out in s.25(1). In the case of C, she has a right under court rules to be separately represented from her Guardian ad Litem, but she does not have a right that her wishes and feelings prevail over all other considerations. C's wishes and their frustration by social work intervention are just one element in a wider consideration of her welfare. It is this wider consideration that the Guardian ad Litem is bound to bring before the court in evidence. In this instance that wider consideration included the opinion of a consultant paediatrician at a strategy meeting held on 20 December 2000 who stated that unless something was done to protect C she could die as a result of her high-risk lifestyle. This opinion was delivered in the light of C's continued involvement in sex work and hard drug use regardless of whether she was accommodated by the local authority or living with her father.

This case undoubtedly posed dilemmas for the social workers involved. Here was a young person who had abandoned her infant son in hospital and thereafter had continued to act in ways which put her at risk of significant harm. In this situation practitioners were left to fulfil two opposing imperatives set out in the GSCC *Code of Practice for Social Care Workers*. According to paragraph 3.1 they ought to be 'promoting the independence of service users and assisting them to understand and exercise their rights'; yet at the same time, by virtue of paragraph 4.3, to be taking 'necessary steps to minimise the risks of services users from doing actual or potential harm to themselves or other people'. Of course these conflicting obligations are also reflected in the Children Act 1989 with the requirement under s.22(3) to promote a child's welfare while seeking to restrict his or her liberty under s.25(1). The reconciliation between these apparently conflicting stipulations is that in certain circumstances the restriction of a child's liberty is the only way to preserve their welfare and protect them from harm. Furthermore, for social workers who find themselves having to act against the wishes of parents, children, users or carers, this does not preclude informing them about their rights and enabling them to avail of them. In this particular case it would have been important for the social worker acting at the Guardian ad Litem (now a Children's Guardian) to inform C that she was entitled to be separately represented in court and to instruct her own solicitor.

The case of C brings together two legal principles, first the obligation to take into consideration a child's wishes and second the status of a *Gillick* competent child. As a 15-year-old of sufficient age and understanding, C was entitled to instruct her own solicitor and have separate legal representation in court from her Guardian ad Litem with whom she vehemently disagreed. Where older children are involved in Family or Care Proceedings it is sometimes necessary for them to have their own legal counsel. It goes without saying that social workers should endeavour to work in partnership with children, negotiating their preferences and when at all possible incorporating these into care plans. But, as with C, there will be occasions when the imperatives of safeguarding children override those of the child's wishes. In these circumstances, social workers should facilitate children to avail of advocacy services and ultimately of their own legal advice and representation if they are *Gillick* competent.

Right to a fair trial

The basis of C's resort to the Court of Appeal was not that her wishes were contravened by the Magistrates' (and subsequently the High Court's) judgement, but that she was not permitted sufficient time with her solicitor to prepare her case. In fact C met her solicitor for the first time in relation to the hearing on Secure Accommodation on 11 January 2001, the very morning the case itself was to be heard in the Family Proceedings Court. Ms Pattni had not been served with notice of the court case as had C's parents and her Guardian ad Litem on 9 January. This was of course because Ms Pattni had not been instructed to represent C until the following day, 10 January. Serving notice of an upcoming court case is much more than just a matter of indicating the time and venue of the hearing. It involves exchanging documents which set out the reasons for the hearing and allowing each party who is notified to prepare their evidence if they wish to oppose the course of action proposed by the local authority.

Ms Pattni did not receive these papers and therefore arrived on the day of the hearing without all the requisite information. The *Family Proceedings Courts (Children Act 1989) Rules 1991* regulates the conduct of the court when hearing cases relating to children which are governed by the Children Act 1989. Rule 4(1) requires a minimum of one day for notice to be served; however, rule 8(8) gives discretion to the court to dispense with this in exceptional circumstances. Representations made by the local authority's solicitor in court led the magistrates to consider that the case was of such urgency that it could not be postponed. In the circumstances the hearing was rescheduled from the morning to the afternoon of 11 January to permit Ms Pattni sufficient time to familiarise herself with the case and to take instruction from C.

At the Court of Appeal hearing Mr De Mello, junior counsel acting for C, argued that as the case concerned C's detainment in secure accommodation, for the purposes of article 6 of the European Convention on Human Rights the original hearing by a bench of Magistrates sitting as a Family Proceedings Court should be treated as a criminal case. In other words Mr De Mello was equating a custodial sentence with detainment in secure accommodation. The reason why Mr De Mello sought to equate custody with secure accommodation was because of the precise wording of article 6, which is reproduced in the box below.

Key legislation

European Convention on Human Rights

Article 6

1 In the determination of his civil rights and obligations or of any criminal charge against him, everyone is entitled to a fair and public hearing within a reasonable time by an independent and impartial tribunal established by law . . .

2 Everyone charged with a criminal offence shall be presumed innocent until proved guilty according to law.

3 Everyone charged with a criminal offence has the following minimum rights:

   (a) to be informed promptly, in a language which he understands and in detail, of the nature and cause of the accusation against him

   (b) to have adequate time and facilities for the preparation of his defence

It was Mr De Mello's contention before the Court of Appeal that C had not been given 'adequate time and facilities for the preparation of [her] defence'. This legal argument was dismissed by Lord Justice Thorpe who countered that the Family Proceedings hearing falls within the civil jurisdiction and cannot sensibly be construed as a criminal trial. He observed that secure accommodation is protective not penal and therefore cannot be equated with a form of custodial sentence. Lord Justice Thorpe was also of the opinion that it was unnecessary for Mr De Mello to try to contort Family Proceedings in respect of secure accommodation into a form of criminal proceedings to enable C to avail of rights under article 6(3) of the European Convention. Since, as a child subject to proceedings under the Children Act 1989, the law already afforded C the right to be notified of the proceedings, while she held common law rights which entitled her and her counsel adequate time to prepare for a hearing, whether within the civil or criminal court system.

In deciding on this particular legal point, Lord Justice Thorpe had sight of the original evidence presented in the Magistrate's Court and noted that the evidence-in-chief presented by Ms Johnson was largely a matter of record, bearing in mind that Ms Pattni had acted for C in relation to the care proceedings involving her son R. She was therefore already familiar with most of the facts of the case. Records of the Family Proceedings

Court hearing also revealed that Ms Pattni had cross-examined Ms Johnson, the solicitor for the local authority, at length, indicating that she had a good grasp of the facts-at-issue despite only taking instruction from C on the morning of the hearing. Perhaps the most significant fact was that even after taking instruction from C during the morning, Ms Pattni did not ask for an adjournment of the case in order to take further instruction from C, to call additional witnesses or to better prepare herself for a court hearing. In other words, apparently neither C nor her solicitor at the time of the original hearing thought that they were being so disadvantaged by circumstances as to insist upon rescheduling the hearing for a later date. Given these facts Lord Justice Thorpe concluded that, notwithstanding the very short period of time afforded to Ms Pattni before the hearing commenced, no injustice had been done.

The notion of a fair trial involves many different aspects, one of which is highlighted in the circumstances surrounding C and her proposed detention in a secure unit. A fair trial is measured not only by the fairness of court procedures during the trial itself, but by the processes which lead up to the hearing. The ability to present good evidence in court and call witnesses to testify depends on having sufficient notice of the hearing. In short, a fair trial requires that the parties to it have sufficient opportunity before the day of the hearing to gather evidence and collate it in order to convince a judge (or jury in a criminal case) of their standpoint. It was only because C's solicitor was already familiar with her circumstances, having represented C in previous Care Proceedings, that the judge concluded she had received a fair trial despite the lack of notice. However, as the judgement related to C makes clear, in normal circumstances local authority social workers would have to ensure that those directly affected by their decisions had ample notice and therefore opportunity to gather evidence and present this in court. Only in situations of dire emergency which necessitate ex parte Emergency Protection Orders are the normal rules of a fair trial temporarily suspended. However, as previous judgements demonstrate, such situations are in practice very exceptional.

Judgement in *Re C (A Child) (Secure Accommodation Order: Representation)*

The bench of judges sitting on the Court of Appeal case concluded that C's article 6 right had not been violated. They were of the opinion that despite the short period before the original Family Proceedings hearing for C to instruct her legal representative, given all the other circumstances of the case, C had received a fair trial. While the Court of Appeal judges decided to dismiss the appeal, Lord Justice Brooke added a rider (para. 41):

> Even though we are dismissing this appeal, it has given this court an opportunity to stress how important it is that fair procedures should be followed before a secure accommodation order is made. Even if the availability of such orders is a manifestation of the wish of a benevolent state to protect its children from harm, they will not be seen in this light by young people of C's age and maturity. It is most important that they should feel they have been treated fairly, and that they have had a fair opportunity of putting their side of things to the court before a substantive order is made.

? Critical questions

1 A central issue in this case was whether C had been given sufficient time to prepare for the case and instruct her solicitor. Do you think this case was correctly decided? If so, why; if not, what ruling do you think the judge ought to have made?

2 The GSCC Code of Practice requires social workers to promote the independence of users and to assist them to take appropriate risks. This creates a considerable professional dilemma when a user, in this case a young person, decides to take risks which cause them or threaten to cause them significant harm. Do you think social workers made the right decision in this case? If not, what other courses of action do you think they could have pursued?

3 If you were faced with similar circumstances to those of the social workers intervening with C, how would you personally handle the professional dilemmas raised?

 Perspectives

Young people in secure accommodation

O'Neill (2001) in her study of young people in secure accommodation found pronounced gender differences in their paths into the system. Boys predominantly came into secure accommodation because they were on remand pending trial or because they had already been convicted of a criminal offence. By contrast, girls were much more likely to have been admitted to secure accommodation through the care system. Many of the girls in this study were already the subject of a Care Order or had been *looked after* under s.20 of the Children Act 1989. For children who came into secure accommodation through the welfare route, girls tended to be admitted due to repeated absconding from local authority accommodation and their exposure to sexual harm. Conversely, boys who were already *looked after* were more likely to be admitted to secure accommodation due to absconding and the risk of offending. Self-harm, violence towards others and drug or alcohol abuse were also reasons why young people of both sexes had been admitted to secure accommodation.

O'Neill (2001) found that for those young people who had been admitted through the criminal justice system – predominantly boys – secure accommodation was viewed as a form of punishment. Conversely, those admitted through the welfare route were often confused and unsure as to why they were in secure accommodation. For example one girl told the researcher:

> The staff keep telling me that it's not a punishment, it's to give me a break . . . it feels like a punishment because you are permanently watched, the staff listen carefully to everything you say, waiting for you to slip up on everything, and this can lead to being jeopardized as to when you get out.

In addition because of the close monitoring and restrictions on choice and action, many young people found that they could not employ their normal coping mechanisms. Another girl in secure accommodation observed that:

> Being in secure makes you think about things more because whereas if you're in an open unit you can run away from your problems, you can get drunk, you can take drugs and your problems have gone, in here you've got to think about your problems all the time.

Many young people reported increased incidents of self-harm due to raised levels of distress in secure accommodation. Deprivation of liberty, the removal of possessions and the violation of privacy were major causes of the depression and frustration reported by the young people. The use of sanctions and restraint combined with poor therapeutic engagement were also major sources of resentment among both girls and boys in secure accommodation.

CASE 4
R (on the application of J) v. Caerphilly County Borough Council [2005] 2 FLR 860

Importance of the case

It illustrates the duties which local authorites owe to children who leave the care system and the difficulty of partnership working with young people. The case also explores the potential conflict in roles when social workers are employed by Children's Services, but are also acting as an advocate for a young person leaving care.

History of the case

The apparent failure of Caerphilly Social Services to produce a Pathway Plan and identify accommodation for J, a 17-year-old under a Care Order and just released from a Young Offender Institution, resulted in an application to the Queen's Bench Division of the High Court for a judicial review of the local authority's action. This case was actually brought by the Howard League for Penal Reform acting as J's litigation friend.

Facts of the case

J was born in 1987 and had been abused by his mother's stepfather since he was four. He became addicted to drugs having first been introduced to these by his abuser. His first offence for burglary was committed when he was only 10 years old, after which there followed a string of offences for theft. In September 2002 the local authority was granted a full Care Order for J. He remained *in care* for the following four years, during which time he committed a number of offences and spent periods in secure accommodation, culminating in a custodial sentence in Ashfield Young Offender Institution. He was released in January 2005 having served half of his sentence. At the time of the High Court case in April 2005 J was 17 years old and therefore still a child under the Children Act 1989. He had been assessed as having a reading age of 13 and had difficulty with numeracy. On release from Ashfield Youth Offender Institution J was technically a child leaving care and therefore the local authority retained legal responsibilities in relation to him. J alleged that the local authority had failed to fulfil its statutory duties towards him in respect of a pathway plan. For its part, the local authority contended that J had missed numerous appointments and generally made partnership working with him to develop the pathway plan impossible.

Key people in the case

J – 17-year-old young person
Mr S – J's personal advisor
Mr Justice Munby – presiding judge in High Court case
Mr Wise – legal counsel instructed by Howard League

Discussion of the case

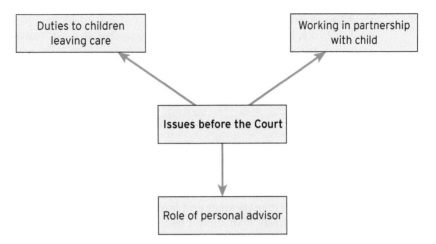

Duties to children leaving care

The Children (Leaving Care) Act 2000 amended the Children Act 1989 by inserting new sections into this statute which are set out in the box below. The new provisions within the Children Act 1989 were designed to impose additional duties on local authorities towards children leaving local authority care. It was intended that these new obligations would enhance the life chances of vulnerable young people by ensuring they were properly prepared for leaving care and continued to receive support from the local authority as they adapted to independent living in the community. The Children (Leaving Care) Act 2000 applies equally to children who are *accommodated* and those *in care* as long as they meet the qualifying period of actually being *looked after* by the local authority. For most children this means they become an 'eligible child' for the purposes of the Children (Leaving Care) Act 2000 if they are aged between 16 and 17 years and have been *looked after* for at least 13 weeks since they were aged 14 years. Of course the statute also applies to those young people who qualified as an 'eligible child' but have now left local authority care. The provisions of the Children (Leaving Care) Act 2000 also apply to children subject to a Care Order who are (or have been) detained in hospital under the Mental Health Act 1983 or are/were detained in a remand centre or Young Offender Institution.

Key legislation

Children (Leaving Care) Act 2000 amendments to Children Act 1989

Sch.2 para. 19A 'It is the duty of the local authority looking after a child to advise, assist and befriend him with a view to promoting his welfare when they have ceased to look after him.'

- Sch.2 para. 19B(4) imposes a duty on the local authority to make an assessment of needs for advice, assistance and support for those aged 16 and 17 years.
- Sch.2 para. 19B(4) and 19B(5) requires a Pathway Plan to map out a route to independence to be regularly reviewed (Reg. 9 – at least every 6 months).
- S.23E requires the local authority to provide personal and practical support to *looked after* 16 and 17-year-olds or care leavers to meet the objectives of their Pathway Plan.

- S.23B(8) requires the local authority to maintain a care leaver and to provide him or her with suitable accommodation.
- Sch.2 para. 19C requires the local authority to allocate a personal advisor to each young person to participate in the assessment and review of the Pathway Plan and to coordinate the provision of services.
- S.24 and S.24B impose a duty on each local authority to maintain contact with care leavers until at least the age of 21 years or up to 24 years of age if they are in education or training.

In order to facilitate the implementation of the amendments to the Children Act 1989 listed in the box above, Department of Health (2001c) *Children (Leaving Care) Act 2000: Regulations and Guidance* issued under s.7 of the Local Authority Social Services Act 1970 gives directions to management and frontline professionals. This policy guidance makes clear that the Pathway Plan should be initiated 'well before a young person leaves care' and should complement the Care Plan for the young person and extend it until they are at least 21 years of age (Department of Health, 2001c: 27, 40). Since the Care Plan for each *looked after* child is based on the *Framework for the Assessment of Children in Need and their Families*, there is a direct relationship between this assessment framework and the Pathway Plan which is set out in the policy guidance and reproduced below.

The Assessment Framework, and the Assessment of Needs and Pathway Plans

Framework for the Assessment of children in need	Children (Leaving Care) Act Regulations	
	Needs Assessment	Pathway Planning
Health	Health and development	Health needs, including health promotion and mental health needs, how they are to be met
Education	Education, training, employment	A detailed plan for education or training, or assistance in employment
Emotional and behavioral development including identity	Health and development	Health needs, health promotion, mental health needs, how they are to be met
Family and social relationship	Family and other social relationships	Support to develop and sustain family and social relationships Nature and level of personal support
Social presentation and self-care skills	Practical and other skills necessary for independent living	Programme to develop practical and other skills to live independently
Parenting capacity		
Basic care, ensuring safety, stimulation, guidance and boundaries, stability	Support available from family Support to sustain other relationships	Family and social relationships Nature and level of personal support Cotingency plans
Family and environmental factors		
Family history and wider family	Support available from family and other social relationships	Support to maintain family and social relationships

(Continued)

Framework for the Assessment of children in need	Children (Leaving Care) Act Regulations	
	Needs Assessment	*Pathway Planning*
Housing	Care, support, accommodation	Details of accommodation
Employment	Education, training and employment	Assistance to employment
Income	Financial needs	Financial support
Family's social integration	Support available from family and other social relationships	Support to develop and sustain family and other social relationships
Community resources	Support available from within the community	Community resources to provide support

Department of Health (2001c) *Children (Leaving Care) Act 2000: Regulations and Guidance*, London: Stationery Office.

Dissatisfied with the local authority's preparation for his imminent release from Ashfield Youth Offender Institution at the age of 17 years, J telephoned the Howard League for Penal Reform on their advice line in November 2004. The Howard League contacted the local authority who responded that a needs assessment and Pathway Plan had been completed, but was awaiting review on J's release in January 2005. As the High Court was to discover, in fact these documents were incomplete, unsigned and undated. Mr Justice Munby expressed his suspicion that the assessment of need and Pathway Plan had not been drafted until contact was made by the Howard League. This plainly contravened the stipulations in Department of Health (2001c) *Children (Leaving Care) Act 2000: Regulations and Guidance*. This was of course policy guidance and therefore social workers were obliged to follow it.

In any event, as Social Services were to admit in a letter (later submitted as evidence) neither the assessment nor the pathway plan had been shared with J. A review of the pathway plan was scheduled to take place on 14 February 2005, a month after J's release from Ashfield Youth Offender Institution, but this did not happen. It therefore appeared that the local authority had neither commenced the assessment of need nor the drawing up of the Pathway Plan in good time as required by policy guidance. Neither apparently had there been discussion with J about his plans for the future. This meant of course that no services had been put in place to meet the objectives of a Pathway Plan, nor had suitable accommodation been arranged for J on his release. In these circumstances J was granted permission to seek a judicial review of the local authority's action on the grounds that it had failed to:

- Correctly appoint a personal advisor.
- Follow the correct procedures to assess J's needs or produce a Pathway Plan for him.
- Produce an adequate assessment of need or Pathway Plan for J.

As J was a vulnerable young man leaving care and his clash with the local authority raised legal issues likely to affect other young people in similar circumstances, the Howard League for Penal Reform agreed to act as J's litigation friend and pursue the judicial review on his behalf. The box on next page explains what it means to act through a litigation friend in court proceedings.

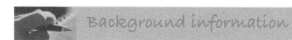

Litigation friend

In law neither children nor adults lacking mental capacity as defined by the Mental Capacity Act 2005 can bring or defend legal proceedings. Any such individual must have a litigation friend to act on their behalf. In proceedings under the Children Act 1989, children usually have an appointed Children's Guardian who performs the same function as a litigation friend. However, in legal proceedings where a Children's Guardian is not normally appointed, such as for a judicial review, these instances require the appointment of a litigation friend.

The Practice Direction on Litigation Friends, which provides instruction on court procedure, requires a litigation friend to conduct proceedings on behalf of a child or incapacitated adult 'fairly and competently' (Rule 21.4). This means that the person acting as the litigation friend must have no conflicting interests with that of the person they are representing. At all times they must conduct proceedings to the benefit of the child or adult in question. Usually a parent or guardian will be a suitable litigation friend to act on behalf of their child. Similarly, a long-term partner or carer would be considered an appropriate litigation friend for an adult who lacks capacity. Outside these categories someone with whom the child or incapacitated adult is and has been residing with for an extended period of time is also likely to be a suitable litigation friend.

The court has the power to direct that a person cannot act as a litigation friend for a particular individual or to terminate the appointment of a litigation friend if he or she fails to conduct legal proceedings 'fairly and competently'. Where a child reaches the age of 18 years or an adult regains capacity during the course of legal proceedings the appointment of the litigation friend will cease.

The Children (Leaving Care) Act 2000 increased the legal duties which local authorities owe to *looked after* children beyond the time they are actually in the direct care of Children's Services. Local authorities are required to assist young people about to leave their care to prepare for independent living and to support them thereafter to attain the goals set out in their Pathway Plans. Young people leaving care have lower educational attainments, higher rates of offending and a higher prevalence of mental health problems and teenage pregnancy than the rest of the population. These are often manifestations of adverse childhood experiences, sometimes compounded by multiple moves between foster carers and/or residential homes while being *looked after* by the local authority. For these reasons they require ongoing support from the local authority after leaving the care system. Social workers in Youth Offending Teams and in voluntary sector organisations offering youth services will often be working with young people who remain entitled to services from their local authority despite being 18 years of age or over. Therefore it is not just social workers in local authority Leaving Care Teams who will have responsibilities for care leavers.

Role of personal advisor

Although a personal advisor was appointed for J as far back as March 2004, almost ten months prior to J's release from Ashfield, it was J's contention that the advisor's position as an employee of the local authority was inconsistent with his role as J's personal advisor. Mr Wise, legal counsel instructed by the Howard League and acting for J as the claimant, argued before the High Court that the local authority should not have appointed Mr S, one of its employees, as a personal advisor as this created a conflict of interest. In addition,

Mr Wise contended that Mr S, a social worker, had misunderstood his role as a personal advisor and acted incorrectly in relation to the preparation of J's Pathway Plan. Mr Justice Munby dealt swiftly with Mr Wise's first point. There was, according to Justice Munby, nothing in the Children (Leaving Care) Act 2000 or in related government guidance which prohibited the appointment of an officer of the local authority as a personal advisor for a young person leaving the care of that same local authority. But, as Justice Munby conceded, in circumstances where the personal advisor was also a social worker employed by Children's Services, then there must be a clear understanding of the distinction between these two roles. In J's case, Mr S was both his personal advisor and a social worker on the Leaving Care Team. The functions of a personal advisor are set out in the box below. From this list it becomes obvious why there can potentially be a conflict of interest if personal advisors are also employed by Children's Services.

Key legislation

Children (Leaving Care) Act 2000

Regulation 12

(1) A personal adviser shall have the following functions [towards children leaving care] . . .

(2) The functions are -

    (a) to provide them with advice (including practical advice) and support

    (b) to participate in their assessment and the preparation of their pathway plans

    (c) to participate in reviews of their pathway plans

    (d) to liaise with the responsible local authority in the implementation of the pathway plan

    (e) to co-ordinate the provision of services to them, and to take reasonable steps to ensure that they make use of such services

    (f) to keep informed about their progress and wellbeing

    (g) to keep a written record of any of the adviser's contacts with them.

In documentary evidence presented to the High Court it became apparent that Mr S who had attended the Looked After Children Review Meeting on 1 April 2004, a point at which Pathway Planning should have commenced, had signed the record of the meeting as a member of the Leaving Care Team and not as J's personal advisor. In other words Mr S, and indeed other local authority staff, had conflated Mr S's role as a leaving care social worker with that of his role as J's personal advisor. Personal advisors have important tasks to perform together with and on behalf of the young person as set out in Regulation 12 in the box above. Specifically, personal advisors are required to 'participate' and 'liaise' with the local authority in drawing up the Pathway Plan; they are not responsible for actually producing the plan, as this is the duty of the local authority as the budget holder. In fact Mr S produced the pathway plan himself. This is a crucial point which goes to the core of Mr Wise's legal argument. Obviously there can be a conflict of interest between a local authority as the budget holder and the young person for whom they are providing the services which flow from the Pathway Plan. It is precisely to circumvent this potential clash in roles that Department of Health (2001c: 48) *Children (Leaving Care) Act 2000: Regulations and*

Guidance states that 'in order to avoid setting up conflicts of interest, the personal advisor should not also be the budget-holder'.

The local authority appointed one of its officers as J's personal advisor, but subsequently that personal advisor failed to ensure that he acted exclusively in this role and avoided taking on a role as a member of the Leaving Care Team, that is, as the budget-holder. As Justice Munby concluded, 'part of the personal advisor's role is, in a sense, to be the advocate or representative of the child in the course of the child's dealings with the local authority' (para. 30). It is for exactly this reason that the professional who conducts the assessment of the child's need and then draws up his or her Pathway Plan should not be the same one who acts as the child's personal advisor. It is simply not feasible for the same person to be the budget-holder responsible for allocating the resources required to meet the Pathway Plan while at the same time advocating on behalf of the child when there is disagreement about the assessment of need and provision of services. Since Department of Health (2001c) is guidance issued under s.7 of the Local Authority Social Services Act 1970 by contravening it, Mr S and his local authority employer had misapplied the law. For although policy guidance can be lawfully departed from in exceptional circumstances, there were none in this instance to justify such an extraordinary course of action.

Social workers perform a variety of statutory roles in relation to children and young people. These are outlined in primary legislation and often elaborated through secondary legislation and government-issued guidance. Social workers are well positioned in Children's Services and through their generic vocational training to perform a wide range of tasks within the ambit of different roles. However, practitioners need to be clear as to what capacity they are acting in with respect to a particular child or young person in a given instance. Guidance often lays down rules concerning which functions or roles can be undertaken by the same person. These rules are designed to prevent conflicts of interest and to meet the standards of best practice. A local authority social worker acting for the budget-holder who also then acts as an advocate for a young person in disagreement with the agency is hardly in a position to act non-prejudicially. The social worker's good intentions are unavoidably compromised. As was the case with J, such conflicts of interest can cause unnecessary mistrust between social workers and the people they seek to assist.

Working in partnership

Regulation 6 of the Children (Leaving Care) (England) Regulations 2001 identifies the people that the local authority must endeavour to consult and involve in assessing the child's needs and drawing up the pathway plan. This is reproduced in the box on the next page. Regulation 6 of the Children (Leaving Care) (England) Regulations 2001 is elaborated in policy guidance which states that, 'each young person will be central to drawing up their own plan, setting out their own goals and identifying with their personal advisor how the local authority will help them. The authority should work to ensure that the Plan is owned by the young person and is able to respond to their changing needs and ambitions' (Department of Health 2001c: 40). The guidance also notes that 'young people should be central to discussions and plans for their future. It will be exceptional for decisions to be made without their full participation' (Department of Health, 2001c: 27).

In March 2004 Mr S was appointed as J's personal advisor and attempted to meet with J who failed to keep nine separate appointments between March and May 2004. Indeed, it was not until J was detained at Ashfield Youth Offender Institution after a period on the run, when his address was unknown, that Mr S was finally able to meet him face-to-face.

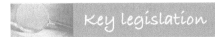

Key legislation

Children (Leaving Care) (England) Regulations 2001

Regulation 6

(1) The responsible local authority in carrying out an assessment and in preparing or reviewing a pathway plan, shall to the extent that it is reasonably practicable -

    (a) seek and have regard to the views of the child or young person to who it relates; and

    (b) take steps to enable him or her to attend and participate in any meetings at which his or her case is to be considered.

(2) the responsible local authority shall without delay provide the child or young person with copies of -

    (a) the results of his or her assessment,

    (b) his or her pathway plan,

    (c) each review of his or her pathway plan and shall so far as reasonably practicable ensure that the contents of each document are explained to him or her.

Records of *looked after* children reviews for 2004, which were presented to the court in evidence, consistently referred to the difficulty of working in partnership with J and his unwillingness to engage with the local authority or other agencies. Justice Munby accepted that J had demonstrated an uncooperative attitude despite repeated attempts by the local authority to help him (para. 33). However, in Justice Munby's opinion, this did not excuse the failure of Children's Services to appoint a personal advisor for J or draw up a Pathway Plan for him until months after these things should have been done. Nor did J's lack of engagement with the local authority justify its failure to share the contents of the Pathway Plan, which it apparently drew up without his input in November 2004. Finally, J's hostile attitude towards the local authority did not account for the inadequacy of either the assessment of his needs or the poor detail in the Pathway Plan. Justice Munby was particularly critical of the Pathway Plan, which reflected a set of aspirations rather than a series of practical actions carefully formulated to achieve measurable objectives in J's life on leaving care (para. 38–43).

In addressing the very real difficulties which confronted Children's Services in trying to work in partnership with J Mr Justice Munby conceded (para. 55) that he had:

> considerable sympathy with the local authority, faced as it is with a child who, as I readily acknowledge, has for a long time been, and who continues to be, remarkably uncooperative and unwilling to engage – indeed who on occasions refuses to engage – not merely with the local authority but also with a number of other agencies who are trying to help him.

Justice Munby then added a rider to this acknowledgement by pointing out (paras 56–7) that:

> The fact that a child is uncooperative and unwilling to engage, or even refuses to engage, is no reason for the local authority not to carry out its obligations under the Act and the Regulations. After all, a disturbed child's unwillingness to engage with those who are trying to help is often merely a part of the overall problems which justified the local authority's statutory intervention in the first place. The local authority must do its best . . . If the local authority is hindered in carrying out its duties under the Act and the Regulations by the child's lack of engagement then that should be documented, clearly and in detail, in the assessment and the pathway plan.

Throughout the court hearing, legal counsel for the local authority emphasised the diffi-culty which social workers had experienced trying to work with J. While partnership working with children is a basic requirement of safeguarding them and promoting their welfare, it is often easier said than done. Children and young people can on occasion be exceptionally uncooperative. Their behaviour may be attributable to: traumatic events in their childhoods, later adverse experiences in the care system, or simply opposition to what is being proposed by professionals. Inevitably such behaviour can make it all but impossible for social workers to constructively engage with the young person concerned. Despite this, practitioners must endeavour to follow guidance on partnership working with children to the best of their ability. Where the relationship has broken down entirely social workers should ensure that children and young people are still informed and kept up to date with any plans being made on their behalf. It remains the responsi-bility of the practitioner to enable and facilitate children and young people to re-engage with assessment and care planning processes once they feel able or motivated to do so.

Judgement in *R (on the application of J)* v. *Caerphilly County Borough Council*

Mr Justice Munby concluded that while J presented the local authority with particular challenges because of his uncooperative behaviour this did not account for or justify the failure of the local authority to comply with the requirements of the Children (Leaving Care) Act 2000 and its associated guidance. The judge found that the local authority had acted unlawfully and granted relief to J as the claimant. This relief required the local authority to produce a detailed assessment and Pathway Plan in accordance with the Act.

 Critical questions

1 This case focussed on the conflict of two roles which a social worker was required to perform in relation to a young person leaving care. Can you think of other situations in which as a practi-tioner you might be obliged to carry out two functions which have the potential to conflict with one another? How would you handle this kind of role conflict?

2 A major challenge for the social workers attempting to engage with J was his general lack of cooperation and his failure to attend appointments to discuss his future plans. These difficulties were clearly recorded on the case file. How realistic was the judge's ruling in this case? How can partnership working be achieved with a child or parent who does not want to engage with future planning?

 Perspectives

Looked after children reviews

The Children Act 1989 s.26(1) and (2) places a duty on local authorities to ensure that *looked after* children have a review within 4 weeks of their initial placement and then a second review within 3 months and are reviewed every 6 months thereafter. This innovation in the Children Act 1989 is designed to ensure that care planning takes place for *looked after* chil-dren and they are not simply abandoned or left to drift within the care system. Statutory reviews also constitute a regular forum at which the child (if of sufficient age and understand-ing), parents or guardians and professionals can discuss and progress the care plan.

Boylan and Braye (2006) conducted focus groups and individual interviews with *looked after* children to ascertain their experiences of attending statutory reviews. Many children said that they were talked about rather than talked to during the meeting. As one young person put it, the review is 'a place where your social worker and them bosses get to talk about you to see where you're going to end up in the future'. Another young person complained, 'they talk about you as if you're not there – it's like they're talking about you but they don't realise you're there' (Boylan and Braye, 2006: 238). In another study conducted by Thomas and O'Kane (1999: 226) while 67% of *looked after* children reported being listened to during review meetings, only 28% thought they could substantively influence the outcome. The same research revealed that only 17% of children liked going to review meetings, with most describing them as 'boring', 'scary', 'horrible', 'intimidating' and 'upsetting' (Thomas and O'Kane, 1999: 226-7). At the same time, children from these studies expressed the view that they valued the opportunity to participate in decisions about their own future.

Even the use of child advocates at review meetings to assist children's participation was problematic as children were often not given the opportunity to build up a relationship with the advocate, who could be a different person at each of their reviews. Child advocates could only offer limited confidentiality and would disclose what had been said to them by a young person if he or she appeared to be at risk of harm. This served to inhibit children from fully confiding in their advocates in relation to statutory reviews. One young person expressed the thoughts of many *looked after* children when she told the researchers, 'we just want somebody who's going to listen and, like, at least . . . make an effort to understand' (Boylan and Braye, 2006: 243).

CASE 5

Re MJ (A Child) (Adoption Order or Special Guardianship Order) [2007] 1 FLR 691

Importance of the case

This explores adoption and special guardianship. It considers the nature of consent by birth parents to adoption and what is meant by the child's welfare in the context of adoption.

History of the case

This was an appeal by a mother to the Civil Division of the Court of Appeal against an order for adoption of her 3-year-old son made by a County Court.

Facts of the case

M gave birth to MJ in June 2003. Both MJ's birth mother and father were alcohol and drug dependent. MJ was born, having suffered growth retardation in the womb, and was subsequently admitted to hospital on a number of occasions due to failure to thrive. As a result in December 2003 the child was moved into foster care by Social Services with the mother's agreement. Six months later, in June 2004 the local authority commenced care proceedings. At this time SJ, the mother's half-sister indicated to the local authority that if the mother was unable to care for her son then she would be willing to adopt him. Throughout 2004 and into early 2005 the mother had regular contact with her son, but was often under the influence of alcohol. In March 2005 the local authority was granted a Care Order on the basis of a care plan submitted to the court which provided for the rehabilitation of the child with his mother on condition that she successfully completed treatment and detoxi-fication programmes. The care plan included a contingency plan whereby failure by the mother to end her drug and alcohol addiction would result in her child being placed for adoption with SJ, who was M's maternal half-sister. In the event, the mother was found to have taken heroin in May 2005 after the completion of the first stage of her treatment pro-gramme and this triggered the adoption proceedings. The child was moved from his foster placement into the care of his aunt SJ in August 2005. During the adoption proceedings at the County Court the mother conceded that she was not in a position to take care of her son and that his welfare was best served by remaining with his aunt. However, she opposed the making of the Adoption Order and instead had requested that the court make a Special Guardianship Order which would not deprive the mother of parental responsibility for her son. When the County Court dispensed with the mother's consent and made an Adoption Order despite her objection, she appealed against the decision to the Court of Appeal.

Key people in the case

MJ – 3-year-old boy
M – mother of MJ
SJ – maternal half-sister of M and aunt of MJ
Dr Wenban-Smith – forensic psychologist
Dr Jamil – consultant psychiatrist

Discussion of the case

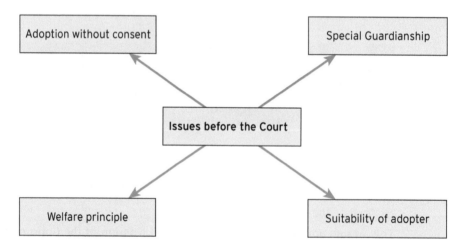

Adoption without consent

The Adoption and Children Act 2002 repealed the Adoption Act 1976 and introduced a new two-stage format in the adoption process. This comprised placement for adoption and of proceedings for adoption itself. The idea of having two distinct stages for an adop-tion was to prevent birth parents from withdrawing their consent at the last moment just as the adoption was about to go through. This was not uncommon under the old Adop-tion Act 1976, with devastating consequences for children who had become attached to their prospective adopters. Consent for adoption is only required from parents holding parental responsibility. Therefore, unmarried fathers who have not acquired parental responsibility through any of the available legal routes have no rights in the adoption process and their consent to the adoption is not necessary. The Adoption and Children

Act 2002 also makes provision for a situation in which parents with parental responsibility refuse consent to an adoption when this refusal is plainly detrimental to the welfare of their child. The adoption agency, which may be the local authority or a private or charitable registered adoption agency, can place a child for adoption:

- with the consent of parents or guardians who have parental responsibility (s.19);
- with a Placement Order if parental consent is refused or there is a dispute regarding the proposed adoption (s.21);
- where the local authority does not hold a Care Order but the threshold for a Care Order is met and the local authority has successfully applied for a Placement Order (s.21);
- where the child has no parent or guardian (s.21).

This means that if parents with parental responsibility consent to the adoption of their child, he or she can be placed for adoption. The consent given by the parents under s.19 can be in respect of specific named adopters or a general consent that their child can be placed for adoption. In the latter case the adoption agency has discretion in identifying suitable adoptive parents for the child. Where birth parents do not consent to the adoption of their child the Adoption and Children Act 2002 makes provision for this consent to be dispensed with. The power of the State to deprive parents permanently of their children is plainly one which interferes with article 8 of the European Convention on Human Rights, which guarantees citizens of signatory States respect for their private and family life. Although article 8 is a qualified right which can be justifiably contravened by the State, in order to ensure that the Adoption and Children Act 2002 is compliant with the Convention the nature of consent is also legally defined by the statute and is set out in the box below.

Key legislation

Adoption and Children Act 2002

s.52(1) The court cannot dispense with the consent of any parent or guardian of a child, to the child being placed for adoption or to the making of an Adoption Order in respect of the child unless the court is satisfied that –

    (a) the parent or guardian cannot be found or is incapable of giving consent, or

    (b) the welfare of the child requires that consent to be dispensed with.

- s.52(5) defines consent as 'given unconditionally with full understanding of what is involved'.
- Reg.14 of the Adoption Agencies Regulations 2005 requires adoption agencies to provide counselling to parents to ensure they are fully informed of the consequences of giving their consent.
- s.52(7) provides that consent must be given in writing on the prescribed form.
- s.102 requires that parental consent must be witnessed by an officer of CAFCASS.
- s.52(3) makes consent given by a mother within 6 weeks of giving birth to the child ineffective.
- s.52(4) provides that the withdrawal of consent will be ineffective after the application for an Adoption Order.
- s.47 provides that exceptionally where there has been a material change in circumstances the court may give permission for a parent with parental responsibility to oppose the making of an Adoption Order. Permission is subject to the paramount consideration of the child's welfare.

In the present case M, the mother, had signed a 'contract of expectations' with Social Services agreeing to the stipulation in the care plan which would result in her son being placed for adoption with SJ, her half-sister, in the event of M's failure to successfully complete the prescribed treatment programmes and thereafter stay drug free. During the County Court case the judge had praised the mother's decision not to contest the Care Order and her recognition that her child's best interests lay in being cared for by the mother's sister SJ. The County Court judge observed 'her acceptance at the end of her evidence that MJ's interests and welfare dictated that he should remain with SJ was a courageous and selfless act' (para. 11). Yet, despite what had appeared to be the mother's consent to the contingency plan, it transpired in the County Court that she had always harboured the expectation that she would ultimately care for her own child. Consequently, although she had originally consented to the adoption of her son by her sister, when it came to the point she was not willing to accede to this course of action.

It was established by the County Court that while the boy had been moved to live with his aunt in August 2005 after the instigation of adoption proceedings, by January 2006 the mother had informed the local authority that she no longer consented to the adoption. At the same time she admitted to the local authority that she was not in a position to care for her son herself. By April 2006 there had been a further change in M's position as she expressed doubts to the local authority about her sister's ability to take care of the child and meet his emotional needs. The legal effect of the mother's unexpected withdrawal of consent was to scupper what should have been the final hearing for the adoption on 20 and 21 April 2006. In addition to this the mother had not informed her sister of her change of mind, despite the fact that the two sisters were in fortnightly contact with each other. This state of affairs was described by the County Court judge as having 'a devastating impact' on their relationship, making contact between the two sisters 'strained and difficult from the adults' perspectives'. Furthermore, the behaviour of M during her periods of contact with her son and her sister after January 2005 had 'led to feelings of great insecurity and anxiety, and a belief that (the mother) will try and undermine MJ's placement' (para. 11).

Here was a situation in which MJ's birth mother had at first consented to the adoption of her son by her half-sister (albeit as a contingency measure), had then sought to withdraw that consent and subsequently questioned the suitability of SJ to be the adoptive parent of her son. This all occurred after the boy had been placed with his aunt preparative to the adoption going ahead with the mother's consent. In the present case the original application for adoption was made under the old Adoption Act 1976 and the mother was permitted to oppose in court the making of the Adoption Order. Consequently MJ, as the 3-year-old child concerned, automatically became a party to the proceedings. His best interests were represented by a Children's Guardian from CAFCASS who is always appointed if a birth parent does not consent to an adoption. As the prospective adopter, SJ was also made a party to the court case. The child's unmarried father did not have parental responsibility and was therefore not a party to the proceedings. The birth mother, who was refusing to give consent to her child's adoption, was a party to all the legal proceedings regarding the adoption.

The mother's unanticipated change of mind and her decision to oppose her son's adoption at a point in time when he had already been placed for adoption was precisely the situation that the new two-step process introduced by the Adoption and Children Act 2002 is designed to prevent. Under the Adoption and Children Act 2002 if each parent with parental responsibility consents to the adoption, then the child can simply be placed with prospective adopters. However, where a parent with parental responsibility refuses to consent to the adoption or the child is the subject of a Care Order the local authority must in the first instance apply for a Placement Order. It is at this court hearing that the judges consider evidence as to whether a parent's consent should be dispensed with. This means that legal argument over the adoption is heard at an earlier stage in the proceedings (than under the Adoption Act 1976) and before an application is actually made for the adoption itself. If a parent's consent is dispensed with at this stage then the local authority can proceed to the second stage of the process, which is to apply to the court for the Adoption Order itself. It is this latter order which actually permits the child to be adopted by new parents. The box below outlines the initial placement phase of this new two-step process.

Key legislation

Adoption and Children Act 2002

Placement for Adoption

1 An adoption agency has parental responsibility where it is authorised to place a child for adoption or a Placement Order is in force (s.19).

2 Prospective adopters have parental responsibility when the child is placed with them.

3 If a Placement Order is in force it supersedes any care, supervision or S.8 orders (s.29(3)).

4 The court may make a Contact Order for a child placed or authorised to be placed (s.26).

5 An adoption agency may refuse contact with parents and relatives or friends if necessary to safeguard or promote the child's welfare (s.27(2)).

6 Residence Orders and Special Guardianship Orders can be applied for during adoption proceedings (s.47).

7 Children authorised to be placed for adoption are categorised as *looked after* and thus have legal entitlements under the Children Act 1989 (s.53).

8 No one can remove children who have been placed for adoption except the adoption agency (s.30).

9 No one can remove a child accommodated by the local authority during an application for a Placement Order (s.30).

10 Exceptionally a parent or guardian may remove a child placed for adoption if that child is not subject to a Care Order and they withdraw consent (ss. 31–32).

To prevent a birth parent derailing the adoption hearing, under the Adoption and Children Act 2002 once a Placement Order is made or if parents with parental responsibility consent up to the point of the local authority's application for adoption, the parents will not be permitted to oppose the adoption of their child. At least they cannot do so unless there has been an extraordinary change in circumstances such as to persuade the court to make a parent with parental responsibility a party to the final adoption hearing under s.47 of the Adoption and Children Act 2002. Therefore, under this statute, adoption hearings are normally heard without being contested. The box on the next page sets out the effects of an Adoption Order.

Key legislation

Adoption and Children Act 2002

Making an Adoption Order

1 Adoption Orders may not be made for someone who is or has been married or is not under 18 years (s.47(9) and s.49(4)).

2 Adoption by a married, unmarried or same sex couple requires that at least one of them must be domiciled in the British Islands and have been habitually resident for one year, both must be over 21 years or one over 18 years if birth parent (s.50 and s.144(4)).

3 In determining the suitability of a couple to adopt a child regard will be had to the stability and permanence of their relationship (s.45).

4 If the adoption is by a single person then he or she must be:
   - over 21 years, not married and domiciled in the British Islands
   - partner of the birth parent
   - separated from their partner
   - person whose partner due to ill-health is incapable of making any application (s.51).

5 An adoption agency must submit to the court a report on the suitability of the applicants and on any other matters relevant to the welfare checklist for adoption (s.43).

6 An application for adoption can be made when a child has lived with prospective adopters for ten weeks after initial placement with them (s.42).

7 Before making an Adoption Order the court must consider whether arrangements for the child's contact with any other person should be made (s.46(6)).

8 The parent or guardian must consent to the making of an Adoption Order or that consent can be dispensed with (s.47(2)).

9 Parents or guardians cannot oppose the making of an Adoption Order unless they have the leave of the court. Leave will only be given if there has been a change since the consent of the parent or guardian to the placement for adoption (s.47(7)).

10 An Adoption Order discharges all other orders made under the Children Act 1989.

11 An Adoption Order confers parental responsibility upon the adoptive parents and extinguishes the parental responsibility of everyone else including the birth parents (s.46).

12 An Adoption Order treats the adopted child in law as if he or she were a child born to the adoptive parents (s.67).

For children *in care* adoption has become a major aspect of permanency planning. The adoption process is not just a matter for social workers employed by adoption agencies. Any practitioner working with children *in care* will need to consider the possibility of adoption where rehabilitation back with their families appears unlikely and long-term arrangements for their care need to be made. At the same time, social workers need to appreciate the traumatic decision which those with parental responsibility are being asked to make. For some birth parents sustained partnership working can help to prepare them for surrendering their legal relationship with their child so as to ensure that he or she receives stable, consistent and suitable care. Given the magnitude of the consequences for birth parents when their children are put up for adoption, it is not surprising that a number seek to oppose the adoption or initially consent and then seek to withdraw it. For all of these reasons the Department of Health (2001d: Appendix D) *National Adoption Standards* requires social workers and allied professionals to attend to the needs of birth parents.

 Key guidance

National Adoption Standards

Appendix D

1 Agencies will work with birth parents and significant birth family members to enable effective plans to be made and implemented for their child(ren).

2 Every effort will be made to ensure that birth parents and significant birth family members have a full understanding of the adoption process, the legal implications, and their rights.

3 Birth parents will have access to a support worker independent of the child's social worker from the time adoption is identified as the plan for the child.

4 Birth parents and birth families (including siblings) will have access to a range of support services both before and after adoption, including information about local and national support groups and services.

5 Birth parents will have the opportunity to give their account of events, and to see and comment on what is written about them in reports for the adoption panel, and in information passed to the adopters.

6 Birth parents and families will be supported to provide information that the adopted child needs.

7 Where it is in the child's best interest for there to be ongoing links, including contact, with birth parents and families (including siblings separated by adoption) birth families will be involved in discussions about how best to achieve this and helped to fulfil agreed plans, e.g. through practical or financial support.

Section 46(6) of the Adoption Act 2002 requires the court to make provision for continued contact between adopted children and their birth families where this is consistent with their welfare and does not jeopardise the adoption itself. As the standards set out in the box above make clear, birth parents remain entitled to support and services after the Placement and Adoption Orders are made. As in many other areas of practice, social workers involved in adoption proceedings may find themselves not only acting in opposition to birth parents, but actively seeking to dispense with their consent to their child's adoption. It is in recognition of this untenable position that the *National Adoption Standards* require birth parents to have a support worker, who is not the child's social worker, during the adoption process. While only around 3,000 Adoption Orders are made annually, it is not a narrow specialism within social work, but an important consideration for practitioners involved in permanency planning for children *in care*.

Suitability of adopter

At a crucial stage in the adoption process M not only withdrew her consent, but began to question the suitability of her half-sister to bring up MJ. Those who wish to be considered as adoptive parents are subject to a rigorous process of assessment under the Suitability of

Adopters Regulations 2005 SI 2005/1712 which is a statutory instrument issued under the Children and Adoption Act 2002. This includes:

- Interviews with prospective adopters exploring their relationships, health and lifestyle.
- Inspection of the prospective adopters' home.
- Interviews with referees provided by the prospective adopters.

On completion of this stage a report is written for consideration by the agency's Adoption Panel. It is this body, described in the box below, which approves or rejects the application of a person to become an adopter.

Background information

The Adoption Panel

Each adoption agency is legally required to set up an Adoption Panel comprising two experienced social workers in childcare, a local councillor, a medical expert and a number of lay people, to include if possible one adopter and one adopted individual. This panel obtains wide-ranging assessments on the birth parents or guardians, children and prospective adopters in order to make recommendations regarding:

1 Whether adoption is in the best interests of the child.

2 The suitability of individuals or couples to be adopters.

3 The suitability of a particular prospective adoptive parent for a specific child.

4 The post-adoption support which should be provided.

The Adoption Panel is required to make its recommendations in writing to the adoption agency and under Department of Health (2003a: para. 13.3) this decision must also be conveyed to the child, the parents or guardian and the prospective adopters. Since adoption requires a court order, the decision of the adoption agency will ultimately be subject to that of the court.

On approval of the applicant by the Adoption Panel discussions will take place between the adoption agency, Children's Services and the approved adopters in order to match them with children awaiting adoption. SJ would have already gone through this process and been approved as an adopter before the adoption proceedings commenced. For this reason it was unlikely that M's insinuations that her half-sister was an unsuitable parent for her son would succeed. Indeed, M produced no convincing evidence in court to substantiate her allegations against SJ. Aside from the established suitability of SJ as an adoptive parent, the court still had to deliberate on whether there was an effective match between SJ as an adoptive parent and MJ as a child awaiting adoption. This requirement is detailed in the *National Adoption Standards* which are excerpted in the box below.

Key guidance

Adoption: National Minimum Standards

Department of Health (2003a) *Adoption: National Minimum Standards* sets out standards for adoption agencies which are responsible for recruiting potential adopters. This guidance requires adoption agencies to ensure that:

Para. 2.2 Children are matched with adopters who best meet their assessed needs. Wherever possible this will be with a family which:
   (a) reflects their ethnic origin, cultural background, religion and language; and
   (b) allows them to live with brothers and sisters unless this will not meet their individually assessed needs.

Para. 2.3 In matching children with approved adopters, the adoption agency takes into account the view and feelings of the child as far as these can be ascertained based on his age and understanding, the child's care plan and recent written assessments of the child and his birth family, potential adoptive parents and their children.

Para. 4.1 Prospective adopters are involved in a formal, thorough and comprehensive assessment, preparation and approval process.

SJ had been formally assessed and approved by the Adoption Panel and as MJ's aunt met the requirements of matching set out in para. 2.2 of the Department of Health's (2003a) statutory guidance. At the time of the adoption hearing before the County Court MJ was just 3 years old and was therefore not of sufficient age or understanding to participate meaningfully in the ultimate decision about his future. However, MJ was closely observed and account taken of the strength of his attachment to his aunt and the stress he appeared to suffer when there was confusion about his primary carer or place of residence. In this regard the County Court judge observed (para. 12):

> Turning to MJ, currently he is a vulnerable child, small for his age, and despite his many changes of carer, had developed a strong and secure attachment to SJ, whose parenting skills are obviously of a high calibre. Any disruption of that attachment would have a highly detrimental effect upon him . . .

Both the County Court and the Court of Appeal on the submission of reports found SJ to be an entirely suitable prospective adopter for MJ. Although M had questioned SJ's parental ability, this was not questioned by either court. Confronted by the weight of evidence which deemed SJ a fit adoptive parent, in the end M conceded that MJ should live with SJ. But her legal counsel argued that this arrangement should be under a Special Guardianship Order which would preserve M's parental responsibility as the birth mother and not under an Adoption Order which would extinguish it.

Special Guardianship

Special Guardianship Orders were created under the Adoption and Children Act 2002 and are principally designed to cater for older *looked after* children and some children from ethnic minority backgrounds who do not want to sever the legal relationship with their birth parents. Unlike with an Adoption Order, which is irrevocable, there remains the possibility of discharge or variation of a Special Guardianship Order by subsequent court proceedings. The Adoption and Children Act 2002 amended the Children Act 1989 by creating the new status of Special Guardianship through the insertion of sections 14A through to 14G. The main changes introduced by the amendment are set out in the box on next page. As the creation of Special Guardianship Orders is by way of amendment to the Children Act 1989, a court considering this order is bound by all the provisions of the Children Act 1989. The court will therefore be applying the welfare checklist, the *no order principle*, the *non-delay principle* and has the discretion to consider the making of any other order provided for by the Children Act 1989.

Key legislation

Adoption and Children Act 2002

Special Guardianship provisions

1 The special guardian must be over 18 years and not a parent of the child (s.14A).

2 S.8 orders can continue concurrently with a Special Guardianship Order.

3 An individual must notify the local authority if he or she intends to apply for Special Guardianship and the local authority must then investigate that individual's suitability and prepare a report for the court (s.14A(8)).

4 A Special Guardianship Order gives parental responsibility to the applicant which he or she may exercise, but to the exclusion of any other person with parental responsibility apart from another special guardian (s.14C).

5 The local authority is required to make counselling, advice and financial support available to special guardians on assessment of their needs (s.14F).

As various provisions of the Adoption and Children Act 2002 had come into force during the period over which the events concerning MJ took place, it became possible for M to ask the court to make a Special Guardianship Order as against an Adoption Order. The White Paper *Adoption: A New Approach* makes clear that the intention of the Adoption and Children Act 2002 is to create increased opportunities for permanence for *looked after* children. Special Guardianship was to be an alternative route whereby children for whom adoption was not suitable could still avail of a legally secure long-term placement. Department for Education and Skills (2005b: 4) *Special Guardianship Regulations 2005: Special Guardianship Regulations* issued under s.7 of the Local Authority Social Services Act 1970 details the purpose of a Special Guardianship Order, which is to:

- Give the carer clear responsibility for all aspects of caring for the child and for taking the decisions to do with their upbringing.
- Provide a firm foundation on which to build a lifelong permanent relationship between the child and their carer.
- Be legally secure.
- Preserve the basic link between the child and their birth family.
- Be accompanied by access to a full range of support services including, where appropriate, financial support.

It is clear from the White Paper and statutory guidance that the intention of Special Guardianship is to create permanence and stability for a child who for one reason or another cannot continue to live with his or her birth parents. A Special Guardianship Order in favour of SJ would give her parental responsibility for the child while the mother would still retain her parental responsibility. However, under s.14C inserted into the Children Act 1989 the birth parent's responsibility can only be exercised subject to that of the Special Guardian's. Thus SJ would be in a position to make decisions about the child's welfare without reference to his mother, and if necessary to overrule her. But, on hearing evidence, the suspicion of both the County Court and the Court of Appeal was that the mother would seek to use her retention of parental responsibility in ways which would disrupt her sister's relationship with MJ and create divided loyalties for the child (para. 11). Additionally the mother would be in a position to go back to court at a later date to seek the variation or discharge of the Special Guardianship Order, albeit subject to the court's permission. This plainly could not occur were an Adoption Order made, as such an order is irrevocable and extinguishes the birth mother's rights as a parent.

Under s.17(1) of the Children Act 1989 local authorities have a statutory duty to safeguard and promote the welfare of *children in need,* and where consistent with this, to promote their upbringing within their own families. In situations where children in need are living away from their family home, but are not in local authority accommodation, Sch. 2 (para. 10) of the Children Act 1989 applies. This provision requires local authorities to provide a range of services to support rehabilitative interventions to facilitate family reunification. In the present case, MJ was living away from his parental home and residing with his aunt under a Care Order. Social Services Inspectorate and Department of Health (1995: para. 2.16–7) *The Challenge of Partnership in Child Protection* defines 'family' as consisting essentially of birth parents and their partners, siblings and grandparents. Department of Health (2003a: 5) *Adoption: National Minimum Standards* reiterates that 'it is best for children where possible to be brought up by their own birth family'. Preference is given to children being brought up by their birth parents both by statute and common law. In the present case the court was being asked to adjudicate on whether MJ should be permanently removed from the care of his birth mother to that of his aunt. This dilemma can only be resolved by reference to the welfare checklist for adoption proceedings.

Welfare principle

While emphasising the importance of children being brought up by their birth families, Department of Health (2003a: 5) *Adoption: National Minimum Standards* stresses that 'the child's welfare, safety and needs will be at the centre of the adoption process'. This child-focussed approach to adoption is also highlighted in Department for Education and Skills (2005c: 1) *Adoption and Children Act 2002: Adoption Guidance* issued under s.7 of the Local Authority Social Services Act 1970, which directs that 'the focus is firmly on the needs of the child, whose interests will be paramount in all decisions relating to adoption'. In order to balance the preference for children to be brought up by their birth parents against the imperative to protect them, the Adoption and Children Act 2002, like the Children Act 1989 contains a welfare checklist. The court must consider each item in the list and if necessary weigh one against another. The two checklists are very similar, but an important difference is the obligation upon the court contained in s.1(2) of the Adoption and Children Act 2002 to consider the likely effect of the adoption on the child *throughout his or her life*. Like the Children Act 1989 the Adoption and Children Act 2002 also incorporates the *non-delay* and *no order principles*.

Key legislation

Adoption and Children Act 2002

s.1(2) The paramount consideration of the court or adoption agency must be the child's welfare, throughout his life

s.1(3) The court or adoption agency must at all times bear in mind that, in general, any delay in coming to the decision is likely to prejudice the child's welfare s.1(4) The court or adoption agency must have regard to the following matters (among others) –

(a) The child's ascertainable wishes and feelings regarding the decision (considered in the light of the child's age and understanding)

(b) The child's particular needs

(c) The likely effect on the child (throughout his life) of having ceased to be a member of the original family and become an adopted person

(d) The child's age, sex, background and any of the child's characteristics which the court or agency considers relevant

(e) Any harm (within the meaning of the Children Act 1989) which the child has suffered or is at risk of suffering

(f) The relationship the child has with relatives and any other relevant person in relation to whom the court or agency considers the relationship to be relevant,

  (i) the likelihood of any such relationship continuing and the value to the child of its doing so

  (ii) the ability and willingness of any of the child's relatives, or of any such person, to provide the child with a secure environment in which the child can develop, and otherwise to meet the child's needs

  (iii) the wishes and feelings of any of the child's relatives, or of any such person, regarding the child

s.1(5) In placing the child for adoption, the adoption agency must give due consideration to the child's religious persuasion, racial origin and cultural and linguistic background

s.1(6) The court or adoption agency must always consider the whole range of powers available to it in the child's case (whether under this Act or the Children Act 1989); and the court must not make any order under this Act unless it considers that making the order would be better for the child than not doing so.

Adoption proceedings fall under family proceedings and therefore the menu of orders principle applies, meaning that a court can make any order even if the original application is for adoption. In the present case all parties to the proceedings before the Court of Appeal perceived the issue to be whether SJ's care of MJ should be under an order for adoption or one for Special Guardianship. It was of course in the power of the court to go beyond this sort of consensus and consider other living arrangements for the child, for example a Residence Order in favour of SJ. This would result in SJ obtaining parental responsibility for MJ and MJ residing with her. In the present case the Court of Appeal was in agreement with both parties that the only feasible arrangement for MJ, which would both promote and safeguard his welfare, was living with his aunt either under an Adoption or Special Guardianship Order. Consequently no other living arrangements or alternative orders were discussed at the court hearing.

Dr Wenban-Smith, a chartered forensic psychologist, was instructed to assess 'MJ's future placement needs, his attachments, and further contact needs'. A second expert witness, Dr Jamil, a consultant psychiatrist was jointly instructed by the parties to the County Court case to assess the mother's parental capacity and other relevant matters. The Children's Guardian appointed to represent MJ also produced a report for the court detailing his best interests. The local authority social worker and SJ as the prospective adopter also gave oral evidence at the original County Court hearing on the adoption. The written and oral evidence given by Dr Wenban-Smith, the Children's Guardian, the local authority social worker and the prospective adopter all indicated that MJ despite having a number of different carers had formed a strong attachment to SJ. Precisely because of his past and the changes of mind of his mother, who apparently still harboured a belief that SJ would be a temporary caretaker for her son who would eventually return to M's care, it was agreed that MJ required stability and security of placement.

Evidence from Dr Jamil highlighted and corroborated the perception of the local authority that M was an extremely impulsive, though intelligent, woman, who was liable to undermine the stability of MJ's placement if the opportunity presented itself. Commenting on M's presentation of herself during the proceedings in the County Court, the judge concluded, 'she displayed little insight in her evidence until the very end of the consequences of removal of MJ from SJ's care . . . it was clear in her evidence that this mother sees herself very much as a victim, and much of her evidence focused on her own feelings of rejection and isolation from her family' (para. 11). The County Court established that M was not a suitable carer for MJ and indeed, as M conceded in court, she was still not in a position to care for M although she was refusing her consent to his adoption.

The County Court judge then turned to the welfare checklist of which one item at s.1(4)(c) requires the court to consider 'the likely effect on the child (throughout his life) of having ceased to be a member of the original family'. In this instance, as the judge noted, since MJ would be adopted by his mother's maternal half-sister he would continue to be an integral part of his own biological family. The one change, however, of an Adoption Order would be that legally his aunt would become his mother and his biological mother would become his aunt. As the County Court judge acknowledged 'this was not an insignificant factor' (para. 16). But set against this was the consensus of all parties to the court case, with the exception of M, that 'notwithstanding those factors, the guardian, the local authority and the jointly instructed expert Dr Wenban-Smith, all maintain that adoption is the placement option which most accords with MJ's welfare' (para. 16).

As the case of MJ demonstrates the *welfare principle* is a legal concept which has wide applicability and can be invoked to resolve a variety of dilemmas. It is not a single consideration for the court, but is broken down into constituent parts by the welfare checklist. This list directs both social workers and the courts to consider a range of matters which collectively comprise the welfare of the child. It is by weighing the different elements of the welfare checklist against one another that the court can arrive at a considered decision which serves the best interests of the child. Social workers involved in permanency planning for *looked after* children must be conversant with the welfare checklist if they are to formulate effective long-term care plans and produce convincing evidence in court when these are opposed by parents or others.

Judgement in *Re MJ (A Child) (Adoption Order or Special Guardianship Order)*

Having revisited the legal reasoning behind the original judgement of the County Court, the three justices presiding over the Court of Appeal case agreed unanimously with its decision and dismissed the appeal by M against the granting of an Adoption Order.

 Critical questions

1 Adoption of a child without the birth mother's consent was at the heart of this case. In a context of such complete disagreement between a social worker and a parent, how would you manage partnership working?

2 The court was asked to deliberate on whether it would be in the child's best interests to grant an Adoption Order or a Special Guardianship Order. What do you perceive to be the advantages and disadvantages of these orders for parents, special guardians and children? How might your judgement be affected by the different characteristics of the parents, special guardians and child, such as age, ethnic background, and so forth? Are there particular family circumstances in which you perceive a Special Guardianship Order to have particular advantages over an Adoption Order for those concerned?

3 In this case both social workers and ultimately the judge had to weigh different considerations in the welfare checklist against one another. Do you think they got the balance right? If so why; if not, what do you think would have been the correct balancing of the elements in the welfare checklist in the Adoption and Children Act 2002?

Perspectives

Practitioners and the Adoption and Children Act 2002

The White Paper *Adoption: A New Approach*, which preceded the Adoption and Children Act 2002, highlighted the Government's conviction that children are best brought up in a family and not within the care system. To this end Department of Health (2000f) *Adoption: A New Approach* explicitly states that the Adoption and Children Act 2002 is intended to:

- Increase the number of *looked after* children adopted.
- Reduce the time children spend in the care system before being adopted.
- Increase the pool of potential adopters.
- Reduce delays in the adoption process.
- Minimise breakdowns in adoption by providing support to all those involved in the adoption process.

The Government also issued guidance setting out targets for the achievement of these goals. For example, LAC (2001) 33 requires local authorities to ensure that once adoption is deemed in the best interests of a *looked after* child, 95% of them should be placed for adoption within one year of that decision being made (Department of Health, 2001a).

Sagar and Hitchings (2007) interviewed social workers from three teams dealing with adoption about their experiences of working under the Adoption and Children Act 2002 and the impact of Government targets. Generally social workers considered that targets were 'totally unrealistic'. One observed that they are 'not in the interests of the child . . . we are not making up school numbers . . . we are dealing with little people here and we are not seeing the other side - the breakdowns' (Sagar and Hitchings, 2007: 203). Social workers also expressed concern that prospective adopters often demonstrated misconceptions about the children available for adoption as few of them were infants and many of them had complex needs. One practitioner observed that, 'parents have fairly standard sets of ways of trying to manage behaviour and for children who have been abused and neglected that can often make the situation worse . . . [adopters need] a lot of training on how to deal with a lot of behavioural issues and to deal with the emotional trauma that lies underneath' (Sagar and Hitchings, 2007: 205-6).

Social workers also expressed concern that insufficient training and support services were available to prospective and existing adopters. One practitioner revealed 'we try and work with the families and the children but if we can't resolve the issues then we pass them on to the Children and Adult Mental Health Service . . . which is now acknowledging that they haven't got the skills to deal with kids who have attachment disorders. The next step up is therapy . . . and then we are into resource issues – it's very expensive' (Sagar and Hitchings, 2007: 206). These findings also echo those of Thoburn (2003: 400) who concluded:

> If the need to be adopted and to be adopted quickly takes precedence over other needs, it is inevitable that some children will be placed with families who cannot meet some important identified needs. There is ample evidence that some children are harmed by avoidable delay. But there is also evidence that children are harmed when they are placed too quickly with families who cannot meet important identified needs, and their expressed wishes are overruled. Both delayed placements and rushed placements can result in avoidable placement breakdown . . .

Learning points

- Children may be in the care system either under voluntary agreement with their parents or due to compulsion as the result of a court order.
- Working in partnership with children and parents is an essential aspect of practice even when there is disagreement between them and the professionals concerned.
- Local authorities have a range of legal duties towards *looked after* children and children leaving care which are set out in the Children Act 1989 as amended.
- Agency resources and government policy influence decisions about a child's placement and have to be set alongside promoting a child's welfare.
- Social workers are responsible for safeguarding and promoting the welfare of *looked after* children and need to have the skills to effectively investigate allegations of abuse.
- Social workers gathering evidence from children for court proceedings must also consider their therapeutic needs, while not prejudicing the evidence.
- National Minimum Standards for fostering and adoption provide a benchmark for social work practice and service provision.
- Both parents and children may act in ways which are harmful to themselves or others. At times it is necessary to act directly against their wishes in seeking a court order for compulsory intervention in their lives.
- Social work activity which takes place against the wishes of parents and children must be compliant with the European Convention on Human Rights.
- The *welfare*, *non-delay* and *no order* principles underpin the Adoption and Children Act 2002 as well as the Children Act 1989.

Further reading

Allen, N. (2003) *Making Sense of the New Adoption Law: A Guide for Social and Welfare Services,* Lyme Regis: Russell House. This short book provides an introduction to and overview of the Adoption and Children Act 2002. It explains the main provisions of this statute.

Frazer, L. and Selwyn, J. (2005) 'Why are we waiting? The demography of adoption for children of black, Asian and black mixed parentage in England', *Child and Family Social Work* 10: 135–47. This article examines the problems encountered by children from ethnic minority backgrounds in the care system. In particular it focusses on problems around adoption and permanency planning.

Morgan, R. and Lindsay, M. (2006) *Young People's Views on Leaving Care: What Young People in and formerly in Residential and Foster Care think about Leaving Care,* London: Commission for Social Care Inspection. This publication presents the views of *looked after* children and care leavers on their experiences of the care system.

Smith, F. (2004) *Fostering Now: Current Law including Regulation, Guidance and Standards,* London: British Agency for Adoption and Fostering. This publication provides an easy-to-follow overview of the law relating to fostering. It also presents information on the main government issued guidance relating to this area of practice.

Useful websites

www.everychildmatters.gov.uk This is a government website which also has a section specifically on fostering.

www.baaf.org.uk This is the site of the British Association for Adoption and Fostering. It provides easily accessible material on both adoption and fostering.

http://nchacti01.uuhost.uk.uu.net/carelaw/ This is the site of Carelaw which provides information for children and young people in the care system. It offers downloads of easy-to-follow guides on the rights of *looked after* children.

www.childrensociety.org.uk/ This site is run by the Children's Society, which is a national charity working to safeguard children and enhance childhood. It is a campaigning organisation which also offers legal advice to young people and service providers working with children.

5

YOUTH JUSTICE

Fact file

- Total number of Anti-social Behaviour Orders (ASBOs) given to 10-17-years-olds during 1999-2007 - 6,000
- Total number of Acceptable Behaviour Contracts (ABCs) made 2003-07 - 30,000
- Average number of Parenting Orders issued each year - 1,500
- Average number of custodial sentences given to 10-17-year-olds each year - 3,500
- Around 60% of 10-17-year-olds have breached their (ASBOs)

Source: Hansard.

Overview of relevant legislation

As is demonstrable from the figures in the Fact File above, a considerable number of children and young people are involved in the youth justice system each year. Social workers in Youth Offending Teams are obviously the most likely to be working directly with young offenders. However, it would be a mistake to imagine that young offenders, children at risk of significant harm and *children in need* fall neatly into separate categories necessitating the inputs of different agencies. As some of the cases in this chapter demonstrate, often a young offender is also a *child in need* or a child about whom there are safeguarding concerns. So a social worker acting under an Education Supervision Order, or the named worker for a disabled child or a child at risk of significant harm may simultaneously be working with a young offender.

Precisely because a *child in need* or a child at risk of significant harm can at the same time be either a young offender or a child on the margins of the youth justice system, close working between different agencies with responsibilities for children is imperative. Social workers practising in the areas of education, disability or child protection still need to understand the workings of the youth justice system and the protocols in place for liaison and joint working with colleagues in Youth Offending Teams. A number of the cases in this chapter highlight the multi-agency nature of effective work with young offenders.

As the Fact File above reveals, increasingly the parents of young offenders are also subject to court orders in connection with their children's offending behaviour. This means that professionals in Youth Offending Teams, including social workers, are often required to work with parents on aspects of their parenting, as well as working with the young offender. The Crime and Disorder Act 1998 introduced key changes in the youth justice system including the establishment of Youth Offending Teams and the creation of new court orders designed to reduce anti-social behaviour. For this reason the statute is summarised in the table below and is frequently referred to throughout this chapter.

Crime and Disorder Act 1998	Key sections
Part I - Prevention of Crime and Disorder	s.1 Anti-social behaviour orders ss.2-3 Sex offender orders ss.8-10 Parenting orders ss.11-13 Child safety orders ss.14-15 Local child curfews
Part II - Criminal Justice System	s.39 Youth offending teams
Part IV - Dealing with Offenders	ss.65-66 Young offenders reprimands and warnings ss.67-68 Reparation orders ss.69-70 Action plan orders ss.71-72 Improvements to supervision order ss.73-79 Detention and training orders
Part V - Miscellaneous and Supplemental	ss.97-98 Remands and committals of children and young people

The Crime and Disorder Act 1998 was intended to create Youth Offending Teams to coordinate work with young offenders and those at risk of entering the youth justice system. It is aimed at the prevention of re-offending and repeat low level criminal activity. But it is not underpinned by a set of statutory principles as is true for the Children Act 1989. However, a number of policy and practice guidance documents have been issued by the Government to direct the implementation of the Crime and Disorder Act 1998 and these are summarised in the table below and referred to in this chapter.

Guidance document	Outline of content
HM Government (2006a) *Working Together to Safeguard Children*	Provides policy guidance on inter-agency collaboration to safeguard children to all agencies working with children including Youth Offending Teams.
Home Office, Youth Justice Board and Department for Constitutional Affairs (2004) *Parenting Contracts and Orders Guidance*	This provides guidance to professionals on Youth Offending Teams on implementing Parenting Contracts and Parenting Orders.
Home Office (2003) *A Guide to Anti-social Behaviour Orders and Acceptable Behaviour Contracts*	This provides guidance to professionals responsible for tackling anti-social behaviour and explains the procedures for applying and supervising ASBOs and ABCs.

(Continued)

Guidance document	Outline of content
Youth Justice Board (2006) *Criminal Justice Act 2003, 'Dangerousness' and the New Sentences for Public Protection: Guidance for Youth Offending Teams*	This provides guidance to professionals on Youth Offending Teams regarding the assessment of risk of harm to the pubic posed by a young offender and the implications of designating them a 'dangerous' offender.
Youth Justice Board (2004) *National Standards for Youth Justice Services*	This sets out 12 minimum standards for professionals involved in delivering youth justice services. The standards cover preventative work with young offenders as well as supervising sentences handed down by the courts.
Department for Communities and Local Government (2006) *Homelessness Code of Guidance for Local Authorities*	This code regulates the allocation of social housing to individuals and families. It must be followed by Local Authority Housing Departments.
Youth Justice Board, Ministry of Justice and Department for Children, Schools and Families (2008) *When to Share Information: Best Practice Guidance for Everyone Working in the Youth Justice System*	This is addressed to professionals in Youth Offending Teams and provides guidance on sharing confidential information about young people when working with other agencies or when a referral to another professional is indicated.

Overview of the cases

This chapter examines the events relating to five court cases. The first case came before the European Court of Human Rights in Strasbourg while the other four cases were tried in the domestic courts of the United Kingdom. A brief overview of each case is provided below.

Case 1 *T* v. *United Kingdom* and *V* v. *United Kingdom* [2000] 30 EHRR 121 explores the:

- Meaning of a fair trial.
- Special measures available to children in court.
- Dilemma of providing therapy to young defendants.
- Definition of degrading treatment under the European Convention.

Case 2 *R (on the application of M)* v. *Inner London Crown Court* [2003] EWHA 301 explores the:

- Range of court orders available for young offenders.
- Application of Parenting Orders.
- Application of Compensation Orders.
- Protections for family life offered by the European Convention.

Case 3 *R (on application of M (a child))* v. *Sheffield Magistrates' Court* [2004] EWHC 1830 explores the:

- Procedure for applying for an Anti-social Behaviour Order (ASBO).
- Role conflict for social workers of *looked after* children subject to ASBO proceedings.
- Challenges of multi-agency work with *looked after* children who are also young offenders.

Case 4 *R* v. *H* [2007] EWCA Crim 2330 explores the:

- Risk assessment of young offenders.
- Legal definition of dangerousness.
- Nature and importance of the Pre-Sentence Report.
- Need to balance a child's welfare against the need to punish and protect the public in deciding on an appropriate sentence for a young offender.

Case 5 *R (on the application of AB)* v. *Nottingham City Council* [2001] EWHC Admin 235 explores the:

- Importance of following policy guidance in completing assessments.
- Centrality of inter-agency collaboration in assessment and care planning.
- The role of housing authorities in assisting Children's Services.
- The need for joint working between Youth Offending Teams and Children's Services.

CASE 1
T v. United Kingdom and V v. United Kingdom [2000] 30 EHRR 121

Importance of the case

It concerns two children who, both aged 10 years of age, murdered the toddler James Bulger. There followed considerable outrage and media coverage of the subsequent Crown Court trial of the two defendants. This case examines the impact of this media coverage on the two children and how this affected the fairness of their trial.

History of the case

Two children, T and V, were convicted in a Crown Court of the murder of a 2-year-old toddler in 1993. T and V argued that their trial in an adult criminal court and the manner of their sentencing had violated their rights under articles 3, 5 and 6 in conjunction with article 14 of the European Convention on Human Rights. T and V brought their case before the European Court of Human Rights.

Facts of the case

T and V were both aged 10 years when on 12 February 1993, a day that they were both truant from school, they abducted a 2-year-old boy named James Bulger from a shopping centre. They took James two miles away from the shopping precinct before battering him to death and placing his body on a railway line to be run over by a passing train. Shortly after committing the crime, T and V were arrested. They were brought to trial aged 11 years in Preston Crown Court during November 1993 in a case which lasted three weeks and attracted intense media coverage. The public and press were allowed into the court room and the vehicles ferrying T and V to and from the Crown Court were frequently attacked by members of the public. The dock was raised so that T and V as defendants were viewable to everyone in the courtroom throughout each day's hearing. In almost all respects procedures followed those for adult defendants with the exception that T and V were seated beside their social workers, and their parents were seated nearby, although not with them in the dock. The judge also permitted shortened daily hearings and ten-minute adjournments every hour to reflect the children's more limited ability to concentrate on and comprehend the proceedings. No therapeutic work was conducted with the children prior to or during the trial. Expert evidence indicated that both children experienced high levels of distress and were suffering from post-traumatic stress syndrome throughout the period of the trial. Expert opinion suggested that the boys' mental state meant they were unable to properly instruct legal counsel or effectively comprehend the Crown Court's proceedings. The trial judge sentenced the children to 'detention during Her Majesty's pleasure' with a recommendation that they both serve eight years. This tariff was widely publicised by the media and met with a storm of protest. This took the form of petitions signed by thousands of members of the public and letters by constituents to their MPs demanding an increase in the length of the custodial sentences for the two boys. In July 1994 the Home Secretary fixed the tariff at 15 years. T and V sought a judicial review of both the increase in their custodial sentence and also the action of the Home Secretary, who appeared to be acting as a judge, in setting it. This case was appealed through a succession of judicial review hearings up to the House of Lords, which decided that the Home Secretary had acted unlawfully in setting the tariff and quashed his decision. However, no alternative tariff was set, leaving T and V facing an indeterminate sentence *during Her Majesty's pleasure*. As the Human Rights Act 1998 was not in force at the time (see p. 509) T and V appealed to the European Court of Human Rights in Strasbourg on the grounds that they were subjected to inhuman and degrading treatment, denied a fair trail and were being deprived of their liberty by a custodial sentence not amenable to review by a judicial body.

Key people in the case

James Bulger – murdered toddler
V – boy convicted of murdering James
T – boy convicted of murdering James
Dr Bailey – consultant psychiatrist
Dr Bentovim – specialist at the Great Ormond Street Hospital for Children
Dr Vizard – consultant child and adolescent psychiatrist
Michael Howard – Home Secretary
Lord Goff – Law Lord presiding in House of Lords judicial review

Discussion of the case

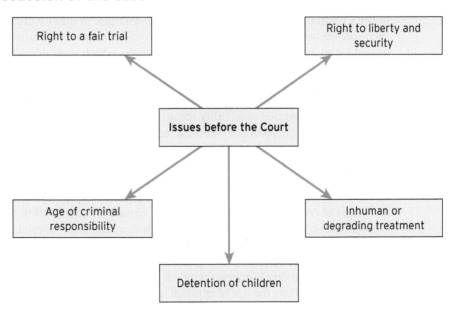

Age of criminal responsibility

Article 3 of the European Convention on Human Rights declares that 'no one shall be subjected to torture or to inhuman or degrading treatment or punishment'. This is an absolute right and is not qualified in any way within the Convention. In other words under no circumstances, not even to protect the public, can a person be subjected to torture or inhuman treatment. Nor can anyone be subjected to degrading forms of punishment for criminal offences. As the judiciary and the police are extensions of the State this means that they were prohibited from inflicting upon T and V treatment which was inhuman or degrading. In submission by their legal counsel to the European Court of Human Rights, T and V argued that article 3 had been violated on a number of counts.

1 That the criminal age of responsibility, which is 10 years in England and Wales, was arbitrary and discriminatory.
2 That the imposition of an indeterminate sentence, potentially lifelong, under the rubric of *detention during Her Majesty's pleasure* took no account of each child's individual circumstances and was not subject to review.
3 That it was inhuman to punish T and V, aged 10 at the time of their crime, as if they were adults.
4 That the conduct of the trial in open court amidst the glare of publicity and using adult criminal procedures was intimidating and humiliating.

The European Court of Human Rights considered legal argument on each of these contentions in turn. The Children and Young Persons Act 1933 s.50 creates an irrebuttable assumption that a child of less than 10 years of age is unable to commit a criminal act. This is referred to as the *doli incapax* rule, which means 'incapable of evil'. Children under 10 years are treated in English law as not having sufficient understanding to differentiate between right and wrong for legal purposes. They therefore cannot be prosecuted in a court of law. However, they could still be held in secure accommodation or a secure psychiatric unit under the Children Act 1989 or Mental Health Act 1983 respectively, if they posed a danger to themselves or others. Persistent offending by children under the age of 10 years, which places them and others at risk, has been construed by the courts as a 'child's being beyond parental control' and as such meeting the threshold under s.31(2) of the Children Act 1989 for the grant of a Care Order. In other words, while young children cannot be prosecuted for acts which would amount to criminal behaviour if committed by an adult, there are other statutes under which their offending behaviour may be addressed. In the present case T and V were 10 years of age when they murdered James Bulger and could therefore be tried by a criminal court.

Barristers for the two boys argued that 10 years as the age of criminal responsibility was extremely low given that most other countries who were members of the Council of Europe had set a higher age. In particular France had an age of 13 years, Germany 14 years, Spain 16 years, and Belgium 18 years for criminal responsibility. Deliberating on this point, judges at the Court of Human Rights observed that there was no agreed standard as to the age of criminal responsibility among Member States of the Council of Europe, with this being influenced by each country's history and culture. In fact, Ireland, Cyprus and Switzerland have even lower ages of criminal responsibility than the United Kingdom. While article 40 of the UN Convention on the Rights of the Child requires signatory States to establish a minimum age of criminal responsibility, the age itself is not stipulated in the Convention. In other words there was no internationally recognised age of criminal responsibility, nor was there consensus even among European nations. Given these facts, the Court of Human Rights concluded that setting the age of criminal responsibility in the United Kingdom at 10 years of age was not of itself tantamount to inhuman or degrading treatment.

The age at which children can be prosecuted for a criminal offence affects what action can be taken against them if they infringe the law. Social workers, regardless of which user group they are working with, will invariably come into contact with young people who are in danger of becoming caught up in the youth justice system. Children in need or children at risk of significant harm can also be children who are young offenders. Sometimes those exposed to neglect or abuse act out their traumatic experiences through offending behaviour. Children of any age who repeatedly offend may be found by a court to be beyond parental control, which is a criteria for a Care Order under s.31(2)(b)(ii) of the Children Act 1989. Therefore children coming before a Magistrates' Court or Crown Court are often also children from deprived backgrounds and are themselves at risk of significant harm or require supportive social care provision. For children below the age of criminal responsibility Care Orders, Child Safety Orders and the use of curfew powers may form a range of interventions deployed by social workers attempting to address the offending behaviour of children under the age of 10 years. Such youngsters are likely to be vulnerable and at risk of committing more serious crimes.

Detention of children

Detention during Her Majesty's pleasure is a mandatory sentence for children convicted of murder and is imposed under s.53(1) of the Children and Young Persons Act 1933 (as amended). This form of detention was originally introduced as an alternative to the death penalty or life imprisonment, which were sentences liable to be imposed on adults convicted of murder. As a mandatory punishment, a judge must sentence defendants under the age of 18 years to *detention during Her Majesty's pleasure* if they are found guilty of murder by a jury. Barristers for T and V argued before the European Court of Human Rights that such a sentence is imposed regardless of the child's age or mitigating circumstances, that it is a life-long sentence, which even on release from custody places the offender on licence and makes them liable to be recalled to prison. Legal counsel for the two boys pointed out that the UN Convention on the Rights of the Child, to which the United Kingdom is a signatory, requires detention of children to be for the shortest appropriate period to be determined by the child's welfare rather than for purposes of retribution. The barristers for the two boys drew the courts' attention to article 3 and article 37 of the UN Convention of the Rights of the Child 1989, which are reproduced in the box below.

 Key legislation

UN Convention on the Rights of the Child 1989

Article 3

(1) In all actions concerning children, whether undertaken by public or private social welfare institutions, courts of law, administrative, authoritative, or legislative bodies, the best interests of the child shall be a primary consideration.

Article 37

(a) No child shall be subjected to torture or other cruel, inhuman or degrading treatment or punishment, neither capital punishment nor life imprisonment without the possibility of release shall be imposed for offences committed by persons below 18 years of age.

(b) No child shall be deprived of his or her liberty unlawfully or arbitrarily. The arrest, detention or imprisonment of a child shall be in conformity with the law and shall be used only as a measure of last resort and for the shortest appropriate period of time . . .

Legal counsel for the British Government countered that T and V had committed the gravest of offences and that a custodial sentence was entirely appropriate. Through their barristers, the Government also submitted that T and V were not in reality subject to life sentences. The State, charged with protecting the public, was entitled to punish wrong-doing and to detain children until able to determine that they were no longer a danger to others. In view of this it was reasoned that a custodial sentence incorporating a tariff specifying a minimum period of imprisonment for retribution and deterrence, and there-after for account to be taken of the dangerousness posed by T and V to the public, could not be construed as inhuman treatment. At the end of the tariff period, be it the original 8 years recommended by the judge or the 15 years suggested by the Home Secretary, T and V could expect to be released unless it was determined that they still posed a danger to the public. In the Government's view the sentence imposed on the two boys was by no means lifelong and in effect account had been taken of their status as children.

Furthermore, according to article 3 of the Convention, decisions taken by courts of law regarding children were to be guided by the best interests of the child as 'a primary consideration' and not as *the* primary consideration. This wording of article 3(1) thus permits scope for the incarceration of children as a means of both retribution and deterrence to others. While T and V were subject to a custodial sentence, this was initially to be in a local authority secure children's home before transfer to a Young Offender Institution on reaching the age of 18 years, with transfer to an adult prison at the age of 21 years. Therefore account was being taken of the welfare of T and V in terms of detaining them in institutions with children of a similar age and in establishments which took account of their needs as children. Current provision for children and young people given custodial sentences by criminal courts is summarised in the box below. The European Court of Human Rights agreed with the Government's perspective on this point and dismissed argument of the applicants' legal counsel that the nature of the custodial sentence handed down to the children amounted to inhuman or degrading treatment.

 Background information

Detention of children

Ideally if a young person is arrested and charged with a crime they should be given police bail to live at home with their parents or guardian. However, if there is a risk of them absconding before their court appearance or if they pose as a risk to themselves or others they may be remanded to local authority accommodation, which may be secure. Older children will be remanded to a Young Offender Institution to await trial.

Children convicted of a crime by the court will be held in different secure institutions during their custodial sentence, depending on their age, gender and vulnerability. As children get older or become less vulnerable they are liable to be moved between the different types of custodial accommodation:

- Boys and girls under 12 years are placed in a local authority secure children's home.
- Boys and girls aged 12-14 years are placed in a local authority secure children's home or a privately run secure training centre.
- Girls aged 15-17 years may be sent to a Young Offender Institution, but are usually given priority for placement in a local authority secure children's home or privately run secure training centre if available.
- Boys aged 15-17 years are normally placed in a Young Offender Institution, but vulnerable 15-16 year old boys may be placed in a local authority secure children's home or privately run secure training centre.

Since the beginning of the nineteenth century there has been a commitment by the State to treat adults and children separately within the criminal justice system. Their differential treatment recognises the:

- Dramatic developmental changes which normally occur during childhood.
- Differences in understanding between adults and children.
- Need to prevent children given custodial sentences from mixing with adult criminals who could exert malign influences upon them.

For this reason children over the age of 10 years who are found guilty of serious offences are incarcerated in institutions with other young people as opposed to adults. Such children, precisely because they are children, still fall under the provisions of the Children Act 1989 and social workers may therefore continue to be responsible for the welfare and protection of children who are given custodial sentences. Obviously in such circumstances social workers will be required to exercise their duties and powers under the Children Act 1989 subject to the conditions of the children's imprisonment. Younger children who persistently offend, but who cannot be convicted of a crime, may still be the subject of a Secure Accommodation Order or Care Order depending on the nature of their offending behaviour. Therefore children of all ages may be detained in connection with their offending behaviour if certain legally prescribed criteria are met. A proportion of these children may either be detained in local authority accommodation or local authorities will continue to have responsibilities for them under the Children Act 1989 even though they are in Young Offender Institutions or secure training centres.

As the Probation Service normally deals with adult offenders and has been split away from social work, practitioners are most likely to be working with young offenders in local authority care or Young Offender Institutions. Those social workers who are members of Youth Offending Teams may also be responsible for supervising offenders released from custody on licence. Social workers within Children's Services may be responsible for arranging the resettlement of young people who have served their sentence and are not subject to any further restrictions on their liberty. For young offenders detained in local authority secure accommodation, social workers will continue to have direct responsibility for their care and safety as well as that of the public. Therefore practitioners have a number of different roles and tasks in relation to children sentenced to custodial sentences, depending on the age of the child and the terms of their detainment and release.

Inhuman or degrading treatment

Finally it fell to the court to determine whether the trial itself, conducted as it was in a blaze of publicity, constituted inhuman or degrading treatment. In paragraph 2 of the summary of its judgement the Court of Human Rights set out the parameters of article 3:

> Ill-treatment must attain a minimum level of severity if it is to fall within the scope of Article 3. The assessment of this minimum is, in the nature of things, relative. It depends on all the circumstances of the case, such as the nature and context of the treatment or punishment, the manner and method of its execution, its duration, its physical or mental effects and, in some cases, the sex, age and health of the victim.

> Treatment has been held to be 'inhuman' because, inter alia, it was premeditated, was applied for hours at a stretch and caused actual bodily injury or intense physical and mental suffering, and 'degrading' because it was such as to arouse in its victims feelings of fear, anguish and inferiority capable of humiliating and debasing them. In order for a punishment or treatment associated with it to be 'inhuman' or 'degrading', the suffering or humiliation involved must in any event go beyond that inevitable element of suffering or humiliation connected with a given form of legitimate treatment or punishment.

This judicial interpretation of article 3 of the European Convention on Human Rights raised two issues. First, whether T and V had experienced 'suffering or humiliation' above and beyond that which would inevitably accompany a court case in conjunction with recognition and remorse for their crime. Secondly, whether their age had a bearing on what could be defined as inhuman or degrading treatment. In essence, barristers for the applicants put it to the Court of Human Rights that:

> the cumulative effect of the age of criminal responsibility, the accusatorial nature of the trial, the adult proceedings in a public court, the length of the trial, the jury of 12 adult strangers, the physical lay-out of the courtroom, the overwhelming presence of the media and public, the attacks by the public on the prison van which brought him to court and the disclosure of his identity, together with a number of other factors linked to his sentence gave rise to a breach of Article 3. (para. 63)

A key claim deployed by legal counsel for T and V was that they should have been tried in a Youth Court and not a Crown Court. Had they been tried in a Youth Court, less formality and public attention during the trial would have prevailed. For example, in a Youth Court there is no raised dock and defendants normally sit with their parents, who are encouraged to attend hearings. Members of the public are not permitted in the Youth Court and although members of the press can attend they are normally not permitted to report any information which could identify the accused. In exceptional circumstances under s.49(4A) of the Children and Young Persons Act 1933, Magistrates can lift reporting restrictions relating to criminal charges, but this is at their discretion and not that of the press. In effect the only people permitted in a Youth Court are those directly involved in the case in some way. By contrast in a Crown Court the defendant is isolated off from the rest of the courtroom and placed in the dock. There is a presumption in favour of permitting full reporting of the case, including the naming of defendants. However, in the case of T and V, the judge exercised his discretion and prohibited the naming of the children prior to and during the trial, although this reporting restriction was lifted after the trial ended. Currently, s.44 of the Youth Justice and Criminal Evidence Act 1999 prohibits the press from identifying anyone under the age of 18 years prior to the commencement of court proceedings, whether they are witnesses, victims or defendants. This is regardless of which court is trying the offence.

Rebutting the claims of the barristers acting for T and V, the British Government argued that a number of modifications had been made to the physical layout and procedures of the Crown Court to take account of the children's ages. These included raising the dock so that they could see all the proceedings, creating regular rest periods and permitting the children to spend time with their parents throughout the trial period, when the hearing itself was not in progress. According to the State, not only was judicial procedure not designed to deliberately inflict suffering or humiliate the defendants, it had in fact been specially adapted to some of their needs. Having heard argument from both parties to the case, the European Court of Human Rights delivered its verdict on this issue bearing in mind that to meet the criteria of 'inhuman' and 'degrading' the treatment had to reach a level of severity and be beyond the suffering which would necessarily attend prosecution for a criminal act. The Court of Human Rights concluded (para. 2) that:

> The criminal proceedings against the applicant were not motivated by any intention on the part of the State authorities to humiliate him or cause him suffering. Indeed, special measures were taken to modify the Crown Court procedure in order to attenuate the rigours of an adult trial in view of the defendants' young age. Even if there is evidence that proceedings such as those applied to the applicant could be expected to have a harmful effect on an 11-year-old child, the Court considers that any proceedings or inquiry to determine the

circumstances of the acts committed by T and the applicant, whether such inquiry had been carried out in public or private, attended by the formality of the Crown Court or informally in the Youth Court, would have provoked in the applicant feelings of guilt, distress, anguish and fear.

Inhuman and degrading treatment is prohibited under article 3 of the European Convention on Human Rights, but what constitutes inhuman treatment is not defined. It is left to the courts to decide whether certain forms of conduct, given the victim's developmental age and any other relevant circumstances, amount to degrading treatment. This means, in effect, that what constitutes degrading treatment within one set of circumstances might not be so considered given a different set of circumstances. In relation to T and V the European Court of Human Rights concluded that the threshold of inhuman or degrading treatment had not been crossed. But it is crucial that practitioners working with children and young people within the youth justice system are aware of the need to ensure that their treatment during trial and incarceration does not violate their human rights. Social workers who discover that children for whom they are responsible are being ill-treated must report this to their employer. The GSCC *Code of Practice for Social Care Workers* at para. 3.2 obliges practitioners to use 'established processes and procedures to challenge and report dangerous, abusive, discriminatory or exploitive behaviour and practice'. Professionals working for public bodies who treat service-users in degrading or dehumanising ways are likely to find themselves in breach of article 3 alongside their employers who will be vicariously liable for their conduct.

Right to a fair trial

The right to a fair trial guaranteed by article 6 of the European Convention on Human Rights, which is reproduced in the box below, was also evoked on behalf of T and V. This revolved around whether procedures designed to safeguard the rights of adults during a criminal trial equally protected children.

Key legislation

European Convention on Human Rights

Article 6 - Right to a Fair Trial

1. In the determination of his civil rights and obligations or of any criminal charge against him, everyone is entitled to a fair and public hearing within a reasonable time by an independent and impartial tribunal established by law. Judgement shall be pronounced publicly but the press and public may be excluded from all or part of the trial in the interests of morals, public order or national security in a democratic society, where the interests of juveniles or the protection of the private life of the parties so require, or to the extent strictly necessary in the opinion of the court in special circumstances where publicity would prejudice the interests of justice.

Article 6 is an unqualified right and therefore there are no circumstances in which States can derogate from providing defendants with a fair trial. Its wording endorses public access to court proceedings because this is crucial to ensuring that justice is both done and seen to be done. It is the openness of judicial procedure to scrutiny by the press, and hence the public, that is an integral aspect of a functioning democracy regulated by the rule of law. However, article 6 does permit the press to be excluded from court hearings where this is necessary for the protection of private life or to safeguard the process of a fair trial. The British Government argued in the Court of Human Rights that it was compliant with article 6 in permitting press coverage of the Crown Court case, in which there was substantial public interest. Judgement by the Court of Human Rights highlighted the distinction to be made between 'public clamour' and 'public interest', suggesting that the State had capitulated to 'public clamour'. Widespread moral repugnance at the notion of two young children killing a toddler led to sustained public focus on, and desire for, details of the trial. The British Government maintained that the Crown Court's decision to forbid publication of the names of the defendants prior to and during the trial (although the name of the victim was in the public domain) under s.39 of the Children and Young Persons Act 1933 meant that the State had complied with article 6. Interpreting article 6, the Court of Human Rights (para. 153) observed that:

> It is an essential element of 'fairness' in Article 6 that the trial process provides for the effective participation of the defendant in that process, which requires in principle that a defendant should be present during the proceedings and should be able to hear and follow them, and to give instructions where necessary to his or her lawyer. This cannot mean that a defendant must necessarily be able to understand the intricacies of law or procedure, his interests in this regard being adequately protected by having a competent legal adviser to represent him. But it does mean, in my view, that a defendant should have some ability to comprehend what is going on and to contribute effectively to his own defence.

Legal counsel for V and T argued that the presence of the press in the courtroom together with members of the public in conjunction with the raised dock greatly increased the sense of intimidation felt by the defendants. Expert opinion described the effect of the trial arrangements on the two boys. Dr Bentovim, a specialist at the Great Ormond Street Hospital for Children, found that V exhibited post-traumatic stress syndrome coupled with 'extreme distress and guilt'. Dr Bailey, a consultant psychiatrist concurred with this conclusion in her report placed before the Crown Court. It mentioned that V 'had cried inconsolably and shown signs of distress' on each occasion he met with the psychiatrist. Both consultants were of the opinion that V was unable to discuss the events surrounding James Bulger's murder in any meaningful way. After the trial V also informed Dr Bentovim that 'most of the time he had not been able to participate in the proceedings and had spent time counting in his head or making shapes with his shoes because he could not pay attention or process the whole proceedings'. Dr Bentovim concluded that 'whether . . . he had an understanding of the situation such that he could give an informed instruction to his lawyer to act on his behalf . . . is, in my view, very doubtful given his immaturity' (para. 17).

Dr Vizard, a consultant child and adolescent psychiatrist, had examined T and found that he showed signs of post-traumatic stress disorder. Although Dr Vizard agreed that T was fit to stand trial she was of the opinion that, 'This disorder, combined with the lack of any therapeutic work since the offence, limited his ability to instruct his lawyers and testify adequately in his own defence' (para.11). Both defendants reported being terrified by the media and public presence in the court room, a fear of being stared at or recognised outside the courtroom and an inability to concentrate on the proceedings.

The police and judiciary had adopted a number of measures to reduce the anxiety experienced by the children, which had included not only modification of adult court procedures, but also the use of taped audio-visual interviews of V and T giving evidence-in-chief. This meant that V and T did not experience the trauma of having to repeat this evidence in court for a second time. The pre-recording of evidential interviews with children was originally introduced by the Criminal Justice Act 1991. After the trial of V and T, the Youth Justice and Criminal Evidence Act 1999 brought in a series of *special measures* which are exceptional arrangements designed to serve two purposes. The first is to protect children and vulnerable or intimidated adults when giving evidence in civil and criminal proceedings. The second is to ensure that best evidence is obtained and placed before the court. *Special measures* are generally availed of at the direction of the judge, who can also decide not to admit evidence obtained through *special measures* if it appears contaminated or would deprive a defendant of a fair trial. These *special measures* span both pre-trail investigations and the examination of witnesses during a court hearing and are listed in the box below.

Key legislation

Youth Justice and Criminal Evidence Act 1999

Special Measures for children, vulnerable adults and intimidated witnesses

s.23 *Screens* – shield witness from defendant who cannot then identify them.

s.24 *Live Link* – consisting of closed circuit television cameras which enable witness located in another room or building to give evidence before the court.

s.25 *Evidence given in private* – the public and press are excluded from the court in cases involving sexual offences or intimidation.

s.26 *Removal of wigs and gowns* – judges and barristers take these off to reduce formality and any additional anxiety they may cause.

s.27 *A video recorded interview* – a pre-trial audio-visual taped interview of evidence-in-chief.

s.28 *Video recorded cross-examination* – audio-visual taped interview of cross-examination.

s.29 *Examination of the witness through an intermediary* – person appointed by the court to assist a witness give evidence if eligible for special measures on the grounds of being a child or due to incapacity.

s.30 *Aids to communication* – witness is facilitated to give best evidence through used of an interpreter or communication aid, but only available to those eligible for special measures on the grounds of being a child or due to incapacity.

ss.34 and 35 *Mandatory protection of witness from cross-examination by the accused in person* – prohibition on an unrepresented defendant cross-examining vulnerable child or adult victims in cases involving sexual offences.

s.36 *Discretionary protection of witness from cross-examination by the accused person* – in cases not involving sexual offences the judge may exercise discretion to prevent cross-examination by the accused in person.

s.41 *Restrictions on evidence and questions about complainant's sexual behaviour* – restricts the ability of the defence to cite in evidence the previous sexual behaviour of the complainant in cases involving sexual offences.

As most of the *special measures* set out in the Youth Justice and Criminal Evidence Act 1999 were introduced after T and V were tried for murder, they were unavailable to these two particular child defendants. Consequently, judges at the European Court of Human Rights came to the conclusion that although some *special measures* were adopted during the trial, these were insufficient to shield the defendants from intense media intrusion and public outrage. Indeed, evidence indicated that the raised dock had the effect of inhibiting greater participation by the children in the proceedings rather than enhancing it. The result was to leave the defendants feeling intensely intimidated and exposed to the point where they could not concentrate properly on the proceedings nor adequately instruct their lawyers (para. 3). Referring directly to V, but equally applicable to T, the European Court of Human Rights decided that article 6 had been violated on the grounds that:

> although the applicant's legal representatives were seated 'within whispering distance', it is highly unlikely that he would have felt sufficiently uninhibited, in the tense courtroom and under public scrutiny, to have consulted with them during the trial or, indeed, that given his immaturity and his disturbed emotional state, he would have been capable outside the courtroom of co-operating with his lawyers and giving them information for the purposes of his defence. (para. 3e)

Special measures apply not only to children but also to vulnerable adult witnesses, for example a person with a learning difficulty. They are designed to protect children and vulnerable adults as witnesses, but can also be used to ensure a fair trial where they are the defendant. All children are automatically entitled to *special measures*, but social workers may need to advocate on behalf of vulnerable adults to ensure that they are recognised as such and afforded *special measures* by the court. As there is a balance to be struck between the right of the defendant to a fair trial and the need to protect and gain best evidence from vulnerable witnesses, judges will weigh these competing aspects of justice. Social workers may need to present evidence to judges which demonstrates the necessity of *special measures* where practitioners are involved with court cases concerning child protection, adult protection or young offenders.

Children because of their stage of development and level of understanding are likely to require additional support from their parents or guardians and social workers if they are to effectively defend themselves in criminal proceedings. Children's Guardians are not appointed in criminal proceedings against children, and the child's welfare, although a consideration, is not the paramount consideration of the court. This means that children are solely dependent on their legal counsel and do not have a dedicated adult to represent their interests as is true of Care Proceedings and disputed private law proceedings. Therefore the child's social worker, as in the case of T and V, may have a particularly important role to play in offering social and emotional support to a child at a time of immense personal crisis. To do this effectively social workers themselves, although not lawyers, must nevertheless have a working knowledge of the youth and criminal justice systems.

Right to liberty and security

The right to liberty guaranteed under article 5 of the European Convention on Human Rights, which is reproduced in the box on the next page, is not an absolute right. It is qualified and explicitly excludes 'the lawful detention of a person after conviction by a competent court'. It follows that those accused of and found guilty of an offence through the process of a fair trial are not guaranteed liberty. If they were it would mean that no State could imprison anyone regardless of the danger they posed to society at large. Legal counsel for the defendants did not dispute the legality of the arrest and conviction of V and T, but they did dispute the failure to ensure that the two boys were given a means to challenge their continued detention. While article 5 does not secure the liberty of those convicted of an offence, it does provide a number of protections to those subject to arrest or detention by the State.

European Convention on Human Rights

Article 5 - Right to Liberty and Security

2. Everyone who is arrested shall be informed promptly, in a language which he understands, of the reasons for his arrest and of any charge against him.

3. Everyone arrested or detained in accordance with the provisions of paragraph 1.c of this article shall be brought promptly before a judge or other officer authorised by law to exercise judicial power and shall be entitled to trial within a reasonable time or to release pending trial. Release may be conditioned by guarantees to appear for trial.

4. Everyone who is deprived of his liberty by arrest or detention shall be entitled to take proceedings by which the lawfulness of his detention shall be decided speedily by a court and his release ordered if the detention is not lawful.

5. Everyone who has been the victim of arrest or detention in contravention of the provisions of this article shall have an enforceable right to compensation.

Lawyers for the defendants argued before the Court of Human Rights in Strasbourg that the British Government had contravened article 5(4) by failing to provide a mechanism by which T and V could challenge the length of their detention. This arose out of a House of Lords court case relating to the way in which the tariff had been set for T and V. The judge at the Crown Court trial, who can only make a recommendation, suggested a tariff of eight years for each boy to reflect retribution and deterrence. Thereafter their continued detention would depend upon the danger they posed to society at large, which would be assessed by the Parole Board whose functions are described in the box on the next page. However, the public outrage at the perceived low tariff resulted in Michael Howard, the then Home Secretary, whose legal responsibility it was to set the tariff for those detained *during Her Majesty's pleasure*, deciding to raise it to 15 years. The House of Lords found this to be unlawful as Michael Howard, instead of being impartial, had been strongly influenced by the view of the public rather than the developmental and welfare needs of the children which had to be set against retribution and deterrence.

The House of Lords judgement resulted in decisions on the length of the tariff being handed over to the Lord Chief Justice on the recommendation of the trial judge. The Home Secretary, who is inevitably susceptible to political pressures, is no longer responsible for setting the tariff for children subject to *detainment during Her Majesty's Pleasure*. Unfortunately this did not happen until after the court proceedings concerning V and T. Consequently, the effect of the House of Lords decision handed down in June 1997 declaring that the increased tariff set by the Home Secretary was unlawful was that no tariff at all was set. The contention of V and T before the European Court of Human Rights was that by failing to set a new tariff the State had in effect passed an indeterminate custodial sentence on the two boys which could be indefinite. Counsel for V and T, as the applicants to the Court of Human Rights case, argued that they had been deprived of their right under article 5(4) of the European Convention to have their continued detention reviewed. For without a tariff, and therefore a minimum sentence to be served before release, their custody could not be reviewed by the Parole Board. The Court of Human Rights, noting that V and T had by that stage been detained for 5 years without

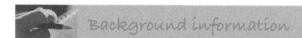
Background information

The Parole Board

Members of the Parole Board are appointed by the Home Secretary, but the Board is an independent public body which operates at arm's length from the Government. The Parole Board nationally comprises around 170 experts with backgrounds in the judiciary, psychiatry and work with offenders. At local level three experts at a time sit on a Parole Board Panel to deliberate on prisoner release. The primary purpose of the Parole Board is to protect members of the public by assessing the risk to their safety posed by the release of prisoners back into the community. In coming to its decisions, the Parole Board is required to take into consideration the importance of rehabilitation for both prisoners and society. It is responsible for deliberating on several different types of cases.

Prisoners with indeterminate sentences

This category includes prisoners sentenced to life imprisonment or subject to *detention during Her Majesty's pleasure* and those given indeterminate sentences in order to protect the public. In relation to these prisoners the Parole Board is required to decide whether they are safe to be released into the community on serving their tariff, that is, the minimum period of imprisonment fixed at the time of their conviction. The Parole Board is also responsible for re-examining the decision of the Secretary of State when a released prisoner is recalled to prison for breach of their life licence conditions. These conditions can include reporting regularly to the police and observing restrictions on freedom of movement. The Parole Board has the power to re-release the prisoner.

Prisoners with determinate sentences

This category includes discretionary conditional release prisoners and those given extended sentences for public protection. The Parole Board is charged to decide whether such offenders having served the minimum time specified at the time of their conviction and sentencing are now safe enough to be released into the community. Prisoners serving sentences of more than four years are normally eligible for parole halfway through their sentences. These prisoners on release from custody are subject to any licence conditions imposed by the Parole Board. As with released life sentence prisoners, the breach of conditions can result in immediate recall to prison by the Secretary of State. The Parole Board is also responsible for deciding whether the recall was justified and if the prisoner should be re-released back into the community.

the setting of a tariff, concluded that in the absence of a tariff period V and T had in fact no effective recourse to challenge their continued detention as per their entitlement under article 5(4).

Judgement in *T* v. *United Kingdom* and *V* v. *United Kingdom*

Ruling on the case, the European Court of Human Rights sitting in Strasbourg found that the British Government had violated the rights of the applicants T and V in relation to articles 5(4) and 6(1). The two boys had not received a fair trial, although it was not sufficiently flawed to place in doubt the legality of their conviction. Nor were the applicants given access to a judicial process through which they could challenge their continued detention. However, the court concluded that there was no violation of article 3 as the suffering experienced by T and V during the trial was largely attributable to their crime and the inevitable judicial process which followed upon it.

? Critical questions

1 Social workers in Youth Offending Teams are involved in work with young people who come before the Youth Court and occasionally the Crown Court. Given the difficulties which V and T encountered during their trial, what actions should a child's social worker take to ensure that he or she receives a fair trial?

2 Judges in sentencing children are legally required to consider their welfare alongside the need to punish them and protect the public. Do you think the original trial judge who sentenced V and T to serve eight years in prison was correct? If so why; if not, what sentence do you think should have been handed down to V and T and why?

3 No therapeutic work was undertaken with V and T in the period leading up to or during their trial. Given that V and T were the perpetrators of a violent crime and not the victims of one, what is your view on providing children in this situation with therapeutic support? Returning to the discussion in Chapter 4 concerning the risk of contaminating evidence by providing therapy, how can a social worker minimise this hazard?

CASE 2
R (on the application of M) v. Inner London Crown Court
[2003] EWHA 301

Importance of the case

It explores the extent to which parents can be held legally accountable for the offending behaviour of their children. This is examined within the context of the right to family life guaranteed under the European Convention on Human Rights.

History of the case

The mother of a girl aged 13 years of age at the time of her conviction for wounding another child was made the subject of Parenting and Compensation Orders by a Youth Court. The mother appealed this decision to the Crown Court, which dismissed her appeal. The mother then sought a judicial review in the High Court of the Crown Court's decision, on the grounds that the Parenting Order contravened article 8 of the European Convention on Human Rights and that the making of both the Parenting and Compensation Orders was irrational.

Facts of the case

M, a girl aged 13 years, together with a friend attacked a third girl also aged 13 years in July 2000. During the attack M held down the victim while her friend inflicted a wound to the victim's forehead. M came before Camberwell Youth Court in June 2001 which, on convicting her of the offence, made an Action Plan Order requiring her to be under supervision for three months. The Magistrates also imposed a one-year Parenting Order and a Compensation Order amounting to £30 on M's mother, AM. Both mother and daughter appealed this judgement to the Inner London Crown Court in March 2002, but their appeal was dismissed. As decisions made by the State which appear to contravene the European Convention on Human Rights is a ground for judicial review, the mother then pursued an action against the Parenting Order through the judicial review process in the Queen's Bench Division, Divisional Court of the High Court.

Key people in the case

AM – applicant in the High Court case
M – daughter of applicant
Mr Hardie – legal counsel for applicant
Mr Crow – legal counsel for Government
Mr Justice Henriques – presiding judge in High Court

Discussion of the case

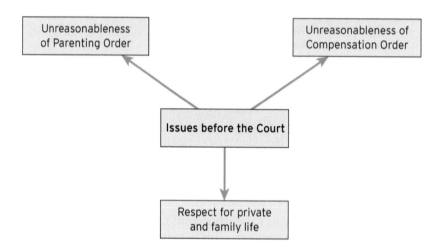

Unreasonableness of Parenting Order

Mr Hardie, acting for the mother, AM, argued that the Youth Court had been wrong in law to issue a Parenting Order against her. A Parenting Order is just one of the many orders which has been introduced by a series of statutes and can be issued by Magistrates during civil proceedings or in a Youth Court. These orders have a diversity of functions and duration. Magistrates making an order will take into consideration the nature of the offence, the age and present circumstances of the offender while balancing the requirements of retribution, deterrence, crime prevention and rehabilitation in deciding which order to apply. The table on the next page sets out the orders most commonly made by civil and Youth Courts.

The terms of a Parenting Order are defined under s.8(4) of the Crime and Disorder Act 1998 which requires the parent or guardian named to comply with its directions such as closer supervision of their child and to attend parenting classes or counselling sessions.

Type of court order	Applicable age group	Duration of court order	Requirements of court order
Referral Order PCC(S)A 2000 ss.16-20	10-17 years	3-12 months	Must be given to young person who pleads guilty and is in court for the first time. Young offender is referred to Youth Offender Panel which decides the sentence and draws up a contract with the young person and their parents. The Referral Order can include elements of reparation, community work, curfew, mediation, contact with victims, and education courses or other specified activities.
Action Plan Order PCC(S)A 2000 ss.69-72	10-17 years	3 months	Short intensive order to examine offending behaviour and how it is triggered. Supervision is by Youth Offending Team (YOT). Can include elements of counselling, education, victim awareness, and community work.
Attendance Centre Order PCC(S)A 2000 s.60	10-17 years	4-24 hours	Must spend time at local Attendance Centre staffed by police officers to undertake prescribed structured activities.
Exclusion Order PCC(S)A 2000	10-17 years	Up to 3 months	Prohibits the offender from entering specified areas or premises at all or during particular times.
Curfew Order PCC(S)A 2000 ss.37-40	12-17 years	Up to 3 months for children under 16 years and 6 months for those aged over 16 years	The curfew can be electronically tagged and requires offender to remain in a specified place for a specified time from 2-12 hours per day. The offender must consent to the order which should not interfere with work or education. A responsible person must agree to monitor the curfew.
Supervision Order PCC(S)A 2000 ss.63-68	10-17 years	6 months-3 years	Designed to prevent re-offending the order is tailored to the needs of the offender. Supervision is by the Youth Offending Team, social worker or probation officer. Can include elements of: community work; curfew; therapeutic work; and training. Can require offender to live in local authority accommodation.
Youth Community Order CJA 2003 (replaces Curfew, Attendance Centre, Action Plan, Exclusion and Supervision Order)	10-17 years	Up to 3 years	Order made by Magistrate but details of Youth Community Order will be based on assessment by Youth Offending Team. These will be tailored programmes to punish and prevent re-offending, consisting of elements of curfew, surveillance, attendance at specified places and exclusion from specified places.
Community Order CJA 2003 (replaces Community Rehabilitation, Community Punishment, Curfew and Drug Treatment and Testing Orders)	16-17 years	Up to 3 years	Can include elements of prohibited activity, unpaid work requirement, curfew, mental health treatment or treatment for drug addiction, attendance at training programmes, a residence requirement or regular meetings with an appointed supervisor.

(Continued)

Type of court order	Applicable age group	Duration of court order	Requirements of court order
Reparation Order PCC(S)A 2000 ss.73-75	10-17 years	3 months	Requires the offender to make reparation to the victim up to a maximum of 24 hours activity. Can contain elements of apology, repairing damage caused, and voluntary work. Supervision is by a member of YOT, social worker or probation officer.
Anti-social Behaviour Order (ASBO) CDA 1998 s.1	Anyone over the age of 10 years	2 years upwards	Civil order which can be applied for by local authority, police or social landlords or be made by Magistrate against a convicted offender. Issued if person has caused harassment or distress. Can have elements of prohibiting person from specific premises. Breach of order is a criminal offence.
Child Safety Order (CSO) CDA 1998 ss.11-13	Under 10 years	Up to 12 months	Civil order which is the equivalent of an ASBO for those under 10 years and is supervised by a social worker or member of YOT. Can contain elements of curfew, specified activities and requirement for support and care by parent. Comes under family proceedings and therefore s.1 of the Children Act 1989 applies. Breach of a CSO can result in a Parenting Order.
Detention and Training Order CDA 1998 s.73 and PCC(S)A 2000 ss.100-107	12-17 years	4 months to 2 years	Custodial sentence in a secure training centre, young offender institution, youth treatment centre or local authority or other secure accommodation. Supervision in community on release from detention.
Parenting Order CDA 1998 s.8	Parent or guardian	3-12 months	Civil order imposed on parents or guardians of young offenders. Normally issued alongside an ASBO. Parent must attend parenting programme and can be required to more closely supervise child, e.g. ensure they come home at night. Exceptionally a parenting programme can be residential. Breach of the order is a criminal offence.
Compensation Order PCC(S)A 2000 s.137	10-17 years	Not applicable	It specifies an amount to be paid to the victim by the offender or the parent if the offender is under 16 years of age. The amount determined should take account of harm caused to victim and ability of offender to pay.
Child Curfew Schemes CDA 1998 ss.14-15	Under 10 years	Up to 90 days	Bans children from being in a specified public place during specified hours unless under the control of a responsible person over 18 years of age. Police are required to take a child home if found in breach of curfew. Breach of a Child Curfew Scheme triggers s.47 investigation under Children Act 1989.

CDA 1998 = Crime and Disorder Act 1998
PCC(S)A 2000 = Powers of Criminal Courts (Sentencing) Act 2000
CJA 2003 = Criminal Justice Act 2003

This provision is designed to enable the court to direct the parent or guardian to take action so as to prevent repetition of the child's offending behaviour. Under s.8(8) a social worker, probation officer, member of the Youth Offending Team or a person nominated by the chief education officer is required to act as a responsible officer to arrange and supervise the implementation of the Parenting Order. Home Office, Youth Justice Board and Department for Constitutional Affairs (2004) *Parenting Contracts and Orders Guidance*, which is non-statutory guidance, makes it clear that a parent must be assessed for an appropriate parenting programme and not simply assigned to one. Furthermore, the responsible officer must maintain contact and monitor the parent's progress, liaising with the provider where necessary (paras. 8.4–8.5 and 9.5). If the young person is also likely to have involvement from a Youth Offending Team, it is good practice to make the responsible officer for the Parenting Order the same person as that working with the young offender (para. 9.3). This arrangement is likely to facilitate more holistic work with the family. In addition responsible officers, or indeed any other member of the Youth Offending Team, must meet the requirements set out in the National Standards for Youth Justice Services. The requirements which relate specifically to work with parents of young offenders are shown in the box below.

Key guidance

National Standards for Youth Justice Services

8.74 The first contact between the YOT Officer or other responsible officer and the parent(s) must be before the end of the next working day following the court hearing. At this meeting the responsible officer must:

- Explain the requirements of the order
- Check that the parent(s) understand(s) the requirements and consequences of non-compliance
- Agree a draft plan for meeting the requirements of the order and what will be expected
- Make arrangements for other social work agencies, where involved, to be consulted

Imposing a Parenting Order under s.8 is at the court's discretion and depends on whether Magistrates are satisfied that making a Parenting Order is desirable to prevent the commission of further offences by the child. Exceptionally, under s.9(1) and 9(2) where a child is under 16 years of age and has been convicted of an offence – as was the case for M convicted of wounding another child – a Parenting Order must be issued unless there are extenuating circumstances. As the Home Office, Youth Justice Board and Department for Constitutional Affairs (2004: para.7.1) makes clear, 'Before making a parenting order where the child or young person is under the age of 16, the court must obtain and consider information about the parent's or guardian's family circumstances and the likely effect of the order on those circumstances.' In addition under s.8(4) the court must avoid specifying requirements in the Parenting Order which:

- conflict with the parents' religious beliefs,
- interfere with the times of a parent's work or educational commitments.

Although the Youth Court is a criminal court, a Parenting Order is in fact a civil order which can be issued without the person in question having committed a criminal act. It is designed to prevent crime and not to punish crime. However, breach of a Parenting

Order by the parent or guardian, for instance failure to attend a specified training programme or impose a required curfew on their child, would constitute a criminal offence. Thus Parenting Orders, like ASBOs, combine elements of both civil and criminal law.

In her appeal to the High Court, the mother's counsel argued that the decision of the Magistrate's court to impose a Parenting Order was unreasonable and that it had failed to follow the correct considerations under the Crime and Disorder Act 1998. The High Court had to decide whether, given all the facts of the case, a Parenting Order would prevent further offending by the child and what, given the family's circumstances, would be the likely effect of imposing the order. In coming to its judgement on this matter the High Court took into consideration the following (paras. 69–73):

- At the date of the offence M was 14 years old and had previously been of exemplary character.
- A school report indicating that the child's conduct was good in class and she was preparing for her GCSE examinations.
- A report from an educational psychologist which concluded that M 'was of broad average intelligence with no abnormal features of personality'.
- A report from a consultant clinical psychologist indicating that M 'had no anxiety or depression, she enjoyed reading books and had plans for educating herself further and getting a decent job'.
- That the offence arose from a long-standing dispute with a neighbour and aside from this M's conduct had been exemplary.
- A pre-sentence report produced by a member of the Youth Offending Team which stated that the mother would not be receptive to a Parenting Order.

Given all these circumstances the High Court concluded that the making of a Parenting Order by the Magistrates' Court had been unreasonable and failed to take proper account of the material evidence which had been placed before it. Given the nature of the dispute and the exemplary conduct of M up until that point it was clear that she was very unlikely to engage in further offending behaviour. According to reports from her school and expert opinion she was intent on concentrating on her education. Given this state of affairs the High Court concluded that a Parenting Order would not in fact have any affect upon M's offending behaviour because she was most unlikely to offend again in any case. Consequently the High Court quashed the Parenting Order.

Government policy, and therefore legislation to implement it, is increasingly linking standards of parenting to children's offending behaviour. The use of Parenting Orders is a clear example of this. Consequently, social workers involved in working with youth offenders are often required to work with parents who are subject to court orders in connection with their child's behaviour. Practitioners are not only working with the family, but are also responsible for ensuring that both parent and child abide by the conditions of the court orders issued against them. Inevitably, this can create additional tensions and challenges in professional practice. Many parents will resent the imposition of a court order upon them for what they perceive to be the actions of their children over which they often have little control.

Unreasonableness of Compensation Order

A Compensation Order can be made under s.137 of the Powers of the Criminal Courts (Sentencing) Act 2000 where a child aged 10–17 years is convicted of an offence which can attract a fine or the payment of compensation. Where the child in question is aged between 10 and 15 years the parent or guardian can be ordered to pay the amount on the child's behalf. However, the court cannot issue a Compensation Order under s.137 unless it is satisfied, given all the circumstances, that it is reasonable to compel the parent or guardian to make such a payment. As is true of Parenting Orders, the imposition of a Compensation Order is not a form of criminal sentence although it is a form of financial penalty against the young offender or their parent.

Mr Hardie insisted that a Compensation Order should not have been imposed on the mother, AM, by the Magistrates' Court as she was in no way at fault or responsible for the offence committed by her daughter, M. In arguing this position, Mr Hardie sought to rely on judicial precedent created in *TA* v. *Director of Public Prosecutions* [1997] 1 Cr App R (S) 1 and *R* v. *Sheffield Crown Court ex parte Clarkson* [1986] Cr App R (S) 454 as in both cases the judge concluded that it would be unreasonable, given the surrounding circumstances, to make a Compensation Order against the parent. However, Justice Henriques distinguished between the facts in these two previous cases and those in AM's. In *TA* v. *Director of Public Prosecutions* the parent in question was not living with the offender at the time of the crime. This differed from the present case where AM lived with her daughter M together with two other children in the same household. Furthermore, as Justice Henriques observed, judgement in *TA* v. *Director of Public Prosecutions* explicitly stated that had the mother been living with the young offender a Compensation Order would have been reasonable.

In *R* v. *Sheffield Crown Court* it was accepted that the mother had done all she could to prevent her son committing offences and that the imposition of a £299 Compensation Order would result in the mother taking two-and-a-half years to pay it, given the state of her finances. These facts differed from those of the present case where there was no evidence of the mother being involved in dissuading her daughter from the offence, and the fine imposed was just £30. This was a sum well within the means of the mother to pay. Justice Henriques effectively challenged Mr Hardie's interpretation of the precedents created by these two previous cases and their applicability to AM's circumstances. He also observed that s.137 of the Powers of the Criminal Courts (Sentencing) Act 2000 did not require the court to establish any fault on the part of the parent or guardian for the acts of their child as a criterion for imposing a Compensation Order. The court only had to establish that it was not unreasonable given all the circumstances of the case to require the parent or guardian to pay the compensation on behalf of the child. In the present case Justice Henriques concluded that Mr Hardie had not offered convincing evidence that AM's situation was exceptional such as would make the issuance of a Compensation Order unreasonable.

Respect for private and family life

Since the incompatibility of a statute or individual statutory provision with the European Convention on Human Rights is a ground for a judicial review (see p. 34), AM was granted permission to take her case before the High Court. Mr Hardie at the start of his submission on behalf of AM reminded the High Court of the legal principle that when the State interferes with a Convention right, the burden of proof is on the State to demonstrate that the interference is justified. Interference with a Convention right is only legally justifiable if it accords with the conditions which qualify that right as stipulated in the European Convention. In addition the action taken by a government to restrict the right must be proportionate to achieve a lawful objective. In this case Mr Hardie claimed that AM's article 8 right to respect for private and family life had been violated by the imposition on her of the Parenting Order. As article 8 is a qualified right and not an absolute one, it does permit the State to restrict the rights of parents in certain circumstances. Two of these circumstances are to protect 'public safety' and 'for the prevention of disorder or crime', both of which are directly relevant to the present case.

Mr Hardie contended that the Parenting Order imposed on AM, which required her to attend counselling sessions two hours a week for three months, was a disproportionate interference in her family life in order to prevent further offending by her daughter. Such a prescriptive order prohibited the mother from making her own choices as a parent as to how best to control her child. It also created a situation in which any parent could be the subject of a Parenting Order if their child offended, regardless of how scrupulous the parent's care and control of their child and regardless of their actual conduct as a primary carer. Mr Hardie was in essence arguing that s.8 of the Crime and Disorder Act 1998 creating a Parenting Order was incompatible with article 8 of the European Convention on Human Rights, which guaranteed family life.

Responding to legal argument put before the High Court by Mr Hardie, legal counsel for the Secretary of State submitted that in determining whether State interference in a Convention right was lawful the court had to answer three crucial questions (para. 53):

1 Does the interference pursue a legitimate objective?
2 Is it in accordance with the law?
3 Is it necessary in a democratic society, is it proportionate?

In relation to point 1, Mr Crow acting for the Government reminded the High Court that the prevention of juvenile crime was a legitimate objective and fell within the conditions under which a parent's article 8 right could be interfered with or restricted. Indeed there was no dispute on this issue between the parties to the present case. As to point 2, Mr Crow claimed that the interference was in accordance with national laws, in this case the Crime and Disorder Act 1998, which was primary legislation and was sufficiently clear as to the circumstances under which a Parenting Order would be imposed. Clarity of the law is plainly integral to the rule of law as citizens need to know what constitutes a civil wrong or crime if they are to regulate their conduct so as to avoid committing one. Again there was no dispute between the parties on this issue. The contention between the mother and the State centred on whether a Parenting Order was necessary in a democratic society and a proportionate response to reducing re-offending by children and young people.

As to proportionality regarding qualified rights under the Convention on Human Rights, Mr Crow argued that, given the pressing and legitimate objective of reducing juvenile crime, Parenting Orders did constitute the minimum necessary intervention. Section 8 of the Crime and Disorder Act 1998 limited their duration to up to one year only and prescribed that the maximum counselling input was once a week for a period of not more than three months. Mr Crow also submitted research evidence to the High Court comprising an evaluative study of Parenting Orders conducted by the Policy Research Bureau in 2002 on behalf of the Youth Justice Board. The Board, whose functions are summarised in the box on the next page, monitors the delivery of youth justice services, supports research and promotes good practice. The study conducted by the Policy Research Bureau found that in instances where Parenting Orders were imposed, re-offending by children dropped by 50 per cent as between the year before the parent attended a parenting programme and the year after they completed it.

According to Mr Crow, findings from research studies supported by the Youth Justice Board and a number of other organisations demonstrated that Parenting Orders directly contribute to the objective of reducing re-offending and to an overall reduction in youth crime. Mr Crow's contention was in short that Parenting Orders were a very limited form of interference in parents' right to respect for their family life and constituted the minimum necessary for the prevention of crime. Justice Henriques, presiding over the High

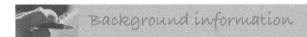

Background information

Youth Justice Board

The National Youth Justice Board was set up under s.41 and Sch. 2 of the Crime and Disorder Act 1998 and is part of the Home Office. Comprised of ten to twelve members, it has special responsibility for overseeing the effective operation of Youth Offending Teams. Under s.41 the National Youth Justice Board is required to:

- Monitor the delivery of youth justice services.
- Develop National Standards for Youth Justice Services.
- Commission research.
- Promote good practice.
- Disseminate information through publication.

Court case, found Mr Crow's legal argument convincing, and concluded that Parenting Orders are necessary in a democratic society. He explicitly recognised in his judgement that article 8 requires the rights of parents to be balanced against those of the wider public (para. 62). On this interpretation there are competing interests between the rights of parents to respect for their family life and the rights of the public to protection of life and property. It was for the High Court to decide on hearing the evidence from both parties if the State in enacting s.8 of the Crime and Disorder Act 1998 had achieved the correct balance in terms of limiting parental rights to the minimum necessary to protect the public.

Even when it is established that the State is entitled to interfere in the family life of a citizen in pursuance of a lawful objective, the issue of proportionality still arises. In this High Court case, legal counsel for the Government produced research findings to demonstrate the efficacy of Parenting Orders in reducing re-offending rates. Social work intervention should be grounded in evidence-based practice and therefore research which links inputs to successful outcomes. Professional activity in connection with youth offending, like that in other areas of practice, requires justification and validation through research. Where studies are authoritative, courts will accept these in evidence so as to support a particular line of legal reasoning (also see Case 5 in Chapter 2). In the present case, Mr Crow very effectively deployed research findings to justify the proportionality of interference in family life through the use of Parenting Orders. In other words, he was able to convince the High Court of the linkage between the intervention of Parenting Orders and a lawful objective which was the reduction of offending and thus protection of the public.

Judgement in *R (on the application of M)* v. *Inner London Crown Court*

The High Court decided that there had been no violation of either the mother's article 6 or article 8 rights under the European Convention on Human Rights. The judgement handed down recognised the responsibility of the State to protect its citizens as a whole from harm in ways which could occasion the curtailment of the rights of individual citizens. The court concluded that the curtailment of AM's right through the imposition of a Parenting Order was the minimum necessary and a proportionate response to the legitimate aim of protecting the public at large. However, the High Court found that there were surrounding circumstances which made the imposition of the Parenting Order unreasonable. The High Court therefore overruled the decision of the Youth Court which issued a Parenting Order. As regards the Compensation Order for £30, the High Court concluded that the Magistrate at the original hearing in the Youth Court had correctly decided to impose it.

Critical questions

1 Social workers as members of Youth Offending Teams may be designated as the *responsible officer* for overseeing a Parenting Order and a court order against the young offender. If a parent has been served with a Parenting Order and/or a Compensation Order because of their child's offending, what additional challenges might this present for a practitioner working with the family?

2 Legislation makes parents responsible for aspects of their children's offending behaviour. Consider the facts of this case and the precedents cited concerning Compensation Orders. Do you think there are circumstances in which parents should be held accountable for their children's offending behaviour? If so what are they? If not, why should parents not be penalised for their children's conduct?

3 Read back through the descriptions of the different court orders which can be issued against children and young people in the table at the beginning of this case. Applying your knowledge of the European Convention on Human Rights, identify the tensions between some of these orders and the human rights of children.

 Critical commentary

Parenting Orders

Parenting Orders can now be imposed not just in conjunction with an Anti-social Behaviour Order, but also alongside a Referral Order, Child Safety Order, Sex Offender Order or because of the failure of parents to comply with a School Attendance Order. In 2000-01 approximately 1,000 Parenting Orders were issued, rising to 1,500 by 2004-05. Currently over 2,000 Parenting Orders are made annually and this number is likely to increase further (Walters and Woodward, 2007: 8). Although the trend is upwards, compared to the much larger number of ASBOs made against young offenders these figures evidence some reluctance on the part of the courts to make Parenting Orders. This is probably because where parents are willing to address their children's offending behaviour, this is best done on a voluntary basis and where they are indifferent it is unlikely that a Parenting Order will have any effect (Arthur, 2005: 240).

There has been considerable criticism of Parenting Orders from criminologists who argue that making parents responsible for their children's offending behaviour and punishing them amounts to the criminalisation of inadequate parenting or parenting in difficult circumstances (Arthur, 2005; Walters and Woodward, 2007). Their opposition to the use of Parenting and Compensation Orders is based on consistent research findings which link juvenile delinquency to a range of factors beyond parenting style. Poverty, family breakdown, living in social housing and conditions of deprivation are found to be strongly positively correlated with rates of offending (Arthur, 2005: 238-9). This is not to deny that family conflict, inadequate child-rearing skills, inconsistent disciplining, poor supervision and neglect by parents are similarly positively correlated to offending (Arthur, 2005: 237).

Research reveals a complex web of interdependent factors which both contribute to initial offending and thereafter tend to sustain offending behaviour. It is the complexity which scholars such as Arthur (2005) and Walters and Woodward (2007) argue is not addressed through the use of Parenting Orders, which despite Government rhetoric to the contrary, are in reality a punitive approach to low income families. Arthur (2005: 245) argues that offending would be more effectively addressed through preventative social work under the Children Act 1989 and thus within a welfare paradigm. The criminalisation of inadequate parenting, which may itself be attributable to rearing children in conditions of deprivation, focusses on offending behaviour while ignoring the social and structural factors perpetuating it.

CASE 3
R (on application of M (a child)) v. *Sheffield Magistrates' Court* [2004] EWHC 1830

Importance of the case

This considers the contradictions which arise when a local authority with parental responsibility for a young person then takes that young person to court for offending behaviour. The case also examines the challenges of multidisciplinary work with young offenders.

History of the case

This was an application made by the grandmother of M acting as his litigation friend for a judicial review of a local authority's decision to apply for an ASBO against M. A Youth Court had already imposed an ASBO on M and the judicial review came before the High Court.

Facts of the case

M was born in 1989 and at the age of 6 years was the subject of a Care Order and became *looked after* by Sheffield City Council. He was placed in a series of different residential homes up until 1999 when he was placed with his maternal grandmother, JW. The boy lived with his grandmother for a while before moving to reside with his paternal aunt where he frequently engaged in offending behaviour. Consequently, M was again placed by the local authority in a number of residential homes. He absconded from each of these homes, usually returning to the home of a family member. In February 2001 M was once more placed with his maternal grandmother. Over the next two-year period he engaged in a catalogue of offending behaviour ranging from attempting to steal a car to common assault. In December 2002 a Statutory Review noted that his current placement with his grandmother was not meeting his needs for control and protection. The Statutory Review meeting gave consideration to providing M with a residential placement, although this proposal was not acted upon at the time. In May 2003 he was placed on a Supervision Order which was breached by further offending. Following a conviction for common assault in October 2003 the Supervision Order was revoked and he was made the subject of a Curfew Order. In February 2003 the ASBO panel agreed in principle to apply for an ASBO against the boy. This meeting was attended by representatives from the police, the local authority Housing Department, and M's social worker. In May 2003 the ASBO panel approved the application for the ASBO. An interim ASBO was imposed on M by Sheffield Magistrates' Court in March 2004. At this time his grandmother, acting as her grandson's litigation friend, applied on his behalf to the High Court for a judicial review concerning the interim Anti-social Behaviour Order.

Key people in the case

M – child subject to an ASBO
JW – maternal grandmother of child
Mr Justice Newman – judge presiding over High Court case

Discussion of the case

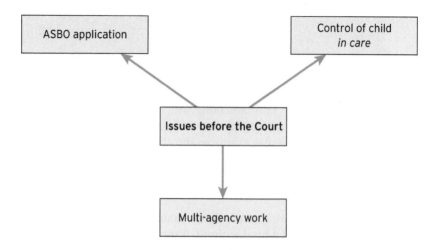

ASBO application

M was under a Care Order, which automatically gave the local authority parental responsibility without depriving his birth mother of her parental responsibility. Although living with his grandmother, who did not have parental responsibility for him, M was still legally *in care*. Since parental responsibility must be exercised consistent with a court order, even though his birth mother retained parental responsibility this could only be exercised subject to the Care Order in place. The boy's offending behaviour became persistent after he moved, aged 11 years, to live with his aunt and thereafter on moving back to reside with his grandmother. It was at the beginning of 2003 that formal consideration was first given to applying for an ASBO against him. The legal basis for issuing an Anti-social Behaviour Order is set out in the box below.

 Key legislation

Crime and Disorder Act 1998 (as amended)

1(1) An application for an order under this section may be made by a relevant authority if it appears to the authority that the following conditions are fulfilled with respect to any person aged 10 or over, namely –

    (a) that the person has acted, since the commencement date, in an anti-social manner, that is to say, in a manner that caused or was likely to cause harassment, alarm or distress to one or more persons not of the same household as himself; and

    (b) that such an order is necessary to protect relevant persons from further anti-social acts by him

1(4) If, on such an application it is proved that the conditions mentioned in subsection (1) above are fulfilled, the magistrates' court may make an order under this section (an 'anti-social behaviour order') which prohibits the defendant from doing anything described in the order.

Under s.1 'relevant authority' is defined as a local authority, the police or registered social landlord and 'relevant persons' is defined as anyone living in the local authority area.

Judgement in *R (McCann)* v. *Crown Court* at Manchester; *Clingham* v. *Kensington and Chelsea Royal Borough* [2002] UKHL 39 confirmed that ASBOs are civil orders. However, this House of Lords decision also established that a heightened standard of proof was to be applied given the serious ramifications of such an order being made. This heightened standard of civil proof equates with that for criminal cases. In effect a *relevant authority* (such as a local authority or social landlord) bringing an application for an ASBO before a Magistrates' Court has to produce evidence to prove *beyond a reasonable doubt* that the defendant had 'caused or was likely to cause harassment, alarm or distress to one or more persons'. Since breach of an ASBO is a criminal offence, the Crown Prosecution Service must prove *beyond a reasonable doubt* that after the making of the Anti-social Behaviour Order the defendant continued to 'cause harassment, alarm or distress'. Anyone found guilty of breaching an ASBO can be jailed for up to 5 years and/or required to pay a fine. As a Youth Court is a criminal court, any application for an ASBO will be brought before either a Magistrates' Court acting in its civil judicial capacity or a County Court. However, because the breach of an ASBO is a criminal offence, such cases would be brought before a Youth Court or Crown Court depending on the age of the defendant and the seriousness of the alleged offence resulting in the breach.

Under s.1E of the Crime and Disorder Act 1998 any *relevant authority* making an application for an ASBO must consult with the other *relevant authorities*. This means that a local authority or social landlord considering applying for an ASBO must consult with the police and vice versa. Non-statutory guidance Home Office (2003) *A Guide to Anti-Social Behaviour Orders and Acceptable Behaviour Contracts* sets out the procedures for consultation between *relevant authorities*. Home Office (2003: 22) emphasises that,

> A fully co-ordinated approach is essential if anti-social behaviour is to be tackled. Effective defence of communities depends on all agencies – including housing organisations, social services, education authorities and youth services – accepting that promoting safe and orderly neighbourhoods is a priority and working together to agree a response to unacceptable behaviour . . . A multi-agency approach should be adopted so that all agencies that could hold information on the individual in question are involved in the process at an early stage. Such agencies include the probation service, social services, health services, the youth offending team and voluntary organisations, all of which may have come into contact with the individual or members of their family.

Home Office (2003: 23) requires *relevant authorities* to put in place protocols which ensure multi-agency consultation, information sharing, coordinated action and effective case management. In Sheffield the statutory requirement for partnership under s.1E of the Crime and Disorder Act 1998 was implemented through case conferences of the ASBO panel. At the case conference meeting of 4 February 2003, which first considered an ASBO application regarding M, present were representatives from the Housing Department of Sheffield City Council (which wished to initiate ASBO proceedings), police officers and M's social worker. Representatives from both the Youth Offending Team and the boy's school had been invited, but did not attend. Home Office (2003: 24) stipulates that 'any agency should be able to request a case management meeting' which 'should be held within two weeks of the identification of a case'. The guidance also notes that while Youth Offending Teams and educational establishments are not *relevant authorities* under the Crime and Disorder Act 1998, in the interests of coordinated action, representatives from these agencies should be invited to case conference meetings as a matter of course (ibid.). Home Office (2003: 23) directs that 'case management meetings should be action oriented and outcome focused, the primary objective being to identify and implement appropriate measures to protect communities from anti-social acts'.

It is plain that the ASBO panel meeting of 4 February 2003 did not meet a number of the good practice requirements set out in Home Office (2003). First, there were absences of key professionals from the 4 February 2003 meeting. Secondly, even a month after this panel meeting, the Housing Department, despite consultation with *relevant authorities* regarding its intention to seek an ASBO, had taken little further action. At a second meeting of the ASBO panel on 24 April 2003 it was agreed that the necessity for seeking an ASBO against M had been proved. However, the panel still put off initiating court proceedings, instead opting to wait until it had received a report from Social Services on the boy's circumstances. Home Office (2003: 24) recognises the importance of Children's Services completing an up-to-date assessment on a young person who may be the subject of an ASBO, but emphasises that this can take place in parallel with the application for an ASBO.

In fact the ASBO panel did not make an application for an ASBO until October 2003 and therefore six months after the decision by the panel to seek an order in the first place. Mr Justice Newman, presiding over the present case, observed that there was considerable delay in commencing proceedings for an ASBO despite consultation and an agreement in principle between *relevant authorities* to proceed with this course of action. He noted that this created the rather absurd situation in which the boy went on to commit 21 incidents of anti-social behaviour between April and September 2003, in other words after the point at which the ASBO panel had decided that it had enough evidence to proceed with an application for an order (para. 19). The ASBO panel had plainly failed to protect the public from anti-social behaviour by failing to act promptly on its own decision.

To summarise, there was consistently poor attendance by key professionals at case conferences of the ASBO panel, which was then exacerbated by poor follow through of decisions made at this multi-agency forum. The result was undue delay in actually applying for the ASBO, thus creating the opportunity for M to commit a number of further offences with impunity. Government-issued guidance sets out the framework and appropriate timescales for inter-agency cooperation in relation to Anti-social Behaviour Orders. Professionals from most of the agencies involved with the boy failed to adhere to the guidance with the consequent persistence of M's offending behaviour. Social workers must be clear about their roles and responsibilities in these multi-agency contexts and ensure that they both fulfil their own remit and draw to the attention of more senior colleagues any shortcomings in inter-agency protocols. Working in partnership with professionals from other agencies and disciplines is clearly required by paragraph 6. 7 of the GSCC *Code of Practice for Social Care Workers*.

Multi-agency work

Crucial to the multi-agency process regarding ASBOs is the clarification contained in Home Office (2003: 26) that the consultation requirement under s.1E of the Crime and Disorder Act 1998 is just that. There is no statutory requirement that all *relevant authorities* agree unanimously to making an ASBO application. In the present case M's social worker raised reservations about proceeding with an ASBO at several case conferences of the ASBO panel. While no *relevant authority* can veto the decision of another *relevant authority* to make an ASBO application, Home Office (2003: 26) makes clear that 'the expectation is that any reservations or alternative proposals should be discussed carefully against the background of the overriding need to bring the anti-social behaviour to a speedy end'. All that is required by the court to demonstrate compliance with s.1E is a 'signed document of consultation' which does not include details of how the case conference arrived at its decision. In the present case reservations expressed by the boy's social worker led to drift and inaction by the ASBO panel, rather than a candid exchange of views culminating in an alternative course of action. In this connection Home Office

(2003: 34) reminds *relevant authorities* that while it is ultimately for the court to decide on the conditions to be attached to an ASBO, the agency making the application should make recommendations to the court. In other words there is scope, even where *relevant authorities* initially disagree with each another, to develop agreement through deliberating on the terms of the Anti-social Behaviour Order to be recommended to the court.

One obstacle to taking coordinated action to curb the boy's anti-social behaviour was the parallel processes of statutory reviews under the Children Act 1989 in relation to his care, and the series of case conferences held by the ASBO panel to consider his anti-social behaviour. Often different professionals were present at these two sets of meetings, resulting in gaps in the information being shared. Under s.115 of the Crime and Disorder Act 1998 any person with information pertaining to action under the statute is empowered to disclose that information to the police, local authority, probation service or health authority. This is an important provision, as under the Data Protection Act 1998, data subjects normally have the right under s.10 to prevent disclosure of personal data where this is likely to cause harm or distress to the data subject.

Given these statutory provisions it should not have been problematic for professionals from Children's Services attending the case conferences of the ASBO panel to share sufficient information to gain a holistic picture of the child's needs and family circumstances. Not only were Children's Services directly involved as his corporate parent, but the Youth Offending Team, which is described in the box below, was intensively working with M. This was as a result of the Supervision Order made by Sheffield Magistrates' Court in May 2003. When M was convicted a month later by the same court of interfering with a motor vehicle this was amended to include an Intensive Supervision and Surveillance Programme (ISSP).

Background information

Youth Offending Team (YOT)

Youth Offending Teams were established under s.39 of the Crime and Disorder Act 1998 and removed responsibility for intervention with young people caught up in the justice system away from Social Services Departments. Youth Offending Teams are designed to create a multidisciplinary team of professionals specialised in working with young offenders and young people at risk of offending. There is a minimum statutory requirement that each YOT consist of police officers, social workers, probation officers and nominees from the education and health services. Beyond this, psychologists, housing officers, youth workers, etc. may also be members. Youth Offending Teams have the following functions and responsibilities:

- Assessment of children and young people for rehabilitation programmes.
- Provision of appropriate adults when children or young people are arrested.
- Support for children and young people awaiting trial.
- Provision of court reports in criminal proceedings.
- Provision of *responsible officers* for Parenting Orders and Child Safety Orders.
- Supervision of children or young people subject to a Supervision Order or other forms of community sentence.
- Supervision and support of children and young people serving custodial sentences or on remand.
- Coordination of youth justice services.

This is the most rigorous form of non-custodial sentence which can be imposed on young offenders. It requires as a minimum 25 hours contact time each week, comprising work with members of the Youth Offending Team or attendance at prescribed programmes. At least two surveillance checks per day by the Youth Offending Team are mandatory. Supervision extends over weekends and can include 24-hour monitoring and electronic tagging to follow the movements of the offender. M's ISSP required him to attend a named school (from which he had been truant for many months) and a programme of summer activities.

HM Government (2006a: para. 2.116–7) Working Together to Safeguard Children reminds Youth Offending Teams that, 'A number of the children who are supervised by the YOTs will also be children in need, some of whose needs will require safeguarding. It is necessary therefore for there to be clear links between youth justice and local authority children's social care both at strategic level and at a child-specific operational level.' In the present case there was disjunction between the information held and shared between the three multidisciplinary forums which were involved in decision making in relation to M. These included the Youth Offending Team, the series of Statutory Review Meetings and the case conferences of the ASBO panel. Attendance at the review meetings and ASBO panel were often by different professionals and sometimes by different agencies. As a result there were misunderstandings of the decisions which had been taken by another multidisciplinary meeting and unexplained changes regarding what information was being awaited prior to a final decision being made on the ASBO application. The table below summarises events at the parallel meetings of the ASBO Panel and the Looked After Statutory Review Meetings for M.

Date of meeting	Statutory Review	ASBO Panel
December 2002	*Present*: M's social worker, YOT representative, teacher from school. *Outcome*: need for residential and possibly secure placement.	
February 2003		*Present*: M's social worker, representatives from police and local authority Housing Department, and LEA attendance officer. *Outcome:* agreement in principle to ASBO application and LEA attendance officer to obtain up-to-date assessment of M's needs.
March 2003	*Present*: M's social worker, YOT members, representative from school. *Outcome:* misapprehension that the local authority Housing Department had already applied for an ASBO and M's grandmother to be assessed to become a foster carer.	
April 2003		*Present:* representatives from the police and local authority Housing Department. *Outcome:* evidence justified application for ASBO but panel to await report from Social Services as to whether the ASBO is necessary.

(Continued)

Date of meeting	Statutory Review	ASBO Panel
May 2003		*Present:* representatives from the police, local authority Housing Department and the LEA. M's social worker was not present but sent a report expressing reservations about seeking an ASBO.
		Outcome: Panel approved application for ASBO, but no application was in fact made until October 2003.

Not only did Mr Justice Newman in his judgement criticise the lack of collaboration and coordination of action between different multidisciplinary forums, but he also highlighted the poor quality of information put before the ASBO Panel in May 2003. Professionals from Housing, Social Services and Education were all censured for their poorly detailed responses to the questions in the standard pro forma used by the ASBO Panel. Often their answers consisted of just a few lines which failed to demonstrate that full consideration had been given to the issues at stake. The judge alighted upon a typical example of this poor practice. The professional from the Local Education Authority (LEA) in answer to the question 'What further action are you intending to take or do you think may be appropriate to try and deal with the subject's involvement in anti-social behaviours?' wrote simply 'consideration of an ASBO'. This curt response indicated to Mr Justice Newman that no serious consideration had been given to the alternatives to an ASBO, nor as to why possible alternative courses of action had been ruled out.

Reviewing the facts of this case, a crucial aspect was the objection of M's social worker to the proposal of the Housing Department of Sheffield City Council to apply for an ASBO against the boy at a case conference of the ASBO Panel. Paragraph 6.5 of the GSCC *Code of Practice for Social Care Workers* requires practitioners to work 'openly and co-operatively with colleagues' which includes 'treating them with respect'. In the context of applying for an ASBO, the child's social worker was present at a multi-agency forum constituted to consider whether or not an application should be made for an ASBO. As Home Office (2003) guidance makes clear, this is a consultative forum and not one which required the unanimity of all the *relevant authorities* in order to proceed with an ASBO against a young person. But it is a forum in which professionals are expected to articulate their perspectives and to discuss and negotiate these with one another. Therefore it was entirely correct that M's social worker should have taken this opportunity to voice her concerns about the detrimental aspects of proceeding with an ASBO against the boy. In doing so she acted in an open manner which did not obstruct the working of the case conference of the ASBO Panel.

The problem was that her colleagues in the Housing Department of Sheffield City Council failed to follow procedures laid down in government guidance. In accord with Home Office (2003) once the Housing Department had take into account the perspective of other *relevant authorities* it should have proceeded to make a decision either to apply for the ASBO or in conjunction with other agencies to pursue an alternative course of action. In the present case neither of these things happened. Instead there was procrastination leading to postponement of a decision either way. This illustrates the importance of understanding not only the role of the social worker in a multi-agency context, but also the role, purpose and decision-making powers of the multi-agency setting itself. As social workers were attendees of the case conferences of the ASBO Panel, both as members of the Youth Offending Team and as employees of Children's Services directly involved in work with M, they had a responsibility to ensure that this particular multi-agency forum functioned correctly.

Control of child *in care*

The criticism by Mr Justice Newman of multidisciplinary decision making included the conflict of interest which existed for the child's social worker who was acting on behalf of a local authority with parental responsibility for M under a Care Order. This meant that she was responsible for promoting his welfare and safeguarding him under s.22(3) and for ascertaining his wishes and feelings under s.22(4) of the Children Act 1989. The difficulty for M's social worker was that as a participant at the case conference of the ASBO Panel she was acting in a punitive capacity. Home Office (2003: 40) is explicit that where a young person aged 10–17 years is the subject of an application for an ASBO this should involve an assessment of their circumstances and needs to be conducted using the *Framework for the Assessment of Children in Need and their Families.*

Home Office (2003: 41) reminds Children's Services that where an assessment under the *Framework* indicates the need for social work support or services these should be put in place whatever the stage of an ASBO application. In the first instance Mr Justice Newman expressed concern that M's social worker in her report to the case conference of the ASBO Panel held in May 2003 had used the standard pro forma of the ASBO Panel. This meant that her written responses were constrained by the format of the ASBO Panel pro forma. In fact as per Home Office (2003: 40) she should have either shared the needs identified by a Core Assessment with the ASBO Panel or updated any existing Core Assessment to take account of changes in the boy's circumstances and the likely impact of an ASBO on him.

Aside from the failure to share an up-to-date assessment of M's needs with the ASBO Panel, M's grandmother (acting as his litigation friend) sought to question the conduct of his social worker during the court case concerning the ASBO. M's social worker was summoned to appear, but did not attend court. This meant that the boy and his grandmother attended without anyone with parental responsibility for M accompanying him in court. The Magistrate expressed concern regarding the conduct of the Social Services Department and had to adjourn the court case as a result.

M's social worker was then changed and in February 2004 M's solicitor sought a meeting with the new social worker to ascertain his willingness to act as a defence witness on behalf of M in the upcoming court hearing on the Anti-social Behaviour Order. M's new social worker attended the meeting with his legal representative. On advice from his lawyer M's new social worker refused to act as a witness in his defence. This meant that no one from the local authority which held parental responsibility for the child was going to attend court to support him or his legal defence. M was informed by his solicitor of the position adopted by his new social worker. As a result the boy became distrustful of a social worker who had refused to testify on his behalf and who had, it transpired, expressed his willingness to testify against the boy in relation to the ASBO application. Such a state of affairs destroyed the working relationship between M and his new social worker.

Presiding over the present case Mr Justice Newman acknowledged the dilemma posed for local authorities who were required under one statute to promote the welfare of children and under another to take action to prevent persistent offending and harassment of the public. In the judge's opinion it was self evident that any caring parent, regardless of how much they wished to impose discipline on a recalcitrant child, 'would hesitate to place their child at risk of detention in custody' (para. 44). It was reasonable to suppose that any concerned parent would accompany their child to court and most likely appear as a witness for the defence. This was an expectation and indeed legal entitlement denied to M because he had a statutory parent in the form of the local authority who was the very entity seeking an ASBO against him. Here was M's parent, in the shape of the local authority, pursuing a course of action which could ultimately result in his imprisonment. Faced with this paradox, Justice Newman asked himself 'how the interests of a child in care can be protected when the local authority responsible for the child's care makes an application for an anti-social behaviour order against the child' (para. 33). In posing this question his judgement established a precedent for dealing with exactly this kind of circumstance.

This case presents another example of role conflict for social workers due to the multiple responsibilities which local authorities have for children and young people. Like Case 4 in Chapter 4, here was a child's social worker participating in decision-making processes in respect of two different roles. On the one hand M's social worker was acting to promote the child's welfare in the context of the parental responsibility held for M by the local authority. On the other hand M's social worker was participating in a multi-agency forum as the employee of a *relevant authority* which was deciding whether or not to apply for an ASBO against M. The social worker was plainly caught in a conflict of interests between promoting the child's welfare and acting punitively against him. This conflict became even starker when M's second social worker refused to even attend the Youth Court with him, leaving him without the support of anyone holding parental responsibility. For both of M's social workers this was a situation in which they should have acted in accordance with paragraph 6.3 of the GSCC *Code of Practice for Social Care Workers* which urges practitioners to inform 'your employer or the appropriate authority about any personal difficulties that might affect your ability to do your job competently and safely'. Social workers need to be perceptive and sensitive to the potential conflicts that may arise for them in the course of their work with children, parents and other family members.

Judgement in *R (on application of M (a child))* v. *Sheffield Magistrates' Court*

Mr Justice Newman concluded that a decision to apply for an ASBO for a *looked after* child falls under s.22(4) of the Children Act 1989. In giving judgement he stated that compliance with this provision requires the following take place:

- The local authority consults the child, any parent, person with parental responsibility or other relevant person before making a decision in relation to the child.
- Having consulted all parties under s.22(4) the child's social worker should produce a report on the child's behalf and should not participate in the decision whether or not to pursue an application for an ASBO.
- The agency contemplating an application for an ASBO must take account of the social worker's report.
- Once a decision has been made to apply to court for an ASBO there should be no further contact between the local authority's Social Services Department and the ASBO Panel or team, without the knowledge and consent of the child's solicitor.
- Where the ASBO application relates to a child *in care*, a representative from Social Services must attend court to ensure that its view is taken into consideration by Magistrates in reaching their judgement.

Plainly this was not the procedure adopted by the local authority involved with M. Mr Justice Newman therefore ruled that no application for an ASBO in relation to M could succeed until such times as the local authority acted in accordance with his ruling.

Critical questions

1 Anti-social Behaviour Orders are now a key means by which local authorities, the police and social landlords endeavour to reduce anti-social behaviour, particularly by young people. These are civil orders which result in a criminal offence if they are breached. What are your own personal views about ASBOs? Would this personal view create conflicts with your professional role as a member of a Youth Offending Team? If so, how would it affect your practice and how would you manage this as a qualified social worker?

2 Poor understanding of the functions of a multi-agency forum and inadequate inter-agency collaboration pervade events surrounding M. Reread this case and list the different problems which occurred. If you were a social worker involved in a similar situation how would you contribute to effective inter-agency partnership working?

3 Social workers for M were placed in a difficult position because of their dual role – as employees of the local authority with a legal obligation to protect the public, and as named workers for a child, responsible for promoting his welfare. Although in this case the conflict was particularly extreme, it remains a tension for all social workers involved with young offenders. How would you manage this professional tension?

CASE 4
R v. H [2007] EWCA Crim 2330

Importance of the case

It explores the assessment of risk of re-offending and the legal definition of dangerousness. The case also highlights the role of pre-sentence reports in providing advice to sentencing judges.

History of the case

H was found guilty by a Magistrates' Court of causing grievous bodily harm to another young person. Due to the level of dangerousness she was judged to pose to the public she was then committed to the Crown Court for sentencing. The Crown Court imposed a custodial sentence of two extended to four years. H appealed against this sentence to the Court of Appeal.

Facts of the case

H, then aged 15 years, during an argument with her friend L, then aged 12 years, pushed her to the ground and proceeded to kick and stamp on her. L sustained multiple bruising to her head, including a fracture to the right eye socket. She remained in hospital for four days and was absent from school for a month as a result of her injuries. L also suffered repeated nightmares in the aftermath of the attack. H had no previous convictions, nor history of sudden and ferocious physical attacks on others. Due to the nature of H's offence the Magistrates trying her case considered that she presented a risk to the public and invoked the dangerous offender provisions of the Criminal Justice Act 2003. This required referring the case up to the Crown Court to determine H's sentence. A pre-sentence report submitted by the Youth Offending Team indicated that H had been sexually abused by an adult since she was 9 years of age, had low educational ability and poor social skills. The report incorporated a risk assessment indicating that H was not a danger to the public and advocating a community sentence implemented by way of Supervision and Curfew Orders. The judge at the Crown Court decided that H was dangerous and sentenced her to a two-year custodial sentence as punishment extended to four years to protect members of the public. H appealed against this sentence on the grounds that the judge had failed to consider the Pre-Sentence Report and other evidence indicating that she did not present a significant risk to the public.

Key people in the case

H – girl aged 15 years at time of offence
L – friend of H aged 12 years

Discussion of the case

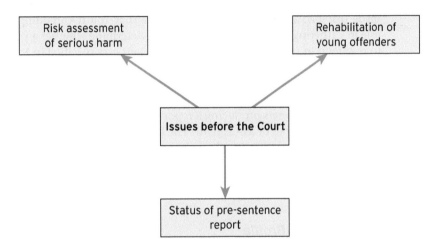

Risk assessment of serious harm

The Criminal Justice Act 2003 introduced two new forms of sentence for certain kinds of sexual and violent offences (specified in Sch. 15) related to an assessment of a convicted offender's 'dangerousness' to the public. These are Detention for Public Protection, which is for an indeterminate period of imprisonment, and the Extended Sentence for Public Protection, which specifies the time to be served in custody by the offender. Both new types of custodial sentence can be handed down to adults or children aged 10–17 years. In the present case the Crown Court sentenced H to two years for her crime and then added a further two years under the Extended Sentence for Public Protection provision of the Criminal Justice Act 2003. The additional two years in custody were designed to take account of the perceived risk of H harming members of the public by engaging in similar unprovoked violent attacks were she released prematurely back into the community.

Only if a person is found guilty of one of the sexual or violent offences listed in Sch. 15 of the Criminal Justice Act 2003 must the court assess their 'dangerousness'. Not all sexual or violent crimes fall under the provisions of the Criminal Justice Act 2003. Where an offender is convicted of an offence specified in Sch. 15 the court must form a judgement as to the likelihood of the offender engaging in further such specified sexual or violent acts were they to be released back into the community. In statutory terms, under s.229(1)(b) of the Criminal Justice Act 2003 the court is required to determine if there is a 'significant risk to members of the public of serious harm occasioned by the commission by [the offender] of further such offences'. This is commonly referred to as the 'significant risk' test. The crucial terms in this provision are 'significant risk' and 'serious harm'. The qualification of *significant* and *serious* indicate that a certain threshold has to be reached before an offender who has committed an act specified in Sch. 15 can be subject to the new sentence provisions of the Criminal Justice Act 2003.

Issues relating to risk assessment and dangerousness are not just matters for judges, they are central to the work of Youth Offending Teams as they prepare reports on children and young people coming before the court accused of sexual and violent crimes. Youth Justice Board (2006) *Criminal Justice Act 2003, 'Dangerousness' and the New Sentences for Public Protection: Guidance for Youth Offending Teams* sets out instructions for practitioners in this area of work. Youth Justice Board (2006: 8) states that, 'The YOT has a significant role to play in contributing to the assessment of dangerousness by providing the court with detailed information and assessment regarding the young person and their level of risk of harm to others. This should be based on a comprehensive assessment made using *Asset.'* It is clear from guidance that Youth Offending Teams play a crucial role in gathering evidence to help the court determine whether a young offender is likely to re-offend in respect of the sexual and violent acts specified in Sch. 15 of the Criminal Justice Act 2003. Furthermore, risk is to be measured by Youth Offending Teams using the assessment framework referred to as *Asset*. This consists of two standardised assessment tools: *Asset – Core Profile* and *Asset – Risk of Serious Harm*. According to Youth Justice Board (2006: 8) practitioners producing a report for the court concerning 'dangerousness', must complete both types of assessment. The box below outlines the *Asset* assessment tool.

 Background information

Asset - Core Profile

Asset - Core Profile is an assessment tool designed as a systematic approach to gathering information on the circumstances and characteristics of young offenders. Based on a collation of the research, it comprises 12 different elements associated with the risk of re-offending. Each element consists essentially of a series of tick boxes and, on completing these, the assessor is required to assign a score from 0 to 4 depending on how strongly associated these aspects of the young offender's background are with re-offending. An *Asset - Core Profile* must be undertaken with every young person who comes into contact with the Youth Offending Team in connection with a Final Warning (verbal warning given by a police officer for a first or second offence), Referral Order or a pre-sentence report. The factors known to be associated with the risk of re-offending and incorporated into *Asset - Core Profile* are:

1 Living arrangements
2 Family and personal relationships
3 Education, training and employment
4 Neighbourhood
5 Lifestyle
6 Substance use
7 Physical health
8 Emotional and mental health
9 Perception of self and others

10 Thinking and behaviour

11 Attitudes to offending

12 Motivation to change

In addition to the tick boxes and scoring system, practitioners completing the *Asset - Core Profile* must justify their scoring by using the evidence boxes incorporated within the assessment tool to support their conclusions. There are also three sections towards the end of *Asset - Core Profile* requiring practitioners to identify positive aspects of the offender's background in terms of Individual, Family and Community Factors which reduce the risk of re-offending. An additional section of *Asset - Core Profile* addresses the vulnerability of the young person and comprises a series of questions exploring his or her experience of bullying, risk taking, stress, loss and self-harm. The sections recording positive factors and vulnerability are not scored.

The *Asset - Core Profile* is under review in order to make it more consistent with the *Framework for the Assessment of Children in Need and their Families*. This should make it easier for professionals responsible for working with young offenders and those safeguarding children to more effectively assess children and understand the interdependencies between offending, risk of harm and welfare needs.

Asset – Risk of Serious Harm must be completed if the practitioner has ticked any of the boxes for 'yes' in answer to the final set of questions contained in the last section of *Asset – Core Profile* entitled *Indicators of serious harm to others*. This supplementary assessment tool focusses on potential harm to others and provides a standardised pro forma for more detailed investigation of the risk factors in the backgrounds of offenders known to have committed sexual or violent crimes. *Asset – Risk of Serious Harm* is divided into a number of sections. These focus sequentially on: the offender's pattern of offending behaviour; the risk factors present within his or her current circumstances; any factors protecting against further offending; future behaviour and likelihood of re-offending. Based on this information the practitioner is then required to judge whether the offending behaviour identified falls within the *Asset* definition of 'serious harm' which means causing to others 'death or injury (either physical or psychological) which is life threatening and/or traumatic and from which recovery is expected to be difficult, incomplete or impossible' (Youth Justice Board, 2005b: 4).

Having concluded that the offence and potential for re-offending does come within this definition, the practitioner must then make a judgement as to whether the offender falls into the category of *low*, *medium*, *high* or *very high* risk (defined in *Asset* guidance) of committing further offences likely to cause 'serious harm'. Youth Justice Board (2006: 10) indicates that normally a young person would be judged as *dangerous* by the court within the terms of the Criminal Justice Act 2003 if he or she was assessed as falling into the category of *very high risk*. Occasionally, if there are particularly concerning aspects of their offending behaviour, young people assessed as presenting a *high risk* will also be judged *dangerous* by the courts. In the present case before the Court of Appeal the pre-sentence report produced by the Youth Offending Team on this 15-year-old girl, H, which incorporated an *Asset* assessment, indicated that she was not a *dangerous* offender within the meaning of the Criminal Justice Act 2003. Yet, despite this, the Crown Court judge still handed down a two-year Extended Sentence for Public Protection. It was on account of the contradiction between the pre-sentence report and the sentence itself that the girl made her appeal to the Court of Appeal.

Pre-sentence reports form a large proportion of the work of members of the Youth Offending Team, including social workers. As is evident from the guidance referred to throughout the discussion of this case, there are assessment tools and instructions to support the completion of pre-sentence reports. Concerning the background to the girl's attack upon her friend, both the Magistrates' Court and Crown Court accepted that the pre-sentence report had been fully researched, correctly completed and duly submitted to the court. It was precisely because the pre-sentence report followed best practice and was properly evidenced, but yet set aside by the sentencing judge, that the Court of Appeal agreed to hear an appeal.

Status of pre-sentence report

As a matter of course, Magistrates have asked for a pre-sentence report on the conviction of a young person where there is the possibility of handing down a custodial sentence. The Criminal Justice Act 2003 now makes this a statutory requirement. Youth Justice Board (2006: 11) *Criminal Justice Act 2003, 'Dangerousness' and the New Sentences for Public Protection: Guidance for Youth Offending Teams* stipulates that both an *Asset – Core Profile* and *Asset – Risk of Serious Harm* must form part of the pre-sentence report where a court is required to make a judgement regarding the risk an offender poses to the public. In addition, a pre-sentence report may draw on specialist assessments by other agencies and professionals, for example a psychiatric report or a Statement of Educational Needs. These supplementary reports will provide further detail on the circumstances and character of an offender pertinent to a decision on sentencing. The format and content of pre-sentence reports are set out in Youth Justice Board (2004) *National Standards for Youth Justice Services* which are excerpted in the box below.

 Key guidance

National Standards for Youth Justice Services

National Standard 7: Reports for Courts and Youth Offender Panels

7.2 All reports, in whatever format, must be:
- balanced
- impartial
- timely
- focused
- free from discriminatory language and stereotypes
- verified and factually accurate
- understandable to the young person

7.3 Reports must be based on:
- an *Asset* assessment
- a minimum of one interview with the young person
- an interview with at least one parent and/or carer where possible
- victim personal statements where available
- information from all relevant sources

7.7 The purpose of a Pre-Sentence Report (PSR) is to provide information to the sentencing court about the young person and the offence(s) committed and to assist the court to come to a decision on a suitable sentence.

7.8 A PSR must be in writing and a copy provided to the young person, his or her parent(s) or carer(s) (if appropriate – there is a need to consider child protection implications), the court, the Crown Prosecution Service and defence.

7.9 A PSR must be produced within 15 working days of request. PRSs concerning persistent young offenders (PYOs) and those young offenders meeting the ISSP criteria must be produced within 10 working days of request.

7.10 A PSR must be written using the following format:
- front sheet
- sources of information, including whether an Asset has been completed
- offence analysis, including impact of the offence on victim(s)
- assessment of young person
- assessment of risk to the community, including the risk of re-offending and harm
- conclusion including proposal for sentencing

While emphasising the crucial contribution of the pre-sentence report to the court's decision on sentencing, Youth Justice Board (2006: 11) makes clear that 'there is no automatic link between the results of a YOT assessment and the final decision of the court . . . the YOTs responsibility in each individual case is to present all relevant information to the court which will then make a determination of dangerousness'. This does not mean that there is no connection between the pre-sentence report and the sentence handed down by a court. The presentation of a pre-sentence report to the court is a statutory requirement and judges are not at liberty simply to ignore it. Youth Justice Board (2006: 17) states that, 'before imposing a custodial sentence or youth community order, the court must take into account all information available to it, including that relating to the offence and the offender. In addition, the courts are now obliged to request and consider a PSR.'

In the present case the argument put by H's barrister was that the Crown Court judge responsible for passing sentence on her had failed to give due weight to the pre-sentence report. The Youth Offending Team had produced a detailed and properly completed pre-sentence report which by all accounts met National Standard 7 (see text box above). This also comprised a neuro-psychological report and an assessment from a mental health clinician. These indicated that the child had been sexually abused since she was 9 years old, had poor social skills and problems with trust, but had not previously exhibited fits of sudden violence. The pre-sentence report ended by recommending a non-custodial sentence for H, consisting of a Supervision Order and Curfew Order. Indeed, the Court of Appeal judge commented, 'the Youth Offending Service worker set out in a report, in a carefully-reasoned, step-by-step approach to the assessment of dangerousness, the reasons for his conclusion that there is no significant risk to members of the public or serious harm occasioned by the commission by H of further specified offences' (para. 8). In the opinion of the Court of Appeal there were no grounds for questioning either the assessment of risk or the conclusions drawn from that assessment regarding the girl's future offending behaviour. Therefore the appeal against her sentence turned on the degree to which the Crown Court judge considered the report and whether there were other factors beyond those contained in the pre-sentence report which accounted for his imposition of an Extended Sentence.

Justifying his assessment of H's dangerousness, the Crown Court judge had stated (para. 5):

The reason I do so consider that there is such a risk is that despite the work that has taken place over the last two months or so with H, the very unpredictability of this attack, combined with the ferocity of it, and the fact that it took place in a way which was apparently uncontrolled, leads me to conclude that there is such a risk.

The Court of Appeal judge in the present case turned to precedent in *R* v. *Lang and Others* [2005] EWCA Crim 2864 in which Lord Justice Rose said at paragraph 17(vi):

> It is still necessary, when sentencing young offenders, to bear in mind that, within a shorter time than adults, they may change and develop. This and their level of maturity may be highly pertinent when assessing what their future conduct may be and whether it may give rise to significant risk of serious harm.

The Court of Appeal concluded that the Crown Court judge had failed to take account of the girl's young age and had not identified any other factors in his judgement which justified overruling the professional opinion set out in the pre-sentence report. In short, a judge departing from the conclusions and recommendations of a pre-sentence report must justify that departure. This, the sentencing judge at the Crown Court had failed to do.

The facts of this case and the conclusions arrived at by the Court of Appeal judge demonstrate the centrality of pre-sentence reports to decisions on sentencing. Here was a situation in which a pre-sentence report had been fastidiously researched and written up by a professional from the Youth Offending Team. Plainly a pre-sentence report cannot determine the sentence which is handed down to a young offender. That is to say, a social worker in a Youth Offending Team cannot dictate to a Magistrate or Crown Court judge as to what sentence he or she should pass. But what the case concerning H does demonstrate is the considerable influence which a pre-sentence report can and should have upon a sentencing judge. A pre-sentence report which follows best practice can neither dictate what sentence is to be handed down, nor can it be ignored by a sentencing judge. It is a powerful means by which social workers can convey the mitigating circumstances or welfare needs of a child or young person involved in a serious crime. Paragraph 4.2 of the GSCC Code also requires social workers to follow 'risk assessment policies and procedures to assess whether the behaviour of service users presents a risk of harm to themselves or others'. To this end social workers must balance the need to protect the public against the welfare needs of children as indeed must sentencing judges.

Rehabilitation of young offenders

Every young person found guilty of an offence confronts the court with a dilemma. Should that individual be treated essentially as a *child in need* within the definition of s.17 of the Children Act 1989, with all the welfare implications that carries, or as a criminal in much the same way as an adult? The youth justice system dates from the Children Act 1908 which established that different considerations should apply in the sentencing of child offenders. A series of statutes enacted since the early twentieth century have changed the weight to be given by sentencing judges to the child's welfare on the one hand and the imperatives of justice and punishment on the other. The Criminal Justice Act 2003, which sets out the current statutory framework for sentencing, stipulates that any sentence needs to take account of the requirement to:

- Punish and rehabilitate the offender.
- Reduce re-offending.
- Deter others from offending.
- Offer reparation by the offender.

- Protect the public.
- Assess the gravity of the offence in conjunction with any aggravating or mitigating circumstances when passing sentence.

This framework is supplemented by the sentencing guidelines issued from time to time by the Magistrates' Association and the Court of Appeal. In relation to children, judges are also bound by a statutory duty under the Children and Young Persons Act 1933 which is reproduced in the box below.

Key legislation

Children and Young Persons Act 1933 (as amended)

s.44 Every court in dealing with a child or young person who is brought before it, either as an offender or otherwise, shall have regard to the welfare of the child or young person, and shall in a proper case take steps for removing him from undesirable surroundings, and for securing that proper provision is made for his education and training.

In contrast to s.1 of the Children Act 1989 which applies in Family and Care Proceedings and makes the child's welfare the court's *paramount* consideration, s.44 of the Children and Young Persons Act 1933 only makes the child's welfare *a* consideration. Therefore the statutory duty to have regard to the child's welfare imposed by the Children and Young Persons Act 1933 sits alongside other statutory duties. These other statutory obligations include that imposed under the Criminal Justice Act 2003 which requires judges to have regard to the 'dangerousness' of offenders when deciding whether to impose a jail term and for how long. The Criminal Justice Act 2003 also codifies the principle of proportionality, with less serious offences meriting fines moving up to community orders and culminating in custodial sentences for the most serious crimes. At the same time, s.37(1) of the Crime and Disorder Act 1998 states that, 'it shall be the principal aim of the youth justice system to prevent offending by children and young persons'. Thus, judges operate within a web of statutory duties and sentencing guidelines.

Re-examining the reasoning of the Crown Court judge in handing down sentence, the Court of Appeal concluded that not only had the judge erred in disregarding the well-evidenced professional opinion contained in the pre-sentence report, but that he had given insufficient consideration to H's welfare. While a custodial sentence would of course punish her for her offence, it would not address her welfare. The Youth Offending Team had recommended that H be given a Supervision Order detailing arrangements for her education and other programmes of instruction and treatment, including counselling. This was to be supplemented by a Curfew Order which was designed as a punishment for the attack on L and would confine H to her home during the evenings. By addressing her educational needs and deficits in her social skills in conjunction with the need for punishment the Youth Offending Team was attending to H's welfare within the context of the youth justice system.

Judges sentencing convicted defendants are required to take a range of factors into consideration in determining whether to hand down a community or custodial sentence or how long to make a term of imprisonment. For children, there are additional considerations concerning their welfare, the stage of their development at which they committed a serious crime, and how a particular sentence might affect their future development. Social workers responsible for writing pre-sentence reports must also consider the same range of factors and advise sentencing judges accordingly. Consequently, practitioners are also required to balance matters relating to the welfare of a young offender against the need to punish and protect the public

Judgement in *R* v. *H*

The Court of Appeal quashed the extended sentence imposed on H by the Crown Court and substituted the original custodial sentence with a three-year Supervision Order and a three-month Curfew Order. This closely followed the sentence recommended in the pre-sentence report. However, the Court explicitly recognised the tension between punishment and welfare, capturing this dilemma in the closing paragraphs (paras 10 and 12) of its judgement:

> In the unusual circumstances of this case, we have concluded that the interests of the public and the interests of H will be served better by a non-custodial sentence. Whereas a sentence of detention and training would punish her, it would not achieve anything by way of the provision to her of the guidance and help that she needs to overcome her particular problems . . . We would conclude this judgement by expressing the hope that L and her parents will understand that, by taking the course that this court has taken, we do not in any way minimise the seriousness of the attack to which L was subjected . . . we consider it necessary not only to punish H, but to provide her with such help as we can to ensure that she has the opportunity of leading a useful and fulfilling life.

 ## Critical questions

1 Given what you know of the facts of this case, do you think it was correctly decided? If not, what sentence do you think should have been handed down to H and why? What does this tell you about your own perceptions and understanding of young offenders?

2 A fundamental dynamic in this case was the tension between H's welfare, the need to punish her for an offence and the need to protect the public from further re-offending by H. If you were working for a Youth Offending Team and responsible for writing pre-sentence reports for children and young people, how would you manage this tension?

3 More serious offences tend to result in an assessment of the risk of serious harm to others. Applying your knowledge of anti-oppressive practice, how might perceptions of black males, lone mothers, drug users or individuals with a mental health problem affect assessments of risk for young offenders falling into these groups or family circumstances?

 ### Critical commentary

Asset assessment tools

Asset was introduced to improve the quality of assessments conducted by the youth justice service and to provide better evaluations of risk in relation to re-offending and harm to the public alongside more appropriate prevention programmes. The Youth Justice Board designed it to enable practitioners to gather information from a range of sources in a systematic and practical way. The scoring system provides a means of measuring the likelihood of re-offending and of predicting the nature of future offending behaviour. In her research based on 300 completed assessments Baker (2008) found that *Asset - Risk of Serious Harm* had improved the quality of the data collected. The imposition of a tightly structured and standardised approach to assessment also reduced the temptation of some practitioners to rely on professional experience and 'gut feeling' to justify their assumptions (Baker, 2008: 1471). *Asset – Risk of Serious Harm* forced assessors to produce clear evidence for their conclusions. Conversely, the same study found that the enhancement of the information obtained was not matched by improved levels of analysis. Research reveals the tendency of practitioners to use the tick boxes as a form of rapid assessment while under-using the evidence boxes provided in each section to justify their rating score, synthesise the information gathered and draw accurate inferences from it.

A number of studies of practitioners' attitudes to *Asset* reveal widespread scepticism about its value in assessment. Many perceived it to be essentially a management tool designed to collect data for quality assurance purposes. Other practitioners objected to the way in which the use of a prescriptive tick-box approach to assessment undermined professional judgement. Of particular concern to them was the emphasis on negative risk factors and the failure to permit positive factors to be scored. This meant that *Asset* contained a built-in bias as to the likelihood of re-offending. Youth Offending Teams were also concerned by the scoring system which gave the appearance of mathematical objectivity when it was in fact highly dependent on each assessor's subjective judgement. The danger of this was to obscure behind a mathematical calculation the real nature of professional judgement in assessment (Smith, 2003: 101; Burnett and Appleton, 2004: 33).

CASE 5
R (on the application of AB) v. *Nottingham City Council*
[2001] EWHC Admin 235

Importance of the case

It explores the implications for inter-agency collaboration when a young person is both a youth offender and a *child in need*. The case also highlights the requirement to follow policy guidance when assessing a *child in need*.

History of the case

AB and her son SB, the claimants, sought a judicial review in the Queen's Bench Division of the High Court of the assessment of their needs conducted by the local authority.

Facts of the case

AB was the white 35-year-old divorced mother of SB, who was black and aged 14 years at the time of the High Court Case. In November 1999 the police referred the 14-year-old to Social Services because of concerns over his offending behaviour. He had been excluded from school and had not attended for over a year. In December 1999 a Child Protection Conference was convened and agreed to place SB on the child protection register under the category of neglect. A Child Protection Plan was drawn up requiring multi-agency inputs from the Youth Offending Team and the police to tackle SB's prolific offending. Further specialist assessments were to be undertaken in relation to his health and education needs, which would inform further inputs from other professionals and agencies. In March 2000 consideration was given to making an application for an Anti-social Behaviour Order against SB as he was using his dog to intimidate neighbours. A Child

Protection Review Conference in June 2000 decided to remove him from the Child Protection Register and designate him instead as a *child in need*. In November 2000 the Youth Court made him the subject of a Supervision Order. A Child in Need Review that should have taken place in December 2000 was delayed until January 2001 pending the outcome of the application for an Anti-social Behaviour Order. The boy's social worker prepared an assessment under the *Framework for the Assessment of Children in Need and their Families* for the January Child in Need Review meeting. He recommended that the boy remain designated a *child in need* and this was duly agreed at the January review meeting. Another assessment was undertaken in December 2000, independently of SB's social worker, in relation to the proceedings for an Anti-social Behaviour Order scheduled for April 2001 at the time of the High Court hearing. The mother AB and the son SB alleged that the assessment produced by SB's social worker for the January 2001 Child in Need Review meeting was inadequate and failed to identify or meet their needs.

Key people in the case

SB – aged 14 years and claimant
AB – divorced mother of SB and claimant
Mr Wise – barrister for claimants
Mr Pollard – SB's social worker
Mr Wilson – educational psychologist
Dr Randall – educational psychologist
Ms Read – independent social worker
Mr McNamara – barrister for local authority
Mr Justice Richards – judge presiding in High Court

Discussion of the case

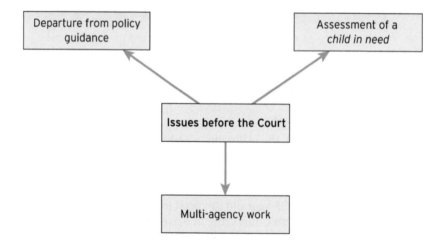

Departure from policy guidance

The mother AB was in the care of the local authority as a teenager and had been the victim of domestic violence at the hands of her former husband, which led to her taking drugs. At the time of this judicial review she had recently suffered a serious sexual assault. As a divorced single mother, she was the primary carer for two sons, one of whom was detained in a Young Offender Institution and due for release in November 2001. Her other son SB (who was also a claimant in the judicial review) was already subject to a

Supervision Order and to ongoing court proceedings in relation to an Anti-social Behaviour Order. Mother and son were living in social housing rented from a local housing trust in Nottingham. As a result of the sexual assault perpetrated against her, the mother felt unsafe living in her house and asked that she and her son be moved to alternative accommodation. Social Services were aware of the involvement of the Youth Offending Team in ongoing work with the son relating to his offending behaviour.

Department of Health (2000d) *Framework for the Assessment of Children in Need and their Families* was identified by the High Court as the applicable policy guidance, a fact not in dispute between the parties. Social Services had initially commenced a s.47 investigation under the Children Act 1989 and a social worker had produced a report for the Child Protection Conference which placed SB on the Child Protection Register in December 1999. As Department of Health (2000d: para. 3.15) makes clear, a s.47 investigation because of suspicions about child maltreatment is not a separate activity from an assessment under s.17 of the Children Act 1989 in order to ascertain a child's welfare needs. The Department of Health (2000d) provides guidance for both forms of assessment. Indeed, according to the guidance the only difference between these two forms of assessment may be the 'pace and scope of the assessment' and both may be ongoing simultaneously. The flowchart contained in Department of Health (2000d: 35, Figure 5) indicates that when a child is placed on the Child Protection Register and then de-registered by a subsequent Child Protection Conference, it must decide whether the case should now be treated as 'no further action' or re-designated as 'children in need of services' which means that the child becomes a *child in need*. At the High Court there was agreement between the claimants and the respondent local authority that when the boy's name was removed from the Child Protection Register by the Child Protection Review Conference in June 2000 he remained a *child in need*.

The argument of Mr Wise, legal counsel for the claimants, was that SB's social worker, Mr Pollard, had failed to carry out a Core Assessment for a *child in need* as outlined in the *Framework for the Assessment of Children in Need and their Families* and further detailed in the supplemental age-appropriate *Core Assessment Records*. As a consequence, Mr Wise contended, the local authority had not provided adequate services to meet the boy's needs or that of his mother as his primary carer. The main criticism of Mr Pollard's assessment was that it lacked the detail required by the Department of Health (2000d) policy guidance which is explicit in the requirement for assessment to cover the three domains of the child's developmental needs, the caregiver's parental capacity and the wider family and environmental circumstances. Working in partnership with parents and children in producing an assessment and devising intervention strategies is also a key requirement of Department of Health (2000d: para. 1.33). For a *child in need* the Core Assessment should also culminate in a *Children in Need Plan* to be reviewed every six months.

Where indicated, a Core Assessment should include reports and specialist assessments by other professionals. Mr Pollard's assessment contained just one short report from Mr Wilson, a senior educational psychologist, which summarised the boy's educational history and indicated that it was not necessary to obtain a Statement of Educational Needs for him. The recommendations of SB's *child in need* assessment were:

- SB be supported to attend school.
- SB be assessed for child therapy.
- Continued work on SB's identity issues with a local project.
- Social Services to liaise closely with the Youth Offending Team, police and housing authority.

These recommendations were adopted by the Child in Need Review meeting, but it appeared that no proper care plan for SB was produced as a consequence. Mr Wise argued that: lack of detail regarding specific actions or the designated personnel to carry them out; the absence of timelines for implementation; the scantiness of specialist reports; and the vagueness of the recommendations, amounted to a failure to follow statutory guidance on assessment. The relevant guidance was the *Framework for the Assessment of Children in Need and their Families*. Of course failure to follow statutory guidance without justification amounts to maladministration under the *Wednesbury* principles.

This case was to centre on the failure of Mr Pollard, SB's social worker, to produce a detailed and adequate assessment of his needs which complied with the requirements of the *Framework for the Assessment of Children in Need and their Families*. This is policy guidance and therefore must be followed by practitioners unless there are exceptional circumstances which justify departure from it. In the High Court the local authority was unable to produce evidence to indicate that there were any extraordinary factors in play. The *Framework*, alongside *Working Together,* are the most important policy guidance for social workers involved in direct or indirect work with children. Failure to follow them inevitably results in: weak multidisciplinary inputs; inadequate assessments; poorly formulated care plans; and ineffective implementation. This is exactly what happened in relation to SB and his mother.

Assessment of a *child in need*

In his argument before the High Court, Mr Wise drew attention to the assessment produced by an independent social worker, Ms Read, in connection with the application for an Anti-social Behaviour Order, which was taking place in parallel to the series of case conferences relating to the boy's protection and welfare. The same assessment included a report by Dr Randall, an educational psychologist. This concluded that SB 'is a boy with learning difficulties and co-morbid conduct and attention deficit disorder. He requires a statutory assessment by the LEA leading to a Statement of Special Educational Needs' (para. 34). The findings of Ms Read's assessment differed significantly from those produced by Mr Pollard. Ms Read was of the opinion that SB's needs required:

- A full psychiatric and psychological assessment which will determine or exclude Attention Deficit Hyperactive Disorder or any other disorder as a diagnosis.
- An assessment of educational special needs which will lead to the identification of an appropriate school for him.
- An interim provision of home tutoring using materials which will focus on learning to read and write.
- An assessment of any identity needs he may have.
- An active effort by his mother to support and involve herself in the operation of the Supervision Order according to the proposals agreed with the Youth Offending team (para. 32).

In addition, following the sexual assault on the mother, Ms Read stated that neither mother nor son could continue to live in their present home. She proposed that the local authority exercise its powers under the Children Act 1989 to assist in the provision of suitable accommodation. Plainly the assessment conducted by Ms Read and supported by the report of Dr Randall described a set of much more grave and urgent needs than those set out by Mr Pollard, SB's social worker. Most of these needs required further investigation by specialists. Ms Read's assessment also sought to place on Social Services a statutory responsibility to identify suitable housing for mother and son. This contrasted with Mr Pollard's assessment, which referred to the need for 'SB and his mother to be supported in accessing safe and appropriate housing' (para. 29). AB and SB had been designated low priority by the housing authority and for this status to change it would require the proactive involvement of Social Services. This matter was directly relevant to a properly conducted Core Assessment, since the living environment of children is one of the three domains that practitioners must explore.

Although the Children Act 2004 was not in force at the time of the events surrounding AB and SB it was designed to address precisely this kind of situation. Section 11 of the Children Act 2004 now places a duty on key agencies, including housing authorities, to have regard to the need to safeguard children and promote their welfare in exercising their normal day-to-day functions. The Department for Communities and Local Government (2006: para. 13.3–5) explains the implications of this statutory duty for housing officers and social workers. The crucial passages from the guidance are reproduced in the box below.

Key guidance

Homelessness Code of Guidance for Local Authorities

Para. 13.3 Where an applicant is eligible for assistance and unintentionally homeless, and has a priority need because there is one or more dependent child in his or her household, the housing authority will owe a main homelessness duty to secure that accommodation is available to them. However, not all applicants with dependent children will be owed a main homelessness duty . . .

Para. 13.4 In each of the above cases, there is a possibility that situations could arise where families may find themselves without accommodation and any prospect of further assistance from the housing authority. This could give rise to a situation in which the children of such families might become children in need, within the meaning of the term as set out in s.17 of the Children Act 1989.

Para. 13.5 In such cases is it important that local authority children's services are alerted as quickly as possible because the family may wish to seek assistance under Part 3 of the Children Act 1989, in circumstances in which they are owed no, or only limited, assistance under the homelessness legislation. This will give local authority children's services the opportunity to consider the circumstances of the child(ren) and family, and plan any response that may be deemed by them to be appropriate.

The excerpt from the *Homelessness Code of Guidance for Local Authorities* set out above instructs housing authorities who discover that a family with children does not qualify for accommodation under the Housing Act 1996 Part VII to alert Children's Services. This is because although the family may not meet the criteria for obtaining accommodation under the Housing Act 1996, they may qualify for it under s.17 of the Children Act 1989. Under s.17 Children's Services have a legal power and not a duty to provide accommodation to a family where there is a *child in need*. In other words Children's Services can exercise a degree of discretion in whether to assist a family to obtain accommodation, for instance by providing the money for a deposit or for rent. Under s.213 of the Housing Act 1996 a housing authority can request the assistance of Social Services concerning the provision of accommodation to a family that presents as homeless or threatened with homelessness within the next 28 days.

In this case, AB and SB had first come to the attention of Children's Services rather than the housing authority. Under s.27 of the Children Act 1989, Children's Services can ask for the housing authority to assist them in carrying out their duties towards children. The obligation of housing authorities to cooperate in such circumstances has been further strengthened by the Children Act 2004 and the additional duties it imposes on key agencies to agree protocols to facilitate inter-agency cooperation. Therefore Mr Pollard should have been proactive in contacting the housing authority and asking them to reassess AB under the Housing Act 1996. The housing authority needed to decide whether she qualified for rehousing in alternative accommodation given that she was under threat of violence where she was presently living. Should the housing authority have concluded that she still did not fall into high priority for social housing (or even if she did, but it would have been some time before alternative accommodation could be found) then Social Services would have needed to decide whether to exercise its power under s.17 of the Children Act 1989. However, because the son's care plan failed to allocate specific tasks to designated professionals to be completed within an agreed timescale, the close liaison which should have taken place between the housing authority and Social Services did not occur.

Mr Justice Richards presiding at the High Court hearing acknowledged that Social Services had closely followed the procedures laid down in the *Framework for the Assessment of Children in Need and their Families*. It had acted correctly in initiating and conducting a s.47 enquiry and then in reviewing the placing of the boy SB on the Child Protection Register. Social Services had also, in Mr Justice Richards' opinion, been right in its approach to later removing him from the Child Protection Register and to treat him as a *child in need*. Furthermore, review meetings had largely been held at the right time, although the judge did admonish the local authority's Social Services for postponing the six-monthly Child in Need Review meeting for four weeks in order to take account of the pending application for an Anti-social Behaviour Order. According to Justice Richards this was a separate matter and should not have been permitted to interfere with the statutory duty to assess a *child in need* under s.17 of the Children Act 1989.

In contrast to his finding that the local authority had adhered to procedure laid down in policy guidance in terms of process, Justice Richards was of the opinion that it had not done so in terms of assessment. The judge pointed out that the *Framework for the Assessment of Children in Need and their Families* consistently emphasises the need for a Core Assessment. Although conceding that the Core Assessment Records are not a prescribed pro forma for a *child in need* assessment, they nevertheless indicate the scope and detail of it. Mr Justice Richards summed up (para. 41) his understanding of the demands of assessment within the policy guidance:

> There should be a systematic assessment of needs which takes into account the three domains (child's developmental needs, parenting capacity, family and environmental factors) and involves collaboration between all relevant agencies so as to achieve a full understanding of the child in his or her family and community context. It is important, moreover, to be clear about the three-stage process: identification of needs, production of a care plan, and provision of the identified services. It seems to me that where an authority follows a path that does not involve the preparation of a core assessment as such, it must nevertheless adopt a similarly systematic approach with a view to achievement of the same objective. Failure to do so without good cause will constitute an impermissible departure from the guidance.

Here was a situation in which local authority social workers were commended by the court for following procedure in terms of safeguarding a child and then recognising when he had become a *child in need*. Unfortunately, although they had closely adhered to the procedures laid down in the *Framework for the Assessment of Children in Need and their Families*, there had been substantial shortcomings in producing an assessment of need at the end of it. Inevitably, an assessment that failed to encompass environmental factors such as the boy SB's housing and the violence suffered by his mother, in turn led to the production of a vague and under-developed care plan, which could not be effectively implemented. Hence the housing authority was never properly engaged in the assessment of the boy's needs and little was done to tackle the underlying problems which threatened his welfare.

Multi-agency work

A major criticism by Mr Justice Richards of the assessment produced by Mr Pollard and adopted by the Child in Need Review meeting was its vagueness as to multi-agency inputs and collaboration between named personnel. SB was a child at high risk of re-offending and of becoming increasingly mired in the youth justice system as he engaged in more serious forms of criminal activity. Yet, he was at the same time a *child in need* with learning difficulties and possibly a conduct disorder. By the time of the High Court hearing he had not attended school for two years and despite being 14 years old he was found to have the reading and numeracy ability of a six-year-old. At the same time he had a mother who had herself been in care and was and continued to be the subject of violence. She was an individual who plainly had needs in her own right. Given that SB's elder brother was already serving a custodial sentence in a Young Offender Institution this was a state of affairs consisting of multiple risk factors related to offending behaviour which required addressing. It was a major failing of the *child in need* assessment completed by Mr Pollard that the Supervision Order to which SB was subject and the nature of his offending behaviour received relatively little attention. There was undoubtedly a linkage between the boy's welfare needs and the preventative work being undertaken by the Youth Offending Team to reduce his offending behaviour.

The original Child Protection Plan drawn up for the boy after the Child Protection Conference convened in December 1999 expressed 'concern that [SB] is at risk of harm as a result of his offending behaviour' and stated that 'the aim of the plan is to engage [SB] in a multi-agency programme of activity including health, education and welfare needs, which will divert him from criminal activity'. At the stage of initial contact with Social Services there was a clear recognition that child protection, welfare needs and education were closely linked to issues surrounding the boy's offending behaviour. Yet, neither when SB was subject to child protection procedures, nor thereafter when he became a *child in need*, was a care plan devised which set out how social workers from Social Services were to work in conjunction with personnel from the Youth Offending Team and the police. Indeed, the disparity of the assessments produced for SB as a *child in need* and in relation to the application for an Anti-social Behaviour Order highlights the lack of common understanding between agencies. Department of Health (2000d: para. 5.68) states that:

> It will be important for YOTs completing Asset to liaise within social service departments about young people with whom social services have had or have contact. Prior assessments of need undertaken by social services departments can inform the work of YOTs. Similarly, assessments undertaken by YOTs will be an important source of knowledge if the young person continues to be worked with as a child in need under the Children Act 1989 or is re-referred to the social services department for help following their involvement with the youth justice system. The dimensions of the Assessment Framework in this guidance are consistent with those of the youth offending assessment profile. The key difference is that Asset concentrates in depth on areas of a young person's life most likely to be associated with offending behaviour.

In addition, the Children Act 2004 enacted after the events in this case, requires relevant partners named in s.10 to cooperate with each other in order to safeguard and promote the welfare of children. Youth Offending Teams, the police and Children's Services are three of the relevant partners referred to in s.10 of the Children Act 2004. These agencies are now under a statutory duty to liaise closely with one another in their work with children and young people. The necessity of close working between Youth Offending Teams and Social Services is also highlighted in Youth Justice Board (2005a: 9, 11) *A Guide to the Role of Youth Offending Teams in Dealing with Anti-Social Behaviour* which identifies Social Services as a crucial partner in multi-agency collaboration and outlines the role of Youth Offending Teams in this type of intervention:

> YOTs therefore, have the skills to assess the needs of young people, and to offer advice to and work with local partners in order to offer comprehensive interventions that will address the factors behind a young person's anti-social behaviour, while providing the appropriate level of protection for the community . . . The YOT, in partnership with local child care agencies, has a key part to play in supporting young people after a decision has been made about using a particular intervention.

Youth Justice Board, Ministry of Justice and Department for Children, Schools and Families (2008) *When to Share Information* sets out best practice for professionals implementing their duties under the Children Act 2004 to collaborate and share information across agency boundaries. This was obviously not a document available to social workers at the time of the events concerning SB. But it provides crucial guidance for present-day practitioners working in youth justice with children who are also children at risk of significant harm or *children in need*. For this reason the key principles for information sharing between professionals working with young offenders and those in other agencies, set out in Youth Justice Board, Ministry of Justice and Department for Children, Schools and Families (2008: 11–12) are reproduced in the box below.

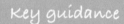
Key guidance

When to Share Information: Best Practice Guidance for Everyone Working in the Youth Justice System

You should explain to children, young people and families at the outset, openly and honestly, what, how and why information will, or could be, shared, and seek their agreement. The exception to this is where to do so would put that child/young person or others at increased risk of significant harm or an adult at risk of serious harm, or if it would undermine the prevention, detection or prosecution of a serious crime, including where seeking consent might lead to interference with any potential investigation.

You must always consider the safety and welfare of a child or young person when making decisions on whether to share information about them. Where there is concern that the child may be suffering or is at risk of suffering significant harm, the child's safety and welfare must be overriding considerations.

You should, where possible, respect the wishes of children, young people or families who do not consent to share confidential information. You may still share information if, in your judgement on the facts of the case, there is sufficient need to override that lack of consent.

You should seek guidance where you are in doubt, especially where your doubt relates to a concern about possible significant harm to a child or serious harm to others.

You should ensure that the information you share is accurate and up-to-date, necessary for the purpose for which you are sharing it, shared only with those people who need to see it and shared securely.

You should always record the reasons for your decision - whether it is to share information or not.

Mr Justice Richards referred in his judgement to the requirement in policy guidance for multi-agency collaboration and the lack thereof in relation to SB's *child in need* assessment and related care plan. He criticised Mr Pollard's care plan for simply mentioning the involvement of other agencies or possible referrals to them as opposed to the formulation of a detailed plan of intervention. Such an approach would have comprised named professionals with specified roles and tasks, together with timelines for work with SB and his mother. In Mr Justice Richards' opinion, the care plan did not evidence multi-agency inputs either in its development or in its proposed implementation.

The multi-agency aspect of this case clearly has wide-ranging implications for social work practice, whether that is in the context of a Youth Offending Team or Children's Services. The Children Act 2004, which has been enacted since the events in this case, places a responsibility on frontline professionals to do more than merely make referrals to other agencies in relation to assessment and care planning. Collaboration necessitates ongoing consultation, appropriate inputs in terms of specialist assessments, and joint working on intervention strategies with children and their families. Many young people, like SB, have multiple problems which span housing, education and offending behaviour. Some of their parents' difficulties, as in this case the fact that the boy's mother was subjected to sexual violence, can be intimately linked to the welfare of the child. It is for this reason that multi-agency working has become so central to effective work with children and young people.

Judgement in *R (on the application of AB)* v. *Nottingham City Council*

The local authority was unable to produce in evidence a document or collection of documents which in Mr Justice Richards' opinion amounted to a systematic assessment of needs as required by the *Framework for the Assessment of Children in Need and their Families*. In view of this, the judge concluded that the local authority had essentially produced a descriptive document which merely reflected the current circumstances of AB and SB rather than an assessment of their needs. The local authority had therefore failed to conduct an assessment of need as stipulated in s.17 of the Children Act 1989. The High Court issued a Mandatory Order requiring the local authority to complete a Core Assessment within 35 days of the order, which is the same time frame for a core assessment as laid down in *Framework for the Assessment of Children in Need and their Families*.

 ## Critical questions

1 Poor inter-agency collaboration was a key issue in this case. If you had been SB's social worker, but in the context of the current legal framework for multi-agency collaboration, how would you have gone about liaising and working with other agencies to assess SB's needs and formulate and implement a *child in need* plan?

2 Look again at the principles contained in *When to Share Information: Best Practice Guidance for Everyone Working in the Youth Justice System* and set out in the text box above. If you had been a social worker in the Youth Offending Team working with SB and you wanted to share information with SB's social worker in Social Services, how would you go about this? What would you do if SB refused to give his consent to your sharing any information with a social worker from another agency? How would you justify your decision and record this in case notes?

3 There was a failure in this case to complete a Core Assessment for SB as required by policy guidance. What factors do you think might make it difficult for a social worker employed by Children's Services to complete a detailed assessment on a *child in need* in accordance with the *Framework for the Assessment of Children in Need and their Families*?

Learning points

- Children and young people who are the subject of criminal proceedings are entitled to a fair trial which may require the use of *special measures*.

- Sentences handed down to children must take account of their welfare in conjunction with the need to punish and protect the public.

- An assessment of risk of harm to the public can result in custodial sentences for children and young people being extended by Crown Court judges to take account of their dangerousness to the public.

- Youth Courts can choose from a wide range of custodial and non-custodial sentences for children and young people, which can be tailored to their particular offence and circumstances.

- Pre-sentence reports normally produced by social workers in relation to young offenders are a crucial source of guidance for judges deciding on sentencing.

- Parents may be held accountable for the conduct of their children through the use of Parenting Contracts, Parenting Orders and Compensation Orders.

- Applications for Anti-social Behaviour Orders for children *looked after* by a local authority must not be pursued by the child's social worker in order to avoid a conflict of interest.

- Multi-agency collaboration between Youth Offending Teams, housing and education authorities, Children's Services and the police is essential to assessment and care planning under the *Framework for the Assessment of Children in Need and their Families*.

Further reading

Arthur, R. (2005) 'Punish parents for the crimes of their children', *The Howard Journal* 44(3): 233-53. This article considers the controversy surrounding making parents accountable for the offending behaviour of their children.

Dugmore, P. and Pickford, J. (2006) *Youth Justice and Social Work*, Exeter: Learning Matters. This publication describes the role of social work within the youth justice system. It also focuses on social work practice with young offenders.

Smith, R. (2007) *Youth Justice: Ideas, Policy and Practice*, Cullompton: Willan. This publication examines the policy drivers behind legislation in relation to youth offending. It also provides an overview of the current youth justice system and critical commentary on recent developments.

Squires, P. and Stephen, D.E. (2005) *Rougher Justice: Anti-social Behaviour and Young People*, Cullompton: Willan. This book examines the political discourses surrounding youth justice and youth offending.

Useful websites

www.crimereduction.homeoffice.gov.uk/ Run by the Home Office this website provides statistics on the use of Anti-social Behaviour Orders and easy-to-read guides on these and other crime reduction strategies introduced by the Government.

www.direct.gov.uk/en/crimejusticeandthelaw/crimeprevention Run by the Government this website provides easy-to-follow guides on dealing with anti-social behaviour and low-level forms of criminal activity.

www.yjb.gov.uk Run by the Youth Justice Board this website offers a range of publications and guides on the youth justice system. It also has many easy-to-read free downloads giving advice to parents, young people and victims of crime.

www.howardleague.org/ The Howard League is a charitable body which campaigns for penal reform and the increased use of community sentences and restorative justice. It provides critical commentary on the present youth justice system and imprisonment of children and young people.

6

MENTAL CAPACITY

Fact file

- Proportion of adults with at least one mental health problem each year - 25%
- Proportion of patients admitted to psychiatric wards that lack capacity - 60%
- Number of people with dementia by 2025 - 1 million
- Number of people who suffer a stroke each year - 130,000
- Number of people in England and Wales estimated to lack the mental capacity to make some decisions for themselves at any given time - 2 million

Source: Office of the Public Guardian (2008); Owen, et al. (2008).

Overview of relevant legislation

As the headline figure in the Fact File reveals, at any one time in England and Wales around 2 million people will be unable to make some decisions for themselves due to: learning disability; dementia; mental disorder; stroke; brain injury; accident; or unconsciousness. Mental incapacity caused by an accident or operation is quite temporary. Other conditions such as a stroke or brain injury may result in mental incapacity during a period of recovery stretching over a number of months. For those with learning difficulties, dementia or mental disorders, many adults may be perfectly capable of making all decisions on their own behalf. The figures in the Fact File indicate that 40 per cent of those admitted to psychiatric wards with a mental disorder actually have full mental capacity. Therefore it is a mistake to assume that mental disorder, dementia or learning difficulty are synonymous with mental incapacity. This would be to negatively stereotype people with a learning disability or mental health problem and possibly to misuse professional power to deprive them of autonomy. Undoubtedly, however, a proportion of people with dementia, learning disabilities, mental disorders, strokes, and brain injuries do lack the mental capacity at certain points in time and in relation to specific matters to make decisions on their own behalf. This chapter explores the definition of mental capacity and what it means to be able or unable to make decisions from a legal perspective.

Historically the law relating to mental capacity has depended on a series of judicial precedents and therefore has been embedded in common law rather than statute law. However, that changed with the passing of the Mental Capacity Act 2005 which is the principal statute dealing with mental incapacity. This legislation only applies to people 16 years of age or over and provides a legal framework for decision making on behalf of individuals who do not have mental capacity. The Children Act 1989 will be the relevant legislation for those under 16 years of age as this statute applies equally to children with a mental disability. The main sections of the Mental Capacity Act 2005 are listed in the table below.

Mental Capacity Act 2005	Key sections
Part I – Persons who lack capacity	s.1 Principles
	s.2 People who lack capacity
	s.3 Inability to make decisions
	s.4 Best interests
	s.5 Acts in connection with care or treatment
	s.9 Lasting powers of attorney
	s.10 Appointment of donees
	ss.11–13 Regulation of attorney powers
	s.15 Power of court to make declarations
	s.16 Powers of court to appoint deputies
	ss.24–26 Advance decisions to refuse treatment
	ss.35–41 Appointment and functions of independent mental capacity advocates
Part II – The court of protection and the public guardian	ss.45–46 Court of protection
	ss.47–49 Powers of court of protection
	ss.50–53 Procedures of court of protection
	s.57 Appointment of public guardian
	s.58 Functions of public guardian
Part III – Miscellaneous and general	s.63 International protection of adults

The principles which underpin the Mental Capacity Act 2005 are set out in s.1 of the statute. Like the principles set out in s.1 of the Children Act 1989, because these form part of the legislation itself, they have statutory force. This means that any court or indeed any practitioner involved in working under the Mental Capacity Act 2005 is legally obliged to act in accordance with these principles. The new Court of Protection, which now hears all cases concerning adults who lack mental capacity, will utilise these principles to inform and direct its judgements. For this reason s.1 of the Mental Capacity Act 2005 is reproduced in the box below.

 Key legislation

Mental Capacity Act 2005

s.1(1) The following principles apply for the purposes of this Act.

s.1(2) A person must be assumed to have capacity unless it is established that he lacks capacity.

s.1(3) A person is not to be treated as unable to make a decisions unless all practicable steps to help him to do so have been taken without success.

s.1(4) A person is not to be treated as unable to make a decision merely because he makes an unwise decision.

s.1(5) An act done, or decision made, under this Act for or on behalf of a person who lacks capacity must be done, or made, in his best interests.

s.1(6) Before the act is done, or the decision is made, regard must be had to whether the purpose for which it is needed can be as effectively achieved in a way that is less restrictive of the person's rights and freedom of action.

In addition to the principles and provisions laid down in the Mental Capacity Act 2005 it is supplemented by a code of practice issued under s.42 of the statute. The *Mental Capacity Act 2005: Code of Practice* has statutory force which means that professionals acting under the provisions of the Mental Capacity Act 2005 are legally required to have regard to it. Failure to comply with the Code of Practice could be used as evidence to show that a practitioner or agency was responsible for maladministration were a complaint to come before the Local Government Ombudsman or a claim to be made for a judicial review before the High Court. Besides the *Mental Capacity Act 2005: Code of Practice* there are a number of Government-issued guidance documents which support and direct the practice of professionals working with vulnerable adults and their families. These additional documents are enumerated in the table below and are referred to in this chapter.

Guidance document	Outline of content
Department for Constitutional Affairs (2007) *Mental Capacity Act 2005: Code of Practice*	This is the statutory code of practice which directs professionals working under the Mental Capacity Act 2005.
Department of Health (2008) *Refocusing the Care Programme Approach: Policy and Positive Practice Guidance*	This provides detailed guidance on the Care Programme Approach including assessment and care planning for people with mental health problems living in the community.
Department of Health (2003c) *Domiciliary Care: National Minimum Standards*	This sets out 27 minimum standards which must be adhered to by providers of domiciliary services to the home of users and carers.
Department of Health (1990: para. 3.25) *Community Care in the Next Decade and Beyond*	This is policy guidance which describes the framework of community care. It also sets out the objectives of this policy and directs agencies and professionals on the delivery of packages of care.
Department of Health (2000d) *Framework for the Assessment of Children in Need and their Families*	This is policy guidance for the assessment of *children in need* and *at risk*. It also sets out procedures for investigating allegations of abuse and neglect.
HM Government (2006a) *Working Together to Safeguard Children*	This is policy guidance and sets out the procedures for inter-agency collaboration to safeguard children. It also outlines the roles of each agency in relation towards children.

Overview of the cases

This chapter explores the issues arising from four different court cases. A brief summary of each case is set out below.

Case 1 *Westminster City Council* v. *C sub nom: KC* v. *City of Westminster Social and Community Services Department* [2008] EWCA Civ 198 explores the:

- Nature of marriage.
- Legal meaning of mental capacity.
- Right to a family life.
- Right to marry and found a family.
- Tension between cultural or religious beliefs and statute law.

Case 2 *Re P (A Child) (Care and Placement Order Proceedings: Mental Capacity of Parent)* [2008] EWCA Civ 462 explores the:

- Situation of a parent representing herself in court.
- Role of McKenzie friends.
- Meaning of *best interests* decisions.
- Nature of a fair trial.
- Dispensing with parent's consent for an adoption.

Case 3 *Local Authority X* v. *M sub nom: MM (An Adult, Re: A Local Authority X* v. *MM)* [2007] EWHC 2003 (Fam) explores:

- Respect for private and family life.
- *Best interests* decisions made by a local authority.
- The tension between autonomy and risk of harm for an adult with limited capacity.

Case 4 *R (on application of A)* v. *East Sussex County Council (No. 2)* [2003] EWHC 167 explores the:

- Rights of social care workers to safe conditions of employment.
- Nature of inhuman and degrading treatment for vulnerable adults.
- Implications of carers making *best interest* decisions for vulnerable adults.

CASE 1
Westminster City Council v. *C sub nom: KC* v. *City of Westminster Social and Community Services Department* [2008] EWCA Civ 198

Importance of the case

It explores the actions of social workers to protect a vulnerable adult without capacity. The case also examines the clash between religious and cultural practices and the law on marriage.

History of the case

The local authority applied for and obtained a declaration from the Family Division of the High Court that IC, a 26-year-old man with severe learning difficulties, did not have the mental capacity to marry. IC's parents appealed against this judgement to the Court of Appeal.

Facts of the case

K and his wife N were born in Bangladesh, but had lived in the UK for many years and were both British nationals. Their son IC was born in the United Kingdom and like his parents was also a British subject. K and N who were both Muslims arranged a marriage for IC with a young woman NK living in Bangladesh, with the intention that she should come to live in the United Kingdom after the wedding. In a transnational telephone call between Britain and Bangladesh in September 2006 a Muslim marriage took place involving the parents of the couple, IC and NK and an officiating Khazi. During the ceremony IC was heard to say 'Yes' and to consent to the marriage. Based on expert evidence submitted to the court by Professor Menski, Professor of South Asian Laws at the University of London, it was accepted by the appeal court that the wedding had taken place in accordance with Islamic religious practice and was legally recognised in Bangladesh. In Prof. Menski's opinion, under Sharia law, K, as IC's marriage guardian, had the authority to act in his best interests and to arrange his marriage as a means of protecting him and securing his future welfare. This was accepted by the presiding judges. Dr Khouja, a consultant psychiatrist and expert witness jointly instructed by the parties to the court case, testified that IC barely possessed the abilities of a 3-year-old and could not be left alone without putting himself at risk. The question before the court was whether the marriage of IC and NK was valid under English law given the nature of the marriage ceremony and IC's severe learning disability. The court was also required to consider whether it had jurisdiction to interfere in the private life of IC and his family.

Key people in the case

IC – vulnerable adult
K – father of IC
N – mother of IC
NK – young woman engaged to IC
Mr Luba – legal counsel for appellants K and N
Dr Khouja – psychiatrist and expert witness
Prof. Menski – expert witness on Sharia law
Lord Justice Wall – presiding judge in Court of Appeal case

Discussion of the case

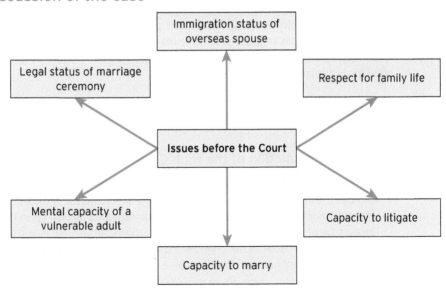

Capacity to litigate

Although IC is 26 years of age he has the developmental age of a 3-year-old. Common law has established a presumption that adults have capacity. This has now been incorporated into legislation through the Mental Capacity Act 2005. Consequently, convincing evidence has to be produced in court for a judge to conclude that an adult does not have capacity and cannot therefore make decisions on his or her own behalf. The test of capacity is defined in the Mental Capacity Act 2005 and is reproduced in the box below.

Key legislation

Mental Capacity Act 2005

s.1(1) . . . A person lacks capacity if at the material time he is unable to make a decision for himself in relation to the matter because of an impairment of, or a disturbance in the functioning of, the mind or brain.

(2) It does not matter whether the impairment or disturbance is permanent or temporary.

s.3(1) . . . a person is unable to make a decision for himself if he is unable -

(a) to understand the information relevant to the decision,
(b) to retain the information,
(c) to use or weigh that information as part of the process of making the decision, or
(d) to communicate the decision.

Section 3(1) of the Mental Capacity 2005 defines incapacity which involves difficulties with several mental processes. These are the ability to understand information, to retain it, to weigh it or to communicate a decision. Of course a decision can be communicated either verbally or non-verbally. A person may also need assistance to understand or weigh information and this need of itself does not mean he or she lacks mental capacity. As regards IC, there were two issues before the court concerning his capacity. The first was his ability to understand and take part in legal proceedings and the second was his ability to make a decision regarding marriage. Dr Khouja's expert evidence established that IC did not have the capacity to understand court proceedings or to instruct his own solicitor. In other words, IC was unable to litigate on his own behalf. In these instances the High Court can invoke its inherent jurisdiction to protect the welfare of adults without capacity. This is explained in the box below.

Background information

Inherent jurisdiction of the High Court

This power derives from a historical precept that the State has a responsibility to protect all its citizens, regardless of their age. Anyone with a direct interest in the welfare of another, such as friends, relatives or local authorities, can instigate proceedings in the High Court. The exercise of inherent jurisdiction enables the High Court to step in and protect the welfare of any child or adult in the United Kingdom. In the present day the High Court can only exercise its inherent jurisdiction where there is no alternative statutory provision to protect the welfare of the individual concerned. The Children Act 1989 has largely negated the need for the High Court to exercise its inherent jurisdiction in relation to children.

As there is no comparable statute to the Children Act 1989, with its comprehensive framework of protections for children, available for vulnerable adults, the High Court uses its inherent jurisdiction to protect them. When this happens the Official Solicitor may be invited to act as the *litigation friend* of the vulnerable or mentally incapacitated adult. A litigation friend (previously known as *next friend*) is someone who is competent to conduct legal proceedings on behalf of the vulnerable person. The Official Solicitor is the litigation friend of last resort and only becomes involved if there is no one else suitable (such as a family member) to act in the interests of the vulnerable adult. The High Court exercises its inherent power through declaratory relief. This consists of statements, known as *declarations*, which set out the legal position and are issued by a High Court judge after hearing a case. These declarations have legal force, and failing to comply with them constitutes contempt of court. Anyone guilty of contempt of court is liable to a fine or custodial sentence.

In relation to very vulnerable adults or those without capacity, the High Court may make any declaration relating to their finances and welfare on the basis of what is considered to be in their 'best interests'. This is usually determined on the basis of the benefits and dis-benefits to the vulnerable adult of any given course of action. Under the Mental Capacity Act 2005 the powers of the High Court in relation to adults *without mental capacity* are now exercised by the new Court of Protection. The new Court of Protection will make declarations of 'best interest' as opposed to giving declaratory relief. Vulnerable adults *with mental capacity* still fall under the inherent jurisdiction of the High Court.

The inherent jurisdiction of the High Court and the new Court of Protection introduced by the Mental Capacity Act 2005 enable social workers concerned about the welfare of a vulnerable adult to intervene to protect them. Precisely because there is no equivalent to the Children Act 1989 for vulnerable adults, social workers do not have comparable statutory powers to safeguard adults as they do for children. The Children Act 1989 gives social workers the right to initiate an investigation if they suspect that a child is at risk of harm in conjunction with a choice of court orders to directly intervene. The protection of adults without mental capacity is more difficult for social workers due to the weaker legislative framework to safeguard them. As a result social workers are largely dependent on applications to the High Court and the use of the new Court of Protection.

Mental capacity of a vulnerable adult

Throughout the court case the Official Solicitor acted as IC's litigation friend and conducted legal proceedings on his behalf. However, incapacity to make decisions in one area does not automatically preclude the ability to make any decision at all in relation to any matter. Established at common law and given legislative expression in the Mental Capacity Act 2005, ss.1 and 3 above, a finding of mental incapacity is relative to the decision to be made by the vulnerable adult. Assessing an adult's mental capacity means assessing their ability to make an informed decision at a particular time about a specific matter. It is not a once-and-for-all assessment of their overall mental capacity. This opens up the possibility of vulnerable people having mental capacity to make their own decisions in one area of their lives, for instance where they live, but not in another, for example about their finances. The *Mental Capacity Act 2005: Code of Practice* identifies professionals, carers and those having daily contact with the vulnerable adult as likely to be involved in assessing his or her mental capacity to make a decision on a specified matter at a given point in time. The Mental Capacity Act 2005 and its associated Code of Practice set out the factors which must be taken into account in any determination of an adult's mental capacity. For any social worker intervening with an adult whose capacity to make decisions for himself or herself is in question, the GSCC Code of Practice gives clear guidance to practitioners, as set out in the table below.

Mental Capacity Act 2005	Practice implications	Related GSCC Code
s.1(2) Legal presumption of capacity	A diagnosis of dementia, a mental disorder or a severe learning difficulty is not of itself grounds to conclude that an adult does not have capacity. The person who alleges incapacity of an adult has to prove it in court.	1.1 Treating each person as an individual 1.3 Supporting the service users' rights to control their lives and make informed choices about the services they receive
s.2(1) Whether an adult has sufficient capacity to make a decision depends on the nature of the decision to be made	An adult may be able to understand and make informed decisions in one area of their life, e.g. where to live, but not have capacity to give informed consent in another area, e.g. life saving treatment.	1.3 Supporting the service-users' rights to control their lives and make informed choices about the services they receive 2.2 Communicating in an appropriate, open, accurate and straightforward way
s.1(3) An adult does not lack capacity unless all practicable steps have been taken to aid him or her to make the decision	A vulnerable adult may require advocacy support or information communicated in Makaton or in other forms to be able to participate in decision making.	3.1 Promoting the independence of service-users and assisting them to understand and exercise their rights
s.1(4) An adult is not treated as lacking capacity because he or she makes an unwise decision	If an adult has the capacity to make a decision for instance about who he or she lives with, then that adult also has the capacity to make the decision to live with someone who is exploitative or abusive.	4.1 Recognising that service-users have the right to take risks and helping them to identify and manage potential and actual risks to themselves and others
s.1(5) Any decision made on behalf of an adult lacking capacity must be in his or her *best interest* s.4(6), (7) the known preferences of the adult before he or she lost capacity, his or her religious and cultural heritage or family obligations and the views of carers or family members must be considered in *best interest* decisions	A balance sheet of benefits and losses encompassing physical, mental, social, and financial welfare is pertinent to any *best interest* decision and those with daily contact with the incapacitated adult should be consulted alongside other professionals.	1.6 Respecting diversity and different cultures and values

(Continued)

Mental Capacity Act 2005	Practice implications	Related GSCC Code
s.1(6) Any decision made on behalf of an adult must result in the least possible constraint on the exercise of his or her autonomy	*Best interest* decisions must be made and implemented so as to minimise interference and restriction in the life of the adult without capacity.	1.2 Promoting the individual views and wishes of both services users and carers 1.4 Respecting and maintain the dignity and privacy of service users 3.8 Recognising and using responsibly the power that comes from your work with service users and carers
The test of capacity is a legal not a medical matter (this is a common law principle left unchanged by MCA 2005)	Where an adult's mental capacity is disputed, this is to be determined by the court after hearing evidence from all parties, including family members and social care workers. The determination of capacity is not solely dependent on the assessment of a medical doctor, although it may constitute expert opinion in court.	6.5 Working openly and co-operatively with colleagues and treating them with respect 6.7 Recognising and respecting the roles and expertise of workers from other agencies and working in partnership with them
High Court hearings on mental capacity take place within the Civil Justice System and the standard of proof for capacity is therefore the *balance of probabilities*	The person alleging incapacity of an adult must prove they lack capacity on the *balance of probabilities*.	6.1 Meeting relevant standards of practice and working in a lawful, safe and effective way

As this table demonstrates there are a series of practice implications which follow from the provisions of the Mental Capacity Act 2005. These in turn invoke various standards and value-based approaches to work with users, set out in the GSCC *Code of Practice for Social Care Workers*. Plainly the interrelationship between sections of this statute, social work practice and the GSCC Code are not necessarily straightforward and raise a number of dilemmas for professionals. Assisting a mentally incapacitated adult and supporting them to exercise autonomy in as many areas of their life as possible will inevitably challenge both personal and professional values. This is particularly true when vulnerable adults who lack mental capacity make choices which put them at risk of harm, or where carers, family members or friends make decisions on their behalf which are clearly against their *best interests*.

Capacity to marry

Although it was established in evidence that IC lacked capacity to understand or participate in litigation, the judge still had to consider, as a separate matter, whether IC could comprehend the nature of marriage. In law, marriage is a contract between a male and female resulting in a series of legal consequences which impinge on their lives and inform their actions. Marriage creates financial obligations towards a spouse; grants rights to live in the matrimonial home; affects the immigration status of a spouse from overseas; and alters benefit and pension entitlements alongside changes to tax liabilities. It also carries the expectation of sexual relations as non-consummation is a ground for declaring a marriage void under s.12 of the Matrimonial Causes Act 1973. In addition to their obligations to one another, couples also have legal duties towards any children of their marriage, which includes maintaining them and ensuring they receive adequate education and medical treatment. The Matrimonial Causes Act 1973 sets out the requirements for a valid marriage under ss.11 and 12 and the grounds for divorce or legal separation under s.1.

Matrimonial Causes Act 1973

Void marriage	Voidable marriage	Divorce and separation
A void marriage has no legal status and therefore the parties to it do not incur any of the rights or responsibilities of a marriage. It is as if the marriage never took place.	A voidable marriage is a valid marriage until one of the parties challenges it and obtains a decree annulling it. Therefore the parties have all the duties and rights of a legally married couple while the marriage endures.	The parties must be married for at least a year before either can petition for divorce or legal separation. The party petitioning to end the marriage must prove it has *broken down irretrievably* on any one of five grounds.
Grounds for a void marriage s.11	*Grounds for a voidable marriage s.12*	*Grounds for a divorce or legal separation s.1*
• The parties are within prohibited degrees of relationship, e.g. siblings, parent and child, uncle and niece, etc. • Either party is under sixteen years of age. • The parties are not married according to the legal formalities of marriage, e.g. solemnisation and registration of marriage, etc. • Either party is already married to someone else (precludes polygamous marriages in UK). • Either party was domiciled in England and Wales when they entered into a polygamous marriage in another country. (Polygamous marriages contracted outside the UK are valid, but only one wife will be permitted to enter the UK under immigration rules.) • The parties are not male and female (transsexuals can legally acquire a gender by a Gender Recognition Certificate issued under the Gender Recognition Act 2004).	• The marriage is unconsummated due to incapacity or wilful refusal by either party. • Due to duress, mistake or unsoundness of mind either party did not validly consent to the marriage. • At the time of the marriage either party was suffering from a mental disorder and unable to fulfil the typical obligations of a marriage. • Either party at the time of the marriage had a communicable venereal disease. • At the time of the marriage the woman was pregnant by another man. • The gender of either party changes during the course of the marriage.	• The respondent has committed adultery and the petitioner finds it intolerable to live with the respondent. • The respondent has behaved in such a way that the petitioner cannot reasonably be expected to live with the respondent. • The respondent has deserted the petitioner for a continuous period of at least two years. • The parties to the marriage have lived apart for a continuous period of two years and the respondent consents to the decree. • The parties to the marriage have lived apart for a continuous period of five years.

None of the grounds under s.11 of the Matrimonial Causes Act 1973 apply to IC, and therefore the marriage is not void. However, under s.12 a marriage can be voided by the court if either party to it was unable to validly consent to the marriage due to 'unsoundness of mind'. This was the ground on which the City of Westminster Social and Community Services Department sought to nullify IC's marriage in order to protect his welfare. Judgement in *Hill* v. *Hill* [1959] 1 All ER 281 established that valid consent to a marriage requires understanding the contract and obligations of marriage. Mental capacity means that an adult, with assistance if needed, is able to: comprehend in a general way (rather than in every detail) the matter requiring a decision; apply rational considerations; and understand broadly the consequences that will flow from his or her decision.

Both IC's parents and the Official Solicitor acting for IC agreed to the appointment of Dr Khouja, a consultant psychiatrist, to conduct the assessment of IC's mental capacity. Expert opinion was then given by Dr Khouja who reported that IC could not meet the test of capacity set out in s.3(1) of the Mental Capacity Act 2005 because IC was unable to understand information regarding the nature of marriage or to retain it or weigh it in deciding whether to marry or not. The Court of Appeal therefore concluded that IC did not have capacity to enter into a marriage and that his utterance of the word 'Yes' during the international telephone call to Bangladesh could not be construed as valid consent. Exercising the court's inherent jurisdiction to protect IC, Lord Justice Thorpe observed in his judgement that:

> there is much expert evidence to suggest that the marriage which his parents have arranged for him is potentially highly injurious. He has not the capacity to understand the introduction of NK into his life and that introduction would be likely to destroy his equilibrium or destabilise his emotional state. Physical intimacy is an ordinary consequence of the celebration of a marriage.

Legal status of marriage ceremony

The Court of Appeal judges concluded that the marriage of IC to NK was voidable in English law because IC could not give valid consent to it. In response Mr Luba QC, the barrister acting for IC's parents, sought to argue that the marriage was valid under both Sharia and Bangladeshi law and should therefore be recognised by English courts. He attempted to rely on the public policy position adopted by British courts, which is a predisposition to uphold the institution of marriage rather than to destroy it, even when the marriage is not contracted according to the tenets of English law. Giving judgement in the court case concerning IC, Lord Justice Wall cited *Cheni (otherwise Rodriguez)* v. *Cheni* [1965] p. 85 as a precedent for recognising marriages contracted outside of English law which depended on 'whether the marriage is so offensive to the conscience of the English court that it should refuse to recognise and give effect to the proper foreign law. In deciding that question the court will seek to exercise common sense, good manners and a reasonable tolerance.' Lord Justice Wall then distinguished between the facts in *Cheni* v. *Cheni* and those before him regarding the marriage of IC and NK. Judgement in *Cheni* v. *Cheni* recognised the marriage in that case, which was between two consenting adults with capacity who married in Egypt according to Jewish rites. But, as Lord Justice Wall highlighted in his own judgement, this was in sharp contrast to the marriage of IC and NK. First, IC did not have capacity and, secondly, evidence indicated that IC's welfare would be harmed if the marriage persisted. In other words the English courts are willing to recognise marriages contracted abroad and outside the formalities required in the United Kingdom. However, they will only do so if the form of marriage accords sufficiently closely to the basic principles and safeguards which underpin English law.

When a marriage is contracted in England according to the rites of other faiths, the marriage must accord with English law in order to be recognised as a marriage by the State. So, for example, a marriage which takes place in England or Wales of a Jewish couple in a synagogue or a Muslim couple in a Mosque is a marriage contracted under English law. Although polygamous marriages are legally permitted in a number of Muslim countries, they are expressly prohibited from taking place in Britain by s.11 of the Matrimonial Causes Act 1973. A Muslim wedding in the United Kingdom therefore creates a monogamous union. If such a marriage does not conform to the formalities laid down under the Marriage Act 1949 then the marriage will be treated as void under s.11 of the Matrimonial Causes Act 1973. In such circumstances a second wife would not be recognised as a wife under English law.

Social workers come into contact with a wide range of people from a diversity of backgrounds, holding a variety of cultural and religious beliefs. Paragraph 1.6 of the GSCC Code stipulates that practitioners must respect 'diversity and different cultures and values'. But, this does not mean adopting a position of cultural relativity whereby all cultural and religious practices, regardless of their harmful affects, are to be equally accepted or tolerated. This case demonstrates some of the limits on cultural diversity embedded in English law. It is also worth noting that while some British Muslims would agree with the choices of IC's family, a proportion would not. A respectful professional stance towards the cultural heritage of users and carers needs to take account of the cultural and spiritual diversity within ethnic communities and not just between ethnic communities in the United Kingdom. In short, social workers have to weigh up the rights of individuals to give expression to their cultural and religious beliefs and the rights of every citizen to be protected from harm.

Some professionals may be of the opinion that in relation to marriage, English law draws the line between valid and invalid marriages in the wrong place as far as respecting cultural diversity is concerned. This will create a tension between the requirements of the GSCC Code to respect cultural diversity and at the same time to practice within the legal framework. Of course the dilemma created by the Matrimonial Causes Act 1973 over the issue of marriage is not unique. There are many statutes which reflect Anglo-centric values rather than multicultural ones. It is inevitable that direct work with children, adults and families from different cultural backgrounds will create ethical dilemmas for professionals committed to compliance with the GSCC Code of Practice.

Critical commentary

Multiculturalism and legal pluralism

Dr Rowan Williams, the Archbishop of Canterbury caused public controversy in February 2008 when he was reported as advocating the incorporation of Sharia law into the British legal system. He faced widespread criticism in the media and calls from within the Church of England for him to resign. In fact his lecture to lawyers in London was a balanced consideration of what Sharia law, a religious and social code guiding Muslims in their daily lives, might offer.

In his lecture the Archbishop explicitly recognised that there are different versions of Sharia law, a number of which undermine the rights of women relative to those of men and can create other inequalities. What the Archbishop actually proposed was an opt-in system whereby practising Muslims would be free to choose under which jurisdiction they wished their dispute to be settled.

A supplementary system of justice has operated for many years with little controversy among Jewish communities. The Beth Din is a Jewish religious court, which in the United Kingdom deals with civil matters including marital and commercial disputes. To use the Beth Din both parties to the dispute must be Jewish and must voluntarily agree to be bound by the decision of the court. Of course either party could refuse to submit to the Beth Din and instead apply to the English courts for a resolution of the marital or business dispute.

Shachar (2001) argues for 'transformative accommodation' within the legal system which by allowing different jurisdictions to compete for clients prevents a supplementary court system from adopting precedents which disadvantage one group of petitioners as against another, since those so disadvantaged will simply vote with their feet and access the formal court system. This form of modified legal pluralism ensures every citizen continues to enjoy exactly the same rights under the law, while having access to a supplementary court system which recognises other aspects of their social and religious identity.

Respect for family life

Mr Luba, representing the parents, next sought to argue that by refusing to recognise IC's marriage the court was interfering in the private marital affairs of IC. In effect this meant that the judiciary, which is part of the State, was violating IC's right to respect for his private and family life (article 8) and the right to marry (article 12) guaranteed under the European Convention on Human Rights. The Convention was created to protect individuals from the immense power of the State in the form of the government, the security forces and the court system, thus ensuring that citizens enjoy fundamental freedoms without unjustified State interference. Mr Luba was relying on the European Convention to exclude the court from interfering in the private life of IC, including the decision of his parents to arrange a marriage for him to NK. Responding to this challenge Lord Justice Wall pointed out that articles 8 and 12 are not absolute rights and are in fact qualified within the wording of the Convention.

European Convention on Human Rights

Convention right	Qualification to Convention right
Article 8 Everyone has the right to respect for his private and family life, his home and his correspondence	There shall be no interference by a public authority with the exercise of this right except such as in accordance with the law and is necessary in a democratic society in the interests of national security, public safety or the economic well-being of the country, for the prevention of disorder or crime, for the protection of health or morals, or for the protection of the rights and freedoms of others.
Article 12 Men and women of marriageable age have the right to marry and to found a family	According to the national laws governing the exercise of this right.

The effect of the qualifications to article 8 means that the court (State) is permitted to intervene in the private life of an individual where it is necessary 'for the protection of health'. In this case the court had already established that IC's welfare would be harmed if his marriage was recognised, and therefore Lord Justice Wall concluded in his judgement that the court's exercise of its inherent jurisdiction to protect vulnerable adults did not violate IC's rights under article 8 of the European Convention. As to IC's right to marry, Lord Justice Wall again alluded to the qualification to this right which states that it must be exercised 'according to the national laws'. In this instance English law codified in the Matrimonial Causes Act 1973 s.12 requires capacity to validly consent to a marriage. As IC did not have capacity, he could not validly consent to the marriage.

Aside from the Matrimonial Causes Act 1973, national laws governing the exercise of the right to marriage include the Sexual Offences Act 2003. Provisions contained in sections 30–33 of this statute, which are discussed in the box below, make it an offence to engage in sexual activity with a person who due to lack of capacity is unable to refuse to participate in that activity. This means in effect that if NK, even were she IC's wife, were to engage in sexual activity with him, she would be guilty of a criminal offence. This is consistent with developments in other aspects of family law. Since 1990 both the courts and Parliament have progressively sought to intervene to protect individuals within the family from violence and abuse. Increasingly, neither judges, nor the government are prepared to accept that marriage, and sexual relations within it, belong to the private and personal sphere which should be exempt from regulation by the law.

Key legislation

Sexual Offences Act 2003

The Sexual Offences Act 2003 creates sexual offences in relation to:

- Non-consensual acts against people who have mental capacity.
- Sexual activity with those who have a mental disorder.
- Offences against children.
- Offences by a person in a position of trust (e.g. a teacher or care worker) against a child.
- Offences by a care worker against a person who has a mental disorder (breach of relationship to care).
- Offences by a family member against a relative.
- Offences in connection with human trafficking.
- Offences in connection with prostitution.

The definition of what constitutes a sexual offence is set out in s.78 of the Sexual Offences Act 2003. It encompasses not only vaginal or anal penetration, but also touch and other forms of sexual activity which includes inducing others to watch sexual acts. Section 79(6) of the Sexual Offences Act 2003 applies the same definition of mental disorder as s.1 of the Mental Health Act 1983, which defines it as a 'mental illness, arrested or incomplete development of mind, psychopathic disorder and any other disorder or disability of mind'. According to Home Office (2004: para. 132) *Guidance on Part 1 of the Sexual Offences Act* 2003 under ss.30-33 a criminal offence is committed against a person with a mental disorder if the perpetrator engages in sexual activity when he or she 'knew or could reasonably have been expected to know that the victim had a mental disorder and that because of it he was likely to be unable to refuse'. Home Office (2004: para. 134) states that:

> . . . a victim is unable to refuse if he lacks the capacity to choose whether to agree to the touching or other activity (whether because he lacks sufficient understanding of the nature of or the reasonably foreseeable consequences of what is being done, or for any other reason or is unable to communicate such a choice to the offender) . . . Other reasons why a person may be unable to refuse might include not understanding that they had a choice through institutionalisation, or because they suffered from a condition that might affect the ability to make a choice.

Offences under ss.30-33 are applicable to everyone who may come into contact with a person who has a mental disorder and is 'unable to refuse' to engage in sexual activity because of it. It is essential to observe that sexual activity with someone who has a mental disorder is not an offence. It is only an offence to engage in sexual activity with a person who has a mental disorder *and* is 'unable to refuse' as defined in paragraph 134 of the guidance excerpted above. However there are offences under the Sexual Offences Act 2003 which apply only to care workers who are in a special relationship with people who have a mental disorder. For health and social care professionals there are more stringent prohibitions on sexual activity with those who have a mental disorder.

Offences under ss.38-41 apply to health and social care practitioners and prohibit any sexual activity with people who have a mental disorder whether or not they consent or are 'unable to refuse'. These provisions outlaw all sexual activity between care workers and those who have a mental disorder whom they come into contact with in the course of their professional role. Physiotherapists, occupational therapists, nurses, doctors, social workers, psychotherapists, personal care assistants and residential care workers are all encompassed by ss.38-41. This means that regardless of the mental capacity of someone with a mental disorder to understand and consent to sexual contact with a care worker, it will be illegal for a care worker to engage in such activity.

Article 14 of the European Convention on Human Rights stipulates that all human rights under the Convention 'shall be secured without discrimination on any ground such as sex, race, colour, language, religion, political or other opinion, national or social origin, association with a national minority, property, birth or other status'. This means that articles 8 and 12 must be applied equally to British citizens from the white majority population as to those from ethnic minority communities in the United Kingdom. In this case the Matrimonial Causes Act 1973 applied to all marriages regardless of where or how they had been contracted. There was no intention by the State to deprive people from Muslim backgrounds of the right to marry. The Matrimonial Causes Act 1973 did establish an across-the-board minimum requirement for marriage which applied to all citizens. To take a different example, the Matrimonial Causes Act 1973 under s. 11 makes void marriages between children under 16 years of age. Yet these are recognised as lawful marriages among some sections of the Romany community. To sum up, no violation of article 14 had occurred and there was no finding of discrimination.

Once again this illustrates the lawful limits on cultural diversity and the tensions which can arise between human rights legislation as codified in the Human Rights Act 1998 and cultural practices accepted by some sections of the population. The Matrimonial Causes Act 1973 seeks to protect all mentally incapacitated adults and all children under 16 years from being forced into the state of marriage for which they are deemed unfitted given its financial, sexual and social obligations. Social workers need to be aware of the possible conflicts that may exist for families between British law, human rights and some cultural practices. They will often be in the forefront of negotiating these differences of perspective, and ultimately may have to forcibly intervene where acceptable compromises to safeguard vulnerable adults or children cannot be reached. The case of IC is one such instance.

Immigration status of overseas spouse

It was the original intention of IC's parents to arrange for NK to travel from Bangladesh to settle in the United Kingdom and to live as IC's wife in his parental home. Under para. 281 of the current immigration rules, if NK was legally married to NK, then she would be entitled to enter the United Kingdom as IC's spouse as long as she met all the requirements to obtain *leave to enter* set out below:

- The applicant for *leave to enter* is married to a person who is settled in the United Kingdom (i.e. ordinarily resident in the UK and not subject to any immigration restrictions).
- The spouses have met.
- The spouses will be able to maintain themselves and any dependants adequately without relying on public funds.
- The spouses have adequate accommodation for themselves and their dependants without relying on public funds.
- The spouses intend to live permanently in the United Kingdom.
- The marriage is valid.

If *entry clearance* or *leave to enter* is given to a spouse, generally it will only be for two years. At the end of this *probationary period* the applicant, in this case NK, may obtain *indefinite leave to remain.* The Social Security (Persons from Abroad) Miscellaneous Amendment Regulations 1996 removed entitlement to non-contributory benefit from people with *limited leave,* which includes spouses from overseas. Once *indefinite leave to remain* is granted the spouse from abroad is free to claim benefits in his or her own right. At this point the spouse will also be free from immigration restrictions in the United Kingdom. He or she however cannot automatically obtain British citizenship as this involves additional requirements and processes. Plainly if IC's marriage to NK was found not to be valid by the courts then NK would have no entitlement to enter the United Kingdom and the plans of both families would be derailed.

Non-British nationals residing in the United Kingdom will have different legal statuses depending on whether they are an overseas spouse, an asylum seeker, a refugee, an unaccompanied minor, or a national of another Member State of the European Union. The legal status of foreign nationals living in the United Kingdom will affect their:

- Right to continue living in Britain.
- Right to work.
- Access to healthcare.
- Access to social care.
- Entitlement to social housing.
- Claim for welfare benefits.

In this particular court case although IC's parents were originally from Bangladesh they had both obtained British citizenship and therefore had exactly the same legal status and concomitant rights and entitlements as any British-born subject. Their son IC was a British born national and as such was entitled to marry an overseas spouse and bring her to live with him. *Leave to enter* the United Kingdom for NK was dependent on IC demonstrating that he and his family could support her for at least two years without recourse to public funds. Even if plans had proceeded as IC's parents intended and NK had entered Britain she would only have been granted *limited leave* which under the Social Security (Persons from Abroad) Miscellaneous Amendment Regulations 1996 would prevent her from claiming non-contributory benefits in her own right for at least two years. Social workers come into contact with an exceptionally diverse population, some of whom are not British nationals. Practitioners therefore need to be aware of how different immigration statuses affect a user's or carer's rights and entitlements.

Judgement in *KC, NNC v. City of Westminster*

The appellants sought to argue that the court was not entitled to interfere in the private life of IC and his family under article 8 and article 12 of the European Convention on Human Rights. The judge pointed out that these were qualified rights and did not prohibit the court from exercising its inherent jurisdiction to protect a vulnerable or mentally incapacitated adult. It was established in expert evidence given by Dr Khouja that IC did not have mental capacity. The common law principle requiring the exercise of inherent jurisdiction on the basis of 'best interests' (now incorporated into s.1(5) of the Mental Capacity Act 2005) taken together with s.12 of the Matrimonial Causes Act 1973 obliged the judges to make a declaration that the marriage was not valid. This had the secondary effect of preventing NK from entering the United Kingdom as she was not recognised under English law as IC's wife.

 Critical questions

1 Do you think this case was correctly decided, and if not, why? What is your own perspective on the cultural and religious beliefs which were the focus of this case? If you had been the social worker working with IC and his family, would your perspective have created conflicts between your personal and professional values? If so, how would you have resolved these?

2 In this case the parents of a vulnerable adult made a decision on his behalf in keeping with their cultural and spiritual beliefs, but which was ultimately harmful to their adult son. What is expected of different family members on the basis of their age, gender or disability is influenced by culture and often by religious belief. If you were working with carers who were putting a vulnerable adult at risk due to the carers' cultural or religious beliefs how would you approach your practice with them so as to comply with the GSCC Code?

CASE 2
Re P (A Child) (Care and Placement Order Proceedings: Mental Capacity of Parent) [2008] EWCA Civ 462

Importance of the case

This examines the meaning of *best interests* and how this is defined when a vulnerable adult objects to a decision being made on their behalf. The case also considers issues relating to mental capacity and parenting in the context of adoption without consent.

History of the case

This was an appeal to the Court of Appeal by a birth mother against the decision of a County Court to dispense with her consent to a Placement Order for her infant daughter in relation to a future adoption.

Facts of the case

The appellant RP is of white British background and had significant learning difficulties. She was aged 23 years at the time of the Court of Appeal hearing and had given birth to a baby daughter KP in May 2006 who was aged 2 years. The father of KP, who was of African Caribbean descent, was aged around 65 years. The birth parents had no ongoing sexual relationship and the father played no part in the child's life, neither was he a party to the Court of Appeal proceedings. The mother appears to have been unaware that she was pregnant until just before the birth of KP. Her baby was born prematurely and remained in hospital for some time due to a number of serious medical conditions. Care proceedings were instigated by Nottingham City Council in September 2006. An Interim Care Order was granted for the infant by Nottingham Magistrates' Court sitting as a Family Proceedings Court and she was discharged from hospital into the care of foster parents in November 2006. The child was still residing with the same foster carers at the time of the Court of Appeal case. Thus at no stage was the child in the care of her birth mother. Nottingham City Council also commenced proceedings under s.21 of the Adoption and Children Act 2002 for a Placement Order prospective to an adoption. This application was consolidated with an application for a full Care Order and because of their complexity, both were transferred up to Nottingham County Court, where the case was heard in August 2007. A consultant clinical psychologist jointly instructed to examine the mother's mental capacity assessed her as incapable of understanding court proceedings, in a report dated 23 October 2006. As a result, throughout the County Court hearing RP was represented by the Official Solicitor who did not oppose the making of the Care Order. The Official Solicitor also accepted on her behalf that she did not have capacity to consent to the making of the Placement Order. Consequently, under s.52(1)(a) of the Adoption and Children Act 2002 the mother's consent to the Placement Order was dispensed with. RP appealed to the Court of Appeal on three principal grounds. First, that she had mental capacity and it was therefore unlawful to appoint an Official Solicitor to act on her behalf. Secondly, the Official Solicitor had not acted in her *best interests* during the proceedings at the County Court. Thirdly, her rights under article 6 of the European Convention on Human Rights had been violated.

Key people in the case

RP – mother and appellant
KP – infant daughter of RP
AP – brother of mother and McKenzie friend
Mr Hemming – Member of Parliament and McKenzie friend
SC – RP's solicitor and later retained by the Official Solicitor
HJ – consultant clinical psychologist
Ms Rogers – barrister for local authority and first respondent
Mr Jackson – barrister for Official Solicitor and second respondent
Her Honour Judge Butler – judge in County Court case
Lord Justice Wall – judge in Court of Appeal case

Discussion of the case

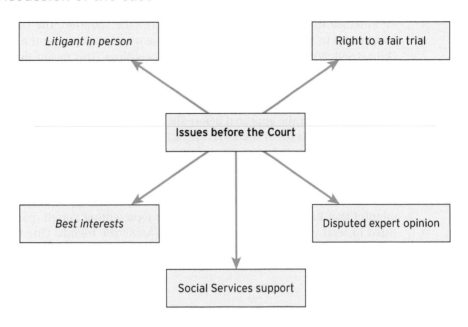

Litigant in person

During the consolidated care proceedings in August 2007 concerning the full Care Order and Placement Order, RP had been represented by the Official Solicitor. This had occurred because an evaluation report commissioned from HJ, a consultant clinical psychologist, had concluded that RP lacked the mental capacity to litigate. RP's contention before the Court of Appeal was that this evaluation report contained many inaccuracies and was incorrect in its conclusion that she lacked the mental capacity to instruct her own solicitor. Furthermore, RP alleged that the Official Solicitor had not acted in her *best interests*, most particularly in relation to the proposed adoption of her daughter. The Official Solicitor had in fact neither opposed the making of the Care Order nor the Placement Order. Common law presumes an adult to have capacity unless there is clear evidence to the contrary. Sections 1 and 3 of the Mental Capacity Act 2005 set out the test to be applied to establish if a litigant lacks capacity. In this instance the psychologist produced a report to the effect that RP lacked mental capacity. This had two major consequences which profoundly affected how the hearing on the Care Order and the Placement Order proceeded. First, the mother was represented throughout by the Official Solicitor acting as her litigation friend. This also meant that her solicitor SC was required to take instructions from the Official Solicitor and not from RP herself. Secondly, as s.52(1)(a) of the Adoption and Children Act 2002 permits the consent of a birth mother to be dispensed with if she is deemed 'incapable of giving consent' this meant that RP's objection to the Placement Order was overridden.

These events left RP in a difficult legal position. She had been deemed mentally incapable of conducting her own litigation by a consultant clinical psychologist, an expert opinion which had been accepted by Her Honour Judge Butler who presided over the County Court case. This was an expert opinion which RP sought to dispute. In addition, during the County Court case she had been represented by the Official Solicitor who, acting in her *best interests*, had not opposed the Care Order or Placement Order for her child. RP intended to claim that by failing to oppose the adoption, the Official Solicitor had failed to act in her *best interests*. Therefore she was also disputing the competence of the Official Solicitor to represent her in court proceedings. This meant that in order to bring her appeal before the Court of Appeal either RP had to find another solicitor willing to take her instruction or she had to represent herself. Although RP did initially consult solicitors who gave her pro bono assistance (free legal advice) she chose to represent herself, which means that she appeared before the court to conduct her own legal action. When a litigant conducts his or her own case rather than being represented in court by a solicitor or barrister this is known as appearing as a *litigant in person*. In these circumstances judges are obliged to conduct the hearing in such a way as to ensure fairness despite the unequal legal knowledge and competence of those arguing the case for each party before the court. Lord Justice Wall presiding over the Court of Appeal hearing was particularly mindful that RP was also a vulnerable adult representing herself (para. 33). She was assisted in legally representing herself by two McKenzie friends. One was her brother AP and the other was Mr Hemming, a Member of Parliament. The box below outlines the role of a McKenzie friend.

 Background information

McKenzie friend

A McKenzie friend is an individual who is not legally qualified, but who sits with a party to a court case to offer them support, advice and assistance. He or she does not have a right to address the court and therefore cannot legally represent the *litigant in person*. It follows that a McKenzie friend cannot take the place of the litigant and attend the court hearing instead of him or her. The litigant must be present in court in order for his or her McKenzie friend to attend as well. Although a McKenzie friend cannot conduct the case for a litigant he or she can assist a litigant to conduct their own case.

There is an established presumption within the court and tribunal system that a litigant is entitled to bring a person of their own choosing with them to a hearing to act as a McKenzie friend. While a litigant is required to give the presiding judge notice of the attendance of a McKenzie friend at the hearing, their presence is normally permitted. A judge would require strong and sound reasons for refusing permission for a McKenzie friend to attend court. Such a refusal would be based on the likelihood of their interference with the administration of justice.

A McKenzie friend is likely to be called upon when a party to legal action at court or before a tribunal would commonly expect to have legal representation, but for some reason does not. There is a clear legal distinction between a litigation friend who legally represents minors or adults without capacity and a McKenzie friend who provides assistance to a litigant in person, but does not legally represent them. To be able to assist a litigant in person to conduct his or her case a McKenzie friend will need access to a number of legal documents. Judgement handed down in *Re O (Children); Re W-R (A Child); Re W (Children)* [2005] EWCA Civ 759 a Court of Appeal hearing on three separate cases, which concerned the attendance of McKenzie friends at family proceedings hearings, established that they are entitled to see all the relevant court documents. This will include witness statements and expert reports to-gether with any assessments, care plans or exchanges of correspondence which bear upon the case.

Occasionally social workers may act as the McKenzie friend of a service-user if he or she was to be involved in tribunal or court proceedings. For example if a user brought an action be-fore an Employment Tribunal or County Court in relation to discrimination. Alternatively a service-user may bring a McKenzie friend along to a Child Protection Case Conference where legal action is pending.

Mr Hemming MP and AP, the appellant's brother, acting as McKenzie friends, made a number of claims. These allegations constituted the facts-at-issue, meaning the matters in dispute between the parties to the case which the Court of Appeal was required to address. Lord Justice Wall summarised these at paragraph 21 of his Court of Appeal judgement:

1 The appointment of the Official Solicitor in the case was unlawful. RP throughout under-stood what the case was about, and in any event family members were available to repre-sent RP.
2 The expert who had been appointed, notwithstanding her duty to the court, had wrongly and unlawfully failed to properly address the question of RP's capacity . . . In so doing, the expert had given the appearance of bias.
3 The decision to make a Placement Order had been plainly wrong, and had been made in breach of RP's article 6 right to a fair trial.
4 RP accepted that the process of re-uniting her with KP would be gradual. However, RP had the mental capacity to conduct the proceedings, and should have been permitted to do so.

Issues of mental capacity do not exist in isolation from other aspects of the law. In this case RP was not only a vulnerable adult herself with learning difficulties, but also a mother confronted by adoption proceedings. The events surrounding RP illustrate how the Official Solicitor acts on behalf of adults without mental capacity (and occasionally for children) in court proceedings. In effect the Official Solicitor instructs lawyers on be-half of the mentally incapacitated adult on the basis of outcomes which would be in his or her *best interests*. Inevitably social workers employed in Adult Services or working in residential homes for adults or with voluntary agencies such as Age Concern will come into contact with mentally incapacitated adults. It is equally true that social workers in-volved in direct work with children will also find themselves drawn into issues concern-ing adults and mental capacity, as this case amply demonstrates. As is also apparent from this Court of Appeal hearing, simply because adults are deemed not to have capacity to engage in court proceedings this does not deny them strong feelings and opinions, some-times of anger and opposition, towards what is being done in their *best interests*.

Disputed expert opinion

RP alleged in her initial submission to the Court of Appeal (para. 13) that:

I was not allowed to speak at the final hearing to refute any claims made against myself or to provide evidence to support my case, the case was very short and I was basically a spec-tator . . . My legal representative was changed or 'ordered' to take instructions from an official solicitor, this was based on a psychological report by [HJ]. I wish to refute this report in any further granted case, I also intend to get my own evaluation report done, as I didn't have an opportunity to refute the report before, as this very report crippled my case and this stopped me from defending myself or instructing my legal team to do so, which stopped me having a 'fair trial' which is a human right as specified under article 6 of the Human Rights Act . . . Parties in the case gave misleading, exaggerated facts and lies in their reports knowingly, these reports were used as evidence and I did not get the chance to refute these during the final hearing, and I wish to argue that point at any new hearing.

From the above excerpt, in which RP sets out her grounds for seeking an appeal, it is clear that the fundamental fact-at-issue was the content of the evaluation report produced by HJ, a consultant clinical psychologist. She had been engaged by the parties to the consolidated care proceedings to assess RP's competence to instruct a solicitor. HJ interviewed RP as part of this assessment and completed her report in October 2006. At paragraph 3.1 she wrote:

Because of the difficulties (RP) has in understanding, processing and recalling information, I believe that she will find it very difficult to understand the advice given by her solicitor. She will not be able to make informed decisions on the basis of this advice, particularly when this involves anticipating possible outcomes. It would be appropriate for the Official Solicitor to become involved.

It was on receipt of this report that the district judge of Nottingham County Court invited the Official Solicitor to conduct legal proceedings on behalf of RP. Mr Hemming MP, one of RP's McKenzie friends, alleged that HJ was in the pay of the local authority and had produced a biased report. In fact HJ had been a jointly appointed expert, her costs were equally apportioned between the parties to the court case and she was required to produce an objective opinion. On examining her credentials Lord Justice Wall found that HJ held a number of relevant qualifications in clinical psychology, including a doctorate. She had been in practice since 1990 and had specialised in assessing the capabilities and support needs of parents with leaning disabilities. Thus Lord Justice Wall concluded that HJ was 'eminently qualified' to carry out the assessment of RP, an assertion not disputed by any of the parties to the Court of Appeal case.

HJ's report on RP, which was made available to the Court of Appeal, showed that she had applied the Wechsler Adult Intelligence Scale, a widely accepted standard psychological questionnaire to assess mental capacity. Again none of the parties to the court case disputed the aptness of the psychological instrument chosen by the clinical psychologist. In this connection it is significant that at no stage during her appeal did RP engage another psychologist or psychiatrist to make an independent assessment of her mental capacity. RP had claimed that she was not afforded the opportunity to refute the conclusions of the clinical psychologist's report in the County Court. Yet, in the Court of Appeal when offered the chance to do so, she failed to engage another professional to give a second opinion, produce an alternative expert witness, or to demonstrate bias in HJ's report. Lord Justice Wall therefore determined that the report produced by the consultant clinical psychologist was impartial and in accordance with her position as a jointly appointed expert.

Since the coming into force of the Mental Capacity Act 2005, which occurred soon after the events at Nottingham County Court, there are now provisions to assist vulnerable people in RP's situation to challenge assessments of their mental capacity. Under paragraph 4.65 of the Department for Constitutional Affairs (2007) *Mental Capacity Act 2005: Code of Practice*, a person assessed as lacking capacity can challenge this either by insisting on a second opinion or via direct application to the Court of Protection for a determination on the matter. In other words, there is now a formal legal mechanism by which adults assessed as lacking mental capacity in relation to a particular matter can dispute the finding. The role and functions of the new Court of Protection are set out in the box below.

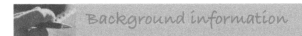

Background information

Court of Protection

The new Court of Protection was set up under s.45 of the Mental Capacity Act 2005. It is a specialist court created to deal with decision making for adults (and occasionally children aged 16-17 years) who lack the mental capacity to make their own decisions. The old Court of Protection was restricted to matters concerning the property and finances of people who lacked capacity. This meant that previously disputes over the care or treatment of a person without capacity had to be addressed under the inherent jurisdiction of the High Court. Now the new expanded Court of Protection introduced under the Mental Capacity Act 2005 can address a much wider range of issues and build up expertise in dealing with decisions affecting people without mental capacity. The new Court of Protection has the same powers as the High Court and as a superior court can create judicial precedent to bind the rulings of lower courts. It is bound by the *best interests* principle contained in the Mental Capacity Act 2005 and therefore the Court of Protection must make all its decisions in compliance with this overarching consideration. According to paragraphs 8.13-8.17 of the Code of Practice the new Court of Protection can:

- Make declarations on the mental capacity of a person or on their mental capacity to make a particular decision, give consent or take a particular action.
- Make a declaration as to whether a specific act relating to a person's care or treatment is lawful. This can include the failure to provide care or treatment that the person needs.
- Make declarations, decisions and orders on financial and welfare matters affecting people who lack capacity.
- Appoint deputies to make decisions for people who lack capacity to make those decisions.
- Remove deputies or attorneys who act inappropriately.
- Deliberate on matters concerning Lasting and Enduring Powers of Attorney.

In the present case, RP and her McKenzie friends did challenge the clinical psychologist's report in the Court of Appeal, but they did so without producing any evidence to substantiate their allegations. It is therefore exceptionally unlikely, even if the *Mental Capacity Act 2005: Code of Practice* had been in operation at the time of the County Court hearing, that either a second opinion from another clinical psychologist or application to the Court of Protection would have contradicted the conclusions arrived at by HJ in her original assessment. What this case does demonstrate is the importance of engaging an expert witness who is appropriately qualified and demonstrably competent in their area of assumed expertise. The local authority's legal team together with the social workers involved in the care and adoption proceedings had plainly taken time and effort to engage a clinical psychologist with a specialism in assessing parents with learning difficulties. It was for this reason that her expert evidence stood up under criticism from RP and her McKenzie friends and to scrutiny by the Court of Appeal. This highlights the crucial role of experts in court proceedings concerning issues of capacity.

Best interests

At the Court of Appeal, RP, through her McKenzie friends, took the view that even if she had been found incapable of instructing her solicitor, a family member should have been appointed as her litigation friend instead of the Official Solicitor. It was RP's view that a family member would have been better placed to act in her *best interests* than the Official Solicitor. Lord Justice Wall duly considered this point. He observed that both AP's brother and her parents had put themselves forward as possible candidates to adopt RP's daughter. This meant that at some stage in the future they might themselves become party to court proceedings concerning RP. Litigation friends are legally required to act 'fairly and competently' on behalf of the incapacitated adults they are representing. For this reason they must not have any conflicting interests with the vulnerable adult in question. Plainly if RP's brother or parents might be prospective adopters for her child, they could not act objectively on RP's behalf in a court case connected with the adoption of her daughter KP. This was the more so in a case where RP had consistently voiced her opposition to any such adoption and sought the return of KP to her care. This conflict of interest effectively ruled out RP's brother and parents, who were the only family members conceivably able to act as a litigation friend. As Lord Justice Wall observed in his judgement, had they been proposed as litigation friends at the time of the County Court case, Her Honour Judge Butler would have had no choice but to refuse their appointment. She was obliged, given all the circumstances, to appoint the Official Solicitor to act as RP's litigation friend (para. 133).

As the Official Solicitor was appointed to act on behalf of RP due to her lack of mental capacity, RP did not address the court directly. It was therefore left to the Official Solicitor to set before Nottingham County Court RP's position regarding the care proceedings and prospective adoption of her infant daughter. The Official Solicitor represented RP's position in the following terms (para. 19):

> [RP believes] that she would be able to provide appropriate care for KP; and that she had developed the skills necessary to parent KP . . . [and] that KP should be returned to her care, but that if she was not able to care for KP, that she would want KP to be cared for by family members. It is [RP's] position that she has shown a commitment to contact and that there is a close and loving bond between her and her daughter. If [RP] is unable to care for [KP], she would like to have continuing direct contact with her. [RP] has commented on the position taken by the other parties and feels that the local authority has not given her a chance to acquire the skills necessary to provide care to her daughter. [RP] feels that she should have the right to a family life and that if [KP] were to reside in her care, there would be no risk of significant harm.

After setting out RP's perspective and wishes the Official Solicitor then proceeded to exercise the responsibility of a litigation friend to conduct proceedings on behalf of the incapacitated adult 'fairly and competently' and to his or her benefit. The Official Solicitor interpreted this as 'a duty to conduct this case on [RP's] behalf and in her best interests' (para. 20). In consequence, at the hearing before Nottingham County Court, the Official Solicitor adopted the following positions:

1 The threshold criteria under section 31 of the Children Act 1989 were satisfied.
2 He could not oppose a Care Order being made in relation to KP.
3 RP was not in a position to consent or refuse her consent to the Placement Order.
4 He could not oppose the local authority's application for such an order.

Effectively this meant that all the parties to the consolidated proceedings before the County Court were agreeing to the granting of a Care Order and Placement Order. This was in opposition to the articulated view of RP who wanted the return of her daughter into her care and was trenchantly against the making of either court order. It was on this point that RP argued the Official Solicitor had failed to act in her *best interests*. Under s.1(5) of the Mental Capacity Act 2005 'an act done, or decision made, under this Act for or on behalf of a person who lacks capacity must be done, or made, in his best interests'. The statute does not legally define 'best interests' because the circumstances under which someone may be acting for a person without capacity varies so widely. However, the Code of Practice issued under s.42 of the Mental Capacity Act 2005 does list the considerations which comprise *best interest* decisions on behalf of mentally incapacitated adults. These are set out in the box below.

Key guidance

Mental Capacity Act 2005: Code of Practice

Pages 65-66: A person trying to work out the best interests of a person who lacks capacity to make a particular decision ('lacks capacity') should:

Encourage participation - do whatever is possible to permit and encourage the person to take part, or to improve their ability to take part, in making the decision. Identify all the relevant circumstances - try to identify all the things that make the person who lacks capacity would take into account if they were making the decisions or acting for themselves.

Find out the person's views - try to find out the views of the person who lacks capacity.

Avoid discrimination - not make assumptions about someone's best interests simply on the basis of the person's age, appearance, condition or behaviour.

Assess whether the person might regain capacity - consider whether the person is likely to regain capacity (e.g. after receiving medical treatment). If so can the decision wait until then?

If the decision concerns life-sustaining treatment - not be motivated in any way by a desire to bring about the person's death. They should not make assumptions about the person's quality of life.

Consult others - if it is practical and appropriate to do so, consult other people for their views about the person's best interests and to see if they have any information about the person's wishes and feelings, beliefs and values.

Avoid restricting the person's rights - see if there are other options that may be less restrictive of the person's rights.

Take all of this into account - weigh up all of these factors in order to work out what is in the person's best interests.

As paragraph 5.2 of the Code of Practice makes clear the *best interests* principle covers all aspects of financial, personal welfare and healthcare decision making and actions. It applies to anyone making decisions or acting under the provisions of the Act, including:

- Family carers, other carers and care workers
- Healthcare and social care staff
- Attorneys appointed under a Lasting Power of Attorney or registered Enduring Power of Attorney

- Deputies appointed by the court to make decisions on behalf of someone who lacks capacity, and
- The Court of Protection

Strictly speaking the acts complained of by RP regarding the conduct of the Official Solicitor took place prior to the coming into force of the Mental Capacity Act 2005. However, as Lord Justice Wall alluded during his judgement, he was mindful of the provisions contained in the Mental Capacity Act 2005, which had been introduced since the hearing at Nottingham County Court. Under the Code of Practice issued under the Mental Capacity Act 2005 the Official Solicitor was obliged to ascertain the wishes of RP. This, the Official Solicitor plainly did, and by all accounts brought to the attention of the County Court the implacable opposition of RP to the adoption of her child. The Official Solicitor also informed the same court that RP wished to have the care of KP, but was willing to contemplate her care by another family member. So undoubtedly the Official Solicitor did ascertain and convey RP's wishes accurately and in full to Nottingham County Court and in accordance with the *best interests* principle. But conveying a client's wishes is one thing, actually arguing for his or her position in court is another.

As is made explicit in the *Mental Capacity Act 2005: Code of Practice,* considerations of *best interests* are not confined to court cases. They are equally applicable to professionals and carers making day-to-day decisions on behalf of incapacitated adults. In so far as this is true, social workers are also bound by the guidance set out in pages 65–66 of the Code of Practice and extracted in the box above. The need to differentiate out what is really in the *best interests* of an incapacitated adult and what is expedient for a professional in terms of risk management or a carer in terms of convenience are matters which require serious reflection. The peril intrinsic to making *best interests* decisions is that of imposing what is in the *best interests* of others upon the incapacitated adult. This raises the issue of professional power and invokes paragraph 3.8 of the GSCC Code which reminds social workers of the need to use 'responsibly the power that comes from your work with service users and carers'.

 Critical commentary

Best interests

As para. 4.4 of the *Mental Capacity Act 2005: Code of Practice* makes clear, mental incapacity is to be understood in terms of an inability to make a decision in relation to a particular matter at a specific point in time. This means that those with the profoundest cognitive impairments will be incapacitated in relation to a greater number of matters. Substitute decision-making, whether concerning a single matter such as proposed medical treatment or innumerable daily routines, requires a carer or professional to make decisions for the incapacitated user or patient. This begs the question as to what guiding principles should be applied by the substitute decision maker. Section 1(5) of the Mental Capacity Act 2005 requires that the basis for any decision on behalf of mentally incapacitated adults is that of their 'best interests'. What constitutes the 'best interests' of an incapacitated person is not legally defined. The Mental Capacity Act 2005, s.4 does set out a checklist of considerations which must inform the determination of a person's 'best interests'. This checklist concerns the *process* of reaching a decision on 'best interests' and not the *outcome* or actual decision.

Under the Mental Capacity Act 2005 the 'best interests' principle relates to a person's over-all welfare and embraces his or her health, education, occupation, social life, sexuality, leisure, personal dignity and overall quality of life. One understanding of a person's 'best in-terests' is that they can be objectively determined. This is achieved by drawing up a list of possible alternative outcomes on any given matter and then identifying the benefits and dis-benefits to the incapacitated adult of each outcome. The course of action which would be in the 'best interests' of the incapacitated person will be the one which generates the greatest benefit and causes the least harm. This is referred to in common law as the 'balance sheet' approach. A subjective perspective on 'best interests' sets it within the context of an inca-pacitated adult's personal history, their former or current values, preferences and aspira-tions. This is essentially the approach adopted in the Mental Capacity Act 2005. It is of limited application for those with life-long profound learning difficulties and who are unable to articulate values, aspirations or wishes. Although their preferences may be expressed through non-verbal behaviour, which may in turn require interpretation by others.

In situations where adults with profound cognitive impairments are looked after by family members, it may be extremely difficult to disentangle the 'best interests' of the incapaci-tated adult from those who care for him or her. For example, parents ask for their incapaci-tated daughter to be sterilised because they are uncomfortable with her emerging sexuality. At the same time it is recognised that their daughter is unable to keep herself safe and that pregnancy would be a deeply distressing experience for her. Another difficulty surrounds the time frame of 'best interest' decisions. Are they purely about the present or ought they to be future oriented and if so how are the dis-benefits of the present to be offset against the po-tential benefits of the future? For example, insisting that a young incapacitated adult attends a college they dislike, so as to optimise their cognitive abilities.

For those with profound and life-long cognitive impairment, family members, informal carers and practitioners will continue to make 'best interest' decisions on their behalf. These deci-sions will inevitably reflect professional or lay notions of 'best interests' based on concerns about safety and ideas regarding a worthwhile life. For professionals, these decisions may be inextricably bound up with their preoccupation with risk management in relation to self-harm and protecting others. For carers, there is an understandable propensity for them to make 'best interest' decisions which relieve rather than add to their caring responsibilities. In this connection, s.5 of the Mental Capacity Act 2005 protects substitute decision makers from prosecution for acts detrimental to the incapacitated adult, as long as they reasonably believed they were acting in his or her 'best interests'. This provision gives professionals and carers considerable scope for developing their own interpretation of another's 'best interest'.

Right to a fair trial

On a number of occasions RP had complained to SC, her solicitor, that she did not feel any-one was fighting her corner. SC was in a difficult position. She was originally engaged by RP in relation to the first hearing in Nottingham Family Proceedings Court, but once the Offi-cial Solicitor was appointed she began to take instructions from him. In a record of a meet-ing in August 2007, SC records that RP said 'she did not feel that her voice was being heard and that nobody was fighting for her'. In a sense this was true. By this point in time RP had been found to be mentally incapable and SC was legally obliged to take instructions from the Official Solicitor and not RP. But the Official Solicitor had informed both RP and SC that he would not contest the making of a full Care Order or Placement Order.

Of course RP's position was that she opposed the granting of Care and Placement Orders. She claimed that in accordance with her Convention Right to a fair trial, she was entitled to be represented in court by legal counsel who would contest the orders on her behalf. This she was deprived of by the intervention of the Official Solicitor. Lord Justice Wall presiding in the Court of Appeal had to adduce from the evidence put before him if indeed RP had been denied a fair trial and the opportunity to argue her claims before Nottingham County Court. Article 6 (1) of the European Convention on Human Rights declares that 'in the determination of his civil rights and obligations everyone is entitled to a fair and public hearing within a reasonable time by an independent and impartial tribunal established by law'. RP's unequivocal position was that her child should be returned to her care and failing this into the care of one of her family members. Both her brother and parents had already put themselves forward as possible substitute carers. The County Court heard expert evidence as to the unsuitability of RP or other family members to care for KP.

Social workers from the local authority placed before the Court in evidence their assessment of RP, her brother and parents conducted in accordance with the *Framework for the Assessment of Children in Need and their Families*. The assessment of RP, supported as it was by specialist reports, demonstrated to the Court's satisfaction that the child would be at significant risk of harm if returned to the care of her mother. Further assessments also presented in evidence revealed that neither RP's brother nor her parents were suitable carers for a child who was disabled and continued to have substantial medical needs. There was no allegation by the local authority that any of the family members would deliberately harm the child. But the assessments completed on different family members (and particularly that for RP) indicated that through no fault of their own, they did not possess the parenting capacity necessary to meet the care needs of the infant. The evidence put before the County Court by the local authority met the threshold criteria set out in s.31 of the Children Act 1989 for the granting of a Care Order. To ensure stability for the child in the future (given that none of her family members was deemed able to provide for her care) the local authority had drawn up a care plan based on adoption.

Removing a child not only from his or her birth parents, but from the birth family entirely, permanently and irrevocably, under an Adoption Order is an exceptionally extreme course of action. It can only be undertaken after thorough assessment. In this case social workers produced detailed assessments supported by expert reports which complied with the *Framework for the Assessment of Children in Need and their Families*. Neither the County Court, nor the Court of Appeal called into question the thoroughness and appropriateness of the way in which social workers had conducted their assessments. Therefore the conclusions arrived at by social workers regarding adoption were not questioned by the courts either. This yet again demonstrates the importance of following policy guidance in relation to assessment, not simply to ensure that the assessment stands up to scrutiny in a court of law, but to ensure that it fully considers all the relevant matters that touch upon a decision to permanently remove a child.

The issue for RP was that once the matter came to court she was not properly represented by a lawyer prepared to argue her point of view. While the courts found the assessments produced by social workers to be thorough and professional, at the same time these were not being challenged by the Official Solicitor who was representing RP. For of course the Official Solicitor had concluded that the adoption of RP's daughter was in RP's *best interests*. Regardless of how properly assessments are conducted or care plans developed, a fair trial would seem to demand that a user or parent who fundamentally disagrees with them should be given the opportunity to have that position effectively argued in court.

Social Services support

RP argued at the Court of Appeal that she had not been given a fair trial in relation to the adoption and care proceedings in Nottingham County Court. As evidence put before the Court of Appeal was to show, adoption was not the initial plan for KP's care. Social Services produced evidence detailing how social workers had endeavoured to meet the wishes of RP and support her to care for her infant daughter. The first care plan for the infant was produced in September 2006, about four months after her birth. As she had been born prematurely with medical complications she required hospital treatment over an extended period and up until September 2006 had remained in hospital. The overarching objective of this initial care plan was 'to identify how the local authority will keep KP alive and safe in a home environment whilst her birth mother is given the opportunity to develop her care skills. RP has been assessed as being unable to have sole care of KP.'

At this stage the intention of social workers was to identify a short-term foster care placement for the infant on her discharge from hospital and to work with the mother to improve her parenting capacity. This is why the original application by the local authority in November 2006 to Nottingham Family Proceedings Court had been for an Interim Care Order and not a full Care Order. In fact the local authority had endeavoured to accommodate the infant under s.20 of the Children Act 1989, that is to say under a voluntary agreement with the mother. This accords with the principles laid down in *Working Together to Protect Children* and *The Challenge of Partnership in Child Protection*. These emphasise the importance of working in partnership with families and avoiding recourse to the courts where this is possible without endangering the health or safety of the child concerned. The mother refused to contemplate such an arrangement, stating that she wanted her child discharged from hospital directly into her care in 'the belief that KP would be fine once she had breathed fresh air' (para. 151).

The Framework for the Assessment of Children in Need requires that the assessment of *children in need* be conducted along three dimensions – that of the child's developmental needs, parenting capacity and family and environmental factors. In this instance the infant had health needs which placed demands on parenting capacity above and beyond those of a child without disabilities. As a mother with learning difficulties the mother's parenting capacity was hampered by her inability to fully comprehend the implications of her daughter's health needs. In addition, social workers had discovered on further exploration of RP's background that there were incidents of violence and conflict within the wider family network (para. 132). This of course raised doubts for social workers as to the level of support close relatives could realistically provide to RP in looking after her daughter at home. So there were family and environmental factors which were more likely to detract from, rather than positively contribute to, RP's ability to take care of her daughter.

The way in which these initial concerns expressed by professionals began to play out is clear from the documentation produced in court by Social Services covering the period between the granting of the Interim Care Order and their application for a full Care Order and Placement Order. Placed before the Court of Appeal was the original case synopsis which the solicitor representing the local authority had compiled for Nottingham Family Proceedings Court and which set out the situation as at September 2006. This stated (para. 149) that RP:

> lacks practice and expertise in completing basic care tasks and the more complicated skills required to deal with KP's oxygen dependence. The hospital and social services have devised a list of requirements that RP needs to be able to demonstrate satisfactorily before KP can be discharged into her care. Whilst this has been discussed with her on three occasions,

she had difficulty in understanding the seriousness of the situation. RP is confident that she is able to care for KP upon discharge from hospital. She is unable to articulate what KP's medical needs are or what has caused them. She has expressed the view that KP will only require oxygen for four weeks post discharge because when she 'breaths fresh air' she will be OK. She does not comprehend KP's vulnerability and the fact that she may die if care is inadequate.

Notwithstanding these substantial difficulties there was an unequivocal commitment from Social Services to reunite mother and child. This is evidenced in a contemporaneous note kept by RP's solicitor in which she observed that 'it is our understanding that the local authority do want to continue to work with RP in the hope that one day KP may be returned to her care' (para. 150). However, the problems identified in the case synopsis relating to RP's mental capacity to understand the severity of KP's medical condition and her ability to acquire the skills necessary to meet KP's critical health needs persisted. Inputs were arranged from social workers and other care professionals to improve aspects of RP's parenting capacity, most particularly in relation to giving her daughter oxygen. This was absolutely imperative as the infant's lungs were under-developed and without regular access to oxygen she would die.

It was agreed by Social Services to devise a training programme for RP to teach her how to care for the baby and improve her parenting capacity. HJ, the consultant clinical psychologist was to be involved in approving the teaching methods to be used. In November 2006 a local children's resource centre commenced an assessment of RP's capacity 'to learn and consistently sustain the necessary child care skills to care for KP'. In the succeeding months social workers recorded that the mother continued to maintain that she needed no assistance to look after the baby. In June 2007 HJ reported on the progress of the training for RP. She explicitly endorsed the approach of Social Services, noting at paragraph 2.1 of her report that RP 'has been given every opportunity to learn and demonstrate [parenting] skills'. HJ went on to conclude (para. 156) that:

1.1 As I have indicated previously RP has a significant learning disability, and she will always need a high level of support in caring for KP. If she were not receiving this support she would pose a high level of risk to KP's well-being, which is not due to any desire on her part to hurt KP, but to her limitations, which are too extensive to allow her to parent KP successfully on her own.

1.2 If she were receiving a high level of support this risk could be reduced. The level of support which would be needed for this to happen would be for another competent adult to be present at all times, to prompt and assist RP in her care of KP. Essentially this means that RP would need to be living with a partner or family member who could appropriately provide this level of support.

The matter of real concern to social workers was that throughout the period of teaching, observation and assessment relating to her parenting capacity, neither RP nor her family were willing to cooperate with Social Services. While every effort was made by professionals to work in partnership with RP, at no stage was she able to recognise the life-threatening nature of her baby's condition, let alone acquire the skills to manage her health needs. This situation was exacerbated by a hostile family network which understandably (though unhelpfully) regarded Social Services as unjustifiably interfering in their private family life. Reading through the documentation presented by the local authority at the Court of Appeal, Lord Justice Wall commended the thoroughness of the work which had been attempted with RP. He also praised the comprehensiveness of the assessments and reports produced by social workers and other professionals in relation to her abilities (para. 158).

Lord Justice Wall then turned to the report of the Children's Guardian, who provided separate representation for the infant KP at Nottingham County Court. She concluded in her submission (para. 159) that:

> Whilst I acknowledge the high level of commitment shown by [RP] to her daughter during these proceedings and am very clear that she loves [KP] dearly, the sad fact is that the evidence clearly leads to the conclusion that KP's needs cannot be safely met by RP or by any member of the family.

As the Children's Guardian is charged to represent the *best interests* of the child and is an officer of CAFCASS and not the local authority, this was yet another independent opinion. In other words, Judge Butler sitting in Nottingham County Court had before her a number of expert opinions which endorsed the decision of the local authority to apply for Care and Placement Orders.

The series of assessments, case notes and expert reports presented in evidence before the Court of Appeal amply demonstrated the commitment of social workers to engage with RP and her family in trying to reunite mother and child. They point up the dilemmas posed for social workers who are at one and the same time required to support families to bring up children, and to protect children from significant harm. In this case social workers attempted to reconcile these two imperatives by endeavouring to improve RP's parenting capacity alongside encouraging other family members to support her. Unfortunately the inability of RP to appreciate the life-threatening nature of her daughter's condition, the hostility of family members to social work intervention and the unsuitability of any relative to take over parenting responsibilities resulted in adoption proceedings. The professional dilemmas faced by practitioners in relation to RP are paralleled in the GSCC Code of Practice. On the one hand this requires social workers to promote the views and wishes of users and to assist them to control their lives. On the other hand they must act to minimise the risks of users harming others. The events surrounding RP and the adoption of her daughter highlight the conflict which there can be between these two stipulations. Social workers are called upon not to choose one imperative over the other, but like the practitioners working with RP, to make every effort to meet both imperatives.

 Perspectives

Parents with learning difficulties

There are no accurate statistics available on the number of children of parents with learning difficulties who are taken into public care in the United Kingdom. Research from other European countries and small-scale studies conducted in Britain indicate that 30–50% of children are removed from parents with learning difficulties (Booth et al., 2005: 8). A study by Booth et al. (2005) of County Court care proceedings during 2000 in Sheffield and Leeds found that parents with learning difficulties comprised 15% of all parents involved in care proceedings even though they make up less than 1% of the total population of parents in the United Kingdom.

Booth and Booth (2005) interviewed parents with learning difficulties from 20 households where at least one of their children had been the subject of care proceedings. Only in five instances did parents report being assessed at home. Most had received a focussed out-of-home assessment of their parenting capacity in the unfamiliar surroundings of a family centre or residential assessment unit (Booth and Booth, 2005: 112). Parents complained that their advocates were rarely a party to the parenting assessments, which were often determinant as to whether their children remained with them or were taken into care. Most parents with learning difficulties expressed cynicism about the whole assessment process, epitomised in one response which described the social worker as 'there for taking kids, not helping us' (Booth and Booth, 2005: 116).

Case Conferences, which are generally intimidating for all parents, are particularly so for those with learning difficulties. One such parent recalled 'all I was getting really was negative vibes from everybody. It was negative, negative' while another stated that 'I feel nervous because most of the time I don't understand what they're talking about. I can't understand big words' (Booth and Booth, 2005: 118). Many parents were very dependent on their advocate in order to understand what professionals were saying. As one parent explained, 'they talk fast and then I have to wait for Kath [my advocate]. I say, I didn't understand that Kath, did you?' Yet another parent with learning difficulties concluded that professionals at Case Conferences 'don't mind if they hurt our feelings' while another described crying at a Case Conference which felt like being back in court all over again (Booth and Booth, 2005: 118).

Parents with learning difficulties felt most resentful about what they regarded as the inaccurate things said and written about them by professionals. One interviewee summed this up, 'they're asking questions and you've got to think what you say before you answer because half the time they twist it, to say something what they want to say and not what you said' (Booth and Booth, 2005: 119). Another added, 'they kept saying I wasn't a fit mother. I didn't like that. It just told 'em I am a fit mother. I know I've got learning disabilities but I am a good mum' (Booth and Booth, 2005: 119).

Often these parents perceived their solicitors as doing their utmost to argue the parents' case, even when ultimately the children concerned were taken into care. The many positive views of solicitors are best summed up by one parent who stated 'she did it so I understood. If there was something I didn't understand my solicitor put it in shorter sentences and explained it more clearly' (Booth and Booth, 2005: 122). For those who attended court, their typical experiences are best captured by the recollections of two other parents. One reported, 'Terrified. Each time, terrified. All the time I was right scared. When I first went in front of magistrates I nearly passed out.' Another said of attending a court hearing, 'I couldn't take in what was happening. It's a different language an' all. It was mumbo jumbo to me' (Booth and Booth, 2005: 122).

Judgement in Re P (A Child)(Care and Placement Order Proceedings: Mental Capacity of Parent)

Lord Justice Wall reproached RP and her McKenzie friends for putting their case in such a way that it focussed exclusively on the rights of RP as a parent and ignored the rights of KP as a child. Under the Children Act 1989 Her Honour Judge Butler was legally obliged to give paramount consideration to the child's welfare. In the opinion of Lord Justice Wall the evidence before Judge Butler at Nottingham County Court was 'overwhelmingly in favour of care and placement orders' and the Official Solicitor had no choice but to concede that this was the correct course of action. Lord Justice Wall concluded that while the Official Solicitor could and did set before the court RP's wishes, the Official Solicitor could not reasonably advance an argument that she be given custody of KP in the face of such persuasive evidence to the contrary.

Critical questions

1 In this case an adult assessed as not having mental capacity was represented by the Official Solicitor who conceded in court that it was in RP's *best interests* for her child to be put up for adoption. Arguably this would be the equivalent of a lawyer engaged by mentally competent birth parents conceding in court that the local authority was right to put their child up for adoption and there was no point in engaging in legal argument to the contrary. Do you think that RP received a fair trial in relation to the consolidated care and adoption proceedings? If you think RP did not receive a fair trial, how might parents, deemed mentally incapacitated in relation to litigation, be better represented in care proceedings?

2 This case concerned the meaning of *best interests* in relation to a mentally incapacitated adult. How can social workers avoid making *best interests* decisions which are professionally expedient rather than ones which truly reflect a mentally incapacitated adult's care needs and preferences?

3 RP as a vulnerable adult and KP as a disabled child with a life-threatening condition had conflicting needs. Having read the facts of this case, what is your reaction to social work intervention with this family? Is there anything else you think social workers ought to have done to support this birth parent?

Perspectives

Practitioners and parents with learning difficulties

Booth et al. (2006: 997–8) note that the number of parents with learning difficulties coming to the attention of social and healthcare practitioners has been steadily increasing. In their study they interviewed 31 professionals ranging from social workers to psychologists and solicitors who had experience of parents with learning difficulties caught up in the child protection system. Booth et al. (2006:1000) observe that those with learning difficulties experience particular problems around time, attention and memory. Their study examined how child protection procedures interact with these aspects of learning disability.

A major problem for social workers was the pressure on their time and the lack of opportunity for really getting to know parents with learning difficulties. As one social worker put it, 'We don't do relationships, we do intervention. We get in there, do the stuff and then we leave. I pick up a case, I slog through the care proceedings and then there's the goodbye at the end.' A social work manager admitted, 'to work effectively with that family you need time and space. There are pressures on the workers at the moment. They're not in a position to provide that. It's very frustrating at times because what takes ten minutes for someone without learning disabilities can take an hour, sometimes longer, for someone with learning disabilities' (Booth et al., 2006: 1002).

The separation of Children's Services and Adult Social Services was identified by numerous professionals as a major barrier to getting the right support to parents with learning difficulties. A director of a Learning Disabilities Service, which is located in Adult Social Services, claimed: 'We don't find out, help's not put in, and all of a sudden it's a child protection issue and it goes to court. Whereas if there was more time and more people involved in the prevention, they might prevent a crisis arising.' Looking at the same situation from the standpoint of Children's Services, a childcare social worker observed, 'It seems to me they fall between . . . I've tried to get Emily her own adult worker from the Learning Disability Team and I've not really been successful. I've flagged it up but as far as I know they've not allocated a worker. I suppose I keep thinking if they find out she's got some significant problems that I'll be able to get it passed on to the Disability Team. I hope they might be better than me because they'll be more used to dealing with learning disability' (Booth et al., 2006: 1003).

Criticising the tight timescales set out in the *Framework for the Assessment of Children in Need and their Families* one child protection social worker insisted, 'At the end of the day you need a quality piece of assessment, don't you, and to do it on thirty five days with a family with learning disabilities is just totally unethical, unachievable. That isn't possible.' Moreover because of the paramountcy given to the child's welfare, as one social worker admitted, 'the focus would be on the child and their needs. To a certain degree the parents would be ignored' (Booth et al., 2006:1006, 1010). For other social workers the splitting of parents' rights away from those of children's was contradictory. As one practitioner in Children's Services explained, 'Look at the UN Convention and you'll see that the child has a right to grow up with mum and dad as well as a right to protection from abuse and neglect. You get this fight between the issues around adults and the issues around children. They're never seen as issues around families' (Booth et al., 2006: 1010).

CASE 3
Local Authority X v. MM (by her litigation friend, the Official Solicitor) [2007] EWHC 2003 (Fam)

Importance of the case

Focus is on the nature of mental capacity and the operation of the Mental Capacity Act 2005 in practice. The case considers the conflict between a vulnerable adult's right to a private and family life and the decisions made in her *best interests* by a local authority which restrict her freedom to pursue a private and family life.

History of the case

The local authority applied to the High Court for an exercise of its inherent jurisdiction to make a declaration requiring MM to live in supported accommodation and for contact with her long-term partner to be severely limited.

Facts of the case

MM was born in August 1968 and was 39 years old at the time of the High Court case. She was sexually abused by her older brother and removed into care at the age of 13 years. MM had a diagnosis of paranoid schizophrenia alongside moderate learning difficulties and lacked functional literacy. By the time of the High Court case KM had been her partner for 15 years. He had previously been diagnosed with a personality disorder and was known to misuse alcohol. KM had been violent towards MM and had stabbed her in the leg in the past for which he received a short prison sentence. It was also suspected that he used her welfare benefits to purchase alcohol for himself. The local authority believed that KM encouraged MM to disengage from psychiatric care, leading to deterioration in her mental health. KM tended to move from address to address and often MM followed him, likewise moving from place to place. In March 2006 MM accepted supported accommodation at

W unit. There was an agreement between her and staff that KM would not be permitted on the premises and MM would inform staff if she was leaving the unit and would return there by 8.30 pm each evening. However, MM left the unit without informing staff and often did not return for some days, during which time she appeared to be with KM and sleeping rough. In June 2006 the local authority discovered that KM intended to take MM to stay with his brother in another part of the United Kingdom. The local authority applied for and obtained an ex parte interim declaration from the High Court that 'MM lacked the capacity to decide where she should reside and with whom she should associate and that it was not in her best interests to be removed from the W unit or to have unsupervised contact with KM' (para. 7). A court order was issued to prevent her being removed from W unit, and the Official Solicitor was appointed to act on MM's behalf in subsequent legal proceedings. The court ordered that KM be restricted to supervised contact with MM twice a week for two hours. In early July 2006 MM went missing from the W unit and some weeks later was found by the police and returned there. MM was abusive towards staff on her return to the W unit and on 10 October 2006 was subject to detainment for assessment under s.2 of the Mental Health Act 1983. On 30 October MM was discharged to an adult family placement where, by court order, she was only permitted to see KM once a week for two hours. He was prohibited from approaching within 100 yards of the premises, contacting MM's carers or removing her from the adult family placement. This placement broke down in December 2006 at which time MM was moved to an emergency placement at a residential care home and from there to an independent supported living placement in March 2007. MM remained in this placement at the time of the final High Court hearing pursuant to the original interim declarations made in June 2006.

Key people in the case

MM – vulnerable adult
KM – partner of MM
PR – MM's allocated social worker
Dr Milne – consultant psychiatrist
Mr Fowler – social work consultant
Ms Amiraftabi – barrister for the claimant local authority
Mr Sachdeva – barrister for MM
Mr Justice Munby – judge presiding in High Court case

Discussion of the case

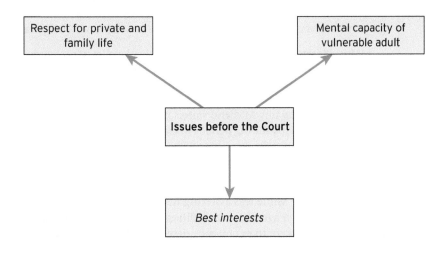

Mental capacity of vulnerable adult

Dr Milne, a consultant psychiatrist, in her expert evidence contained in a report for the High Court (paras. 26 and 28) stated that:

> [MM] has only limited insight into her own care needs and has no appreciation of the fact that living with KM has repeatedly led to a situation where her own mental and physical health is at risk. Her history indicates that she has repeatedly disengaged from involvement with services which are essential to her well being . . .
>
> At interview it was clear that MM understood the nature of sexual intercourse and that she additionally had an understanding of the risks of this including the risks of pregnancy and sexually transmitted diseases. She also would be capable of verbally refusing sexual intercourse although she may not always appreciate that she is in a risky situation . . .
>
> When examining the capacity of MM to marry she was able to give me a list of words which she told me was what marriage meant. However she did not understand these words or the concepts that they represented. Asking her to explain what a single item from the list of words meant resulted in her repeating the list by rote. It is unlikely that she will in the future understand the duties and responsibilities of marriage in the future.

Dr Milne concluded (para. 25) that MM:

(i)   Lacks the capacity to litigate.
(ii) Lacks the capacity to decide where she should live and with whom.
(iii) Lacks the capacity to decide with whom she should have contact.
(iv) Lacks the capacity to marry.
(v)   Lacks the capacity to manage her finances.
(vi) Does have the capacity to consent to sexual relations.

Deliberating on the implications of these conclusions, Mr Justice Munby turned to the Mental Capacity Act 2005. Although there is a presumption at law that adults have mental capacity, this can be refuted if adequate evidence is produced to show that the person is not capable of making informed decisions. In this instance MM had been assessed by a consultant psychiatrist who had been formally appointed to examine her mental capacity. Dr Milne's findings were accepted by the High Court. However, as Mr Justice Munby pointed out, citing para. 4.4 of the Code of Practice issued under the Mental Capacity Act 2005, 'An assessment of a person's capacity must be based on their ability to make a specific decision at the time it needs to be made, and not their ability to make decisions in general.' So, although Dr Milne had established that MM did not have mental capacity to make a wide range of decisions, she also needed to offer expert opinion as to the time periods involved. This she did in a report dated 12 March 2007, stating (para. 30):

> MM is 38 years of age. She is no longer in the developmental period and therefore her underlying level of ability will not increase. In time it may decrease. The available information indicates that MM's level of intellectual functioning is very significantly impaired. She would not be capable of living independently without significant assistance. In addition to her learning disability MM also suffers from a psychotic mental illness. This will have two main effects. Firstly during periods of exacerbation of that illness her intellectual functioning and ability to make decisions will be further impaired. Secondly over time patients with severe mental illness can experience an overall deterioration in intellectual functioning outside of periods of acute exacerbation of the illness.

In other words Dr Milne was asserting that not only did MM lack capacity in a number of areas, but due to her age and mental illness she would not gain mental capacity in the future and indeed was likely to experience deterioration in her ability to understand and make informed decisions over time. This expert evidence tended to support the local authority's position that MM was a vulnerable adult who would never be able to make decisions to protect her own health and safety. A situation which the local authority argued required the court to decide on her behalf where she should reside and with whom she should have contact. The new Court of Protection situated within the High Court is empowered by s.16 of the Mental Capacity Act 2005 to make decisions regarding an incapacitated person's welfare. Section 17(1), which is reproduced in the box below, lists the precise powers which the Court of Protection can exercise.

Key legislation

Mental Capacity Act 2005

s.17(1) The powers under section 16 as respects P's personal welfare extend in particular to -

   (a) deciding where P is to live
   (b) deciding what contact, if any, P is to have with any specified persons
   (c) making an order prohibiting a named person from having contact with P
   (d) giving or refusing consent to the carrying out or continuation of a treatment by a person providing health care for P
   (e) giving a direction that a person responsible for P's health care allow a different person to take over that responsibility

s.27(1) Nothing in this Act permits a decision on any of the following matters to be made on behalf of a person -

   (a) consenting to marriage or a civil partnership
   (b) consenting to have sexual relations

The implication of s.17 and s.27 taken together is that while the Court of Protection can decide on behalf of incapacitated adults where they are to live and with whom they may have contact, it cannot give consent on their behalf to a marriage or civil partnership. Entering into a marriage or civil partnership requires the informed and valid consent of the partners under both the Matrimonial Causes Act 1973 and the Civil Partnership Act 2004. Nor can the Court of Protection consent on behalf of vulnerable adults to their having sexual relations as this would contravene the Sexual Offences Act 2003 which prohibits sexual activity with people who lack mental capacity. Since Dr Milne found that MM did have capacity to consent to sexual relations this placed the local authority in a considerable quandary. Not only could MM validly consent to sexual relations, she had a long-established sexual relationship with her male partner KM.

The Mental Capacity Act 2005, s.2(1) stipulates that, 'a person lacks capacity in relation to a matter if at the material time he is unable to make a decision for himself in relation to the matter because of an impairment of, or a disturbance in the functioning of, the mind or brain'. As s.2(3) makes clear 'a lack of capacity cannot be established merely by reference to a condition of, or an aspect of, his behaviour, which might lead others to make unjustified assumptions about his capacity'. In this case MM had a diagnosis of paranoid schizophrenia, but a mental disorder which is a 'condition' does not mean that a person automatically lacks mental capacity. MM also behaved in ways that placed her at risk of violence and exploitation by KM, but this 'behaviour' cannot of itself lead to a presumption that she lacked capacity. To draw such conclusions would be an act of discrimination against people with a mental illness. Social workers acting in compliance with paragraphs 5.5 and 5.6 of the GSCC Code of Practice must neither discriminate themselves against users nor condone discrimination by others.

Practitioners who are Care Coordinators under the Care Programme Approach, or Approved Mental Health Professionals, will be working with mental health users, the majority of whom *have* mental capacity. However, some users may lack mental capacity in respect of specific matters or areas of their lives. Others may usually have mental capacity but lose it during periods of acute episodes of illness associated with their mental disorder. Social workers who are charged to protect the rights of users must be alert to the widespread prejudice that people diagnosed with a mental disorder lack mental capacity. As in the circumstances concerning MM, mental capacity is something which must be professionally assessed. Not only that, but each area in which a person exercises choice must be separately investigated and the medium to long term prospect of their regaining mental capacity explored. The involvement of Dr Milne, a specialist, was the correct approach to establishing what kinds of decisions MM had the mental capacity to make for herself.

 Critical commentary

The assessment of mental capacity

The *Mental Capacity Act 2005: Code of Practice*, page 41, provides only very broad guidance to clinicians assessing capacity and in the following terms:

- Does the person have a general understanding of what decision they need to make and why they need to make it?
- Does the person have a general understanding of the likely consequences of making, or not making, this decision?
- Is the person able to understand, retain, use and weigh up the information relevant to this decision?
- Can the person communicate their decision (by talking, using sign language or any other means)?

This confers upon clinicians considerable discretion as to how they assess a person's capacity. There are standard instruments for measuring mental capacity, which may or may not be used as there is no requirement in the Code of Practice that they be systematically applied. So, different clinicians can employ different modes of assessment. Indeed, it is not necessary that it be a clinician who makes the decision regarding capacity. Para. 4.38 of the Code of Practice states that 'the person who assesses an individual's capacity to make a decision will usually be the person who is directly concerned with the individual at the time the decision needs to be made'. Thus a family member, care worker, doctor, social worker or solicitor could be making an assessment as to capacity. Research conducted by Hotopf (2005: 582) found high agreement between clinicians using the same psychological instruments for measuring capacity. The same study found poor agreement between assessors when they employed different means to assess capacity, e.g. if one uses an interview and another a standardised questionnaire. This has obvious implications if many people are assessing the mental capacity of an individual at different points in time for different purposes.

The broad criteria for assessing capacity laid down in the Code of Practice do not define a threshold of understanding other than 'general understanding'. Nor do the criteria distinguish between more and less serious consequences of decision making. The implication is that the same threshold of understanding should be applied across the full range of decisions. Hence the level of understanding needed to decide on simple daily routines would be the same as that required for consenting to marriage or major surgery. It could be argued that setting different threshold levels depending on the severity of the consequences of poor decision making would enhance the autonomy of people who lack capacity.

Despite the cautionary note at para. 4.7 in the Code of Practice, that judgements as to a person's mental capacity must not be based on 'assumptions about their condition or any aspect of their behaviour' there is a commonplace misconception that mental illness and mental incapacity are synonymous. Those with a mental health problem are particularly at risk of discriminatory and adverse assessments as to their mental capacity. According to Hotopf (2005: 583) the likelihood of a finding of mental incapacity increases if a person with a mental illness refuses medical treatment or is defined as uncooperative by mental health professionals.

In further research Hotopf (2005: 582) in a study of acute general medical patients admitted to hosptial found that 31% lacked mental capacity. Similar studies collated by Hotopf (2005: 582) evidenced mental incapacity ranging from 9% up to 52% among patients admitted for treatment of physical illness. A comparative study of acute psychiatric patients admitted to hospital, also conducted by Hotopf (2005: 582), discovered that of these 44% lacked capacity. The point illustrated by such studies is that those suffering from acute physical and mental illnesses exhibit similar rates of mental incapacity. It is therefore prejudicial to associate mental incapacity with mental illness. Incapacity is in fact more properly associated with acute and chronic states of impaired physical and psychological functioning.

Best interests

Section 1(5) of the Mental Capacity Act 2005 requires that any decision made on behalf of an incapacitated adult is made in his or her *best interests*. The Code of Practice issued in connection with this statute provides further guidance as to how an adult's *best interests* are to be determined. In Dr Milne's expert opinion it was not in MM's *best interests* to live with KM either with or without a support package. Dr Milne concluded in her report dated 12 March 1997 that, 'it is in MM's best interests to remain in accommodation where she has the opportunity to acquire new skills and she is protected from exploitation' (para. 32). During cross-examination of her oral evidence at the High Court hearing Dr Milne conceded that, 'MM gets pleasure from her contact with KM and that they care for each other deeply. If her long-standing sexual relationship with KM were to be stopped, it would be very, very distressing for MM' (para. 35). In view of both the strength of MM's bond with KM and at the same time the hazard he posed to her health and safety, Dr Milne recommended that there be 'maintenance contact only to be supervised at all times'. Mr Fowler, a social work consultant who also presented expert evidence to the court in his report dated 14 November 2006 largely concurred with Dr Milne, stating (paras 36–38):

> It is my view that MM should not move to reside either temporarily or permanently with KM. MM has not accessed appropriately medical or social work support systems when she has been living with KM and I do not believe that they would accept any form of support package designed to support and monitor them living together in the community. I cannot imagine any package of support which could appropriately safeguard and promote MM's welfare if she was living in the community with KM. There is in my view significant

historical evidence to demonstrate the power which KM exercises over MM and the extent to which she is influenced by his behaviour and comments. That influence does not serve her best interests . . . I believe that overtly or covertly he will attempt to undermine MM's placement within local authority arranged accommodation because his primary goal is to be reunited with MM . . . If direct contact is supervised the possibility of KM compromising MM's placement is greatly diminished. At the moment MM enjoys seeing KM and I would be reluctant to prevent that from happening . . . MM responded positively to KM's tactile behaviour and positive comments. There was evidence of a significant emotional connection to him. There must be times when she feels cared for and cared about by him in ways she has never previously experienced. It is likely that she has seen the abusive aspect of their relationship as a price worth paying for these positive emotional feelings.

In his second report, dated, 22 January 2007, which was presented in evidence to the High Court, Mr Fowler dissented from the opinion of Dr Milne. Instead he recommended more substantial ongoing contact between MM and KM and set out the arrangements (para. 41), which in his opinion would meet MM's best interests:

- The continued prevention of telephone contact with the attached penal notice, is likely to be breached and has probably already been so. I feel telephone contact should be allowed to take place on a regular basis, but should perhaps be time limited.
- Restricting actual contact to once a week for a two hour supervised period as a medium and long term strategy prevents any normality being possible within their relationship. It is likely to create ongoing resentment.
- It is my opinion that 'managed' periods of unsupervised contact are the most appropriate way forward. For example, a period of unsupervised contact of between 2 and 4 hours could be permitted each week.

Given this evidence, the local authority accepted in court that 'there should be direct, unsupervised, contact between MM and KM once per week for up to four hours, and such further contact as might be agreed between the allocated social worker, MM and KM' (para. 23). This, the local authority claimed would be in MM's *best interests* as it protected her from exploitation by KM and ensured she was accommodated in a protective environment. The Official Solicitor who was legally representing MM's *best interests* (see pp. 318–19) took a rather different view from the local authority as to what they actually were. He made a separate statement before the Court of Protection which (para. 52) contended:

It is my submission, if the court finds it is in MM's best interests that her contact with KM should be regulated, that the court should adopt a cautious approach. In conducting the balance sheet exercise, weight must be given not only to MM's need for care and protection but also to the fact that her relationship with KM has endured for a significant period of time, that it is a relationship which is important to her, and that the relationship has included a number of lengthy periods of cohabitation . . . I question whether the court should so restrict and regulate the terms of a relationship, in circumstances where MM has capacity to consent to a sexual relationship with KM, to the extent that such regulation may result in the breakdown of that relationship or impose a change in the nature of the relationship.

This was a submission to the court which emphasised MM's right to exercise choice over her contact with others and autonomy in respect of her sexual relations. It contrasted with the local authority's heavy focus on the need to protect MM from the adverse consequences of her relationship with KM. Indeed, the local authority linked the protection of MM to her *best interests*. Mr Justice Munby observed that MM in oral evidence before the High Court had clearly articulated her desire to live with KM and her strong affectionate bond with him. In acknowledging this, Justice Munby turned to the *Mental*

Capacity Act 2005: Code of Practice which at page 65 requires those making *best interests* decisions to 'try and find out the views of the person who lacks capacity', including:

- The person's past and present wishes and feelings – these may have been expressed verbally, in writing or through behaviour or habits.
- Any beliefs and values (e.g. religious, cultural, moral or political) that would be likely to influence the decision in question.
- Any other factors the person themselves would be likely to consider if they were making the decision or acting for themselves.

By citing the Mental Capacity Act 2005 and its associated Code of Practice, Justice Munby was drawing attention to the fact that *best interests* decisions, even for incapacitated adults, cannot be made in ways which are completely divorced from their views and feelings about a proposed course of action. There was ample evidence before the court from expert witnesses as well as the vulnerable adult concerned, that a curtailment of MM's relationship with KM would cause her substantial mental distress and unhappiness.

The local authority and the social workers involved in the care of MM were caught on the horns of a dilemma. On the one hand Department of Health (2000a) *No Secrets* Policy Guidance required the local authority to intervene to protect MM who was a vulnerable adult and furthermore lacked mental capacity regarding most aspects of her life. She was almost certainly not in a position to protect herself from exploitation or abuse by KM. Paragraph 3.2 of the GSCC Code of Practice demands that social workers use 'established processes and procedures to challenge and report dangerous, abusive, discriminatory or exploitive behaviour'. On the other hand paragraph 3.1 of the same Code urges practitioners to promote the independence of service users. Similarly, at page 66 the *Mental Capacity Act 2005: Code of Practice,* professionals are directed when working with mentally incapacitated adults to 'avoid restricting the person's rights' and to 'see if there are other options that may be less restrictive of the person's rights'.

In this instance the local authority and the social workers it employed had at one and the same time to protect MM from abuse while acting to maximise her self-determination. This necessitated an incredibly precarious balancing act which pitted the high risk to MM's mental health and physical safety against her deep desire to continue her relationship with KM; a relationship which both the social and healthcare professionals who came into contact with MM acknowledged also made a positive and essential contribution to her well-being and quality of life. MM's circumstances are far from unique. Many adults who lack mental capacity are in danger of exploitation and abuse by family members. Yet those same individuals may offer these vulnerable, often stigmatised, adults some much-needed affection and assistance. Relationships are rarely all good or all bad in terms of their effect upon a vulnerable adult. It is this which makes it so difficult to discern what is really in a mentally incapacitated person's *best interests*, rather than in the interests of professionals. Professionals are subject to pressure from public opinion and in turn from their agency to act in ways which minimise risk of harm, but which simultaneously impose restrictions upon those they seek to protect from harm. In the midst of these kinds of pressures it can be difficult to bear in mind that positive risk taking is both an element of the Care Programme Approach and an imperative set out in the GSCC Code of Practice.

Right to private and family life

The local authority in formulating the *best interests* of MM (or indeed any other vulnerable adult) was obliged to comply with the European Convention on Human Rights. As the Official Solicitor reminded the High Court in his statement, there is 'the need to have regard to questions of proportionality in terms of balancing MM's Article 8 rights and her *best interests* as regards contact with KM' (para. 53). Article 8 of the European Convention on Human Rights states that, 'everyone has the right to respect for his private and family life, his home and his correspondence'. This is a qualified right which in fact permits the State to lawfully interfere with this right in circumstances where it is necessary 'for the protection of health'. This can include interfering in the sexual lives of mentally incapacitated adults to protect them from exploitation and abuse. All parties to the court case, with the exception of MM and KM themselves, accepted that there was lawful justification for interfering in MM's rights to decide with whom to live. Even in circumstances where the State may lawfully interfere with a Convention Right, such interference must be proportionate, meaning that it must be the minimum necessary to secure a lawful end; in this instance the protection of MM's health. The question before the High Court became whether the restrictions on MM's contact with KM were a proportionate response to protect her health.

Mr Justice Munby turned to persuasive precedent decided by the European Court of Human Rights in *Pretty* v. *United Kingdom* [2003] 35 EHRR 1 para. 61 for guidance as to what constitutes private and family life for the purposes of article 8 of the European Convention:

It covers the physical and psychological integrity of a person. It can sometimes embrace aspects of an individual's physical and social identity. Elements such as, for example, gender identification, name and sexual orientation and sexual life fall within the personal sphere protected by Article 8. Article 8 also protects a right to personal development, and the right to establish and develop relationships with other human beings and the outside world. Though no previous case has established as such any right to self-determination as being contained in Article 8 of the Convention, the court considers that the notion of personal autonomy is an important principle underlying the interpretation of its guarantees.

Mr Justice Munby interpreted this to mean that article 8 protects 'both the private life lived privately and kept hidden from the outside world and also the private life lived in company with other human beings or shared with the outside world' (para. 106). The form of supervised and regulated contact which the local authority sought to impose on MM violated both these private spheres. Mr Justice Munby was also acutely aware that KM, as MM's partner of over 10 years, was her family. In view of this he reasoned (paras 116 and 118):

that the longer a vulnerable adult's partner, family or carer have looked after her without the State having perceived the need for its intervention, the more carefully must any proposals for intervention be scrutinised and the more cautious the court should be before accepting too readily the assertion that the State can do better than the partner, family or carer . . . the court must be careful to ensure that in rescuing a vulnerable adult from one type of abuse it does not expose her to the risk of treatment at the hands of the State which, however well intentioned, can itself end up being abusive of her dignity, her happiness and indeed of her human rights.

Since MM had mental capacity to have sexual relations the restrictions which the local authority sought to impose on her had the effect of prohibiting her from engaging in sexual contact with KM. He was banned from the supported local authority accommodation in which she lived because of his abusive conduct towards staff, and his contact with KM had been severely curtailed by the interim declarations issued by the High Court in June 2006. At one point it had been reduced to just one supervised face-to-face meeting a month in conjunction with a prohibition on all telephone contact. On the one hand the local authority argued that it was protecting MM from exploitation and other detrimental consequences of her association with KM. On the other hand the local authority was preventing MM from exercising self determination over her sexual relations, which it acknowledged she had the mental capacity to decide for herself. In effect the paternalism of social workers and their understandable desire to protect MM was denying her sexual freedom. As Justice Munby was to conclude, Social Services was violating MM's article 8 rights. Commenting on this state of affairs, he observed (para. 120):

> . . . we must avoid the temptation always to put the physical health and safety of the elderly and the vulnerable before everything else. Often it will be appropriate to do so, but not always. Physical health and safety can sometimes be bought at too high a price in happiness and emotional welfare. The emphasis must be on sensible risk appraisal, not striving to avoid all risk, whatever the price, but instead seeking a proper balance and being willing to tolerate manageable or acceptable risks as the price appropriately to be paid in order to achieve some other good – in particular to achieve the vital good of the elderly or vulnerable person's happiness. What good is it making someone safer if it merely makes them miserable?

The key to resolving the dilemma for the local authority, caught as it was between protecting MM and supporting her autonomy, was to resort to the European Convention on Human Rights. The local authority had attempted to come down on one side of the dilemma. It sought to protect MM by severely restricting her contact with KM to the point where social workers were complicit in actively destroying their relationship. Article 8, which safeguards the right to a family life of every citizen regardless of mental capacity, permits interference with that right to protect health. Interference by the State, in this case by the Social Services Department of a local authority, must be proportionate to achieving the legitimate purpose of protecting health. However, as the judge pointed out, the interference in MM's sex life was so excessive and draconian as to virtually constitute an abuse of itself. It threatened to undermine her mental health and to exclude her from the companionship and physical comfort of her long-term partner. Social work intervention has to be viewed as a two-edged sword. On the one hand it can serve to protect individuals from abuse, but on the other in so doing can expose them to other more covert forms of abuse. In these situations it is simply not enough for practitioners to claim that the infliction of distress and unhappiness is somehow in the *best interests* of the vulnerable adult who suffers it.

Judgement in *Local Authority X v. MM (by her litigation friend, the Official Solicitor)*

Mr Justice Munby accepted, given the evidence put before him, that MM as an incapacitated and vulnerable adult needed to be protected from exploitation and abuse by KM. However, interference in their relationship should be the minimum necessary to achieve the lawful objective of protecting MM's health. Delivering his ruling, Mr Justice Munby concluded (para. 154) that the local authority had:

> placed too much weight and emphasis on the need to protect MM from various risks and far too little weight on the emotional and other benefits that MM derives from the relationship [with KM]. It failed to strike the balance proportionately, fairly and . . . even humanely between the proper need to minimise the risks to MM's physical and mental health and safety and the equally pressing need to further her emotional welfare – her happiness.

According to Justice Munby, what was being proposed by Social Services constituted 'a wholly disproportionate interference by the local authority both with the family life which exists as between MM and KM' (para. 142). On the basis of this judgement Social Services was required to go back and draw up a new care plan for MM which would both enable her to live in local authority supported accommodation while being able to continue her sexual relationship with KM. Mr Justice Munby acknowledged that this requirement may necessitate the local authority paying for MM and KM to have private time together in a hotel if they could not do so at MM's residential placement.

 ## Critical questions

1 The enactment of the Mental Capacity Act 2005 introduced important safeguards for vulnerable adults, making decisions around mental capacity issue and time specific. As this case demonstrates, this new concept of capacity can also result in distressing contradictions. MM was assessed as having mental capacity to conduct sexual relationships and yet not the capacity to decide who to associate with, who to live with or even to marry. Thus in the eyes of the law, society and the church her sexual relationship could never be legitimated. Do you think this case was correctly decided, and if not, why not? What alternative interventions, if any, do you think could have been pursued by professionals in this situation?

2 The Mental Capacity Act 2005 fails to define *best interests*, leaving carers and professionals to decide this for themselves in any given situation. What is your understanding of the concept of a person's *best interests*? If a social worker was required to decide on a vulnerable adult's *best interests* how might the agency context in which he or she worked influence their professional judgement?

3 How would you reconcile the right of a person who lacks mental capacity to a private and family life with their *best interests*? How do you think these two concepts relate to each other? What might be some of the practice situations in which these two imperatives would appear to be in conflict with each other? What strategies might you employ or actions would you take to resolve conflicts between best interest decisions and the set of rights granted under the European Convention on Human Rights?

CASE 4
R (on application of A) v. *East Sussex County Council (No. 2)* [2003] EWHC 167

Importance of the case

This explores the tension between the rights of social care workers to the protection of their health, and the needs and preferences of users. It also examines inhuman and degrading treatment in relation to social care provision. Finally, consideration is given to the implications of carers expressing the preferences of users on their behalf.

History of the case

This was a judicial review brought before the High Court by the Official Solicitor acting as a litigation friend for A and B, two sisters who had multiple disabilities. The judicial review concerned the assistance being provided by the local authority to enable the sisters to mobilise in their own home.

Facts of the case

A was born in 1976 and B in 1980 and were in their twenties at the time of the High Court case. Both sisters had severe physical disabilities and each required the assistance of a carer to mobilise. They also had profound learning difficulties and neither had mental capacity. The sisters lived together with their mother X and stepfather Y who were their full-time carers. Social Services became involved with the family during the 1990s and since then there had been dispute between the parents and the local authority as to how A and B should be assisted to mobilise. At the time, East Sussex County Council had in place under its *Safety Code of Practice: Manual Handling* for care workers a policy of no manual lifting. Both parents maintained that their daughters required manual lifting, while the local authority insisted that lifting equipment operated by personal care assistants was necessary. In July 2000 Mr Wall, an independent social worker employed by Personal Care Consultants Ltd., conducted assessments of needs for both sisters, and prepared a care plan. As part of this process several occupational therapists also employed by the same agency carried out manual handling risk assessments. Meanwhile East Sussex County Council also engaged professionals to produce specialist assessments culminating in the production of a community care assessment dated 28 September 2001. The care plan linked to this assessment stated that all lifting was to be undertaken with a hoist and not manually. As a result, judicial review proceedings were commenced on behalf of A and B on the grounds that continuous use of the hoist constituted inhuman and degrading treatment under article 3 of the European Convention on Human Rights. Acting as a litigation friend for A and B the Official Solicitor sought an order to quash the community care assessments dated 28 September 2001 together with the care plans based on them.

Key people in the case

A – claimant woman aged 26 years at time of High Court case
B – claimant woman aged 22 years at time of High Court case
X – claimant mother of A and B
Y – claimant stepfather of A and B
Mr Hunt – legal counsel for the parents
Mr Justice Munby – judge presiding in High Court case

Discussion of the case

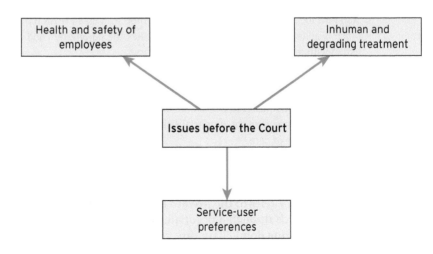

Health and safety of employees

This was a judicial review which concerned the provision of personal care to two young adults in their own home. Both the needs assessment and care delivery were required to comply with the National Minimum Standards for domiciliary care. These are detailed in Department of Health (2003c) *Domiciliary Care: National Minimum Standards* and have to be met for a domiciliary service provider to continue to be registered and permitted to operate by the Commission for Social Care Inspection. There are 27 standards in all, which cover matters ranging from the quality of personal care and the protection of vulnerable adults to the organisation and management of the domiciliary service itself. The box below sets out the standards most directly relevant to the facts-at-issue in the High Court hearing.

 Key guidance

Domiciliary Care: National Minimum Standards

Standard 3: The registered person is able to demonstrate the capacity of the agency to meet the needs (including specialist needs) of individuals accepted by the agency.

Standard 4: Each service user is issued with a written contract (if self-funding) provided by the agency within seven days of commencement of the service.

Standard 5: Care and support staff respect information given by service users or their representatives in confidence and handle information about service users in accordance with the Data Protection Act 1998.

Standard 6: Staff are reliable and dependable, are able to respond flexibly to the needs and preferences of service users.

Standard 7: A personal service user plan outlining the delivery arrangements for the care is developed and agreed with each service user, which provides the basis for the care to be delivered and is generated from the care needs assessment.

Standard 8: Personal care and support is provided in a way which maintains and respects the privacy, dignity and lifestyle of the person receiving care at all times.

Standard 9: Managers and care and support workers enable service users to make decisions in relation to their own lives, providing information, assistance and support where needed.

Standard 10: The registered person ensures there is a clear, written policy and procedure which is adhered to by staff and which identifies the parameters and circumstances for assisting with medication and health related tasks.

Standard 11: The registered person ensures that the agency has systems and procedures in place to comply with the requirements of the Health and Safety legislation.

Standard 12: The registered person ensures that an assessment is undertaken by a trained and qualified person, of the potential risks to service users and staff associated with delivering the package of care.

Standards 6 and 7 refer to the need to meet service user preferences and to respond flexibly to their needs through a negotiated care plan. Standard 8 complements these stipulations by requiring domiciliary care to be provided in a way which is consistent with a user's dignity and lifestyle choices. At the same time Standards 11 and 12 oblige providers of domiciliary services to ensure that the way in which social care is delivered complies with health and safety legislation; that is to say, that care is provided in a manner which protects the health of care workers as well as ensuring safety for users. As Standard 12 indicates, how care is actually provided on a day-to-day basis is to be determined by conducting a risk assessment in relation to both the user and the care worker. In addition, Standard 12 requires employers of social care workers going into people's homes and other community settings to ensure that they are properly trained for the care tasks they are undertaking.

East Sussex County Council in an effort to comply with legislation on health and safety appeared to instruct social workers, acting as care managers, not to write care plans which included manual lifting by care workers. This policy was contained in the *Safety Code of Practice: Manual Handling* issued by the local authority and it appeared to prohibit any manual lifting by care workers. Such a blanket policy conflicts with Standards 6–8 which clearly envisage negotiation and agreement in the delivery of packages of care. Although in the run-up to the High Court hearing the local authority modified its position in prohibiting all manual lifting of users, it still maintained that the two physically disabled sisters A and B should always be lifted by a hoist.

Mr Justice Munby presiding at the High Court was confronted by a mass of reports and witness statements from occupational therapists, physiotherapists, psychiatrists and specialists in lifting techniques who had been commissioned by the various parties to the court case. With each report either a claimant or the defendant sought to justify their position before the court. Rather than examine these reports in detail the judge turned to setting out the legal principles which must guide a local authority in determining how its employees or those contracted from private or voluntary sector agencies are to provide personal assistance to disabled service-users. The health and safety of workers is covered by a vast number of different statutes. In this instance the most important statute is the Health and Safety at Work etc. Act 1974 which under s.2(1) makes it 'the duty of every employer to ensure, so far as is reasonably practicable, the health, safety and welfare at work of all his employees'. This duty is equally applicable to social workers as employees as it is to personal care assistants.

The Health and Safety at Work etc Act 1974 is a parent act which has given rise to two pieces of secondary legislation relevant to the High Court case. The first is the Management of Health and Safety at Work Regulations 1999 (SI1999/3242), which obliges employers to assess what the risks are to the health and safety of employees during the course of their work. On completing this assessment the employer must then take such measures as are necessary to comply with statutory requirements to protect the health and safety of employees e.g. providing proper training to operate a piece of equipment. Additionally, employers must assess the risks to the health and safety of people who are not employees, but who are affected by the operations of the employer. In the context of a local authority employer, such as East Sussex County Council, it must not just be concerned with care workers which it directly employs, but also those it contracts from the private or voluntary sectors. This duty also extends to service-users who are directly affected by how personal care assistants carry out their tasks. The text box on the next page sets out the provisions of Manual Handling Operations Regulations 1992 (SI1992/2793), which is the second statutory instrument relevant to this case.

The *Safety Code of Practice: Manual Handling* was produced in the context of these statutory provisions and was plainly designed to protect the health and safety of care workers

Key legislation

Manual Handling Operations Regulations 1992 (SI1992/2793)

Reg.2(1) defines 'manual handling operations' as meaning 'any transporting or supporting of a load (including the lifting, putting down, pushing, pulling, carrying or moving thereof) by hand or by bodily force'.

Reg.4(1) each employer shall –

(a) so far as is practicable, avoid the need for his employees to undertake any manual handling operations at work which involve a risk of their being injured; or

(b) where it is not reasonably practicable to avoid the need for his employees to undertake any manual handling operations at work which involve a risk of their being injured –

   (i) make a suitable and sufficient assessment of all such manual handling operations to be undertaken by them

   (ii) take appropriate steps to reduce the risk of injury to those employees arising out of their undertaking any such manual handling operations to the lowest level reasonably applicable

regardless of whether they were employed directly by the Council or contracted from another agency. In compliance with reg.4(1)(a) of the Manual Handling Operations Regulations 1992 the *Safety Code of Practice* was also intended to reduce the necessity for care workers to manually handle service-users, by standardising the use of a hoist. The local authority was caught between its statutory obligations as an employer to protect the health and safety of its workers or contracted workers and the preference of A and B for manual lifting, which appeared to put staff at risk of injury. It is significant that as the two sisters were mentally incapacitated their preferences were actually being articulated through their parents (and carers) and legally represented by the Official Solicitor. The claimants were to argue that the issue over manual lifting concerned more than service-user or carer preferences. The central contention of both claimants was that the excessive use of equipment to lift A and B was inhuman and degrading. This assertion moved the argument beyond an issue over health and safety on the one hand and user preferences on the other to the arena of human rights.

Statute law makes it an employer's responsibility to ensure there is compliance with health and safety regulations in the day-to-day work of employees and those it contracts as workers. On the other hand, the Care Standards Act 2000 in the form of Department of Health (2003c) *Domiciliary Care: National Minimum Standards* clearly envisages that user preferences, lifestyle choices and dignity will be accommodated through negotiated packages of care and agreement as to how they are delivered. Department of Health (1990: para. 3. 25) *Community Care in the Next Decade and Beyond* requires care managers to develop the 'most cost effective package of services that meets the user's care needs taking account of the user's and carer's own preferences'. In this instance cost was not an issue, as manual lifting was deemed as cost effective as using a hoist. The care package therefore turned on the tension between maintaining the safety of care workers and the preferences of users. As this case demonstrates, social workers when acting as care managers, can be caught in the middle when user preferences and worker safety appear to conflict with one another. Of course the issue of manual lifting and the risk of injury it presents is just one example of how workers can be put in danger by the tasks they are required to carry out. Where users (or indeed their carers) engage in challenging or violent behaviour many of the same principles and issues raised in this case will be equally applicable.

Inhuman and degrading treatment

Article 3 of the European Convention on Human Rights stipulates that 'no one shall be subjected to torture or to inhuman or degrading treatment or punishment'. This is an absolute right which means that it cannot be lawfully violated in any circumstances. In order to spell out what qualifies as ill-treatment for the purposes of article 3, Mr Justice Munby presiding over the High Court case cited precedent in *A* v. *United Kingdom* [1998] 27 EHRR 611 at 629 para. 20 which states that:

> ill-treatment must attain a minimum level of severity if it is to fall within the scope of Article 3. The assessment of this minimum is relative: it depends on all the circumstances of the case, such as the nature and context of the treatment, its duration, its physical and mental effects and, in some instances, the sex, age and state of health of the victim.

Justice Munby added that 'thoughtlessness, uncaring and uncharitable actions can be quite as damaging and distressing to the victim as the vicious, wilful or malicious' (para. 89). In other words an act does not have to be deliberately intended to humiliate or degrade the victim in order to come within the scope of article 3.

Justice Munby also referred to a case which came before the European Court of Human Rights in Strasbourg and concerned the week-long imprisonment of a disabled woman for contempt of court connected to civil proceedings. The woman had no limbs as the result of thalidomide and used an electric wheelchair to mobilise. She also suffered from a number of related health problems. The prison authorities prohibited her from taking the battery charger for her wheelchair into her cell, which had the effect of immobilising her. No concession was made to her disability, which meant that she could not properly use the bed or toilet which were designed for able-bodied prisoners. The result was that within days of her incarceration she suffered from the cold and had to be attended by a doctor. Quoting directly from the ruling in *Price* v. *United Kingdom* (2002) 34 EHRR 53 at 1294 para. 30, Mr Justice Munby recited that:

> There is no evidence in this case of any positive intention to humiliate or debase the applicant. However, the Court considers that to detain a severely disabled person in conditions where she is dangerously cold, risks developing sores because her bed is too hard or unreachable, and is unable to go to the toilet or keep clean without the greatest of difficulty, constitutes degrading treatment contrary to Article 3.

The reason why Justice Munby chose to bring this precedent to the attention of the parties to the High Court case was that A and B as severely physically disabled individuals who also lacked mental capacity required measures to compensate for their disabilities. He observed that 'this brings out the enhanced degree of protection which may be called for when the human dignity at stake is that of someone who is, as A and B are in the present case, so disabled as to be critically dependent on the help of others for even the simplest and most basic tasks of day-to-day living' (para. 93). However, Justice Munby also qualified his comments by reminding the parties to the High Court case (paras 121–2) that:

> insistence on the use of dignified means cannot be allowed to obstruct more important ends. On occasions our very humanity and dignity may itself demand that we be subjected

to a certain amount – sometimes a very great deal – of indignity. Dignified ends may sometimes demand the use of undignified means. The immediate dignity of a person trapped in a blazing building is probably the very last thing on his mind or in the mind of the fireman who bundles him undignified out of the widow to save his life . . .The other point is this. One must guard against jumping too readily to the conclusion that manual handling is necessarily more dignified than the use of equipment. A disabled person or invalid may prefer manual handling by a relative or friend to the use of a hoist but at the same time prefer a hoist to manual handling by a stranger or a paid carer. The independently minded but physically disabled person might prefer to hoist himself up from his bath or chair rather than to be assisted even by his devoted wife.

In the above excerpt from his judgement, Mr Justice Munby highlights that dignity is a subjective experience and not an objective fact. The acts an individual considers humiliating will to a degree depend on the ends they are designed to achieve. Moreover, how people with disabilities experience their treatment will also depend on the extent to which they are enabled to exercise choice over their intimate personal care. In the case of A and B, the sisters were being frequently lifted in order to enable them to carry out basic activities of daily living. There was no intention to subject them to degrading treatment. A mere lack of malicious intent to humiliate is not of itself sufficient to protect vulnerable adults. Mr Justice Munby emphasised that a balancing exercise was required in circumstances where the rights of different individuals potentially conflicted.

In this instance the statutory obligations of the local authority as an employer to protect care workers from injury caused by manual lifting was in tension with the right of A and B not to be subjected to inhuman or degrading treatment. As Justice Munby observed, not all lifts required to mobilise A and B constituted a risk to the health and safety of care workers. Where particular manual lifts did present a hazard the local authority as the employer needed to carry out a risk assessment. Once this was completed the local authority needed to formulate protocols to ensure that any manual lifts were carried out so as to minimise the risk of injury to the care workers and reduce indignity to the disabled person. However, at paragraph 154 of his judgement Justice Munby did identify circumstances in which care workers would be expected to take additional risks to their health and safety. These comprised a specific set of situations where failure of a care worker to act was likely to constitute a breach of article 3. Where a disabled person required manual lifting and refusing to lift them would:

(a) Allow them to remain sitting in the bath for any really appreciable time without lifting them out.
(b) Leave them sitting on the lavatory for a long time.
(c) Leave them in a chair or elsewhere with the risk that bedsores will develop.
(d) Fail to pick them up if they fall and remain lying.
(e) Leave them sitting in bodily waste for any appreciable time.

According to Justice Munby all of these situations constitute inhuman and degrading treatment. It is the responsibility of local authorities to assess risk, and to reduce it through the provision of training and equipment. Where risk of injury is an inherent aspect of care work, it is the responsibility of local authority employers to develop lifting protocols which reduce the risks of injury and discomfort to the care worker and the disabled person to the greatest possible extent. As Justice Munby concluded, 'this is not a situation in which the disabled person's rights trump those of the carer, though equally, I should emphasise, the carer's rights do not trump those of the disabled person' (para. 129). Although this case focussed on lifting, Mr Justice Munby elaborates a number of principles which plainly have wider applicability:

- To treat a disabled person in the same way as an able-bodied person may in certain circumstances amount to inhuman and degrading treatment.
- The rights of care workers to a safe working environment have to be balanced against the rights of users to be treated in ways which respect their dignity and preferences.
- The balancing of the rights of workers and users has to be conducted on a case-by-case basis and not implemented through a blanket policy.
- What constitutes dignity for a user is a subjective matter which has to be inquired into and not assumed.
- Users may have to choose whether to sacrifice a degree of dignity in the pursuit of other objectives which they value.

As care managers, social workers are likely to be in the forefront of incorporating these principles into care planning. They require professionals to find out what risks to the health and safety of care workers might be raised by a particular package of care. If health and safety issues are implicated, they will need to make arrangements for an appropriate assessment of risk to be undertaken. At the same time practitioners should discuss users' preferences, particularly around personal care, and discuss how these can be carried out in ways consistent with a user's perceptions of his or her dignity. Where there are conflicts between user needs or preferences and the health or safety of care workers, practitioners may need to negotiate these with the user. However, the case of A and B presents care managers with additional challenges in negotiating a care package. Like many vulnerable adults with whom social workers in Adult Social Services come into contact, neither of the sisters had mental capacity. The practical effect of this was that their carers, in this case their parents, articulated the views of the sisters on their behalf. This meant that social workers found themselves actually negotiating with the carers as opposed to the users. This raises some additional considerations for practitioners working with mentally incapacitated adults and their carers.

Service-user preferences

The High Court case was further complicated by the lack of capacity of A and B. This meant that in terms of the balancing exercise the service users were unable to verbally express their preferences in terms of how they wanted to be lifted. In these situations, as Justice Munby observed citing precedent in *Re S* [2003] 1 FLR 292 at 306 para. 49:

> the devoted parent who . . . has spent years caring for a disabled child is likely to be much better able than any social worker, however skilled, or any judge, however compassionate, to 'read' his child, to understand his personality and to interpret the wishes and feelings which he lacks the ability to express.

People unable to verbally express themselves can still communicate non-verbally, as an expression of distress or discomfort does not require language. For this reason Justice Munby cautioned that relatives cannot have the last word as to how an incapacitated service-user wishes to be treated. This responsibility ultimately rests with the care worker involved. It is Justice Munby's considered opinion (para. 134) that:

> in the final analysis the tasks of deciding whether, in truth, there is a refusal or fear of other negative reaction to being lifted must . . . fall on the carer, for the duty to act within the framework given by the employer falls upon the employee. Were the patient not incapacitated, there could be no suggestion that the relative's views are other than a factor to be

considered. Because of the lack of capacity and the extraordinary circumstances in a case such as this, the views of the relatives are of very great importance, but they are not determinative.

In this instance, social workers did not challenge the needs and preferences expressed by X and Y on behalf of their daughters, who lacked the mental capacity to articulate these for themselves. But is it not difficult to envisage situations in which parents or carers claim to speak on behalf of users and make assertions about their *best interests* which are detrimental to the welfare of the users concerned. The Mental Capacity Act 2005 permits family members, care workers and professionals to make decisions on behalf of adults who lack mental capacity regarding day-to-day routines and more far reaching matters such as their finances and place of residence. In doing so, the Mental Capacity Act 2005 also protects such persons from liability if their actions are carried out in compliance with the stipulations of s.5, which is reproduced in the box below.

Key legislation

Mental Capacity Act 2005

s.5(1) If a person ('D') does an act in connection with the care or treatment of another person ('P'), the act is one to which this section applies if -
  (a) before doing the act, D takes reasonable steps to establish whether P lacks capacity in relation to the matter in question, and
  (b) when doing the act, D reasonably believes -
      (i) that P lacks capacity in relation to the matter, and
      (ii) that it will be in P's best interests for the act to be done.

s.5(2) D does not incur any liability in relation to the act that he would not have incurred if P -
  (a) had had capacity to consent in relation to the matter, and
  (b) had consented to D's doing the act.

s.5(3) Nothing in this section excludes a person's civil liability for loss or damage, or his criminal liability, resulting from his negligence in doing the act.

The effect of this provision is that broadly speaking as long as a carer or practitioner carries out an act in the belief that the person on whose behalf they are acting lacks mental capacity and that they are acting in his or her *best interests* they will not be liable to being sued for carrying out that act. So, for example, it would be an act of trespass for a social worker to enter a house without the permission of the owner or tenant. It could be a form of physical assault if a care worker undressed or toileted an individual without his or her consent. A person who lacks mental capacity cannot give consent for people to enter his or her dwelling or provide personal care. For this reason s.5 of the Mental Capacity Act 2005 permits these sorts of acts to be undertaken as if the person without mental capacity had in fact consented to them.

However, as s.5(3) makes clear, this does not mean that for instance a social worker who left the door wide open of a user's home which was subsequently burgled would be immune from prosecution. On the contrary, carrying out acts on behalf of an adult who lacks mental capacity in a negligent manner or in ways which injure that person will constitute criminal or civil offences. Inevitably these will result in either prosecution in a criminal court or an action being brought in a civil court for damages. Aside from harm caused maliciously or through negligence, the Mental Capacity Act 2005 does provide considerable protection from liability for those acting in the *best interests* of adults who lack mental capacity. The statute balances the immunity by empowering the Court of Protection to take action when someone acting on behalf of a mentally incapacitated adult is not acting in their *best interests* or where there is a dispute over their *best interests*. These powers enable the Court of Protection to step in to protect an incapacitated adult and are described in the *Mental Capacity Act 2005: Code of Practice*, which is excerpted in the box below.

Key guidance

Mental Capacity Act 2005: Code of Practice

Para. 8.30 The Court of Protection can determine the validity of an LPA [Lasting Power of Attorney] or EPA [Enduring Power of Attorney] and can give directions as to how an attorney should use their powers under an LPA. In particular, the court can cancel an LPA and end the attorney's appointment. The court might do this if the attorney was not carrying out their duties properly or acting in the best interests of the donor. The court must then decide whether it is necessary to appoint a deputy or take over the attorney's role.

Para. 8.31 Sometimes it is not practical or appropriate for the court to make a single declaration or decision. In such cases, if the court thinks that somebody needs to make future or ongoing decisions for someone whose condition makes it likely they will lack capacity to make some further decisions in the future, it can appoint a deputy to act for and make decisions for that person. A deputy's authority should be as limited in scope and duration as possible.

Para. 8.32 It is for the court to decide who to appoint as a deputy. Different skills may be required depending on whether the deputy's decisions will be about a person's welfare (including healthcare), their finances or both. The court will decide whether the proposed deputy is reliable and trustworthy and has an appropriate level of skill and competence to carry out the necessary tasks.

Para. 8.33 In the majority of cases, the deputy is likely to be a family member or someone who knows the person well. But in some cases the court may decide to appoint a deputy who is independent of the family (for example, where the person's affairs or care needs are particularly complicated). This could be for example, the Director of Adult Services in the relevant local authority . . .

The above excerpt from the Code of Practice refers to Enduring and Lasting Powers of Attorney. These are people appointed by the vulnerable adult, at a point in time when they still had mental capacity, to take over the running of their affairs. For instance, a solicitor or accountant could be given Enduring Powers of Attorney by a person diagnosed with Alzheimer's disease while they still retained capacity, to administer their financial affairs once they became mentally incapacitated. Lasting Powers of Attorney created under s.9 of the Mental Capacity Act 2005 enable the attorney, often referred to as a donee, to make decisions relating not only to the finances of the incapacitated adult, but also in respect of their welfare, medical treatment and residence. Precisely because these are such broad powers, as paragraph 8.30 indicates, the Court of Protection can remove the attorney and either make decisions itself on behalf of the incapacitated adult or appoint a deputy to do so. Of course in the case concerning A and B, they had severe learning difficulties from birth and therefore had never been in a position to legally vest Lasting Powers of Attorney in their parents.

As the excerpted paragraphs from the Code of Practice set out above indicate, the Court of Protection is not only concerned with monitoring Lasting Powers of Attorney, it also has the power to step in to make a single declaration or direction regarding the care of a person who lacks mental capacity. So, for example, in a situation where local authority social workers were of the opinion that a carer's decision to move an adult without mental capacity to a different town was not in their best interests they could apply to the Court of Protection for a one-off declaration specifying where that incapacitated adult should live. Likewise were there to be a dispute between family members over the care of a mentally incapacitated adult in relation to their medical treatment, place of residence or finances, the Court of Protection could step in to make a declaration. Occasionally the local authority itself, in the person of the Director of Adult Social Services, may be appointed as a deputy to make ongoing decisions about the care of an adult who lacks mental capacity.

The events surrounding the care of A and B took place before the Mental Capacity Act 2005 was enacted and in any case do not directly invoke the matters dealt with by the Court of Protection. It was accepted by all parties to this High Court case that X and Y were acting in the *best interests* of their daughters and articulating their views in so far as they could be known. The juxtaposing of the Mental Capacity Act 2005 with the events surrounding A and B is intended to demonstrate the potential for disputes to arise between social workers, carers, users and members of the wider family network as to what constitutes the user's *best interests*. At the same time, this discussion of both the High Court case and the Mental Capacity Act 2005 identifies the avenues open to social workers confronted by carers who appear not to be acting in the *best interests* of a mentally incapacitated adult for whom the practitioner holds care management responsibilities.

Judgement in *R (on application of A)* v. *East Sussex County Council (No. 2)*

Having used his judgement to set out the principles to guide a balancing exercise between the rights of care workers and those of service users, Justice Munby directed that these be incorporated into the formulation by East Sussex County Council of new care plans for A and B.

 ## Critical questions

1 The events concerning A and B centred on manual lifting and the balance to be struck between the health and safety of care workers on the one hand and the needs, preferences and dignity of users on the other. Try to identify other situations in which the health and safety of care workers and professionals might be at risk. How would you apply the principles identified by Justice Munby in this case and those set out in the GSCC Code of Practice to design a care package which would resolve potential conflicts between the needs of user and worker?

2 In this case the instances of inhuman and degrading treatment were focussed on the consequences of not providing manual assistance to users. What other examples of non-deliberate inhuman and degrading treatment can you think of which could take place in a person's home or in a residential setting? Drawing on your knowledge of National Minimum Standards for different care providers and the GSCC Code of Practice, as a practitioner, how would you go about dealing with an instance of inhuman or degrading treatment caused by the care offered by a local authority or a provider contracted by the local authority?

3 How might issues connected to culture, religious belief, gender, sexual orientation and age affect your understanding of dignity? If dignity is a subjective experience how would you explore these aspects with a service-user for whom you were arranging a care package?

Carers for people without mental capacity

Carers typically exercise informal decision-making powers on behalf of the incapacitated adults they care for. These can range from simple daily routines such as what to eat through to deciding when to arrange a consultation with a medical practitioner. Section 5 of the Mental Capacity Act 2005 legitimates these often daily decisions by protecting carers in this role from prosecution even if their decision has negative consequences for the person they care for. This protection can only be availed of if a carer 'reasonably believes' he or she was acting in the cared for person's best interests. This is quite a low threshold and opens up the possibility of poor decision making by some carers with no recourse to the courts by those concerned for an incapacitated adult receiving deficient informal care. Such a legal position can be exacerbated by assumptions on the part of busy professionals that carers because of their intimate knowledge of the user are best positioned to make decisions concerning his or her welfare (Keywood, 2003: 357).

Informal carers are widely acknowledged as essential to enabling vulnerable adults to access health and social care services (Keywood, 2003: 360). Often such informal or family carers are responsible for monitoring changes in the cared for person and alerting social workers of the need to review a care plan or a medical practitioner to treat him or her. Carers therefore act as gatekeepers for a range of resources to which the cared for person is entitled, but to which he or she is unlikely to have access without the carer bringing him or her to the attention of professionals. This places considerable power in the hands of carers.

Research reveals that lack of training or adequate professional support can make it difficult for carers to know when to call in specialists for the incapacitated adult they look after. The stigmatising effects of contact with mental health and Adult Social Services can also inhibit carers from accessing help for those they care for (Keywood, 2003: 360-1). The Mental Capacity Act 2005 increases the legal responsibilities of carers, whether in their informal role or as appointed attorneys or deputies, expanding their decision making beyond financial matters and into the realms of health and welfare. Yet this expansion in expectation has not been accompanied by any public spending commitment to increase training or support.

As advocates, carers have long spoken up for the welfare needs of those they care for, representing them to health and social care professionals. Often they have fought public sector bureaucracy and delay in obtaining services for the vulnerable adults for whom they care. Undoubtedly carers are uniquely placed to offer opinions on the preferences and best interests of incapacitated adults. For the first time section 4(7) of the Mental Capacity Act 2005 requires professionals making decisions in relation to a mentally incapacitated adult to consult with their carers. However, the relationship between a mentally competent carer and a mentally incapacitated adult remains one of unequal power. This can permit carers, acting as advocates, to determine and sometimes narrow the opportunities of those they look after. Carer attitudes towards normalisation, sexuality and conjectures regarding the ability of a vulnerable adult can have wide-reaching effects on that adult's quality of life. Despite the benign assumptions about carers as decision makers for incapacitated adults, which underpin much of the Mental Capacity Act 2005, professionals must be aware that such power can be used to restrict the lives of those with profound learning difficulties (Keywood, 2003: 364).

Learning points

- The Mental Capacity Act 2005, which is underpinned by five principles, is the major statute which is applicable in situations where a person over the age of 16 years of age may lack the mental capacity to make decisions.

- Mental capacity is not a global assessment of a person's ability to make decisions. It is an assessment made in relation to a specific decision about a precise matter at a particular point in time.

- The legal definition of capacity under the Mental Capacity Act 2005 means that an adult may regain capacity during periods of time or may exercise capacity in relation to some matters in their lives, but not in relation to others.

- The *best interests* decisions on behalf of an incapacitated adult can sometimes be biased by professional concerns about risk and carers' concerns about avoiding additional difficulty in relation to caring.

- Human rights legislation has an important role to play in offering protection against disproportionate intervention by local authorities which interferes with the private and family life of adults who are mentally incapacitated.

- The cultural and religious beliefs of people from ethnic minority backgrounds can come into conflict with legislation based on Anglo-centric values or human rights law. Practitioners may face dilemmas concerned with balancing respect for diversity against safeguarding vulnerable adults.

- In certain circumstances where adults with physical or mental disabilities are given the same standard of care as able-bodied adults, this may amount to inhuman and degrading treatment.

- The rights of adults with disabilities to assistance have to be weighed against the rights of care workers to a safe working environment. This may result in compromises being made concerning the dignity of users and the preferences of their carers.

Further reading

Brown, R., Barber, P. and Martin, D. (2009) *The Mental Capacity Act 2005: A Guide for Practice*, Exeter: Learning Matters. This publication provides an overview of the Act and explains it main provisions. It also includes the complete text of the legislation as an appendix.

Dimond, B. (2008) *Legal Aspects of Mental Capacity*, Oxford: Blackwell. This book provides a detailed explanation of the Mental Capacity Act 2005, supported by a number of worked examples of practice under the Act.

Mental Health Foundation (2008) *Engaging with Black and Minority Ethnic Communities about the Mental Capacity Act,* London: The Mental Health Foundation. This publication reflects black and ethnic minority views on mental capacity legislation and their perspectives on how its operation could be improved. Issues of culture in the context of mental capacity and the law are explored.

Rapaport, J., Manthorpe, J. and Stanley, N. (2009) 'Mental health and mental capacity law: some mutual concerns for social work practice', *Practice: Social Work in Action* 21(2): 91-105. This article considers the implications of the reforms to the law on mental capacity and mental health for social work practice. It also examines the differences of approach embedded in these two areas of the law.

Useful websites

www.officialsolicitor.gov.uk Run by the Official Solicitor this website explains the role of the Official Solicitor in legal proceedings. It also provides information and guidance for people concerned with litigation which involves the Official Solicitor.

www.scie.org.uk/publications/mca/index.asp Run by the Social Care Institute for Excellence this site provides accessible guides and information about the Mental Capacity Act 2005. It offers resource materials for student social workers and professionals who need to understand more about mental capacity and its legal implications.

www.mentalhealth.org.uk Run by the Mental Health Foundation, which is an established charity, this website offers accessible guides on the Mental Capacity Act 2005. It also highlights research studies in relation to learning difficulty and mental capacity.

www.publicguardian.gov.uk/ Run by The Office of the Public Guardian this website provides information on the role and functions of both the public guardian and the Court of Protection.

7

ADULTS WITH DISABILITIES

Fact file

- Number of new contacts received by Adult Social Services - 2.1 million
- Number of first assessments completed by Adult Social Services - 661,000
- Total number of adults receiving services - 1.8 million
- Number of adults receiving community care services - 1.53 million
- Number of adults in independent sector residential care - 199,000
- Number of adults in local authority residential care - 25,000
- Number of adults in nursing care - 102,000
- Number of people receiving direct payments - 67,000
- Number of carers assessed or reviewed - 378,000
- Number of carers assessed or reviewed who received services - 336,000
- Number of people in receipt of equipment or adaptations - 240,000

All statistics given are for England for 2007-08

Source: The Information Centre for Health and Social Care (2008)

Overview of relevant legislation

As the figures in the Fact File above reveal, community care is provided to a large proportion of the population. Local authority Adult Social Services deal with a huge number of new contacts from people requesting services each year. Also significant is the fact that the vast majority of adults with disabilities receive care in their own home or in sheltered accommodation in the community as opposed to in residential or nursing care. It is worth noting that local authorities now only provide a relatively small proportion of residential placements for adults compared to the independent sector. Although the use of direct payments may appear small at 67,000 compared to the total number of people receiving community care services, this figure represents a 38 per cent increase on the previous year. This is important as direct payments are a key aspect of the Government's new personalisation agenda which, as this chapter will explain, is transforming the existing system of care management for the delivery of community care services.

A raft of statutes enacted since the end of the Second World War oblige local authorities to either provide or arrange social care for adults experiencing mental or physical disabilities, learning difficulties, frailty due to old age or problems caused by the misuse of drugs or alcohol. The NHS and Community Care Act 1990 established the present system for supporting people with disabilities to live as independently as possible in the community as opposed to residence in long-stay hospitals or other institutions. This overarching statute sets out how entitlement to services under legislation enacted since 1945 is assessed and delivered. Additional legislation entitles the carers of disabled adults and children to social care services. Different statutes are applicable to different categories of people and provide for different types of services as shown in the table below. However, children with disabilities generally do not fall under community care legislation as their needs are met under the provisions of the Children Act 1989.

Statute	User group	Services
National Assistance Act 1948	Individuals over 18 years with a mental disorder, physical disability or learning difficulty who are substantially and permanently handicapped	• Residential accommodation for those in need due to illness or disability • Facilities for rehabilitation, employment and recreation • Domiciliary services • Social work advice and support
Health Services and Public Health Act 1968	Individuals who are frail due to age	• Domiciliary services
Chronically Sick and Disabled Persons Act 1970	Individuals of any age with a mental disorder, physical disability or learning difficulty who are substantially and permanently handicapped	• Domiciliary services • Home adaptations • Assistance for recreational and educational activities
Mental Health Act 1983	Individuals of any age with a mental disorder or impairment who have been compulsorily detained in hospital	• After-care in the community • Residential accommodation • Domiciliary services
National Health Services Acts 2006	Individuals of any age and includes those with addictions, expectant and nursing mothers, those with mental or physical disabilities or illnesses which *may not be* substantial or permanent	• Domiciliary services • Prevention, care and aftercare services • Day care and training facilities • Social work support
Carers and Disabled Children Act 2000	Carers aged 16 years or over and parents of disabled children	• Entitlement to separate assessment • Domiciliary services • Respite services • Direct payments and vouchers to purchase services
Carers (Equal Opportunities) Act 2004	Carers aged 16 years or over and parents of disabled children	• Entitlement to information and separate assessment • Cooperation between public authorities in provision of services • Right of carers to have their commitments to employment, education, training and social life taken into account in assessments

The underlying principle of community care is set out in the forward to Department of Health (1990) *Community Care in the Next Decade and Beyond: Policy Guidance*. This states that 'community care is about providing the services and support which will enable people affected by ageing or disability to live as independently as possible. The aim is to support people in their own homes or in "homely" surroundings wherever this can be done.' To this end 'service provision should as far as possible, preserve or restore normal living' (Department of Health, 1990: para. 3.24). The same paragraph in the Policy Guidance also sets out the order of preference in terms of living arrangements for those with disabilities:

Support for the service-user in his or her own home

A move to sheltered housing

A move to the home of relatives or friends or an adult fostering scheme

Residential care

Nursing home care

Long-stay care in hospital

Guidance document	Outline of content
Department of Health (1990) *Community Care in the Next Decade and Beyond: Policy Guidance*	Explains the objectives of care management and describes the system for implementing it.
Department of Health and Social Services Inspectorate (1991) *Care Management and Assessment: Practitioner's Guide*	This is addressed to frontline professionals and provides a step-by-step approach to care management.
Department of Health (2002c) *Fair Access to Care Services: Guidance on Eligibility Criteria for Adult Social Care* (LAC (2002) 13)	This is a local authority circular with policy guidance setting out the scheme for determining users' eligible needs.
Department of Health (2002b) *The Single Assessment Process*	This guidance describes the assessment framework for older people, which is designed to simplify complex, multidisciplinary assessments.
Department of Health (2001e) *National Service Framework for Older People*	This sets out standards for service delivery to older people by the National Health Service and Adult Social Services.
Department of Health (2003b) *Care Homes for Adults (18-65)*	This document sets out the National Minimum Standards which have to be met by care homes providing residential accommodation to adults.
Department of Health (2001a) *A Practitioner's Guide to Carers' Assessments under the Carers and Disabled Children Act 2000*	This guidance is addressed to practitioners undertaking assessments of carers and provides a step-by-step approach to care planning for carers.
Department of Health (2003e) *Direct Payment Guidance, Community Care, Services for Carers and Children's Services (Direct Payments) Guidance England*	This document details the direct payments scheme and explains the rules governing the provision of payments to both users and carers.
Department of Health (2000a) *No Secrets: Guidance on Developing and Implementing Multi-agency Policies and Procedures to Protect Vulnerable Adults from Abuse*	This is policy guidance and is directed both to management and practitioners. It sets out the framework for safeguarding vulnerable adults.

Overview of the cases

This chapter explores the issues arising from four court cases and one case which came before the Local Government Ombudsman. These are briefly summarised below:

Case 1 *R v. Gloucestershire County Council ex parte Barry* [1997] 2 WLR 459 explores the:

- System of care management.
- Assessment of need.
- Impact of local authority finances on service provision.

Case 2 *R (on the application of Chavda)* v. *Harrow London Borough Council* [2007] EWHC 3064 explores the:

- Distinction between care needs and eligible needs.
- Impact of the introduction of Fair Access to Care Services (FACS) on people with disabilities.
- Disability Equality Duty.

Case 3 *R (on the application of Ireneschild)* v. *Lambeth London Borough Council* [2007] EWCA Civ 234 explores the:

- Housing needs of people with disabilities.
- Issues raised by multidisciplinary Comprehensive Assessments.
- Exercise of professional judgement by social workers conducting assessments.
- Use of information provided by users.
- Nature of risk in the context of lifestyle choices.

Case 4 *R (on the application of Khana)* v. *Southwark London Borough Council* [2001] EWCA Civ 999 explores the:

- Effect of immigration status on the right to services.
- Distinction between user and carer preferences and their social care needs.
- Cultural aspects of community care assessment and care planning.
- Role of carers in the design of care packages.

Case 5 Ombudsman Report Complaint No. 03/B/18884 against London Borough of Bromley 9 December 2004 explores the:

- Failure of adult protection systems.
- Failure to investigate an allegation of abuse.
- Importance of review in the care management process.

CASE 1

R v. Gloucestershire County Council ex parte Barry [1997] 2 WLR 459

Importance of the case

This explores the relationship between local authority budgetary constraints and their duty to provide services under community care legislation. It resulted in a landmark judgement which permitted local authorities thereafter to take their finances into account in planning services for their area.

History of the case

The applicant, who had physical disabilities, brought a judicial review in the Queen's Bench Division of the High Court against the decision of Gloucestershire County Council to withdraw services due to resource constraints. The High Court ruled that the local authority was entitled to take into consideration its resources in reassessing social care needs. The applicant then appealed this judgement to the Court of Appeal which reversed the decision of the lower court, ruling that the local authority was not entitled to take its resources into account in assessing the care needs of the applicant. Gloucestershire County Council in turn appealed the decision of the Court of Appeal to the House of Lords.

Facts of the case

Mr Barry, born in 1915, was in his eighties and sight impaired, he had also suffered a minor stroke and a number of heart attacks when his care needs were assessed by Gloucestershire County Council in September 1992. His care package was to consist of home assistance for shopping, laundry, cleaning, meals-on-wheels and collecting his pension. In August 1993 after a routine visit by a social worker his needs were assessed as being the same. Then a year later, in September 1994, Gloucestershire County Council informed Mr Barry by letter, together with 1,500 other service-users, that due to a reduction in funding from central government, the local authority would be withdrawing laundry and cleaning services. Mr Barry and a number of other users sought a judicial review of Gloucester County Council's decision. The High Court handed down judgement in June 1995, finding that a local authority was entitled to take account of its financial resources in both assessing and meeting needs, but could only withdraw services after a reassessment of needs. In Mr Barry's case and that of the other applicants for a judicial review, the local authority had not reassessed the care needs of users before withdrawing services from them. Therefore the High Court found that Gloucester County Council had acted unlawfully. Mr Barry then appealed this judgement to the Court of Appeal on the grounds that the High Court decided a local authority could take into account its resources in assessing needs. At a hearing in June 1996 the Court of Appeal decided that a local authority was *not* entitled to take its resources into account when arranging to meet an adult's social care needs. Gloucester County Council in turn appealed this decision up to the House of Lords, which in final judgement on the case ruled that a local authority was not entitled to take its resources into account when assessing or reassessing the needs of people with disabilities, but was entitled to take account of its resources when deciding whether it was necessary to meet those needs.

Key people in the case

Mr Barry – applicant
Mr Richard Gordon – barrister for Mr Barry
Mr Patrick Eccles – barrister for Gloucester County Council
Lord Lloyd of Berwick – judge in House of Lords court case

Discussion of the case

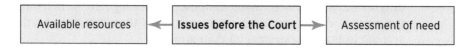

Assessment of need

This case, although pursued by Mr Barry, plainly affected a large number of older people and adults with disabilities living in Gloucestershire. They were dependent on the provision of domiciliary services to continue living at home and to avoid more substantial interventions, such as hospital admission due to deterioration in their health. In order to restore normal living and support independence in the community, the Department of Health (1990: para. 3.5) *Community Care in the Next Decade and Beyond: Policy Guidance* identifies a number of key approaches, which are set out in the box below.

 key guidance

Community Care in the Next Decade and Beyond

Para. 3.5 . . . Care management systems should aim to:

- Respond flexibly and sensitively to the needs of users and their carers
- Allow a range of options
- Intervene no more than is necessary to foster independence
- Prevent deterioration
- Concentrate on those with the greatest needs

Department of Health and Social Services Inspectorate (1991: para. 11) *Care Management and Assessment: Practitioner's Guide*, which is practice guidance, defines 'need' as 'the requirements of individuals to enable them to achieve, maintain or restore an acceptable level of social independence or quality of life, as defined by the particular care agency'. Lord Lloyd of Berwick, presiding in the House of Lords case concerning Mr Barry, afforded further clarification, observing that 'to need is not the same as to want. "Need" is the lack of what is essential for the ordinary business of living.' Section 47 of the NHS and Community Care Act 1990, which is reproduced in the box below, sets out the circumstances under which local authorities have a duty to assess the care 'needs' of individuals and provide social care.

 key legislation

NHS and Community Care Act 1990

s.47(1) . . . where it appears to a local authority that any person for whom they may provide or arrange for the provision of community care services may be in need of any such services, the authority –

    (a) shall carry out an assessment of his needs for those services; and

    (b) having regard to the results of that assessment, shall then decide whether his needs call for the provision by them of any such services.

Section 47(1) of the NHS and Community Care Act 1990 incorporates an extremely low threshold, which stipulates that if a person merely *appears* to be in need of services then the local authority's duty to assess is triggered. There was agreement between the parties to the

House of Lords case that Mr Barry *appeared* to have care needs and was entitled to the provision of services. The issue in dispute was the range of services to which Mr Barry was entitled and whether these could be justifiably curtailed on the basis of their cost to the local authority. Department of Health and Social Services Inspectorate (1991: 58–9) *Care Management and Assessment: Practitioner's Guide* requires Comprehensive Assessments to encompass needs associated with: mental health; physical disability or illness; medication; housing; transport; finance; social networks and risk in the context of self-care, coping mechanisms, lifestyle and culture alongside any existing service provision and the needs of carers. In addition, professionals must inquire into users' and carers' perception of their own needs. *Care Management and Assessment: Practitioner's Guide* details the stages of care management, which are described in the box below.

Key guidance

Care Management and Assessment: Practitioner's Guide

Stages in Care Management

1 Publishing information - the local authority is required to provide easily understandable guidance as to its services, eligibility for those services and how to access them. Practitioners are responsible for ensuring that these reach potential users and carers.
2 Determining the level of assessment - this may range from a Simple Assessment for a single uncomplicated care need, e.g. a free bus pass for an older person, to a Comprehensive Assessment for complex needs such as those of an individual with advanced dementia.
3 Assessment of user and carer needs - this involves face-to-face interviewing which encourages participation by the user and carer and incorporates their perspectives, priorities and preferences into care planning. The assessment must be recorded in writing.
4 Development of the care plan - the care plan is based on the identification of needs during stage three and is a written document which contains clear objectives and timescales for the provision of different services and may include behavioural change by the user or carer. At this point services are costed and alternative means of meeting identified care needs considered.
5 Implementation of the care plan - this should be the minimum intervention required to meet the objectives of the care plan. At this stage the care manager negotiates with providers and oversees the integration of different services to produce a seamless care package for the user and/or carer.
6 Monitoring the care plan - this includes coordinating the service inputs over time, obtaining feedback from the user and/or carer and checking the quality of provision. At this stage the care plan should also be fine-tuned and the budget monitored alongside service delivery.
7 Reviewing the care plan - LAC (2002) 13 stipulates that an initial review should be held within 3 months of implementation of the care plan and at least once a year thereafter. Reviews should identify any changes in needs or required adjustments to the care package alongside progress towards the objectives of the care plan.

In the present case Mr Barry's needs were assessed and a care plan produced in September 1992 in accordance with stages three, four and five of the care management process (see text box above). Mr Barry's care package consisted of home assistance for shopping, laundry, cleaning, meals-on-wheels and collecting his pension. In August 1993 his needs were reviewed in line with stage seven of the care management process. These were found to be the same and the care package consequently remained unaltered. Then unexpectedly in September 1994 the local authority unilaterally withdrew Mr Barry's laundry and cleaning services without any review of his needs. In other words, without ascertaining whether or not Mr Barry's care needs had changed, the local authority modified (or rather reduced) the provision of services included in his original care package. The issue before the House of Lords was whether the local authority could lawfully do this on the grounds that it did not have the resources to deliver the provision identified in Mr Barry's care plan. Given that all local authorities have a finite budget and all have a duty to deliver social care to people who are ill or disabled, the outcome of Mr Barry's court case had wide applicability to local authorities across England and Wales. The complexity of health and social care needs for older people like Mr Barry has since led to the introduction of the Single Assessment Process, which modifies care management procedures for people over 65 years.

The complexity of the mental, physical and social care needs of older people led to the publication of Department of Health (2002b) *The Single Assessment Process* which amended the approach to care management for older people. This guidance introduced the Single Assessment Process for Older People. This approach to care management requires the National Health Service and local authorities providing or arranging social care to develop a common assessment which pulls together information thus ensuring that older people are not subject to a series of assessments by professionals from different health and social care agencies. Annex A page 2 of Department of Health (2002b), which is reproduced in the box below, describes the Single Assessment Process as a person-centred approach.

 Background information

The Single Assessment Process

- The older person seeking help from health and social care services experiences a single assessment process where:
  - Information about needs is given once, no matter that the assessment and subsequent care planning and service delivery involves a number of professionals and agencies.
  - Professionals work together in the best interests of the older person (as defined by the older person or those close to them).
- The older person's views and wishes are central to the assessment process, and the assessment takes account of the strengths the older person can bring to bear on their needs, and external or environmental factors that are causing or exacerbating needs.
- Assessment builds a rounded picture of older people's needs and circumstances, including not only health and social care issues but also relevant housing, benefits, transport and other issues.
- The depth and detail of the assessment is proportionate to an individual's needs.
- Each older person is informed of, and consents to, information about their needs and circumstances being collected and shared.
- Key decisions and issues are copied in writing, or other appropriate formats, to the older person.

Available resources

In this case, Mr Barry had been provided with domiciliary services under s.2(1)(a) of the Chronically Sick and Disabled Persons Act 1970. While this section of the statute defines the duty of local authorities regarding the provision of services to those who are 'substantially and permanently handicapped by illness, injury or congenital deformity' it makes no mention of the financial context. Mr Richard Gordon QC acting for Mr Barry sought to argue that this meant the local authority was legally obliged to provide services to those who were assessed as needing them regardless of the cost. The Law Lords presiding over the House of Lords court case agreed that where there is doubt or disagreement as to the construction of a statutory provision, White Papers, Policy Guidance and Practice Guidance can be invoked to interpret the intentions of Parliament. Later statutes which amend or alter the implementation of earlier Acts can also be relied upon to clarify the law.

Mr Patrick Eccles QC, the barrister acting for Gloucester County Council, noted that in this instance the Chronically Sick and Disabled Persons Act 1970 was amended by the NHS and Community Care Act 1990. Section 47(1)(a) of this later statute states that local authorities must carry out an assessment of need (if it appears that the person is in need of services). Then s.47(1)(b) goes on to state that 'having regard to the results of that assessment' the local authority 'shall then decide whether his needs call for the provision by them of any such services'. This means that a local authority is only obliged to 'have regard' to the assessment of need and 'then decide whether' to provide services. So there is not a strict correlation between needs and services. Instead, the NHS and Community Care Act 1990 introduced an aspect of evaluation and judgement in the provision of services relative to assessed needs. For example, a disabled person's care needs may be met by a family member, by a simple change in user or carer behaviour, or by the ability to purchase services privately, or the needs may not be 'essential to the ordinary business of living'. In each of these circumstances the assessed need would not be met by the provision of services by the local authority.

Since Policy Guidance is also a source which judges can utilise to aid statutory interpretation, Mr Eccles also argued that *Community Care in the Next Decade and Beyond* was pertinent to the interpretation of s.2(1)(a) of the Chronically Sick and Disabled Persons Act 1970. Department of Health (1990: para. 3.25) *Community Care in the Next Decade and Beyond* explicitly states that:

> The aim shall be to secure the most cost effective package of services that meets the user's care needs taking account of the user's and carer's own preferences . . . However, local authorities also have a responsibility to meet needs within the resources available and this will sometimes involve difficult decisions where it will be necessary to strike a balance between meeting the needs identified within available resources and meeting the care preferences of the individual.

This unambiguous statement pits service-user preferences against the finite resources of the local authority with the task falling to practitioners (acting as care managers) to resolve any conflicts between the two. Plainly, local authorities are under a duty to meet the care needs of people ordinarily resident in their area. They are at the same time obliged to design cost-effective care packages, which ultimately may not reflect the wishes of particular users or carers. In practice, service-user choice is just one factor among a number of others which social workers are obliged to take account of in formulating care plans. On this point the Law Lords agreed broadly with the barrister acting for Gloucester County Council.

This does not imply that social workers (or other professionals) in their role as care managers can simply ignore people's care needs if the local authority has insufficient resources to meet them. On the contrary, as Lord Lloyd of Berwick stressed in his judgement, needs must be identified independently of any resource considerations. Local authorities cannot simply cite limited resources as a pretext for reducing the assessed needs of disabled people, which they have a statutory duty to meet under s.2 of the Chronically Sick and Disabled Persons Act 1970. If this were so, then a local authority could assess disabled individuals as having no needs because it did not have the funds for services to meet them. This creates the possibility of unmet needs whereby a practitioner conducts an assessment as per stage three of the care management process, but the care plan does not reflect the means to address all the identified needs.

Both legislation and guidance indicate that social workers employed by local authorities to arrange social care services are required to take into consideration the cost-effectiveness of providing those services. In circumstances of severe budgetary cutbacks among local authorities this can pose substantial professional dilemmas for social workers. Paragraph 1.3 of the GSCC *Code of Practice for Social Care Workers* requires practitioners to support 'service users' rights to control their lives and make informed choices about the services they receive'. This stipulation sits in tension with local authority budgetary constraint, user preferences as distinct from user needs, and the notion of unmet needs. When the cost of a service denies users their preference for a service and where social workers are unable to satisfactorily negotiate an acceptable compromise with a user, then they may need to act as advocates or brokers for a particular service. They also have the option of bringing the matter to the attention of their employers. Paragraph 3.4 of the GSCC Code enjoins social workers to bring 'to the attention of your employer or the appropriate authority resource or operational difficulties that might get in the way of the delivery of safe care'.

Judgement in *R v. Gloucestershire County Council ex parte Barry*

The Law Lords openly sympathised in their judgement with the difficult position of local authorities across Britain created by funding constraints imposed by central government and the dilemmas this posed for local councils trying to meet the needs of vulnerable adults. They concluded that local authorities were entitled to take their resources into account in deciding which assessed needs to meet. However, local authorities were not permitted to take their resources into account when actually assessing or reassessing a person's care needs. The House of Lords ruling also endorsed the judgement of the lower courts that services once arranged could only be reduced after a further assessment of need. This judgement resulted in the introduction of *Fair Access to Care Services* which is discussed in the next case.

 Critical questions

1 Local authorities had been left in a very difficult position as a result of increased demand for social care services but a failure by central government to make more funding available to keep pace with this. The response of local authorities was to cut services to existing users and to impose more stringent criteria for the provision of services to new users. These dynamics continue to underlie community care. Do you think local authorities could respond in a more constructive way to this problem and, if so, how?

2 This was a landmark judgement which made the cost of provision a lawful consideration in the delivery of services to meet social care needs. In this case social workers, as care managers, were in the forefront of reducing services to older people. In your practice how would you reconcile the imperatives of government guidance and your GSCC Code of Practice to maintain and promote people's independence in the community and at the same time to work for a local authority which was either reducing services or raising the criteria to obtain them?

Perspectives

Care management

A major finding from research into the implementation of care management arrangements has been the frequent changes in care manager for people receiving medium to long-term care provision (Challis et al, 1999). For users with learning disabilities short-termism in the provision of services was particularly detrimental to realising their full potential (Department of Health, 1998b). Restrictive and tight eligibility criteria to determine access to services was another factor which impaired the effectiveness of care management in supporting independent living in the community (Department of Health, 1998b). Lack of real budgetary control by care managers (or even by their direct line managers) meant that they were often unable to make financial decisions and thus innovate in terms of service provision (Xie, 2008: 161).

Parry-Jones and Soulsby (2001) found that social and health care professionals were highly committed to needs-led assessment and the development of individually tailored care plans. In practice, resource constraints forced them to allocate established standardised services and curtail choice for individual users. Although policy has sought to align health and social care provision, Worth (2001) and Vernon et al. (2000) discovered that nurses and social workers acting as care managers tend to conduct assessments from a single disciplinary standpoint. Nurses focussed on diagnostic and treatment issues while social workers centred their assessment on social factors. Professionals from both health and social care backgrounds believed that their assessments were holistic, when in fact they contained clear disciplinary biases.

While the Single Assessment Process for older people with complex care needs was intended to resolve a number of the problems identified by research, this too has faced obstacles to effective implementation. Christiansen and Roberts (2005) found that despite this innovation to care management practice, the geographical separation of nurses and social workers impeded genuine multidisciplinary assessment and care planning. Diverse IT systems and record keeping acted as a barrier to good communication between NHS agencies and Adult Social Services. The result was that the health and social care needs of users tended to be addressed in relative isolation from one another. In the study conducted by Christiansen and Roberts (2005) practitioners were clear that the concept of a Single Assessment Process was the right one for users and carers. However, they were universally of the opinion that to be effectively implemented it required joint health and social care budgets, integrated service provision and additional training for frontline staff.

CASE 2
R (on the application of Chavda) v. Harrow London Borough Council [2007] EWHC 3064

Importance of the case

It explores the introduction of eligibility criteria and the creation of a legal distinction between user needs and eligible needs. It also examines the implications of this for the disability equality duty owed by local authorities.

History of the case

This was a judicial review brought before the Queen's Bench Division of the High Court by three claimants with disabilities. They sought a court order to quash the decision of Harrow London Borough Council to restrict social care provision to those with critical needs only.

Facts of the case

Following the issuance of LAC (2002) 13 *Fair Access to Care Services* by the Department of Health, Harrow London Borough Council adopted a set of standardised eligibility criteria which were duly applied to disabled persons living in its area who appeared to be in need of services. The first claimant, Ms Chavda, had mental health problems and back trouble. Her needs had been assessed by the local authority as being substantial. The second claimant, Mrs Fitzpatrick, who was 81 years old and lived alone, was housebound as a result of multiple disabilities and several illnesses. Mrs Fitzpatrick, whose needs had been assessed as being critical, was represented by her daughter acting as a litigation friend. The third claimant, Mr Moas, suffered from depression, anxiety and a number of phobias. His needs had been assessed by Harrow London Borough Council as critical in relation to harm to himself or others and substantial as regard sustaining his independence, occupational activity and social network. Harrow London Borough Council had experienced consider-able overspend of its social care budget, which it attributed to: growing demand for social care provision; increasingly complex needs; and additional costs caused by the withdrawal of the local Primary Care Trust from joint funding arrangements. Faced with prospective funding shortfalls of £6.7 million in 2008/9 and £7.5 million for 2009/10 the Council's cabinet decided in December 2006 to begin a formal consultation process on a proposal to limit social care services only to those assessed as having critical needs. A consultation process duly took place with users, carers, voluntary sector organisations and healthcare providers. Although the consultation produced overwhelming support for retaining the council's existing policy of providing services to those assessed as having substantial or crit-ical needs, in July 2007 the Council's cabinet decided to restrict social care provision funded by the local authority to those with critical needs. The three claimants contended that the council's consultation process was flawed and that the decision to confine provi-sion to those with critical needs violated the local authority's equality duty towards dis-abled people under the Disability Discrimination Act 1995.

Key people in the case

Ms Chavda – first claimant
Mrs Fitzpatrick – second claimant
Mr Moas – third claimant
Mr Cragg – barrister for all three claimants
Mr McCarthy – barrister for Harrow London Borough Council
Mr Mackie – judge presiding in High Court case

Discussion of the case

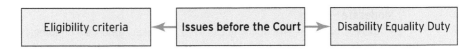

Eligibility criteria

Following the judgement in *R* v. *Gloucestershire County Council ex parte Barry* and a host of subsequent judicial reviews linked to the funding available for community care, central government produced policy guidance to instruct local authorities on eligibility criteria for provision. This policy guidance was issued as a local authority circular. Department of Health (2002c) *Fair Access to Care Services* (LAC (2002) 13) sets out a framework for determining the entitlement of individuals to adult social care services funded by local government. The first paragraph of LAC (2002) 13 directs that:

> Councils should ensure that they can provide or commission services to meet eligible needs, subject to their resources and, that within the council area, individuals in similar circumstances receive services capable of achieving broadly similar outcomes . . . councils should be aware that this guidance neither says that different councils should make identical decisions about eligibility, nor prescribes what services should be available to service users who have similar needs.

Fair Access to Care Services (FACS) creates four bands or categories of need which are determined on the basis of the risk to an individual's independence. It is for councils to decide, based on their financial position, which bands of needs they are able to meet. Effectively it is no longer the *assessed* needs of disabled persons which will be met by the local authority, but only their *eligible* needs as framed by FACS. The bands are detailed in the box below.

Key guidance

Fair Access to Care Services

Critical - when
- life is, or will be, threatened; and/or
- significant health problems have developed or will develop; and/or
- there is, or will be, little or no choice and control over vital aspects of the immediate environment; and/or
- serious abuse or neglect has occurred or will occur; and/or
- there is, or will be, an inability to carry out vital personal care or domestic routines; and/or
- vital involvement in work, education or learning cannot or will not be sustained; and/or
- vital social support systems and relationships cannot or will not be undertaken.

Substantial - when
- there is, or will be, only partial choice and control over the immediate environment; and/or
- abuse or neglect has occurred or will occur; and/or
- there is, or will be, an inability to carry out the majority of personal care or domestic routines; and/or
- involvement in many aspects of work, education or learning cannot or will not be sustained; and/or
- the majority of social support systems and relationships cannot or will not be sustained; and/or
- the majority of family and other social roles and responsibilities cannot or will not be undertaken.

Moderate - when
- there is, or will be, an inability to carry out several personal care or domestic routines; and/or
- involvement in several aspects of work, education or learning cannot or will not be sustained; and/or
- several social support systems and relationships cannot or will not be sustained; and/or
- several family and other social roles and responsibilities cannot or will not be undertaken.

Low – when

- there is, or will be, an inability to carry out one or two personal care or domestic routines; and/or
- involvement in one or two aspects of work, education or learning cannot or will not be sustained; and/or
- one or two social support systems and relationships cannot or will not be sustained; and/or
- one or two family and other social roles and responsibilities cannot or will not be undertaken.

The introduction of *Fair Access to Care Services*, which was fully implemented in 2003, meant that councils could examine their financial position and decide ahead of time which bands of needs they could afford to meet through the provision of adult social care services. In effect councils could, based on their resources, decide only to fund services to meet specified bands or categories of needs. In 2003 Harrow London Borough Council duly set eligibility criteria which meant it would provide services for assessed needs falling into the *critical* and *substantial* bands. Subsequently, the Council was confronted with a running shortfall in its finances and decided in July 2007 that eligible needs would be confined to needs classified as *critical*. So even if adults ordinarily resident in the Harrow borough were assessed as having needs which fell into the *low*, *moderate* or *substantial* bands, the local council was not going to meet these through the provision of publicly funded services. Furthermore, when a local authority changed its eligibility criteria for meeting the care needs of disabled adults, *Fair Access to Care Services* permitted it to withdraw existing services from previously assessed adults, albeit that this could only occur after a reassessment.

Prior to Harrow London Borough Council's decision in July 2007, Ms Chavda, the first claimant, had been assessed as having *substantial* needs. Mrs Fitzpatrick, the second claimant, was assessed as having *critical* needs, while the third claimant, Mr Moas, was assessed as having *critical* needs concerning some aspects of his life and *substantial* needs in relation to others. Despite the fact that all three claimants had been previously assessed and a care package put in place for each to meet their needs, the effect of the July 2007 decision by Harrow Council meant that these could be removed on reassessment. Since Mrs Fitzpatrick had *critical* needs and the local authority proposed to designate these eligible needs, her services were protected from reduction. However, Ms Chavda stood to have her whole care package removed after reassessment as her needs were *substantial* and not *critical*. Mr Moas on the other hand was likely to have his services reduced as some of his needs were previously assessed as *substantial* and others as *critical*. In effect, what had once been *eligible* needs falling into the *substantial* category were, by a decision of the Council, now rendered *ineligible* needs, which the local authority was no longer obliged to meet. Of course, Mr Moas and Ms Chavda were far from being the only adults with disabilities affected by the decision of Harrow London Borough Council. Given that *Fair Access to Care Services* permits local authorities to change which bands constitute eligible needs and also allows them to reassess and withdraw services, Mr Cragg, the barrister acting for the claimants, had to identify other grounds for attacking the decision of Harrow London Borough Council.

This case, perhaps more than any other, brings into stark relief the very difficult policies which social workers, acting as care managers, are required to implement. The introduction of *Fair Access to Care Services* and the resource-constrained circumstances of local authorities have resulted in either more stringent eligibility criteria being applied to new users or, after reassessment, the withdrawal of services from existing users. Social workers in Adult Services will inevitably be undertaking assessment and care planning within this context. Plainly, professionals in these circumstances are going to find themselves caught between the budgetary imperatives of their local authority employer and the social care needs of users and carers. This may be a situation in which practitioners need to comply with paragraph 3.7 of the GSCC Code of Practice and help 'users and carers to make complaints, taking complaints seriously and responding to them'. Unfortunately, in circumstances where services are withdrawn but where a user's actual needs have not changed, pursuing a complaint may be the only option left for those with unmet needs. It is precisely because the care management approach does not appear to be delivering on user choice that the Government is in the process of introducing the personalisation agenda which is explained in the box below.

Background information

The personalisation agenda

Care management has not delivered on needs-led assessment and personally tailored care planning in the context of user choice as was intended. This system of care provision has also absorbed an increasingly large proportion of local authority finances resulting in the prioritising of assistance to users at high risk rather than the delivery of preventive services under FACS. Confronted by these failings the Government published its White Paper entitled *Our Health, Our Care, Our Say: A New Direction for Community Services* in 2006. This set out what is called the 'personalisation agenda', which is designed to give users and carers better access to and more control over health and social care provision.

The personalisation agenda involves greatly increasing the numbers of users and carers currently availing of direct payments. It also introduces the concept of personal budgets which comprise an allocation of funding to users based on a community-care assessment. Users can take their personal budget in the form of a direct payment and arrange their own services, thus taking on responsibility for paying care assistants, meal preparation and so forth. Alternatively they will have the option of asking a care manager to arrange services and manage their personal budget. Users will also be encouraged to adopt a combination of these approaches where they wish to take on responsibility for some aspects of their care package, but not others. Local authorities are required to reconfigure their social care finances to produce personal budgets over the period 2008-11.

In the longer-term *Our Health, Our Care, Our Say* paves the way for the introduction of individual budgets which will bring together money currently in separate income streams which include: a local authority's social care budget; Community Equipment; Access to Work; Independent Living Fund; Disability Facility Grant; and Supporting People. Presently, funding from all these budgets involves a separate application. Under the Government's plans for individual budgets these different funding streams will be amalgamated to give a disabled person access to a single individual budget. The user will then be able to draw on the monies in this budget in order to arrange their own services in ways which best meet their needs and preferences.

The reorientation of services detailed in the White Paper *Our Health, Our Care, Our Say* will mean that although community care assessments will continue to be undertaken the commissioning and arrangement of services will be increasingly undertaken by users themselves. The personalisation agenda reduces the necessity of care management as this passes to users. However care management is likely to be retained for people who are seriously ill, lack mental capacity, or who simply do not want the additional responsibilities that go along with the self-management of services.

Disability Equality Duty

Mr Cragg, legal counsel for the claimants, next sought to argue that the council's deliberations failed to take account of their Disability Equality Duty. This comprises a set of related duties imposed on public authorities by the Disability Discrimination Act 2005, which amended the earlier Disability Discrimination Act 1995. These additional duties require local authorities while performing their functions to consider the need to eliminate discrimination against people with disabilities and to promote their rights. These duties are detailed in s.49A of the amended statute.

Key legislation

Disability Discrimination Act 1995 (as amended)

s.49 A Every public authority shall in carrying out its functions have due regard to -
  (a) the need to eliminate discrimination that is unlawful under this Act;
  (b) the need to eliminate harassment of disabled persons that is related to their disabilities;
  (c) the need to promote equality of opportunity between disabled persons and other persons;
  (d) the need to take steps to take account of disabled persons' disabilities, even where that involves treating disabled persons more favourably than other persons;
  (e) the need to promote positive attitudes towards disabled persons; and
  (f) the need to encourage participation by disabled persons in public life

In addition to the provisions of s.49A, the Disability Rights Commission (now subsumed into the Commission for Equality and Human Rights) issued a statutory Code of Practice. Disability Rights Commission (2005) *The Duty to Promote Disability Equality*, while not legally binding upon local authorities, nevertheless constitutes compelling guidance for the conduct of their affairs. Paragraph 2.34 of *The Duty to Promote Disability Equality* interprets 'due regard' in s.49A as requiring public authorities to do more than just give cursory consideration to issues of equality and disability when deliberating on particular issues. It requires them to make a tangible effort to discover the effect of their policy decisions on disabled people. To this end the Code of Practice directs local authorities to carry out a full impact assessment to establish the likely effects of policy changes and to modify their decisions in the light of the findings from such surveys. Mr Cragg, representing the claimants at the High Court, argued that Harrow London Borough Council had failed to conduct an impact assessment or have 'due regard' to the list of duties comprising s.49A of the Disability Discrimination Act 1995.

Responding to this claim, Mr McCarthy, barrister for the defendant council, contended that it had indeed conducted an impact assessment and had given 'due regard' to matters cited in s.49A in coming to its final decision in July 2007. Substantiating this assertion, Mr McCarthy produced as evidence the summary report of an Equality Impact Assessment carried out under the Comprehensive Equality Scheme. This had been appended to documentation brought to the attention of councillors before their decision of July 2007 restricting eligible needs to the *critical* category. The summary report presents a breakdown of the proportions of people with different types of disability potentially affected by the local authority's change of policy on eligibility. The report also draws attention to the likelihood that users with less severe disabilities would have their services withdrawn as a consequence of the decision. A short bullet point in one section of the report refers to 'a potential conflict with DDA 1995' and notes that 'a change in criteria could be seen as limiting access for some people to services'.

Mr Cragg in turn criticised the Equality Impact Assessment which covered the impact of the council's decision on all minority groups including those distinguished by race and age. Disability in fact received relatively little coverage in the summary report of the Equality Impact Assessment given that the policy change directly affected this group in particular. According to Mr Cragg, the summary report merely mentioned that the policy change being pursued by Harrow London Borough Council was potentially in conflict with the Disability Discrimination Act 1995. Indeed, the report did not elaborate on this and consequently did not reflect any detailed consideration of the Disability Equality Duty or the extent to which the proposed changes might contravene it. In conclusion Mr Cragg argued that the Council had not in fact given 'due regard' to the Disability Equality Duty set out in s.49A of the Disability Discrimination Act 1995. He claimed that as the local authority was contemplating a policy change related to its function of delivering adult social care services, which was bound to intimately affect large numbers of disabled people, it was incumbent upon the Council to conduct an impact assessment focussed on disability.

The Disability Equality Duty is imposed on local authorities and therefore on their employees in the day-to-day performance of their public functions. Consequently, social workers are bound by the equality duty, not only in relation to disability but across the range of equality duties imposed on public bodies by the Equality Act 2006. This includes promoting social inclusion and good community relations alongside working towards the elimination of discrimination against people on the grounds of race, religion, gender and sexual orientation. The Equality Duty is complemented by the imperatives of anti-discriminatory practice contained in the GSCC Codes of Practice for both social care workers and their employers.

Judgement in *R (on the application of Chavda)* v. *Harrow London Borough Council*

Ruling in the High Court case, Judge Mackie acknowledge that a local authority was entitled to change its eligibility criteria after completing a consultation process with various stakeholders. However, in contemplating a policy change which directly affected disabled people, Harrow London Borough Council should have paid specific attention to its Disability Equality Duty. As detailed in the related Code of Practice, this required the Council to do more than merely consider the impact on people with disabilities. It obliged the local authority to actively engage with its duties under s.49A of the Disability Discrimination Act 1995. This in Judge Mackie's opinion the local authority had failed to do and consequently he ruled that its decision in July 2007 to restrict eligible needs to those falling to the *critical* band was unlawful.

 Critical questions

---

1 Policy and practice guidance makes clear that community care should centre on supporting people to live in their own homes for as long as possible. Preventative service provision is clearly envisaged in these guidance documents as an important aspect of that objective. This case demonstrates how FACS is being deployed by cash-strapped local authorities to spread services thinner and further among more people. How might the personalisation agenda address this problem?

2 In this case, the local authority was only found to have acted unlawfully because it failed to sufficiently take into consideration the impact of changing the eligibility criteria on people with disabilities. But the judgement did not rule that the local authority had breached its Disability Equality Duty by reducing services. In other words, local authorities are still free to reduce services to people with disabilities as long as they give 'due regard' to the impact of such a policy change. This raises the question as to whether the Equality Duty has any real practical effect. Go back to the text box detailing the Disability Equality Duty. How might you implement this in your day-to-day practice with disabled users?

Critical commentary

Fair Access to Care Services

By 2000-01 approximately 9 out of every 10 local authority Social Services Departments were experiencing year-on-year overspend (Association of Directors of Social Services et al., 2001). There was an ever-widening gap between the central government formula for allocating funding for Social Services and the actual local government spend. For example in 2004-5 the total overspend was £840 million, but by 2005-6 this had jumped to £1,800 million, representing a doubling of the gap between central government allocated funding and spend by local government on Social Services (Local Government Association and Society of County Treasurers, 2005). Local authorities had to make up this shortfall by identifying additional monies from other sources, resulting in service cutbacks in other areas. It was in the context of these colossal funding shortfalls that *Fair Access to Care Services* was introduced. It was designed to ensure the equitable rationing of finite resources across local authorities with provision concentrated on those most at risk of abuse or loss of independence. Local authorities were, however, given discretion as to which bands of *eligible needs* they would fund, creating inequality in service provision as between different local authority areas.

By 2005 only 6% of local authorities were meeting the needs of users who fell into the *low* band, and just 36% were meeting those falling into the *moderate* category (Local Government Association and Society of County Treasurers, 2005: 8). The concentration of provision on people falling within the *critical* and *substantial* bands meant that preventative services were no longer being put in place by most local authorities. This reality runs directly counter to the programme set out in the government's White Paper HM Government (2006b) *Our Health, Our Care, Our Say: A New Direction in Community Services*, which emphasises health promotion, better access to community care services and improved user choice.

Newton and Browne (2008) have compiled the most recent research to date on the impact of *Fair Access to Care Services* on users and practitioners. This revealed a number of important findings. Department of Health (2003d) *Fairer Charging Policies for Home Care and other Non-residential Social Services: Guidance for Councils with Social Services Responsibilities* introduced guidance as to how local authorities should charge for non-residential social care provision, including short-term respite care. This guidance permitted considerable discretion and there is wide variation in charging policies across local authority areas. Research collated by Newton and Browne (2008) also reveals that generally people who are required to pay the cost of their service (and therefore who make their own arrangements) were given little assistance by Social Services. Similarly those in the *low* and *moderate* categories of needs, who were not entitled to services in most local authority areas, received scant attention from care managers.

Social workers responsible for assessments often did as much as they could for users in very difficult circumstances. Many were generous in their assessments in order to place users in a higher category where their needs would be eligible for service provision (Newton and Browne, 2008: 239-10). Frontline social workers were confronted by contradictory imperatives which on the one hand obliged them to offer choice and prevent deterioration of people's health and safety and on the other to restrict services to the most seriously at risk. In an effort to square this circle many care managers, despite government guidance and agency level instruction, are exercising their own professional judgement as to what constitutes equal access to care services in an effort to do their best for their users (Newton and Brown, 2008: 245). The overall result of this can be yet more inequity for users within and between different local authority catchment areas.

CASE 3

R (on the application of Ireneschild) v. *Lambeth London Borough Council* [2007] EWCA Civ 234

Importance of the case

It focusses on community care assessments and the use of specialist reports to assist in care planning. The case also examines a situation in which the user is in disagreement with the care plan proposed by a social worker.

History of the case

The claimant brought a judicial review of her community care assessment by the local authority before the Queen's Bench Division of the High Court, which found that the assessment was flawed and unlawful. The local authority then appealed against this decision to the Court of Appeal.

Facts of the case

Ms Ireneschild, the claimant, was in 1982 granted a secure tenancy by the local authority of a two-bedroomed flat located on the first and second floors of a large Victorian house. She resided there with her two adult sons. In 1992 Ms Ireneschild was the victim of a climbing accident which left her unable to stand or move without support, doubly incontinent and in constant pain. She required a wheelchair when outdoors. At this point her two sons became her main carers. In 1996 Ms Ireneschild applied to the local housing authority for transfer to ground-floor accommodation for medical reasons. These included the difficulty of access to the flat as it could only be entered using a staircase leading from the street. In addition, the flat itself had an internal staircase which the claimant was unable to use unaided. Ms Ireneschild applied for a housing transfer on the grounds that she was at risk of falling down the stairs and that her sons were at risk of injury through having to carry her upstairs. Over the next decade there followed a series of assessments of the claimant's care needs. Then in 2006 an occupational therapist assessed the claimant as having *substantial* needs and requiring ground-floor accommodation. However, the social worker conducting the community care assessment placed less priority on this in drawing up the care plan. At this point Ms Ireneschild applied for a judicial review on the grounds that the social worker had ignored the occupational therapist's report, had failed to follow guidance in taking account of risk, and had not permitted the claimant an opportunity to comment on the facts relied upon to determine the care plan. The High Court found in favour of the claimant, ruling that the community care assessment of her needs was unlawful. Consequently, in September 2006, the High Court made a Quashing Order which invalidated the original assessment and required the local authority to conduct a new one within 28 days. Lambeth London Borough Council appealed against this judgement to the Court of Appeal.

Key people in the case

Ms Ireneschild – respondent in Court of Appeal case
Mr Rogerson – occupational therapist
Ms Thorpe – principal medical housing advisor
Ms Williams – social worker
Mr Drabble – barrister for respondent
Mr Béar – barrister for the appellant local authority
Lord Justice Hallett – judge in Court of Appeal case

Discussion of the case

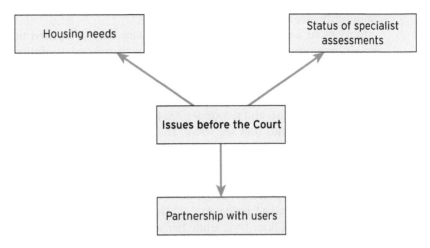

Housing needs

Housing may be rented from the private sector or from social landlords such as housing trusts or housing associations. Throughout the 1980s and 1990s a large proportion of housing stock, previously owned and rented out by local authority Housing Departments, was either sold off to existing tenants or transferred to housing associations or housing action trusts. In the present case the claimant, Ms Ireneschild, held a secure tenancy from the local authority, which owned the property she lived in with her adult sons and was therefore her landlord. Consequently, the terms of her tenancy were regulated under the Housing Act 1985, even though her tenancy actually commenced before the enactment of this statute. The Housing Act 1985 gives secure tenants of local authority Housing Departments a number of important rights. These are generally more advantageous than those held by tenants of private landlords. The rights of secure tenants are outlined in the box below.

Key legislation

Housing Act 1985

Secure tenants are entitled to:

- One succession which enables the original tenant to pass on the tenancy as of right to a family member.
- Be charged a reasonable rent.
- Buy the rented property at a discounted rate.
- Take in lodgers.
- Security of tenure which restricts the local authority's right as a landlord to evict the tenant.

Under the provisions of the Housing Act 1985 Ms Ireneschild had considerable security of tenure. As long as she abided by the terms of her tenancy agreement, such as paying the rent and not causing a nuisance to neighbours, the Housing Department of the local authority was, broadly speaking, unable to evict her. The problem for Ms Ireneschild was that after her climbing accident in 1992 her flat, located as it was on the first and second floors of a large Victorian house, became unsuitable. There was considerable dispute between the parties to the Court of Appeal case as to the urgency and importance of Ms Ireneschild's housing needs. There was also apparent disagreement between the professionals who examined Ms Ireneschild's housing requirements and whose reports contributed to the claimant's community care assessment.

In 1999 an assessment and related care plan were completed under s.47 of the NHS and Community Care Act 1990. This care plan referred to difficulties stemming from Ms Ireneschild's accommodation and the need for contact to be made with the housing department of the local authority. Little else was done to progress the matter until in 2003 Mr Rogerson, an occupational therapist, carried out an assessment of Ms Ireneschild's housing requirements and recommended that she be rehoused in accommodation without stairs, on the grounds that she was at risk of falling. Despite this further specialist assessment nothing happened. As a result of continued inaction Ms Ireneschild engaged a solicitor to pursue the matter. Her solicitor obtained a copy of a community care assessment in February 2005 which stated that 'the risk to [Ms Ireneschild's] independence is substantial'. The assessment proposed modification to the interior of the double-storey flat to convert it into two self-contained living spaces. This would give Ms Ireneschild accommodation all on the one first-floor level while her sons occupied the second floor. Failing this, the assessment report warned that the 'current care arrangement is likely to break down and [Ms Ireneschild] will require an extensive package due to high care need. However, it is recognised that this is Housing's decision.' The Housing Grants, Construction and Regeneration Act 1996 provides for Disabled Facilities Grants which fund the adaptation of dwellings occupied by people who have a disability, as outlined in the box below.

 Background information

Disabled Facilities Grants

Social workers from Adult Social Services or Children's Services conducting assessments are required to explore and identify the housing needs of vulnerable individuals and families. This includes recognising when adaptations to a home might improve the quality of life for a child or adult with a disability. Disabled Facilities Grants are allocated and administered by the Housing Department of local authorities. Social Services do not have decision-making powers in relation to Disabled Facilities Grants, but can make a referral to the Local Housing Authority requesting it to carry out an assessment into a disabled person's housing needs.

Social Services may also provide information to the Local Housing Authority in order to support the application for a Disabled Facilities Grant. The grant is available to fund adaptations to the homes of owner occupiers and public, voluntary or private tenants who have a disability as defined by s.29 of the National Assistance Act 1948. That is to say, 'persons aged eighteen or over who are blind, deaf or dumb or who suffer from mental disorder of any description and other persons aged eighteen or over who are substantially and permanently handicapped by illness, injury or congenital deformity'.

According to s.23 of the Housing Grants, Construction and Regeneration Act 1996, Disabled Facilities Grants are available for the following purposes:

- Facilitate access to the dwelling
- Make the dwelling safe
- Facilitate access within the dwelling
- Improve access to basic facilities such as kitchen and bathroom
- Improve the heating system of the dwelling
- Enable better access to power source for lighting, heating, etc.
- Ease movement around the dwelling

Still no action was taken by the local authority and only after further letters from Ms Ireneschild's solicitor in June 2006 did Mr Rogerson complete a second occupational therapist's report. This cited the high risk of Ms Ireneschild falling on the stairs and the risk posed to the health of her informal carers when carrying her up and down stairs. Mr Rogerson assessed the risk to the claimant's independence across a wide range of needs as being *substantial*. However, the High Court judge described this report as being 'short on text and analysis'. This was most significant because under the *Fair Access to Care Services* both *critical* and *substantial* needs were treated as eligible needs by Lambeth London Borough Council. Therefore, if Mr Rogerson's assessment were accepted by the local authority, it would be legally obliged to meet Ms Ireneschild's housing needs. Instead of acting on Mr Rogerson's assessment in July 2006 the Council's Housing Department asked Ms Thorpe, a principal medical housing advisor, to assess Ms Ireneschild's housing needs.

Ms Thorpe visited the claimant at her flat and conducted a thorough assessment of her housing needs. She produced a detailed six-page document which included consideration of all the other reports concerning Ms Ireneschild's accommodation. Ms Thorpe's housing assessment revealed that the claimant had last fallen eight years previously and did not in fact have a history of falls. Regarding the risk of falls and the need for transfer to more suitable accommodation, Ms Thorpe found that to an extent Ms Ireneschild was making choices which put her at greater risk of falls. Ms Thorpe concluded in her report that:

> Ms Ireneschild may require additional assistance with her mobility when she is tired but I also note that she is most likely to be tired when she has stayed up all night 'clubbing'. I would suggest this is a life style choice that Ms Ireneschild makes for herself . . . In recognition that a property with stairs is far from ideal for a person with limited mobility, I have awarded the maximum number of medical points for transfer to a more suitable property, i.e. 25 points. This case does not fit the criteria for an emergency transfer on medical grounds.

This excerpt from Ms Thorpe's report refers to the housing allocation scheme operated by local authorities across England and Wales to ration social housing. This is accommodation available for rent generally below market rents to vulnerable adults and families who are homeless or threatened with homelessness, which includes those living in unsuitable accommodation. Ms Ireneschild's contention was that she was living in unsuitable accommodation which prevented her from mobilising safely in her flat. However, Ms Thorpe used her report to argue that the risk of falls due to mobility difficulties in the flat was a consequence of Ms Ireneschild's lifestyle choices rather than inherent to aspects of the flat layout. It was for this reason that Ms Thorpe would not classify her as a medical emergency. The housing allocation scheme is explained in the box on the next page.

According to the Lambeth Housing Allocation Scheme, Ms Ireneschild could only have been classed as an emergency on medical grounds had she been diagnosed with 'a currently life-threatening illness or disability, whose housing circumstances are, in the opinion of the Medical Advisor, affecting their health very severely'. Plainly, Ms Ireneschild did not fall within this very stringent criterion for an emergency transfer to another property, a fact not disputed by the parties to the Court of Appeal case. The effect of Ms Thorpe's housing assessment was to give Ms Ireneschild additional points for transfer to ground-floor or first-floor accommodation accessible by a lift under the Council's Housing Allocation Scheme. However, because Lambeth Council, in common with local authorities across England and Wales, had far more people applying for social housing than was available, this simply meant that Ms Ireneschild would move up a few places on an already exceedingly long waiting list.

The housing points system

In order to create a fair and transparent approach to the allocation of social housing, local authorities have designed a points system. Under this system the Housing Authority awards individuals and households a number of points depending on their circumstances. For example points can be awarded for:

- Shared accommodation/lodger points
- Lack of facilities
- Overcrowding/lack of bedrooms
- Families who live apart
- Children in one-bedroom flats
- Medical need
- Social need
- Condition of property
- Homelessness waiting points

The greater the number of points accumulated by an applicant for social housing the higher the priority he or she is given on the local authority's housing waiting list. As an applicant for social housing may be adversely affected by a number of the circumstances bullet-pointed above, he or she will be awarded points for each of these circumstances, resulting in accumulated points. The award of points for time spent waiting also means that those waiting the longest receive an increase in priority over time.

Due to shortfalls in social housing caused by the Right-to-Buy Scheme, low levels of build in the social housing sector and the growing demand for social housing there is a chronic shortage of available housing. This means that, in practice, even individuals or households who fall into priority housing categories and are high up the housing waiting list may be waiting for months or several years in temporary accommodation awaiting the allocation of social housing.

To summarise, there was plainly a consensus among professionals who assessed Ms Ireneschild that her accommodation was unsuitable. There was a difference of opinion as to the level of risk the stairs posed to Ms Ireneschild and, consequently, there was disagreement as to the urgency of moving her to a more suitable dwelling. In addition there was variance in the thoroughness of the assessments and the degree of specialism and expertise among those who carried them out. Added to this was the fact that Ms Ireneschild could not obtain a swift transfer to more suitable accommodation under the provisions of the Housing Act 1996 because her circumstances did not amount to an 'emergency'. Of course Ms Ireneschild's circumstances are far from unusual. Invariably social workers acting as care managers or indeed working with children who have a disabled parent are likely to be confronted by similar housing issues.

Many people with disabilities find themselves in unsuitable accommodation designed for people from the majority able-bodied population. The use of grants to carry out adaptations, or ultimately a move to an alternative dwelling, are key ways in which the needs of people with disabilities can be met. The high demand placed on the limited supply of social housing makes it particularly difficult for people with disabilities to move to suitable accommodation. This can mean people with mobility problems living at risk of falls in unsuitable premises over a number of years. Precisely for this reason it is crucial to obtain a detailed and thorough assessment of a user's housing needs. As in the case of Ms Ireneschild, such an assessment needs to have regard to: any parenting responsibilities; issues relating to employment, education or training; risks of further impairment to health and lifestyle choices.

Status of specialist assessments

Unable to obtain transfer to more suitable accommodation in the near future under the Housing Act 1996, Ms Ireneschild now turned to the provisions contained in s.21(1) of the National Assistance Act 1948, which are detailed in the box below.

Key legislation

National Assistance Act 1948

21(1) . . . a local authority may with the approval of the Secretary of State, and to such extent as he may direct shall, make arrangements for providing:

    (a) residential accommodation for persons aged eighteen or over who by reason of age, illness, disability or any other circumstances are in need of care and attention which is not otherwise available to them . . .

Services cannot be provided under the National Assistance Act 1948 until such times as a community care assessment under s.47 of the NHS and Community Care Act 1990 is completed. This task fell to Ms Williams, the social worker who was assigned to conduct a community care assessment at a point in time when Ms Ireneschild had already commenced proceedings for a judicial review of the local authority's failure to move her to ground-floor accommodation. Paragraph 40 of *Fair Access to Care Services* emphasises that an assessment of needs must include a person's: physical and mental health; housing requirements; lifestyle; needs of carers; and any risks posed by the environment.

A Comprehensive Assessment by its very nature encompasses much more that just an individual's housing needs. Drawing together the risks posed to Ms Ireneschild's physical and psychological well-being, activities of daily living and support from carers, she was assessed as falling into the *substantial* category under the *Fair Access to Care Services* policy guidance. In other words, Ms Ireneschild was assessed as having eligible needs. The care plan provided for these needs to be met through support services and not a change of accommodation. In coming to this conclusion Ms Williams relied on the findings of Ms Thorpe, the principal medical housing advisor, rather than those in the report of Mr Rogerson, the occupational therapist. The effect of this was that Ms Williams assessed there being a low risk of falls within Ms Ireneschild's accommodation because, as Ms Thorpe had concluded, there was in fact no history of falls. This meant that Ms Ireneschild did not have *substantial* housing needs.

In order to address the fact that Ms Ireneschild was likely to remain in her current accommodation for quite a long period of time, the care plan proposed 'a need for modest support in her home in order to maintain her independence and ability to function well in her current accommodation'. Rather than being assessed as requiring the provision of residential accommodation under s.21 of the National Assistance Act 1948, Ms Ireneschild was in effect being offered a variety of support services under s.2 of the Chronically Sick and

Disabled Persons Act 1970. Thus Social Services, while explicitly acknowledging there was a housing problem, placed this firmly within the remit of the local authority Housing Department to act upon under the Housing Act 1996. Of course the Housing Department had already acted on this very issue by allocating Ms Ireneschild the maximum number of waiting list points for a non-emergency medical problem.

Mr Drabble, the barrister acting for Ms Ireneschild, argued that under the Wednesbury principles Ms Williams as an employee of a public body had failed to take into consideration relevant facts, namely Mr Rogerson's report, in reaching her decision. Of course Mr Rogerson's report referred to a history of falls and attributed the risk directly to Ms Ireneschild's housing. Direct incorporation of Mr Rogerson's report into the Comprehensive Assessment would most likely have resulted in Ms Ireneschild's housing needs being identified as *substantial*, thus making them eligible needs for the purposes of s.21(1) of the National Assistance Act 1948. This would in turn have qualified her for more suitable accommodation under that section. It was for this reason that the key point of dispute between the parties to the court case was the decision of Ms Williams to rely on Ms Thorpe's report rather than Mr Rogerson's. The question before the court was whether Ms Williams had acted unreasonably in excluding the findings of Mr Rogerson's report from the Comprehensive Assessment.

Presiding in the Court of Appeal case, Lord Justice Hallett reminded the parties that the local authority was entitled to commission whatever reports it wanted and from whomsoever it wanted as long as these decisions were reasonable and not perverse. Mr Drabble contended that the decision of the local authority to first commission an occupational therapist's report from Mr Rogerson and then to subsequently ignore it in completing the Comprehensive Assessment was indeed 'perverse' and no reasonable authority would have acted in this manner. In the opinion of Lord Justice Hallett a reading of the Comprehensive Assessment revealed that Mr Rogerson's report had been considered. However, it was also clear to the judge that Ms Williams, the social worker, had preferred the analysis and findings of Ms Thorpe's report regarding the risks of falls posed to Ms Ireneschild's over that of the occupational therapist's. Given that Ms Thorpe had produced a far more detailed report than Mr Rogerson, which revealed that Ms Ireneschild did not have a history of falls, reliance on Ms Thorpe's report was entirely reasonable. In short, Ms Williams as the social worker responsible for the community care assessment exercised her professional judgement in deciding which elements of which specialist reports to incorporate into the final Comprehensive Assessment. As long as she did not act irrationally in doing so, she was perfectly entitled to exercise this degree of professional judgement.

When acting as care managers, social workers are responsible for commissioning specialist reports and incorporating them into community care plans. In this instance Ms Williams correctly paid attention to all the reports she had received relating to the user, but gave greater weight to a report which was more thoroughly detailed and presented more substantial evidence for its conclusions. Social workers responsible for assessment, care planning and the coordination of service inputs are not automatons who simply accept what is put in front of them. Practitioners are required to exercise professional judgement in collating the information they obtain to develop a cost-effective care package.

Partnership with users

Having found his initial line of argument effectively rebutted by the appellant local authority, Mr Drabble now turned to the issue of procedural unfairness. Ms Ireneschild objected to several assertions made by Ms Thorpe in her report. Of course this was the very report which the social worker, Ms Williams, largely relied upon when assessing Ms Ireneschild's housing needs within the wider context of a community care assessment. In particular, Ms Ireneschild took issue with Ms Thorpe's finding that she had no history of falls and that she only needed assistance on the stairs after going out 'clubbing'. The legal position adopted by Mr Drabble was that Ms Ireneschild should have been informed of the findings of Ms Thorpe's report before the social worker relied on these and integrated them into the community care assessment. For it was this assessment which concluded that Ms Ireneschild had no eligible housing needs. In other words, here was a situation in which the service-user disagreed with the findings of a professional, and yet those findings had not been disclosed to her prior to their incorporation into a community care assessment. Ms Ireneschild had not been given the opportunity to correct or challenge statements made about her, which she believed to be inaccurate.

In raising this issue Mr Drabble, the respondent's barrister, relied on precedent in *R (on the application of Begum)* v. *Tower Hamlets London Borough Council* [2002] EWHC 633 (Admin) [2003] HLR 8 in which at paragraph 34 Justice Burnton ruled:

> when enquiries of third persons yield significant information inconsistent with that provided by the applicant, which will substantially affect the decision of the local authority, the local authority must put that information to the applicant and give him an opportunity to comment on it. In my judgement a local authority is under such a duty. It is supported by the principles of fairness and principles of good administration.

Mr Béar, the barrister acting for the local authority, countered Mr Drabble's line of reasoning by claiming that the information used by Ms Thorpe was not from a third person and was derived directly from her conversations with the service-user. It merely reflected what Ms Ireneschild had told her. In effect this left Ms Ireneschild taking issue with her own account of her care needs. Lord Justice Hallett agreed with Mr Béar, conceding that Ms Thorpe's report was not essentially an account by a third party. Conversely, had Ms Thorpe relied instead on, say, the account of one of Ms Ireneschild's son's, then this would have brought the matter within the scope of the ruling in *R (on the application of Begum)* v. *Tower Hamlets London Borough Council*. As it was Lord Justice Hallett distinguished the facts in the present case from those in *R* v. *Tower Hamlets*, making this precedent inapplicable.

Social workers, regardless of their area of practice, are in the position of gathering information about people. This may be obtained directly from parents, children, users and carers or information may be derived from discussions with third parties who know the person which whom the social worker is directly concerned. Paragraph 3.8 of the GSCC Code obliges social workers to recognise and use 'responsibly the power that comes from your work with service users and carers'. An important source of this power is the selection of information and its incorporation into assessments and care planning. This is not a neutral activity. As Ms Williams' approach to a community care assessment demonstrates, a social worker can have significant authority in deciding what information to give weight to. The Data Protection Act 1998 grants users who are also 'data subjects' under this statute a number of rights regarding the accuracy of the information which is held on them. As the precedent in *R* v. *Tower Hamlets* makes clear, professionals gathering information from third parties should double check its reliability with the person who is the subject of it. Inconsistencies between the perspectives of users or carers and third persons should be highlighted in the write-up of any subsequent assessment.

Judgement in *R (on the application of Ireneschild)* v. *Lambeth London Borough Council*

After hearing evidence, the Court of Appeal decided that there were no grounds for concluding that the local authority had acted irrationally or unreasonably in its reliance on specialist reports in conducting a community care assessment. Consequently, the Court of Appeal overturned the ruling of the High Court which meant that there was no maladministration by Social Services.

 Critical questions

1 Do you think that Ms Williams as the social worker involved dealt correctly with the issue of lifestyle and risk of falls in her assessment? If so why, if not, how do you think the assessment of Ms Ireneschild should have been approached in relation to her lifestyle choices?

2 This court case raised issues surrounding the use of information provided by a user to a professional and provided by third parties to a professional about a user. The ruling concluded that when obtaining vital information from a third party the user should be permitted to see this information and comment on it. But, the court ruled that this was not necessary if the user had supplied the information directly to a professional. Do you think the court was correct to differentiate between these two types of situation? What scope might there be for a practitioner with direct contact with a user to misreport that user through selective use of the information provided in an interview? What do you think best practice is in this situation?

3 Return to Chapter 1 and read the details provided on the Data Protection Act 1998. How would you apply your understanding of the Data Protection Act 1998 to collecting, handling and reproducing information provided by a carer (who is a third party) and a user in a Comprehensive Assessment?

CASE 4

R (on the application of Khana) v. *Southwark London Borough Council* [2001] EWCA Civ 999

Importance of the case

It explores issues of culture in relation to user and carer needs. The case considers the implications of immigration status and entitlement to welfare benefits and community services. The entitlement of carers to assistance is also discussed.

History of the case

The claimants, a married couple, originally applied to the Queen's Bench Division of the High Court for a judicial review of the decision by Southwark London Borough Council to offer the claimants residential care places rather than support to live in the community. The High Court upheld the local authority's decision and one of the claimants then appealed through the Official Solicitor against this judgement to the Court of Appeal.

Facts of the case

Mr Karim aged 71 years and Mrs Khana aged 91 years, who had been married to each other for over 40 years, arrived in the United Kingdom in 1998. Both were Kurds who had been born and brought up in Iraq. They were given leave to enter Britain on condition that they would be supported by their sponsors and have no recourse to public funds. But by September 1999 the couple's sponsors, who were their grandson and their granddaughter's husband, had ceased to support them. This meant that neither Mr Karim, nor Mrs Khana were eligible for either income support or housing benefit. However, they were still entitled to care provision under the National Assistance Act 1948. The couple occupied the sitting room of a second-floor one-bedroom flat which belonged to their daughter Ms Kazal, who slept in the bedroom. Mrs Khana had been diagnosed with paranoid schizophrenia and had sight and hearing impairments. She also suffered from arthritis as a result of which she needed assistance with many personal care tasks. Mrs Khana was found to be mentally unable to manage her own affairs. Mr Karim was his wife's primary carer. He was supported in this role by Ms Kazal, the couple's daughter, who lived with them in the flat, and also by Nazanin, the couple's granddaughter, who visited her grandparents regularly at the flat. Mrs Khana was effectively housebound and the flat was overcrowded and not appropriate to her needs. Mrs Khana frequently experienced hallucinations at night which caused her considerable distress and resulted in others being kept awake through the night. Neither Mrs Khana nor Mr Karim spoke English. Mr Wilson, a social worker, assessed Mrs Khana's care needs and proposed a residential care placement to meet these in January 2000. Mr Karim refused the residential placement and requested assistance to move to appropriate accommodation where he could continue as his wife's primary carer. However, Mr Karim complained of back pain caused by lifting his wife, and Mr O'Meara, an independent social worker, subsequently assessed Mr Karim in April 2000 as being at risk of injury if he continued to provide physical care to his wife. Mr O'Meara recommended that the couple be rehoused as part of Mrs Karim's care plan. In a revised decision in May 2000 Southwark London Borough Council offered a residential placement to both Mr Karim and Mrs Khana to enable them to continue living together as a couple. On refusal of this offer the Council stated that it was prepared to offer personal care assistance to Mrs Khana in the flat, but considered that this would not properly meet her needs. In August 2000 an action was commenced by the claimants for a judicial review of the Council's decision. The High Court found that a care plan which offered joint residential accommodation to the couple was the 'only reasonable option' and that the decision of Mr Karim to decline it was 'objectively unreasonable'. Therefore the High Court found in favour of Southwark London Borough Council and against the claimants. It was this ruling which Mrs Khana acting through the Official Solicitor sought to challenge through an appeal to the Court of Appeal.

Key people in the case

Mrs Khana – claimant and appellant acting through the Official Solicitor
Mr Karim – claimant's husband
Ms Kazal – daughter of claimant
Nazanin – granddaughter of claimant
Mr Wilson – social worker employed by Council
Mr O'Meara – independent social worker
Dr Evans – general practitioner
Dr Jefferys – psychiatrist
Mr Drabble – barrister for the appellant
Mr Harrop-Griffiths – barrister for the respondent local authority

Discussion of the case

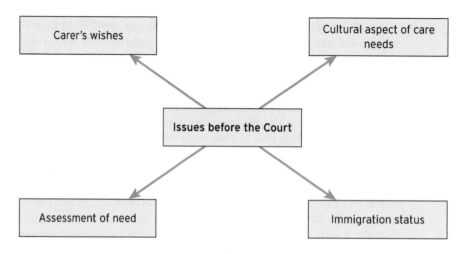

Immigration status

Legislation enacted since the 1990s and changes to immigration rules have progressively removed welfare entitlements from asylum seekers and other non-UK nationals subject to immigration controls. As a result different immigration statuses now attract different entitlements to social care, healthcare, social housing and means-tested benefits. The table below sets out the most common immigration statuses and the welfare entitlements associated with each one.

Immigration status	Restrictions	Welfare entitlements
Citizen of a Member State of the European Union	Citizens of EU Member States have free movement and are not subject to immigration control	• Generally similar entitlements as British citizens, but nationals of States which joined the EU after 2004 have limited welfare rights during their first year of residence in the UK
Refugee	Asylum seekers granted asylum gain refugee status and are normally granted *indefinite leave to remain* free from immigration controls	• Same entitlements as British citizens • A refugee applying for social housing is treated as resident in the local authority area to which he or she was dispersed on first arrival in the UK
Adult asylum seeker	Those awaiting outcome of their application for asylum are subject to strict immigration controls	• Accommodated and financially supported by NAM (New Asylum Model, formerly NASS or National Asylum Support Service) • No entitlement to accommodation by local authority except as a consequence of disability or illness • No entitlement to benefit payments • Entitled to necessary medical treatment

(Continued)

Immigration status	Restrictions	Welfare entitlements
Failed asylum seeker	No right to remain in the United Kingdom and therefore likely to be deported	• No entitlement to accommodation or financial support by NAM (formerly NASS) • No entitlement to welfare benefits • No entitlement to accommodation or support by local authority unless ill or disabled • No entitlement to social care on the grounds of destitution alone • Entitlement to necessary medical treatment
Accompanied minor seeking asylum	Children who are dependents of adults seeking asylum in the UK are treated according to the immigration status of their primary carers	• Fewer entitlements than British children and normally *do not* fall under the Children Act 1989 • Exceptionally if child is disabled then will be treated as 'child in need' under s.17 of Children Act 1989 • Responsibility of NAM (formerly NASS) • Entitled to education and healthcare • local authority can accommodate failed asylum seekers' children under s.20 of Children Act 1989 if they become destitute and are unable to look after their children
Unaccompanied minor seeking asylum	Children arriving in the UK alone are normally granted temporary leave to remain until they are 18 years old	• Treated as 'child in need' with the same entitlements as British children until they are 18 years of age • Children's Services are responsible for their welfare under the Children Act 1989
Overseas spouse or civil partner of people *settled* in the UK	Subject to *entry clearance* for initial two-year probationary period after which foreign spouse may apply for *indefinite leave to remain*	• Overseas spouse or civil partner with *limited leave to remain* are not entitled to means-tested benefits • Entitled to necessary healthcare treatment • Foreign spouses or civil partners obtaining *indefinite leave to remain* after initial probationary period have similar entitlements to British citizens
Overseas dependent adult relatives of people *settled* in the UK	*Entry clearance* is normally for *indefinite leave to remain*	• Prohibited from claiming means-tested benefits for five years from date of entry • Not entitled to accommodation or support from local authority during first five years in UK unless ill or disabled • Entitlement to healthcare

In order for a non-UK national living in Britain to be able to bring their foreign spouse or adult dependant to live with them he or she must be *settled* in the United Kingdom. This means that the person is not subject to any immigration restrictions and is *ordinarily resident* in the UK. In *Shah* v. *Barnet London Borough Council* [1983] 1 All ER 226 p. 236, Lord Scarman interpreted 'ordinarily resident' as meaning that a person 'can show a regular, habitual mode of life in a particular place, the continuity of which has persisted despite temporary absences'. In the present Court of Appeal case Mr Karim's and Mrs Khana's grandson and the husband of their granddaughter were ordinarily resident in the United Kingdom. They were also willing to act as sponsors for the couple, which meant agreeing to provide their accommodation and meet all their living expenses. Under immigration rules Mr Karim and Mrs Khana also had to meet a number of conditions in order to obtain *indefinite leave to remain* in the United Kingdom, which are set out in the box below.

Key guidance

Immigration Rules for Overseas Adult Relatives

Adults other than a spouse or civil partner are only permitted to enter and remain in the United Kingdom if they fulfil *all* of the following three conditions:

1 The dependent adult must fall within one of the following categories:
   (a) Widowed parents or grandparents aged 65 years or over
   (b) Parents or grandparents travelling together at least one of which is over 65 years
   (c) Parent or grandparent under the age of 65 years *or* a son, daughter, sister, brother uncle or aunt over 18 years living alone in exceptional circumstances

2 Overseas adult relatives must show that they are mainly dependent on the sponsor or relatives settled in the United Kingdom

3 Overseas adult relatives must demonstrate that they have no close relatives to turn to for support or assistance in their country of origin

Mr Karim and Mrs Khana were Iraqi Kurds who were both aged over 65 years, were unable to obtain support from close relatives in Iraq, and had a UK sponsor willing to meet their day-to-day needs. This meant that the couple met all three of the conditions required by immigration rules for *indefinite leave to remain* in the United Kingdom. However, it also meant that once Mr Karim and Mrs Khana entered the United Kingdom they were entirely dependent on their grandson and their granddaughter's husband to provide them with accommodation and meet their expenses. For a period of five years from the date of entry by law they were debarred from availing of social housing or receiving non-contributory benefits. Unfortunately for Mr Karim and Mrs Khana approximately a year after they first entered the United Kingdom both their grandson and the husband of their granddaughter ceased to provide support for their accommodation or living expenses. Since neither Mr Karim nor Mrs Khana were entitled to social housing or Income Support, Housing Benefit or any other non-contributory welfare benefit this left them effectively dependent on the goodwill of other relatives. In the circumstances Ms Kazal, the couple's daughter agreed that they could reside in her one-bedroom flat, but this plainly resulted in Mr Karim and Mrs Khana having to share overcrowded accommodation.

Mr Karim and Mrs Khana, although given *indefinite leave to remain* had been in the United Kingdom for less than five years and consequently were still subject to immigration control. This meant that their entitlement to social care services was restricted by s.116 of the Immigration and Asylum Act 1999 which inserted a new section into the National Assistance Act 1948 set out in the box below. The new s.21(1A) inserted into the National Assistance Act 1948 prohibits local authorities from providing accommodation to failed asylum seekers or those subject to immigration control because they are homeless and destitute or due to social care needs arising from that state of affairs. Consequently, a local authority cannot provide any form of residential care for people experiencing physical or mental health problems purely related to their destitution.

Key legislation

National Assistance Act 1948

21(1) . . . a local authority may with the approval of the Secretary of State, and to such extent as he may direct shall, make arrangements for providing:

   (b) residential accommodation for persons aged eighteen or over who by reason of age, illness, disability or any other circumstances are in need of care and attention which is not otherwise available to them . . .

s.21 (1A) A person to whom section 115 of the Immigration and Asylum Act 1999 (exclusion from benefits) applies may not be provided with residential accommodation under subsection 1(a) if this need for care and attention has arisen solely –

   (a) because he is destitute; or,

   (b) because of the physical effects, or anticipated effects, of his being destitute.

29(1) A local authority may, with the approval of the Secretary of State, and to such extent as he may direct in relation to persons ordinarily resident in the area of the local authority shall make arrangements for promoting the welfare of persons to whom this section applies, that is to say persons aged eighteen or over who are blind, deaf or dumb or who suffer from mental disorder of any description and other persons aged eighteen or over who are substantially and permanently handicapped by illness, injury or congenital deformity or such other disabilities as may be prescribed by the Minister.

Mrs Khana was having to live with her daughter and husband in overcrowded accommodation as a result of being ineligible for any form of social housing. However, her mental health problems, though undoubtedly exacerbated by the overcrowded accommodation, were not caused by it. Mrs Khana had been diagnosed as having paranoid schizophrenia. Furthermore, she had sight and hearing impairments and suffered from arthritis which was sufficiently severe for her to require assistance with most personal care tasks. Therefore the physical and mental health problems experienced by Mrs Khana could not be attributed to her deprivation as a result of losing the sponsorship of her grandson and granddaughter's husband and of being unable to access social housing or any welfare benefits. This meant in effect that Mrs Khana was not excluded from assistance by the local authority due to her immigration status. In fact the local authority had a duty to her under s.21 and s.29 of the National Assistance Act 1948 if an assessment of need showed her to require either domiciliary services or residential care.

Social workers, whether as care managers or in their capacity as Approved Mental Health Professionals or named social workers for children, intervene with people from diverse cultural backgrounds. A proportion of the families and individuals with whom social workers come into contact will be migrants from the European Union or from countries beyond its borders. People will have come to the United Kingdom under a range of different circumstances, some on work permits, some as asylum seekers and others as the spouses, partners, children or relatives of those already resident in Britain. A person's country of origin, their period of residency in the United Kingdom and the circumstances under which he or she was permitted to enter Britain will all affect the welfare entitlements of that individual. For this reason it is crucial that social workers are not only aware of a person's immigration status, but of the implications of that status on their rights to welfare benefits, medical treatment and social care in the United Kingdom.

Assessment of need

Neither in the High Court nor in the subsequent hearing before the Court of Appeal was it disputed that Southwark Borough Council owed duties to Mrs Khana under s.21 and s.29 of the National Assistance Act 1948. Instead the dispute between the parties centred on the care package which Southwark Borough Council actually offered Mrs Khana. In January 2000 Mr Wilson, a social worker employed by the local authority, assessed Mrs Khana as requiring support from one person with all personal care activities, all transfers, getting to a standing position and walking short distances. According to his assessment she also needed 'full support with all activities of daily living including maintaining a clean, safe environment, getting help in an emergency, shopping, meal and drink preparation, encouragement and support to eat and drink'. Mr Wilson concluded that in fact Mrs Khana required 24-hour supervision. This he determined could only effectively be provided in a residential care home. The local authority duly offered Mrs Khana a residential placement. This would result in Mrs Khana being admitted to a care home while Mr Karim remained living in the one-bedroom flat with their daughter. Such a care package had the effect of splitting up and separating an elderly married couple. Mr Karim, who was both Mrs Khana's husband and her primary carer, rejected the care plan proposed by Social Services.

Mr Drabble, the barrister representing her, argued that the Council had acted unlawfully because it failed to take account of Mrs Khana's wishes in formulating the care package. In other words, Mr Drabble was alleging that the local authority had failed to take into consideration relevant facts which it was legally obliged to when making its decision. Department of Health (1990: para.3.18) *Community Care in the Next Decade and Beyond: Policy Guidance* makes clear that users and carers must be enabled 'to exercise genuine choice and participate in the assessment of their care needs and in the making of arrangements for meeting those needs'. This is in addition to the requirements set out in paragraph 3.5 which highlight the importance of offering users and carers 'a range of options' and responding 'flexibly and sensitively' to their needs. This accords closely with the GSCC *Code of Practice for Social Care Workers* which in paragraph 1.2 urges social workers to promote 'the individual views and wishes of both service users and carers'.

Another social worker, Mr O'Meara, was engaged by the family to conduct an independent assessment of Mrs Khana's care needs. He concluded that the overcrowded conditions of the flat were likely to have 'a serious detrimental impact on the emotional and mental health of Mrs Khana as well as her physical well-being'. Mr O'Meara also stated in his assessment 'that it would be utterly inappropriate as well as highly detrimental for Mrs Khana to be placed in residential care . . . it would be completely against the expressed wishes of herself and her husband as well as her wider family'. Mr O'Meara concluded his assessment by asserting that Mrs Khana's needs would best be met by the provision of an adapted ground-floor two-bedroom flat alongside domiciliary services. As the court recognised, Mr O'Meara's proposed care package was advanced as an alternative to the offer of a residential care placement for Mrs Khana alone. Dr Evans, a GP, also wrote a letter to Southwark Borough Council in support of Mrs Khana 'being re-housed in the community, in more suitable accommodation'.

On receiving the opinions of Mr O'Meara and Dr Evans, Southwark Borough Council revised the original care package and sent a further letter to the couple in May 2000. This letter reiterated that 'the only way in which Mrs Khana's needs can properly be met is for her to go into a full-time residential home'. It highlighted the physical toll and the risk of injury which Mr Karim's care of his wife posed. The letter concluded that due to the high care needs of Mrs Khana and the health risks posed to Mr Karim as her primary carer that even a move to a ground-floor flat would not properly meet Mrs Khana's identified eligible care needs. However, recognising that the offer of only a residential placement for Mrs Khana would in effect separate her from her husband, Southwark Borough Council now proposed to offer both husband and wife places in a residential home so that they could remain together. The Council also identified a potential residential unit within 200 yards of Ms Kazal's flat, thus enabling her to continue to make regular visits to her parents were they to accept the local authority's offer of residential care.

The letter to Mr Karim and Mrs Khana amending the original care plan went on to state that if they were resolutely against moving into a residential home, Southwark Borough Council would be willing to provide some personal care to support Mrs Khana in the flat. Towards the end of the same letter, the Council added in relation to the offer of personal care assistance that 'it considers that this is not an appropriate response as it would not provide the care and level of support that Mrs Khana needs; it is the view of the local authority that only residential care can provide this'. The assessments of need completed by Mr Wilson and Mr O'Meara, the letter written by Dr Evans, and the correspondence between Southwark Borough Council and the couple revising the original care package were all presented in evidence before the Court of Appeal. So, too, was a further letter from Dr Evans written in October 2000, when she had been made aware of the offer of residential placements for Mrs Khana together with her husband. Despite the offer by Southwark Borough Council of a dual residential placement, the family still refused to accept the prospect of Mr Karim and Mrs Khana going into residential care, partly for cultural reasons.

It is not unusual for care managers to be confronted by users or carers who disagree either with their assessment or with the care plan based upon it. In this case social workers at Southwark Borough Council had recognised the magnitude of distress which would be caused to both Mr Karim and Mrs Khana if after 40 years of marriage they were to be accommodated separately. The offer to provide a residential placement to the couple rather than just for Mrs Khana was a sincere endeavour to work in partnership with the family and promote the wish of the couple to remain together. This is consistent both with Department of Health (1990) and the GSCC *Code of Practice for Social Care Workers*. Unfortunately it was an attempt at compromise and accommodation over the community care plan which the family rejected.

Cultural aspects of care needs

Mr Karim and Mrs Khana were Iraqi Kurds and, apart from a few years in the United Kingdom, had lived all their lives in Iraq. Both of them were practising Muslims. Neither of them spoke English, although Mr Karim had a little basic English vocabulary. At the time of the Court of Appeal case they were living with their daughter and received frequent visits from their granddaughter. But as Kurdish speakers the couple were relatively isolated from the British neighbours among whom they lived. Social workers are of course required to respect 'diversity and different cultures and values' by paragraph 1.6 of the GSCC *Code of Practice for Social Care Workers*. Policy and practice guidance relating to care in the community convey the practical implications of this for day-to-day practice. Department of Health (1990: para. 3.21) *Community Care in the Next Decade and Beyond* recognises the communication needs of people who have a learning difficulty or physical disability or for whom English is not their first language, and requires local authorities to, 'ensure that assessment is accessible to people from black and minority ethnic backgrounds'.

Policy guidance also brings to the attention of social workers and other professionals issues which go beyond language barriers. Department of Health (1990: para. 3.22) acknowledges that 'because of their cultural background, some users may need services of a special type or kind; service geared to the requirements of the majority may not always be appropriate'. An older person's ethnic and cultural background is an explicit consideration in the Department of Health (2001e) *National Service Framework for Older People* which sets out standards for service provision to this user group. These standards must be adhered to by those responsible for commissioning, managing or delivering health and social services to older people. There are eight standards which comprise the *National Service Framework for Older People*. These are set out in the box below.

 Key guidance

National Service Framework for Older People

Standard 1: Rooting out age discrimination – NHS services will be provided, regardless of age, on the basis of clinical needs alone. Social care services will not use age in their eligibility criteria or policies, to restrict access to available services.

Standard 2: Person-centred care – NHS and social care services treat older people as individuals and enable them to make choices about their own care. This is achieved through the single assessment process, integrated commissioning arrangements and integrated provision of services, including community equipment and continence services.

Standard 3: Intermediate care – Older people will have access to a new range of intermediate care services at home or in designated care settings, to promote their independence by providing enhanced services from the NHS and councils to prevent unnecessary hospital admission and effective rehabilitation services to enable early discharge from hospital and to prevent premature or unnecessary admission to long-term residential care.

Standard 4: General hospital care – Older people's care in hospital is delivered through appropriate specialist care and by hospital staff who have the right set of skills to meet their needs.

Standard 5: Stroke – The NHS will take action to prevent strokes, working in partnership with other agencies where appropriate.

Standard 6: Falls – The NHS, working in partnership with councils, takes action to prevent falls and reduce resultant fractures or other injuries in their populations of older people.

Standard 7: Mental health in older people – Older people who have mental health problems have access to integrated mental health services, provided by the NHS and councils to ensure effective diagnosis, treatment and support, for them and for their carers.

Standard 8: The promotion of health and active life in older age – The health and well-being of older people is promoted through a co-ordinated programme of action led by the NHS with support from councils.

Most of the standards in the *National Service Framework for Older People* are directly relevant to Mrs Khana, particularly in relation to her mental health, supporting her to take part in an active life, preventing falls or premature admission to a residential home. Of particular importance to her Kurdish heritage is Standard 2 which requires that:

> Older people and their carers should receive person-centred care and services which respect them as individuals and which are arranged around their needs. Person-centred care requires managers and professionals to:
>
> * Listen to older people
> * Respect their dignity and privacy
> * Recognise individual differences and specific needs including cultural and religious differences
> * Enable older people to make informed choices, involving them in all decisions about their needs and care
> * Provide co-ordinated and integrated service responses
> * Involve and support carers whenever necessary.

Taken altogether the GSCC Code, policy guidance and the relevant National Service Framework oblige social workers to explore the cultural and spiritual aspects of users' daily lives and to develop care plans which accommodate these. On behalf of Mrs Khana, Mr Drabble QC submitted to the court that the local authority in coming to its decision had failed to take account of Mrs Khana's cultural background. A medical report compiled by Dr Jefferys, a psychiatrist commissioned on behalf of Mrs Khana, was presented in evidence. In it Dr Jefferys advocated for a care plan which focussed on rehousing Mrs Khana and her husband in a ground-floor flat, stating that:

> While I welcome Southwark Council's offer to accommodate Mrs Khana and her husband in the same location, there are serious weaknesses in the proposal to place them in a residential home for older people. Southwark does not appear to have access to a home with other Kurdish residents and their proposal would mean that both husband and wife would be socially and linguistically isolated. In addition, other family members are likely to find themselves subject to criticism from the Kurdish community for letting their elderly relatives be moved to 'an institution' outside the Kurdish culture . . . I was told that it would be unacceptable for a single Muslim woman from their culture to live alone in London.

Rebutting this evidence, Mr Harrop-Griffiths, the barrister acting for Southwark London Borough Council, argued that Southwark had been unable to identify a Kurdish-speaking personal care assistant for Mrs Khana. In other words he was claiming that whether the couple were accommodated in a residential home or a flat in the community they would still be 'socially and linguistically isolated'. Secondly, Mr Harrop-Griffiths observed that Ms Kazal the couple's daughter had in fact been living on her own in the flat for some years before being joined by her elderly parents there. This meant that whatever the views of members of her ethnic community, Ms Kazal had lived seemly undisturbed as a single Muslim woman. This plainly undermined the legal argument of Mr Drabble QC who, based on Dr Jefferys' medical report, was trying to convince the court that the move of Mr Karim and Mrs Khana to a residential home would leave Ms Kazal living alone and on the receiving end of vocal disapproval from members of her ethnic community.

Mr Harrop-Griffiths argued that Southwark London Borough Council had assessed Mrs Khana as requiring 24-hour supervision. This could not be provided through domiciliary services to Mrs Khana in her flat on the grounds that it would be prohibitively expensive. As established in *R* v. *Gloucestershire County Council ex parte Barry* (see Case 1) the local authority was lawfully entitled to take cost into account in deciding how to meet the assessed care needs of individuals. In this instance, Southwark London Borough Council had offered to provide 24-hour supervision within the context of a residential care placement. Mindful of separating a married couple, it had gone one step further and offered a second residential place to Mr Karim. Mr Harrop-Griffiths also claimed that Southwark Council had indeed taken account of the wishes of Mrs Khana and her primary carer in developing the care plan. But, according to Mr Harrop-Griffiths, their views amounted to a preference as to how Mrs Khana's care needs should be met. As Department of Health (1990: para. 3.25) *Community Care in the Next Decade and Beyond* makes clear, local authorities are required to implement the 'most cost-effective package of services that meets the user's care needs taking account of the user's and carer's own preference'. In effect the barrister for the local authority was contending that a cost-effective package of care which met both the user's and carer's needs had been offered. However, this had been rejected because it did not meet the needs of user and carer in a way of their choosing.

 Critical commentary

National Service Framework for Older People

The *National Service Framework for Older People* was claimed by the Labour Government to be an evidenced-based 10-year programme of action to ensure an equitable, high quality and integrated approach to health and social services provision for older people. It was designed to promote their health and independence through the development of specialist services for strokes, mental illness and the prevention of falls, all of which disproportionately affect older people. Yet, the *National Service Framework* has been subject to debate among professionals and academics as to whether it has delivered tangible improvement in health and social services for older people (Manthorpe, et al., 2007: 502).

In their nationwide study involving almost 2,000 participants, Manthorpe, et al. (2007) investigated the experiences of older people of health and social services under the *National Service Framework*. They found that few older people had heard of the *National Service Framework* and many thought that its major objectives, such as health promotion, fell within the remit of other public services. Most research participants were unaware of 'intermediate care' provision, which is a central plank of the *Framework*. This is a package of integrated health and social care designed to either forestall hospital admission or to aid independent living after hospital discharge.

Although many older people contributing to the study by Manthorpe, et al. (2007: 504) reported high quality provision, a number complained about poor access to services, hurried or impersonal care and discrimination against older people by professionals. Sometimes this took the form of practitioners assuming that older people were confused or the practitioner deferred to their carer rather than consulting with the user or patient. Analysing the negative and positive views expressed by research participants, Manthorpe, et al. (2007: 504-5) discovered that while most older people experienced faster more efficient services this was frequently at the expense of the quality of provision. For example, a home care package might be put in place quickly, but older people found themselves receiving personal assistance from a number of different care workers rather than a single permanent worker. The fragmentation of health and social care services was another source of lower quality provision for older people (Manthorpe, et al., 2007: 505). Manthorpe and her colleagues concluded that it was difficult to attribute improvements in services directly to the *National Service Framework for Older People* while in some instances changes in health and social care ran directly counter to its directives.

Carer's wishes

On conducting the assessment in January 2000, Mr Wilson, the social worker, stated that 'I am led to conclude that Mr Karim is placing himself and his wife at risk of an accident as there is potential for him to further damage himself and to cause injury to his wife should he drop her while transferring or supporting her to mobilise.' The social worker engaged by the family, Mr O'Meara similarly observed that:

> I am of the firm view that Mr Karim is continuing to place himself at high risk of further damage to his back as he continues to care for and inevitably has to lift and physically support his wife daily. There is also a high risk of [him] having an accident whilst undertaking any of these tasks with a consequent risk of injury to his elderly wife.

Department of Health (1990: para.3.28) *Community Care in the Next Decade and Beyond* states that the 'preferences of carers should be taken into account and their willingness to continue caring should not be assumed'. Subsequent statutes have increased the entitlements of carers. The Carers (Recognition and Services) Act 1995 (as amended) requires practitioners to inform carers of the right to a separate assessment of their needs as carers. The Carers and Disabled Children Act 2000 entitles carers to a needs assessment whether or not the person they care for has agreed to an assessment of needs or to accept services. However, the right to a carer's assessment and services provision for the carer (not the user) is dependent upon the person being cared for being someone for whom the local authority would normally be expected to provide services. The principal provisions of the Carers and Disabled Children Act 2000 are set out in the box below.

Key legislation

Carers and Disabled Children Act 2000

s.1 Provides a free standing right to carers aged 16 years and over who care for a disabled adult if he or she 'provides or intends to provide a substantial amount of care on a regular basis' and 'asks a local authority to carry out an assessment of his ability to provide and to continue to provide care for the person cared for'. Before carrying out the carer's assessment the local authority 'must be satisfied that the person cared for is someone for whom it may provide or arrange for the provision of community care services'.

s.2 Creates a power for local authorities to provide services to carers following an assessment of their needs. Such services can be anything that could 'help the carer care for the person cared for'.

s.3 Enables local authorities to issue vouchers which can be used to obtain respite services.

s.5 Authorises local authorities to provide direct payments to carers based on their carer's assessment.

s.6 Entitles parents of disabled children to a carer's assessment.

The Carers (Equal Opportunities) Act 2004 further enhanced the rights of carers. Section 2 of this statute requires that carers' assessments take account of whether the carer is undertaking or wishes to undertake work, education, training or any leisure activity. This means that a social worker undertaking a carer's assessment is legally obliged to ask what the carer would do if he or she did not have caring responsibilities and what services would enable the carer to achieve a reasonable balance between his or her personal life and caring? In the case before the Court of Appeal, Mr Karim had made clear to both the social workers involved that he wished to continue caring for Mrs Khana. Indeed, he wished her to remain with him in a more suitable flat so that he could continue to provide for her care; though, as noted by Dr Jefferys' in his report, Mr Karim appeared 'to be showing evidence of clinical depression – caused at least in part by his unwillingness to leave his wife alone in the flat for fear of a fall'. Here was a situation in which Mr Karim was providing 'a substantial amount of care on a regular basis', therefore meeting the legal definition of being a carer. Furthermore, providing that care was having a detrimental impact on his own health and in turn undermining his capacity to continue caring for his wife. Such circumstances entitled him to a carer's assessment of his needs and, through this, access to support services in his own right as a carer. Department of Health (2001a: 17–22) *A Practitioner's Guide to Carers' Assessments under the Carers and Disabled Children Act 2000* identifies the elements of a holistic carer's assessment. These are set out in the box below.

Key guidance

A Practitioner's Guide to Carers' Assessments under the Carers and Disabled Children Act 2000

1 Carer's role - how willing or able is the carer to provide care and are there any conflicts between them and the person cared for?

2 Breaks and social life - how often is the carer able to have breaks and pursue other aspects of their social life?

3 Physical well being and personal safety - is the carer in good health and do aspects of their caring role put them at risk?

4 Relationships and mental well being - what impact does the caring role have on the carer's relationships with others and their own mental health?

5 Care of the home - is the carer able to maintain the home?

6 Accommodation - are there any problems arising for the carer from the accommodation in which they care for the user?

7 Finances - are there any difficulties around money?

8 Work - does the carer want to remain in work or return to work?

9 Education and training - does the carer want to develop their skills or are they at risk of having to give up training or education?

10 Current practical and emotional support - who assists the carer and is this sufficient?

11 Wider responsibilities - what other responsibilities does the carer have and are these suffering as a result of their caring role?

12 Future caring role - what factors are likely to affect the ability or willingness of the carer to continue caring into the future?

13 Emergencies/alternative arrangements - what networks does the carer have to assist with caring in an emergency?

14 Access to information and advocacy - does the carer know how to get information?

15 Agreed outcomes - what outcomes does the carer want in terms of their quality of life and the sustainability of caring and are these in conflict with the person being cared for?

16 Complaints and challenges - is the carer aware of the local complaints procedure?

17 Review - when will the assessment be reviewed and by whom?

18 Charging - have any charges for services been assessed and explained to the carer?

Mr Karim was undoubtedly entitled to a carer's assessment which would have given him access to services to relieve some of his caring responsibilities. For example a sitting service (whereby a care worker comes into the home to sit with the user) would have freed Mr Karim to leave the flat and pursue some aspects of his own social life. It transpired during the Court of Appeal hearing that the family had previously refused domiciliary services which relieved Mr Karim of more physically onerous care tasks. At one stage a non-Kurdish care assistant had been provided for one and a half hours each morning to help Mrs Khana. This arrangement had been short lived as Mr Karim and Ms Kazal had decided by October 2000 to refuse the service. The consequence of this state of affairs was that Mrs Khana and Mr Karim were making decisions which placed both of them at risk of a deterioration of their mental and physical health. The GSCC *Code of Practice for Social Care Workers* paragraph 4 states that practitioners 'must respect the rights of service users while seeking to ensure that their behaviour does not harm themselves or other people'. Recognising the right of users and carers to refuse services, despite the increased risk to their own health, can be exceptionally difficult for practitioners committed to reducing risk. The requirements of the Code in relation to risk are clear in these circumstances and are detailed in the box below.

Key guidance

GSCC *Code of Practice for Social Care Workers*

4.1 Recognising that service users have the right to take risks and helping them to identify and manage potential and actual risks to themselves and others.

4.2 Following risk assessment policies and procedures to assess whether the behaviour of service users presents a risk of harm to themselves or others.

4.3 Taking necessary steps to minimise the risks of service users from doing actual or potential harm to themselves or other people.

4.4 Ensuring that relevant colleagues and agencies are informed about the outcomes and implications of risk assessments.

Judgement in *R (on application of Khana) v. Southwark London Borough Council*

Lord Justice Mance, delivering judgement in the Court of Appeal case, concluded that Mrs Khana had a preference to move with her husband and daughter to living in a two-bedroom ground-floor flat as expressed through her representatives. However, according to Lord Justice Mance she did not have a psychological or physical *need* to do so. Furthermore, the judge concluded that Southwark London Borough Council had taken into consideration the beliefs of Mrs Khana, but had correctly decided that a ground-floor flat would still not meet Mrs Khana's care needs for 24-hour supervision. This could only cost-effectively be met in a residential home. Lord Justice Mance ended his judgement by reiterating that 'the local authority is required to assess and meet needs, not to satisfy preferences for, or insistence upon, new accommodation which would meet only some and not all of a person's needs'. According to the Court of Appeal, social workers at Southwark Council had correctly discharged their duty under s.21 and s.29 of the National Assistance Act 1948. The Court of Appeal concluded that it was unreasonable of Mrs Khana through her representatives to refuse the care package offered by Southwark London Borough Council and upheld the verdict of the High Court.

Critical questions

1 In this case Mr Karim refused both domiciliary and residential provision for himself and on behalf of his mentally incapacitated wife. This placed both of them at higher risk of injury and ironically of having to be admitted to a residential placement if either of them suffered a serious accident. There have been a number of high-profile cases in the media of older people refusing social care services and subsequently dying in their home as a result of an accident or neglect. In these instances social workers have been the target of considerable public criticism. As a practitioner striving to abide by the GSCC Code how would you manage these tensions in your work?

2 Policy and practice guidance relating to community care stipulates that cultural factors must be taken into account in assessment and care planning. The new Equality Duty in relation to race and religion also imposes additional duties on local authority employees to eliminate discrimination and promote participation by people from ethnic minority backgrounds. Do you think sufficient consideration was given to cultural issues in this case? If not, how do you think the cultural heritage of Mr Karim and Mrs Khana could have been better accommodated by a care package? How would you distinguish between cultural or spiritual needs and user or carer preferences in conducting an assessment of care needs?

3 In this case Mr Karim, as the carer, made a decision on behalf of both himself and his mentally incapacitated wife to refuse the care package being proposed by Adult Services. Undoubtedly, given the longevity of the couple's relationship, Mrs Khana would have been deeply distressed to have been admitted to a residential placement without her husband. Do you think Mr Wilson, as the social worker involved in this case, was right to permit Mr Karim to refuse the care package on his wife's behalf or do you think he should have adopted a different approach? In this case how would you balance the needs of the carer against the needs of the user? How can care planning help to do this?

 Perspectives

Carers' views of carers' assessments

Research conducted after the enactment of the Carers and Disabled Children Act 2000 found that carers' assessments were under-promoted, with high numbers of carers remaining unsure of their right to an assessment (Seddon and Robinson, 2001; Audit Commission, 2004). Carers UK (2003) in their survey found that 45% of carers were not aware of their entitlement to a separate carer assessment. Seddon, et al. (2007) undertook a retrospective analysis of nine separate research studies on carers spanning the period 1993-2006. This identified many recurrent themes.

Practitioners were frequently reluctant to complete separate carers' assessments which added time and bureaucracy to assessment of needs. Conversely, carers themselves valued a separate assessment and privacy with the care manager. One carer stated, 'I wouldn't say anything detrimental in front of [cared-for-person]. Having a carer assessment in front of the cared-for is a waste of time' (Seddon, et al., 2007:1345). However, some carers remained unsure about the purpose of the assessment and thought they were being evaluated. A carer explained 'I wasn't sure whether they felt I was incapable. I wasn't sure whether they were assessing my abilities or what it was all about' (Seddon, et al., 2007: 1345).

Many carers complained about the lack of priority given to their assessment and the long time delay often involved in obtaining services. Care managers corroborated this experience, with one confessing that before services would be offered to a carer 'things would have to be pretty drastic. The carer would have to be providing a high level of care, night and day, and I'm afraid to say they'd have to be on their hands and knees' (Seddon, et al., 2007: 1346). Most carers who participated in the studies conducted by Seddon and her colleagues decried the task-oriented and practical focus of carer assessments. These largely ignored the impact of stress on carers, including the need for emotional support and supportive relationships. Only 3-4% of carers in England and Wales reported receiving emotional support such as counselling services following their assessment (Seddon, et al., 2007: 1346).

In many of the studies reviewed by Seddon et al. (2007) the common assumption by care managers that as long as carers were *capable* of caring then they were *willing* to care, was deeply resented. As one carer put it, 'I was emphatically not asked about my willingness to continue caring . . . this was taken as read and expected' (Seddon et al., 2007: 1347). Finally, the divide between health and social care was identified as a major impediment to multidisciplinary carers' assessments and the design of optimal care packages for them (Seddon et al., 2007: 1349).

CASE 5
Ombudsman Report Complaint No. 03/B/18884 against London Borough of Bromley 9 December 2004

Importance of the case

This explores an allegation of abuse against a vulnerable service-user and the procedure which should be followed where this occurs. It also considers the consequences for users and carers when there is a failure by professionals to properly investigate allegations of abuse.

History of the case

This was a complaint to the Local Government Ombudsman brought by a mother on behalf of her adult daughter, Ruth, who has Down's syndrome. The complaint related to the failure of Social Services to adequately investigate an alleged sexual assault on Ruth or to provide an adequate care plan for her.

Facts of the case

Ruth was in her twenties at the time of the events to which the complaint relates. She had been diagnosed as having Down's syndrome, epilepsy and scoliosis of the spine. As a result of learning difficulties she could not read or write. Ruth lived at home with her parents, attended a local college and received respite care in a residential facility provided by the local Primary Care Trust. On 10 March 2002 during a period of respite Ruth informed a member of staff at the residential unit that she had been sexually assaulted by another service-user. It was two weeks before staff from the Primary Care Trust informed Adult Social Services of the allegation. At no point was the matter reported to the police. Mrs Davis, Ruth's mother, believed that her daughter's allegation was not taken seriously and hence not properly investigated despite the change in her behaviour and refusal to accept respite care at the facility. In July 2002 Mrs Davis made a formal complaint regarding the lack of an investigation into her daughter's allegation, through the complaints procedure of Social Services.

Ruth was due to finish her education at a local college in the summer of 2002 and attend a day centre instead. When it transpired that Ruth's alleged abuser would also be going to the same day centre it became untenable for her to attend. In the circumstances the local authority agreed to fund Ruth for a further year at college. In September 2002 Adult Social Services sent Mrs Davis a revised care plan to reflect the decision that Ruth was to stay on at college for an additional year. Mrs Davis considered this care plan to be inadequate and it formed part of her complaint to Social Services. Despite a number of subsequent meetings, Mrs Davis's concerns regarding the inadequacy of the care plan continued, culminating in a request for the Local Government Ombudsman to investigate the matter.

Key people in the case

Mrs Davis – complainant
Ruth – complainant's daughter
Officer A – senior care manager for Ruth
Officer E – complaints investigator at Stage Two

Discussion of the case

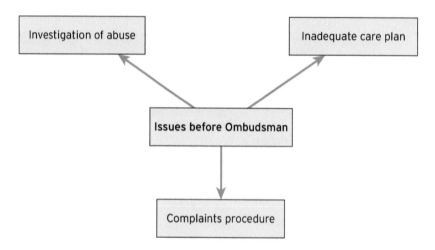

Investigation of abuse

The initial ground of Mrs Davis's complaint in relation to her daughter was the failure of Social Services to properly investigate an allegation of abuse. Aggravating this grievance was the practical effect that Ruth would not attend any facility where she was likely to come into contact with her alleged abuser. This included not just the day centre, which she was due to start attending in the autumn of 2003, but also a weekly dance class from which she had to be withdrawn. Mrs Davis noted a marked change in her daughter after she reported the sexual assault in March 2002. Ruth became greatly agitated and distressed at the prospect of going to the residential unit for respite after March 2002 in contrast to her previous fairly unperturbed attitude to it. She became too upset when in proximity to her alleged abuser for attendance either at the day centre or dance classes to be any longer a workable component of her care plan. The procedure for the investigation of alleged abuse against vulnerable adults is described in Department of Health (2000a) *No Secrets: Guidance on Developing and Implementing Multi-agency Policies and Procedures to Protect Vulnerable Adults from Abuse,* which is issued under s.7 of the local authority Services Act 1970 and is policy guidance. The main elements of this guidance are outlined in the box below.

Key guidance

No Secrets

Department of Health (2000a) *No Secrets* describes a range of abuses against vulnerable adults, and highlights the importance of prevention through inter-agency collaboration. The main categories of abuse identified in the guidance are:

Physical abuse – hitting, pushing, misuse of medication, restraint or inappropriate sanctions.

Sexual abuse – sexual assault or sexual acts to which the vulnerable adult has not or could not consent.

Psychological abuse – emotional abuse, threats of harm, deprivation of contact, humiliation, verbal abuse, intimidation, withdrawal from services.

Financial abuse – theft, exploitation, misuse of property or benefits.

Neglect – ignoring medical or physical care needs, failure to provide access to appropriate services.

Discriminatory abuse – harassment or slurs based on a person's disability, race, gender, etc.

The guidance requires police, housing, education, health and social services authorities to set up inter-agency procedures to both protect vulnerable adults and to handle investigations when an allegation of abuse is made. These inter-agency structures may also include benefits agencies, voluntary organisations, user-led services and carer support groups. In all investigations Social Services is normally expected to take the lead role.

A vulnerable adult is defined in Lord Chancellor's Department (1997) *Who Decides: Making Decisions on Behalf of Mentally Incapacitated Adults* as a person 'who is or may be in need of community care services by reason of mental or other disability, age or illness; and who is or may be unable to take care of him or herself, or unable to protect him or herself against significant harm or exploitation'. Ruth plainly fell within this definition and therefore within the framework set out in *No Secrets*. Paragraph 2.8 of this policy guidance stipulates:

> Some instances of abuse will constitute a criminal offence. In this respect vulnerable adults are entitled to the protection of the law in the same way as any other member of the public . . . Accordingly, when complaints about alleged abuse suggest that a criminal offence may have been committed it is imperative that reference should be made to the policy as a matter of urgency. Criminal investigation by the police takes priority over all other lines of inquiry.

So, in the first instance, either a designated member of staff at the Primary Care Trust or at Adult Social Services should have taken responsibility for informing the police. As Social Services is usually the lead agency for investigation into the abuse of vulnerable adults it should certainly have double checked that the police were aware of the allegation. Paragraph 3.7 of *No Secrets* also makes clear that an agency which is made aware of an allegation of abuse must inform the relevant regulatory body. In this instance the relevant regulatory body was the Commission for Social Care Inspection, which has a statutory duty to ensure compliance with National Minimum Standards for residential care homes. In two important respects health and social care professionals failed to implement the requirements of policy guidance relating to adult protection.

In line with the directions set out in *No Secrets* the Department of Social Services of the local authority developed agency-specific guidance entitled *Bromley Adult Protection Inter-Agency Guidelines*. This emphasised: the high priority to be given to referrals concerning abuse against vulnerable adults; the position of Bromley Social Services as the lead agency in such circumstances; the importance of determining the ongoing risk to the vulnerable; the requirement to assess their care needs; and the necessity of putting in place arrangements to protect them. The Local Government Ombudsman made no criticism of *Bromley Adult Protection Inter-Agency Guidelines,* which complied with the provisions of the *No Secrets* policy guidance. The problem was that social workers failed to follow the agency guidance which implemented *No Secrets* at local level. In fact no investigation into the circumstances surrounding Ruth's allegation of sexual assault was conducted by Adult Social Services. This had several effects:

- Ruth felt that she had not been believed, which exacerbated her sense of fearfulness and resultant agitation.
- Ruth was left at risk of further abuse.
- Ruth rather than the alleged abuser was withdrawn from the proposed day centre and dance classes where she would have met her alleged abuser.
- As the allegations of sexual assault were not treated seriously, Ruth's revised assessment of need failed to reflect this event and its impact upon her.
- Failure to investigate meant that the service-user accused of a sexual assault was left in a position to assault other users at the respite care facility and day centre.
- The lack of a proper investigation meant that a user accused of a sexual assault was not given the opportunity to offer evidence of his possible innocence.

Specialists reporting to Bromley Social Services in November 2002 stated that they had discovered signs of abuse, which had been compounded by the failure of social workers to believe Ruth. The principles which should have guided the conduct of social and health care workers involved in Ruth's care are set out in the box below.

 Key guidance

No Secrets

Paragraph 4.3 lists the principles which should underpin the action of all agencies involved in protecting vulnerable adults.

i. Actively work together within an inter-agency framework.
ii. Actively promote the empowerment and well-being of vulnerable adults through the services they provide.
iii. Act in a way which supports the rights of the individual to lead an independent life based on self determination and personal choice.
iv. Recognise people who are unable to take their own decisions and/or to protect themselves, their assets and bodily integrity.
v. Recognise that the right to self determination can involve risk and ensure that such risk is recognised and understood by all concerned and minimised whenever possible.
vi. Ensure the safety of vulnerable adults by integrating strategies, policies and services relevant to abuse.
vii. Ensure that when the right to an independent lifestyle and choice is at risk the individual concerned receives appropriate help, including advice, protection and support from relevant agencies.
viii. Ensure that the law and statutory requirements are known and used appropriately so that vulnerable adults receive the protection of the law and access to the judicial process.

Social workers in Adult Services as well as those in Children's Services working with parents are often working with vulnerable adults. Precisely because the safeguarding of adults lacks the comprehensive legal framework which has been developed to protect children, professionals are often confronted by situations which can make it exceptionally difficult to intervene. However, the practitioners with responsibility for Ruth's care were not facing such an intractable situation. Ruth was a service-user availing of the same facilities as her alleged abuser. There was ample opportunity for health and social care professionals to act to both protect Ruth and begin an investigation of the allegation. By the professionals failing to do this, both Ruth and other users were plainly left at risk of further harm. This is quite apart from the additional distress caused to both Ruth and her carer by the lack of action and by the need to then remove Ruth from a number of services and amenities. Policy guidance, if followed, facilitates early intervention and remedial action in situations where vulnerable adults are being abused or are at risk of abuse.

 Critical commentary

Adult protection

Adult protection lacks a comprehensive legislative framework such as that which protects children. There is no single statute in adult protection which equates to the Children Act 1989. There is instead a plethora of acts which can be invoked in different contexts. For example, provisions under the Family Law Act 1996 can be used in the case of violence or the threat of violence between associated persons. The Family Law Act 1996 does not cover emotional or financial abuse, both of which fall within the *No Secrets* policy guidance. Nor does the Protection from Harassment Act 1997 protect adult victims of discrimination, emotional or financial abuse.

Alternatively, the Sexual Offences Act 2003 can be used in circumstances where a person with capacity is sexually abused by a care worker or when someone has sexual relations with a mentally incapacitated adult. This statute deals exclusively with forms of sexual abuse. The Mental Capacity Act 2005 offers some defence against financial abuse as the Court of Protection can remove deputies or attorneys appointed to act for incapacitated adults who cease to make decisions in their best interests. The rarely exercised power under s.47 of the National Assistance Act 1948 permits the removal of physically ill or disabled persons with capacity from their home if they are living in unsanitary conditions and are unable to care for themselves. The High Court also retains an inherent jurisdiction to safeguard the welfare of an adult with capacity.

What is apparent from this list of statutes is the fragmentation of adult protection across different Acts of Parliament and the absence of a coherent legal framework to protect vulnerable adults on a par with that for children. *No Secrets* is policy guidance and not legislation. It sets out in fairly broad terms inter-agency arrangements for adult protection, but without the prescription contained in *Working Together to Safeguard Children* or the legal enforceability of inter-agency collaboration under the Children Act 2004. Although, Adult Social Services is the designated lead agency for adult protection, it does not have a statutory duty to investigate allegations of adult abuse or to protect vulnerable adults thereafter. This differs markedly from the duties of social workers in Children's Services, as under the Children Act 1989 s.47 they are legally required to conduct investigations of alleged abuse against children. The Children Act 1989 also gives social workers a range of legally enforceable interventions ranging from supervision of a child under a Supervision Order to temporary removal from their home under an Emergency Protection Order to permanent removal under a Care Order.

Conversely, social workers responsible for adult protection are reliant on statutes based on private law, meaning that their protective provisions can only be invoked if the victim decides to initiate court proceedings. This is to be distinguished from the public law provisions of the Children Act 1989, which permit social workers to intervene in family life, whether parents or children want them to or not. The government is reluctant to apply the principles of child protection to vulnerable adults. It has support among many practitioners who regard such a move as infantilising vulnerable adults and threatening their autonomy (Williams, 2002: 296). An adult protection framework does need to distinguish between vulnerable adults with mental capacity and those without. On the one hand, adults must be permitted to exercise their autonomy and to choose to take risks, even ones which expose them to abuse. On the other hand, adults, especially those without capacity, cannot be left to endure abuse because they are hampered from effectively protecting themselves.

Inadequate care plan

The *No Secrets* policy guidance, which envisages the completion of an investigation, stipulates at paragraph 6.19 that 'once the facts have been established, an assessment of the needs of the adult abused will need to be made. This will entail joint discussion, decision and planning for the person's future protection.' The second element of Mrs Davis's complaint in relation to her daughter was that Social Services after failing to investigate Ruth's accusation against another service-user, then failed to produce a revised care plan which took account of the alleged assault. In September 2002, that is almost six months after Ruth made her allegation, her care manager produced a revised care plan to reflect that she would be remaining on at college for an additional year. According to the Local Government Ombudsman who had sight of the document during their investigation, the second page of the care plan was blank and it appeared to be incomplete. Social Services Inspectorate and Department of Health (1991d: 67) *Care Management and Assessment: A Practitioner's Guide* lists the elements which should be included in a care plan and these are reproduced in the box below.

 Key guidance

Care Management and Assessment: A Practitioner's Guide

A care plan should contain the following:

- The overall objectives
- The specific objectives of:
  - users
  - carers
  - service providers
- The criteria for measuring the achievement of these objectives
- The services to be provided by which personnel/agency
- The cost to the user and the contributing agencies
- The other options considered
- Any point of difference between the user, carer, care planning practitioner or other agency
- Any unmet needs with reasons
- The named person(s) responsible for implementing, monitoring and reviewing the care plan
- The date of the first planned review

Paragraph 4.37 of *Care Management and Assessment: A Practitioner's Guide* requires that:

> care plans should be set out in concise written form, linked with the assessment of need. The document should be accessible to the user; for example, in Braille or translated into the user's own language. A copy should be given to the user but it should also, subject to the constraints of confidentiality, be shared with other contributors to the plan.

As Ruth could not read or write, the care plan completed in September 2002 was shared in written form with Mrs Davis who was her main carer. As Mrs Davis was to complain, this care plan did not reflect the change in Ruth's needs brought about by the traumatising effect of the sexual assault upon her. After Mrs Davis expressed dissatisfaction with Ruth's care manager, she was replaced by Officer A who was to complete a Comprehensive Assessment. This assessment and linked care plan should have ensured a smooth transition from college attendance to day-care centre provision during 2003. However, by April 2003 little progress had been made and at the end of her patience Mrs Davis engaged solicitors to act on her behalf. They wrote to Bromley Social Services to point out that a suitable care package for Ruth had still not been put in place and Mrs Davis was contemplating applying for a judicial review of the local authority's handling of Ruth's care.

Bromley Social Services responded to the threat of legal action by calling a case conference in May 2003 at which social workers broadly accepted a document produced by Mrs Davis which set out her perspective on Ruth's care needs. It was agreed at the meeting that a Comprehensive Assessment would be undertaken and a care plan developed by June 2003, but no such assessment took place. The last community care assessment for Ruth was dated 1997, that is to say almost six years previously. No evidence was presented to the Local Government Ombudsman to show that this original assessment of care needs had been regularly reviewed, something which should have occurred at least once a year. In the succeeding months Officer A, Ruth's new care manager, negotiated several service inputs which included attendance for three days a week at a different day centre from that attended by the alleged abuser, alongside the allocation of a support worker.

However, Mrs Davis complained that the programme of activities to be undertaken between the day centre and the support worker was poorly structured and lacked integration (para. 26). She was also of the opinion that given the symptoms of post-traumatic stress disorder and underlying depression which had been diagnosed in Ruth by health professionals, that her daughter's care package should include psychotherapy (para. 30). There were also problems with public transport and waiting times around the scheduled activities for Ruth (para. 36). Despite the expression on a number of occasions of these concerns by Mrs Davis by November 2003 an updated community care assessment had still not been completed. Thereafter a series of drafted community care assessments and associated care plans passed backwards and forwards between Adult Social Services and Mrs Davis. The lack of face-to-face contact between Ruth's care manager on the one hand and Mrs Davis as the carer and Ruth as the user on the other continued (para. 50). In short there was poor partnership working. At the time of the investigation by the Local Government Ombudsman, Bromley's Adult Social Services was still working on yet another draft of the community care assessment for Ruth.

Social Services had, however, made over to Mrs Davis a weekly sum of money with which to organise more appropriate services for Ruth. The ongoing disagreements between Mrs Davis and the local authority as to the appropriateness of the care package might have been diminished if instead of dealing with this matter on an ad hoc basis the local authority had negotiated a Direct Payment. This scheme was first introduced under the Community Care (Direct Payments) Act 1996 and later extended by the Health and Social Care Act 2001. It permits local authorities to make financial payments to users and carers based on their eligible assessed needs, as opposed to arranging services for them. This frees users and carers to use the money made available to them to set up their own care package in a way that is better tailored to their needs and preferences. Strictly speaking, Bromley London Borough Council could have made Direct Payments to Ruth if she could have managed this with the assistance of her mother or other supporter. As Ruth's main carer, Mrs Davis would also have been entitled to a carer's assessment in her own right. Hence Direct Payments could also have been made to Mrs Davis enabling her to purchase services that met her needs as a carer for rest, work and leisure activities. The box below sets out the main rules governing the making of Direct Payments by local authorities to users and carers.

Key legislation

Health and Social Care Act 2001

Sections 57 and 58 of the Health and Social Care Act 2001 made Direct Payments widely available to users and carers to spend on services of their choice. Department of Health (2003e) *Direct Payment Guidance, Community Care, Services for Carers and Children's Services (Direct Payments) Guidance England* details the regulations relating to direct payments. The main rules which apply to these payments are that:

- The amount paid must be based on users' or carers' assessments under NHS and Community Care Act 1990, Children Act 1989 or Carers and Disabled Children Act 2000.
- The local authority must usually make direct payments if requested by a user or carer aged 16 years or over who meets the eligibility criteria.
- Money is to be paid direct to users or carers for them to purchase their own care package.
- Money from Direct Payments cannot be used to pay a sexual partner or someone normally resident in the user's home to provide care.
- Direct Payments can only be made with the consent of the user or carer and are not mandatory.
- Direct Payments can only be used for non-residential care or short periods in residential care amounting to no more than 4 weeks in any twelve months.
- Direct Payments will only be made if it appears to the local authority that the user or carer is capable of managing the Direct Payment on his or her own or with available assistance.
- Users and carers receiving Direct Payments remain accountable to the local authority as to how they spend that money and must demonstrate that they are using it to meet their assessed needs.

Conducting regular reviews of a care package is stage seven of the care management approach to care planning described in the *Care Management and Assessment: Practitioners' Guide*. As this case demonstrates, it is a crucial aspect of effective care delivery. There had been a major change in Ruth's circumstances as a result of the alleged sexual assault. This change detrimentally affected her mental health and reduced the range of services that she could access because of the presence of her alleged abuser. Such an alteration in her circumstances indicated that a new Comprehensive Assessment needed to be completed with multidisciplinary inputs and multi-agency involvement in care planning. As Social Services Inspectorate and Department of Health (1991d: para. 7.23) *Care Management and Assessment: Practitioners' Guide* points out, 'the interval of reviews should be related to the pace of change in the user's needs as this determines the need to revise the care plans'. Care managers need to be sensitive to changes in the circumstances of users and carers which indicate that a review of the care package is necessary. This may require some minor modification to the original care plan or (as in this case) it may demand a thorough re-evaluation of service provision conducted through a new Comprehensive Assessment.

Complaints procedure

Mrs Davis took her grievance through the statutory complaints procedure for Adult Social Services. As provided by Department of Health (2006) *Learning from Complaints: Social Services Complaints Procedure for Adults* for complaints about more serious matters, Mrs Davis went directly to stage two of the process without having to go through stage one first. Although Mrs Davis lodged her complaint in July 2002, it was not until October 2002, some three months later that Officer E was appointed to investigate the matter. This was in contravention of *Learning from Complaints* which requires that an investigation at stage two should be completed within 25 days, or 65 days if there are extenuating circumstances. During the Local Government Ombudsman's inquiry the Bromley London Borough Council presented no extenuating circumstances and failed to account for the delay in dealing with Mrs Davis's complaint.

When Officer E did complete the independent investigation at stage two, she concluded that Mrs Davis was correct in her contention that there had been no effective inquiry into the assault alleged by her daughter (para. 12). In fact Officer E was unable to ascertain any substantive documentation relating to an investigation into the sexual assault against Ruth (para. 10). Officer E also found that the agency had neither taken the incident seriously nor followed agency adult protection procedures (para. 11). Her findings were set out in a report of her investigation dated 8 January 2003 – that is, ten months after the date of the alleged assault. The stage two report recommended that Bromley Council call a case conference to deal with the financial and practical assistance Mrs Davis and Ruth needed in order to be able to move on from the events surrounding the alleged sexual assault (para. 18).

The stage two report was candid about the shortcomings of the local authority, and resulted in a written apology from the Assistant Director of Social Services addressed to Mrs Davis. The Assistant Director accepted in her correspondence with Mrs Davis that a case conference was required alongside a comprehensive assessment of Ruth's needs. Precisely because the stage two report was so unequivocal in agreeing with the claims made by Mrs Davis, she was satisfied with it and did not pursue her complaint to stage three, which would have involved a Review Panel. Unfortunately for Mrs Davis what appeared a successful outcome to her stage two complaint proved short lived as Bromley London Borough Council failed to follow through on the recommendations of Officer E. The promised case conference was not held until May 2003, 14 months after the alleged sexual assault, and then it failed to produce a community care assessment or an agreed care package.

Strictly speaking, Mrs Davis and Ruth could also have pursued their complaint through the complaints procedure of the care home itself. Department of Health (2003b) *Care Homes for Adults (18–65) and Supplementary Standards for Care Homes Accommodating Young People Aged 16 and 17* stipulates the National Minimum Standards for all residential facilities providing personal or nursing care to adults and young people. This document details the required standards for care delivery in such residential units if providers are to retain their registration with the Commission for Social Care Inspection and hence their authorisation to operate. There are 43 standards in all, covering a wide range of matters from management to quality of care. These are set out in the text box below.

 Key guidance

National Minimum Standards for Care Homes for Adults (18-65)

Standards 1-5: Choice of Home - provision of information about residential homes, introductory visits, needs assessment, meeting identified needs and drawing up a contract.

Standards 6-10: Individual Needs and Choices - development of service-user plan, participation by user, how decisions are made, risk taking and confidentiality.

Standards 11-17: Lifestyle - personal development, education, occupation, leisure, daily routines together with social inclusion and relationships.

Standards 18-21: Personal and Healthcare Support - personal support and healthcare including palliative treatment during terminal stages.

Standards 22-23: Concerns, Complaints and Protection - procedures to protect adults in residential care and enable complaints to be investigated.

Standards 24-30: Environment - common areas, residents' rooms, furniture, bathrooms adaptations and equipment, hygiene.

Standards 31-36: Staffing - recruitment, training, qualifications, roles and supervision.

Standards 37-43: Conduct and Management of Home - day-to-day operations, policies and procedures, record keeping, safe working practices and quality assurance.

Most pertinent to the events surrounding the alleged assault on Ruth at the NHS-run residential unit were Standard 22, which concerns the care home's complaints procedure, and Standard 23, which requires systems to be put in place to protect residents. The whole of Standard 23 from Department of Health (2003b) *Care Homes for Adults (18–65)* is reproduced in the box below.

 Key guidance

National Minimum Standards for Care Homes for Adults (18-65)

23.1 The registered person ensures that service users are safeguarded from physical, financial or material, psychological or sexual abuse, neglect, discriminatory abuse or self-harm or inhuman or degrading treatment, through deliberate intent, negligence or ignorance, in accordance with written policy.

23.2 Robust procedures for responding to suspicion or evidence of abuse or neglect (including whistle blowing) ensure the safety and protection of service users, including passing on concerns to the CSCI [now the Care Quality Commission] in accordance with the Public Interest Disclosure Act 1998 and Department of Health guidance *No Secrets*.

23.3 All allegations and incidents of abuse, and action taken, are recorded.

23.4 Staff who may be unsuitable to work with vulnerable adults are referred in accordance with the Care Standards Act for consideration for inclusion on the Protection of Children and Vulnerable Adults Registers.

23.5 Physical and verbal aggression by a service user is understood and dealt with appropriately, and physical intervention is used only as a last resort by trained staff in accordance with Department of Health guidance, protects the rights and best interests of the service user, and is the minimum consistent with safety.

23.6 The home's policies and practices regarding service users' money and financial affairs ensure for example service users' access to their personal financial records, safe storage of money and valuables, consultation on finances in private, and advice on personal insurance; and preclude staff involvement in making or benefiting from service users' wills.

Standard 23.1 requires that all adult care homes must have a written policy in place designed to protect their vulnerable adult residents from the types of abuse set out in *No Secrets*. Such a policy must comprise procedures which both protect residents and direct the conduct of investigations, including information sharing with other agencies, primarily the police and Adult Social Services. Standard 23.3 makes clear that all allegations of abuse, whether eventually substantiated or not, must be recorded. Officer E, who was appointed to examine Mrs Davis's grievance at stage two of the complaints procedure, informed the Local Government Ombudsman that her investigation was hampered by the lack of written documentation relating to the alleged sexual assault. It seems that neither staff at the residential home nor Adult Social Services kept detailed records of the incident and subsequent follow-ups. This meant that for Officer E it was difficult to trace the sequence of events after Ruth's disclosure of a sexual assault on 10 March 2002. Indeed, it was not until a month later, on 11 April 2002, that there was discussion within Adult Social Services as to whether to launch an adult protection investigation. Of course by this stage it was much more difficult to collect evidence, verify what had actually happened or effectively protect other vulnerable residents. Although as an NHS facility, not part of the Local Government Ombudsman's remit, undoubtedly the lack of prompt action among residential care staff and their failure to follow adult protection procedures could also have constituted grounds for a complaint to the Commission for Social Care Inspection.

The GSCC *Code of Practice for Social Care Workers* requires that users and carers be assisted to 'understand and exercise their rights' and 'to make complaints'. Paragraph 3.7 stipulates that practitioners must take complaints seriously, respond to them or pass them to an appropriate person who will then deal with them. Social workers who are privy to concerns expressed by users or carers about the standards of care they are receiving or an allegation of abuse are obliged by the GSCC Code to inquire further and if appropriate initiate an investigation. For Ruth and her mother the lack of action by professionals to deal with the initial allegation of sexual abuse was compounded by a complaints procedure which found in the complainants' favour but failed to ensure the implementation of stage two recommendations. Taking complaints seriously involves more than listening to users or carers expressing them, or even facilitating them, to avail of the complaints procedure. It necessitates ensuring that the outcome of a complaints process is conveyed to the complainant and then acted upon within an agreed timescale.

Perspectives

Practitioners on adult protection

Northway, et al. (2007) examined the implementation of adult protection policy in Wales, while McCreadie, et al. (2007) investigated it in England. National Assembly for Wales (2000) *In Safe Hands* is the Welsh equivalent of Department of Health (2000a) *No Secrets* and closely follows its framework. Northway, et al. (2007) focussed on health and social care services to people with learning difficulties and spanned the public, private and voluntary sectors. McCreadie, et al. (2007) interviewed around 100 professionals working in health, social care, housing and the police across different user groups.

A social worker participating in the study by Northway et al. (2007: 98) recognised that, 'the policy is only as good as the agency that you work with in terms of implementing it and I think in their interpretation in terms of their priority in responding to an allegation and the cooperation you get in progressing it'. However, because Adult Social Services are the designated lead agency in relation to adult protection, professionals in other agencies tended to downplay their own role. One healthcare worker remarked, 'you know it is the social services' responsibility after that, I don't know it is within that policy, I just know it exists and it is under the social care and housing remit that it goes from there' (Northway, et al., 2007: 98). It was also of concern to the researchers that a number of agencies in the independent sector decided not to participate in the study on the grounds that Social Services 'deal' with matters relating to adult protection (Northway, et al., 2007: 100).

Similar findings emerged from McCreadie, et al. (2008) which also revealed confusion among practitioners as to who qualified as a 'vulnerable adult' although crucial to triggering adult protection procedures under *No Secrets*. A major problem was that *No Secrets* policy guidance defined a vulnerable adult as someone 'who is or may be in need of community care services'. This created paradoxical situations as described by one healthcare professional:

> we felt we had a situation there where there was somebody at home with a carer who was not necessarily acting in the best interests of the patient. So we did contact the social worker . . . the decision by the social worker in that particular instant is that the person doesn't fit into this vulnerable adults . . . we were told, 'well no, the patient's got a carer at home and there's not very much we can do in that respect' (McCreadie, et al., 2007: 252).

A high number of professionals interviewed by McCreadie, et al. (2007) identified difficulties linked to the multi-agency approach set out in *No Secrets*, which lacked the necessary detail. Management in Adult Social Services had not sufficient authority to design policy which allocated precise roles to other agencies or to compel their cooperation in multi-agency investigations. One social worker observed, 'So it is trying to write something that isn't so prescriptive that you're tying people into something that they're not going to do because it doesn't fit in with the way they practise' (McCreadie, et al., 2007: 253). Many professionals outside of local authority Social Services displayed confusion about their role in adult protection. Lack of resources for adult protection, and high workloads, meant that adult protection tended to be relegated within agencies. For example one healthcare practitioner admitted, 'I'm afraid that adult protection amongst everything else in the NHS isn't high, high priority' (McCreadie, et al., 2007: 256). The overall effect of this was that allegations and the outcome of investigations were poorly recorded and tracked over time (McCreadie, et al., 2007: 264-5).

Outcome of Ombudsman Report Complaint No. 03/B/18884 against London Borough of Bromley

The Ombudsman found that the local authority had failed to carry out an investigation of the alleged sexual assault against Ruth, with the result that she was denied access to services which she could have expected to receive. As there was no effective investigation of the matter the service-user against whom the allegations were made could not be removed from any of the facilities. The Council had failed to follow its own adult protection procedures, which amounted to maladministration. The Council subsequently failed to complete a new community care assessment to take account of Ruth's changed needs after the alleged sexual assault upon her. The alterations to the care package which did occur appeared to be service-led rather than needs-led and were not tailored to Ruth's specific requirements. In summary, the Local Government Ombudsman upheld the complaint by Mrs Davis and recommended that Bromley London Borough Council:

- Pay Mrs Davis £5,000 in compensation
- Produce an adequate care plan to meet Ruth's identified needs
- Review its procedures to ensure that the maladministration identified in the Ombudsman's report does not re-occur.

 Critical questions

1 In this case one user made an allegation of sexual abuse against another user. This was never properly investigated. It is possible that no sexual abuse took place. How can social workers responsible for safeguarding vulnerable adults balance the rights of alleged victims against those of alleged perpetrators? How does the *No Secrets* guidance assist practitioners to do this?

2 Given the facts of the case, how might care planning have been improved to both protect Ruth and meet her needs and those of her carer?

3 Go back to Chapter 1 and reread details about the complaints procedure. What difficulties do you think a vulnerable adult in receipt of services might encounter in availing of this procedure? In practical terms how might a social worker assist a vulnerable adult or a carer to use the complaints procedure?

 Critical commentary

The personalisation agenda and adult protection

Fyson and Kitson (2007) consider the implications of the personalisation agenda and its emphasis on independence and choice for those with learning difficulties. They identify some contradictions in this policy. The White Paper, Department of Health (2001f) *Valuing People: A New Strategy for Learning Disability for the 21st Century* proposed a plan of action to improve services for people with learning disabilities; to be driven by four key principles and a set of related strategies:

Rights – through raising awareness of the rights of people with learning disabilities and ensuring they receive the protection of the law.

Independence – through improved housing options and community-based accommodation in tandem with integrated health and social care provision.

Choice - through enhancing the control people with learning difficulties have over their lives, including improved advocacy services, increased uptake of direct payments and more choice over types of support.

Inclusion - through better access to healthcare, education and employment.

Fyson and Kitson (2007) while endorsing the principles behind the Government's White Paper raise crucial questions as to how in practice people with learning difficulties can both be independent and protected from abuse. They focus on independent living and the move away from institutional and family care to private sector accommodation in single and shared housing arrangements. This gives users much greater choice in deciding who to live with and what assistance they want to receive. Fyson and Kitson (2007: 410) highlight the virtual absence of adult protection considerations from *Valuing People*. Yet, as they point out, people with learning disabilities are more likely to be at risk of exploitation and other forms of abuse than those with physical impairments.

The Safeguarding Vulnerable Groups Act 2006 creates an adults' barred list for vulnerable adults - defined as people receiving health or social care in a hospital, residential or home care setting or who are in receipt of Direct Payments. Health and social care workers can be included on this 'barring list' if their conduct harmed or placed at risk of harm a vulnerable adult. Inclusion on the list debars a person from working with vulnerable adults. Employers of care workers are legally required to consult the 'barring list' before contracting anyone. This is in addition to their obligations under the Care Standards Act 2000, which oblige employers to obtain criminal record checks of potential care workers. However, users employing care workers under Direct Payments or in the context of personal or individual budgets are not legally required to request a Criminal Records Bureau check or consult the adults' barred list. This puts people with learning difficulties employing their own personal assistants using Direct Payments at greater risk of abuse from a care worker than those availing of care management arrangements.

Fyson and Kitson (2007: 433) highlight how the policy objectives of independence and choice have become divorced from adult protection for those with learning difficulties. Fyson and Kitson (2007: 433) insist that independence should not be the only measure of quality of life and that the guarantee of a non-abuse environment in one's own home is arguably as important, concluding:

> There should be nothing wrong with acknowledging that, like most of us, people with learning difficulties can hope only to be interdependent rather than independent; that they need the support of others to make choices and to maintain an optimum level of independence. The danger is that, where organizations insist that people with learning disabilities are wholly responsible for their own, independent, choices they ignore the control exerted over them by others.

Learning points

- The law relating to the provision of community care for adults is contained in a number of different statutes. But most services are still made available to disabled children under the Children Act 1989 and to a much lesser extent under the Chronically Sick and Disabled Persons Act 1970.

- Different statutes govern the provision of services for users and carers. Carers are entitled to a separate assessment from users, and for their commitments to employment, education, and social activity to be considered.

- Local authorities are permitted to take the cost of services into consideration in deciding on the eligible needs of users. *Fair Access to Care Services* provides the policy framework for ensuring this is done in a transparent and fair way.

- There is a legal difference between user and carer preferences and their care needs. It is up to local authorities to assess the care needs of users and carers and to meet these through a cost-effective care package.

- Care management is currently being transformed by the introduction of the personalisation agenda which gives users and carers more control over their care budget and therefore more scope to exercise their choices.

- Suitable housing is particularly important to those with disabilities. Care packages need to take account of people's medium to long-term housing requirements as well as their social and healthcare needs.

- Comprehensive Assessments involve multi-agency inputs and need care managers to exercise professional judgement in deciding what weight to give to specialist assessments and how to use these to maximum effect in care planning.

- Assessment and care planning must include attention to the cultural heritage of users and carers and their needs in relation to cultural and spiritual practices.

- There is no comprehensive legal framework to protect vulnerable adults which parallels that for safeguarding children. Professionals are dependent on a range of different statutes to protect vulnerable adults depending on their circumstances.

- Professionals are required to follow government-issued policy guidance on protecting vulnerable adults. This emphasises the importance of timely and thorough investigation of allegations of abuse, alongside action to protect the victim.

Further reading

Commission for Social Care Inspection and Health Care Commission (2006) *Joint Investigation into the Provision of Service for People with Learning Disabilities at Cornwall Partnership NHS Trust*, London: Commission for Healthcare Audit and Inspection. This publication describes abuse against vulnerable adults in residential care and living in the community. It also identifies the failings of health and social care agencies to safeguard vulnerable adults and makes key recommendations to address this problem.

Clements, L. and Thompson, P. (2007) *Community Care and the Law*, London: Legal Action Group (LAG). This is a comprehensive text detailing the law in relation to community care. It provides coverage of issues concerning assessment and care planning and addresses matters relating to mental health, physical health, learning difficulties and addiction.

Mandelstam, M. (2009) *Safeguarding Vulnerable Adults and the Law*, London: Jessica Kingsley. This publication provides details of the law on adult protection. It covers financial abuse as well as sexual and physical abuse. Safeguarding is addressed in relation to vulnerable adults both with and without mental capacity.

Williams, J. (2002) 'Public law protection of vulnerable adults: the debate continues, so does the abuse', *Journal of Social Work* 2(3): 293-316. This article focusses on the differences between the legal protections available to vulnerable adults and those available to children. It discusses the implications of this for the health and safety of vulnerable adults.

Useful websites

www.disability.gov.uk This is the Government Disability Website which offers easy-to-follow guides on the law relating to disability and discrimination.

www.cqc.org.uk/ Run by the Care Quality Commission, which took over the functions of the Commission for Social Care Inspection, this site provides background material on National Minimum Standards and inspection for social care providers and service-users' rights.

www.dh.gov.uk This is the website of the Department of Health which offers free downloads of key policy and practice guidance documents in the area of community care. It also provides information on the entitlements of users and carers.

www.carersnet.org.uk Run by Carersnet this website gives access to downloads of all the major statutes, policy and practice guidance in relation to carers. It also provides details of carers' entitlements.

8

MENTAL HEALTH: HOSPITAL SETTING

Overview of relevant legislation

As the Fact File above reveals, around 50,000 people are compulsorily detained in England in any given year due to the condition of their mental health. However, as these statistics also reveal, only around one-third of those detained are in hospital at any one time. Many mental health patients live in the community, although they may be subject to conditions of compliance with their treatment and liable to recall to hospital if their mental health deteriorates. Fairly even numbers of people are detained for assessment and treatment, with only a few, just 1,000, detained in emergency situations. Allowing for the fact that most people are only detained for a relatively short period of time, counted in weeks and months rather than years, this means that there is a considerable turnover of mental health patients in hospitals. A proportion of these will be repeatedly discharged and admitted back into hospital as their mental health improves for a while and then deteriorates again.

The law related to mental health is contained in one major statute, the Mental Health Act 1983. This piece of legislation was recently amended by the Mental Health Act 2007, which extended mental health law to people with personality disorders and strengthened provisions for the compulsory treatment in the community of people with mental disorders. The Mental Health Act 1983 (as amended) is a comprehensive piece of legislation which sets out legal provisions governing the assessment, treatment and detainment of people with mental disorders, including those within the criminal justice system. It covers people with mental disorders admitted to hospital, in prison or on remand and those living in the community. The main sections of the Mental Health Act 1983 (as amended) are set out in the table below.

Mental Health Act 1983 (as amended)	Key sections
Part I – Definition and applicability	s.1 'Mental disorder'
Part II – Compulsory admission to hospital and guardianship	s.2 Assessment s.3 Admission for treatment s.4 Emergency admission s.5 Patient already in hospital s.7 Application for guardianship s.8 Effect of guardianship s.13 Applications for admission and guardianship s.17 Leave of absence from hospital s.17A Community treatment orders s.18 Patients absent without leave s.19 Transfer of patients s.23 Discharge of patients s.26 Definition of nearest relative s.29 Displacement of nearest relative
Part III – Patients involved in criminal proceedings or under sentence	s.35 Remand to hospital for assessment s.36 Remand to hospital for treatment s.37 Hospital order or guardianship s.41 Restriction orders s.47 Transfer from prison to hospital for treatment
Part IV – Consent to treatment	s.57 Treatment requiring consent and second opinion s.58 Treatment requiring consent or a second opinion s.62 Urgent treatment
Part V – Tribunal	s.66 Application to tribunal s.68 Referral to tribunal by hospital managers s.72 Powers of tribunal s.78 Procedures of tribunal
Part VI – Removal and return of patients within United Kingdom	ss.80–92 Movement of patients between countries of the United Kingdom including Channel Islands and Isle of Man
Part VII – Management of property and affairs of patients	Repealed by Mental Capacity Act 2005
Part VIII – Miscellaneous functions of local authorities and Secretary of State	s.114 Appointment of Approved Mental Health Professional s.115 Power of entry and inspection s.117 Aftercare s.118 Code of Practice

(Continued)

Mental Health Act 1983 (as amended)	Key sections
Part IX – Offences	s.126 Forgery and false statements
	s.127 Ill treatment of patients
	s.128 Assisting patients to absent without leave
	s.129 Obstruction
Part X – Miscellaneous and supplementary	s.130 A Independent mental health advocates
	s.131 Informal admission of patients
	s.132 Duty to give information to patients
	s.133 Duty to inform nearest relative of discharge
	s.134 Correspondence of patients
	s.135 Warrant to search for and remove patients
	s.136 Mentally disordered persons found in public places
	s.137 Conveyance of patients

Source: Adapted from Brammer (2007: 496-7).

The *Mental Health Act 1983: Code of Practice* sets out the guiding principles underpinning this statute and these are detailed in the box below. Unlike the Children Act 1989 (which enshrines its principles in s.1 thus giving them the force of law) the principles underpinning the Mental Health Act 1983 only appear in the Code of Practice and therefore do not have statutory effect. This means that the principles serve to guide mental health professionals, but the courts do not have to rigorously enforce them in coming to their judgements. Even paragraph 1.8 of the Code of Practice diminishes the significance of these standards by stating that 'the principles inform decisions, they do not determine them'. This is a very different position to that under the Children Act 1989, which binds the courts and consequently Children's Services to make the child's welfare their paramount consideration in conjunction with the *non-delay* and *no order principles*.

 Key guidance

Mental Health Act 1983: Code of Practice

Purpose principle

1.2 Decisions under the Act must be taken with a view to minimising the undesirable effects of mental disorder, by maximising the safety and wellbeing (mental and physical) of patients, promoting their recovery and protecting other people from harm.

Least restriction principle

1.3 People taking action without a patient's consent must attempt to keep to a minimum the restrictions they impose on the patient's liberty, having regard to the purpose for which the restrictions are imposed.

Respect principle

1.4 People taking decisions under the Act must recognise and respect the diverse needs, values and circumstances of each patient, including their race, religion, culture, gender, age, sexual orientation and any disability. They must consider the patient's views, wishes and feelings (whether expressed at the time or in advance), so far as they are reasonably ascertainable, and follow those wishes wherever practicable and consistent with the purpose of the decision. There must be no unlawful discrimination.

Participation principle

1.5 Patients must be given the opportunity to be involved, as far as practicable in the circumstances, in planning, developing and reviewing their own treatment and care to help ensure that it is delivered in a way that is as appropriate and effective for them as possible. The involvement of carers, family members and other people who have an interest in the patient's welfare should be encouraged (unless there are particular reasons to the contrary) and their views taken seriously.

Effectiveness, efficiency and equity principle

1.6 People taking decisions under the Act must seek to use the resources available to them and to patients in the most effective, efficient and equitable way, to meet the needs of patients and achieve the purpose for which the decision was taken.

There are a number of government-issued documents which set out guidance for the provision of mental health services and the conduct of mental health professionals acting under the Mental Health Act 1983 (as amended). These are summarised briefly in the table below and are referred to in this chapter.

Guidance document	Outline of content
Department of Health (2008) *Mental Health Act 1983: Code of Practice*	This is the statutory code of practice which directs professionals working under the Mental Health Act 1983 (as amended).
Department of Health (2008) *Refocusing the Care Programme Approach: Policy and Positive Practice Guidance*	This provides detailed guidance on the Care Programme Approach including assessment and care planning for people with mental health problems living in the community.
Department of Health (1999) *The National Service Framework for Mental Health*	This sets out seven standards for the delivery of high quality and accessible mental health services both in a community and hospital setting.

Overview of the cases

This chapter explores the issues raised by the circumstances of two different people whose lives were affected by the provisions of the Mental Health Act 1983. The first cases came before the courts while the second was the subject of a public inquiry. The title of each case and the main issues it addresses are outlined below.

Case 1 *St George's Healthcare Trust* v. *S* and *R* v. *Collins and Others* explores the:

- Definition of mental disorder.
- Meaning of informed consent.
- Treatment which can be given against a patient's wishes.

Case 2 Independent Inquiry into the Death of David Bennett explores the:

- Relationship between offending and mental disorder.
- Criteria for detainment in hospital for treatment.
- Procedures for the administration of treatment against a patient's wishes.
- Use of restraint on detained patients.
- Racial discrimination within the mental health system.
- Care Programme Approach and aftercare provision.

CASE 1
St George's Healthcare NHS Trust v. *S* and *R* v. *Collins and Others* [1998] 3 WLR 936

Importance of the case

It highlights the kind of ethical dilemma that can confront professionals when service users exercise their right of self-determination in ways which place themselves or others at risk of harm. The case illustrates how social workers and medical practitioners can exploit their statutory powers to override the choices of patients and users. Professionals may seek to justify their actions by citing a higher motive, such as acting in the person's best interests or to prevent harm. Or, as in this case, professionals may interpret a user's behaviour in ways which are self-serving and give them more power to make choices on behalf of that individual. At the same time this case also demonstrates the crucial contribution which the *Mental Health Act 1983: Code of Practice* can make to good practice.

History of the case

This was an application by a mother for a judicial review of her compulsory detainment under the Mental Health Act 1983. This was heard alongside her appeal against a declaration by the High Court dispensing with her consent to a Caesarean section which was subsequently carried out against her will.

Facts of the case

MS was born in 1967 and was white. She attempted to register as a new patient at a GP practice in London on 25 April 1996. At that time she was working as a veterinary nurse and was 36 weeks pregnant. The relationship with the father had ended and she was single. She had not previously sought any antenatal care. MS was seen by Dr Chill who quickly diagnosed severe pre-eclampsia and advised her that if she did not agree to admission to hospital for an induced delivery she would endanger both her own life and that of her unborn child. MS was unwilling to accept this advice, but agreed to be seen later that day by Ms Collins, an Approved Social Worker, and Dr Jeffreys, the duty psychiatrist. Both of them repeated the same medical advice given by Dr Chill. MS rejected the opinions of both physicians. An application was made by the Approved Social Work under s.2 of the Mental Health Act 1983 for MS to be compulsorily admitted to Springfield Hospital, a psychiatric institute, for an assessment, which was supported with the signatures of both Dr Chill and Dr Jeffreys. On the same day as she had attempted to register as a new patient MS was admitted to Springfield Hospital and shortly before midnight transferred to St George's Hospital, which was a general hospital. An ex parte application was made by the St George's Healthcare NHS Trust to the Family Division of the High Court for a declaration dispensing with MS's consent to a Caesarean section. This was granted by the High Court and against her will a Caesarean operation was performed on MS in St George's Hospital where on 26 April she was delivered of a baby girl. A few days later she was transferred back to psychiatric care at Springfield Hospital. On 2 May her s.2 detainment there was terminated, whereupon MS immediately discharged herself from Springfield Hospital against medical advice.

Key people in the case

MS – applicant
Dr Chill – General Practitioner
Dr Jeffreys – senior registrar and psychiatrist
Ms Collins – approved social worker
Mr Gordon – barrister representing the applicant MS
Mr Pitt – legal counsel for St George's NHS Healthcare Trust
Justice Hogg – judge presiding in High Court hearing
Lady Justice Butler-Sloss – judge presiding in Court of Appeal hearing
Lord Justice Walker – judge presiding in Court of Appeal hearing

Discussion of the case

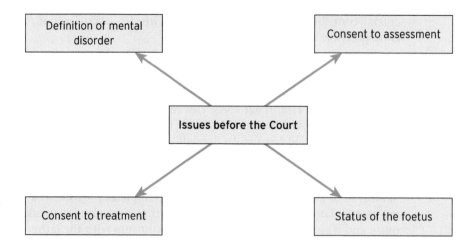

Definition of mental disorder

The Mental Health Act 1983 as amended by the Mental Health Act 2007 is the main legislation concerned with the care of people who have a mental illness or cognitive impairment when their condition places them at risk of injuring themselves or others. Those who do not have a diagnosed mental disability cannot be compulsorily detained or treated under the Mental Health Acts. The box below reproduces the definition of mental disorder contained in the Mental Health Act 1983.

Key legislation

Mental Health Act 1983 (as amended)

s.1(1) The provisions of this Act shall have effect with respect to the reception, care and treatment of mentally disordered patients, the management of their property and other re-lated matters.

s.1(2) In this Act – "mental disorder" means any disorder or disability of the mind; and "men-tally disordered" shall be construed accordingly.

s.1(2A) But a person with a learning disability shall not be considered by reason of that dis-ability to be –

 (a) suffering from a mental disorder for the purposes of the provisions mentioned in sub-section (2B) below; or

 (b) requiring treatment in hospital for mental disorder for the purposes of sections 17E and 50 to 53 below,
  unless that disability is associated with abnormally aggressive or seriously irresponsi-ble conduct on his part.

s.1(3) Dependence on alcohol or drugs is not considered to be a disorder or disability of the mind for the purposes of subsection (2) above.

s.1(4) In subsection (2A) above, "learning disability" means a state of arrested or incomplete development of the mind which includes significant impairment of intelligence and social functioning.

The subsections of the first section of the Mental Health Act 1983 identify a number of important exclusions from the statute. The effect of s.1(2A) is that people with a learning difficulty do not automatically fall under all the provisions of the statute simply because they have a learning difficulty. While they can be subject to short-term detainment under the Mental Health Act 1983, they can only be subject to long-term compulsory detainment in hospital if in addition to having a cognitive impairment they also exhibit 'abnormally aggressive or seriously irresponsible conduct'. Section 1(4) provides a defini-tion of 'learning disability' which excludes an additional group of people from the provi-sions of the Mental Health Act 1983. These are people who do have a learning disability, but whose disability does not include a 'significant impairment of intelligence and social functioning'. This means that someone with a mild learning difficulty who displayed 'abnormally aggressive or seriously irresponsible conduct' would not fall under the provi-sions of the Mental Health Act 1983. They would instead be subject to the same civil and criminal law if they posed a threat of harm to others as for people who do not have a learning difficulty.

Also excluded from the Mental Health Act 1983 under s.1(3) are those whose attempts at self-harm or harm to others is caused by the misuse of drugs or alcohol. Threatening behaviour, causing a nuisance or occasioning actual bodily harm to others will be dealt with under the same civil and criminal offences as are these acts if com-mitted by someone who is not intoxicated or under the influence of drugs. However, a person will fall under the provisions of the Mental Health Acts if their habitual use of alcohol and/or drugs has resulted in a mental disorder, such as a drug-induced psy-chosis. People who misuse alcohol and/or drugs and have developed an associated mental disorder are given a dual diagnosis. The term 'dual diagnosis' refers to both the addiction and the linked mental disorder.

MS did not have a learning disability nor was she addicted to alcohol or drugs. The question before the Court of Appeal was whether she had a mental illness such as to bring her within the scope of the Mental Health Act 1983. MS was a pregnant woman who had been informed by several physicians that unless her baby was delivered by Caesarean section it was likely that the baby would die and that she would either die or suffer severe and lasting disability. On 25 April 1996 when MS was first given this prognosis, she accepted its implications and did not dispute the doctors' opinion. But she also wanted to have a natural birth and was prepared to assume the risks to her health and that of the baby associated with refusing medical intervention. The judges presiding over the Court of Appeal case summed up the dilemma before both the professionals involved in detaining MS and indeed before the court itself in the following terms (page 957):

> The Act cannot be deployed to achieve the detention of an individual against her will merely because her thinking process is unusual, even apparently bizarre and irrational, and contrary to the views of the overwhelming majority of the community at large. The prohibited reasoning is readily identified and easily understood. Here is an intelligent woman. She knows perfectly well that if she persists with this course against medical advice she is likely to cause serious harm, and possibly death, to her baby and to herself. No normal mother-to-be could possibly think like that. Although this mother would not dream of taking any positive steps to cause injury to herself or her baby, her refusal is likely to lead to such a result. Her bizarre thinking represents a danger to their safety and health. It therefore follows that she must be mentally disordered and detained in hospital in her own interests and those of her baby. The short answer is that she may be perfectly rational and quite outside the ambit of the Act, and will remain so notwithstanding her eccentric thought process.

In other words making a choice which is morally repugnant or incomprehensible to the vast majority of people in British society does not mean that the person – merely by virtue of that choice – has a mental disorder. Yet, at the same time it could be argued that someone exercising a choice so eccentric and dangerous must be suffering from a mental illness. The Approved Social Worker (now Approved Mental Health Professional and described in the box on the next page) and the doctors who came into contact with MS were confronted with this paradox. In her assessment, which comprised part of the grounds for compulsorily admitting MS to hospital under the Mental Health Act 1983, Ms Collins, the Approved Social Worker, wrote:

> I attempted to persuade [MS] of the less restrictive option which would have involved her and myself going to the obstetric unit at St George's Hospital where her delivery would have been induced immediately. After many attempts at negotiating this option [MS] continued to refuse, therefore I felt I had no choice but to detain her for assessment to a safe place where there would be general nurses as well as psychiatric nurses to monitor her very severe condition.

As the judges presiding over the Court of Appeal case identified, 'severe condition' referred to MS's pre-eclampsia and not her mental state. In other words the Approved Social Worker was referring to a physical health condition for detaining MS in hospital and not a mental health one. But, of course, provisions under the Mental Health Act 1983 can only be invoked for someone suffering from a mental disorder.

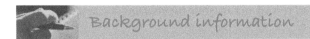

Background information

Approved Mental Health Professional

The Mental Health Act 1983, s.114 created the position of Approved Social Worker (ASW). These were qualified social workers who had undertaken a prescribed programme of training and were appointed by the local authority to perform duties specified under the statute. But the Mental Health Act 2007 amended the law to replace Approved Social Workers with Approved Mental Health Professionals (AMHP). The main effect of this was to open up the position to people other than qualified social workers. So, for example, a community psychiatric nurse or a psychologist could apply to become an AMHP and, having undertaken the prescribed training, be appointed as such by the local authority. Hence an AMHP may be a qualified social worker, but equally he or she may be drawn from another field of the caring professions. Under the Mental Health Act 1983 (as amended by the Mental Health Act 2007) Approved Mental Health Professionals have the same duties and responsibilities as were previously held by Approved Social Workers. These are as follows:

- Interview the person prior to making an application for his or her detainment in hospital.
- Make an application to detain a person in hospital for the assessment or treatment of a mental disorder.
- Consult with the person's *nearest relative* before making an application for his or her detainment in hospital.
- Inform the nearest relative when making an application for the detainment of a person in hospital.
- Produce a Social Circumstance Report where the *nearest relative* makes an application for a person to be detained in hospital.
- Produce a Social Circumstance Report for the Tribunal for Mental Health Review.
- Convey a detained patient to hospital.
- Retake a detained patient who is absent without leave.
- Protect the moveable property of a detained patient.
- Enter premises (other than a hospital) where a mentally disordered patient is living if there is reasonable cause to believe he or she is not receiving proper care.

On the application to detain MS in hospital for assessment under the Mental Health Act 1983 Dr Jeffreys wrote:

> the patient is refusing treatment and will not accept voluntary admission. She appears to be significantly depressed with low self esteem and a profound indifference to the consequences of refusing treatment for her serious physical conditions. She is pregnant and her behaviour is putting her own life and the life of her unborn baby at risk.

It is significant that although Dr Jeffreys refers to MS's depression she makes no plans for her mental health to be assessed. In fact throughout her period of detainment in hospital MS was not given any treatment for depression. This led the judges to conclude that MS's detainment was solely for the purpose of conducting a medical procedure which MS had explicitly refused to undergo. The Court of Appeal was also presented with evidence from MS herself. Shortly after her removal to hospital MS was asked by Dr Jeffreys to record her reasons for refusing a Caesarean. This she did in the following terms:

> (i) I am a qualified veterinary nurse, and am therefore quite able to comprehend the medical terminology used, and feel happy to ask for clarification if an unfamiliar term is used. (ii) I fully understand that pre-eclampsia is a potentially life threatening condition, i.e. that the raised blood pressure may lead to haemorrhage, shock and, if untreated, death; or alternatively death due to total organ failure resulting from inability to compensate. (iii) I have always held very strong views with regard to medical and surgical treatments for myself, and particularly wish to allow nature to 'take its course', without intervention. I fully understand that, in certain circumstances this may endanger my life. I see death as a natural and inevitable end point to certain conditions, and that natural events should not be interfered with. It is not a belief attached to the fact of my being pregnant, but would apply equally to any conditions arising.

As was obvious to the Court of Appeal from this contemporary written explanation of her refusal to accept medical treatment, MS had produced a lucid and rational line of reasoning. Her explanation evidences no disordered thought processes, nor any diagnosable mental illness. Certainly MS's written statement expresses beliefs which may seem extraordinary or eccentric to the vast majority of people living in Britain who daily take advantage of medical treatment to avoid serious illness and death. The point is that an exceptional belief is not of itself a form of mental disorder. This led Lady Justice Butler-Sloss and Lord Justice Walker to conclude that MS had in fact been detained because Ms Collins, Dr Chill and Dr Jeffreys disagreed with her decision to refuse medical treatment and not because she had a mental illness. In other words, MS was detained under the Mental Health Act 1983 due to her strongly held views against medical intervention rather than because she had a mental disorder. Essentially this means that MS was detained because of what she believed, that is to say on the grounds of ideology, rather than on grounds related to her mental health.

The 'respect principle' set out in paragraph 1.4 of the *Mental Health Act 1983: Code of Practice* requires mental health professionals to 'respect the diverse needs, values and circumstances of each patient' and to 'consider the patient's views, wishes and feelings'. This is echoed in the GSCC *Code of Practice for Social Care Workers* at paragraph 1.6 which stipulates that social workers must respect the 'diversity and different cultures and values' which they encounter among users and carers. The same Code at paragraph 1.2 requires that this respect include 'where appropriate, promoting the individual views and wishes of both service users and carers'. Any social worker performing statutory duties as an Approved Mental Health Professional is bound by both these Codes of Practice. However, the notion of 'respect' is a rather vague term. What does it mean to 'respect' a value or wish or decision of a user which is different from one's own as a professional?

In the case concerning MS, 'respect' meant recognising that she held distinctly different opinions regarding medical intervention in her pregnancy from those of most other people. While her beliefs did not have a religious basis, they were nevertheless deeply held. To respect another's belief or value system must necessitate permitting them to act upon that belief or make decisions in keeping with their values. Of course such respect is not indiscriminate. Social workers are not required by the Code of Practice to respect values which are plainly self serving and operate to the detriment of others, such as the self-justifying beliefs of a child molester.

For those acting within the law, there is a wide range of spiritual and personal values and beliefs which may be objectionable to individual practitioners. Nevertheless, users and carers are entitled to act upon their understanding and beliefs about the world, even to their own detriment. Respect for diversity in such circumstances means ensuring that users and carers are given all the relevant information, as indeed Ms Collins, the Approved Social Worker, provided to MS. It then means permitting a choice or an outcome with which one, as a practitioner, disagrees. The issue in this case is that Ms Collin on failing to dissuade MS from her course of action, without further evidence interpreted her refusal of a Caesarean as symptomatic of mental illness. In other words, the mental health professionals involved pathologised MS's conduct because they disagreed with it. This was an interpretation of MS's behaviour which permitted them to substitute her decision with their own.

Consent to assessment

The Mental Health Act 1983 sets out the conditions under which people can be detained against their will and forced to undergo a psychiatric assessment without their consent. These provisions are contained in section 2 of the Act which is reproduced in the box below.

Key legislation

Mental Health Act 1983

2(2) An application for admission for assessment may be made in respect of a patient on the grounds that –

    (a) he is suffering from mental disorder of a nature or degree which warrants the detention of the patient in a hospital for assessment (or for assessment followed by medical treatment) for at least a limited period; and

    (b) he ought to be so detained in the interests of his own health or safety or with a view to the protection of other persons.

2(3) An application for admission for assessment shall be founded on the written recommendations in the prescribed form of two registered medical practitioners, including in each case a statement that in the opinion of the practitioner the conditions set out in subsection (2) above are complied with.

2(4) . . . a patient admitted to hospital in pursuance of an application for admission for assessment may be detained for a period not exceeding 28 days beginning with the day on which he is admitted, but shall not be detained after the expiration of that period unless before it has expired he has become liable to be detained by virtue of a subsequent application, order or direction under the following provisions of this Act.

In order to compulsorily detain a person under s.2 of the Mental Health Act 1983 (as amended):

- Either an Approved Mental Health Professional or the person's *nearest relative* must make an application by completing statutory form A1 or A2 (HO1 and HO2 in Wales) respectively.
- The application must be supported on statutory form A3 (HO3 in Wales) by two registered medical practitioners. At least one of these physicians must be approved under s.12 of the Mental Health Act 1983 (as amended) as 'having special experience in the

diagnosis or treatment of mental disorder'. Therefore at least one doctor completing form A3 is normally a psychiatrist.

- Both medical practitioners must have either jointly or separately examined the person to be detained. On form A3 (or HO3 in Wales) each doctor must set out his or her reasons for proceeding with the detainment.

In relation to the circumstances surrounding MS's compulsory admission to hospital, Ms Collins, the Approved Social Worker (now AMHP) applied on form A1 while Dr Chill, a GP and Dr Jeffreys (who was a s.12 approved doctor and psychiatrist) completed the statutory form A3. This permitted MS to be compulsorily detained in hospital for up to 28 days for the assessment of her mental disorder. While the correct forms were completed and submitted by duly qualified practitioners, the question before the Court of Appeal was whether MS actually met the criteria to be forcibly admitted to hospital under s.2 of the Mental Health Act 1983. There are in fact three related criteria in s.2 which have to be met:

- The person is suffering from a mental disorder.
- The mental disorder is of a nature or degree which warrants their detainment in hospital.
- The person poses a danger to their own 'health and safety' or that of others.

Dr Chill wrote on the A3 form: 'patient depressed and self neglectful refusing voluntary treatment. Has pre-eclampsia with potential severe physical complications which needs assessment, monitoring and treatment. Potential risk of self-harm or harm to unborn child if not treated.' Dr Jeffreys wrote in similar terms (see page 415 above). But what stood out for the judges (page 944) was the emphasis in both accounts on MS's physical rather than her psychological condition and the need to administer medical treatment in relation to her pregnancy. Both doctors refer to the potential harm that MS might do to herself and the unborn child by refusing medical intervention for her physical condition. Mr Gordon, QC acting for MS before the Court of Appeal insisted that the s.2 application to detain MS was unlawful. He contended that Ms Collins, the ASW (now an AMHP) had 'acted for a collateral motive, that is to save MS and the unborn child rather than for the purpose of assessing MS's mental condition' (page 959). As the judges presiding over the Court of Appeal case recognised, although this was a humane motive, it was not a lawful one, and did not bring MS within the ambit of the Mental Health Act 1983.

Neither, Ms Collins nor the two doctors had clearly established that MS was suffering from a mental disorder or of one sufficiently serious to necessitate detainment. In other words, while MS's behaviour was placing both herself and her unborn child at risk of harm, she did not have a depressive illness and therefore did not meet the criteria contained in s.2(2)(a) of the Mental Health Act 1983. As Court of Appeal judges observed, even if a person has a mental disorder it must be 'of a nature or degree which warrants the detention of the patient in a hospital for assessment'. So for instance being 'a bit depressed' or 'feeling fed-up' indicate fairly mild and transient mental states which do not bring a person within the ambit of s.2 of the Mental Health Act 1983. It was never established that MS experienced anything more than feeling indifferent to her pregnancy and the prospect of having a baby she did not want. Such feelings are not constitutive of a mental disorder for the purposes of the Mental Health Act 1983.

It is the Approved Mental Health Professional who carries the primary responsibility under the Mental Health Act 1983 (as amended) to ensure that an application for the compulsory detainment of a person in hospital is correctly made. The duties of the AMHP in this respect are set out in s.13 which is reproduced in the box below. He or she is required to both interview the patient and be satisfied that detainment is the most appropriate course of action given all the surrounding circumstances. While two registered medical practitioners are required to support the application for a person's compulsory admission to hospital, the application is actually made by the Approved Mental Health Professional (formerly the Approved Social Worker).

Key legislation

Mental Health Act 1983 (as amended)

13(1) If a local social services authority have reason to think that an application for admission to hospital or a guardianship application may need to be made in respect of a patient within their area, they shall make arrangements for an approved mental health professional to consider the patient's care on their behalf,

13(1A) If that professional is –

(a) satisfied that such an application ought to be made in respect of the patient; and

(b) of the opinion, having regard to any wishes expressed by relatives of the patient or any other relevant circumstances, that is it necessary or proper for the application to be made by him,

he shall make the application.

13(2) Before making an application for the admission of a patient to hospital an approved mental health professional shall interview the patient in a suitable manner and satisfy himself that detention in a hospital is in all the circumstances of the case the most appropriate way of providing the care and medical treatment of which the patient stands in need.

Section 13(1A)(a) requires the AMHP to have 'regard to any wishes expressed by relatives of the patient or any other relevant circumstances'. The judges concluded that 'the necessary care and treatment for MS's pregnancy would not fall within section 13' and did not constitute a 'relevant circumstance'. In effect Ms Collins had applied for the detainment of MS on grounds which conflated the need to assess her mental state with the need to compel her to receive urgent medical treatment for her pre-eclampsia. Returning to the Wednesbury principles (see above, page 35) Ms Collins had taken into consideration a matter which she should not have in making the application for MS's compulsory admission to hospital for an assessment. The fact that MS was refusing medical treatment for herself and her unborn child was not a relevant matter of itself. It could only be relevant in so far as it indicated an underlying mental disorder, which was never established.

Paragraph 3.8 of the GSCC *Code of Practice for Social Care Workers* enjoins social workers to recognise and use 'responsibly the power that comes from your work with service users and carers'. Social workers appointed as Approved Mental Health Professionals occupy a particularly powerful position. By virtue of holding duties, powers and responsibilities under the Mental Health Act 1983, they must ensure complete adherence to the criteria set out in the statutory provisions under which they act. As this case demonstrates, statutory provisions, such as section 3 of the Mental Health Act 1983, do not consist merely of a single threshold. Commonly, they incorporate multiple thresholds each one of which must be met before a social worker can exercise their statutory

duties or powers. Such thresholds are designed to protect citizens from excessive interference by the State and to preserve the freedoms enshrined in the European Convention on Human Rights. As the practitioner responsible for actually making an
application for the compulsory detainment of someone in hospital, social workers are
directly involved in determining the limits of user autonomy. In this situation it is crucial that social workers avoid using or threatening to use their statutory powers to
impose their own values or deciding an outcome in the 'best interests' of a user or
patient. It is imperative that Approved Mental Health Professionals clearly distinguish
their own personal values from those required of them as professionals and set out in
the Codes of Practice.

In the case concerning MS, both the Approved Social Worker and the doctors
superimposed their beliefs regarding medical treatment upon a woman who was entitled by law to make choices for herself. 'Supporting service users' rights to control
their lives and make informed choices about the services they receive', as required by
para.1.3 of the GSCC Code of Practice, obliges social workers to promote user self
determination. The promoting of user autonomy cannot simply be confined to those
decisions with which a practitioner agrees. It must mean 'supporting service users'
rights' even when the exercise of these rights appear to have detrimental consequences or fly in the face of a social worker's own value system. As the circumstances
surrounding MS's decision demonstrate, it can be immensely difficult for social workers to stand back and permit someone to make what seems a perverse and self-
destructive decision without resorting to an exploitation of their own statutory
powers to prevent it.

Consent to treatment

Under British law a person with mental capacity is entitled to refuse medical treatment
regardless of the consequences for his or her health. Common law is very clear on this
point, leading Lady Justice Butler-Sloss and Lord Justice Walker to cite a number of
precedents in their deliberations. In *Airedale NHS Trust* v. *Bland* [1993] AC 789, which
went before the House of Lords, the judgement drew attention to the fact 'that it is
unlawful, so as to constitute both a tort and the crime of battery, to administer medical
treatment to an adult, who is conscious and of sound mind, without his consent'. In *Re
F (Mental Patient: Sterilisation)* [1990] 2 AC 1 Lord Keith of Kinkel giving judgement
stated (page 857):

> It is established that the principle of self-determination requires that respect must be
> given to the wishes of the patient, so that if an adult patient of sound mind refuses,
> however unreasonably, to consent to treatment of care by which his life would or
> might be prolonged, the doctors responsible for his care must give effect to his wishes,
> even though they do not consider it to be in his best interests to do so . . . To this
> extent, the principle of the sanctity of human life must yield to the principle of self-
> determination.

Department of Health (2008a) *Mental Health Act 1983: Code of Practice* provides guidance
to practitioners carrying out duties under the Mental Health Acts. While the Mental
Health Act 1983 does not impose a legal duty on doctors, nurses or Approved Mental
Health Professionals to comply with the Code they must have regard to it. Paragraph iv
of the Code states that 'the reasons for any departure should be recorded. Departures
from the Code could give rise to legal challenge, and a court, in reviewing any departure
from the Code, will scrutinise the reasons for the departure to ensure that there is

sufficiently convincing justification in the circumstances.' Plainly this means that there must be exceptional circumstances for a practitioner to depart from the Code of Practice. The box below details instruction to doctors and Approved Mental Health Professionals concerning s.2 of the Mental Health Act 1983.

 Key guidance

Mental Health Act 1983: Code of Practice

Para.6.7 The purpose of the appropriate medical treatment test is to ensure that no-one is detained (or remains detained) for treatment, or is an SCT [Supervised Community Treatment] patient, unless they are actually to be offered medical treatment for their mental disorder.

Para.6.8 This medical treatment must be appropriate, taking into account the nature and degree of the person's mental disorder and all their particular circumstances, including cultural, ethnic and religious considerations. By definition, it must be treatment which is for the purpose of alleviating or preventing a worsening of the patient's mental disorder or its symptoms or manifestations.

Para.6.9 The appropriate medical treatment test requires a judgement about whether an appropriate package of treatment for mental disorder is available for the individual in question. Where the appropriate medical treatment test forms part of the criteria for detention, the medical treatment in question is treatment for mental disorder in the hospital in which the patient is to be detained.

It is clear from the Code of Practice that the medical intervention which can be compulsorily administered to a patient detained under s.2 of the Mental Health Act 1983 must relate to his or her mental disorder. MS found herself subject to medical interventions which had little to do with treatment for a mental disorder. Within a few hours of her admission to Springfield Hospital, a psychiatric unit, she was transferred to St George's, which by contrast was a general hospital. At this time MS recorded in writing that she had an 'extreme objection to *any* medical or surgical intervention' and that it 'is against my wishes and I shall consider it an assault on my person'. She also made clear to medical staff when arrangements were being made to move her to St George's that she was 'not prepared to consent to admission to St George's Hospital for obstetric treatment' (page 945).

On 26 April, shortly after her arrival at St George's Hospital, MS was again examined by Dr. Jeffreys, the psychiatrist who had completed the A3 form for her detainment. Dr Jeffreys recorded that MS fully understood the proposed Caesarean operation and the consequences of her refusal to have it. The psychiatrist also noted that MS's 'mental state is not affecting her capacity to consent'. In other words, MS was acknowledged to have mental capacity. Indeed, on the same day MS conducted a perfectly rational half-hour telephone conversation with her solicitors who assured her that she was entitled to refuse consent to the Caesarean section. As MS had mental capacity, she did not fall under the Mental Capacity Act 2005 and consequently hospital staff could not lawfully carry out a medical intervention in her 'best interests'. Faced with these circumstances a decision was taken by staff at St George's Hospital to make an application to the High Court. This requested that the court exercise its inherent jurisdiction and make a declaration directing medical staff to conduct a Caesarean section in MS's 'best interests'. This would in effect legally override her objection to medical treatment.

Mr Pitt, acting as legal counsel for St George's NHS Healthcare Trust before the High Court inadvertently led Justice Hogg into believing that MS had been in labour for 24 hours and that both she and her unborn baby were at immediate risk of death. He also informed the judge that MS had been diagnosed with 'moderate depression'. In fact MS had not started labour and neither her death, nor that of her unborn child, was imminent, although both were undoubtedly in danger. As is usual in such exceptionally urgent circumstances a hearing was arranged for that very day, 26 April. The hearing was ex parte, meaning that MS was not legally represented at it to put her side of the matter, and the normal rules of evidence were suspended. This meant that Mr Pitt quickly obtained a Declaratory Order from the High Court directing that:

> notwithstanding the purported refusal to consent of [MS] it is declared that: (1) all necessary investigations for the purposes of diagnosing the cause of and treating her severe pre-eclampsia may be performed . . . (3) there be leave to carry out such treatment to mother and foetus as may be deemed necessary following such investigations, including Caesarean section by general anaesthetic.

The judges presiding over the Court of Appeal case roundly criticised both Mr Pitt and Justice Hogg for failing to: concern themselves with the fact that MS possessed mental capacity; inform themselves that MS had already instructed solicitors; and ascertain whether MS was aware of the High Court hearing. It was to transpire that MS had not been informed by staff at St George's that an application was being made to the High Court. The decision to conduct ex parte proceedings and not to inform MS of them plainly contravenes her right to a fair trial guaranteed under article 5 of the European Convention on Human Rights. No subsequent documentary evidence was ever tendered to the High Court to confirm the assertions made by Mr Pitt.

MS was subjected to a Caesarean operation on 26 April against her will after being shown the High Court declaration, which she asked to be faxed to her solicitors. After the successful delivery of her baby, MS remained at St George's hospital, receiving post-natal care until 30 April when she was transferred back to Springfield Hospital. There she was assessed by Dr Fisher, her Responsible Medical Officer (now known as the Responsible Clinician, described in the box below) and consultant psychiatrist who could detect no symptoms of mental illness. On 1 May Dr Fisher discharged the s.2 order and MS discharged herself from Springfield Hospital that same day. From the point of view of Lady Justice Butler-Sloss and Lord Justice Walker these events provided further evidence that s.2 had been used for unlawful ends – that is, to force a pregnant woman of sound mind to undergo a Caesarean operation she expressly did not want.

 Background information

Responsible Clinician

The position of Responsible Clinician has a statutory definition which is set out in the Mental Health Act 1983 (as amended) and the role is further elaborated in the Code of Practice. Professionals acting as Responsible Clinicians must have been approved by their health authority. Once approved, a Responsible Clinician, who is normally a psychiatrist, is the professional who has the overall responsibility for a mental health patient. This includes overall clinical responsibility for in-patients and for out-patients living in the community and still receiving treatment for their mental disorder. However, Responsible Clinicians cease to hold clinical responsibility for hospital or community patients who have been formally discharged. A professional designated as a Responsible Clinician for a particular patient exercises the following functions:

- Discharging a patient from compulsory detainment in hospital.
- Granting a patient s.17 leave from hospital.
- Recalling a patient on s.17 leave to hospital.
- Making a Community Treatment Order.
- Varying the conditions of an existing Community Treatment Order.
- Recalling a patient to hospital who is on a Community Treatment Order.
- Discharging a patient from a Community Treatment Order.
- Discharging a patient from guardianship.

Having decided that MS was suffering from a mental illness and compulsorily admitting her to hospital for assessment under s.2 of the Mental Health Act 1983 all the mental health professionals involved in her care were then legally obliged to adhere to both the statute itself and the related Code of Practice. Both the statute and the Code are clear, that only treatment for a mental disorder may be given to a person admitted to hospital under the Mental Health Act 1983. The one circumstance in which treatment for a physical aliment may be given without consent is if they lack mental capacity. However, those who lack mental capacity now fall under the provisions of the Mental Capacity Act 2005. Although MS was suspected of having a depressive disorder, it was widely acknowledged by medical staff at the hospital that she had mental capacity. Unable to legally override her refusal to accept medical treatment for a physical rather than a mental disorder without application to the court, the hospital managers at St George's did just this.

The lawyer acting for St George's inadvertently misled the High Court judge into believing that MS's death was imminent. The judge by agreeing to an ex parte hearing of which MS was not informed and at which consequently she had no legal representative deprived her of a fair trial. Her side of the argument was never put before the court before a Declaratory Order was made to override her objection to a Caesarean operation. MS was deprived of one of her human rights. Social workers are enjoined to comply, not only with the GSCC Code of Practice and that issued under s.118 of the Mental Health Act 1983, but with the European Convention on Human Rights when carrying out public or statutory functions.

No social worker was directly involved in the application to the High Court, yet this certainly was a situation in which a social worker could have assisted MS, a detained patient and service user, to 'understand and exercise their rights' as required by paragraph 3.1 of the GSCC Code of Practice. Instead MS was forced to rely solely upon contact with her solicitors in circumstances of great illness and distress. Faithful adherence to the GSCC Code of Practice necessitates that practitioners are proactive in their approach to implementing it. Promoting the rights and autonomy of users, while balancing these against potential harm to the user or others, is not a passive endeavour. It requires attentiveness to the circumstances which threaten to deprive users of their entitlements, self-determination and control over those events which intimately involve them.

Status of the foetus

Under 2(2) of the Mental Health Act 1983 two criteria have to be met for a person to be detained. First, the patient has to be 'suffering from mental disorder of a nature or degree which warrants the detention' and secondly the patient needs to be 'detained in the interests of his own health or safety or with a view to the protection of other persons'. The Approved Social Worker and the two doctors who supported the s.2 application all referred to the risk posed by MS to her unborn child if she was not detained and did not receive treatment for her pre-eclampsia. They were making one of the grounds for detaining MS the risk of harm she presented to 'other persons'. The social worker and physicians implied that MS should be detained under s.2 in order to protect her unborn child. There is a problem with this ground for detainment because an unborn child does not have the same legal status within the British justice system as a newly born baby. The status of the foetus has been long established at common law. A foetus is not a legal person, nor is it treated as having a separate existence from its mother. Giving judgement in *MB (Caesarean Section), Re* [1997] 2 FLR 426; [1997] 2 FCR 541 (pages 553, 561) Lady Justice Butler-Sloss said:

> A competent woman who has the capacity to decide may, for religious reasons, other reasons, for rational or irrational reasons or for no reason at all, choose not to have medical intervention, even though . . . the consequence may be death or serious handicap of the child she bears, or her own death. She may refuse to consent to the anaesthesia injection in the full knowledge that her decision may significantly reduce the chance of her unborn child being alive. The foetus up to the moment of birth does not have any separate interests capable of being taken into account when a court has to consider an application for a declaration in respect of a Caesarean section operation.

In view of the position established at common law the judges in the Court of Appeal case were bound to conclude that:

> an unborn child is not a separate person from its mother. Its need for medical assistance does not prevail over her rights. She is entitled not to be forced to submit to an invasion of her body against her will, whether her own life or that of her unborn child depends on it. Her right is not reduced or diminished merely because her decision to exercise it may appear morally repugnant.

Plainly these precedents mean that whatever the circumstances in which a woman finds herself, if she has mental capacity, she retains the right to determine what happens to her body. This remains so, even if she is pregnant and her decision whether or not to avail of medical treatment will affect her foetus. In the situation concerning MS, the protection of the unborn child did not fall within s.2(2)(b) of the Mental Health Act 1983 regarding the 'protection of other persons'. Therefore the Approved Social Worker and the two doctors who supported the s.2 application took into consideration a matter which they should not have in reaching their decision. It follows that they contravened one of the Wednesbury principles (see above, pages 35–6) and thus acted unlawfully.

The status of the foetus has long been a matter of particular concern to different religious faiths. It can be particularly difficult for social workers who believe in the personhood of the foetus and its possession of a soul to come to terms with the different view of British law. Paragraph 6.1 of the GSCC Code of Practice obliges social workers to operate in 'a lawful, safe and effective way'. This of course means acting in accordance with statute and case law. The foetus does not have a legal status under British law and for this reason it is not possible for someone to be arraigned before a court for the injury or murder of a foetus (although if a person stabbed a pregnant woman so as to cause the death of the child she was carrying, such an offender could be tried for assault upon the mother). This is yet another example of the degree to which the personal values of individual social workers may differ significantly from those of users or indeed from the law itself. It is incumbent upon practitioners to examine their belief systems and to ensure that they do not deliberately or inadvertently abuse their power so as to impose their personal values and preferred outcomes upon those they are charged to help. Paragraph 2.6 of the GSCC Code of Practice obliges social workers to declare 'issues that might create conflicts of interest and make sure that they do not influence your judgement or practice'.

Judgement in *St George's Healthcare NHS Trust* v. *S* and *R* v. *Collins and Others*

The Court of Appeal had two chief matters to determine, first the lawfulness of the original s.2 application for MS's detainment and, second, the status of the Declaratory Order issued by the High Court permitting medical intervention against MS's will. On the first issue Lady Justice Butler-Sloss and Lord Justice Walker found that Ms Collins, Dr Chill and Dr Jeffreys had each 'failed to maintain the distinction between the urgent need of MS for treatment arising from her pregnancy and the separate question whether her mental disorder (in the form of depression) warranted her detention in hospital' (page 962). The judges concluded that although the requirements of s.2(2)(b) may have been fulfilled in that MS's behaviour was endangering her health and safety (although not that of the foetus) s.2(2)(a) was not. That is to say, having heard all the evidence the Court of Appeal was not convinced that MS ever suffered from a 'mental disorder of a nature or degree which warrants the detention of the patient in a hospital for assessment'.

Regarding the exercise by the High Court of its inherent jurisdiction, Lady Justice Butler-Sloss and Lord Justice Walker allowed the appeal by MS, finding that the High Court had decided wrongly. The two judges concluded that, since a Declaratory Order should not be made 'without adequate investigation of the evidence put forward by either side, it follows that a declaration (especially one affecting an individual's personal autonomy) ought not to be made on an ex parte basis' (page 965). As the High Court had exercised its inherent jurisdiction in a manner that had prevented MS from making any representations to it and which ignored the fact that she had capacity, the Court of Appeal ruled that the Caesarean section 'amounted to trespass' on MS and awarded her damages against St George's Healthcare Trust.

❓ Critical questions

1 In this case a pregnant woman held a belief that even though her life was in danger, there should be no medical intervention and nature should take its course. How would you go about deciding whether a belief is symptomatic of a mental disorder or simply a deviant or eccentric viewpoint? If a person objected to medical intervention for religious reasons how would this influence your understanding of mental disorder?

2 If you had been the Approved Mental Health Professional who first came into contact with MS what personal and professional dilemmas would her situation present to you? How would you resolve these for yourself?

3 What pressures might the social workers and medical professionals involved in this case have been under to intervene to save MS's life and that of her unborn child? What might have been the consequences for these professionals had they not intervened and permitted MS to exercise her self-determination in this matter?

4 If after giving birth to a sickly baby, MS then objected to any medical treatment of her daughter on the grounds that she believed nature should take its course, how might this case have been decided differently?

CASE 2
Independent Inquiry into the Death of David Bennett
December 2003

Importance of the case

It outlines the linkage between the criminal and civil provisions of the Mental Health Act 1983 and illustrates the way in which service users can pass to and fro between the criminal justice and mental health systems. The lack of attention given by professionals to the ethnicity and culture of a mental health patient is examined in conjunction with the Codes of Practice and their directions to practitioners on this issue. Also explored are the detrimental consequences of poor follow-up and liaison between mental health professionals and between practitioners and carers once a patient leaves hospital to return to the community. This is set within the context of aftercare services and Practice Guidance relating to community care for those with a mental disorder.

History of the case

A psychiatric patient died at the hands of medical staff in hospital while he was being restrained. An independent inquiry was set up by the strategic health authority to examine the circumstances surrounding his death.

Facts of the case

David Bennett was born in Jamaica in 1960 and immigrated to the United Kingdom in 1968 to join his family. He was of African-Caribbean heritage and a Rastafarian. When he was 20 years old David first developed symptoms of what was later diagnosed as schizophrenia, believed to have been induced by cannabis use. From 1980 onwards David spent periods in and out of psychiatric hospitals and was imprisoned for six months on one occasion. He was known to make apparently unprovoked physical assaults on others. On returning home to the council flat in which he lived alone, he often stopped taking his medication and was consequently re-admitted to hospital. A pattern of minor criminal offending emerged while David was back in the community, resulting in frequent police involvement. As an in-patient David was frequently transferred to more secure accommodation as he physically attacked nursing staff on a number of occasions. Several times he also absconded from hospital after being detained under the Mental Health Act 1983 or failed to attend for out-patient appointments. Yet, throughout David's involvement with the mental health system he continued to have contact with members of his immediate family. During in-patient treatment David complained of being over medicated and was reluctant to take the anti-psychotic drugs prescribed for him. During his last admission to the Norvic Clinic Medium Secure Unit as an in-patient an altercation took place between David and another patient on the evening of 30 October 1998 during which they punched each other. David appeared agitated afterwards and was transferred to another ward that same evening. On reaching the ward to which he had been moved David hit a nurse several times at which point other nursing staff attempted to physically restrain him. While David was being held down on the floor by several psychiatric nurses he suffered cardiac and respiratory failure and died.

Key people in the case

David Bennett – mental health patient
Dr Joanna Bennett – sister of David Bennett
Winifred Bennett – sister of David Bennett
Dr Sagovsky – consultant psychiatrist
Dr Stanley – consultant psychiatrist
SN Hadley – staff nurse at the Norvic Clinic

Discussion of the case

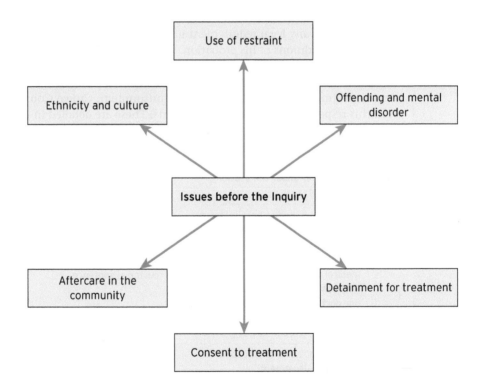

Offending and mental disorder

In November 1984 David appeared before a Magistrates' Court where he was found guilty of several minor criminal offences. Before sentencing, David's solicitor obtained a psychiatric report which recommended that he be admitted to hospital for treatment. Under s.157 of the Criminal Justice Act 2003 (which was enacted after the events of this inquiry) before passing sentence the court is required to:

- Obtain a medical report on an offender who appears to be mentally disordered.
- Consider the impact of any sentence on their mental condition.
- Take into account the effect of the sentence on treatment for the mental disorder.

In the case of David Bennett, on reading the psychiatric report the Magistrates agreed to make a Probation Order attaching a requirement for medical treatment instead of passing a custodial sentence. Probation Orders were abolished by the Criminal Justice Act 2003 and replaced by Community Orders. Like the present day Community Order, a Probation Order can contain directions to an offender which prohibit or require him or her to do something. In this instance the Probation Order required David to attend hospital as an in-patient and accept treatment.

David was admitted to Peterborough District Hospital for psychiatric treatment, but he quickly discharged himself. Since this was a breach of his Probation Order (now a Community Order) he again appeared before the Magistrates' Court and was subsequently sentenced to six months' imprisonment for his offences. David Bennett's admission to hospital as an informal patient for psychiatric treatment was a condition of his Probation Order. He was not subject to compulsion under s.3 of the Mental Health Act 1983. It was for this reason that he could discharge himself. Consequently, although he had not violated any legal requirement under the Mental Health Act 1983, he had contravened the conditions of his probation. It was this which landed him back in the Magistrates' Court and led to his imprisonment. However, the courts do have powers under the Mental Health Act 1983 to compulsorily admit a defendant to hospital for assessment or treatment or as an alternative to imprisonment. Crown Courts have wider powers in this respect than do Magistrates' Courts. These are detailed in the table below.

Criminal provisions of the Mental Health Act 1983

Sections of the Mental Health Act 1983	Effect of order under the section	Power of Magistrates' Court	Power of Crown Court
s.35 Remand to Hospital for Report	• Remands accused to hospital for a psychiatric assessment and report to the court • Patient's consent required for all medical treatment • Requires oral or written evidence of one doctor of possible mental disorder • Maximum duration 28 days renewable for up to 12 weeks	• Used if person has been convicted of an offence which is punishable by a custodial sentence	• Used if person is awaiting trial or arraigned before the court
s.36 Remand to Hospital for Treatment	• Remands accused to a hospital for psychiatric treatment • Patient's consent is not required for most treatments • Requires oral or written evidence of two doctors that accused is suffering from a mental disorder • Maximum duration for 28 days renewable for up to 12 weeks		• Used if person is in custody awaiting trial for an offence punishable by imprisonment • Used instead of remanding an accused person in custody

(Continued)

Criminal provisions of the Mental Health Act 1983 *(continued)*

s.37 Hospital Order	• Compulsory admission of offender to hospital • Patient's consent is not required for most treatments • Requires oral or written evidence of two doctors that accused is suffering from a mental disorder • 6 months duration and renewable yearly	• Used if a person is convicted of an offence punishable with imprisonment	• Used if a person is convicted of an offence punishable with imprisonment for which there is not a fixed sentence prescribed by law
s.37 Guardianship Order	• Offender is placed under the guardianship of the local social services authority or a person specified in the order • Guardian has power to specify where offender lives, require them to attend specified places for treatment, education or occupation and to require that professionals be given access to offender • Offender must consent to any medical treatment • Requires oral or written evidence of two doctors that offender is suffering from a mental disorder • Maximum duration is for six months renewable	• Used if a person is convicted of an offence punishable with imprisonment	• Used if a person is convicted of an offence punishable with imprisonment for which there is not a fixed sentence prescribed by law
s.38 Interim Hospital Order	• Used when it is unclear if a full Hospital Order should be made • Compulsory admission of offender to hospital • Patient's consent is not required for most treatments • Requires oral or written evidence of two doctors that accused is suffering from a mental disorder • 12 weeks duration and renewable for 4-week periods thereafter up to a one-year maximum	• Used if a person is convicted of an offence punishable with imprisonment	• Used if a person is convicted of an offence punishable with imprisonment for which there is not a fixed sentence prescribed by law
s.41 Restriction Order	• Can only be used in conjunction with a s.37 Hospital Order • Requires offender to remain in hospital • Used if offender is at risk of committing more offences which cause serious harm to the public if released from hospital • Requires oral or written evidence of two doctors that accused is suffering from a mental disorder and at least one doctor must give evidence in person • Requirement to remain in hospital can be specified or without limit	• Refer matter to Crown Court for determination	• Where a Hospital Order is made court may make a Restriction Order if offender presents a risk of serious harm to the public on completion of Hospital Order

It is significant that Dr Joanna Bennett told the independent inquiry into her brother's death that when she visited David in prison he appeared very mentally unwell and stated that he had been picked on and bullied. It is therefore not surprising that within a month of his release from prison David was admitted to a psychiatric ward at Peterborough Hospital. After physical assaults on a number of staff he was transferred to St Andrew's, a private hospital with medium secure facilities and from there to the Norvic Clinic. He was discharged home in January 1986, but again committed a series of minor offences resulting in his arraignment before a Magistrates' Court in November 1986. This time, instead of trying David, the court exercised its powers under s.35 of the Mental Health Act 1983 and remanded him to hospital for a psychiatric report. By this time David had been given a clear diagnosis of schizophrenia. Once again David found himself at St Andrew's hospital, where he was remanded, although an assessment was not completed due to his mental state. A year later David was transferred to Peterborough District Hospital, but there he was violent and absconded on several occasions resulting in his transfer back to St Andrew's, which had medium secure facilities. Over the succeeding years David was to move backwards and forwards between his home, Peterborough Hospital, St Andrew's and the Norvic Clinic. During this period he would also come to the attention of the police from time to time in connection with minor criminal acts.

Social workers who are members of Youth Offending Teams or trained as Approved Mental Health Professionals are likely to come into contact with offenders who have a mental disorder. The interaction of the criminal justice system with the mental health system can occur either when an accused person is first arraigned before a court or as an aspect of the sentence handed down by a court to an offender. A person accused of an offence punishable by imprisonment may be temporarily remanded in hospital under s.35 of the Mental Health Act 1983 for an assessment of his or her mental state. If it appears to the court that an accused person requires treatment he or she can be remanded to hospital under s.36. On being convicted an offender could be subject to a Community Order which requires attendance at a facility for treatment of his or her mental disorder. Alternatively the court having received a medical report may conclude that the offender has a mental disorder of such seriousness that they require medium to long-term hospitalisation for treatment and so make a Hospital Order under s.37. If the same offender on the termination of the Hospital Order still presents a serious risk of harm to others he or she may be subject to a s.41 Restriction Order which will extend detainment in hospital for an indefinite period if necessary.

David Bennett passed backwards and forwards between the criminal justice system and the mental health system. He was subject both to short-term detainment in hospital under the criminal provisions of the Mental Health Act 1983 and to conditions of probation which required him to comply with treatment for his mental disorder. The independent inquiry identified a lack of follow-up and supervision of David in the community by mental health professionals. As a result he quickly failed to keep to the conditions of his probation relating to treatment for his mental disorder. This in turn led to a prison sentence, which appeared to further undermine his mental health. Effective liaison and inter-agency work between the police, probation officers, mental health professionals and social workers within mental health teams is crucial to ensure that offenders, just like any other mental health user, receive the assistance that they need to access treatment and aftercare services. In this case effective intera-gency work could have prevented David's return to court and subsequent custodial sentence, which arguably exacerbated his mental disorder.

Detainment for treatment

During 1992 David failed to take his anti-psychotic medication, and his mental state deteriorated. On two occasions during that year he was admitted to hospital under s.3 of the Mental Health Act 1983. The process for applying for a person's detainment for treatment under s.3 is similar to that for detainment under s.2 for assessment (see above, page 417). Hence detainment under s.3 requires that an Approved Mental Health Professional or the *nearest relative* must make the application which has to be supported by two doctors, one of whom must be appointed under s.12 of the Mental Health Act 1983. Both doctors must have seen and examined the person to be detained. The criteria for the use of s.3 are set out in the box below.

Key legislation

Mental Health Act 1983 (as amended)

3(2) An application for admission for treatment may be made in respect of a patient on the grounds that –

    (a) he is suffering from mental disorder of a nature or degree which makes it appropriate for him to receive medical treatment in hospital; and

    (b) . . . [repealed]

    (c) it is necessary for the health or safety of the patient or for the protection of other persons that he should receive such treatment and it cannot be provided unless he is detained under this section; and

    (d) appropriate medical treatment is available for him

3(3) An application for admission for treatment shall be founded on the written recommendations in the prescribed form of two registered medical practitioners, including in each case a statement that in the opinion of the practitioner the conditions set out in subsection (2) above are complied with;

3(4) In this Act, references to appropriate medical treatment, in relation to a person suffering from mental disorder, are references to medical treatment which is appropriate in his case, taking into account the nature and degree of the mental disorder and all other circumstances of this case.

s.145(4) Any reference in this Act to medical treatment in relation to mental disorder shall be construed as a reference to medical treatment the purpose of which is to alleviate, or prevent a worsening of, the disorder or one or more of its symptoms or manifestations.

In the case of David Bennett, he had already been diagnosed as having schizophrenia and thus had a mental disorder 'of a nature or degree which makes it appropriate for him to receive medical treatment in hospital'. He was also someone with a history of physical attacks on others and deemed liable to commit more. David therefore met the s.3(2)(c) criterion for detainment. As regards the third criterion, set out in s.3(2)(d), which requires that 'appropriate medical treatment is available', this was an amendment introduced by the Mental Health Act 2007. It replaced the 'treatability test' which was in force at the time of the events leading up to David Bennett's death.

The effect of the amendment to the Mental Health Act 1983 brought in by the Mental Health Act 2007 is to lower the threshold of the treatment criterion from that 'likely to alleviate or prevent a deterioration' to 'the purpose of which is to alleviate or prevent a worsening of' the mental disorder. In other words, under the Mental Health Act 2007 amendment medical practitioners now no longer have to prove that the treatment to be given to patients detained under s.3 is *likely* to improve or prevent a deterioration of their mental condition, only that it was *intended* to do so. David had been diagnosed with a well-recognised disorder for which anti-psychotic drugs were known to reduce its symptoms. Consequently, under both the original Mental Health Act 1983 and the amendment introduced by the Mental Health Act 2007 David's condition would have met the criteria for treatment. Further direction is given to practitioners in the Code of Practice which is reproduced in the box below.

 Key guidance

Mental Health Act 1983: Code of Practice

Para. 4.4 Before it is decided that admission to hospital is necessary, consideration must be given to whether there are alternative means of providing the care and treatment which the patient requires. This includes consideration of whether there might be other effective forms of care or treatment which the patient would be willing to accept, and of whether guardianship would be appropriate instead.

Para. 4.5 In all cases, consideration must be given to:

- the patient's wishes and view of their own needs;
- the patient's age and physical health;
- any past wishes or feelings expressed by the patient;
- the patient's cultural background;
- the patient's social and family circumstances;
- the impact that any future deterioration or lack of improvement in the patient's condition would have on their children, other relatives or carers, especially those living with the patient, including an assessment of these people's ability and willingness to cope; and
- the effect on the patient, and those close to the patient, of a decision to admit or not to admit under the Act.

Para. 4.9 When a patient needs to be in hospital, informal admission is usually appropriate when a patient who has the capacity to do so consents to admission.

Para. 4.10 However, this should not be regarded as an absolute rule, especially if the reason for considering admission is that the patient presents a clear danger to themselves or others because of their mental disorder.

Para. 4.11 Compulsory admission should, in particular, be considered where a patient's current mental state, together with reliable evidence of past experience, indicates a strong likelihood that they will have a change of mind about informal admission, either before or after they are admitted, with a resulting risk to their health or safety or to the safety of other people.

Paragraph 4.4 of the Code of Practice draws attention to the requirement that professionals involved in making an application for a s.3 detainment should endeavour to discuss with the person concerned alternatives to compulsory admission to hospital. These alternatives include treatment in the community or informal admission to hospital for treatment. Paragraph 4.5 of the Code of Practice requires social workers and healthcare professionals considering detainment of a patient under s.2 or s.3 to consider the impact of this on the patient, their family and the progress of their mental disorder. As paragraph 4.9

of the Code indicates, compulsion under the Mental Health Act 1983 is normally a last resort. However, there are a few circumstances detailed in paragraphs 4.10 and 4.11 where despite the apparent willingness of the patient to be admitted informally, detainment is indicated. David had a history of violence against others and it was known that he absconded from hospital or failed to take his medication. Therefore the Code of Practice was complied with in deciding to use s.3 to admit him compulsorily for treatment.

At the time of the events surrounding David Bennett's death, leave of absence from hospital under s.17 of the Mental Health Act 1983 was the predominant means used to compel patients detained under s.2, s.3 or s.37 to comply with their treatment once back living in the community. Any patient conditionally discharged from hospital under s.17 who subsequently failed to take their medication or meet some other specified requirement could at the discretion of the Responsible Medical Officer (now Responsible Clinician) be recalled to hospital. Once back in hospital, as they were still a detained patient, they could be compelled to accept medical intervention. The Mental Health Act 2007 amended the Mental Health Act 1983 to create a new form of compulsion for patients such as David, that is to say, formerly detained patients, who on returning to the community were unlikely to take their medication, triggering deterioration of their mental health which in turn would endanger their own safety or that of others. The new s.17A of the Mental Health Act 1983 creates Community Treatment Orders (also known as supervised community treatment). A Community Treatment Order (CTO) cannot be made unless a patient would meet the criteria for detainment under s.3 or s.37.

This means that a CTO can be used either for individuals who would meet the s.3 criteria for detainment or those who have already been detained under this section and are ready for discharge from hospital. David had of course already been detained on a number of occasions under s.3 and on returning to the community had failed to take his prescribed anti-psychotic drugs. As a result his mental health had deteriorated leading to re-admission to hospital under a new s.3 application. The effect of a Community Treatment Order is to permit a Responsible Clinician to recall patients to hospital if they fail to take their medication while in the community, or breach any other condition of the CTO. This means that under the Mental Health Act 1983 (as amended) there is a wide range of powers to compulsorily detain those who have or appear to have a mental disorder, for assessment or treatment. Such powers can also be applied to mental health patients recently discharged from hospital or still living in the community. The sections of the Mental Health Act 1983 (as amended) which authorise the use of these powers are outlined in the table below.

Civil provisions of the Mental Health Act 1983

Sections of the Mental Health Act 1983	Requirements to apply the section	Effect of the section
s.2 Detainment for Assessment	Application by AMHP or *nearest relative* supported by two doctors	• Detainment in hospital for assessment, treatment can be given without consent for mental disorder • Duration 28 days renewable
s.3 Detainment for Treatment	Application by AMHP or *nearest relative* supported by two doctors	• Detainment in hospital for treatment which can be given without consent for mental disorder • Duration 6 months renewable

(Continued)

Civil provisions of the Mental Health Act 1983 *(continued)*

Sections of the Mental Health Act 1983	Requirements to apply the section	Effect of the sections
s.4 Detainment in an Emergency	Application by AMHP or *nearest relative* supported by one doctor	• Detainment in hospital, treatment can only be given with patient's consent • Duration 72 hours
s.5 Detainment of patient already in hospital	Holding power exercised by doctor or nurse	• Can only be used for in-patients receiving treatment in hospital • Prevents a patient from leaving the hospital • Treatment can only be given with patient's consent • Duration 72 hours if doctor's holding power and 6 hours if nurse's holding power
s.7 Reception into Guardianship	Application by AMHP or *nearest relative* supported by two doctors	• Patient under care of named guardian which can be the local authority • Patient must consent to treatment • Duration six months renewable for six months and yearly thereafter
s.17 Leave from Hospital (largely superseded by s.17A)	Granted by Responsible Clinician	• Leave with conditions, e.g. taking prescribed drugs granted to detained patients • Permits detained patients to leave hospital and live in community • Leave can be for specified period or up to the next renewal date • Patient is liable to recall to hospital for breaching conditions • Recall is by notice in writing to the patient
s.17A Supervised Community Treatment (Community Treatment Order)	Must be agreed by both the Responsible Clinician and an AMHP	• Treatment in the community with possibility of recall to hospital if failure to comply • Duration six months renewable for six months and yearly thereafter
s.135 Warrant to search for and remove patient	Application by anyone to Justice of the Peace (a Magistrate), but warrant is executed by a police officer accompanied by a AMHP	• Power to search and remove to a place of safety a person suspected of suffering from a mental disorder • Patient must consent to treatment • Duration 72 hours
s.136 Police Power to Remove Person to Place of Safety	Power exercised by a police officer	• Power to remove to a place of safety a person found in a public place who appears to be suffering from a mental disorder • Person must consent to treatment • Duration 72 hours non-renewable
s.137 Retaking of a patient subject to detainment or guardianship	Power exercised by a police officer or AMHP	• Power to retake a patient using reasonable force if they are detained and abscond, have been recalled to hospital or are subject to guardianship

While the Mental Health Act 1983 (as amended) grants mental health professionals wide ranging powers of compulsion these must be exercised in compliance not only with the statute itself, but also with the related Code of Practice. Paragraph 1.3 of the Code describes the *least restriction principle*, which requires that those using compulsory powers do so in a manner which seeks 'to keep to a minimum the restrictions they impose on the patient's liberty'. In this instance the Approved Social Worker who applied to detain David under s.3 for treatment in hospital ensured that he met all the threshold criteria listed in this section of the Mental Health Act 1983. However, the *least restrictive principle* requires Approved Mental Health Professionals to do more than merely ensure that all of the threshold criteria for detainment are met. It enjoins them to choose the treatment option which imposes the fewest restrictions on the patient's liberty. Unfortunately David consistently failed to take his anti-psychotic drugs while in the community, resulting in deterioration of his mental health and violence towards others. In these circumstances, paragraph 4.10 of the Code of Practice permits social workers to use detainment as opposed to informal admission to re-admit a patient to hospital for the treatment of a mental disorder. For this reason the Approved Social Worker was justified in resorting to compulsion under s.3. This approach is consistent with paragraph 4.3 of the GSCC *Code of Practice for Social Care Workers* which obliges practitioners to take 'necessary steps to minimise the risks of service users from doing actual or potential harm to themselves or other people'.

Introduced after David Bennett's death, the intended effect of the Community Treatment Order created by the Mental Health Act 2007 is that this will constitute a less restrictive measure than detainment in hospital. Therefore Approved Mental Health Professionals and Responsible Clinicians now have an additional option when deciding whether to admit a person for treatment or to discharge an inpatient from detainment in hospital. At the same time a Community Treatment Order, because of the range of conditions which can be imposed upon a mental health patient living in the community, can of itself severely restrict liberty. As paragraph 25.33 reminds mental health professionals, even the conditions of Community Treatment Orders must 'restrict the patient's liberty as little as possible while being consistent with achieving their purpose'.

Critical commentary

Guardianship under the Mental Health Act 1983

Guardianship was incorporated into the Mental Health Act 1983 with the intention that it should be used to provide long-term support, supervision and guidance to those living in the community with an enduring mental illness or mental impairment. It empowers the guardian (who may be a local authority) to require the patient to: live in a specified place; attend specified facilities or programmes; and permit monitoring by mental health professionals. There are around 1,000 people with a mental disorder subject to guardianship in England and Wales in any given year. As is demonstrable from this small figure, guardianship is not often invoked under the Mental Health Act 1983. Instead Responsible Clinicians tend to use s.17 (leave of absence from hospital) which permits them to attach conditions. The introduction of Community Treatment Orders is unlikely to change the apparent unpopularity of guardianship relative to other means of control under the Mental Health Act 1983. A number of studies have investigated the reasons for the underuse of guardianship.

Shaw, et al. (2000) investigated the variation in the use of guardianship across 130 local authorities. On average each Social Services Department was found to be responsible for administering approximately five guardianships which is an exceptionally low figure compared to the total numbers of individuals receiving mental health services in the community. Indeed of the 130 local authorities surveyed just over one-quarter had no guardianship cases at all. Hatfield, et al. (2004: 206) found that guardianship tended to be used most in circumstances where there was a history of self-neglect or exploitation by others of the mental health patient. It was also sometimes invoked where there was potential risk of violence towards others in the community. Once established, guardianship tended to involve ongoing contact from support staff rather than mental health professionals, with an emphasis on taking medication and practical help rather than on rehabilitative activity (Hatfield, et al., 2004: 206).

Guardianship tends to be used for those perceived as having high welfare needs, particularly in relation to accommodation, relationships and daytime activities. This contrasts with the use of other forms of conditional discharge from hospital for patients perceived to be at a higher risk of harming themselves or others. In this regard it is notable that patients of African-Caribbean heritage were over-represented among forms of conditional discharge and under-represented in guardianship under the Mental Health Act 1983 (Hatfield, et al., 2001: 513-4). It would appear from this study that one of the main reasons why guardianship is underused is that it is perceived as a welfare measure rather than an effective means of managing risk in the community. Given that policy drivers in mental health converge on the supposed danger which mental health patients in the community pose to members of the public it is not surprising that conditional discharge as a form of risk management is favoured over guardianship with its greater emphasis on welfare.

Consent to treatment

As set out in the box below, s.63 of the Mental Health Act 1983 permits a wide range of treatments for detained patients against their will if the purpose 'is to alleviate or prevent a worsening of' the mental disorder. However, s.63 does not apply to all forms of treatment for mental disorders. For particularly invasive forms of medical intervention such as neurosurgery or electro-convulsive therapy (ECT) under s.57 and s.58A respectively, the consent of the patient is required. Although as s.62 (detailed in the box below) indicates, such treatments are permitted without consent in an emergency.

 Key legislation

Mental Health Act 1983 (as amended)

s.62(1) Section 57 and 58 above shall not apply to any treatment –
    (a) which is immediately necessary to save the patient's life; or
    (b) which (not being irreversible) is immediately necessary to prevent a serious deterioration of his condition; or
    (c) which (not being irreversible or hazardous) is immediately necessary to alleviate serious suffering by the patient; or
    (d) which (not being irreversible or hazardous) is immediately necessary and represents the minimum interference necessary to prevent the patient from behaving violently or being a danger to himself or to others.

> s.63 The consent of a patient shall not be required for any medical treatment given to him for the mental disorder from which his is suffering, not being a form of treatment to which section 57, 58 or 58A above applies, if the treatment is given by or under the direction of the approved clinician in charge of the treatment.

David was not subject to any of the invasive treatments specified under s.57 or s.58A, but he was detained for long periods of time in hospital and compelled to accept medication to which he objected. Detained patients receiving any form of treatment for a mental disorder for more than three months are provided with an additional safeguard under s.58 of the Mental Health Act 1983. As can be seen from s.63 set out *above*, normally all that is required for the compulsory administration of medication for a mental disorder is the approval of the clinician in charge of the treatment. However, under s.58 once a detained patient has received such compulsory treatment for three months continued administration of it requires either:

The consent of the patient to further treatment and the approval of the clinician in charge of it or a second opinion appointed doctor (SOAD), normally a psychiatrist of at least 5 years experience who is approved by the Care Quality Commission (formally the Mental Health Act Commission).

or

If the patient refuses to consent to further treatment but it is deemed appropriate for the treatment to continue, then a SOAD must approve the treatment after consultation with two other people professionally involved in the patient's treatment, one of whom must be a nurse, but neither of whom can be the Responsible Clinician or the clinician in charge of the treatment.

David was often subject to periods of detainment under s.3 beyond three months between 1991 and his death in 1998. Records examined by the Independent Inquiry and the statements of witnesses showed that David thought his medication was excessive and he objected to it during a number of admissions to hospital. In compliance with the requirements of s.58 a SOAD approved the continuation of David's anti-psychotic medication when it was indicated and on occasion sanctioned an increase in the dosage, overriding David Bennett's objections to this.

Dr Sagovsky, a consultant psychiatrist who joined Peterborough District Hospital in 1990, told the inquiry (page 11) that 'the levels of medication that David Bennett was on were higher than almost any other patient she had known'. When questioned, she denied that this was attributable to his perceived aggressiveness and unpredictable attacks on professional staff. Although in evidence to the inquiry Dr Sagovsky did concede that 'because of his violence, which the staff often saw as unprovoked, and because he was a very athletic young man, the staff were quite frightened of him' (page 10). The post-mortem conducted on David during October 1998 in the Norvic Clinic revealed that while he was on a high dosage of anti-psychotic drugs these were within prescribed therapeutic limits. Amendments to the Mental Health Act 1983 introduced since David Bennett's death now provide for Independent Mental Health Advocates (IMHA). These are people who are recognised supporters for detained patients and those subject to Community Treatment Orders.

Independent Mental Health Advocates can represent patients in their dealings with mental health professionals. In David Bennett's case an IMHA could (but only with

David's permission) have accessed his medical records and advocated for a reduction in the dosage of the drugs being administered to him. IMHAs have a number of rights and functions which are set out in the box below.

Key legislation

Mental Health Act 1983 (as amended)

Under s.130B Independent Mental Health Advocates are required to assist patients in obtaining information about the:

- Section of the Mental Health Act under which the patient has been detained
- Conditions or restrictions which apply to the patient
- Treatment being considered or given to the patient
- Legal rights of the patient

In order to carry out these tasks alongside advocacy work on behalf of detained patients Independent Mental Health Advocates are (with the consent of a patient who had capacity) entitled to:

- Visit and interview the patient in private
- Visit and interview anyone professionally involved in the patient's care
- Inspect any records relating to the detention or treatment of the patient in hospital.
- Inspect any records in relation to aftercare services provided under s.117 of the Mental Health Act 1983
- Inspect any records held by Social Services relating to the patient

Many drug regimes have unpleasant side effects. Anti-psychotic drugs, which are usually strong tranquillisers, can result in poor concentration and excessive tiredness. It is understandable that mental health patients (who are often also parents and employees) will seek to avoid the additional detriment to their mental health which neuroleptic medication can cause. The *participation principle* described in paragraph 1.5 of the Code of Practice stipulates that 'patients must be given the opportunity to be involved, as far as is practicable in the circumstances, in planning, developing and reviewing their own treatment and care'. Evidence from the Independent Inquiry into David Bennett's death indicates that there was little consultation with him regarding his medication and no notice was taken of his complaints about the dosage.

While it is the Responsible Clinician and sometimes a SOAD who prescribes the treatment regime for a mental disorder, this does not preclude social workers from advocating on behalf of mental health service-users. Psychiatric wards are widely acknowledged to be disempowering settings for patients. Social workers liaising with psychiatric colleagues continue to have an important role under the GSCC Code of Practice to promote the 'views and wishes of both service users and carers' in accordance with paragraph 1.2. Social workers may also be instrumental in assisting mental health users to avail of the services of Independent Mental Health Advocates. Ultimately, regardless of whether a user is in hospital or living in the community, practitioners remain bound by paragraph 1.3 of the GSCC Code to continue 'supporting service users' rights to control their own lives and make informed choices about the services they receive'. This includes their treatment for a mental disorder, which may include not only medication but rehabilitation services.

Perspectives

Users' views of consent to treatment

Paragraph 20.31 of the *Mental Health Act 1983: Code of Practice* defines 'consent' as 'the voluntary and continuing permission of a patient to be given a particular treatment, based on a sufficient knowledge of the purpose, nature, likely effects and risks of that treatment, including the likelihood of its success and any alternatives to it. Permission given under any unfair or undue pressure is not consent'. Paragraph 23.37 reminds clinicians that 'although the Mental Health Act permits some medical treatment for mental disorder to be given without consent, the patient's consent should still be sought before treatment is given, wherever practicable'.

Larkin, et al. (2009) conducted semi-structured interviews with seven detained patients in a medium secure psychiatric hospital to investigate their experiences of consenting to and refusing consent to treatment for their mental disorder. Jimmy in his responses typified the confusion that mental health patients sometimes experience in obtaining information about treatment. His decision to accept treatment he did not comprehend illustrates the extent to which acquiescence or compliance by mental health patients can be interpreted as informed consent by professionals. Jimmy told the researchers:

> You don't always see it when it's explained to you the first time . . . sometimes you have to talk to somebody else about it, and say, 'well, what was that they meant?' Did they, you know, explain it maybe more? Some people explain better . . . sometimes you don't see it at all, and then sort of just agrees with it, and that's it. (Larkin, et al., 2009: 178)

For patients detained for longer than three months continued treatment required the approval of a Second Opinion Appointed Doctor (SOAD) under s.58 of the Mental Health Act 1983. However, many patients like William thought that 'it is somewhat of a mechanistic rubber-stamping process'. They were convinced that SOADs rarely if ever questioned the opinion of the Responsible Medical Officer (Larkin, et al., 2009: 179). Many drug regimes have unpleasant side effects and other patients used their knowledge of a particular treatment to engage in successful non-compliance. Andrew explained:

> I've refused all my medication at some time . . . you know, the lithium as well, and they've said, 'well I can't force you to take lithium'. Because he knows he can't squeeze it in between your teeth . . . and you can't get an injection for them, so I've refused to take that. (Larkin, et al., 2009: 179)

Corroborating the perspectives of patients in the study, a Responsible Medical Officer at the same psychiatric unit admitted:

> Of course if you have detained patients, there is no such thing as freely given consent . . . Even with the patients that are consenting to take the medication, they're not really consenting patients because they are detained and they know the system, and they know if they refuse the medication they're likely to get second-opinioned, and they're to get given the medication anyway, and that if they refuse oral medication they're likely to get given intra-muscular medication . . . They know that taking medication regularly and in a compliant manner is likely to lead to their swift discharge from hospital. So, the whole system's coercive. (Larkin, et al., 2009: 179)

Use of restraint

David Bennett had been known to attack members of the public on occasion. He also had a documented history of physical assaults on nursing staff both at Peterborough District Hospital and at the Norvic Clinic. Indeed the major reason why he was transferred so many times between Peterborough District Hospital, St Andrew's Hospital and the Norvic Clinic, a specialist psychiatric unit, was because of his violence and the need for secure accommodation. A number of these attacks had involved punching and kicking. On the night that he died David had punched a fellow male patient during an altercation over the use of a telephone on Drayton Ward in the Norvic Clinic. On this occasion the patient punched him back. It was at this point that nursing staff intervened and David was moved to Thorpe Ward, where he repeatedly punched Staff Nurse Hadley. This led to other nursing staff becoming involved in order to halt his assault on Staff Nurse Hadley and prevent further physical violence. At one point in this struggle David began to strangle one of the other nurses attempting to restrain him. It was during the time that David was pinned to the ground in a prone position (lying on his front face downwards) by four nurses that he died on the floor of Thorpe Ward. The *Mental Health Act 1983: Code of Practice* identifies the matters to be considered in the use of physical restraint. These are set out in the box below.

Key guidance

Mental Health Act 1983: Code of Practice

Para. 15.5 Factors which may contribute to disturbed behaviour include:

- Boredom and lack of environmental stimulation
- Too much stimulation, noise and general disruption
- Excessive heating, overcrowding and lack of access to external space
- Personal frustrations associated with being in a restricted environment
- Difficulties in communication
- Emotional distress, e.g. following bereavement
- Antagonism, aggression or provocation on the part of others
- The influence of alcohol or drugs
- Physical illness
- An unsuitable mix of patients

Para. 15.6 All hospitals should have a policy on the recognition and prevention of disturbed, or violent, behaviour, as well as risk assessment and management, including the use of de-escalation techniques, enhanced observation, physical intervention, rapid tranquilisation and seclusion. Local policies should suit the needs of the particular groups of patients who may be treated in the hospital.

Para. 15.7 The primary focus of any policy for managing patients who may present with disturbed or violent behaviour (or both) should be the establishment of a culture which focuses on early recognition, prevention and de-escalation of potential aggression, using techniques that minimise the risk of its occurrence.

Para. 15.8 Interventions such as physical restraint, rapid tranquilisation, seclusion and observation should be used only where de-escalation alone proves insufficient, and should always be used in conjunction with further efforts at de-escalation; they must never be used as punishment or in a punitive manner.

Para. 15.9 Any such intervention must be used in a way that minimises any risk to the patient's health and safety and that causes the minimum interference to their privacy and dignity, while being consistent with the need to protect the patient and other people.

After hearing evidence the Independent Inquiry concluded that physical restraint had been necessary at the time of the attack on SN Hadley. At that particular moment it was the only viable means of preventing further acts of violence by David Bennett. The inquiry panel also heard evidence on how restraint should be employed and concluded that nursing staff had incorrectly applied the technique in a way which contributed to David's death. Most importantly, no nurse had been positioned at David's head for the period he was on the floor, from where they would have detected early signs of any respiratory difficulties. Secondly, there were too many nurses restraining David at the one time, which led to excessive pressure on his body as staff lay on top of him in an effort to restrain him. Finally, David Bennett was involved in a prolonged struggle with staff in the prone position lasting up to twenty minutes which at the post-mortem was found to have caused his death by placing too much stress on his heart (page 32). The approach taken to restraining David plainly contravened guidance contained in paragraph 15.9 of the Code of Practice.

Good practice, set out in paragraphs 15.7 and 15.8 of the Code of Practice, emphasises the importance of identifying potential situations of violence and intervening early to de-escalate them. According to the report of the inquiry, unfortunately this did not happen on the night of David's death. He had been involved in an exchange of punches with a fellow patient who had racially abused him when David had asked to use the telephone. Yet, it was David and not the other patient who was made to move from Drayton Ward to Thorpe Ward. Furthermore, the other patient was not reprimanded for his behaviour either at the time or afterwards. This led to David feeling resentment and a sense of injustice, which escalated on arriving at Thorpe Ward where one of his first actions was to attack a nurse. Paragraph 15.13 reminds those working under the Mental Health Act 1983 that a 'patient's behaviour should be seen in context. Professionals should not categorise behaviour as disturbed without taking account of the circumstances under which it occurs. ' The inquiry concluded that there had been a missed opportunity to de-escalate the situation earlier when nursing staff failed to address the provocative conduct of the patient who exchanged punches with David.

Guidance set out in the *Mental Health Act 1983: Code of Practice* directs professionals to be vigilant and alert to early signs of disturbance or agitation of a patient. Where this is observed they must take action to de-escalate any potentially violent situation. As the circumstances surrounding David's aggression towards others demonstrates, violence can be directed at members of the public, professionals or other patients. Practitioners may be called upon to de-escalate a potentially violent incident in any of these contexts. Where de-escalation has been unsuccessful or when aggression is sudden and unprovoked, professionals acting in compliance with the Code of Practice must choose the least interventionist course of action consistent with protecting the patient and others from injury. Often this will depend on the availability of alternatives. For instance on Thorpe Ward the seclusion room in which David could have been secured until he calmed down was just a few paces away from where he attacked Staff Nurse Hadley. The ferocity of his violence and the imminent danger to nurse Hadley of sustaining serious injury was such that, at least initially, nursing staff had little choice but to use the prone position.

Social workers will not be directly involved in physically restraining mental health patients, but like Independent Mental Health Advocates they are likely to have a role in listening to users' viewpoints and relating these back to medical staff. The *Mental Health Act 1983: Code of Practice* makes clear that more often than not aggression in a hospital setting is related to environmental factors. Proactively engaging with mental health users often means that social workers (whether in their role as Care Co-ordinator or Approved Mental Health Professionals) are the first person to whom a user turns to discuss the problems they are experiencing in a medical setting. These may relate directly to the list of factors outlined in paragraph 15.5 of the Code, which contribute to incidents of violence on psychiatric wards. Social workers who are privy to information which plainly affects the quality of service received by users should be active in sharing this with healthcare professionals. Paragraph 6.7 of the GSCC Code requires social workers to recognise the expertise of professionals from other agencies while working closely with them. Effective multi-agency work means that social workers need to recognise that users do not cease to be their concern simply because they are admitted to hospital. The disclosure of adverse experiences by mental health patients demands tact from social workers when addressing these with professionals from other agencies.

Ethnicity and culture

It is significant that the precipitating incident which culminated in David's death was racial abuse from a fellow patient. Referring to this, the inquiry panel wrote, 'We conclude that the staff did not appreciate the need to speak to either patient in order to attempt to de-escalate the incident. They also did not appreciate the importance of doing this because they were unaware of the corrosive and cumulative effect of racist abuse upon a black patient' (page 27). Throughout the inquiry the panel was struck by the lack of attention given to David's African-Caribbean background, his spiritual beliefs and his experiences as a black patient in a predominantly ethnically white environment. David had previously reported to Dr Joanna Bennett, his sister, that at St Andrew's Hospital he was subject to racial abuse and taunts (page 8). It was observed by the inquiry that there were no black members of staff at the Norvic Clinic which was a matter of concern to David who brought it to the attention of the management (page 9). The inquiry panel also noted that the Norvic Clinic appeared to have taken few tangible measures to remedy this situation.

An underlying principle of mental health law, which is set out in paragraph 1.4 of the *Mental Health Act 1983: Code of Practice*, is that 'people taking decisions under the Act must recognise and respect the diverse needs, values and circumstances of each patient, including their race, religion, culture, gender, age, sexual orientation and any disability'. More specifically, paragraph 15.12 of the Code requires that 'services and their staff should demonstrate and encourage respect for racial and cultural diversity and recognise the need for privacy and dignity'. A patient's cultural background is also a consideration when deciding whether to admit a patient to hospital for assessment or treatment in the first instance, as indicated in paragraph 4.5 of the Code (see box above on page 432). The place accorded to culture and race in guidance to professionals and the lack of attention given to it in David Bennett's care was a matter of concern to the Independent Inquiry.

None of the evidence presented to the inquiry indicated that there had been deliberate racism on the part of any professional involved in David's care. Medical staff appearing before the inquiry did admit that racial abuse sometimes occurred between patients and was difficult to tackle because of the fragile mental state of the individuals concerned. There was no policy at the Norvic Clinic on recording racist incidents between patients. Consequently, neither the doctors nor nursing staff could be sure of the extent to which David had encountered racism on the ward. In the opinion of the panel none of the professionals directly involved in David's care had given sufficient thought to his experiences as often the only black patient on the ward in a situation where almost all the staff were also white.

There was some evidence that individual staff members had endeavoured to take account of David's ethnic background. For instance, the Norvic Clinic did obtain from London, especially for David, *The Voice*, an African-Caribbean newspaper. But there were very obvious lapses as well. For example, Dr Stanley, the consultant psychiatrist who took over as David's Responsible Medical Officer (Responsible Clinician) at the Norvic Clinic in January 1998, was aware that he was a practising Rastafarian. However, she did not inquire into his spiritual beliefs or requirements or the ramifications for him of being a black man of African-Caribbean heritage in an environment which was predominantly white. Apart from permitting David to put up posters relating to his faith there was little consideration given to his ethnic or religious background or his experiences of racism. While the panel found no examples of overt racism by professionals towards David, it did identify their obliviousness to his needs as a person of African-Caribbean heritage (pages 23–25). After hearing all the evidence the panel concluded (page 24) that:

> we do not find any instance of deliberate racism in The Norvic Clinic. Nor can we find any instance of deliberate racism in respect of David Bennett's earlier treatment at other mental health institutions. But there certainly was insufficient attention paid to his cultural, social and religious needs. Individually, the nurses impressed us as being kind, considerate and helpful, and often generous with their time and money in looking after David Bennett.

The independent inquiry focussed on the treatment of David within a hospital setting and was critical of the lack of attention given to his African-Caribbean heritage in this context. The social workers who came into contact with David appeared not to have built up a sufficiently trusting relationship with him to have become involved in addressing some of these issues on his behalf with healthcare colleagues. The GSCC Code of Practice is clear at paragraph 1.6 that social workers must respect 'diversity and different cultures and values'. While the word 'respect' lacks specificity on what this means in practice, at a minimum it does involve finding out about the cultural background, spiritual beliefs and religious observances of mental health users. For patients such as David, who move backwards and forwards between hospital and the community, it is particularly important for social and healthcare professionals to liaise and agree on how best to meet their cultural and spiritual needs. This approach is consistent with the *respect principle* which enjoins mental health professionals to 'respect the diverse needs, values and circumstances of each patient, including their race, religion, culture, gender, age, sexual orientation and any disability'.

Paragraph 5.5 of the GSCC *Code of Practice for Social Care Workers* prohibits practitioners from discriminating against users, carers or colleagues. It also obliges practitioners to take a step further than just respecting diversity or not engaging in discrimination, it requires social workers to adopt a proactive anti-oppressive stance. Paragraph 5.6 is unequivocal in stating that social workers must 'not condone any unlawful or unjustifiable discrimination by services users, carers or colleagues'. Silence in the presence of racial abuse, or the inadequate response to it which characterised the conduct of healthcare staff who came into contact with David Bennett, is tantamount to condoning that abuse. For this reason practitioners have to be mindful not only of their own prejudicial attitudes or behaviours, but also those of others. The new Equality Duty imposed on public bodies includes the National Health Service and local authorities. This means that professionals employed by these organisations are under a statutory duty to work towards the elimination of discrimination and the promotion of equal opportunity for people regardless of their colour, ethnic origin or religion.

Perspectives

Views of African and African-Caribbean mental health users

Sproston and Nazroo (2002) conducted a large-scale national study of mental health problems among ethnic minorities in the United Kingdom. They found no statistically significant differences in the incidence of psychotic illnesses among ethnic minority communities as compared to the white majority population. Despite this finding, men of African-Caribbean heritage are five times more likely to be diagnosed with schizophrenia than are white British males (Mason, 2000: 98). They are also three times more likely than their white counterparts to be detained under the Mental Health Act 1983 (Smaje, 1995: 66). In her overview of the research, Laird (2008: 14-5, 111-12) reveals that people of African-Caribbean descent are less likely than those from the white majority to receive 'talking treatments' such as psychotherapy or counselling. Yet those of African-Caribbean backgrounds are more likely than individuals from the white majority population to:

- Be compulsorily detained.
- Have police involvement in their detention under s.136.
- Be identified as violent.
- Be kept in a secure psychiatric unit.
- Receive anti-psychotic drugs or electro-convulsive therapy.
- Receive higher dosages of drugs.
- Be subject to the forcible administration of medication.
- Be subject to physical restraint.

Secker and Harding (2002) interviewed 24 mental health users, 18 of whom described themselves as of African-Caribbean heritage and 6 of African descent. Most had a diagnosis of schizophrenia and experience of multiple hospital admissions. Many interviewees complained of being sectioned and medicated with little attention paid by professionals to helping them understand and manage their mental health problem. Two research participants typify the experiences of many:

'After about four weeks of being in hospital I was sectioned, under section three, and I felt that there was no need for that . . . they could have explained to me exactly what were the problems that they found, the symptoms that I was having . . . but they sectioned me and injected me and shipped me off to a closed ward unit.'

'I asked to see a psychologist and they point blank refused to let me see a psychologist at any time at all . . . I thought if I could get to talk to somebody instead of having all this injection and medication that used to make me feel terrible and really paranoid and horrible and terrible feeling . . .' (Secker and Harding, 2002: 162-3)

Several male interviewees described their encounters with racism within the psychiatric system:

'I found that the staff didn't fully understand, and this is because of my colour and my upbringing, didn't fully understand my concerns about my own well-being and the problems of being black and still being in the mental health system . . . and knowing that the treatment that you got seemed to be very different from those of your, of white people that were in the mental health services as well.'

'I've never, in 15 years, I never put my hand on anybody patient or nurse. Yet they perceive me as being aggressive so I can't work that quite out. I think it, it's just to do with black people, you know. It's like, they don't . . . understand, or like, and do want to suppress black people. That's my experience. It's very racist, the nurses, the doctors . . . I think at the time it was appalling what happened to me. If I was white and middle class or something you wouldn't, they wouldn't have done that to me.' (Secker and Harding, 2002: 163-4)

> For those African and African-Caribbean interviewees who reported beneficial experiences, having the opportunity to talk about their problems rather than being medicated for them was a key aspect of positive interactions with mental health professionals. One research participant (Secker and Harding, 2002: 164) described this:
>
>> 'I am seeing the same psychiatrist so I did build up a good relationship with him . . . It's good to have somebody you can talk to, who can hold things confidential to you. Things that you can't tell friends and family, my psychiatrist is always there as a counsellor . . . He doesn't treat me as if I am insane. He treats me like a normal person and just having somebody there to guide you and to support you with things you do in your personal life, you know give you advice.'

Aftercare in the community

David Bennett's experience as a mental health patient, like that of many others, was characterised by successive admissions to hospital followed by discharges back into the community and subsequent re-admissions to hospital. The potential for the deterioration of a patient's mental health on returning home makes aftercare on leaving hospital a vital component of healthcare planning. Precisely for this reason s.117 of the Mental Health Act 1983, which is reproduced in the box below, places a duty on primary care trusts and local social services to provide care in the community on the discharge of a detained patient. This duty does not apply to informal patients or those detained for short periods under s.2, s.4, s.5, s.135 or s.136. It does include patients detained under the civil and criminal provisions of the Mental Health Act 1983 for treatment. It also includes patients receiving supervised community treatment who were detained in hospital and discharged subject to a Community Treatment Order under s.17A. For such patients aftercare under s.117 may extend beyond the termination of their Community Treatment Order if they still require support from services.

 Key legislation

Mental Health Act 1983 (as amended)

s.117(1) This section applies to persons who are detained under section 3 above, or admitted to a hospital in pursuance of a hospital order made under s.37 above, or transferred to a hospital in pursuance of a hospital direction made under section 45A above or transfer direction made under section 47 or 48 above, and then cease to be detained and (whether or not immediately after so ceasing) leave hospital.

s.117(2) It shall be the duty of the Primary Care Trust or Local Health Board and of the local social services authority to provide, in co-operation with relevant voluntary agencies, aftercare services for any person to whom this section applies until such time as the Primary Care Trust or Local Health Board and the local social services authority are satisfied that the person concerned is no longer in need of such services; but they shall not be so satisfied in the case of a community patient while he remains such a patient.

The s.117 duty is imposed on both health and local authority social services which share the costs of aftercare provision. A formerly detained patient receiving services under s.117 is entitled to refuse them. Therefore negotiation with patients and their carers is a crucial aspect of setting up and maintaining an effective package of care for people with ongoing mental health problems. Community Mental Health Teams, which are multidisciplinary and staffed by social workers, community psychiatric nurses and often psychologists and occupational therapists, are responsible for coordinating these care packages. While the principles underpinning provision for people with mental health problems are similar to those for people with physical disabilities, they are translated into practice through a set of separate guidance documents. Department of Health (2008b) *Refocusing the Care Programme Approach: Policy and Positive Practice Guidance* provides detailed instruction to mental health professionals arranging or delivering services to adults in the community. In effect this means that there are two parallel systems of delivery assistance to those with mental health problems and those with physical disabilities. The Care Programme Approach, which is outlined in the box below, has many similarities to care management.

Key guidance

Refocusing the Care Programme Approach

Statement of Values and Principles

- The approach to individuals' care and support puts them at the centre and promotes social inclusion and recovery.
- Care assessment and planning views a person 'in the round' seeing and supporting them in their individual diverse roles and the needs they have, including: family; parenting; relationships; housing; employment; leisure; education; creativity; spirituality; self-management; and self-nurture; with the aim of optimising mental and physical health and well-being.
- Self-care is promoted and supported whenever possible. Action is taken to encourage independence and self determination to help people maintain control over their own support and care.
- Carers form a vital part of the support required to aid a person's recovery. Their own needs should also be recognised and supported.
- Services should be organised and delivered in ways that promote and co-ordinate helpful and purposeful mental health practice based on fulfilling therapeutic relationships and partnerships between the people involved.
- Care planning is underpinned by long-term engagement, requiring trust, team work and commitment. It is the daily work of mental health services and supporting partner agencies, not just the planned occasions where people meet for reviews.

The Care Programme Approach is focussed on people with complex mental health needs or whose needs range across a number of interdependent areas such as health, housing, education and social care. In such circumstances a multidisciplinary assessment of need is required followed by multi-agency cooperation to implement the resulting care plan. This requires the appointment of a key worker (also known as the Care Co-ordinator) who will hold the responsibility to coordinate the assessment, pull together the care plan, and implement and review services to the user.

In the case of David Bennett, a case conference held at the Norvic Clinic in July 1997 which was attended by his: doctor; social worker; community psychiatric nurse;

physiotherapist; occupational therapist; and a primary nurse involved with his care agreed that he required a Care Programme Approach to his care on discharge back into the community. The box below sets out the characteristics of people requiring the Care Programme Approach. David's history of substance misuse, violence against others, contact with the criminal justice system and non-attendance at appointments clearly met the requirements for the Care Programme Approach.

Key guidance

Refocusing the Care Programme Approach

Table 2: Characteristics to consider when deciding if support of (new) CPA needed

- Severe mental disorder (including personality disorder) with high degree of clinical complexity
- Current or potential risks including:
  - Suicide, self harm, harm to others (including history of offending)
  - Relapse history requiring urgent response
  - Self neglect/non-concordance with treatment plan
  - Vulnerable adult, adult/child protection
- Current or significant history of severe distress/instability or disengagement
- Presence of non-physical co-morbidity e.g. substance/alcohol/prescription drugs misuse, learning disability
- Multiple service provision from different agencies, including housing, physical care, employment, criminal justice, voluntary agencies
- Currently/recently detained under Mental Health Act or referred to crisis/home treatment team
- Significant reliance on carers or has own significant caring responsibilities
- Experiencing difficulty or disadvantage as a result of:
  - Parenting responsibilities
  - Physical health problems/disability
  - Unsettled accommodation/housing issues
  - Employment issues when mentally ill
  - Significant impairment of function due to mental illness
  - Ethnicity (e.g. immigration status, race/cultural issues; language difficulties; religious practices) sexuality or gender issues

The aggression which David displayed towards staff became a major focus of interaction with him during periods of in-patient care, while in the community failure to comply with treatment regimes was a key area of concern for mental health professionals. Department of Health (2008b: 20) *Refocusing the Care Programme Approach: Policy and Positive Practice Guidance* highlights the centrality of risk assessment in aftercare provision. It also asserts that, 'the philosophy underpinning this framework is one that balances care needs against risk needs, and that emphasises: positive risk management; collaboration with the service user and others involved in care; the importance of recognising and building on the service user's strengths'. It was a complaint of members of the Bennett family appearing before the Independent Inquiry that they were not consulted by mental health professionals about David's care and were rarely contacted by them during the periods when David was hospitalised. Linked to wider considerations surrounding risk assessment is crisis prevention and crisis management. Department of Health (2008b:19) states that:

> All care plans must include explicit crisis and contingency plans. This will include arrangements so that the service user or their carer can contact the right person if they need to at any time, with clear details of who is responsible for addressing elements of the care and support.

Such crisis planning also requires the input of carers and family members where they have contact with the patient. Both Winifred and Joanna kept in contact with their brother, David, by phone and visits, but were never given any information to assist with crisis prevention.

According to paragraph 27.12 of the Code of Practice aftercare under s.117 requires the active involvement of hospital staff, primary care professionals, members of the community mental health team and the family or carers of the mental health user. Paragraph 27.5 of the Code of Practice explicitly states that care plans must do more than address risk management and crisis prevention in conjunction with meeting a user's health and social care needs. Instead, 'aftercare should aim to support [patients] in regaining or enhancing their skills, or learning new skills, in order to cope with life outside the hospital' (Department of Health, 2008a: 27.5). The criticism made by the Independent Inquiry of the aftercare provision for David was the lack of effort to involve his family with whom David continued to have contact both while in hospital and in the community (page 47). Indeed, Dr Joanna Bennett in her evidence explained that the family would have willingly assisted mental health professionals in the 'provision of clothing, money and advice on culture and social issues' had they known that this information would have been helpful to supporting David. In fact the family was not even made aware of the treatment David was receiving. Paragraph 27.13 of the Code of Practice, which is reproduced in the box below, details the elements of a care plan under s.117.

Key guidance

Mental Health Act 1983: Code of Practice

Para. 27.13 A thorough assessment is likely to involve consideration of:

- Continuing mental healthcare, whether in the community or on an out-patient basis
- The psychological needs of the patient and, where appropriate, of their family and carers
- Physical healthcare
- Daytime activities or employment
- Appropriate accommodation
- Identified risks and safety issues
- Any specific needs arising from, for example, co-existing physical disability, sensory impairment, learning disability or autistic spectrum disorder
- Any specific needs arising from drug, alcohol or substance misuse
- Any parenting or caring needs
- Social, cultural or spiritual needs
- Counselling and personal support

- Assistance in welfare rights and managing finances
- The involvement of authorities and agencies in a different area, if the patient is not going to live locally
- The involvement of other agencies, for example the probation service or voluntary organisations
- For a restricted patient, the conditions which the Secretary of State for Justice or the Tribunal has imposed or is likely to impose on their conditional discharge
- Contingency plans (should the patient's mental health deteriorate) and crisis contact details

Apart from the duties and powers of social workers acting as Approved Mental Health Professionals, it is the aftercare provisions of s.117 of the Mental Health Act 1983 which most directly involve social workers in the area of mental health. Working in multidisciplinary Community Mental Health Teams, social workers alongside their colleagues are responsible for assisting those discharged from detainment in hospital. They are also likely to have additional responsibilities with the introduction of Community Treatment Orders in supervising patients in the community in collaboration with healthcare professionals. Community Mental Health Teams may also have responsibility for users admitted as informal patients to psychiatric wards and for others whose mental state necessitates treatment although not admission to hospital. For this reason care in the community and aftercare in the community under s.117 are major areas of social work involvement in the provision of mental health services.

Unfortunately for David Bennett there was poor partnership working with his family and poor liaison between social and healthcare professionals and between hospital- and community-based teams. This meant that David often found himself without consistent aftercare provision; though it is also true that David frequently disengaged from what services and supervision was provided to him in the community. There is a comprehensive list of matters identified by paragraph 27.13 of the Code of Practice which should be addressed in any care plan. As was evident to the inquiry panel, there was in practice little focus on anything except David's compliance with his medication. This was an entirely deficient approach to care planning.

The *participation principle* set out in the *Mental Health Act 1983: Code of Practice* stresses that 'the involvement of carers, family members and other people who have an interest in the patient's welfare should be encouraged'. Of course this may not always be feasible or desirable, for example if there is abuse or exploitation. It also has to be recognised that mental health users may not want to avail of aftercare services. Nevertheless, it is crucial to have as a foundation for service provision a properly considered and formulated care plan, which incorporates inputs from both the user and his or her carers. The failure to effectively implement a Care Programme Approach is most likely to result in poor and fragmented service provision, which will in turn contribute to multiple hospital admissions and discharges back into the community.

No matter how committed mental health professionals are or how well conceived and negotiated a care plan with users and carers, it cannot succeed without the existence of high-quality and accessible provision. A year after David Bennett's death the Government introduced a new policy framework for the delivery of services under the Mental Health Act 1983 whether in hospital or the community. These services now have to be consistent with the policy objectives set out by Department of Health (1999a) *The National Service Framework for Mental Health*. This identifies the priorities for the care of people with mental health problems. It also elaborates seven standards designed to ensure that services provided to those with a mental disorder are of a high quality and responsive to the needs of users and carers. The standards for service provision stipulated by central government are outlined in the box below.

Key guidance

The National Service Framework for Mental Health

Standard One: Health and social services promote mental health for all, working with individuals and communities; combat discrimination against individuals and groups with mental health problems, and promote their social inclusion.

Standard Two: Any service user who contacts their primary health care team with a common mental health problem should have their mental health needs identified and assessed; be offered effective treatments, including referral to specialist services for further assessment, treatment and care if they require it.

Standard Three: Any individual with a common mental health problem should be able to make contact round the clock with the local services necessary to meet their needs and receive adequate care; be able to use NHS Direct, as it develops, for first-level advice and referral on to specialist helplines or to local services.

Standard Four: All mental health service users on CPA should receive care which optimises engagement, anticipates or prevents a crisis, and reduces risk; have a copy of a written care plan . . . be able to access services 24 hours a day, 365 days a year.

Standard Five: Each service user who is assessed as requiring a period of care away from their home should have timely access to an appropriate hospital bed or alternative bed or place which is in the least restrictive environment consistent with the need to protect them and the public; as close to home as possible; a copy of a written care plan agreed on discharge.

Standard Six: All individuals who provide regular and substantial care for a person on CPA should have an assessment of their caring, physical and mental health needs, repeated on at least an annual basis; have their own written care plan which is given to them and implemented in discussion with them.

Standard Seven: Local health and social care communities should prevent suicides [by implementing standards one to six].

In terms of David Bennett's care, and that of patients who like him find themselves going from the community to hospital and back to the community, Standard Four is particularly relevant. This stresses the importance of accessible mental health services which not only react to crisis but offer preventive engagement by professionals who work with users to develop strategies to forestall a worsening of their condition. Standard Six emphasises the requirement for ongoing contact with mental health users living in the community to ensure that their care plans are meeting their needs. Of course a problem revealed by the Independent Inquiry was that when David returned to the community from hospital there was little further contact with him until he was re-admitted or once again detained. This meant that he experienced a succession of mental health crises which brought him in contact with the most restrictive and compulsory forms of mental health treatment. The *National Service Framework for Mental Health* is aimed at redressing the kinds of dislocation in mental health care experienced by users such as David Bennett.

Findings of the Independent Inquiry into the Death of David Bennett

The terms of reference of the inquiry ranged further than examining the particular circumstances of David Bennett's care and death. The inquiry was to make broad recommendations based on its findings for the care of patients diagnosed with schizophrenia and those from black and ethnic minority communities. The main recommendations of the inquiry which also have implications for social work practice are as follows (pages 67–8):

- All who work in mental health services should receive training in cultural awareness and sensitivity.
- All mental health services should set out a written policy dealing with racist abuse, which should be disseminated to all members of staff and displayed prominently . . . If any racist abuse takes place by anyone, including patients in a mental health setting, it should be addressed forthwith and appropriate sanctions applied.
- Every CPA care plan should have a mandatory requirement to include appropriate details of each patient's ethnic origin and cultural needs.
- All psychiatric patients and their families should be made aware that patients can apply to move from one hospital to another for good reason, which would include such matters as easier access by their family, a greater ethnic mix, or a reasoned application to be treated by other doctors.

 ## Critical questions

1 A number of people with a mental disorder also engage in offending behaviour. What dilemmas or challenges would confront you in supporting a mental health user who was also caught up in the criminal justice system? How would you manage these difficulties from a personal and professional standpoint?

2 David Bennett, in common with many mental health users, was unhappy about his medication. As a social worker how would you go about assisting a patient in this situation? What professional or inter-agency difficulties might you encounter and how would you deal with these?

3 If you were a professional involved in the care of someone with an African-Caribbean heritage how would you go about finding out about his or her cultural and spiritual needs and ensuring that they were met in a hospital setting or within a Care Programme Approach in the community? As a practitioner, how would you address racial abuse by other professionals or mental health users towards a person you are working with?

4 David Bennett had a documented history of violence towards others and, understandably, social and healthcare professionals were afraid of him. A number of people with mental health problems can be verbally abusive, physically threatening or violent on occasions. As a social worker what measures would you take to ensure your safety when working with a user known to be aggressive or violent? How might these measures be perceived or experienced by the mental health user and how might this impact on your working relationship with them?

5 Aftercare for David Bennett lacked coordination between the NHS and Social Services and there was poor follow-up once he was discharged from hospital back into the community. What are the challenges of multi-agency work with a user involved in the criminal justice system, who objects to the conditions of discharge from hospital and who is liable to disengage from services? What sort of strategies or interventions could facilitate successful multi-agency work with an involuntary and reluctant service-user?

Critical commentary

Community Treatment Orders

Community Treatment Orders were introduced by the Mental Health Act 2007 and over the coming years will largely supplant s.17 leave of absence provisions. Under the new s.17B of the Mental Health Act 1983 a Community Treatment Order (CTO) can be applied to anyone meeting the criteria to be detained under s.3 or s.37. It can include any condition which the Responsible Clinician and Approved Mental Health Professional deem necessary for the purposes of:

- ensuring that the patient receives medical treatment,
- preventing risk of harm to the patient's health or safety,
- protecting other persons.

Paragraph 25.34 of the Code of Practice states that these conditions can stipulate 'where and when the patient is to receive treatment in the community; where the patient is to live; and avoidance of known risk factors or high-risk situations relevant to the patient's mental disorder'. Section 17E empowers the Responsible Clinician to recall a patient to hospital even if they comply with all the conditions of their CTO. This provision permits a Responsible Clinician to require a fully compliant patient to be detained in hospital if the patient needs treatment in hospital for the mental disorder and 'there would be a risk of harm to the health or safety of the patient or to other persons if the patient were not recalled to hospital'.

In effect Community Treatment Orders are a form of compulsory treatment in the community. Potentially this extends coercive measures beyond the hospital population of detained patients to people with mental health problems living in the community. Research conducted in Australia, where similarly framed Community Treatment Orders were recently introduced, found that increased numbers of people with a mental disorder were subject to compulsion (O'Reilly, 2004). This evidence suggests that CTOs were being used to cast the net of compulsion ever wider to an even larger population of people with mental disorders. As Kinderman and Tai (2008) conclude, if CTOs are to be a viable alternative to detainment in hospital then they have to be founded on improved community provision and the increased availability of psychotherapeutic and rehabilitative services. The danger is of resorting to compulsion in the community as a substitute for high-quality mental health provision in community settings.

The amendments to the Mental Health Act 1983 mean that CTOs can be renewed on a yearly basis, consequently patients can be subject to compulsion in the community more or less indefinitely. Since any conditions can be applied as long as they are necessary in relation to medical treatment, protecting the patient or others, this can result in someone being compelled to live in a specified place or avoid known risk factors for a lifetime. CTOs can permit intrusive monitoring not only of outpatients' compliance with medication but also of their conduct. In effect CTOs can be used as a form of psychiatric ASBO with mental health professionals replacing the police and probation services as agents of control. Surveillance in the community becomes a vehicle to recall people with a mental disorder to the custody of a hospital if they act in an aggressive manner (Kinderman and Tai, 2008: 482). Finally, as the range of conditions attached to a CTO encompass not only treatment, but residence and a person's association with others, such an Order can directly threaten the rights to privacy and family life guaranteed under article 8 of the European Convention on Human Rights.

Learning points

- The Mental Health Act 1983 applies to people of any age who have a mental disorder. But the statute can only be used to compulsorily administer medical treatment for a mental disorder and not for physical illness.

- The Mental Health Act 1983 is underpinned by five principles which according to the related Code of Practice must guide the decisions and actions of mental health practitioners.

- The operation of the five principles underpinning mental health legislation often create tensions and conflicts for mental health professionals, which must be resolved by simultaneous reference to a number of relevant statutes and their related Codes of Practice, Policy Guidance and Practice Guidance.

- The Mental Health Act 1983 demands that practitioners ensure the condition and circumstances of someone with a mental disorder fulfils *all* the criteria stated in the applicable section in order to be detained and that all relevant persons have been fully informed of their rights under the Act.

- Social workers have a primary responsibility to promote the independence and autonomy of people with a mental disorder through: consideration of their wishes and feelings; involving them in decisions which concern them; informing them of their rights; and acting to enhance their control over their own lives.

- Respect for the diversity among mental health users of cultural values, religious beliefs and lifestyle choices is not straightforward. It requires a proactive anti-discriminatory stance combined with the recognition that some beliefs and practices can pose dangers to self or others.

- Practitioners need to be aware of the anxiety and fear which many people with mental health problems can experience, including anger towards professionals. They therefore need to be alert to the potential for verbal abuse or physical violence and de-escalate a situation before this occurs.

Further reading

Browne, D. (1996) 'The black experience of mental health law', in T. Heller, J. Reynolds, R. Gomm, R. Muston and S. Pattison (eds) *Mental Health Matters,* Milton Keynes: Open University. This article examines user experiences of mental health services provision and in particular the operation of compulsory provisions under the Mental Health Act 1983.

Campbell, J. (2008) 'Stakeholders' views of legal and advice services for people admitted to psychiatric hospital', *Journal of Social Welfare and Family Law* 30(3): 219-32. This article offers perspectives from users, carers and solicitors involved in Mental Health Review Tribunals. It examines some of the shortcomings of this system and makes recommendations for improvement in the tribunal system to make it more accessible and fair to mental health patients.

Department of Health (2005) *Delivering Race Equality in Mental Health Care: An Action Plan for Reform Inside and Outside Services,* London: Stationery Office. This details how Standard One of the National Service Framework for Mental Health is to be implemented to eliminate discrimination in the NHS towards people from black and ethnic minority communities.

Fennell, P. (2008) *Mental Health: The New Law,* Bristol: Jordan Publishing. This provides an in-depth and technically detailed exploration of the amendments introduced by the Mental Health Act 2007. It also provides a comprehensive guide to current mental health law.

Useful websites

www.mind.org.uk Run by the national mental health charity MIND, this site provides information across a range of mental health issues. It offers a service-user's perspective in conjunction with fact-sheets and publications on different aspects of mental health.

www.sane.org.uk Run by Sane, a charity which focusses on carers' perspectives in relation to mental health issues. This site provides accessible information for carers, and discussion on caring for someone with a mental health problem.

www.yourrights.org.uk Run by Liberty, this site takes a human rights perspective on a wide range of issues including mental health. It provides easy-to-read guides on the rights of mental health service-users.

www.dh.gov.uk/en/healthcare/mentalhealth This is a section of the National Health Service website which offers access to information on mental health. It provides information on policy changes and their implementation in mental health services. There are also publications available to guide mental health professionals in their day-to-day practice.

9

MENTAL HEALTH: COMMUNITY SETTING

Overview of relevant legislation

The Information Centre for Health and Social Care (2009) *Adult Psychiatric Morbidity in England* shows the results of a survey among households, which revealed the prevalence of treated and untreated mental disorders among people in the general population. The broad findings of this study are set out in the Fact File above. This shows that around 15 per cent of people in the general population suffer from common mental disorders, defined as anxiety and depression. One-quarter of people with these conditions will be receiving treatment, predominantly medication, for them. An equally high proportion of people in the general population had considered committing suicide at some point in their lives, while 6 per cent had actually attempted suicide. This high prevalence rate both for common mental disorders and suicidal impulses demonstrates the need for community-based mental health services and preventative intervention.

Although people with drug and alcohol addictions do not fall under the Mental Health Act 1983 purely on account of their addiction, the proportion of people defined as drug or alcohol dependent are at risk of developing drug-related psychosis. Such a dual diagnosis would bring these people within the ambit of mental health law. As the Mental Health Act 1983 is as applicable to people with mental health problems living in the community as it is to those in a hospital setting, the table of its key sections is replicated from Chapter 9. The sections of the statute relating to the discharge of patients, Community Treatment Orders and Guardianship are particularly relevant for the care of people with mental disorders in the community.

Mental Health Act 1983 (as amended)	Key sections
Part I – Definition and applicability	s.1 'Mental disorder'
Part II – Compulsory admission to hospital and guardianship	s.2 Assessment s.3 Admission for treatment s.4 Emergency admission s.5 Patient already in hospital s.7 Application for guardianship s.8 Effect of guardianship s.13 Applications for admission and guardianship s.17 Leave of absence from hospital s.17A Community treatment orders s.18 Patients absent without leave s.19 Transfer of patients s.23 Discharge of patients s.26 Definition of nearest relative s.29 Displacement of nearest relative
Part III – Patients involved in criminal proceedings or under sentence	s.35 Remand to hospital for assessment s.36 Remand to hospital for treatment s.37 Hospital order or guardianship s.41 Restriction orders s.47 Transfer from prison to hospital for treatment
Part IV – Consent to treatment	s.57 Treatment requiring consent and second opinion s.58 Treatment requiring consent or a second opinion s.62 Urgent treatment
Part V – Tribunal	s.66 Application to tribunal s.68 Referral to tribunal by hospital managers s.72 Powers of tribunal s.78 Procedures of tribunal
Part VI – Removal and return of patients within United Kingdom	ss.80–92 Movement of patients between countries of the United Kingdom including Channel Islands and Isle of Man
Part VII – Management of property and affairs of patients	Repealed by Mental Capacity Act 2005

(Continued)

Mental Health Act 1983 (as amended)	Key sections
Part VIII - Miscellaneous functions of local authorities and Secretary of State	s.114 Appointment of Approved Mental Health Professional s.115 Power of entry and inspection s.117 Aftercare s.118 Code of Practice
Part IX - Offences	s.126 Forgery and false statements s.127 Ill treatment of patients s.128 Assisting patients to absent without leave s.129 Obstruction
Part X - Miscellaneous and supplementary	s.130 A Independent mental health advocates s.131 Informal admission of patients s.132 Duty to give information to patients s.133 Duty to inform nearest relative of discharge s.134 Correspondence of patients s.135 Warrant to search for and remove patients s.136 Mentally disordered persons found in public places s.137 Conveyance of patients

Source: Adapted from Brammer (2007: 496-7).

The *Mental Health Act 1983: Code of Practice* sets out the guiding principles underpinning this statute. These are as relevant and crucial to practice with mental health users in the community as for those who are detained in hospital. For this reason the principles which underpin the Mental Health Act 1983 (as amended) are also replicated from the beginning of Chapter 9 and are once again detailed in the box below.

Key guidance

Mental Health Act 1983: Code of Practice

Purpose principle

1.2 Decisions under the Act must be taken with a view to minimising the undesirable effects of mental disorder, by maximising the safety and well-being (mental and physical) of patients, promoting their recovery and protecting other people from harm.

Least restriction principle

1.3 People taking action without a patient's consent must attempt to keep to a minimum the restrictions they impose on the patient's liberty, having regard to the purpose for which the restrictions are imposed.

Respect principle

1.4 People taking decisions under the Act must recognise and respect the diverse needs, values and circumstances of each patient, including their race, religion, culture, gender, age, sexual orientation and any disability. They must consider the patient's views, wishes and feelings (whether expressed at the time or in advance), so far as they are reasonably ascertainable, and follow those wishes wherever practicable and consistent with the purpose of the decision. There must be no unlawful discrimination.

Participation principle

1.5 Patients must be given the opportunity to be involved, as far as practicable in the circumstances, in planning, developing and reviewing their own treatment and care to help ensure that it is delivered in a way that is as appropriate and effective for them as possible. The involvement of carers, family members and other people who have an interest in the patient's welfare should be encouraged (unless there are particular reasons to the contrary) and their views taken seriously.

Effectiveness, efficiency and equity principle

1.6 People taking decisions under the Act must seek to use the resources available to them and to patients in the most effective, efficient and equitable way, to meet the needs of patients and achieve the purpose for which the decisions was taken.

There are a number of government-issued documents which set out guidance for the provision of mental health services and the conduct of mental health professionals acting under the Mental Health Act 1983 (as amended). As mental health issues also intersect with housing needs, government guidance on homelessness is an important source of guidance for those working under the Mental Health Act 1983. These documents are summarised briefly in the table below.

Guidance document	Outline of content
Department of Health (2008) *Mental Health Act 1983: Code of Practice*	This is the statutory code of practice which directs professionals working under the Mental Health Act 1983 (as amended).
Department of Health (2008) *Refocusing the Care Programme Approach: Policy and Positive Practice Guidance*	This provides detailed guidance on the Care Programme Approach including assessment and care planning for people with mental health problems living in the community.
Department of Health (2007) *Best Practice in Managing Risk: Principles and Evidence for Best Practice in the Assessment and Management of Risk to Self and Others in Mental Health Services*	This describes best practice in risk assessment and risk management. It also offers guidance on inter-agency cooperation to manage the risk posed by users to themselves or others.
Ministry of Justice (2008) *Mental Capacity Act 2005 Deprivation of Liberty Safeguards: Code of Practice to Supplement the main Mental Capacity Act 2005 Code of Practice*	This sets out the safeguards for vulnerable adults without mental capacity who are liable to be or have been admitted to hospital, residential care or a nursing home.
Department for Communities and Local Government (2006) *Homelessness Code of Guidance for Local Authorities*	This is the statutory code of practice which governs professional practice under Part VII of the Housing Act 1996 which deals with homelessness and the allocation of social housing.

Overview of the cases

This chapter explores the issues arising from four different cases. Two of these concern complaints brought before the Local Government Ombudsman and two came before the courts. A brief summary of each case is set out below.

Case 1 Ombudsman Report Complaint No. 99/B/03564 and No. 99/B/05735 against Reading Borough Council 7 February 2002 explores the:

- Procedures for detainment under s.2 or s.3.
- Definition of the *nearest relative*.
- Powers of the *nearest relative*.
- Safeguards for those with a mental disorder who lack capacity.
- Charges for residential accommodation.

Case 2 Ombudsman Report Complaint No. 97/B/2696 against Suffolk County Council June 1999 explores:

- Appeal against detainment in hospital.
- Mental disorder in the context of lifestyle choices.
- Working in partnership with the family.

Case 3 *Local Authority X* v. *M* [2007] EWHC 2660 (Fam) explores:

- Conditional discharge from hospital.
- Risk assessment.
- Inter-agency cooperation.

Case 4 *Carter* v. *Wandsworth London Borough Council* [2004] EWCA Civ 1740 explores the:

- Housing needs of people with mental health problems.
- Definition of homelessness.
- Procedure for appealing against the decision of a housing authority.

CASE 1
Ombudsman Report Complaint No. 99/B/03564 and No. 99/B/05735 against Reading Borough Council
7 February 2002

Importance of the case

The role of the *nearest relative* is explored together with the responsibilities of Approved Mental Health Professionals to involve them in deliberations concerning the compulsory admission to hospital of a family member. This case also identifies the conflict of interest which can arise between a user, their *nearest relative* and other family members who may also be carers. The relationship between mental disorder and mental capacity is examined within the framework of mental health legislation.

History of the case

Mr Tudor used the Social Services Complaints Procedure to object to the refusal of Reading Borough Council to compulsorily admit his elderly mother to hospital under the Mental Health Act 1983. When his objection was rejected both at stage two and stage three of the

Social Services investigation into the matter, Mr Tudor made an application to the Local Government Ombudsman to examine the circumstances surrounding his mother's care.

Facts of the case

In 1997 Mrs Tudor was 90 years old. She was a widow and lived alone in Reading, receiving visits and some assistance from her sister Mrs Stuart, her sister-in-law and friends living in the vicinity. Her son Mr Tudor lived and worked abroad, but had regular telephone contact with his mother and with Mrs Stuart. He also visited Mrs Tudor several times a year. During two separate visits which Mr Tudor made to his mother in 1997 he observed a dramatic deterioration in her condition and contacted Mrs Tudor's GP and Social Services informing them that Mrs Tudor 'was becoming confused, her memory and social skills were impaired and she appeared to be finding it increasingly difficult to cope with routine household chores' (para. 19). Dr B, a consultant in Old Age Psychiatry visited Mrs Tudor in November 1997 and diagnosed her as having Alzheimer's disease. At this point Social Services became actively involved with the appointment of a care manager for Mrs Tudor. She refused a place at a day centre but accepted domiciliary services. In April 1998 Mrs Tudor was found wandering in the street and an assessment meeting was convened in her home on 30 April 1998 attended by the GP, Dr B, Mrs Tudor, Mrs Stuart, the care manager and the Approved Social Worker (now Approved Mental Health Professional). The decision of the meeting was *not* to compulsorily admit Mrs Tudor to hospital under the Mental Health Act 1983. In May 1998 Mrs Tudor was again found wandering in the street and Mr Tudor informed health and social care professionals that Mrs Tudor now agreed that she could not manage at home. Mrs Tudor's GP arranged for her informal admission to Lancaster Park Hospital where she was admitted on 23 May 1998. A few months later Mrs Tudor was transferred to the Elderly Mentally Infirm Unit of a nursing home where she died in November 2000. Mr Tudor complained through the Social Services Complaints Procedure that his mother met the criteria for compulsorily admission to hospital in April 1998 and should have been admitted at that time under the Mental Health Act 1983. When this complaint was not upheld by the Review Panel, Mr Tudor made an application to the Local Government Ombudsman.

Key people in the case

Mr Tudor – complainant and son of Mrs Tudor
Mrs Tudor – mother of Mr Tudor
Mrs Stuart – sister of Mrs Tudor
Dr B – consultant in Old Age Psychiatry

Discussion of the case

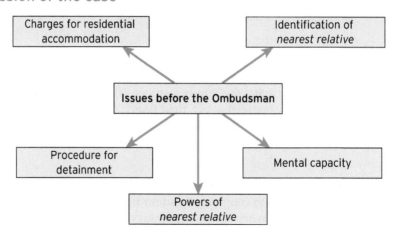

Procedure for detainment

Mr Tudor believed that on 30 April 1998 his mother had met the threshold criteria for admission to hospital under either s.2 or s.3 of the Mental Health Act 1983. In evidence to the Local Government Ombudsman he stated that his mother met the criteria on the following grounds:

- Mrs Tudor had been diagnosed with Alzheimer's disease, a form of dementia which clearly constituted a 'disability of the mind' and was therefore a mental disorder under s.1(2).
- Mrs Tudor had been found wandering the streets and needed to be detained in the interests of her 'own health or safety' either under s.2 for a full assessment of her condition or under s.3 for treatment of her mental disorder.

However, Mr Tudor contended that his mother had not been compulsorily admitted to hospital due to a flawed decision-making process. This, he claimed, had resulted in her remaining at home when she should have been removed to hospital. The procedure to detain someone under s.2 or s.3 of the Mental Health Act 1983 involves the participation of two doctors (one appointed under s.12), the Approved Mental Health Professional and the *nearest relative*. All these people were present at the assessment meeting on 30 April 1998, as was Mrs Tudor herself. While Mr Tudor referred to the wording of the Mental Health Act 1983 and the related Code of Practice in his complaint to Social Services and his submission to the Ombudsman, his reliance on these was rather selective.

In fact both s.2 and s.3 require that a person be 'suffering from mental disorder of a nature or degree' which 'warrants the detention of the patient in a hospital for an assessment' or 'makes it appropriate for him to receive medical treatment in a hospital' respectively. In other words, whether the hospital admission is for assessment under s.2 or treatment under s.3 the mental disorder must be of 'a nature or degree' which justifies this. It is not enough for a person merely to have a mental disorder. In addition, paragraph 4.4 of the Code of Practice requires mental health professionals to consider 'whether there are alternative means of providing the care and treatment which the patient requires' before resorting to compulsory admission under s.2 or s.3. Paragraph 4.5 also obliges practitioners to consider 'the patient's wishes and view of their own needs'.

The Local Government Ombudsman was given sight of the Mental Health Assessment Form completed by the Approved Social Worker (now AMHP) on the day of the assessment meeting. This recorded that:

> Mrs. [Tudor] gave a good account of herself and participated in the discussion, although because of her deafness it was necessary to speak loudly in order to be heard. Mrs. [Tudor] was appropriately dressed and the house was clean and tidy . . . There is some concern about Mrs. [Tudor] going out into the street inappropriately dressed although this has only happened on one occasion . . . Mrs. [Tudor] would benefit from a higher level of domiciliary support and in fact agreed to have Meals on Wheels five days a week.

At the end of the Mental Health Assessment form under the heading *Explanation of Outcome* the Approved Social Worker concluded that 'Mrs [Tudor's] illness is not of a nature or degree that warrants her retention in hospital against her will. She is prepared to accept some extra domiciliary services . . .' In line with the additional requirements of s.2 and s.3 of the Mental Health Act 1983 the Approved Social Worker (now the AMHP) had found that while Mrs Tudor had a mental disorder this was not of a nature to warrant her detention. This was because Mrs Tudor:

- Could plainly maintain her self care, although she required some assistance.
- Was able to participate in decisions about herself.

- Being inappropriately dressed in the street on one occasion was not of itself sufficiently serious to place her health and safety at serious risk.
- Clearly expressed a view that she did not wish to be admitted to hospital, a crucial consideration for mental health professionals under para. 4.5 of the *Mental Health Act 1983: Code of Practice*.
- By agreeing to additional social care provision made it possible for her mental health needs to be met through increased domiciliary support in her own home as opposed to admission to a hospital.

Mrs Tudor's GP and her consultant psychiatrist, who were both present at the assessment meeting, concurred with the opinion of the Approved Social Worker. It is important to appreciate that the GSCC *Code of Practice for Social Care Workers* is also engaged. Social workers are required to:

Para. 1.3 support 'service users' rights to control their lives and make informed choices about the services they receive'.

Para. 3.1 promote 'the independence of service users and assist them to understand and exercise their rights'.

Para. 4.1 recognise 'that service users have the right to take risks and [help] them to identify and manage the potential and actual risks to themselves and others'.

Mrs Tudor was clear at the assessment meeting that she wished to remain at home and was agreeable to additional domiciliary support. She was adamantly opposed to hospital admission or placement in residential care. Undoubtedly there would have been less risk to Mrs Tudor's health and safety in a residential facility where she could be cared for on a 24-hour basis and her behaviour monitored. This would have been against Mrs Tudor's wishes and would also deny her the positive aspects of risk taking. These include retaining capabilities for longer and a sense of mental well-being derived from exercising personal choice in familiar surroundings. The decision of the Approved Social Worker (now an AMHP) not to apply for the detainment of Mrs Tudor under s.2 or s.3 complied with the Mental Health Act 1983 and the related Code of Practice while being consistent with the GSCC *Code of Practice for Social Care Workers*.

Social workers acting as Care Co-ordinators or as Approved Mental Health Professionals often work in partnership with vulnerable people who are at risk of harm and yet want to continue living in the situation which puts them at risk of that harm. Social workers are required under the Care Programme Approach and by virtue of paragraph 4.1 of the GSCC Code to assist users to identify and manage risks as positive aspects of self-care which can enhance quality of life. By not applying for s.2 or s.3 detainment the Approved Social Worker acted to preserve Mrs Tudor's autonomy, albeit at the expense of an increased risk of harm posed by her living with progressive dementia at home. By persuading Mrs Tudor to accept additional domiciliary services the social worker reduced the immediacy of that risk to Mrs Tudor's health and safety. The action of the Approved Social Work clearly complies with the *least restriction principle* set out in the *Mental Health Act 1983: Code of Practice*.

Approved Mental Health Professionals and Care Co-ordinators would be in contravention of their Codes of Practice if they simply acted to reduce risk, rather than to assist users and carers to successfully manage risk. The exercise of choice and of control over a situation is integral to a sense of personal well-being and good mental health. Interventions which interfere in the personal autonomy of users, particularly those resulting in dramatic changes to their lives (such as admission to hospital) also pose risks to their welfare. Ill-conceived and premature interventions which fail to weigh up the risks inherent to intervention itself may have greater adverse consequences for users and carers alike than taking no action or at least a less invasive one.

Identification of *nearest relative*

The crux of Mr Tudor's complaint against Social Services was that the Approved Social Worker (now the AMHP) had failed to properly follow procedures in assessing his mother. One of the grounds of Mr Tudor's allegation was that the Approved Social Worker had failed to properly involve either Mrs Stuart or Mr Tudor himself as a *nearest relative* in the decision-making process. The family member designated as the *nearest relative* has a number of responsibilities under s.11 and s.23 of the Mental Health Act 1983 relating respectively to the detainment and discharge of patients. The legal provisions contained in s.11 regarding the role of the *nearest relative* when consideration is being given to the compulsory admission of a person to hospital are set out in the box below.

 Key legislation

Mental Health Act 1983 (as amended)

s.11(1) Subject to the provisions of this section, an application for admission for assessment, an application for admission for treatment and a guardianship application may be made either by the nearest relative of the patient or by an approved mental health professional.

s.11(3) Before or within a reasonable time after an application for the admission of a patient for assessment is made by an approved mental health professional, that professional shall take such steps as are practicable to inform the person (if any) appearing to be the nearest relative of the patient that the application is to be or has been made and of the power of the nearest relative . . .

Mr Tudor initially protested through the Social Services Complaints Procedure that he had not been recognised as Mrs Tudor's *nearest relative* when he was in fact her son. As the *nearest relative* has important responsibilities under the Mental Health Act 1983, the statute also sets out which family member is to be recognised as the *nearest relative*. Section 26(1) sets out a rank ordered list of relatives and requires Approved Mental Health Professionals to ensure that they identify the correct *nearest relative* by selecting the family member who is highest in the list. The list, which is shown below, priorities a spouse or civil partner over an adult child, and an adult child over a parent or sibling and so forth down to the bottom of the list. Essentially this means that an Approved Mental Health Professional would recognise the civil partner of a patient as the *nearest relative* as opposed to the adult son of the patient. If the civil partner of the patient was deceased then the adult son would become the designated *nearest relative* as they appear next in rank order on the list:

(a) husband or wife or civil partner
(b) son or daughter
(c) father or mother
(d) brother or sister
(e) grandparent
(f) grandchild
(g) uncle or aunt
(h) nephew or niece
(non-kin if co-resident for not less than five years)

In the case of Mrs Tudor, her husband was dead so plainly the position of *nearest relative* passed to adult children, who are next on the list above. Mr Tudor therefore appeared to be his mother's *nearest relative*, but he lived overseas. Section 26 of the Mental Health Act 1983 also enumerates legal rules which have to be applied in order to distinguish who is the *nearest relative* when there appear to be several family members who would qualify. In summary these rules are:

- An illegitimate child is to be treated as the legitimate child of the mother and of the father only if the father has parental responsibility for that child.
- Whole-blood relationships are given precedence over half-blood ones.
- The eldest relative in any category is given precedence.
- If the patient 'ordinarily resides with or is cared for by' a relative, he or she will have precedence over other relatives.
- If there is a person co-resident with the patient he or she will normally be given precedence unless there is a blood relative also co-resident.
- A person living as a partner with the patient for no less than six months will be treated as if they were the person's spouse or civil partner for the purposes of the Act.
- A person not normally resident in the United Kingdom will be excluded as a *nearest relative*.
- A partner who has separated from the patient will normally be excluded as a *nearest relative*.

In the present case Mrs Stuart provided care to her sister on a regular basis while Mr Tudor lived overseas and although he visited his mother several times a year was obviously not a carer. This meant, given the rules for identifying the *nearest relative* detailed in s.26 of the Mental Health Act 1983 (as amended), the Approved Social Work had in fact correctly recognised Mrs Stuart as the *nearest relative*. The practitioner had also correctly ensured that Mrs Stuart was present at the assessment meeting of 30 April 1998 which considered detaining Mrs Tudor in hospital. Although Mr Tudor formally complained that he had not been informed of the importance of the assessment meeting, nor of the role of the *nearest relative*, this was not a requirement under the Mental Health Act 1983 or the related Code of Practice. As the Review Panel at stage three of the Social Service Complaints Procedure concluded, it was not reasonable to require the Approved Social Worker to keep in contact with every member of Mrs Tudor's family, including those living abroad.

The *nearest relative* has a statutory definition contained in s.26 of the Mental Health Act 1983 and there can be disagreement within families as to who qualifies for this designation. In this case the Approved Social Worker (now an AMHP) correctly identified and involved Mrs Stuart as her sister's *nearest relative*. Social workers are required by paragraph 1.2 of the GSCC Code of Practice to promote not only the views of service-users but also those of their carers. But social workers need to be alert to the fact that carers, particularly if they are close family members, can fundamentally disagree about the care of a vulnerable relation. In these instances social workers will need to act as mediators and sometimes as arbiters between competing and contradictory points of view. Fortunately in respect of Mrs Tudor the Approved Social Worker was able to rely on statutory provisions which give unambiguous instruction as to who was qualified to act as the *nearest relative*. This is yet another example of how knowledge of the precise detail of a section in a statute can provide clear direction to social workers confronted by conflicting demands.

Powers of *nearest relative*

It is a requirement under paragraph 4.64 of the *Mental Health Act 1983: Code of Practice* to consult with the *nearest relative* when detainment is being contemplated (see box on next page).

As Mrs Stuart was at the assessment meeting she was not only consulted but was clearly a party to the decision not to admit her sister to hospital under s.2 or s.3 of the Mental Health Act 1983.

Key guidance

Mental Health Act 1983: Code of Practice

Para. 4.64 When consulting nearest relative AMHPs should where possible,

- Ascertain the nearest relative's views about both the patient's needs and the nearest relative's own needs in relation to the patient.
- Inform the nearest relative of the reasons for considering an application for detention and what the effects of such an application would be.
- Inform the nearest relative of their role and rights under the Act.

A further aspect of the complaint made by Mr Tudor was that Mrs Stuart as the *nearest relative* was not fully informed of her rights under the Mental Health Act 1983. As paragraph 4.64 of the Code in the box above indicates, an Approved Mental Health Professional is required to consult with the *nearest relative* when making an application for the compulsory admission of a person to hospital under s.2 or s.3. In addition the AMHP must inform *nearest relatives* of their statutory rights under the Mental Health Act 1983. These statutory rights concern a wide range of different matters as outlined below:

- Right to be given information by hospital managers about a patient's detention and its legal implications (s.132).
- Right to be given seven days' notice of the discharge of the patient by hospital managers (s.133).
- Right to be consulted by the Approved Mental Health Professional before he or she makes a s.3 application (s.11).
- Right to request that an Approved Mental Health Professional make an assessment of the person to decide whether an application should be made for his or her detainment in hospital (s.13).
- Right to object to an application for treatment under s.3 in which case the application cannot proceed unless the Approved Mental Health Professional successfully applies to the County Court for the displacement of that *nearest relative* by another one or by the local authority itself (s.11 and s.29).
- Right to apply for admission of a person under s.2 or s.3, even when an Approved Mental Health Professional refuses to do so, although the application must still be supported by the recommendations of two registered medical practitioners (s.11).
- Right to apply for guardianship under s.7 even when an Approved Mental Health Professional refuses to do so, although the application must still be supported by the recommendations of two registered medical practitioners (s.11).
- Right to apply for the discharge of a patient detained for assessment or treatment (s.23).
- Right to apply for the discharge of the guardianship of a patient (s.23).
- Right to apply to the Tribunal to review the patient's case (s.66).

As Mrs Stuart was present at the assessment meeting she was a party to the decision not to detain her sister and was therefore clearly consulted. Furthermore, she assented to this decision, albeit that the Mental Health Assessment Form completed by the Approved Social Worker records that Mrs Stuart 'feels that her sister should not be left on her own and feels the need for some respite herself from Mrs Tudor's telephone calls'. But Mrs Stuart's view that her sister required more supervision was not tantamount to arguing that her sister should be detained in hospital. In fact the increase in domiciliary services agreed by Mrs Tudor at the assessment meeting provided additional assistance to her, offered some relief from caring to Mrs Stuart and permitted monitoring of Mrs Tudor's condition.

It was precisely this arrangement which presented a viable alternative to hospitalisation under s.2 or s.3 and fully acknowledged Mrs Tudor's wish to continuing living in her own home. Mr Tudor attempted to contend before the Local Government Ombudsman that the Approved Social Worker had failed to inform Mrs Stuart in writing of her right under s.11 to apply for the detainment of Mrs Tudor if she disagreed with the Approved Mental Health Professional. As the Ombudsman observed, since Mrs Stuart was both present at the assessment meeting and a party to its decision not to apply for a compulsory hospital admission, Mr Tudor's allegation that Mrs Stuart was deprived of her rights under s.11 as the *nearest relative* was plainly false.

In fact the social worker involved with Mrs Tudor had acted correctly. The social worker as required by both the Mental Health Act 1983 and the related Code of Practice consulted Mrs Stuart as the *nearest relative*. She had also reflected the views of Mrs Stuart as her sister's carer in the Mental Health Assessment Form. Mrs Stuart's exhaustion from meeting some of her sister's care needs at a time when she was also looking after a seriously ill spouse were taken into consideration in persuading Mrs Tudor to accept additional domiciliary services. These obviously helped to relieve Mrs Stuart of some of her caring responsibilities. Faced with disagreement among carers or family members the GSCC Code of Practice can only give very broad guidance. Practitioners in such difficult situations must instead closely follow the relevant statute law, related Code of Practice and Policy or Practice Guidance. In doing so, they will be best protected against unjustified complaints from carers or relatives, angry that their opinion was not acted upon. In this case the issue in dispute between family members was Mr Tudor's view, contrary to Mrs Stuart's, that his mother should have been compulsorily admitted to hospital and not simply provided with more assistance in her home.

Mental capacity

In pursuing his grievance, Mr Tudor also alleged that his mother had in effect been involuntarily admitted to hospital when her GP arranged for her admission to Lancaster Park Hospital where she was conveyed on 23 May 1998. In his submissions to the Local Government Ombudsman Mr Tudor (para. 24) recalled that:

> On May 23rd the paramedic ambulance arrived to convey Mrs Tudor to the hospital, and she was told that she was to be taken to Lancaster Park. The ambulance crew noted that Mrs Tudor refused to travel. Shortly thereafter Mr Tudor arrived and his mother adamantly persisted in her refusal. Mr Tudor was obliged, without assistance from those present, to physically remove his mother from her home and force her to leave.

Mrs Tudor's well-documented preference to remain at home is unequivocally reflected in Mr Tudor's account of her removal to Lancaster Park Hospital. Even allowing for the deterioration in her mental condition (possibly resulting in mental incapacity), to what extent could it be said that she had voluntarily agreed to admission to Lancaster Park Hospital? Under s.131 of the Mental Health Act 1983 a person can voluntarily decide to be admitted to hospital and is referred to as an informal patient. Informal patients retain the right to refuse all medical treatment, whether for a physical illness or a mental disorder, which can only be administered with their consent. However, an informal patient can be subject to short-term detainment in hospital under a doctor's or nurse's holding power exercised under s.5 of the Mental Health Act 1983. Thereafter they could be detained under s.2, s.3 or s.4. Given Mrs Tudor's opposition to residential or hospital care at the point of being taken to hospital, even if she lacked mental capacity could she sensibly be described as an informal patient? This was the question which came before the European Court of Human Rights in *HL* v. *United Kingdom* [2004] 40 EHRR 761. In a groundbreaking decision, which has become known as the Bournewood judgement, the court case resulted in a major change to British law, as outlined in the box below.

 Background information

HL v. *United Kingdom* [2004] 40 EHRR 761

The case concerned L who was 48 years old at the time and had autism. He was unable to agree to or refuse medical treatment or give valid consent to admission to hospital. L became disruptive at a day centre which he regularly attended and was admitted to hospital as an informal patient. This meant that he did not have to meet the criteria for detainment set out in s.2 or s.3 of the Mental Health Act 1983. However, his carers who wanted L returned to their care argued that L was in effect detained under the Mental Health Act 1983. Legal counsel for the Bournewood Community and Mental Health NHS Trust (in whose hospital L was an inpatient) responded that L was not detained against his will and had simply made no attempt to leave the hospital. In other words the NHS Trust was maintaining that L was free to leave the hospital, but did not choose to do so.

The European Court of Human Rights took a different view from the NHS Trust, which as a public body was part of the State. The State was obliged by the European Convention on Human Rights to ensure that L's Convention Rights were not violated. L's admission to hospital specifically engaged article 5 which guaranteed him the 'right to liberty and security of the person'. This is of course a qualified right and the State is legally entitled to limit the freedom of citizens under certain circumstances, for example in the case of lawful imprisonment, to prevent the spread of infectious diseases or because of mental disability. However, anyone so detained must, according to article 5(4) be, 'entitled to take proceedings by which the lawfulness of his detention shall be decided speedily by a court and his release ordered if the detention is not lawful'. Patients detained under s.2 or s.3 of the Mental Health Act 1983 have a right to apply to the Mental Health Review Tribunal (now known as the First-Tier Tribunal for Mental Health Review) to determine whether they should continue to be compulsorily detained in hospital. Patients admitted informally have no such right, because of the presumption that they are free to leave the hospital when they wish. But a person who is mentally incapacitated does not have the same ability to exercise choice as does someone who has mental capacity. As the Court of Human Rights highlighted, this created a situation in which mentally incapacitated patients informally admitted to hospital (estimated to be around 22,000 in England and Wales in any year) had less legal protections than a detained patient with mental capacity.

The European Court of Human Rights ruled that because healthcare professionals had complete control over L's day-to-day movements, this amounted to a deprivation of his liberty. Moreover, as there was no formal process for L's detention, as this was on the basis of an informal admission, nor was there any recourse to review his detention, the court concluded his article 5 rights had been violated by the British State. In short the European Court of Human Rights found that there was a lack of procedural safeguards to protect L's liberty, albeit that he was of 'unsound mind' and the State was lawfully entitled to limit his freedom. In response the British Government used the Mental Health Act 2007 to introduce new provisions into the earlier Mental Capacity Act 2005. These are collectively referred to as the *Deprivation of Liberty Safeguards* and are accompanied by an additional Code of Practice to supplement that originally issued under s.42 of the Mental Capacity Act 2005.

At the time of Mrs Tudor's informal admission to hospital the *Deprivation of Liberty Safeguards* were not in place, as they were introduced through a statute passed by Parliament after her death. The Code of Practice attached to these safeguards would have directed both Social Services and the Ombudsman to a number of important considerations surrounding the admission of Mrs Tudor to Lancaster Park Hospital and later her transfer from there to the Elderly Mentally Infirm Unit of a nursing home. Neither the investigation by Social Services nor that by the Local Government Ombudsman directly addressed the issue of Mrs Tudor's mental capacity and her ability to legally consent to removal to hospital or her transfer from there to the nursing home. Had it been in force at the time, the Ministry of Justice (2008) *Mental Capacity Act 2005 Deprivation of Liberty Safeguards: Code of Practice to Supplement the main Mental Capacity Act 2005 Code of Practice* would have directed professionals to a set of important considerations. The box below identifies the people who come under the legal protections provided by the *Deprivation of Liberty Safeguards*.

 Key guidance

Mental Capacity Act 2005 Deprivation of Liberty Safeguards: Code of Practice

Para.1.7 The safeguards apply to people in England and Wales who have a mental disorder and lack capacity to consent to the arrangements made for their care of treatment, but for whom receiving care or treatment in circumstances that amount to a deprivation of liberty may be necessary to protect them from harm and appears to be in their best interests. A large number of these people will be those with significant learning disabilities, or older people who have dementia or some similar disability, but they can also include those who have certain other neurological conditions (for example as a result of a brain injury).

Para.1.8 In order to come within the scope of a deprivation of liberty authorisation, a person must be detained in a hospital or care home, for the purpose of being given care or treatment in circumstances that amount to a deprivation of liberty. The authorisation must relate to the individual concerned and to the hospital or care home in which they are detained.

Para.1.9 For the purposes of Article 5 of the ECHR, there is no distinction in principle between depriving a person who lacks capacity of their liberty for the purpose of treating them for a physical condition, and depriving them of their liberty for treatment of a mental disorder. There will therefore be occasions when people who lack capacity to consent to admission are taken to hospital for treatment of physical illnesses or injuries, and then need to be cared for in circumstances that amount to a deprivation of liberty.

The safeguards provided under the new sections 4A and 4B inserted into the Mental Capacity Act 2005 by the Mental Health Act 2007 only apply to people who are not compulsorily detained in hospital. This is because people detained under the Mental Health Act 1983 already have a number of protections by virtue of application to the First-Tier Tribunal, formerly called the Mental Health Review Tribunal. However, people like L in the Bournewood case and Mrs Tudor not only lacked mental capacity but they also did not meet the threshold criteria of s.2 or s.3 of the Mental Health Act 1983 for compulsory detainment in hospital. L had been disruptive in the day centre he attended and Mrs Tudor was wandering into the street inappropriately dressed. Yet, neither of these actions could be said to warrant detention in the interests of their 'own health or safety or with a view to the protection of other persons'. Their actions were simply not of sufficient seriousness.

Undoubtedly Mrs Tudor was at substantial risk of harm in her own home as her dementia progressed and her carers were unable to provide sufficient supervision to keep her safe. It is people in precisely this situation that the *Deprivation of Liberty Safeguards* are designed to protect. They prevent such people being cajoled or threatened into apparently voluntary admissions to psychiatric hospitals, general hospitals, nursing homes or residential care through processes which treat them as consenting when in fact they are mentally incapable of giving valid consent. The *Deprivation of Liberty Safeguards* introduce a raft of procedures and protections which must be complied with before someone such as Mrs Tudor can be admitted to hospital or residential care. The box below sets out the safeguards for people without capacity who are admitted to health or social care institutions regardless of whether they are in the private, voluntary or public sectors.

 Background information

Deprivation of Liberty Safeguards

When an adult without capacity is either deprived of their liberty or at risk of being deprived of it within a hospital or care home, the managing authority of that institution must apply in writing for an authorisation of *deprivation of liberty* to the relevant supervisory body. In the case of a hospital, the supervisory body will be the Primary Care Trust which commissioned the medical care or treatment. For a care home the supervisory body will be the local authority for the area in which the person concerned is ordinarily resident. A supervisory body is responsible for:

- Deliberating on applications for authorisations.
- Commissioning the necessary six assessments.
- Authorising the *deprivation of liberty* if all six assessments agree.

The six assessments which must be completed before a supervisory body can give consideration to authorising the *deprivation of liberty* of a person are set out in Ministry of Justice (2008: paras. 4.23–4.76) *Mental Capacity Act 2005 Deprivation of Liberty Safeguards: Code of Practice to Supplement the main Mental Capacity Act 2005 Code of Practice.*

Age Assessment - Confirmation that the person is aged 18 years or over.

No Refusal Assessment - Establish whether an authorisation would conflict with another existing authority for decision making for the person, e.g. an advance decision to refuse treatment.

Mental Capacity Assessment - Establish if the person lacks capacity to decide whether or not to be in a hospital or residential care or to be given treatment there.

Mental Health Assessment - Establish whether the person has a mental disorder within the meaning of the Mental Health Act 1983.

Eligibility Assessment - A person is not eligible for authorisation if they are detained as a hospital inpatient under the Mental Health Act 1983 or if the authorisation would be inconsistent with directions already in place for those under guardianship or on conditional discharge from hospital living in the community.

Best Interests Assessment - Establish if it is in the best interests of the person to be deprived of their liberty, if it is necessary to prevent harm to themselves and if it is a proportionate response to the seriousness and likelihood of harm.

Only if all six assessments produce a positive result can the supervisory body authorise the *deprivation of liberty*. Any healthcare or social care professional who in the course of their work with users thinks that an authorisation for *deprivation of liberty* is required should inform the relevant managing authority for the hospital or care home.

The *Deprivation of Liberty Safeguards* not only offer protections to vulnerable adults at the point of admission into hospital, nursing or residential accommodation, but also once they have passed all six assessments and entered care. Once a *deprivation of liberty* authorisation has been issued by a supervisory body it must appoint a *relevant person's representative*. Anyone can be appointed as a *relevant person's representative* including relatives of the vulnerable adult as long as they are over 18 years of age and have no financial interest in the managing authority or supervisory body concerned with the vulnerable adult's care. Ministry of Justice (2008: para. 7.2) *Mental Capacity Act 2005 Deprivation of Liberty Safeguards: Code of Practice to Supplement the main Mental Capacity Act 2005 Code of Practice* sets out the role of the *relevant person's representative* which is to:

- Maintain contact with the relevant person.
- Represent the relevant person in matters concerning the deprivation of their liberty and the legal safeguards.
- Where indicated trigger a review of the authorisation for the *deprivation of liberty* by using the complaints procedure of the care provider or through application to the Court of Protection.

As the *Deprivation of Liberty Safeguards* were not in place at the time of Mrs Tudor's admission to hospital and later her transfer to a nursing home, the precise nature of how she came to be admitted to these institutions were not matters considered by Social Services or the Local Government Ombudsman. The reason why the issue of Mrs Tudor's compulsion featured so prominently in Mr Tudor's complaint was not in relation to her mental capacity as such, but the financial implications which flowed from the circumstances under which she was admitted to Lancaster Park Hospital.

The enactment of the Capacity Act 2005 together with the *Mental Capacity Act 2005: Code of Practice* and the *Mental Capacity Act 2005: Deprivation of Liberty Safeguards Supplementary Code of Practice* place additional responsibilities upon social workers. As Mrs Tudor's situation illustrates, a social worker may first come into contact with a user when he or she has mental capacity, but due to a progressive condition loses it at a later date. Social workers as care managers, Care Co-ordinators or Approved Mental Health Professionals may come into only temporary contact with a user. This may be in a community, hospital, residential or day-care setting. Wherever it occurs, if a social worker has grounds to believe that a user has lost capacity they must make it known to the correct authorities. This accords with paragraphs 3.1 and 3.2 of the GSCC Code of Practice, which require practitioners to both assist users to exercise their rights and to challenge 'abusive, discriminatory or exploitive behaviour'. Service-users without capacity, and who have not been recognised as such, run the risk of having no safeguards in place to protect them from abuse or exploitation. Being pressured, threatened or physically forced by a family member or professional to agree to major life changes when the user does not possess the mental capacity to give informed consent is plainly a form of abuse.

Charges for residential accommodation

Mr Tudor argued that his mother should not be liable to make a financial contribution towards her care in the nursing home as, given her refusal to enter the ambulance into which she was ultimately manhandled, she had in effect been compulsorily admitted to Lancaster Park Hospital. From there she had been transferred a few months later to an Elderly Mentally Infirm Unit of a nursing home. Mrs Tudor's transfer to an Elderly Mentally Infirm Unit was residential accommodation provided under s.21(1) of the National Assistance Act 1948 as she was an adult who met the criteria set out in this section. As someone experiencing advanced symptoms of dementia, Mrs Tudor had become a person 'who by reason of age, illness [or] disability' was 'in need of care and attention not otherwise available'. Social Services had sought to support her to live independently at home for as long as possible by providing a package of care consisting of assistance with cleaning and meals. This was also consistent with Mrs Tudor's expressed preference to remain at home rather than enter residential care. Over time, Mrs Tudor's Alzheimer's made it increasingly difficult for her to manage alone at home, even with domiciliary services.

Mr Tudor lived abroad, while Mrs Stuart was already looking after her ill husband. This meant that at a point when Mrs Tudor required 24-hour support to remain safe, there were no available informal carers. In other words, 'care and attention' was 'not otherwise available' to her in the community at the point when she was ready for discharge from Lancaster Park Hospital. For this reason she qualified for the provision of accommodation under s.21 of the National Assistance Act 1948. However, s.22 of the same statute stipulates that anyone accommodated under s.21 must contribute to the cost of their care if they have the resources to do so. In the case of Mrs Tudor, she owned her house and consequently this was an asset which could be sold to raise money toward the cost of her care. It transpired in evidence which came before the Local Government Ombudsman that this was also property which Mr Tudor might have inherited on his mother's death. The box below outlines the provisions for making a charge against a person's capital and income for their residential care.

 Background information

Charges for accommodation under s.22 of the National Assistance Act 1948

- If the individual has capital and income above the upper figure £20,500 they will be liable to pay at the standard rate which represents the full cost of providing the accommodation.
- If a person cannot pay at the standard rate because they have insufficient resources then they will be financially assessed and charged at a lower rate in order to make a contribution towards the cost of their care.

- Disregarded capital is the name given to assets which are automatically excluded from the financial assessment of the person's resources. Disregarded capital includes the value of: personal possessions and the value of a home if:
  - it is occupied by a partner
  - it is occupied by a family member who is over 60 years or under 16 years *and* is incapacitated or is liable to be maintained by the person moving into residential care
  - the local authority also has discretion to disregard the value of a home if occupied by other categories of people.
- Notional capital is the name given to capital which an individual deliberately disposes of to avoid paying the standard rate. For example transferring ownership of their home to a relative in anticipation of entering residential care.

Mrs Tudor's husband was dead at the time of her admission to a nursing home and she had lived alone, so plainly under the rules for financial assessment regarding s.22 of the National Assistance Act 1948 the value of Mrs Tudor's home could be taken into consideration. However, the National Assistance Act 1948 is not the only statute under which long-term residential care can be provided. It can also be provided under the aftercare provisions contained in s.117 of the Mental Health Act 1983. But the crucial difference is that common law has established that local authorities cannot levy a charge for accommodation provided to a person with a mental disorder under this section. So, if Mrs Tudor had been detained under s.3 of the Mental Health Act 1983 when she was admitted to Lancaster Park Hospital she would have be eligible for s.117 aftercare, which in her case would have comprised a long-term placement in an Elderly Mentally Infirm Unit of a nursing home. This went to the core of Mr Tudor's complaint. According to him, in the first instance Mrs Tudor should have been admitted to Lancaster Park Hospital under the Mental Health Act 1983 on 30 April 1998 for compulsory treatment which would have made her eligible for s.117 aftercare. Alternatively, according to Mr Tudor, her admission to Lancaster Park Hospital on 23 May 1998 should be treated as a compulsory admission, which would again entitle her to free aftercare under s.117, including that of long-term residential care, if under s.3.

Social workers cannot assume that the interests of users and carers are the same. They may be in direct conflict with one another, as was true between Mrs Tudor who wished to remain at home and her son Mr Tudor who wanted her to be compulsorily admitted to hospital. Sometimes there can be a genuine disagreement between users and carers, with the latter seeking outcomes which they deeply believe to be in the best interests of the person they look after. Equally, ulterior motives may influence the perspectives of carers or relatives. Considerations related to money can loom large in many families. However understandable these considerations may be, given the circumstances of individual family members, they must not be permitted to exert undue pressure upon users or to direct the decisions of professionals. If practitioners are to have insight into the motivations of users and carers when choices about service provision have financial implications, then they must have sufficient knowledge of the legislation to understand the monetary costs of different courses of action. In this case, knowing that accommodation under s.21 of the National Assistance Act 1948 incurred a charge while that provided under s.117 of the Mental Health Act 1983 did not was crucial to understanding Mr Tudor's ultimate motivations.

Ombudsman's Decision in Complaint No. 99/B/03564 and 99/B/05735 against Reading Borough Council

The investigating officer at stage two and the Review Panel at stage three of the Social Services Complaints Procedure had effectively rejected all the grounds of Mr Tudor's complaint and dismissed it. The Local Government Ombudsman endorsed both the investigation conducted by Social Services into the matter and the outcome of its deliberations. The Local Government Ombudsman therefore dismissed the complaint made by Mr Tudor concluding that:

- The Approved Social Worker had correctly decided not to admit Mrs Tudor to hospital under the Mental Health Act 1983 at the assessment meeting.
- Mrs Stuart had been correctly identified as Mrs Tudor's *nearest relative*.
- Mrs Tudor met the criteria under s.21(1) of the National Assistance Act 1948 for transfer into residential care on discharge from hospital.
- A charge had been properly placed on Mrs Tudor's assets, including her home, to help pay towards the cost of her long-term care.

 Critical questions

1 The Approved Social Worker intervening with Mrs Tudor had a difficult decision to make in terms of assessing her vulnerability and capacity to look after herself in a community setting. Which factors is it important to take into consideration as an Approved Mental Health Professional when deciding whether a mental disorder is of a nature or degree to warrant a person's detention in hospital?

2 Disputes between carers, who are usually family members, and users over how they should be looked after are common. These can be particularly acute when the Mental Health Act 1983 is invoked as the *nearest relative* has statutory rights under this Act. In the situation which confronted the Approved Social Worker in this case how might you have acted differently to negotiate the differences of opinion and perspective between Mrs Tudor, Mrs Stuart and Mr Tudor?

3 Mrs Tudor had Alzheimer's disease which ultimately resulted in a loss of mental capacity. The exact point at which this happened was poorly understood and undoubtedly Mrs Tudor became subject to the will of others, both professionals and family members. In circumstances such as Mrs Tudor's, were you an Approved Mental Health Professional or a Care Co-ordinator how would you intervene to ensure that a vulnerable adult availed of and *continued* to avail of the protections laid down in the Mental Capacity Act 2005?

4 The charge for Mrs Tudor's residential care, which was levied against the house she owned, became a major issue in this case. What do you know about welfare entitlements and charges for residential or domiciliary care? How might a more detailed knowledge of welfare entitlements and charges for care improve your practice with users and carers?

 Perspectives

Users and carers' views on the *nearest relative*

The interplay of roles and powers between the *nearest relative*, Approved Social Worker (ASW) and registered medical practitioner introduced under the Mental Health Act 1983 was designed to safeguard individuals from premature or unfounded admission to

▶

473

psychiatric hospital. The role and powers of the *nearest relative* are retained within the amended Mental Health Act 1983. But patients have been granted the right to replace their *nearest relative* with someone else by application to the County Court under s.29 of the amended Mental Health Act 1983. The Approved Mental Health Professional can also apply for the displacement of a *nearest relative* who is deemed 'unsuitable' to fulfil the functions of that role.

Rapaport (2004) investigated the experiences of users, carers and Approved Social Workers regarding the exercise of powers held by the *nearest relative* under the Mental Health Act 1983. One service-user, in a contribution which clearly endorses the new right of patients to displace their *nearest relative*, said 'it seems jolly unfair that you might have one relative that is prepared to take responsibility who's not necessarily your closest but the nearest relative that is closest won't take responsibility'. For other users the powers exercisable by their *nearest relative* were a source of fear and anxiety. One female user described how her husband had exploited his position as her *nearest relative* to have her detained in an attempt to obtain sole custody of their children.

Some Approved Social Workers in the study also described situations in which they believed that a spouse was trying to compulsorily admit a partner to hospital for ulterior motives (Rapaport, 2004: 386). Conversely several also recalled situations in which the *nearest relative* had acted to prevent detainment in hospital. Rapaport (2004: 389) provides a typical example from an ASW,

> I had one recently where a nearest relative objected and so I supported him against the doctors and luckily with a lot of consultation we managed to work through an alternative plan of action which was quite involved in terms of this person . . . and we managed to get a care package together with a consultant in the area . . . and it worked. It did work.

A number of research participants who acted as a *nearest relative* for a family member described the sometimes harrowing experience of having to admit them to hospital. One carer recounted signing the application to detain her son in hospital, describing it as her 'worst nightmare' (Rapaport, 2004: 387). Relating similar experiences, a *nearest relative* in a study by Campbell (2008: 224) explained:

> the GP wanted me to sign, and said that he could get an ASW as an alternative, but that this would take hours, I reluctantly agreed, just to cut the pain . . . I signed for my son but never again . . . I felt that I had 'put him away'. It is much better that this should be done by someone like an ASW who can then take the blame.

This is not to deny that some close family members felt that acting as the applicant for a compulsory admission to hospital was an aspect of their caring role. As one parent put it, 'I felt responsible for my son, so I thought it was OK for me to sign the form' (Campbell, 2008: 224). Other carers were deeply ambivalent about the necessity and effect of compulsory admission upon their relative. In the study by Campbell (2008: 224) one relative voiced this in the following way:

> It was not really beneficial – it solved an immediate problem but the experiences were so painful, the experience of going through the mental health system can be so degrading, ending up with very low self-esteem – compulsion is part of this – my brother would refer to it as the way the world had harmed him.

CASE 2
Ombudsman Report Complaint No. 97/B/2696 against Suffolk County Council June 1999

Importance of the case

This case considers the right of patients to appeal against their detainment. It also illustrates the tensions and conflicts which can arise between mental health users and their *nearest relatives*. The relationship between lifestyle choices, risk of harm and mental disorder is explored. In this connection disagreement between the Approved Mental Health Professional and the Responsible Clinician is considered alongside its implications for multidisciplinary work.

History of the case

This was a complaint regarding the decision of an Approved Social Worker brought by parents whose adult daughter was discharged from a psychiatric ward against their wishes. The complaint had initially been pursued through the Social Services Complaints Procedure, but dissatisfaction with the outcome of this led to an application to the Local Government Ombudsman.

Facts of the case

Erica Brewer was born in 1959 and first experienced mental health problems in 1976 when she consulted a homeopathic doctor. In the early 1980s she developed anorexia and her weight dropped to six stone, but she refused any psychiatric treatment. In 1987 she left her parental home in the belief that God had called her to become a missionary in China. However, some months later she was deported back to the United Kingdom from Switzerland. Her parents lost contact with her, but in 1988 they received news of Erica when she was hospitalised in France where she refused to accept treatment. Erica returned to the United Kingdom again in January 1989 and stayed with her parents for a year before leaving there once more in February 1989. Mr and Mrs Brewer had no contact with their daughter until almost three and a half years later in June 1992 when she was admitted as an in-patient to a hospital in the United Kingdom. Her parents arranged to meet Erica on her discharge from hospital, but she disappeared before they could do so. In May 1993 Erica landed at Heathrow airport having been deported from Austria. She refused her parents help and again disappeared. In November 1995 the Foreign Office contacted Mr and Mrs Brewer to inform them that Erica was being deported from Algeria where she had been living for the past two years. Although Mr and Mrs Brewer met their daughter at the airport she again disappeared and they had no further contact with her until February 1997 when she was admitted to West Suffolk Hospital. Erica was detained in hospital under s.2 of the Mental Health Act 1983 having initially been held by the police under s.136 of the same statute. Although the Responsible Medical Officer (now the Responsible Clinician) wanted to proceed with a s.3 detainment, the Approved Social Worker did not. Consequently, Erica was discharged from hospital and disappeared again before Mr and Mrs Brewer could take any action. Both parents complained against the decision of the Approved Social Worker through the Social Services Complaints Procedure. When they were dissatisfied by the outcome of this complaint they pursued the matter through the Local Government Ombudsman. At the time of the investigation by the Ombudsman Erica's whereabouts remained unknown.

Key people in the case

Erica Brewer – vulnerable adult
Mr Brewer – Erica's father
Mrs Brewer – Erica's mother
Mr Bodie – Approved Social Worker (AMHP)
Ms Taylor – Approved Social Worker (AMHP)
Consultant psychiatrist – Responsible Medical Officer (Responsible Clinician)

Discussion of the case

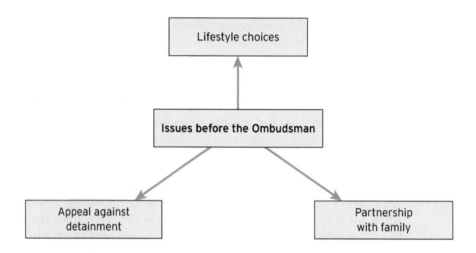

Appeal against detainment

The police initially detained Erica under s.136 of the Mental Health Act 1983 on 3 February 1997. This power permits a police officer to remove to a place of safety a person found in a public place who appears to be suffering from a mental disorder. In this instance the police had been contacted because Erica had lit a fire in the garden of a private residence. It also transpired that she had been living rough in the Thetford Forest for some weeks. This power lasts only for 72 hours and a person subject to it has no right of appeal. The power is non-renewable, which means that at the end of 72 hours if the person has not been detained under longer-term provisions such as s.2 or s.3 of the Mental Health Act 1983, then he or she must be permitted to leave the place of safety. For someone believed to be suffering from a mental disorder an appropriate place of safety will normally be a psychiatric hospital or the psychiatric ward of a general hospital.

Soon after being detained under s.136 by a police officer Erica was taken to West Suffolk Hospital where she was seen by Mr Bodie, an Approved Social Worker (now an Approved Mental Health Professional). After interviewing Erica, Mr Bodie concluded that her mental disorder was of 'a nature or degree' which warranted her detention 'in a hospital for an assessment' and that it was necessary to detain her in the interests of her 'own health or safety'. Mr Bodie's application for a s.2 detainment was also supported by the recommendations of two registered medical practitioners, who like the Approved Social Worker, had concluded that Erica's mental state met the conditions of s.2 for her compulsory admission to hospital for assessment. Erica was absolutely opposed to her detainment and had in fact refused to give any information about herself to Mr Bodie. Mental health patients detained under longer-term provisions have a right to appeal to a Tribunal to review their continued detainment. This is a protection against unlawful detainment and also provides an opportunity for patients to be represented and to argue for their discharge from hospital. The rights of appeal to the Tribunal for patients detained under different sections of the Mental Health Act 1983 (as amended) are set out in the table below.

Sections of Mental Health Act 1983 (as amended)	Period of detainment	Right to appeal to Tribunal
s.2 Detainment for assessment	Maximum 28 days Non-renewable	Within first 14 days
s.3 Detainment for treatment	Maximum six months Renewable for six months Renewable annually thereafter	Once within the first six months and thereafter once within each renewal period
s.4 Detainment in an emergency	Maximum 72 hours	No right of appeal
s.5 Detainment of hospital in-patient	Nurse's holding power: Maximum 6 hours Non-renewable Doctor's holding power: Maximum 72 hours Non-renewable	No right of appeal
s.17A Community Treatment Order	Maximum six months Renewable for six months Renewable annually thereafter	Once within first six months of making of Community Treatment Order and once during each period of extension
s.35 Remand to hospital for report	Maximum 28 days Renewable for further 28 days up to 12 weeks in total	No right of appeal
s.36 Remand to hospital for treatment	Maximum 28 days Renewable for further 28 days up to 12 weeks in total	No right of appeal
s.37 Guardianship	Maximum six months Renewable for six months Renewable annually thereafter	Once within the first six months and thereafter once within each renewal period
s.37 Hospital Order	Maximum six months Renewable for six months Renewable annually thereafter	Once within second six months and thereafter once within each renewal period
s.37/41 Hospital Order with a Restriction Order	Variable	Once within second six months and thereafter once within each renewal period
s.136 Police power in public place	Maximum 72 hours Non-renewable	No right of appeal

Erica was first detained under s.136 by the police and had no right of appeal to the Tribunal. At West Suffolk Hospital where she was taken by a police officer she was then detained under s.2 for assessment. This section allows for a maximum period of compulsory detainment in hospital for 28 days during which time most forms of treatment for the mental disorder can be administered without the patient's consent. Precisely because this section involves a much longer potential period of compulsory hospitalisation patients have a right of appeal against their continued detainment to the Tribunal. In this instance, on admission Erica applied immediately for discharge from hospital to what used to be referred to as the Mental Health Review Tribunal, but is now a First-Tier Tribunal within the Health Education and Social Care Chamber. The Tribunal cannot review the circumstances under which a mental health patient was originally detained in hospital, but it can decide whether their continued detainment is necessary. Any patient who wants to challenge the legality of their original detainment has to do so through using the judicial review procedure as in the case of MS in *St George's Healthcare NHS Trust* v. *S* and *R* v. *Collins and Others* [1998] 3 WLR 936. The remit of the Tribunal is set out in the box below.

 Background information

The Tribunal

Part V of the Mental Health Act 1983 (as amended) which comprises ss.65-79 sets out the powers of the Tribunal. The conduct of The First-Tier Tribunal is governed by the Health Education and Social Care Chamber Rules which are provided for under the Tribunals, Courts and Enforcement Act 2007. These two statutes taken together regulate the First-Tier Tribunal and the system of appeals from it to the Upper Tribunal. From there appeal for mental health patients or their *nearest relatives* will be to the High Court using judicial review procedures. The proceedings of the Chamber in respect of Mental Health Review are normally conducted in private and take place where the patient has been detained. The Tribunal is presided over by a panel of three, which must include a lawyer who chairs the hearing, a psychiatrist and a lay person. Appeal to the First-Tier Tribunal will usually involve the attendance of: the patient; the Responsible Clinician; the Approved Mental Health Professional; the patient's solicitor; the *nearest relative* or next of kin; and a psychiatric nurse who knows the patient.

All mental health patients are entitled to legal representation at the First-Tier and Upper Tier Tribunals for Mental Health Review. The burden of proof is on those who argue that the patient should remain detained. This means that it is for the Responsible Clinician and/or Approved Mental Health Professional to prove before the Tribunal panel on the *balance of probabilities* (see Chapter 1) that the patient is suffering from a mental disorder which warrants their continued detention. It is not necessary for patients or their legal representative to demonstrate that they are not suffering from a mental disorder which necessitates their continued detainment. The decision of the Tribunal is generally made directly after the hearing.

The Tribunal *can*

- Decide if the patient should continue to be detained based on his or her condition and circumstances at the time of the hearing.
- Determine if the patient should be transferred to a different hospital or psychiatric unit.
- Consider whether a patient should be given leave from hospital under s.17 with attached conditions.
- Consider whether a patient should be released from hospital subject to a Community Treatment Order under s.17A.
- Transfer a patient into guardianship.
- Order the discharge of a patient from detainment in hospital.

The Tribunal *cannot*

- Change the treatment of a patient.
- Make a Community Treatment Order.
- Alter the conditions of an existing Community Treatment Order.
- Deliberate on whether the patient was lawfully detained when they were originally admitted to hospital.

On admission to hospital Erica Brewer would have been given information about the legal status of her detainment and her rights under the Mental Health Act 1983 as required by the Code of Practice excerpted in the box below. On being informed of her rights Erica applied to the Tribunal within the first 14 days of her s.2 detainment for treatment. It is a requirement that such an application be heard within 7 days and this duly happened. The Tribunal took medical evidence from the Responsible Clinician (formerly known as the Responsible Medical Officer) who was the consultant psychiatrist in charge of Erica's care. He argued that Erica should continue to be detained under s.2 for treatment. Erica, in her evidence before the panel, refused to concede that she was suffering from a mental illness and asserted that her actions were being directed by God. The Tribunal decided that Erica was a vulnerable adult who was suffering from a mental disorder which warranted her continued detention in hospital given the risk to her own safety caused by her behaviour.

 Key guidance

Mental Health Act 1983: Code of Practice

Para. 2.7 Wherever possible, patients should be engaged in the process of reaching decisions which affect their care and treatment under the Act. Consultation with patients involves assisting them in understanding the issue, their role and the roles of others who are involved in taking the decision. Ideally decisions should be agreed with the patient. Where a decision is made that is contrary to the patient's wishes, that decision and the authority for it should be explained to the patient using a form of communication that the patient understands.

Para. 2.8 The Act requires hospital managers to take steps to ensure that patients who are detained in hospital under the Act, or who are on supervised community treatment (SCT), understand important information about how the Act applies to them. This must be done as soon as practicable after the start of the patient's detention or SCT.

Para. 2.9 Information must be given to the patient both orally and in writing.

Para. 2.11 Patients must be informed:

- Of the provisions of the Act under which they are detained or on SCT, and the effect of those provisions.
- Of the rights (if any) of their nearest relative to discharge them (and what can happen if their responsible clinician does not agree with that decision).
- For SCT patients, of the effect of the community treatment order, including the conditions which they are required to keep to and the circumstances in which their responsible clinician may recall them to hospital.

The right of appeal to a Tribunal, which is held by patients subject to detainment under the Mental Health Act 1983, is a vital check on whether they are being justifiably deprived of their liberty. The compulsory confinement of a person to an institutional setting directly impinges on article 6 of the European Convention on Human Rights which guarantees citizens a fair trial. The Tribunal is the first opportunity at which patients can be legally represented and before which they can present their arguments against continued detainment. For this reason the *Mental Health Act 1983: Code of Practice* emphasises the importance of ensuring that detained patients are fully informed of their rights, especially their entitlement to appear before the Tribunal. Likewise, the GSCC Code of Practice highlights the obligations of social care workers to inform service-users of their rights and to support users in availing of them. Plainly social workers acting as Approved Mental Health Professionals have a direct responsibility to advise patients of their rights and most particularly their recourse to the Tribunal if they disagree with their detainment.

Lifestyle choices

Section 2 provides for a relatively short-term period of detainment of a patient for assessment. Consequently, after the decision of the Tribunal not to discharge Erica, the Responsible Clinician in charge of Erica's care at West Suffolk Hospital began to complete a s.3 application. This would have permitted him to detain Erica for up to six months with the option of renewable periods of detainment in hospital thereafter. This course of action would provide for the longer-term treatment of Erica's mental disorder. Although both the Responsible Clinician and Erica Brewer's GP were willing to support a s.3 application and had completed the paperwork for this, it required Ms Taylor as the Approved Social Worker (now AMHP) to actually make the application. The Mental Health Act 1983 (as amended) places duties on the AMHP when considering a s.2 or s.3 application. These are elaborated in the Code of Practice excerpted in the box below.

Key guidance

Mental Health Act 1983: Code of Practice

Para. 4.48 AMHPs may make an application for detention only if they:

- Have interviewed the patient in a suitable manner;
- Are satisfied that the statutory criteria for detention are met; and
- Are satisfied that, in all the circumstances of the case, detention in hospital is the most appropriate way of providing the care and medical treatment the patient needs.

Para. 4.51 Although AMHPs act on behalf of a LSSA [Local Social Service Authority], they cannot be told by the LSSA or anyone else whether or not to make an application. They must exercise their own judgement, based on social and medical evidence, when deciding whether to apply for a patient to be detained under the Act. The role of AMHPs is to provide an independent decision about whether or not there are alternatives to detention under the Act, bringing a social perspective to bear on their decision.

In accordance with the requirements of the Mental Health Act 1983 as set out in paragraphs 4.48 and 4.51 Ms Taylor, who was the Approved Social Worker on duty on 28 February 1997, duly interviewed Erica in West Suffolk Hospital. She had access to both the Tribunal's decision on Erica's appeal against her detainment under s.2 and the medical recommendations of the Responsible Clinician and the GP. However, Ms Taylor came to a different conclusion from the two medical professionals. In her assessment, written up after her interview with Erica Brewer, she concluded:

> Erica looked extremely healthy although unkempt which I think illustrated her lifestyle. She has been 'on the road' for the past ten years and has set herself specific moral and physical targets to achieve her goal of becoming a missionary . . . Erica seemed to fully understand and accept the risks involved in living a lone nomadic life. She also accepts that because of her lifestyle she flouts social boundaries.

In view of this, Ms Taylor believed that an application for further detainment of Erica in which she would be compelled to accept treatment for her mental disorder was not warranted. Therefore Ms Taylor declined to pursue the s.3 application despite the recommendations of the two registered medical practitioners. In coming to this decision the Approved Social Worker was also taking into account the wishes of the patient and the likely impact that continued detainment would have on her (see page 432 above). Furthermore, she was incorporating into her assessment the degree to which interfering with Erica's choice through confinement in hospital would cause Erica considerable additional distress. While Erica's decision to live 'wild' was unusual, eccentric and possibly impracticable in a post-industrial country such as Britain, it certainly was not of itself constitutive of a mental illness (see page 412 above), although clearly it was recognised by both the Approved Social Worker and the doctors that Erica did have some mental health problems.

As the Responsible Clinician was to tell the Local Government Ombudsman in oral evidence, faced with the refusal of Ms Taylor to make the s.3 application, it remained open to him to seek a second opinion from another Approved Social Worker who might be willing to proceed. This, the Responsible Clinician decided not to do on the grounds that the original s.2 detainment had in his opinion been 'borderline'. For although Erica plainly had mental health problems there was no definitive diagnosis. Moreover, while her behaviour placed her at risk, the fact remained that she had lived with that risk for the previous ten years and had remained physically healthy, if dishevelled. As the Responsible Clinician was to concede in his evidence 'he did not consider that there was a real suggestion of potential harm to Erica or to others' (para. 45). He also stated that 'there had been a body of opinion among medical practitioners on the wards that the hospital was exerting excessive control over Erica and preventing her living her chosen life' (para. 45). The Responsible Clinician also expressed the view to the Ombudsman that he had worked alongside Ms Taylor as a colleague for some years and respected her professional opinion. In the circumstances the Responsible Clinician decided not to pursue the s.3 application and instead discharged Erica Brewer from the s.2 detainment for assessment as provided for under s.23 of the Mental Health Act 1983 (as amended) which is reproduced in the box below.

 Key legislation

Mental Health Act 1983 (as amended)

s.23 (1) . . . a patient who is for the time being liable to be detained or subject to guardianship under this Part of this Act shall cease to be so liable or subject if an order in writing discharging him absolutely from detention or guardianship is made in accordance with this section.

s.23(1A) . . . a community patient shall cease to be liable to recall under this Part of this Act, and the application for admission for treatment cease to have effect, if an order in writing discharging him from such liability is made in accordance with this section.

s.23(2) An order for discharge may be made in respect of a patient –

(a) where the patient is liable to be detained in a hospital in pursuance of an application for admission for assessment or for treatment by the responsible clinician, by the managers or by the nearest relative of the patient

(b) where the patient is subject to guardianship, by the responsible clinician, by the responsible local social services authority or by the nearest relative of the patient.

(c) where the patient is a community patient, by the responsible clinician, by the mangers of the responsible hospital or by the nearest relative of the patient.

Erica Brewer was given an absolute discharge by the Responsible Clinician and there were therefore no conditions attached to her release from hospital. On being informed of her discharge Erica immediately left the psychiatric ward to which she had been admitted at West Suffolk Hospital and disappeared again, her whereabouts still remaining unknown at the time of the Ombudsman's investigation. This meant that Mr and Mrs Brewer, as Erica's parents, were once more in the situation of not knowing their daughter's where-abouts and feeling extremely anxious as to her health and safety. It was the lack of com-munication between mental health professionals and Mr and Mrs Brewer which formed the basis of their complaint to the Local Government Ombudsman.

Ms Taylor as the Approved Social Worker was faced with the contradictory require-ments of the principles set out in the *Mental Health Act 1983: Code of Practice*. On the one hand she was obliged to follow the *least restriction* and *respect* principles which would in-dicate that Erica's lifestyle choice should be tolerated and supported as an aspect of her autonomy and entitlement to take risks with her health and safety. Similarly the GSCC Code of Practice highlights the importance of user independence and of (at para-graph 4.1) 'recognising that service users have the right to take risks and helping them to identify and manage potential and actual risks to themselves and others'. At the same time the *purpose principle* requires that 'decisions under the Act must be taken with a view to minimising the undesirable effects of mental disorder, by maximising the safety and wellbeing (mental and physical) of patients'. Undoubtedly Erica's decision to live a no-madic life and to move through different countries appeared to exacerbate her mental disorder and to put her physical health at risk. Likewise paragraph 4.3 GSCC Code of Practice charges social care workers take 'necessary steps to minimise the risks of service users from doing actual or potential harm to themselves or other people'.

Ms Taylor, as the Approved Social Worker responsible for making a s.3 application if Erica was to be detained for treatment, had to negotiate these competing principles and requirements of good practice. This she did by considering the extent to which Erica's lifestyle choice presented a serious risk to her health and safety and the degree to which she comprehended the implications of her choice. As Ms Taylor observed in her notes, Erica had lived a nomadic lifestyle for ten years without serious harm to herself or others. This meant that although Erica had a mental disorder, it was not such that warranted her detainment. Diversity, cultural practices and lifestyle choices do not attract automatic re-spect and non-interference. Their abuse, exploitive or harmful impacts have to be consid-ered and weighed against other imperatives embedded in the *Mental Health Act 1983: Code of Practice* and the GSCC *Code of Practice for Social Care Workers*.

Although the Approved Social Worker (now AMHP) is ultimately responsible for mak-ing a s.2 or s.3 application for detainment, this can only be done in concert with health-care professionals. Such applications therefore involve multidisciplinary collaboration. In this instance Ms Taylor disagreed with the two medical practitioners who wished to proceed with the application. Paragraph 6.7 of the GSCC Code of Practice stresses the importance of 'recognising and respecting the roles and expertise of workers from other agencies and working in partnership with them'. It is obvious from the Responsible Clinician's evidence to the Ombudsman that he thought that his opinion had been considered by Ms Taylor, although not acted upon. Respect for colleagues from different disciplines or working in other agencies does not mean slavishly doing their bidding. But it does necessitate taking seriously their concerns, viewpoints and the information which they have to contribute to any decision. Good practice in multidisciplinary work also obliges social workers who disagree with the opinion of colleagues to openly acknowledge the disagreement and to explore the reasons for it. At the same time social workers must be clear about the nature of their own role, particularly when this is defined by statute, and take responsibility for the decisions they hold the ultimate authority to make.

Partnership with family

Approved Mental Health Professionals are required by the Mental Health Act 1983 (as amended) to identify and communicate with the *nearest relative* when they are considering a s.2 or s.3 application. Their responsibilities in this regard are set out in paragraph 4.64 of the *Mental Health Act 1983: Code of Practice* (see box on page 465). Hospital managers are required by s.132 and s.133 of the Mental Health Act 1983 to inform the *nearest relative* about the detainment and discharge of the person who has the mental disorder. As Erica was neither married nor in a civil partnership and had no children, according to the rank ordered list set out in s.26(1) of the Mental Health Act 1983 (see page 463) Mr and Mrs Brewer, as her father and mother, were next in the list as her *nearest relatives*. As such there were additional responsibilities laid upon the Approved Social Worker (now AMHP) to inform them about the decisions regarding Erica's detainment in hospital.

Mr and Mrs Brewer complained to the Local Government Ombudsman that they had not been properly informed either by Ms Taylor, the Approved Social Worker, or medical staff at West Suffolk Hospital regarding the s.3 application and discharge of their daughter. Erica's parents argued that had they known in time about Ms Taylor's decision not to make an s.3 application, that Mr Brewer as the *nearest relative* would have made an application instead as provided for in the Mental Health Act 1983. Furthermore, had Mr and Mrs Brewer been made aware that the Responsible Clinician was going to discharge Erica from hospital on 28 February 1997, Mr Brewer informed the Ombudsman that he would have acted immediately to pursue a s.3 application to prevent his daughter being released from hospital.

In response to the complaint made by Mr and Mrs Brewer, Ms Taylor explained that she had attempted to contact them by telephone on 28 February, but received no reply. She then phoned Erica's uncle whose contact details were on the hospital notes and spoke to him, explaining why she did not propose to make a s.3 application to detain Erica further for treatment. In his evidence Erica's uncle described Ms Taylor as having already made her decision and merely asking him to pass it on to Erica's parents. He stated that he urged Ms Taylor at the time to speak to Mr and Mrs Brewer directly about the matter, but Ms Taylor responded that she was about to go off duty. Linked to Ms Taylor's refusal to make an application for s.3 detainment was the decision of the Responsible Clinician to rescind the original s.2 detainment for Erica which still had 48 hours left to run. Since Ms Taylor was of the opinion that a s.3 application was not warranted, the Responsible Clinician concluded that there was no rationale for holding Erica in hospital for an additional 48 hours simply for the sake of it. He therefore discharged her under s.23, but failed to inform the *nearest relative* of his action. This of course meant that by the time Mr Brewer had been made aware of the situation and arrived at the West Suffolk Hospital, Erica had already left it.

The *Mental Health Act 1983: Code of Practice* refers to the requirement for mental health professionals to contact, consult and inform *nearest relatives* of their rights. It also consistently emphasises the importance of involving family members and other carers in the decisions which are being made about someone with a mental disorder. Likewise *Refocusing the Care Programme Approach* lays emphasis on partnership working with family members and carers in setting up and maintaining effective care plans for those with a mental disorder. It is plain from the evidence given to the Local Government Ombudsman that in fact both the Approved Social Worker and the Responsible Clinician failed in their duties to inform Mr and Mrs Brewer of the decisions which were being made regarding their daughter's detainment under the Mental Health Act 1983. Indeed the Ombudsman criticised the social worker for her shortcomings in making contact with Erica's parents.

Mr Brewer was absolutely opposed to Erica's discharge from hospital and it was his stated intention to apply for a s.3 detainment as her *nearest relative*. It is obvious that had Ms Taylor properly informed Mr Brewer, as Erica's father, she would then have been faced with a confrontation between user and carer. Despite this possibility, paragraph 2.2 of the GSCC Code of Practice requires practitioners to communicate 'in an appropriate, open, accurate and straightforward way'. So the onus is on social workers to consult with carers, even if this may lead to disagreement between them and those they look after. It will then be for the practitioner to mediate and negotiate between conflicting perspectives, needs, wants and objectives.

Ombudsman's Decision in Complaint No. 97/B/2696 against Suffolk County Council

Mr and Mrs Brewer sought to complain both about the way in which Ms Taylor had gone about the decision not to apply for a s.3 detainment of their daughter and the fact that she was not detained under s.3. In other words they sought to complain both about the process by which the decision was made and the outcome of the decision. The Local Government Ombudsman can only address issues of maladministration and therefore declined to adjudicate as to whether Erica Brewer should have been compulsory detained in hospital under s.3 of the Mental Health Act 1983.

As to the conduct of the Approved Social Worker, the Ombudsman concluded that Ms Taylor had failed to make sufficient effort to contact and consult with Mr Brewer as Erica's *nearest relative*. This constituted maladministration as she had failed to fulfil her duty under s.11(4)(b) of the Mental Health Act 1983 to consult with the *nearest relative* regarding a s.3 application. Given that the there was still 48 hours left to run of the s.2 under which Erica had originally been admitted to hospital, there was no immediate urgency and a further two days remained during which Ms Taylor could have made additional efforts to contact Erica's parents. The Ombudsman concluded that by not doing so the Approved Social Worker had in effect deprived Mr Brewer as Erica's *nearest relative* of exercising his right to make a s.3 application himself. Consequently, the Local Government Ombudsman awarded Mr and Mrs Brewer a payment of £1,000 against the local authority's Social Services Department.

 Critical questions

1 The Tribunal is a crucial safeguard for people detained in hospital against their will or subject to intrusive conditions in the community. What are some of the weaknesses of the Tribunal system for mental health review? How do you think the Tribunal system might be improved? As a professional how might you support a mental health patient to take full advantage of an opportunity to appear before the Tribunal?

2 Ms Taylor, as the social worker, had a difficult decision to make as Erica had a mental disorder and her behaviour was putting her health and safety at risk. If you were an Approved Mental Health Professional what factors would influence your decision on whether or not to detain someone in hospital for treatment?

3 There was a clear disagreement between Mr Brewer, as the *nearest relative,* and the Approved Social Worker as to the necessity of detaining Erica. It is not uncommon for the *nearest relative* to disagree with the Approved Mental Health Professional. Had you been in Ms Taylor's position how would you better have addressed the difference of opinion between you and the *nearest relative*?

4 The Approved Social Worker in this case disagreed with two medical opinions and decided against making an application for a s.3 detainment on the grounds that Erica as an autonomous individual was entitled to make lifestyle choices, even if they jeopardised her safety. What difficulties or challenges might you encounter as a social worker on a Community Mental Health Team if you disagreed with the opinion of medical professionals?

 Critical commentary

Mental Health Act 2007

The amendments introduced by the Mental Health Act 2007 broadened the categories of people who could be detained in hospital and compelled to accept treatment. Under s.1 of the un-amended Mental Health Act 1983 a person could only be detained for treatment if diagnosed as having a mental illness, psychopathic disorder, mental impairment or severe mental impairment. From these definitions s.1(3) expressly excluded 'promiscuity or other immoral conduct, sexual deviancy or dependence on alcohol or drugs'. This meant that a person could not be deemed to have a mental disorder solely because they were homosexual, worked as a prostitute, had a heroin addiction or sexually abused children.

Consistent with these exclusions from the original Mental Health Act 1983 was what became known as 'the treatability test'. This was contained in the un-amended version of s.3 which required that an individual could only be detained for treatment where 'in the case of psychopathic disorder or mental impairment, such treatment is likely to alleviate or prevent a deterioration of the patient's condition'. Thus, even if someone with a psychopathic disorder or mental impairment constituted a risk to themselves or the public, they could not be detained for treatment in hospital. Medical treatment for a mental disorder could only be given if it alleviated or prevented deterioration of the patient's condition. It is widely acknowledged within the psychiatric profession that personality disorders are not amenable to medical treatment.

The amendments of the Mental Health Act 2007 replaced the four separate definitions of mental disorder and redefined mental disorder in s.1 to mean 'any disorder or disability of the mind'. This clearly broadened the applicability of the now amended Mental Health Act 1983 to a wider group of people, including those with a personality disorder. The amendments also did away with the exclusions of sexual deviancy and immoral behaviour, potentially bringing paedophiles and rapists within the scope of the Mental Health Acts. This has the effect of making those who were previously 'bad' and dealt with under criminal law into those who are 'mad' and are to be dealt with under mental health legislation. It also brings conduct such as consensual sado-masochism and transvestism (which are mental disorders in DSM-IV diagnostic criteria) within the ambit of mental health legislation.

In line with these changes 'the treatability test' has been done away with. In the amended Mental Health Act 1983 a person with a mental disorder, including those with personality disorders

▶

or mental impairments, may be detained in hospital for treatment as long as 'appropriate medical treatment is available'. What constitutes 'appropriate' is not defined in the amended s.3 of the Mental Health Act 1983 and instead this is left to the professional discretion of clinicians.

The Mental Health Act 2007 needs to be seen in relation to the government's pre-occupation with managing risk in terms of 'dangerousness' to the public. The underlying intention of the amendments is to extend mental health law to encompass sex offenders and those persistently aggressive individuals who are often convicted of many offences (Fennell, 2007: 46). But the difference between the effect of criminal law and that of mental health legislation is that within the criminal justice system a person can only be arrested, convicted and incarcerated after they have committed an offence. Under mental health law an individual with a personality disorder can be diagnosed and incarcerated before they commit any offence. All that is required under the amended s.3 of the Mental Health Act 1983 is that treatment in hospital be necessary 'for the protection of others'.

The wide-ranging amendments instigated by the Mental Health Act 2007 illustrate that the dividing line between immorality, deviancy, criminality and madness is a fluctuating one. It shifts over time to reflect changes in society's attitudes to morality and the public's perception of risk. What counts as mental disorder at a given point in time is what is actually given expression in mental health legislation. The definition of mental disorder is itself contingent upon wider societal discourses which are currently bound up with concerns about dangerousness, itself a phenomenon of sensationalist media coverage.

CASE 3
Local Authority X v. M, F, E, J and D (Represented by Children's Guardian EF) [2007] EWHC 2660 (Fam)

Importance of the case

This considers protecting young people under the Children Act 1989 while managing the risk posed by a person with a mental disorder under the Mental Health Act 1983. It also investigates failings in inter-agency cooperation between healthcare professionals in the NHS and social workers employed by the local authority. How poor inter-agency collaboration can increase the likelihood of harm to others is also explored.

History of the case

The local authority applied to the Family Division of the High Court for Care Orders on three children E, J and D, but this application was opposed by their parents M and F.

Facts of the case

F and M, a married couple, are the parents of three daughters, E, J and D who all lived together in the same household. F had a long-standing diagnosis of schizophrenia. At the end of 2003 F had subjected E, his daughter, to disinhibited sexualised behaviour, which had included climbing naked into the bath with E and embracing her. He had also exposed himself on occasions to both E and J. F had also physically assaulted his wife. It appeared that F's behaviour towards both his wife and children was related to his mental disorder and deterioration in his mental health when he failed to comply with drug treatment while in the community. On release from prison in August 2004, after a short jail term, there was a lack of follow-up by community mental health services, and the family received no psychiatric support. Consequently, F's mental health again deteriorated until he was admitted to hospital initially under s.2 and thereafter under s.3 in 2007. At the time of the High Court hearing he was still subject to s.3 detainment in hospital. A review of F's detainment was due and the Responsible Clinician, Dr I, intended to discharge F from hospital subject to conditions which would also address child protection concerns. It was F's intention to return to the family home on his discharge from hospital. In the light of this, the local authority and the Children's Guardian sought Care Orders on all three children so as to remove them from the family home. In response M and F both sought Supervision Orders and the continued care of their children.

Key people in the case

M – mother of E, J and D and first respondent
F – father of E, J and D and second respondent
E, J and D – children of F and M and third, fourth and fifth respondents
Ms S – social worker
Ms X – Children's Services team manager
EF – Children's Guardian
Dr I – consultant psychiatrist
Ms Auld – barrister for M
Ms Bazley – barrister for F
Mrs Justice Macur DBE – judge presiding over High Court case

Discussion of the case

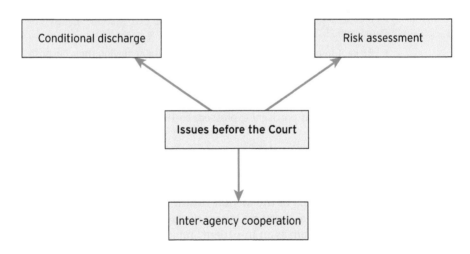

Conditional discharge

Patients subject to s.2 detainment are free to leave the hospital on the expiry of the statutory time limit of 28 days. Those detained under s.3 for assessment can discharge themselves after 6 months if there is no further renewal of their detention for treatment. In both circumstances patients are not subject to any conditions on returning to live in the community. If their mental health deteriorates an Approved Mental Health Professional or the *nearest relative* would have to make a completely new application for detainment. However, a Responsible Clinician has the power to discharge a patient from hospital before the expiry of the time period for a s.2 or s.3 detainment either conditionally or unconditionally. A patient with an absolute discharge is able to return to the community without any imposed conditions regulating their lives. On the other hand a patient who is given s.17 leave of absence from hospital or who is subject to a Community Treatment Order (CTO) under s.17A returns to the community only on condition that they comply with the requirements specified in their s.17 leave from hospital or CTO. Responsible Clinicians in agreement with an Approved Mental Health Professional can impose any combination of the following conditions in a CTO – to:

- Live at a specified place.
- Comply with a treatment regime.
- Permit examination by the Responsible Clinician or SOAD.
- Attend an outpatient's appointment for treatment.
- Remain in the custody of a specified person.
- Avoid situations associated with risk to the patient's mental health.

According to paragraph 25.30 of the *Mental Health Act 1983: Code of Practice* any imposed conditions must be necessary to ensure that the patient either receives the treatment he or she needs or for the protection of his or her health and safety or that of others. In addition to paragraph 25.30 the conditions must be consistent with paragraph 25.33 of the Code of Practice which is reproduced in the box below.

Key guidance

Mental Health Act 1983: Code of Practice

Paragraph 25.33 The conditions should:

- Be kept to a minimum number consistent with achieving their purpose
- Restrict the patient's liberty as little as possible while being consistent with achieving their purpose
- Have a clear rationale, linked to one or more of the purposes in paragraph 25.30
- Be clearly and precisely expressed, so that the patient can readily understand what is expected.

At the time of the High Court hearing F was still in hospital where he was detained for treatment under s.3 of the Mental Health Act 1983. But Dr I, the Responsible Clinician, had concluded that it was no longer necessary for the purpose of treating his mental disorder for F to remain as an in-patient. Yet given that F had engaged in disinhibited sexual behaviour and violence, linked to his mental disorder, once in the community he would pose a risk to the health and safety of others. It was for this reason that Dr I, the Responsible Clinician, intended to proceed with a conditional discharge from hospital under s.17 of the Mental Health Act 1983 rather than an absolute discharge. Dr I intended that leave of absence from hospital under s.17 should specify:

- Residence at a supported unit.
- Regular outpatient reviews.
- Administration of medication.

The changes brought about by the Mental Health Act 2007 mean that s.17 leave of absence will largely be superseded by Community Treatment Orders. The Code of Practice now requires Responsible Clinicians to consult with social workers acting as Approved Mental Health Professionals (AMHPs) in order to agree the conditions, if any, to be imposed on patients discharged from hospital. Social workers have wider duties under the Children Act 1989 relating to the welfare and protection of children. Those with a mental disorder may either be children who are at risk or adults who put children at risk of significant harm. Practitioners working with individuals who have mental health problems are operating not only within the framework of the Mental Health Act 1983, but also within other legal contexts. Most commonly these will be the Children Act 1989, Mental Capacity Act 2005, the National Assistance Act 1948 and the Human Rights Act 1998. This is a far from exhaustive list and when working with young offenders social workers will be operating both within criminal law and mental health legislation.

In this case F had a mental disorder linked to disinhibited sexualised behaviour, but was also the father of three daughters. This situation necessitated close liaison and cooperation between medical practitioners and child protection social workers in formulating conditions which would comply with the *purpose principle*. That is say, conditions which both minimised the 'undesirable effects of mental disorder' and protected 'other people from harm'. To this end the conditions needed to promote F's mental health while protecting his children from sexual abuse by him. At the same time whatever conditions were imposed had to be compliant with article 8 of the European Convention on Human Rights and the right to respect for a family life. In other words the conditions imposed had to be proportionate to the legitimate purpose of protecting both F's health and the safety of his children.

 Perspectives

Users' views of conditional discharge from hospital

The Mental Health (Patients in the Community) Act 1995 created Supervised Discharge Orders (SDO) which could be applied for by the Responsible Medical Officer as a form of supervised aftercare in the community. Supervised Discharge Orders have now been replaced by Community Treatment Orders. Like Guardianship under s.7, Supervised Discharge Orders impose conditions on mental health users living in the community. These can require them to: reside in a specified place; attend a facility for treatment; and permit access to health and social care professionals. This makes research on Guardianship and Supervised Discharge Orders directly relevant to other forms of conditional discharge such as the recently introduced Community Treatment Orders.

Canvin, et al. (2002) conducted in-depth interviews with 20 mental health service-users subject to Guardianship or a Supervised Discharge Order. Service-users tended to perceive these as forms of control or punishment. For instance Carl told the researchers 'I was a pest, a nuisance, they wanted to get rid of me, I was always in court, lots of prison' (Canvin, et al., 2002: 363). Another user, referred to as Barry, characterised his SDO as 'protecting the people from me and me from the people' (Canvin, et al., 2002: 363). Others described the restrictive nature of SDOs and Guardianship Orders. Diane stated, 'I can't do things I want to do. Travel, get a job, things like that.' Mark, along with other users participating in the study, thought that the conditions imposed on him were actually designed to make matters easier for mental health professionals. He reflected 'I know where I have to be at certain times, a lot more regimented, more tabs on me and more contact with general medical profession' (Canvin, et al., 2002: 364).

▶

Although many research participants expressed deep resentment towards mandatory surveillance by mental health professionals, some perceived benefits to Guardianship and SDOs. Kevin described his experience in the following terms, 'You get a lot of help. You're supervised in the community, so you don't get worn down and lose control of yourself. They can stop something serious from happening' (Canvin, et al., 2002: 364). Ultimately all research participants felt they had little choice but to comply with their conditions for fear of being detained in hospital, which they universally viewed as even worse than supervision in the community (Canvin, et al., 2002: 366). In the face of this some adopted a fatalistic outlook epitomised in Barry's response when he said 'I don't like the CPN [Community Psychiatric Nurse] and social worker coming here and I don't like having to go to the doctor, but I have no choice' (Canvin, et al., 2002: 364).

For some users the discipline, regular contact and support from mental health services were experienced as protective. For them the prospect of discharge from Guardianship or the termination of their Supervised Discharge Order was a source of apprehension. Jo explained, 'They wanted to take me off it, but I said I didn't want to. Maybe a couple of years when I get employment. It's a bit too early to come off it just yet.' Mark admitted, 'I'm worried about coming off it, the last thing I want is to go back into prison or hospital' (Canvin, et al., 2002: 365).

Given the ambivalence of most research participants towards the conditions under which they were compelled to live in the community, acts of resistance and self-determination became focussed around attendance and medication. Lee informed the researchers 'I didn't take my medication sometimes because of the side-effects' (Canvin, et al., 2002: 366). Diane conceded, 'I do muck about with my medication a bit, I suppose. I take extra or not enough . . . I don't feel well sometimes and think it might help, or I don't need it.' Mark resisted by failing to turn up for scheduled meetings with mental health professionals. He explained, 'I haven't attended a Care Programme Approach meeting once, I haven't always stuck to the right days here [day unit], I've missed appointments with my psychologist. I haven't been perfect. Forty per cent not attending' (Canvin, et al., 2002: 367).

Risk assessment

Given F's sexualised behaviour towards his daughters and his physical assault upon his wife, any conditions under s.17 would need to be based on a risk assessment of the danger he posed to the health and safety of family members. As this case involved risks in relation to mental health and child abuse, a risk assessment was necessary by both mental health professionals and child protection social workers. The assessment for a Child Protection Plan would have been completed under the *Framework for the Assessment of Children in Need and their Families* by Ms S, the social worker allocated to the family. Due to F's history of sexualised behaviour towards his children and the documented failure of M to supervise his contact with them whilst living at home, social workers concluded that a Child Protection Plan based on F's return to the family home was unworkable. Since F intended to return home on discharge from hospital, which was also desired by M, any Child Protection Plan had to address this eventuality. It was precisely because Children's Services were satisfied that F's return home would mean that his children were 'likely to suffer significant harm' that the local authority applied for Care Orders on all three children.

Dr I as the Responsible Clinician was required to ensure that a full risk assessment was conducted in relation to F's mental health and any danger he posed to himself or others. Department of Health (2007) *Best Practice in Managing Risk* provides guidance for mental health professionals in this respect. It defines the nature of risk and sets out a number of fundamental principles which should underpin any risk management strategy. In the first instance mental health professionals, regardless of whether they are social workers, psychiatric nurses or medical doctors, need to assess the nature of the risk and of a negative event occurring. According to Department of Health (2007:13) this includes estimating:

- How likely it is that the event will occur.
- How soon it is expected to occur.
- How severe the outcome will be if it does occur.

Information has to be gathered from a variety of sources to assist in making accurate estimates as to the likelihood of the negative event occurring and the harm it is likely to cause. Department of Health (2007: 13) suggests that these sources should at a minimum include 'information about the service user's history of violence, self-harm or self-neglect, their relationships and any recent losses or problems, employment and any recent difficulties, housing issues, their family and the support that's available, and their more general social contacts'. *Best Practice in Managing Risk* also comprises a range of risk assessment tools which clinicians are encouraged to use in order to conduct a systematic risk assessment.

Specifically in relation to F, social workers and healthcare professionals needed to determine the probability of F not complying with his treatment leading to a deterioration of his mental health and a greater probability of his molesting his children and assaulting his wife. There was also the need to consider the degree to which M was prepared to take seriously the threat which F posed to their children, and her willingness to ensure his contact with them in the home was supervised. Obviously the higher the probability of F not complying with his treatment, or his wife not supervising his contact with their daughters, then the greater the chance that the children would be sexually abused. In addition professionals needed to assess the severity of harm to the children and the likelihood of F's behaviour escalating to more serious forms of sexual abuse. Department of Health (2007: 5) identifies the principles which must guide any risk management strategy, and these are reproduced in the box below.

 Key guidance

Best Practice in Managing Risk

1 Best practice involves making decisions based on knowledge of the research evidence, knowledge of the individual service user and their social context, knowledge of the service user's own experience and clinical judgement.

2 Positive risk management as part of a carefully constructed plan is required competence for all mental health practitioners.

3 Risk management should be conducted in a spirit of collaboration and based on a relationship between the service user and their carers that is as trusting as possible.

4 Risk management must be built on a recognition of the service user's strengths and should emphasise recovery.

5 Risk management requires an organisational strategy as well as efforts by the individual practitioner.

6 Risk management involves developing flexible strategies aimed at preventing any negative event from occurring or, if this is not possible, minimising the harm caused.

Having completed a risk assessment through the application of the *Framework for the Assessment of Children in Need and their Families* social workers had concluded that given: the lack of cooperation between M and Children's Services in the past; the antagonism of all three children towards social workers; and the failure of M to ensure that F was supervised in the home during contact with the children, that the children could not be protected from sexual abuse if F returned to the home. It was for this reason that Children's Services applied for Care Orders on the three children. In her evidence EF, the Children's Guardian, informed the High Court that the children would be much more vulnerable to abuse if a Supervision Order were made instead of a Care Order. Ms Auld and Ms Bazley, the barristers acting for the father and mother argued that the court should issue a Supervision Order which would of course provide for the children remaining at home with their parents but under statutory supervision by social workers. Ultimately the use of Care Orders would reduce the risk of the children being abused by their father to zero as they would be removed into care. According to Department of Health (2007: 10), of fundamental importance in the development of a risk management strategy is the notion of 'positive risk management' which is elaborated in the box below.

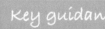

Key guidance

Best Practice in Managing Risk

Positive risk management means being aware that risk can never be completely eliminated, and aware that management plans inevitably have to include decisions that carry some risk. This should be explicit in the decision-making process and should be discussed openly with the service-user. Positive risk management includes:

- Working with the service user to identify what is likely to work
- Paying attention to the views of carers and others around the service-user when deciding a plan of action
- Weighing up the potential benefits and harms of choosing one action over another
- Being willing to take a decision that involves an element of risk because the potential positive benefits outweigh the risk
- Being clear to all involved about the potential benefits and the potential risks
- Developing plans and actions that support the positive potentials and priorities stated by the service-user, and minimise the risks to the service-user and others
- Ensuring that the service-user, carer and others who might be affected are fully informed of the decision, the reasons for it and the associated plans
- Using available resources and support to achieve a balance between a focus on achieving the desired outcomes and minimising the potential harmful outcome.

Reflecting on the position adopted by Children's Services, Mrs Justice Macur DBE presiding over the High Court case reflected, 'whilst I do not underestimate the nature and degree of the risk potentially presented by the father, I balance that risk against the undoubted adverse and pernicious effect on the well being to the present family structure in the event of a Care Order being made' (para. 19). The recognition that removing children into care and breaking up a family unit of itself constitutes serious harm is consistent with the principles laid down in the Children Act 1989 and which judges are obliged to consider by virtue of s.1 in arriving at decisions under that statute. In other words Justice Macur was articulating the fact that a child's welfare can be damaged by removal from his or her family, just as it can be damaged by sexual abuse within the home. Decisions relating to children must balance these conflicting risks to their welfare. Positive risk management involves weighing up the likelihood of harm inherent to different courses of action and requires that identified risks are minimised through effective strategies.

Mrs Justice Macur considered that M's agreement that the children attend an NSPCC project and her acknowledgement in court of the potential of F to sexually abuse their children were protective factors. Moreover they were protective factors which could be used to enhance risk management strategies. For example, the children could be taught assertiveness skills and assisted to formulate actions to protect themselves, such as informing their mother or ensuring they were not alone with their father for extended periods of time. Similarly the eventual acceptance by M that her husband did pose a danger could act as a foundation for joint work with Ms S to develop strategies within the household to protect the children. This approach would minimise, although not eliminate, the risk which F posed to his children.

Perhaps more than any other area of social work practice child protection and mental health involve risk assessments associated with the potential for serious harm to self and others. While the GSCC Code of Practice both obliges social workers to protect users and others from risk of harm and to assist users to take such risks, it gives no guidance as to how to negotiate these conflicting imperatives. This is because the weighing up of the likelihood of harm through positive risk taking and the unintentional (but often foreseeable) harm caused by intervening to eliminate risk can only be conducted on a case-by-case basis. For F and M, the High Court became the final arbiter between the risk of harm induced by sexual abuse and the risk of harm induced by the removal of three children from their parental home. It is normally social workers, alongside their healthcare colleagues, who on a daily basis assess this type of risk and weigh up the likelihood of harm and the degree of its severity within the context of care planning.

 Critical commentary

Mental health law and risk

Since the nineteenth century people with mental disorders have been confined in large geographically isolated institutions. It is only since the 1980s that care in the community for people with mental health problems or mental impairments has been a primary aim of service provision. For this reason most media coverage of mental health issues prior to the 1980s tended to centre on institutional abuse. Those with mental health problems were represented as the vulnerable and powerless victims of abuse by staff in psychiatric hospitals. By the 1990s media focus shifted to incidents of homicide committed by people living in the community who were known to mental health services. This change was fuelled by the public inquiries into the murders of Isabel Schwarz, Jonathan Newby and Jonathan Zito committed by people with diagnosed mental illnesses living in the community and known to mental health agencies. The disproportionate media coverage which such inquiries attract has resulted in mental illness (particularly schizophrenia) being associated in the public mind with unpredictable and random acts of violence directed against complete strangers (Peay, 1996).

Media portrayals of people with mental health problems, particularly in newspapers, have significantly contributed to perceptions of them as dangerous. There are frequent references in the tabloids to 'nutters', 'psychos' and 'maniacs'. Glasgow Media Group (1993) found that two-thirds of the articles appearing in the newspapers surveyed linked mental illness with violence towards others. The same study revealed that two-thirds of readers of these newspapers associated mental illness with violence and cited newspaper portrayals as their main source of information. Ward (1997) arrived at similar findings with 75% of press articles, and 70% of BBC and ITV news being found to associate mental distress with violent behaviour. This is despite the fact that a large-scale national study of homicides committed by people with mental illness reveals that these have actually decreased with the advent of community care (Department of Health, 1999a).

Throughout the 1990s government policy with regard to mental health was driven by widespread public fears of people with mental health problems. As a result the risk posed by people with a mental disorder rather than their welfare became the major policy driver behind changes to mental health law (Brown, P., 2006). The creation of Supervised Discharge Orders in 1995 was an attempt to impose compulsion to accept aftercare services, which under s.117 had up until that point been optional for those discharged from detainment under the Mental Health Act 1983. The more recent introduction of Community Treatment Orders under the Mental Health Act 2007 increases levels of compulsion and the range of conditions which can be imposed on people with mental disorders living in the community. Under both Guardianship and Supervised Discharge users could refuse to accept treatment in the community. Under Community Treatment Orders, complying with medication is now compulsory and failure to do so can result in a patient being recalled to hospital.

Inter-agency cooperation

Department of Health (2007: 6) *Best Practice in Managing Risk* reminds social workers and healthcare professionals that 'risk management plans should be developed by multidisciplinary and multi-agency teams operating in an open, democratic and transparent culture that embraces reflective practice'. Clearly in the case of F and M if the children were to be protected from abuse by their father while at the same time ensuring that he received treatment for his mental disorder, Children's Services and the Community Mental Health Team would have to work in close collaboration. The failure of inter-agency cooperation in the past was in Justice Macur's opinion a major contributing factor to the drift in F's care management in the community. It was also in her estimation the reason why working relationships between Children's Services and M were so poor. Mrs Justice Macur, giving judgement, criticised both the Mental Health Team and the Children, Schools and Families Team for their lack of communication and cooperation with each other. According to her, this had undoubtedly increased the risk of harm to the children (para. 6).

A letter written by Dr I dated 5 November 2007 recording the decision of a Professionals' Meeting and presented in evidence, stated (para. 5) that:

> the Community Mental Health Team and the Forensic Mental Health Services will work together to assess the father's mental health needs on an ongoing basis and address his needs. These teams will also work in liaison with the Children, Schools and Families Team so that the access to children will be arranged properly and that the welfare and the safety of the children are protected.

Justice Macur expressed some satisfaction that Dr I had agreed to preside over and coordinate the discharge of F into the community. Such discharge arrangements would involve integrating a Child Protection Plan for E, J and D with a Care Programme Approach in conjunction with a risk-management strategy. This would demand that social workers liaised closely with Dr I and his staff to formulate both the conditions of hospital discharge and a care plan, which would prevent a deterioration of F's mental health and protect the children from harm.

Interagency collaboration and joint working, most particularly between hospital-based medical staff and members of the Community Mental Health Team, is plainly essential to delivering effective mental health services. As is illustrated by this case, social workers from Community Mental Health Teams must also liaise with colleagues in other agencies concerned with protecting children. Likewise, people with mental disorders may have sensory impairments or other physical disabilities or a learning difficulty. Any one of these will require mental health social workers to liaise and consult with specialists in other fields in order to formulate care packages which best meet the needs of those with a mental disorder. For this reason paragraph 6.1 of the GSCC Code, which requires practitioners to work in a lawful way, also requires them to develop a broad working knowledge of the law across different areas of practice. It is this more comprehensive knowledge which informs social workers as to the 'roles and expertise of workers from other agencies' and better facilitates working in partnership with them.

 Perspectives

Practitioners' views on managing risk in mental health

Warner (2006) identifies the hindsight bias of independent inquiry reports and the blame attributed to mental health professionals as major influences upon social work practice. As Warner (2006: 224) explains, hindsight bias means that a poor outcome (such as a homicide by a person diagnosed with a mental illness) is associated with poor decision making. This fallacy assumes that somehow all the factors acting upon a person can be known to the decision maker before an adverse event occurs. In others words, it assumes that with sufficient vigilance and good practice a person's violent behaviour can be predicted and thus averted. For this reason inquiry reports tend to blame named mental health professionals for their alleged failing to prevent a preventable calamity, as in the murder of Jonathan Zito by Christopher Clunis.

Warner (2006) conducted semi-structured interviews with 39 Approved Social Workers employed by a local authority in England. She found that two-thirds of the social workers interviewed identified inquiry reports, along with the intense and sensationalist media coverage they attracted, as having a negative impact on them personally and professionally. One admitted, 'I am much more anxious now and have reason to be as it is so easy to come under the public spotlight, with all the things that result from that.' Another added, 'I think the ultimate fear is to have an inquiry into one of your cases.' As a result there was increasingly 'more emphasis on covering your back' through the fear of 'ending up on the front page of the evening paper' (Warner, 2006: 227-8). Many research participants identified a fundamental shift in the definition of 'high-risk' within mental health social work. One Approved Social Worker elaborated on this:

> I think it is very easy to just forget the people who are risks to themselves who aren't necessarily a risk to anyone else and it is easier to rate them at a lower risk generally . . . I suppose I feel the issue of risk is violence to others rather than to themselves . . . I think that is part of a number of reasons, partly to do with, if you like, the kind of whole society type thing of the media, the inquiries and everything, which are very much focused on the injuries to other people, the murders

of the public, injuries to the public, rather than the attention that is given to the numbers of mentally ill who commit suicide or commit serious self-harm. I think that is part of the human defensiveness part of our job, protecting society is probably higher than protecting individuals from themselves. (Warner, 2006: 228)

The culture of blame perpetuated by inquiry reports and the very public nature of their findings produces defensive practice. One Approved Social Worker told the researcher, 'I find myself constantly thinking "will we be criticised for this decision?" ' As a result she said 'that is probably what led me to decide to section [the user] rather than not section him. Because I thought if I make a decision not to section him - which I could have made - if that led to a major inquiry, would I be personally made to take the blame?' (Warner, 2006: 232). Another interviewee regretted being 'much less likely to take even calculated risks now in support of a client than I would have been 10 years ago' (Warner, 2006: 232). In a poignant reflection on what actually constitutes good practice, an interviewee aware that his case records could become evidence before an inquiry said he always asked himself, 'Have I covered myself in a way that makes it quite clear that I have done my job? Which is rather different from doing the job. It is about slowing down really and doing less in order to keep clearer records' (Warner, 2006: 232).

Judgement in *Local Authority X* v. *M, F, E, J and D (Represented by Children's Guardian EF)*

Bearing in mind that under s.31(2) of the Children Act 1989 the threshold for a Supervision Order and a Care Order is exactly the same, Mrs Justice Macur DBE described the case as 'extremely finely balanced'. Given the acknowledgement of M that F did pose some risk to their children and the agreement of the Community Mental Health Team and Children, Schools and Families Team to work closely together in both formulating and managing the overall care plan on F's discharge from hospital, the judge (para. 21) concluded:

> In this context I view the balance as tipping in favour of a Supervision Order. In making a Supervision Order I do not reflect a diminished risk and make clear that in the event of the mother permitting the father's return to the home before adequate assessment or obstructing the social workers access to the children in any sense, I anticipate that the Local Authority would seek the Court's approval, by application, for the ultimate sanction of removal of the children.

In expressing this view within her judgement Mrs Justice Macur DBE was making clear to F and M that although she was granting a Supervision Order, which is what they wished, if they failed to comply with the conditions of discharge or the Child Protection Plans, F and M should expect the court to grant Care Orders for the children on any subsequent application by the local authority.

 Critical questions

1 Conditional discharges from hospital can involve onerous requirements upon mental health users on their return to the community and cause considerable resentment. This is despite the fact that such conditions may appear essential to maintaining their mental health. How might the conditions imposed on mental health patients discharged into the community violate their human rights?

2 A risk assessment was a key element in this case. What were the crucial factors in assessing risk in this situation? What general principles of risk assessment and risk management are revealed by this case?

3 Public sentiment and government policy is increasingly risk adverse. Yet social workers are required to assist users to take positive risks. What strategies might you employ to resist some of the pressures to minimise risk in practice situations, as opposed to deciding with users and carers which risks it is important for them to live with and manage?

4 Both intervention and non-intervention by professionals carry adverse risks. Often the general public do not appreciate the negative effects of premature or disproportionate interference in the lives of others. Given the facts of this case, how would you go about weighing up the beneficial and harmful consequences of a professional decision?

 Critical commentary

Parents, mental illness and human rights

The prejudicial linking of mental disorder with inadequate parenting means that those with a diagnosed mental illness, like those with a learning difficulty, are particularly liable to having their children removed by the State. But parents, like their children, also have recourse to human rights law. Prior (2003) in her overview of judgements by the European Court of Human Rights, which have persuasive precedent in British courts, discovered that a static model of mental illness pervades professional decision making in the context of child protection.

In *E.P. v. Italy* [1999] Application no. 31127/96 a mother repeatedly brought her daughter to the attention of medical professionals. She was diagnosed as having a psychosis described as 'vicarious hypochondria' centred on her child (i.e. Munchausen's Syndrome). The authorities in Rome removed the child into foster care. All contact between mother and daughter was prohibited. The mother underwent hospital treatment and her mental health improved. Eight years after the child was taken into care she was adopted by her long-term foster parents. The European Court decided that it would not be in the child's best interests to be returned to her mother, but that the ban on contact between mother and child violated article 8 and had made reunification impossible.

In *K and T v. Finland* [2000] Application no. 25702/94, K the mother of four children was diagnosed with schizophrenia. Two of the mother's children were removed from her, one at birth, in 1993. A year later both children were placed in long-term foster care with a view to their adoption. In 1995 K and her male partner T had a child together which they successfully parented. Both K and T demanded the return of the two older children to their care. Although K's mental state improved, by that time the two children had been in foster care for some years and established bonds with their carers. The European Court held that the decision to remove K's child at birth was excessive and unnecessary. Although the Court held that article 8 had been violated it did not dispute the decision of the Finnish authorities to refuse to return the two children to their mother's care.

In *H v. UK* [1987] Application no. 9580/81 both parents had received psychiatric treatment as in-patients and there was a history of drug abuse and violence. In 1975 the mother's baby daughter was removed into foster care after birth. A year later the mother left the father due to domestic violence. On divorcing him she married another man who provided a stable and positive relationship. However, Social Services decided that the best interests of the child were served by terminating all contact with the mother. The child was adopted in 1980 against the mother's wishes. The European Court did not question the decision of Social Services to place the child for adoption. However, it did find a violation of article 6 and article 8. The ban on contact between mother and daughter combined with a prolonged decision-making process had brought about a *fait accompli*. By denying the mother access to her daughter inevitably the child bonded with other parental figures. This jeopardised any prospect of family reunification.

In all these cases the mental health of the mother improved and there was good evidence to suppose that she would have been able to adequately parent. The *Framework for the Assessment of Children in Need and their Families* emphasises that assessment is a process and not a one-off event. As these cases demonstrate, the common practice across Europe of permanency planning means that a child's best interests can relatively quickly be perceived to lie with long-term foster care or adoption. The rapidity with which decisions regarding children's futures can be made grossly disadvantages parents with a mental illness whose mental health changes over time. These cases evidence a tendency to make snapshot assessments of parental capacity which fail to build into care plans the prospect of an improvement in the mental health of a parent over time and their potential to resume parenting.

CASE 4
Carter v. Wandsworth London Borough Council [2004] EWCA Civ 1740

Importance of the case

It explores the process of deciding whether a homeless person should be treated as in priority need and allocated accommodation by the local authority. The criteria for being treated as in priority need are examined in relation to disability alongside the obligations of local housing authorities to vulnerable people.

History of the case

A homeless woman applied to the local Housing Authority claiming to be homeless and in priority need of accommodation due to her mental health problems. On being refused priority status she requested a review of this decision. When the reviewing officer upheld the original decision she then applied to the County Court. The County Court upheld the decision of the Housing Authority and the claimant then appealed against this judgement to the Court of Appeal.

Facts of the case

In February 2003 Mrs Carter claimed she was homeless and applied to Wandsworth Housing Authority for accommodation, arguing that she should be treated as in priority need. The local Housing Authority provided Mrs Carter with interim accommodation in a hotel while it proceeded to investigate her application. In May 2003 Mrs Carter's GP wrote to the Housing Authority to inform it that Mrs Carter had epilepsy and 'would become clinically depressed were she to remain in the hotel'. The report written by the GP was passed to the Independent Medical Advisor employed by the local authority, who concluded that Mrs Carter did not have any medical problems which had a bearing on her housing needs. In August 2003 the Housing Authority wrote to Mrs Carter informing her that while it accepted she was homeless and eligible for some assistance, it did not regard her as in priority need. Mrs Carter sought a review of this decision and her GP provided a further report to the reviewing officer. In October 2003 the original decision of the Housing Authority was upheld by the review. Mrs Carter appealed this decision to the County Court on the grounds that the reviewing officer had not given due consideration to the medical evidence and had failed to furnish her with an adequate explanation of the reasons for refusing to treat her as in priority need. When the County Court upheld the decision of the reviewing officer, Mrs Carter then appealed to the Court of Appeal.

Key people in the case

Mrs Carter – homeless person and appellant
Dr Jeffcote – Mrs Carter's General Practitioner
Dr Bolade – Mrs Carter's General Practitioner
Dr Keen – Independent Medical Advisor
Mr Adelaja – Reviewing Officer for local Housing Authority

Discussion of the case

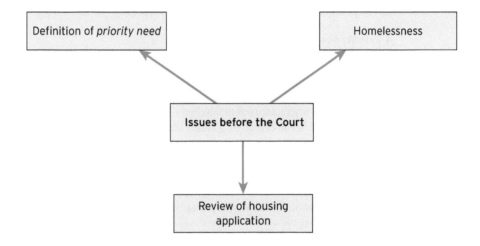

Homelessness

Part VII of the Housing Act 1996 imposes a statutory duty on local housing authorities to provide advice, assistance and in limited circumstances accommodation for people who are homeless. A local housing authority only has a duty to provide accommodation (as opposed to advice and assistance) to applicants who meet *all* four of the criteria set out in the statute which is outlined in the box below

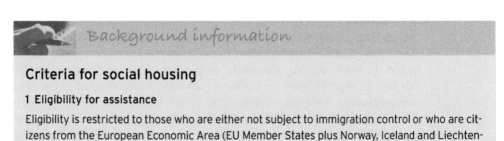

Background information

Criteria for social housing

1 Eligibility for assistance

Eligibility is restricted to those who are either not subject to immigration control or who are citizens from the European Economic Area (EU Member States plus Norway, Iceland and Liechtenstein). Those from the EEA may only be eligible if they meet habitual residency requirements.

2 Homeless

Individuals are defined as homeless under s.175 of the Housing Act 1996 if they, together with anyone they can reasonably be expected to live with, have no accommodation that they are entitled to occupy. This definition includes those threatened with homelessness within the next 28 days. A person will also be treated as homeless if it would be unreasonable to expect him or her to continue to occupy a dwelling due to the threat of violence or overcrowding or because the accommodation is unsuitable or in poor condition.

3 Not intentionally homeless

Under s.191(1) and s.196(1) of the Housing Act 1996 a person is intentionally homeless if:

- He or she ceases to occupy accommodation due to deliberate action or inaction.
- There is accommodation available for that person to occupy.
- It was reasonable for the person to continue to occupy the accommodation.

Deliberate actions include loss of accommodation due to the sale of a house or eviction from rented accommodation due to anti-social behaviour. Non-deliberate actions would include non-payment of rent due to poverty or mental incapacity.

4 Priority need

The following groups are defined in legislation as being in priority need:

- a pregnant woman or a person with whom she resides or might reasonably be expected to reside;
- a person with whom dependent children reside or might reasonably be expected to reside;
- a person who is vulnerable as a result of old age, mental illness or handicap or physical disability or with whom such a person resides or might reasonably be expected to reside;
- a person who is homeless or so threatened due to an emergency;
- a person fleeing domestic, racial or other forms of violence;
- a person with an institutionalised background e.g. foster care, prison;
- Unintentionally homeless 16- and 17-year-olds who are not owed a duty under s.17 or s.20 of the Children Act 1989.

Mrs Carter's situation had to be assessed against the four criteria set out in Part VII of the Housing Act 1996. In the first place Mrs Carter was a white British citizen and consequently not subject to any immigration controls. She had been ordinarily resident in the Wandsworth local authority area for some years although she was now homeless. All parties to the court case therefore readily acknowledged that Mrs Carter was entitled to apply to Wandsworth London Borough Council for social housing. Secondly, the local authority conceded that Mrs Carter was not an owner or tenant of any dwelling which she could have occupied and was therefore genuinely homeless. Thirdly, Mrs Carter had become homeless through no fault of her own and had not deliberately failed to pay rent or otherwise jeopardised her occupation of accommodation. Mr Beglan, legal counsel for the local authority, acknowledged in the court that she was *unintentionally homeless*. Indeed, the letter which the Housing Authority sent to Mrs Carter in August 2003 (and which was to be presented in evidence) explicitly accepted that she was homeless and eligible for assistance. In short, there was no dispute between the parties to the court case as to the fact that Mrs Carter met the requirements of the first three criteria contained in the Housing Act 1996. From the outset, there was disagreement between Mrs Carter and the local Housing Authority as to whether she was in *priority need* of accommodation and therefore whether the authority was under a duty to provide it.

If a local housing authority 'has reason to believe' that an applicant may meet all four of the criteria, but needs time to carry out further enquiries, under s.188 of the Housing Act 1996 it has a duty to provide interim accommodation. In the present case, because Mrs Carter plainly met most of the criteria after preliminary inquiries, Wandsworth London Borough Council did provide her with interim accommodation in a hotel. This enabled the local Housing Authority to meet the immediate housing needs of Mrs Carter while giving it time to investigate her claim that she was in *priority need*. The provision of short-term bed and breakfast accommodation is a typical way in which local housing authorities meet their s.188 duty. However, for Mrs Carter the nature of this accommodation was far from ideal and, according to her General Practitioner, began to detrimentally affect her mental health. This meant that the Wandsworth London Borough Council came under pressure from Mrs Carter both to recognise her as being in *priority need*, and also to do so relatively quickly.

Definition of *priority need*

The Housing Act 1996 by virtue of s.184 imposes a duty on a local housing authority to carry out enquiries if it 'has reason to believe' that the applicant for housing may be homeless or threatened with homelessness in the next 28 days. It was during Mrs Carter's temporary stay at a local hotel that the Housing Authority conducted further investigations into her background to establish if she could be treated as in *priority need*. Section 189(1) of the Housing Act 1996 lists groups of people defined as in *priority need*. This list includes 'a person who is vulnerable as a result of old age, mental illness or handicap or physical disability'. Mrs Carter sought to convince the Housing Authority that she was vulnerable due to her epilepsy and depression, thus making her a vulnerable person for the purposes of the Housing Act 1996. She also brought to the attention of the Housing Authority that she was in receipt of incapacity benefit. It was specifically on the issue of her degree of disability that the Housing Authority and Mrs Carter were in dispute.

In conducting their enquiries housing authorities may liaise with a number of different agencies including Adult Social Services, Children's Services and Primary Care Trusts. Department for Communities and Local Government (2006) *Homelessness Code of Guidance for Local Authorities* is statutory guidance for local housing authorities assessing applications for social housing. An excerpt from this guidance in relation to vulnerability is set out in the box below.

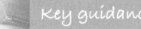
Key guidance

Homelessness Code of Guidance for Local Authorities

Para.10.13 It is a matter of judgement whether the applicant's circumstances make him or her vulnerable. When determining whether an applicant . . . is vulnerable, the local authority should consider whether, when homeless, the applicant would be less able to fend for him/herself than an ordinary homeless person so that he or she would suffer injury or detriment, in circumstances where a less vulnerable person would be able to cope without harmful effects.

Para.10.16 Housing authorities should have regard to any advice from medical professionals, social services or current providers of care and support. In cases where there is doubt as to the extent of any vulnerability authorities may also consider seeking a clinical opinion. However, the final decision on the question of vulnerability will rest with the housing authority. In considering whether such applicants are vulnerable, authorities will need to take account of all relevant factors including:

(i) the nature and extent of the illness and/or disability which may render the applicant vulnerable

(ii) the relationships between the illness and/or disability and the individual's housing difficulties

(iii) the relationship between the illness and/or disability and other factors such as drug/alcohol misuse, offending behaviour, challenging behaviours, age and personality disorder.

Para.10.17 Assessment of vulnerability due to mental health will require close co-operation between housing authorities, social services authorities and mental health agencies. Housing authorities should consider carrying out joint assessments or using a trained mental health practitioner as part of an assessment team.

In Mrs Carter's case, because the disputed matter revolved around her mental and physical health, the local Housing Authority obtained a report in March 2003 from Dr Jeffcote who was Mrs Carter's General Practitioner. This stated that Mrs Carter had epilepsy, was on anti-depressants and would become clinically depressed if she remained living in the interim accommodation provided by the council. The GP urged the Housing Authority to rehouse Mrs Carter as soon as possible in order to prevent further deterioration of her mental health. The General Practitioner's report was passed to Dr Keen, the Independent Medical Advisor to the Housing Authority, who concluded that while Mrs Carter had some health problems, these were not relevant to her housing application. According to s.185(3)(b) on completing its enquiries as to eligibility a housing authority must notify the applicant of its decision in writing and also explain the reasons for this decision. The Housing Authority duly wrote a letter to Mrs Carter which stated, 'I am not persuaded that you, when homeless, are any less able to fend for yourself than the ordinary homeless person.'

In other words, Wandsworth Housing Authority made the necessary enquiries regarding Mrs Carter's health, but concluded that although she did have a disability, this did not make her vulnerable under s.189(1)(3) of the Housing Act 1996, for this section requires that applicants be either disabled or mentally ill *and* that their condition makes them vulnerable. It is not enough that they just have a physical disability or a mental disorder. In effect s.189(1)(3) contains two criteria which an applicant has to meet before they qualify as being in *priority need*. They have to have both a disability and that disability has to make them vulnerable for the purposes of s.189(1)(3) of the Housing Act 1996. Mrs Carter was of course dissatisfied with the decision of Wandsworth Housing Authority. However, s.203(4) of the Housing Act 1996 gives all applicants an automatic right to the review of a decision. Mrs Carter used this section of the Act to demand a reconsideration of her application for social housing.

Although mental health professionals were not directly involved with Mrs Carter, it is obvious from her circumstances that housing needs can be particularly acute for people who have a mental health problem. Indeed, their mental disorder may mean that certain types of accommodation are unsuitable, for example if they are overcrowded or located in neighbourhoods with high noise levels. These factors may be sources of disproportionate psychological stress for people already managing a mental health problem. Homelessness can also be caused if people are harassed or threatened and are forced to leave their accommodation or if in such circumstances it would be unreasonable for them to remain in occupation. People with a known mental disorder are vulnerable to stigmatisation and social exclusion alongside verbal and physical abuse. For this reason identifying the housing needs of people with mental health problems, and working collaboratively with housing authorities to meet these, can be a vital aspect of successful care planning by mental health professionals.

Review of housing application

Mr Adelaja, the Reviewing Officer in the local Housing Authority, obtained a further medical report in September 2003 from Dr Bolade who was by then Mrs Carter's new GP. This stated:

> Subsequent visits to this practice showed that she was clinically very depressed and agitated for which I started her on Prozac and Valium . . . Mrs Carter is a very vulnerable person and evicting her from her current accommodation would only worsen her clinical state of mind and body. The Council could actually do well in helping to improve her housing condition, i.e. by providing her with better accommodation, which would be stress free or near stress free for the patient.

Despite indications that Mrs Carter's mental condition had worsened, when the report was referred to Dr Keen, the Independent Medical Advisor, he advised the Housing Authority that the depression had been 'treated at low level throughout with single minor anti-depressant drugs (Prozac or Dothiepin), has not necessitated psychiatric referral and is not considered significant or severe . . . there is nothing to impede reasonable functions nor any risk of harm from homelessness'. On receiving this assessment from Dr Keen the Reviewing Officer endorsed the original decision of the Housing Authority. As required by s.203(4) of the Housing Act 1996 he notified Mrs Carter, as the applicant, in writing of the outcome of the review and the reasons for it. Once again the decision had gone against Mrs Carter. At this point an applicant normally has to accept rejection of their application.

Exceptionally, and only on a point of law, under s.203(5) and s.204(2) of the Housing Act 1996 is there a right of appeal against the decision of a Reviewing Officer to the County Court. This meant that Mrs Carter could not appeal to the County Court simply because she was aggrieved at the rejection of her housing application. She could only pursue an appeal to the County Court if she was able to convincingly claim that Mr Adelaja had proceeded incorrectly in some way when deliberating on her application. Legal counsel for Mrs Carter tried to argue before the County Court that the Reviewing Officer had failed to give his reasons for upholding the original decision on Mrs Carter's housing application. This contention was rejected by the County Court judge, but Mrs Carter was given permission to pursue her case up to the Court of Appeal. On coming before the Court of Appeal the notification which the Reviewing Officer had sent out to Mrs Carter was presented in evidence. This explained that:

> In Dr Bolade's letter he states 'it is undoubtedly clear that Ms Carter is a very vulnerable person' . . . Vulnerability for the purpose of this application is a matter of law . . . It is not a matter of your GP's opinion or based on the assessments made by the Social Security Service. However due regard has been given to this opinion in consideration of your ability to fend for yourself . . . I am satisfied that you do not suffer from any illness that could render you vulnerable on the basis of mental or physical disability.

On examining this explanation the judges presiding over the Court of Appeal hearing concluded that it did not fully comply with s.203(4) of the Housing Act 1996 which requires the Reviewing Officer to give reasons for his or her decision. This was a situation in which there was disagreement between Mrs Carter's General Practitioner and Dr Keen, the Housing Authority's Independent Medical Advisor. The Court of Appeal concluded that while it was correct for Mr Adelaja to assert that is was not for a General Practitioner to decide whether an applicant was 'vulnerable' for the purposes of the Housing Act 1996, as a Reviewing Officer he still had to explain why he accepted Dr Keen's medical assessment as against that of Dr Bolade. In other words, the Reviewing Officer was confronted by conflicting medical evidence and he appeared to resolve this by ignoring aspects of Dr Bolade's report. Instead, as suggested by paragraph 10.17 of the *Homelessness Code of Guidance,* he should have asked for a joint assessment of Mrs Carter's mental health to be conducted involving other professionals or agencies. This would have been one feasible way of addressing the differences in medical opinion.

Housing authorities are placed in a difficult position as they are responsible for allocating a limited stock of social housing to a much larger number of people who are recognised as being homeless either because they have nowhere to live or because their present accommodation is unsuitable for their needs. Early contact with the Community Mental Health Team by personnel at the Housing Authority might have resulted in an early resolution of Mrs Carter's actual housing needs and the severity of her mental disorder. Understandably, in a situation of very restricted availability of social housing relative to the demand for it, housing authorities seek to ensure that those who are in the severest need are placed highest in the priority waiting list. It is conceivable that had the Community Mental Health Team been involved with Mrs Carter, a care plan could have been developed to address her housing needs in the wider context of managing her day-to-day mental health.

Judgement in *Carter v. Wandsworth London Borough Council*

The Court of Appeal concluded that the Reviewing Officer had failed to adequately explain his reasons for upholding the original decision of the Wandsworth London Borough Council in rejecting Mrs Carter's housing application. The Court of Appeal made a Quashing Order setting aside the decision of the local authority to reject Mrs Carter's housing application on the grounds that she was not in *priority need*. At the same time it issued a Mandatory Order requiring Wandsworth London Borough Council to reconsider Mrs Carter's application for social housing.

 Critical questions

---

1 This was a case which essentially involved housing officers of a local authority rather than mental health professionals. But the case did reveal a potential for inter-agency collaboration which was not acted upon. How might collaboration, in accordance with the *Homelessness Code of Guidance for Local Authorities*, between the Housing Authority and the Community Mental Health Team have provided an alternative approach to Mrs Carter's application to be treated as in *priority need*?

2 Due to the chronic shortage of social housing, even when people are categorised as being in *priority need* they may still be on the waiting list for months or years before being rehoused. For this reason people can be in interim accommodation for extended periods of time. How might the Care Programme Approach be successfully used to address the needs of someone in similar circumstances to Mrs Carter?

3 Mrs Carter used the Housing Authority's review procedure to pursue an appeal against the outcome of her application to be treated as in *priority need*. What difficulties might a person with a mental disorder encounter in availing of this appeal procedure and how might you as a mental health practitioner assist someone to access it?

Learning points

- The Mental Health Act 1983 is equally applicable to mental health users living in the community as it is to people detained in hospital. Many of the provisions of this statute directly address issues concerning discharge from hospital back into the community.

- Mental health law frequently intersects with other statutes which must be adhered to when taking action under the Mental Health Act 1983. These include the Children Act 1989 and the Mental Capacity Act 2005.

- The *Mental Health Act 1983: Code of Practice* and the *Code of Practice for Social Care Workers* require that mental health professionals seek to identify and then actively support beneficial risk taking by users. At the same time they must act to reduce the risk of harm to users and others. The dilemma presented by these apparently oppositional imperatives has to be resolved on a case-by-case basis.

- Lifestyle choices, which may place a user or their carer at risk of harm, have to be distinguished from a diagnosis of a mental disorder. Mental health professionals are often required to differentiate between recognising the legitimate rights of users to exercise their autonomy and recognising when dangerous conduct is the symptom of a mental disorder.

- Partnership working with families, particularly in the light of the special place of the *nearest relative* in mental health law, can create conflicts between users and carers. Practitioners have to be able to arbitrate between different viewpoints and demands while acting within the remit of the GSCC Code of Practice.

- Partnership working with healthcare professionals is a fundamental and essential aspect of social work practice under the Mental Health Act 1983. This requires both respect and the open exchange of opposing views. It obliges social workers to consult with, listen to and justify their disagreements with colleagues from other disciplines and agencies.

- Whilst acting within the legal framework, social workers must be aware of the wider controversies which surround and influence their day-to-day practice. These include the perspectives of service-users and carers caught up in the mental health system, the pressures upon them arising from negative public perceptions of mental illness, and the policy drivers behind recent legislative amendments to the Mental Health Act 1983.

- People with mental health problems, like those with physical disabilities, can have particular needs around housing. Conditions of homelessness can exacerbate mental health problems. Liaison between mental health professionals and housing authorities can be particularly important.

- Mental health legislation permits people to be confined in an institution against their will, to be given treatment without their consent and to subject them to conditions in the community for long periods which fundamentally interfere with their private and family life. Timely recourse to the Tribunal is essential to ensure a fair hearing.

Further reading

Clements, L. and Thompson, P. (2007) *Community Care and the Law,* London: Legal Action Group (LAG). This provides a comprehensive guide to the law relating to provision for people with physical and mental disabilities living in the community. It also indicates the interrelationships between statutes which are focussed on different users groups, but where user groups overlap.

Darlington, Y., Feeney, J.A. and Rixon, K. (2005) 'Practice challenges at the intersection of child protection and mental health', *Child and Family Social Work* 10(3): 329–45. This article examines the challenges of inter-agency work in the context of mental health and child protection. It highlights a number of important practice issues in the area of work.

Fennell, P. (2008) *Mental Health: The New Law,* Bristol: Jordan Publishing. This provides an in-depth and technically detailed exploration of the amendments introduced by the Mental Health Act 2007. It also provides a comprehensive guide to current mental health law.

Richardson, G. (2002) 'Autonomy, guardianship and mental disorder: one problem, two solutions', *Modern Law Review* 65(5): 702–23. This article explores issues concerning the use of Guardianship under the Mental Health Act 1983. It examines some of the dilemmas this poses in terms of user choices and self-determination.

Yeates, V. (2007) 'Ambivalence, Contradiction, and Symbiosis: Carers' and Mental Health Users' Rights', *Law and Policy* 29(4): 435–59. This article considers the whole range of carers' rights under a number of different statutes including the Mental Health Act 1983 and the Mental Capacity Act 2005. It also examines the increasing scope for conflict between the rights of users and the rights of carers as the legal rights of the latter are gradually extended.

Useful websites

www.antipsychiatry.org/ This site is run by The Antipsychiatry Coalition which is an international organisation of psychiatric system survivors and their supporters. The site provides information on the damage caused to users by the psychiatric system. This site also provides access to research and other links.

www.rethink.org Run by the charity Rethink which was formerly called the Schizophrenic Fellowship this site tends to reflect carers' perspectives and offers a range of easy-to-follow guides relating to mental health and service provision.

www.youngminds.org.uk Is run by a charity called Young Minds, which focusses on the mental health of children. It provides accessible guides and information both to parents and young people.

www.mentalhealth.org.uk Is run by the Mental Health Foundation and offers a number of publications relating to the mental health of adults and children. It also examines current trends in mental health law and service provision.

10

LESSONS FOR PRACTICE

Overview of chapter

This final chapter identifies the cross-cutting themes to emerge from what, at first, may appear to be distinctive and discrete areas of law and practice. It highlights the common issues and dilemmas which these raise for practitioners. The broad approaches of the courts to these matters and their implications for social work activity are explored. The chapter takes each emergent theme in turn and summarises both the legal and practice aspects of it.

Essential legal concepts

There are a number of basic legal concepts which underpin the working of the law. Most fundamental is the distinction between case law and statute law and the way in which the operation of Parliamentary Sovereignty, statutory interpretation and judicial precedent mediates the relationship between these. For social work practice the separation between civil and criminal jurisdictions within the justice system is also of crucial importance to working within a legal framework. Social workers are regularly required to move backwards and forwards between civil courts and criminal courts in their work with children and families, both in relation to safeguarding and with young offenders. Without a full understanding of how these different aspects of the law fit together it is difficult to practice effectively within a legal context.

In addition to comprehending basic legal concepts is it also vital to understand the role and place of codes of practice, policy guidance and practice guidance in day-to-day professional activity. The GSCC *Code of Practice for Social Care Workers* issued by the General Social Care Council under the Care Standards Act 2000 stipulates standards of professional conduct from social care practitioners regardless of what area of practice they are engaged in. Aside from this overarching code related to all aspects of professional activity, a number of statutes, for example the Mental Health Act 1983 and the Mental Capacity Act 2005, have codes of practice which instruct practitioners working under these pieces of legislation. The government has also issued policy and practice guidance documents which are usually linked to specific Acts of Parliament or areas of professional practice. For example, the *Children (Leaving Care) Act 2000 Guidance* relates directly to the Children (Leaving Care) Act 2000 and provides direction to both managers and frontline professionals on implementing the provisions of this statute. Conversely, *Working Together to Safeguard Children* draws on statutory provisions of both the Children Act 1989 and the Children Act 2004, but is focussed on inter-agency collaboration to protect children. In other words it addresses an area of practice rather than the implementation of a specific statute.

Application of government policy and practice guidance

Various cases have demonstrated the legal implications of failing to follow either policy or practice guidance. In the **Second Serious Case Review: Baby Peter** the Chair of the initial Child Protection Case conference failed to follow advice set out in para. 5.82 of *Working Together to Safeguard Children* regarding the attendance of a doctor to present and explain the medical evidence. As a result the medical evidence of Peter's non-accidental injury was gradually discounted. In *R (on the application of AB)* v. *Nottingham City Council* a social worker was criticised by the judge for failing to follow policy guidance. The guidance in question was the *Framework for the Assessment of Children in Need and their Families,* providing instruction on assessment and care planning for children and young people. The court ruled that failure to follow the guidance amounted to maladministration and directed the local authority to undertake a properly detailed assessment and produce a related care plan. Conversely in *R (on the application of Ireneschild)* v. *Lambeth London Borough* the social worker was found to have been thorough in her approach to producing a Comprehensive Assessment of care needs which drew appropriately on specialist assessments.

Adherence to government policy and practice guidance facilitates transparency, standardisation and general fairness in the assessment and care planning processes. It also provides instruction to frontline professionals which assists them to perform their tasks competently in a particular area of activity. Many practice guidance documents, such as *Assessing Children in Need and their Families,* draw on research evidence and promote best practice as well as advice on how to approach an area of professional activity. Therefore a working knowledge of relevant policy and practice guidance are crucial both to working lawfully and to developing best practice.

National Minimum Standards and National Standards

The Care Standards Act 2000 introduced a raft of National Minimum Standards across a range of social care provision. These incorporate standards of care and also provision for complaints procedures. Although none of the cases explored in this book related to an offence under the Care Standards Act 2000 for failure to meet National Minimum Standards many have demonstrated how these should inform social work practice. The **Independent Inquiry Report into the Circumstances of Child Sexual Abuse by two Foster Carers in Wakefield** pointed up the extent to which social workers involved in the provision of fostering services had failed to meet National Minimum Standards. In other contexts, such as **Local Government Ombudsman Complaint No. 03/B/18884 against London Borough of Bromley** and *R (on application of A)* v. *East Sussex*

County Council (No. 2), reference to National Minimum Standards assists to inform exploration of the duties and responsibilities of service providers.

Outside the Care Standards Act 2000 there are other service standards, for instance those set by the Home Office for the youth justice system. The National Standards for those providing youth justice services featured in the exploration of *R* v. *H*. This demonstrated how adherence to National Standards and the production of a detailed pre-sentence report could be used to successfully challenge the severity of a judge's sentence handed down to a young offender. National Standards in other areas of social work activity are equally vital to ensuring good practice. These together with National Minimum Standards for social care delivery under the Care Standards Act 2000 direct practice and set minimum requirements for service providers.

Overarching statutory frameworks

There are a number of overarching statutes which apply to social work activity regardless of the setting, user group or practice context. Such statutes include the Data Protection Act 1998 and the Care Standards Act 2000. These statutes apply equally to practitioners in the private, voluntary and public sectors. They will apply to those working in a community or residential context and they will govern practice regardless of whether it is with children or adults, with those experiencing mental health problems, physical illness, or learning disability. Several other statutes are just as encompassing in their scope but are more dependent on context. For example the Human Rights Act 1998 is applicable only to State action and therefore strictly speaking only concerns social workers employed by local authorities or other emanations of the State. However, in many circumstances users availing of facilities or services in the independent sector will still have recourse to human rights legislation if their care was arranged by local authority social workers.

Likewise complaints procedures, resort to the Local Government Ombudsman and use of the judicial review procedure are normally avenues available to all parents, children, users and carers where there is evidence of maladministration by a local authority. Such maladministration may relate to the: assessment, arrangement, denial or provision of services. Given the huge range of activities undertaken by local authorities in the areas of education, housing and social care this links State action to a considerable range of services. In this connection the GSCC *Code of Practice for Social Care Workers* obliges social workers to assist parents, children, users and carers in obtaining information about their rights and exercising them.

Human rights

The Human Rights Act 1998 and the force of law which it gives to the European Convention on Human Rights is another example of a piece of overarching legislation which affects many areas of social work practice. The right to a fair trial has featured in a number of cases. In *T* v. *United Kingdom* and *V* v. *United Kingdom* the trial for murder of two boys in an adult criminal court dissected the provisions made for the children and their impact on their ability to properly instruct their defence lawyers. In *Re C (A Child) (Secure Accommodation Order: Representation)* a *Gillick* competent child argued that she and her solicitor had not been given sufficient time to prepare for a court hearing to oppose the making of a Secure Accommodation Order. An adult assessed as lacking capacity to conduct legal proceedings also alleged that she did not have a fair trial in *Re P (A Child) (Care and Placement Order Proceedings: Mental Capacity)* when she was represented by the Official Solicitor who refused to argue against the adoption of her child expressly against her wishes.

Inevitably the right to a private and family life has been invoked in many of the cases concerning care proceedings and the removal of children from their parental home. It has also been relied upon in a number of cases concerning adults, such as *KC, NNC* v. *City of Westminster Social and Community Services* where local authorities have intervened to prevent a marriage from succeeding. This was a situation in which the right to marry and found a family was also invoked. In other cases the nature of inhuman and degrading treatment has been an issue. Both *T* v. *United Kingdom* and *V* v. *United Kingdom* and *R (on application of A)* v. *East Sussex County Council (No. 2)* considered the threshold for inhuman and degrading treatment. As reference to *T* v. *United Kingdom* and *V* v. *United Kingdom* and *KC, NNC* v. *City of Westminster Social and Community Services* reveals, sometimes State intervention impinges upon more than one human right. A number of these cases have invoked the concept of proportionality or weighted the competing rights of different individuals to reconcile the necessity of State action in the face of inherent human rights.

Interrelated areas of law and practice

The law has often been treated on social work curricula and in texts as a succession of discrete areas of practice. Many of the cases in this book illustrate the close interrelatedness of different areas of the law. In *Carter* v. *Wandsworth London Borough Council* a person with a mental health problem was also homeless; while in *R (on the application of Ireneschild)* v. *Lambeth London Borough Council* a user, denied alternative housing under the Housing Act 1996, sought to rely on the National Assistance Act 1948 for suitable accommodation. The **Independent Inquiry into the Death of David Bennett** demonstrated the linkage between the law on mental health and the criminal law. *R (on the application of M (a child)* v. *Sheffield Magistrates Court* and *R (on the application of AB)* v. *Nottingham City Council* examined the relationship between the law relating to *looked after* children and that regarding young offenders. *Re P (A Child) (Care and Placement Order Proceedings: Mental Capacity of Parent)* brought together the law relating to child protection, adoption and mental capacity. Likewise *Local Authority X* v. *M, F, E, J and D (Represented by Children's Guardian EF)* considered the issue of child protection in relation to the discharge home from hospital of a parent detained for treatment under the Mental Health Act 1983.

These many examples of cross-cutting issues spanning child protection, mental health, mental capacity, physical disability and homelessness demonstrate the necessity for understanding the interlocking nature of different areas of practice and hence the law relevant to them. Often practitioners will find themselves operating simultaneously under a number of statutes which bear upon their work with individuals and families. Poor knowledge of the law in one area can result in poor practice in another. For example in *Local Authority X* v. *M, F, E, J and D (Represented by Children's Guardian)* the judge criticised the lack of joint working between professionals in the Community Mental Health Team and those in the local authority responsible for safeguarding children. While this points to inadequate inter-agency collaboration it is arguably also an example of practitioners failing to appreciate the interlinked aspects of the legal contexts in which they are working.

Principles in statute law and government guidance

Many statutes are explicitly underpinned by guiding principles which play a central role in the determination of practice and court rulings. Most notably the *welfare principle*, the *no order principle* and the *non-delay principle* enshrined in s.1 of the Children Act 1989, which are determinative of decisions made under that statute. Other statutes such as the Mental Health Act 1983 have a related statutory code of practice which sets out the principles that must guide practice under the legislation. Policy and practice guidance related to specific statutes or areas of practice may elaborate principles into practice at quite a detailed level, for example the child-centred approach of the *Framework for the Assessment of Children in Need and their Families*. Many of the principles which guide the implementation of statute law complement those set out in the GSCC *Code of Practice for Social Care Workers*.

Principles guiding social work practice and the rulings of judges in matters coming before the court are not straightforward in their application. For example in the **Ombudsman Report Complaint against Suffolk Council** the Approved Social Worker had at one and the same time to follow the *least restriction* and *respect* principles which pointed to non-intervention, and the *purpose principle* to minimise risk which argued for compulsory intervention. It was for the social worker exercising professional judgement to weigh up these conflicting imperatives and to make a decision. Likewise, *The Challenge of Partnership in Child Protection* requires practitioners to work in partnership with parents whose children are at risk of significant harm. Yet, as in the **Second Serious Case Review: Baby Peter,** partnership working in these circumstances which lacked sufficient boundaries or challenge to a neglectful and abusive parent resulted in the tragic death of a child. At times working in partnership with parents and child-centred practice can be in conflict with each other. Again, it is the use of professional judgement in the context of good supervision and multi-agency collaboration which enables a balance to be struck between what can be seemingly contradictory objectives.

The nature of proof

When issues are not resolvable through partnership working or voluntary agreement, recourse to the courts becomes necessary. At this point the nature of evidence becomes crucial as the judge and sometimes a jury is called upon to determine the truth of a matter and come to a decision. Distinguishing between civil and criminal jurisdictions and understanding the implications for practice which follow from it is vital. This is pointed up in the area of child protection and youth offending, where aspects of the same case often involve both jurisdictions. In the **Independent Inquiry Report into the Circumstances of Child Sexual Abuse by two Foster Carers in Wakefield** the children's social workers failed to appreciate the potentially criminal nature of what was taking place alongside the safeguarding considerations. Consequently, evidence was lost which should have formed part of the criminal case, and children were not properly protected.

Issues of evidence revolve around collecting it, preserving it and ensuring that it meets the different standards of proof in civil and criminal courts. For practitioners pursuing care proceedings in relation to children this can be particularly exacting. In *Re C and B (Children) (Care Order: Future Harm)* local authority social workers failed to produce convincing evidence that two children would suffer future harm on the basis of harm caused to another child. Conversely, in *Re P (A Child) (Care and Placement Order Proceedings: Mental Capacity of Parent)* the judge found that social workers had offered convincing expert reports together with thorough and detailed assessments, and endorsed a lower court's decision to grant a Care and Placement Order on the appellant mother's child.

Expert evidence

Crucial to judges' rulings on many of the cases explored, particularly to those concerning children, has been expert evidence. In *Re M (A Child) (Contact: Domestic Violence)* expert evidence produced by consultant child psychiatrists regarding the impact on child and mother of continued contact with a violent partner was critical to the court's ruling on the father's application for a Contact Order. In *Re P (A Child) (Care and Placement Order Proceedings: Mental Capacity of Parent)* social workers commissioned an expert report on the parenting ability of the appellant mother. The mother and her McKenzie friends disputed the content of the report and the competence of the expert who wrote it. Enquiry by the court into the professional qualifications and experience of the expert witness quickly established her competency and thus the robustness of the evidence presented in her report.

Where experts disagree as in *Re M (A Child) (Contact: Domestic Violence)* or where medical evidence does not appear to be conclusive as in *Re U (A Child) (Serious Injury: Standard of Proof)* judges will weigh up expert evidence as they would any other piece of evidence. In the first case one expert was found to lack expertise in child psychiatry and to express views not widely held within his discipline. In the second case equivocal medical evidence was corroborated by evidence from family members and assessments of the mother's mental health. In both cases expert evidence constituted a crucial factor in the judge's ruling. For this reason the selection of a specialist to inform a broader multidisciplinary assessment or an expert specifically to produce evidence for a court case must be based on careful consideration of the competency of that expert in the area on which they are to give an opinion.

Statutory criteria and thresholds

Attention to the criteria set out in statutory provisions, and the thresholds required to trigger them, have featured in many of the cases. Criteria and thresholds are elemental considerations when taking action to compulsorily intervene with families under the Children Act 1989. In *Re O (A Minor) (Care Proceedings: Education)* the local authority applied for a Care Order under s.31 on the grounds that the child had been largely absent from school for two years and her development was being impaired. A central issue was whether the intellectual and social impairment she was experiencing as a result amounted to *significant* harm as opposed to just a degree of harm. Social workers produced evidence to show that the developmental harm crossed the threshold of being *significant*, that is to say of a sufficiently grave nature. They also demonstrated that this harm was caused by the inadequate care of the parents, which is the criteria that had to be established to obtain a Care Order.

Similarly the Mental Health Act 1983 had criteria and thresholds which have to be met for a person to be compulsorily admitted to hospital. In *St George's Healthcare Trust* v. *S and R* v. *Collins and Others* a pregnant woman was detained on the grounds that she had depression, but this was found not to meet the threshold criteria of constituting a mental disorder of a nature or degree which warranted detention for treatment. Many provisions in the Children Act 1989 and the Mental Health Act 1983, in common with other statutes, contain a number of criteria and thresholds which have to be simultaneously met for lawful action to be taken under them. As in *St George's Healthcare Trust* v. *S and R* v. *Collins and Others* the individual met several of the conditions under s.2 of the Mental Health Act 1983, but not all of them. Without meeting all the conditions the section could not be lawfully invoked. Ensuring that a situation meets *all* the conditions of a statutory provision and that this can be substantiated through evidence to a court if necessary is an important aspect of practising within the law.

Representation in court

The recognition that families are composed of individuals who can have competing rights and interests is reflected in the provision for the separate legal representation of children in both private and public law proceedings. Parents may also be separately represented from each other if they are in dispute over the care of their children. The use of Children's Guardians and Guardians ad Litem to represent children in court ensures that their interests are not subsumed into those of the parents: or in public law proceedings, those of the local authority. These Guardians instruct the solicitor on behalf of the child, but they do so on the basis of the child's best interests and not on the basis of the child's wishes, although these do of course impinge on a *best interests* decision. This means that with the exception of *Gillick* competent children, who may directly instruct their own solicitor as in *Re O (A Minor) (Care Proceedings: Education)*, children's representation is funnelled through *best interests* decisions by the Children's Guardian or Guardian ad Litem. This can create the situation as in *Re O* of a child's solicitor and the solicitor representing the Children's Guardian being in conflict and on opposing sides in a court case.

Adults who are vulnerable due to illness or disability may choose to directly instruct their own solicitor. Alternatively they may be represented by a litigation friend, usually a relative or friend, who acts on their behalf to instruct a solicitor and generally oversee the court proceedings. However, in circumstances where a person is mentally incapacitated and there is no appropriate person to act as their litigation friend the Official Solicitor is appointed in this role. Like Children's Guardians, the Official Solicitor must also act on the basis of the vulnerable adult's best interests. *Re P (A Child) (Care and Placement Order Proceedings: Mental Capacity of Parent)* aptly demonstrates that the *best interests* of an incapacitated adult are not necessarily the same as her wishes, feelings and preferences. As in *Re P*, adults represented by the Official Solicitor can find themselves in direct opposition to legal positions advanced on their behalf and supposedly to their benefit. The idea that children and vulnerable adults are separately and fairly represented in court needs to be tempered by the way in which that representation is mediated by *best interests* decisions.

Best interests

The *welfare principle* ensures that children's rights are placed over and above those of parents, but at the same time courts have been forced to recognise an aspect of interdependency between the welfare of parents and their children. In *Re M (A Child) (Contact: Domestic Violence)* expert evidence demonstrated the need for consideration to be given to the effects on a parent of continued contact between a child and a violent ex-partner. Similarly, in *Re C and Re F (A Child) (Immunisation: Parental Rights)* it was necessary to rebut the position of the mothers' barristers that forcing them to have their children immunised would cause the mothers such distress as to detrimentally affect the children's welfare. In this case it was important for the court not to allow itself to be threatened by parents who argued through their legal representatives that interfering in their family life would have such adverse consequences for their mental health as to detrimentally affect the welfare of their children. Although these were both private law cases the implications for public law proceedings are plain. Compulsory intervention in families, even to safeguard children, can of itself increase parental distress, impair parental capacity and in consequence detrimentally affect children's welfare. It was for this reason in *X Local Authority* v. *B (Emergency Protection Orders)* that the presiding judge stipulated that social workers pursuing without notice applications for court orders must consider their impact on the parents as well as on the children.

Equally, the interpretation of what is in the *best interests* of mentally incapacitated adults can be bound up with the best interests of those most closely involved in their care. This can include professionals as well as family members and other informal carers. Inevitably in circumstances of great strain informal carers may make *best interests* decisions on behalf of the person they look after in terms that minimise their caring responsibilities or at the very least do not increase them. As *Re Local Authority X* v. *MM (by her litigation friend, the Official Solicitor)* illustrated, professionals also can be guilty of making *best interests* decisions which do not at all reflect the wishes and feelings of mentally incapacitated adults, but which best serve agency pressures to minimise risk. The notion of a person's *best interests* is not an objective fact but relies on the judgements and sometimes the biases of those charged with the care of the mentally incapacitated adult.

Presumption of non-intervention

Many of the statutes which are central to social work practice are underpinned by principles which emphasise the necessity to choose the least interventionist form of action when working with individuals and families. The Children Act 1989 embeds the *no order principle* as a statutory provision, which requires the court not to issue a court order unless it can be clearly demonstrated that this would achieve a benefit over and above not making any order at all. For social workers involved in public law proceedings this means not seeking a court order if voluntary agreement can be achieved with children and families to bring about the same ends. However, this is not to deny that a court order may be necessary in situations of apparent agreement where there are doubts that an individual will abide by the agreement, as demonstrated by the behaviour of Peter's mother in the **Second Serious Case Review: Baby Peter**.

Similarly, under the Mental Health Act 1983, Approved Mental Health Professionals are required to act in accordance with the *least restriction principle* and to negotiate informal admission to hospital where this is feasible as opposed to resorting to compulsory detainment. The Mental Capacity Act 2005, like the Children Act 1989 embeds its principles within the statute itself. Section one of the Mental Capacity Act 2005 requires those making decisions on behalf of mentally incapacitated adults to ensure that any act or decision is the one which results in the least restrictions on the person's rights and freedoms. In the case of both children and adults the presumption is against compulsory intervention and for a course of action which will result in the least restrictive consequences for the adults concerned. As with intervention to safeguard children, this does not mean that restrictions on a person's freedoms are needless. It does mean, as in *Re Local Authority X* v. *MM*, that professionals seeking to curtail the rights and freedoms of others must be able to prove the necessity of doing so, and the absence of other viable and less restrictive courses of action.

An aspect of avoiding compulsory intervention is partnership working with individuals and families. This is emphasised in policy and practice guidance relating to safeguarding children, care management and the care programme approach to work with adults diagnosed with a mental disorder. This is consistent with the GSCC *Code of Practice for Social Care Workers* which emphasises the importance of supporting user independence, choice and positive risk taking. However, as the **Ombudsman Report Complaint No. 97/B/2696 against Suffolk County Council** reveals, this can mean negotiating disagreements between users and carers. On the other hand the **Second Serious Case Review: Baby Peter** demonstrated the limits of partnership working with parents where children are at risk of *significant harm*.

Working with diversity

In *KC, NNC* v. *City of Westminster Social and Community Services Department* cultural and religious practices were at the centre of a family's dispute with social workers who intervened to safeguard a vulnerable adult. Culture also featured in *R (on the application of Khana)* v. *Southwark London Borough Council* where it was argued that a range of cultural needs should be met by a care package. This case also rested on the immigration status of the couple concerned. In the **Independent Inquiry Report into the Circumstances of Child Sexual Abuse by two Foster Carers in Wakefield** the sexual orientation of foster parents appeared to have influenced how social workers reacted to an allegation of sexual abuse. In *R (on the application of Chavda)* v. *Harrow London Borough Council* the degree to which the local authority was meeting its Disability Equality Duty to residents within the council boundaries was under scrutiny. The ability of practitioners to take into account aspects of diversity in their work is both a requirement of the GSCC Code of Practice, and also of a number of policy and practice guidance documents, many of which have been cited.

Some cases, such as *KC, NNC* v. *City of Westminster Social and Community Services Department* also explore the boundaries of cultural diversity and the way in which the law operates to place limits on cultural or religious practices which appear to be exploitive or abusive. Conversely, as illustrated in the **Independent Inquiry Report into the Circumstances of Child Sexual Abuse by two Foster Carers in Wakefield**, sometimes social workers engaging with diversity can overcompensate and through fear of being accused of discrimination fail to act to safeguard the vulnerable. These two cases demonstrate the complexity of work with diversity. On the one hand practitioners are required to work in ways which are respectful of diversity. On the other they must be alert to the possibility of, for example, a cultural practice being used to justify abusive or exploitive behaviour. At the same time they need to be aware of how diversity can occasionally be used by individuals from minority groups to repel criticism and intimidate professionals with accusations of homophobia, racism or disablism.

Collection and use of information

The collection and collation of information for the purposes of assessment and care planning feature in many cases. In a number of instances users have sought a judicial review on the grounds that assessment by social workers has been insufficiently detailed and care planning therefore flawed. In other instances, such as *R (on the application of Ireneschild)* v. *Lambeth London Borough Council* users have challenged assessments on the basis of the specialist reports which have been included or ignored. Indeed, these specialist reports themselves have been the subject of court action in a number of the cases explored in this book. Aside from care planning, the collection of accurate information has been shown to be crucial to child protection and the detection of crime both in the **Independent Inquiry Report into the Circumstances of Child Sexual Abuse by two Foster Carers in Wakefield** and the **Second Serious Case Review: Baby Peter.**

While gathering information, analysing it and synthesising it to produce a care plan is central to social work practice, whether with children or adults, many of these cases also demonstrate how crucial the collection of information is for evidential purposes. The **Independent Inquiry Report into the Circumstances of Child Sexual Abuse by two Foster Carers in Wakefield** illustrated how vital evidence could be lost as a result of inadequate investigative approaches by social workers. In other instances, such as *Re C and B (Children) (Care Order: Future Harm)* local authority social workers were found to have produced insufficient evidence to justify the granting of Care Orders. Therefore, information gathering has both an evidential aspect, particularly in relation to safeguarding children and work with vulnerable adults, and a care planning aspect.

Inter-agency collaboration

As many cases in the text have illustrated, inter-agency collaboration is often central to both assessment and the implementation of care plans. As in the **Second Serious Case Review: Baby Peter** it can also be crucial to safeguarding a child, or in *Local Authority X v. M, F, E, J and D (Represented by Children's Guardian EF)*, crucial to managing risk in relating to child protection. The cases explored in the book reveal instances both of effective multi-agency assessment and of poor practice in this regard. They reveal as much about the nature of good inter-agency cooperation as of its inadequacies and failings. The **Ombudsman Report Complaint No. 97/B/2696** shows the degree of respect and trust that can exist between health and social care professionals even when they are in disagreement with each other. Conversely, in the **Second Serious Case Review: Baby Peter**, lack of respect and inadequate communication between professionals from different disciplines contributed to the failure to protect an infant.

Dilemmas and professional judgement

Taken altogether, what these cases demonstrate, more than almost anything else, are the professional dilemmas, the balancing acts, the weighing of factors and often the pitting of one imperative against another. Working within a legal context, while meeting the requirements of the GSCC *Code of Practice for Social Care Workers*, is a tall order for any practitioner, especially in the face of adverse media attention and the risk averse biases of many government policies. These aspects of professional practice can bring to bear their own pressures upon social workers. The financial constraints with which local authorities are constantly wrestling are a further dimension of practice which confronts social workers with considerable challenges in relation to care planning for children and adults alike. It is precisely this complexity which continues to place a premium on professional judgement in negotiating human rights, safeguarding and welfare within the law.

Bibliography

Adams, S. (2007) 'In Practice: Parents' Rights v Children's Needs in Private Cases', *Family Law*, 37: 257–72.

Allen, N. (2003) *Making Sense of the New Adoption Law*: *A Guide for Social and Welfare Services*, Lyme Regis: Russell House.

Allen, N. (2005) *Making Sense of the Children Act 1989*, Chichester: John Wiley and Sons.

Arthur, R. (2005) 'Punish parents for the crimes of their children', *The Howard Journal*, 44 (3): 233–53.

Association of Directors of Social Services, Local Government Association Society of County Treasurers and Society of Municipal Treasurers (2001), *Local Authority Social Services Budget Position: Executive Summary*, www.adss.org.uk/committee/resources/budjulexec.shtml (accessed 25 May 2009).

Audit Commission (2004) *The Effectiveness and Cost-Effectiveness of Support and Services to Informal Carers of Older People*, London: Audit Commission.

Baker, K. (2008) 'Risk, uncertainty and public protection: assessment of young people who offend', *British Journal of Social Work*, 38 (8): 1463–80.

Barlow, A., Duncan, S., James, G., Park, A. (2001) 'Just a piece of paper? Marriage and cohabitation in Britain', in A. Park, J. Curtice, K. Thomson, L. Jarvis and C. Bromley (eds), *British Social Attitudes: The 18th Report*, London: Sage.

Beckett, C., McKeigue, B. and Taylor, H. (2007) 'Coming to conclusions: social workers' perceptions of the decision-making process in care proceedings', *Child and Family Social Work*, 12: 54–63.

Booth, T and Booth, W. (2005) 'Parents with learning difficulties in the child protection system', *Journal of Intellectual Disabilities*, 9 (2): 109–29.

Booth, T., Booth, W. and McConnell, D. (2005) 'The prevalence and outcomes of care proceedings involving parents with learning difficulties in the family courts', *Journal of Applied Research in Intellectual Disabilities*, 18: 7–17.

Booth, T., McConnell, D. and Booth, W. (2006) 'Temporal discrimination and parents with learning difficulties in the child protection system', *British Journal of Social Work*, 36: 997–1015.

Boylan, J. and Braye, S. (2006) 'Paid, professionalised and proceduralised: can legal and policy frameworks for child advocacy give voice to children and young people?' *Journal of Social Welfare and Family Law*, 28 (3–4): 233–49.

Brammer, A. (2007) *Social Work Law*, Harlow: Pearson.

Bretherton, H. (2002) '"Because it's me the decisions are about" – Children's experiences of private law proceedings', *Family Law* 32: 450–7.

Brown, P. (2006) 'Risk versus need in revising the Mental Health Act 1983: conflicting claims, muddled policy', *Health, Risk and Society*, 8 (4): 343–58.

Brown, R., Barber, P. and Martin, D. (2009) *The Mental Capacity Act 2005: A Guide for Practice*, Exeter: Learning Matters.

Browne, D., 'The black experience of mental health law', in T. Heller et al., *Mental Health Matters*, Milton Keynes: Open University.

Buchanan, A., Hunt, J., Bretherton, H., and Bream, V. (2001) *Families in Conflict – perspectives of children and parents on the Family Court Welfare Service*, Bristol: Policy Press.

Burnett, R. and Appleton, C. (2004) *Joined-up Youth Justice: Tackling Youth Crime in Partnership*, Lyme Regis: Russell House.

Campbell, J. (2008) 'Stakeholders' views of legal and advice services for people admitted to psychiatric hospital', *Journal of Social Welfare and Family Law*, 30 (3): 219–32.

Canvin, K., Barlett, A. and Pinfold, V. (2002) 'A "bittersweet pill to swallow": learning from mental health service users' responses to compulsory community care in England', *Health and Social Care in the Community*, 10 (5): 361–9.

Carers UK (2003) *Missed Opportunities: The Impact of New Rights for Carers*, London: Carers UK.

Challis D., Darton, R., Hughes, J., Stewart K. and Weiner, K. (1999) 'Mapping and Evaluation of Care Management Arrangements for Older People and those with Mental Health Problems: An Overview of Care Management Arrangements', Discussion Paper, 1519/M009, unpublished.

Chief Secretary to the Treasury (2003) *Every Child Matters* (Cm. 5860), London: Stationery Office.

Christiansen, A. and Roberts, K. (2005) 'Integrating health and social care assessment and care management: findings from a pilot project evaluation', *Primary Health Care Research and Development*, 6: 269–77.

Cleaver, H. and Freeman, P. (1995) *Parental Perspectives in Cases of Suspected Child Abuse*, London: HMSO.

Clements, L. and Thompson, P. (2007) *Community Care and the Law*, London: Legal Action Group.

Collier, R. (2005) 'Fathers 4 Justice, law and the new politics of fatherhood', *Child and Family Law Quarterly* 17(4): 511.

Commission for Social Care Inspection (2005) *'Getting the Best from Complaints' – the Children's View*, London: Commission for Social Care Inspection.

Commission for Social Care Inspection and Health Care Commission (2006) *Joint Investigation into the Provision of Service for People with Learning Disabilities at Cornwall Partnership NHS Trust*, London: Commission for Healthcare Audit and Inspection.

Conservative Party (1987) *The Next Moves Forward: The Conservative Manifesto 1987*, London: Conservative Central Office.

Corby, B., Millar, M. and Young, L. (1996) 'Parental participation in child protection work: rethinking the rhetoric', *British Journal of Social Work*, 26 (4): 475–92.

Dale, P. (2004) '"Like a fish in a bowl": parents' perceptions of child protection services', *Child Abuse Review*, 13: 137–57.

Darlington, Y., Feeney, J. A. and Rixon, K. (2005) 'Practical challenges at the intersection of child protection and mental health', *Child and Family Social Work* 10(3)329–45.

Department for Children, Schools and Families and Office for National Statistics (2007) *Children Looked After in England, Year Ending 31 March 2007*, SFR 27/2007, London: Stationery Office.

Department for Communities and Local Government (2006) *Homelessness Code of Guidance for Local Authorities*, London: Department for Communities and Local Government.

Department for Constitutional Altars (2005, 2006) *Judicial Statistics for England and Wales (2004, 2005)*, London: HMSO.

Department for Constitutional Affairs (2007) *Mental Capacity Act 2005: Code of Practice*, London: Stationery Office.

Department for Education and Skills (2001) *Special Educational Needs: Code of Practice*, Annesley: DfES Publications.

Department for Education and Skills (2002) *National Minimum Standards for Private Fostering*, London: Department for Education and Skills.

Department for Education and Skills (2005a) *Replacement Children Act 1989 Guidance on Private Fostering*, London: Department for Education and Skills.

Department for Education and Skills (2005b) *Special Guardianship Regulations 2005: Special Guardianship Regulations*, London: Stationery Office.

Department for Education and Skills (2005c) *Adoption and Children Act 2002: Adoption Guidance*, London: Stationery Office.

Department for Education and Skills (2006) *Getting the Best from Complaints: Social Care Complaints and Representations for Children, Young People and Others*, London: Department for Education and Skills.

Department for Education and Skills and Department of Health (2004) *Stand up for Us: Challenging Homophobia in Schools*, London: Stationery Office.

Department of Health (1989) *Caring for People*, White Paper (Cm. 849), London: HMSO.

Department of Health (1990) *Community Care in the Next Decade and Beyond: Policy Guidance*, London: HMSO.

Department of Health (1991a) *The Children Act 1989 Guidance and Regulations: Family Placements*, 3, London: HMSO.

Department of Health (1991b) *The Children Act 1989 Guidance and Regulations: Family Support, Day Care and Educational Provision for Young Children*, Vol. 2, London: HMSO.

Department of Health (1991c) *The Children Act 1989 Guidance and Regulations: Residential Care*, Vol. 4, London: HMSO.

Department of Health and Social Services Inspectorate (1991d) *Care Management and Assessment: Practitioner's Guide*, London: HMSO.

Department of Health and Social Services Inspectorate (1995) *The Challenge of Partnership in Child Protection: Practice Guide*, London: HMSO.

Department of Health (1998a) *Modernising Social Services: Promoting Independence, Improving Projection, Raising Standards*, Cm. 4169, London: Stationery Office.

Department of Health (1998b) *Moving into the Mainstream: The Report of a National Inspection of Services for Adults with Learning Disability*, London: Department of Health.

Department of Health (1999a) *The National Service Framework for Mental Health*, London: HMSO.

Department of Health (1999b) *Objectives for Children's Services*, London: Stationery Office.

Department of Health (2000a) *No Secrets: Guidance on Developing and Implementing Multi-agency Policies and Procedures to Protect Vulnerable Adults from Abuse*, London: Stationery Office.

Department of Health (2000b) *Assessing Children in Need and their Families: Practice Guidance*, London: Stationery Office.

Department of Health (2000c) *Data Protection Act 1998: Guidance to Social Services*, London: Stationery Office.

Department of Health (2000d) *Framework for the Assessment of Children in Need and their Families*, London: Stationery Office.

Department of Health (2000e) *Framework for the Assessment of Children in Need and their Families: Guidance Notes and Glossary for: Referral and Initial Information Record, Initial Assessment Record and Core Assessment Record,* London: Stationery Office.

Department of Health (2000f) *Adoption: A New Approach,* Cm. 5017, London: Stationery Office.

Department of Health (2000g) *Data Protection Act 1998: Guidance to Social Services,* London: Department of Health.

Department of Health (2001a) *A Practitioner's Guide to Carers' Assessments under the Carers and Disabled Children Act 2000,* London: Department of Health.

Department of Health (2001b) *The Children Act Now: Messages from Research,* London: Stationery Office.

Department of Health (2001c) *Children (Leaving Care) Act 2000: Regulations and Guidance,* London: Stationery Office.

Department of Health (2001d) *National Adoption Standards,* London: Stationery Office.

Department of Health (2001e) *National Service Framework for Older People,* London: HMSO.

Department of Health (2001f) *Valuing People: A New Strategy for Learning Disability for the 21st Century,* Cm. 5086, London: Stationery Office.

Department of Health (2001g) *Adoption* (LAC (2001) 33), London: Department of Health.

Department of Health (2002a) *Fostering Services: National Minimum Standards,* London: Stationery Office.

Department of Health (2002b) *The Single Assessment Process,* London: Department of Health.

Department of Health (2002c) *Fair Access to Care Services* (LAC (2002) 13), London: Department of Health.

Department of Health (2003a) *Adoption: National Minimum Standards,* London: Stationery Office.

Department of Health (2003b) *Care Homes for Adults (18–65) and Supplementary Standards for Care Homes Accommodating Young People Aged 16 and 17: National Minimum Standards,* London: Stationery Office.

Department of Health (2003c) *Domiciliary Care: National Minimum Standards,* London: Stationery Office.

Department of Health (2003d) *Fairer Charging Policies for Home Care and other Non-residential Social Services: Guidance for Councils with Social Services Responsibilities,* London: HMSO.

Department of Health (2003e) *Direct Payment Guidance, Community Care, Services for Carers and Children's Services (Direct Payments) Guidance England,* London: Stationery Office.

Department of Health (2004) *Guidance to support implementation of the National Health Service (Complaints) Regulations, 2004,* London: Department of Health.

Department of Health (2005) *Delivering Race Equality in Mental Health Care: An Action Plan for Reform Inside and Outside Services,* London: Stationery Office.

Department of Health (2006) *Learning from Complaints: Social Services Complaints Procedure for Adults,* London: Department of Health.

Department of Health (2007) *Best Practice in Managing Risk: Principles and Evidence for Best Practice in the Assessment and Management of Risk to Self and Others in Mental Health Services,* London: Stationery Office.

Department of Health (2008a) *Mental Health Act 1983: Code of Practice,* London: Stationery Office.

Department of Health (2008b) *Refocusing the Care Programme Approach: Policy and Positive Practice Guidance,* London: Department of Health.

Department of Health and Department for Education and Skills (2005) *Carers and Disabled Children Act 2000 and Carers (Equal Opportunities) Act 2004 Combined Policy Guidance*, London: Department of Health.

Dimond, P. (2008) *Legal Aspects of Mental Capacity*, Oxford: Blackwell.

Disability Rights Commission (2005) *The Duty to Promote Disability Equality: Statutory Code of Practice*, London: Disability Rights Commission.

Dugmore, P. and Pickford, J. (2006), *Youth Justice and Social Work*, Exeter: Learning Matters.

Elliot, C. and Quinn, F. (2004) *English Legal System*, Harlow: Pearson.

Farmer, E. and Owen, M. (1995) *Child Protection Practice: Private Risks and Public Remedies*, London: HMSO.

Fennell, P. (2007) *Mental Health: The New Law*, Bristol: Jordan Publishing.

Ferri, E. and Smith, K. (2003) 'Partnership and parenthood', in E. Ferri, J. Bynner and M. Wadsworth (eds) *Changing Britain, Changing Lives*, London: Institute of Education.

Frazer, L. and Selwyn, J. (2005) 'Why are we waiting? The demography of adoption for children of black, Asian and black mixed percentage in England', *Child and Family Social Work* 10: 135–47.

Freeman, P. and Hunt, J. (1998) *Parental Perspectives on Care Proceedings*, London: The Stationery Office.

Fyson, R. and Kitson, D. (2007) 'Independence or protection – does it have to be a choice? Reflections on the abuse of people with learning disabilities in Cornwall', *Critical Social Policy*, 27 (3): 426–36.

Glasgow Media Group (1993) 'Media images of mental distress', in T. Heller, J. Reynolds, R. Gomm, R. Muston and S. Pattison (eds) *Mental Health Matters: A Reader*, Basingstoke: Macmillan and Open University Press.

Griffiths, R. (1988) *Community Care: Agenda for Action*, London: HMSO.

GSCC (2002a) *Code of Practice for Social Care Workers*, London: General Social Care Council.

GSCC (2002b) *Code of Practice for Employers of Social Care Workers*, London: General Social Care Council.

Hall, C. and Slembrouck, S. (2001) 'Parent participation in social work meetings – the case of child protection conferences', *European Journal of Social Work*, 4 (2): 143–60.

Hall, A. (2008) 'Special Guardianship: A Missed Opportunity – Findings from Research', *Family Law*, 38 (148): 244–48.

Hatfield, B., Shaw, J., Pinfold, V., Bindman, J., Evans, S., Huxley, P. and Thornicroft, G. (2001) 'Managing severe mental illness in the community using the Mental Health Act 1983: a comparison of Supervised Discharge and Guardianship in England', *Social Psychiatry Psychiatric Epidemiology*, 36: 508–15.

Hatfield, B., Bindman, J. and Pinfold, V. (2004) 'Evaluating the use of Supervised Discharge and Guardianship in cases of severe mental illness: a follow-up study', *Journal of Mental Health*, 13 (2): 197–209.

Herring, J. (2007) *Family Law*, London: Pearson.

HM Government (2006a) *Working Together to Safeguard Children*, London: Stationery Office.

HM Government (2006b) *Our Health, Our Care, Our Say: A New Direction for Community Services*, Cm. 6737, London: Stationery Office.

HM Government (2006c) *The Common Assessment Framework for Children and Young People: Practitioners' Guide,* London: Department for Education and Skills.

HM Government (2008) *Safeguarding Children in whom Illness is Fabricated or Induced,* London: Stationery Office.

Home Office, Crown Prosecution Service and Department of Health (2001) *Provision of Therapy for Child Witnesses prior to a Criminal Trial: Practice Guidance,* London: Stationery Office.

Home Office (2002) *Achieving Best Evidence in Criminal Proceedings: Guidance for Vulnerable or Intimidated Witnesses, including Children,* Vols 1 and 2, London: Home Office.

Home Office (2003) *A Guide to Anti-social Behaviour Orders and Acceptable Behaviour Contracts,* London: Home Office.

Home Office (2004) *Guidance on Part 1 of the Sexual Offences Act 2003,* London: Home Office.

Home Office, Youth Justice Board and Department for Constitutional Affairs (2004) *Parenting Contracts and Orders Guidance,* London: Stationery Office.

Hornes, N. and Krawczyk, S. (2006) *Social Work in Education and Children's Services,* Exeter: Learning Matters.

Hotopf, M. (2005) 'The assessment of mental capacity', *Clinical Medicine,* 5 (6): 580–4.

The Information Centre for Health and Social Care (2005) *Guardianship under the Mental Health Act 1983: England 2005,* Leeds: The NHS Information Centre.

The Information Centre for Health and Social Care (2008) *Community Care Statistics 2007–08: Referrals, Assessments and Packages of Care for Adults, England: National Summary,* Leeds: The NHS Information Centre.

The Information Centre for Health and Social Care (2009) *Adult Psychiatric Morbidity in England 2007: Results of a Household Survey,* Leeds: The NHS Information Centre.

Kemp, V., Pleasence, P. and Balmer, N.J. (2005) 'Incentivising disputes: the role of public funding in private law children cases', *Journal of Social Welfare and Family Law,* 27 (2): 125–41.

Keywood, K. (2003) 'Gatekeepers, proxies, advocates? The evolving role of carers under mental health and mental incapacity law reforms', *Journal of Social Welfare and Family Law,* 25 (4): 355–68.

Kinderman, P. and Tai, S. (2008) 'Psychological models of mental disorder, human rights, and compulsory mental health care in the community', *International Journal of Law and Psychiatry,* 31 (6): 479–86.

Kirkham, R. (2005) 'A complainant's view of the Local Government Ombudsman', *Journal of Social Welfare and Family Law,* 27 (3-4): 383–94.

Laird, S. E. (2008) *Anti-oppressive Social Work: A Guide for Developing Cultural Competence,* London: Sage.

Laming, H. (2003) *The Victoria Climbié Inquiry: Report of an Inquiry by Lord Laming,* Cm. 5730, London: HMSO.

Larkin, M., Clifton, E. and de Visser, R. (2009) 'Making sense of "consent" in a constrained environment', *International Journal of Law and Psychiatry,* 32 (3): 178–83.

Leyland, P. and Anthony, G. (2005) *Textbook on Administrative Law,* Oxford: Oxford University Press.

Local Government Association and Society of County Treasurers (2005) *Social Services Finance 2004/05: A Survey of Local Authorities,* London: Local Government Association.

Local Government Ombudsman (2005) *Annual Report 2004–05,* London: Stationery Office.

Local Safeguarding Children Board (2009) *Serious Case Review: Baby Peter: Executive Summary,* Haringey: Local Safeguarding Children Board.

Lord Chancellor's Department (1997) *Who Decides: Making Decisions on Behalf of Mentally Incapacitated Adults,* Cm. 3803, London: Stationery Office.

Lord Chancellor's Department (2000) *A Report to the Lord Chancellor on the Questions of Parental Contact in Cases where there is Domestic Violence,* London: Stationery Office.

Macpherson, W. (1999) *The Stephen Lawrence Inquiry: Report of an Inquiry by Sir William Macpherson of Cluny,* Cm. 4262–1, London: Home Office.

Mail on Sunday (15 June 2008) Lisa Arthurworrey exclusive interview by Eileen Fairweather, Review Supplement.

Mandelstam, M. (2005) *Community Care Practice and the Law,* London: Jessica Kingsley.

Mandelstam, M. (2009) *Safeguarding Vulnerable Adults and the Law,* London: Jessica Kingsley.

Manthorpe, J., Clough, R., Cornes, M., Bright, L., Moriarty, J., Iliffe, S. and OPRSI (2007) 'Four years on: the impact of the National Service Framework for Older People on the experiences, expectations and views of older people,' *Age and Ageing,* 36, 501–7.

Mason, D. (2000) *Race and Ethnicity in Modern Britain,* Oxford: Oxford University Press.

Masson, J. (2005) 'Research – Emergency intervention to protect children: using and avoiding legal controls', *Children and Family Law Quarterly,* 171: 75–96.

McCreadie, C. Matthew, D., Filinson, R. and Askham, J. (2008) 'Ambiguity and cooperation in the implementation of adult protection policy', *Social Policy and Administration,* 42 (3): 248–66.

Mental Health Foundation (2008) *Engaging with Black and Minority Ethnic Communities about the Mental Capacity Act,* London: The Mental Health Foundation.

Ministry of Justice (2008) *Mental Capacity Act 2005 Deprivation of Liberty Safeguards: Code of Practice to Supplement the main Mental Capacity Act 2005 Code of Practice,* London: Stationery Office.

Morgan, R. and Lindsay, M. (2006) *Young People's Views on Leaving Care: What Young People in and formerly in Residential and Foster Care think about Leaving Care,* London: Commission for Social Care Inspection.

National Assembly for Wales (2000) *In Safe Hands,* Cardiff: National Assembly for Wales.

Newton, J. and Browne, L. (2008) 'How fair is Fair Access to Care?' *Practice: Social Work in Action,* 20 (4): 235–49.

NHS (2008) *In-patients Formally Detained in Hospitals under the Mental Health Act 1983 and other Legislation, England: 1997–98 to 2007–2008,* London: The Information Centre for Health and Social Care.

Norfolk, Suffolk and Cambridgeshire Strategic Health Authority (2003) *Independent Inquiry into the Death of David Bennett,* Cambridge: Norfolk, Suffolk and Cambridgeshire Strategic Health Authority.

Northway, R., Davies, R. Mansell, I. and Jenkins, R. (2007) '"Policies don't protect people, it's how they are implemented": policy and practice in protecting people with learning difficulties from abuse', *Social Policy and Administration,* 41 (1): 86–104.

Office of the Public Guardian (2008) *The Mental Capacity Act: A Media Snapshot Guide,* London: Office of the Public Guardian.

Ofsted (2008a) *Ofsted's Inspection of the Experience of CAFCASS Service Users in the Family Courts in South Yorkshire,* London: Ofsted.

Ofsted (2008b) *Children's Experience of Private Fostering,* A Report by the Children's Rights Director for England, London: Ofsted.

Ofsted, Healthcare Commission, and HM Inspectorate of Constabulary (2008) *Joint Area Review: Haringey Children's Services Authority Area,* London: Ofsted.

O'Neill, T. (2001) *Children in Secure Accommodation,* London: Jessica Kingsley.

O'Reilly, R. (2004) 'Why are community treatment orders controversial?' *Canadian Journal of Psychiatry,* 49: 579–84.

Owen, G.S., Richardson, G., David, A.S., Szmukler, G., Hayward, P. and Hotopf, M. (2008) 'Mental capacity to make decisions on treatment in people admitted to psychiatric hospitals: cross sectional study', *British Medical Journal,* 337: a448.

Parry-Jones, B. and Soulsby, J. (2001) 'Needs-led assessment: the challenges and the reality', *Health and Social Care in the Community,* 9: 414–28.

Peay, J. (ed.) (1996) *Inquiries After Homicide,* London: Duckworth Press.

Perri, 6., Raab, C. and Bellamy, C. (2005) 'Joined-up government and privacy in the United Kingdom: managing tensions between data protection and social policy. Part I,' *Public Administration,* 83 (1): 111–33.

Prior, P. M. (2003) 'Removing children from the care of adults with diagnosed mental illnesses – a clash of human rights?' *European Journal of Social Work,* 6 (2): 179–90.

Probert, R. (2007) 'Why couples still believe in common-law marriage', *Family Law Journal,* 37 (403) http://www.lexisnexis.com/uk/legal/delivery/PrintDoc.do?fromCart=falseanddnldFileP accessed 10 June 2008.

Rapaport, J. (2004) 'A matter of principle: the nearest relative under the Mental Health Act 1983 and proposals for legislative reform', *Journal of Social Welfare and Family Law,* 26 (4): 377–96.

Rapaport, J., Manthorpe, J. and Stanley, N. (2009) 'Mental health and mental capacity law: some mutual concerns for social work Practice', *Practice: Social Work in Action* 21 (2): 91–105.

Richardson, G. (2002) 'Autonomy, guardianship and mental disorder: one problem, two solutions', *Modern Law Review* 65 (5): 702–23.

Rivers, I. (2000) 'Social exclusion, absenteeism and sexual minority youth', *Support for Learning,* 15 (1): 13–17.

Rivers, I. (2001) 'The bullying of sexual minorities at school: its nature and long-term correlates', *Education ad Child Psychology,* 18 (1): 33–46.

Sagar, T. and Hitchings, E. (2007) '"More adoptions, more quickly": a study of social workers' responses to the Adoption and Children Act 2002', *Journal of Social Welfare and Family Law,* 29 (3–4): 199–215.

Secker, J. and Harding, C. (2002) 'African and African Caribbean users' perceptions of inpatient services', *Journal of Psychiatric and Mental Health Nursing,* 9: 161–7.

Seddon, D. and Robinson, C.A. (2001) 'Carers of older people with dementia: assessment and the Carers Act', *Journal of Health and Social Care in the Community,* 9 (3): 151–8.

Seddon, D., Robinson, C., Reeves, C., Tommis, Y., Woods, B. and Russell, I. (2007) 'In their own right: translating the policy of carer assessment into practice', *British Journal of Social Work,* 37: 1335–52.

Shachar, A. (2001) *Multicultural Jurisdictions: Cultural Differences and Women's Rights,* Cambridge: Cambridge University Press.

Shaw, J., Hatfield, B., Evans, S. (2000) 'Guardianship under the Mental Health Act 1983', *Psychiatric Bulletin,* 24: 51–2.

Smaje, C. (1995) *Health, 'Race' and Ethnicity: Making Sense of the Evidence*, London: King's Fund Institute.

Smith, F. (2004) *Fostering Now: Current Law including Regulation, Guidance and Standards*, London: British Agency for Adoption and Fostering.

Smith, R. (2003) *Youth Justice: Ideas, Policy and Practice*, Cullompton: Willan.

Social Services Inspectorate and Department of Health (1991) *Care Management and Assessment: A Practitioner's Guide*, London: HMSO.

Social Services Inspectorate and Department of Health (1995) *The Challenge of Partnership in Child Protection: Practice Guidance*, London: HMSO.

Sproston, K. and Nazroo, J. (eds) (2002) *Ethnic Minority Psychiatric Illness Rates in the Community* (EMPIRIC), London: HMSO.

Squires, P. and Stephen, D.E. (2005) *Rough Justice: Anti-social Behaviour and Young People*, Cullompton: Willan.

Sturge, C. and Glaser, D. (2000) 'Contact and Domestic Violence – The Experts' Court Report', *Family Law*, 30: 615–21.

Taylor, H., Beckett, C. and McKeigue, B. (2008) 'Judgements of Solomon: anxieties and defences of social workers involved in care proceedings', *Child and Family Social Work*, 13: 23–31.

The Times (15 February 2008) 'Protection agency staff "left children at risk from abuse" because of errors', Rosemary Bennett, http://women.timesonline.co.uk/tol/life_and_style/women/families/article3372109.ece (accessed 29 June 2008).

Thoburn, J. (2003) 'The risks and rewards of adoption for children in public care', *Child and Family Law Quarterly*, 15: 391–402.

Thomas, N. and O'Kane, C. (1999) 'Children's participation in reviews and planning meetings when they are "looked after" in middle childhood', *Children and Family Social Work*, 4: 221–30.

Trinder, L., Connelley, J., Kellett, J., Notley, C. and Swift, L. (2006) *Making Contact Happen or Making Contact Work? The process and outcomes of in-court conciliation*, London: Department for Constitutional Affairs.

Vernon, S., Ross, F. and Gould, M. (2000) 'Assessment of older people: politics and practice in primary care', *Journal of Advanced Nursing*, 31: 282–7.

Walsh, E. (2006) *Working in the Family Justice System: A Guide for Professionals*, Bristol: Jordan Publishing.

Walters, R. and Woodward, R. (2007) 'Punishing "poor parents": "respect", "responsibility" and Parenting Orders in Scotland', *Youth Justice*, 7 (1): 5–20.

Ward, G. (1997) *Making Headlines: Mental Health and the National Press*, London: Health Education Authority.

Warner, J. (2006) 'Inquiry reports as active texts and their function in relation to professional practice in mental health', *Health, Risk and Society*, 8 (3): 223–7.

White, J. (2007) 'Social welfare and family law issues and the Local Government Ombudsman for England', *Journal of Social Welfare and Family Law*, 29 (1): 77–86.

Williams, J. (2002) 'Public law protection of vulnerable adults: the debate continues and so does the abuse', *Journal of Social Work*, 2 (3): 293–316.

Worth, A. (2001) 'Assessment of the needs of older people by district nurses and social workers: a changing culture? *Journal of Interprofessional Care*, 15: 257–66.

Xie, C., Hughes, J., Challis, D., Stewart, K. and Cambridge, P. (2008) 'Care management arrangements in services for people with intellectual disabilities: results of a national survey', *Journal of Applied Research in Intellectual Disabilities*, 21: 156–67.

Yeates, V. (2007) 'Ambivalence, Contradiction, and Symbiosis: Carers' and Mental Health Users' Rights', *Law and Policy* 29(4): 435–59.

Youth Justice Board (2004) *National Standards for Youth Justice Services*, London: Youth Justice Board.

Youth Justice Board (2005a) *A Guide to the Role of Youth Offending Teams in Dealing with Anti-Social Behaviour*, London: Youth Justice Board.

Youth Justice Board (2005b) *Managing Risk in the Community*, London: Youth Justice Board.

Youth Justice Board (2006) *Criminal Justice Act 2003, 'Dangerousness' and the New Sentences for Public Protection: Guidance for Youth Offending Teams*, London: Youth Justice Board.

Youth Justice Board, Ministry of Justice and Department for Children, Schools and Families (2008) *When to Share Information: Best Practice Guidance for Everyone Working in the Youth Justice System*, London: Youth Justice Board.

Index